The Alabama Catalog
Historic American Buildings Survey

The Alabama Catalog

Historic American Buildings Survey

A Guide to the Early Architecture of the State

ROBERT GAMBLE

The University of Alabama Press

Frontispiece:
Tacon-Gordon House, Mobile
(HABS: Jack Boucher photo, 1974.)

Copyright © 1987 by
The University of Alabama Press
University, Alabama 35487
All rights reserved
Manufactured in the United States of America

Publication of this book has been made possible in part by assistance from the Alabama Historical Commission.

Library of Congress Cataloging in Publication Data

Gamble, Robert S.
   The Alabama catalog.
   Bibliography: p.
   Includes index.
   1. Historic buildings—Alabama—Catalogs.
2. Architecture—Alabama—Catalogs. I. Historic American Buildings Survey. II. Title.
NA730.A2G35   1987   720'.9761   82-20288
ISBN 0-8173-0148-8

To Janet

Faithful friend, co-worker, and student of American history

Contents

Acknowledgments / ix

A Note on Photographers / xi

Foreword / xiii

Introduction / xv

The Historic American Buildings Survey / xix

Part One: Historic Architecture in Alabama
A Primer of Styles and Types, 1810–1930 / 1

Historic Architecture in Alabama / 3

Folk Forms / 23

The High Styles / 44

Epilogue / 169

Part Two: The HABS Catalog / 175

HABS Recording in Alabama / 177

How to Use the HABS Alabama Catalog / 188

A County-by-County Listing / 193

Glossary of Architectural Terms / 371

Brief Bibliography for Alabama Architecture / 395

Appendixes
A. Status of HABS-Recorded Structures in Alabama / 405
B. Mobile Ironwork Survey / 407
C. Mobile Structures Arranged by Street Address / 410
D. Alabama Properties Recorded by the Historic American Engineering Record (HAER) / 417

Index / 419

Acknowledgments

This volume owes its existence to the generous help of very many people. First among these must be mentioned my special assistant, Janet M. Dech, who brought astuteness and remarkable perseverance to the preparation of a long, difficult manuscript.

Vital fieldwork was carried out in the Mobile area by Jeppie Adams Gallalee, Devereaux Bemis, and Patty Fuller; and in central and northern Alabama by James F. Speake and Bernard Hall. These people devoted the better part of a toilsome summer to verifying old information and gathering new data on numerous structures represented in the original HABS recording project of the 1930s. In connection with this and other fieldwork, scores of Alabamians graciously allowed inquisitive strangers to inspect their home, church, or place of business—many times without prior notice. These people are far too numerous to mention, but to each of them is extended a heartfelt thanks.

Several individuals performed a vital service by reading through portions of the manuscript, contributing and correcting information and making a number of worthwhile suggestions. These include Michael Marcuse of Takoma Park, Maryland; Dan Brooks of Camden; Winston Smith, Gwyn Turner, and Mr. and Mrs. Joseph C. P. Turner of Demopolis; Harvie Jones, Frances Cabaniss Roberts, Martha Simms, and Bill Stubno of Huntsville; Mary Ann Neeley of Montgomery; and Robert Mellown of Tuscaloosa. That segment of the catalog dealing with the city of Mobile was reviewed by Caldwell Delaney as well as Elizabeth B. Gould and her staff of the Mobile Historic Development Commission. In addition, Mrs. Gould and Mrs. Nicholas H. Holmes, Jr., provided assistance and advice during the initial stages of field research in the Mobile area. Valuable counsel was also received from my friend John Linley, of the University of Georgia at Athens, and proofreading assistance from Ruth C. Connor of Montgomery.

Others to whom thanks are extended include William Nordan of Abbeville, the Reverend Fletcher Thorington of Andalusia; Judge William Bibb and Grace H. Gates of Anniston; Faye Axford, Bob Dunnavant, Eulalia Weldon, and David Whitehorn of Athens; Alice Cary Pick, David Rosenblatt, and Bill Sumners of Auburn; Ruby Harris and Betty Martin of Bessemer; Teresa Ceravalo, Robert Corley, Miriam Fowler, Mrs. Robert Fry, Madge Hahn, Nita Stuart, Marjorie L. White, and Marvin Whiting of Birmingham; George Alford of Camden; Louise B. Johnson of Columbia; Modelle Davis, the late Mrs. W. Clay McClung, and Mary B. Morgan of Decatur; Steve Fleegal of Dothan; Jeanne Dean and Doug Purcell of Eufaula; Alfred McCroskey, William L. McDonald, and Duane Phillips of Florence; Mary Katherine Rhoads of Forkland; Robert Clotfelter of Gadsden; M. D. Baines, Frances S. Dale, the late Margaret Hobson, Mrs.

George Sledge, and Nancy S. Wright of Greensboro; Tom Braxton and John G. Little of Greenville; Ken Penhale of Helena; Bessie Minge Wendt of Houston, Texas; Linda Bayer and Pat Ryan of Huntsville; Louis Finlay of Jackson; Worden Weaver of Jacksonville; the late Marjorie Andrews of Lafayette; Theodore B. Pearson of Leroy; Nathaniel E. Reed and Bill Stuart of Livingston; Howard Morgan of Luverne; Mary G. Auburtin, W. Stuart Harris, Marshall Knudsen, and Annie Lee Nichols of Marion; Mrs. Palmer Bedsole, Jay Higginbotham, Nicholas H. Holmes, Jr., and Michael V. Thomason of Mobile; Marty and Janice Everse of Montevallo; William Armistead, Mary Seibels Branch, Jim Parker, Mr. and Mrs. Robert Thorington, and Lea Verneuille, all of Montgomery; the late Thomas Pettus of Moulton; Ed "Buck" Whatley of Moundville; Mr. and Mrs. William Junius Jones of Oak Hill; Dale Garrett of Oxford; Agee Broughton of Perdue Hill; Homer D. Teal and Charles Tigner of Seale; Betty Callaway and Jean Martin of Selma; Harold T. Damsgard and C. Wilder Watts of Sheffield; Davida Hastie of Stockton; Grace Bankhead May of Sulligent; the late John Milton Hightower of Sylacauga; Jan Barta, Mrs. Edwin P. Jewell, and Vern Scott of Talladega; Noble Holloway of Tallassee; Mary Helen Andress, Marie Ball, Marvin Harper, Fred R. Maxwell, Jr., and Alex Sartwell of Tuscaloosa; Eleanor F. Holder and the late Mary Wallace Kirk of Tuscumbia; and W. Wat Jones as well as Mrs. Joe Macon of Wetumpka.

Members of the Alabama Historical Commission staff, including Larry Oaks, Cathy Donelson, Ellen Mertins, Jack Stell, and Beverly True, have likewise contributed to this undertaking in various ways. At the Library of Congress I wish to thank Mary Ison and C. Ford Peatross of the Division of Prints and Photographs. Ms. Ison and Mr. Peatross are guardians of the vast HABS collection, and Mr. Peatross has also shared with me his wealth of knowledge about the life and career of William Nichols. Within the National Park Service, I am indebted to S. Allen Chambers, Marlene Bergstrom, Pat Czeka, Jack Boucher, and Collette Miller Eady. And at The University of Alabama Press, I have greatly benefited from the editorial advice of Debbie Davis and from the expertise of the entire Press staff.

Finally, a very personal sense of gratitude is reserved for Mrs. A. Benton Smith, the Reverend and Mrs. O. S. Gamble, Dr. and Mrs. David Wilson, and Marcus A. Gamble, loved ones whose interest and support are deeply felt.

A Note on Photographers

Contemporary Alabama photographers have enriched this volume by supplementing illustrations drawn from the HABS collection and other archival sources. Especially do I wish to thank Duane Phillips of Florence, several of whose fine photographs will be found throughout. Also contributing have been Kerry Akridge of Birmingham, Chip Cooper of Tuscaloosa, Don Fleming of Demopolis, Earl Roberts of Eufaula, Jo Roy and Lewis Kennedy of Birmingham, John Englehardt Scott, Jr., of Montgomery, and Roy Thigpen of Mobile.

Foreword

Nowhere is the rich and diverse heritage of Alabama reflected better than in its wide array of historic structures. Indeed, they serve as a daily, tangible reminder of the people who settled and developed the state; they lead us toward an understanding of our past in a remarkable way that the printed word can never do. Familiarity with this past can, in turn, lead us to a better understanding of the present.

Alabama's architectural legacy offers us a three-dimensional sensory experience in history, from the Creole cottage of the Gulf Coast to the Federal-style plantation houses of the Tennessee Valley. Each type of structure mirrors a time, a set of attitudes and circumstances, that will not exist again.

The state's oldest surviving structures date from the early 1800s. It was at this time that the federal government opened to settlement the interior lands of what is now Alabama. During the 1840s and 1850s the state's booming cotton economy fostered the construction of many noteworthy buildings not only in the Greek Revival style, but also in lesser known styles such as the Gothic Revival and Italianate modes. Architectural developments in the latter part of the century are still expressed by a tapestry of buildings reflecting the eclecticism of the Victorian period. These along with significant structures from our own century forge vivid links leading back through successive stages of Alabama history.

Unfortunately, however, this architectural legacy is being diminished daily by destruction and neglect. For over fifty years now the Historic American Buildings Survey (HABS) has led the way in recording America's architectural resources. And Alabama can proudly lay claim to having hundreds of its early structures represented in the HABS collection.

It is the hope of the Alabama Historical Commission that the HABS Alabama catalog will bring to public attention both the significance of many little-known structures still standing and the plight of those that are now endangered. At the same time, the catalog should prove an invaluable guide to a unique archival resource.

The Alabama Historical Commission is proud to be a part of this effort.

F. Lawerence Oaks
Executive Director,
Alabama Historical Commission

Introduction

It is always pleasant to discover a good book and to be able to share its discovery with others. In this instance the pleasure is heightened by the fact that the subject matter in this particular good book is of great interest to me and its author is a valued friend and colleague. So let me delay your perusal of it for a moment to introduce you to it, and to its author.

The Alabama Catalog, Historic American Buildings Survey is just what it says it is and more. First, it is a listing of those structures and objects recorded by the Survey in Alabama, amply illustrated by the graphic arts of both architect and photographer. Second, it contains a brief history of the survey itself with particular emphasis on its activities in Alabama; and third, it presents a concise but astute chronology of the architecture of the state as it appeared and developed in the nineteenth and first third of the twentieth centuries.

As you will see, there are examples from the Tennessee line to the Gulf of Mexico. The variety of the things recorded is as broad as the needs of man—residences, gardens, hitching posts, navigational aids, ornamental work from the hands of master plasterers, carvers, and smiths, and buildings for education, business, industry, and religion. Some display the sophistication of the skilled professional and some the naïveté of the folk craftsman. Some are refined and understated, and some are bursting with energy, imagination, and, occasionally, exuberant gaucheries.

Together the illustrations will give you just a glimpse of the rich tapestry that constitutes our architectural heritage—and the real subject of this book.

You will note that the quality of the drawings also varies, but all display two common characteristics—they were all prepared by competent architects or architectural students, and all are part of the remarkable collection known as the Historic American Buildings Survey, the H.A.B.S. or HABS.

What is the Historic American Buildings Survey and how did it become involved in the built environment of our state? To answer these questions we must turn back our calendars fifty-one years to the fall of 1933. The country was in the grips of the Great Depression and the construction industry was as dead as a stump. My father's architectural practice netted $1,225.50 in 1931 and then things really got bad. In desperation, FDR was embracing the unbalanced budget and inventing a variety of programs designed to put Americans back to work.

In November of that year a young architect named Charles Peterson, who was employed by the National Park Service, wrote a memorandum that quickly reached the desk of his boss, Harold Ickes, then secretary of the Department of the Interior. It suggested that unemployed architects be hired to measure, draw, and photograph the historic buildings of America.

Within two weeks half a million dollars had been made available. To avoid delays and the need to create new bureaucracies, existing agencies and institutions were pressed into service. The result was the tripartite agreement formally entered into in 1934 by the National Park Service that would administer the program, the American Institute of Architects that would supply both direction and talent, and the Library of Congress that would curate the end results.

In an astonishingly short time, by April 1934, HABS opened its first exhibit of photographs and drawings in Washington, D.C.

I will not dwell on the work performed by HABS in Alabama, in the 1930s, or its rebirth, somewhat altered, in 1957, as Robert Gamble covers these events in depth. But I would like to acknowledge my debt to HABS. My father was one of the unemployed architects who was busy scurrying through all manner of antebellum structures with sketch pad and folding rule in the 1930s, and my son spent a valuable and instructive summer doing the same thing in the governmental buildings of the Cherokee Indian Nation in Talequah, Oklahoma, during the summer of 1975. In partial repayment I have supported HABS through the years, served on its board of advisers, and prepared and donated drawings to the collection.

At present the Survey is no longer a federal give-away program. To get a HABS team to work in your city, you have to raise most of the funds needed. What an astonishing turnaround—a federal program that is largely paid for by private organizations and local governments.

The work has continued since its reanimation in 1957 and by 1983 the survey contained over 41,000 drawings, 80,000 photographs, and 44,000 data pages. It is the most extensive collection of its kind in the world.

Sometimes the value of a collection of this sort is questioned, even though it provided sustenance to the needy during the 1930s and excellent training to the student later. But is there any practical value to a collection of this type or is it primarily useful to researchers, architectural historians, and hopeless romantics pining for earlier and more gracious times and surroundings?

In the 1960s we found the presence of the HABS team in Mobile to be a powerful stimulus to our preservation efforts. The fact that "authorities" from Washington thought our buildings worthy of recording kindled an interest in some segments of our community that did not exist previously.

In north Alabama architect Harvie Jones, FAIA, used HABS drawings to produce a feasibility study in record time that resulted in the preservation of Oak Place, a Greek Revival home designed in 1840 by the noted architect George Steele.

And in Mobile in 1979 City Hall was devastated by the most destructive hurricane, in terms of property damage, ever to hit this country. Our firm was selected to perform the architectural services required to rehabilitate it and the first priority was to secure the building with temporary walls, roofs, and window closures. We were working seven days a week when help arrived from an unexpected source. We knew the complex had been documented by HABS in the 1930s and we obtained copies of the drawings. They saved us a great deal of time and enabled us to protect the buildings quickly to avoid further damage.

But it was rather spooky—son Nicholas the third and I hard at work using HABS drawings made in 1935, by N. H. Holmes, my father.

I first met Robert Gamble in the mid-1970s and learned that he was working to update the HABS survey in Alabama, and furthermore, intended to bring forth a book on the subject. I congratulated him and wished him well—and said to myself "what a monumental slice of work that young fellow has cut out for himself! To bring it off will require talent, knowledge, industry, and perseverance on an equally monumental scale."

Well, we in Alabama are fortunate indeed to have a native son possessed of these qualities. Gamble has produced a work that will serve you as a coffee-table volume, an armchair volume, or an extraordinary guidebook should you choose to take it with you on a building-watching expedition.

As I was concluding these thoughts the postman arrived and with him, a letter from HABS progenitor, Charles Peterson, FAIA, who still practices architecture in Philadelphia and maintains a busy side schedule lecturing and doing research. He wrote that he had recently returned from Italy where he was continuing his study of early cements and concrete. He also stated that HABS photonegative No. 100,000 had just been deposited in the Library of Congress.

Nicholas H. Holmes, Jr., FAIA
Mobile, Alabama

The Historic American Buildings Survey

The Historic American Buildings Survey (HABS) is an ongoing, federally sponsored effort to assemble a national archives of the building art in America. Established more than half a century ago by the National Park Service in collaboration with the Library of Congress and the American Institute of Architects, HABS was the federal government's first major step toward the identification and documentation of historic structures on a nationwide basis. Since that time, over 43,000 measured drawings, 100,000 photographs, and 52,000 pages of written historical and architectural data have been compiled and deposited in the Survey's permanent collection at the Library of Congress. These records cover nearly 19,000 structures and represent every facet of the building art in America, from the pre-Columbian pueblos of the Southwest to the skyscraper era and beyond. The collection embraces the fifty states and Puerto Rico, as well as the U.S. Virgin Islands and other American territories. Intrinsic architectural merit or meaningful association with significant aspects of the American past are the chief criteria for the selection of structures to be documented by HABS. The threatened disappearance of a notable building or building complex may also figure in the selection of sites, as well as in the determination of priorities.

In 1969 the documentary efforts of HABS were joined by those of the Historic American Engineering Record (HAER), a parallel documentary program that focuses upon structures illustrative of technological development. These may include early factories and industrial complexes, railroad stations, or bridges, to cite a few examples. HAER records, too, are on permanent deposit at the Library of Congress. (Appendix D lists Alabama properties thus far recorded by HAER.) In the late 1970s HABS and HAER were brought together as the National Architectural and Engineering Record (NAER), an administrative unit within the National Park Service.

Since HABS and HAER are continuing programs, researchers may wish to consult the central Washington office to learn about current projects. It should also be noted that both HABS and HAER have identified some properties simply by means of brief, standard inventory sheets (usually with a small photo attached). Such inventory sheets are not intended as full documentation, but they do serve to pinpoint properties that may be candidates for future, full-scale recording efforts. Inquiries about either current undertakings or these brief inventory sheets should be addressed to:

> The National Architectural and Engineering Record
> National Park Service
> Department of the Interior
> Washington, D.C. 20240

HABS records may be consulted at the Library of Congress, Prints and Photographs Reading Room. Copies of any material in the collection may be purchased at stated prices by writing to the Prints and Photographs Division, Library of Congress, Washington, D.C. 20540. When ordering such reproductions, one should identify buildings by their historic name (as indicated in the catalog), by the assigned survey number listed immediately after the name given for a structure, and by the building's location; for example: "U.S. Custom House and Old Post Office (AL-830), Mobile, Mobile County, Alabama."

Part One

Historic Architecture in Alabama
A Primer of Styles and Types, 1810–1930

Historic Architecture in Alabama

This essay introduces some of the main folk currents and formal stylistic trends emerging in Alabama architecture from the years shortly before statehood through the early decades of the twentieth century. General physical characteristics associated with a particular style or type are summarized at the end of each section. An asterisk (*) after the name of a structure indicates its inclusion in the Historic American Buildings Survey.

Stylistic labels seem to be a necessary evil of architectural history. Without them the business of sorting, relating, and making sense of hundreds of buildings can become unmanageable. Yet if we take the labels too seriously, we risk becoming oblivious to the more subtle patterns of architectural development. This is especially true when we leave the secure precincts of "high style"—that architecture which reflects the informed taste of the day—and begin to examine the images of folk architecture, images more firmly grounded in custom and practicality than in any abiding concern for fashion.

Both impulses, current fashion and folk custom, were vigorously at work in early Alabama architecture. Together, they produced buildings that often mingled the homespun with the sophisticated. Reflecting the society itself, urbanity and naïveté, bedrock pragmatism and overblown pretension, rudeness and refinement often existed side by side—at times in startling juxtaposition. Behind its elegant neoclassical façade even Gaineswood, the state's grandest pre–Civil War plantation house, represented a curious and somewhat erratic evolution from an open-hall log dwelling. In short, Alabama's was by and large a parochial architecture, with rustic quirks that would have been virtually unheard of in a more cosmopolitan setting.

Yet few would deny that it was these very idiosyncrasies, these architectural "colloquialisms," which enriched the language of building in early Alabama. At the same time they present a dilemma, since again and again they challenge preconceived categories of type and style. Instead of structures that can be neatly tagged as Federal or Greek Revival or Italianate, we repeatedly confront buildings that are neither quite one thing nor the other, structures most conveniently dismissed as "hybrid," "transitional," or "eclectic." Many buildings are too fine to be regarded as folk or vernacular in the strictest sense, yet neither can they be comfortably classified as high style.

It is one thing to label a self-consciously stylish house of the 1840s as Greek Revival, even if it lacks the reassuring columns and triangular pediment. Certain other elements—an entablature perhaps, or maybe just a chaste neoclassical correctness of detail and proportion—can place it squarely within a favorite category of nineteenth-century fashion. The same may be said for a turreted Queen Anne house of the 1890s, or a period English Tudor or Spanish Colonial mansion of the 1920s. In such structures—in their plan and massing

1. *Dr. William Murphey house, Morgan County. Just an abandoned farmhouse to the untrained eye, this 160-year-old dwelling near Decatur is the kind of unprepossessing structure often overlooked for the architectural and social history it represents. Actually, as the conjectural restoration drawing (opposite, top) shows, the house expresses with unusual clarity the architectural carry-over that occurred on the early Alabama frontier. Rural folkways were conservative and changed but slowly. Hence this house, though chronologically belonging to the 1800s, would have been perfectly at home in colonial Virginia, Maryland, or the Carolinas as a humble reflection of high-style Georgian tendencies, filtered down to the level of folk building.*

and detail—we recognize familiar national stylistic currents. They do not surprise or puzzle us. Rather, they conform to an anticipated pattern in the sequence of American high styles.

But what about a tumbledown farmhouse [1] having few if any earmarks of accepted "style," a building in whose lines we nevertheless sense some guiding architectural principle, some forgotten tradition that governed its basic form and layout? If such a structure cannot glibly be inserted into a generalized and preestablished category, neither can it be dismissed. Indeed, as an artifact of *social* history—hinting at the origins of local settlement, the methods of a local builder, or a certain peculiarity of lifestyle—"maverick" buildings of this nature may be more significant than the urbane but predictable embodiment in another structure of the latest architectural fashion from the East.

It follows, then, that the building art in early Alabama must be considered from multiple vantage points, with a sharp eye for the exceptional patterns as well as the anticipated ones. Improved commu-

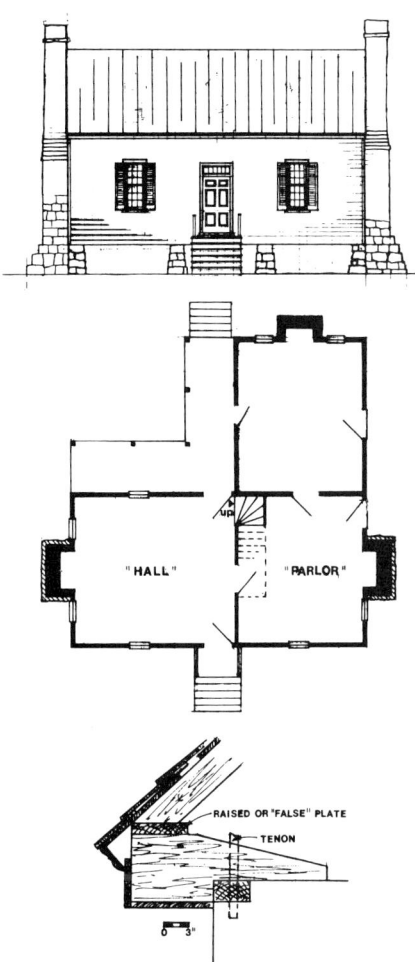

The hall-and-parlor plan (middle) of the Murphey house is likewise a colonial holdover, traceable all the way back to medieval England and seldom seen in Alabama. Bottom: Another rare feature linking the house to colonial antecedents is the raised or "false" plate, which receives the rafters of the roof at the eaves line. Even the rough stone pier-foundation, in lieu of a more refined one of brick or dressed ashlar, represents a reversion to very early practice in English North America. With the massive demographic shifts that began to depopulate some areas of rural Alabama in the 1960s, countless small yet highly significant buildings of this sort are disappearing—for the most part inadequately recorded. (Author's collection.)

nications and the ever more pervasive influence of popular magazines, mass-produced building components, and advances in building technology—not to mention the enhanced professional role of the architect himself—combined to dissolve regionalism and draw American architecture of all types into a common stream around the close of the last century. Except in the more isolated parts of the state, this was as true in Alabama as elsewhere. A new Alabama farmhouse of 1910 was likely to be nearly identical to its counterparts in Kansas or Nebraska. The trend was, of course, much more evident in urban areas. A wide-eaved, Craftsman-style bungalow erected in Birmingham or Montgomery at the beginning of World War I might as easily have been in Duluth or Portland. "The traveler through the South today," concluded *The Architectural Record* in July 1911, "finds less than he expected . . . of local color. . . . Upon the whole the modern Southern house is simply the modern American house."

Through most of the previous century, however, those structures in Alabama and the South that had mirrored national trends of taste were but a minority at one end of an architectural spectrum. At the other end of the same spectrum flourished, simultaneously, several distinct regional modes of building. In between lay numerous other structures influenced by both extremes—folk habit on the one hand, the latest academic fashion on the other. And imposing themselves on even the most ambitious building schemes were powerful social, economic, and geographical constraints that encouraged some tendencies while limiting others.

Foremost among these constraints, perhaps, was the reality of an overwhelmingly rural and semifrontier society, a fact again and again commented upon by travelers from Europe and the Northeast. To be sure, Mobile—Alabama's antebellum metropolis and only port—had by 1860 attained a population of nearly thirty thousand, a fair-sized city according to American standards of the day. But inland for hundreds of square miles, forest, farm, and plantation held sway. Montgomery [2], the state capital and next largest "city" after Mobile, counted fewer than 9,000 people, over half of whom were slaves. Next came the larger market towns—Huntsville, Selma, Tuscaloosa, Eufaula—none with a population above 4,000, of which, again, a large percentage were slaves. Most other Alabamians black and white, roughly 900,000 souls altogether, lived on farms and plantations concentrated along several major rivers: the Alabama and the Tennessee, the Tombigbee, the Black Warrior, the Coosa, the Tallapoosa, and the Chattahoochee. In the northcentral and extreme southern portions of the state, lonely stretches of rocky upland or dense "piney woods" remained a near wilderness. More than half the state's land area, in fact, still lay in the public domain according to the 1850 census.

2. *Montgomery in 1861, as seen from the cotton fields across the Alabama River. The 1851 State Capitol is at the left; the tall spire punctuating the horizon in the middle of this* Harper's Weekly *view is that of St. John's Episcopal Church, completed in 1855. (Alabama Department of Archives and History.)*

The "fine and promising young city of Montgomery," as Frederick Law Olmsted called the state capital, was in the middle of a thriving plantation district. Yet after climbing to the top of the statehouse dome in 1853, Olmsted wrote a friend that he was struck by a surrounding horizon where "the eye falls in every direction upon a dense forest, boundless as the sea, and producing the same solemn sensation of reverence for infinitude."

For the vast majority of Alabamians, then, theirs was a setting and a way of life that fostered conservatism in architecture, as in religion, education, and social attitudes. It was an ambience that preserved folkways and enforced a day-to-day isolation, even for many wealthy families, which our electronic age can scarcely comprehend.

Nevertheless, manufacturing and industrial development slowly gained momentum during the 1840s and 1850s, sparked to no small degree by rising southern nationalism. A South no longer dependent on northern-made goods was one of the arguments advanced for the industrialization of Alabama by Daniel Pratt, a transplanted New Hampshireman whose mill village of Prattville was modeled after similar communities in New England. [3] A smattering of other manufacturing villages, variously utilizing slave and "poor white" labor, were sprinkled across the state by the mid-1800s: among them the Bell Factory in Madison County—dating back to territorial days, Cypress Factory near Florence, Scottsville in Bibb County, Tallassee at the falls of the Tallapoosa, and Autaugaville near Montgomery. These enterprises, however, remained negligible within the total context of a plantation-geared economy.

By the 1850s there were also planing mills and sash, door, and blind factories in several major towns, as well as small foundries at

3. Right: *The Daniel Pratt Cotton Gin Factory at Prattville.* Below: *The Bell textile factory on the Flint River near Huntsville. Architecturally, both complexes mimed developments of a generation or two earlier in New England. The buildings seen here dated from the 1840s and 1850s although, in the case of the Bell factory, some form of manufacturing activity had been carried on at the site since before 1820. The Pratt factory complex still stands today, surrounded by later buildings.* (Archives of Bush Hog–Continental Gin, Inc.; James Record Collection, Huntsville–Madison County Public Library.)

Mobile, Selma, and Montgomery. In 1846 the Janney foundry at Montgomery produced, from north Alabama iron ore, the intricate metal column capitals for the new statehouse. Yet despite such local capabilities, the manufacturers' nameplates on the ornamental iron porches, fences, gates, and even mausoleums that became popular after 1850 were far more likely to bear the insignia of some eastern firm than that of a fledgling Alabama producer. [4]

Moreover, a shortage of both materials and skilled craftsmen for

4. *Cast-iron mausoleum (ca. 1860) of the Hope H. Slatter family, Magnolia Cemetery, Mobile. Illustrating the proliferation after 1850 of prefabricated cast-iron components for all sorts of uses, the Slatter mausoleum is one of at least three identical tombs of this type erected in Alabama. The iron gate and fence, too, followed a standard pattern. Despite growing sentiment for home industry during the years just before the Civil War, Alabamians continued to depend heavily upon northern suppliers for architectural components, just as for other articles of manufacture. Robert Wood and Company of Philadelphia cast the Slatter tomb. (HABS: Jack Boucher photo, 1974.)*

any building enterprise beyond the ordinary persisted outside the larger towns until the Civil War. In 1857 Leonidas Walthall still found it "more economical"—so he informed the architect of his new Italian-style residence near Marion—to order "blinds, sash, doors and hardware, such as nails, glass, locks, [and] weights for windows" from New York, rather than procuring them locally. Walthall's carpenters likewise came from the East and were delighted to find some of their erstwhile employer's neighbors eager to engage them for other house-building schemes.

Contributing to both the scarcity and expense of architecturally related goods and services was the belated development of Alabama's railway system, even when compared to that of neighboring states like Georgia and Tennessee. As early as 1834, the forty-mile Tuscumbia, Courtland, and Decatur Railroad had been constructed by the cotton planters of the Tennessee Valley to circumvent the treacherous Muscle Shoals on the Tennessee River. But the creation of a true rail network began in earnest only after 1850, following years of dilatory starts. During the decades following the Civil War, the lengthening rail lines spurred internal development, and it was no mere happenstance that a landlocked market town like Troy, in the agricultural hinterlands southeast of Montgomery, experienced its first real architectural flowering with the postwar approach of the railroad. At the same time the railroads, in breaking down the isolation between communities and disseminating new ideas and materials, hastened immeasurably the demise of architectural folkways in Alabama. The standardized architectural format represented by the early railroad buildings themselves—the locomotive shops at Huntsville and at Whistler near Mobile for instance—became, in this sense, a sort of metaphor for the general standardization of construction ideas and techniques which the railroads would help to foster. [5]

But if the development, architectural and otherwise, of some regions of Alabama was retarded by the lack of an adequate transportation system, the picture should not be overdrawn. The state as a whole saw a flurry of building activity between 1850 and 1861. During this period cotton production in the best agricultural regions of the state, such as the fertile Black Belt prairielands which extended across southcentral Alabama, nearly doubled. On the eve of the Civil War, Alabama ranked a hefty second in the Union in the number of cotton bales its fields yielded annually for the hungry mills of Lowell and Manchester. Mobile and the inland commercial centers reaped the rewards of this prosperity just as surely as did the country planter. It was cotton that built not only spacious plantation houses but also the mansions of the planter's merchant counterpart, the town-dwelling brokers who shipped the cotton to the outside world. Nondomestic building prospered, too, amid the favorable climate of the fifties as new courthouses, churches, and academies dotted the Alabama countryside.

Ultimately, however, the state's excessive dependence upon a single economic commodity contributed, no less certainly than did the destruction of slavery itself, to the woes of post–Civil War economic recovery. Naturally, these difficulties were reflected by a lapse in building enterprise. At the same time, the surprisingly vigorous construction activity in Reconstruction-era Eufaula and Selma suggests that some private fortunes not only weathered the hard times but prospered as postwar cotton prices soared. Still, it was not until the real estate and industrial boom of the 1880s, centering in the miner-

5. *Machine shops of the Mobile and Ohio Railroad at Whistler, near Mobile, from an 1856 sketch by William M. Merrick. A clerestoried roof, and walls pierced all round by open arches, were standard features of mid-nineteenth-century train sheds and foundry buildings. As Alabama industry and rail transportation slowly developed after 1850, similar structures—used variously as casting sheds, depots, and foundries—appeared elsewhere, notably at Mobile, Montgomery, Selma, and Huntsville, and later in the hilly mineral region of the northeastern part of the state. (Prints Division, New York Public Library.)*

al region about the infant towns of Birmingham and Anniston, that the overall pace of building in the state exceeded its antebellum high.

Tied to the antebellum cotton economy was yet another factor, normally overlooked, which can hardly have failed to affect the course and nature of early Alabama architecture. This was the sheer mobility of the population, the migratory habits not just of the slaveless farmer and day laborer but of the agricultural "gentry" as well. The romantic image of plantation life may be one of stability and rootedness. But in the Old Southwest a cotton planter was an agrarian capitalist in a very real sense—ever looking to the main chance by a prudent investment in land and slaves, as well as by a surprising disposition to move on whenever brighter prospects beckoned, if not to Mississippi or Texas, then to better lands close at hand. Turner Saunders occupied his white-pillared Tennessee Valley plantation house less than ten years before emigrating, for the fourth time since leaving his Virginia birthplace, to the newer cottonlands of Mississippi. That Saunders forsook a columned brick mansion was exceptional. Most planters left behind considerably less impressive abodes.

It could be argued that the heightened architectural activity of the 1850s signified not just prosperity but a general coalescence, the settling-in of a restless and shifting population. This was foreshadowed in 1846 by the permanent fixing of the state capital at Montgomery, after two previous moves in a mere twenty years. Nevertheless, in 1851 an Episcopal clergyman serving the rich cotton-growing region about Livingston could still observe of his genteel flock that there were "very few families now residing in the county of whom it would be safe to assert they will be here this time next year." Little wonder, then, that a surprising number of Alabama's agrarian upper class long contented themselves with rustic domiciles: log houses in most cases, though these might bear such lyrical names as Hill of Howth or Bentwood Park.

The scarcity of professional architectural talent in such a milieu should come as no surprise. Yet in men like Hiram Higgins of Athens and Alexander J. Bragg of Camden, or George Steele of Huntsville, Alabama produced local artisan-designers of no mean accomplishment. There was also the free black carpenter and bridge-builder Horace King, of Girard (now Phenix City), whose exceptional skill earned him a statewide reputation and involved him in the construction of the second Montgomery statehouse, in 1850–51. Finally, there was the occasional gifted amateur like General Nathan Bryan Whitfield, owner and architect of Gaineswood at Demopolis, and a figure who perhaps comes as close as any in Alabama to realizing the *beau ideal* of the southern planter as a Renaissance man.

Much of the talent behind the state's best high-style buildings was, nonetheless, furnished by men who were either nonresident or remained only briefly in Alabama. From 1827 to about 1833, the state enjoyed the services of the English-born architect William Nichols, whose peripatetic career took him from his native city of Bath, first to North Carolina, then to Alabama, and finally on to Mississippi. During the flush times of the mid-1830s, Mobile was fleetingly able to draw upon the New York–honed skills of James Gallier and the brothers Charles and James Dakin, preeminent Greek Revivalists of the Old South. In Montgomery, Stephen D. Button designed the elegant but ill-fated 1846 statehouse and at least one distinguished private mansion before returning east to Philadelphia.

Meanwhile, the pool of locally available architectural expertise remained small. Time and again, nineteenth-century Alabamians turned to out-of-state architects for their grandest schemes: to Samuel Sloan and his partner John Stewart of Philadelphia; to Richard Upjohn and later his son, Richard M. Upjohn, of New York; to Walter T. Downing and Lorenzo B. Wheeler of Atlanta; to Henry Wolters of Louisville and James Freret of New Orleans. Not until the turn of the century did a broadly influential corps of resident professional architects emerge in such figures as William Leslie Welton, William T. Warren, and Harry B. Wheelock of Birmingham; Rudolph Benz, C. L. Hutchisson, and George B. Rogers of Mobile; Frank Lockwood of Montgomery; and Edgar Love of Huntsville.

Thus, until after the Civil War, the evolution of identifiable styles and types in Alabama architecture must be considered largely in terms of the proverbial country builder: frequently itinerant, and all too often nameless. He was a craftsman strongly influenced by his own particular apprenticeship tradition which, in the early 1800s, usually reached back to the South Atlantic seaboard. He was a man for whom "fashion" as such was largely a matter of applying decorative elements gleaned and modified from the pages of available carpenter's handbooks onto the regional forms with which he and his client were comfortable.

The impact of the carpenter's handbook on nineteenth-century southern architecture has yet to be adequately assessed. Clearly, it was considerable. Published in Boston and Hartford, Philadelphia and New York, such handbooks accompanied the westward advance of the nation. Initially, their content was limited in great part to technical matters of structure and joinery. Engraved plates or woodcuts presented one rendition or another of the classical orders: at first Roman; then, especially after 1830, Grecian. Other illustrations showed molding designs, cornices, mantelpieces, door and window treatments, stairways, and other elements. Repeatedly in Alabama one encounters ornamental doorways ("frontispieces" the handbooks called them), window surrounds, plaster ceiling medallions, and mantelpieces based on designs published in the pages of these manuals. [6]

In the earlier books, full elevation drawings and floorplans were few and generally geared to the most formal of structures—prompting builder and client alike to rely upon their own stock of "remembered forms." Yet where technical ability, sufficient means, and personal inclination allowed, these published elevations and plans could and did serve, *in toto,* as models of the latest high style. A case in point was the Huntsville mansion built for ex-Governor Thomas Bibb in the mid-1830s. [7] The stately Greek Revival façade was skillfully adapted, in its entirety, from the pages of Chester Hills' *The Builder's Guide,* published in Hartford, Connecticut, in 1834. Besides Hills, there were also the perennially popular handbooks of Asher Benjamin and Minard Lafever, of Owen Biddle, John Haviland, and Edward Shaw—men who themselves had evolved from carpenters into "stylists" (borrowing heavily from each other in their interpretations, as well as from the latest developments across the Atlantic). They were builders who wrote for fellow builders of similar background and training.

Beginning in the 1840s, the works of still other men—Andrew Jackson Downing, Samuel Sloan, Gervase Wheeler, Calvert Vaux, Thomas U. Walter—joined later editions of the older handbooks. More importantly, the nature itself of these books began to change. Technological advances in printing and engraving enabled their authors to present ever more complete and varied sets of plans, along with beguiling illustrations of a wide variety of dwellings, public buildings, schools, and churches. Following the lead most notably

6. Above: *Doorway of the Cowan-Ramser house, Eufaula, based on Plate 28 (right) from Asher Benjamin's* Practice of Architecture *(1833).*

of Downing, architectural publications became more romantic and philosophical in tone, including essays on the aesthetic and even the moral virtues of this or that particular style, or the merits of one treatment over and against another. Floorplans, elevations, narrative explanations—sometimes even cost estimates—were presented for dwellings exotically labeled as "rural Gothic" or "Tuscan" or "Italian" or simply "bracketed." From New York State, the utopian reformer Orson Squire Fowler added his own theories to the growing tide of architectural eclecticism as he argued the superiority of the octagon-shaped dwelling in his 1848 treatise, *A Home for All.*

If most Alabamians viewed Yankee ideas about social reform with a suspicion that increasingly bordered on paranoia, they were certainly not impervious to new turns of fashion. And under the impact

7. Right: *Front elevation of the Governor Thomas Bibb house, Huntsville, derived from a pair of plates* (below) *published in* The Builder's Guide *(1834) by Chester Hills. Boasting one of the first thoroughgoing Greek Revival domestic façades in the state, the Bibb house was almost certainly designed by local architect-builder George Steele. Elements from the "Doric house" at lower left and the "Ionic house" at lower right were skillfully combined and modified to produce the desired effect. Onto the end-chimneyed arrangement of the Doric house was grafted an Ionic front. The shafts of the columns, however, remained unfluted, in contrast to Hills's schemes. The corner antae flanking the portico were likewise given a molded base—something else missing in the Hills drawings. At the same time, the entire façade was made more monumental by extending the steps the full width of the portico, and by surrounding the doorway with a classical architrave. Subtly, the scale of the house was also enlarged. Thus did the best of Alabama's early builders, starting from standard published formulae, develop their own creative departures in design.* (HABS: *W. R. Van Valkenburgh, delineator, 1934.*)

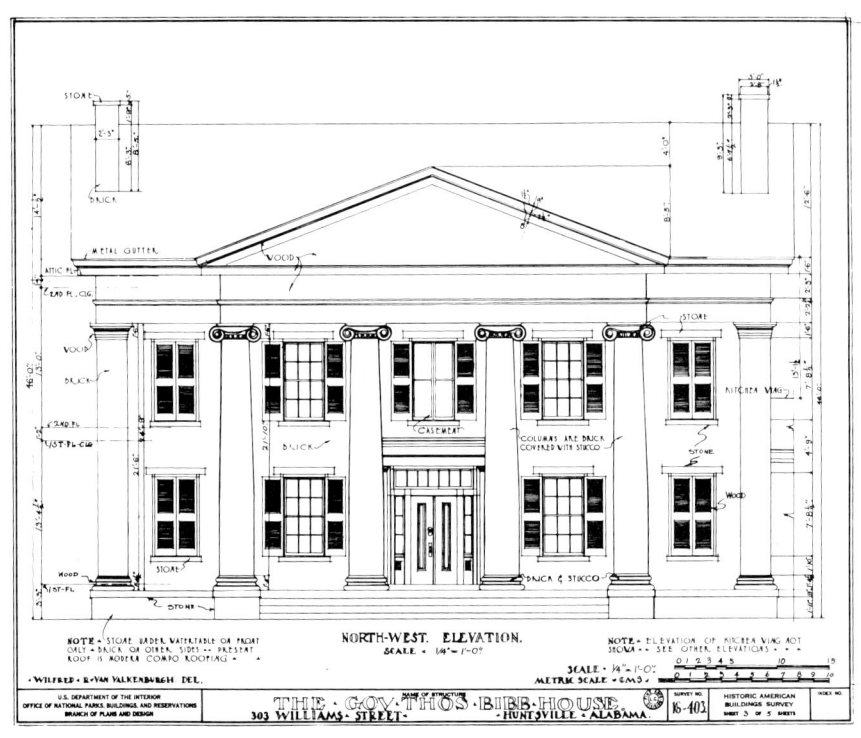

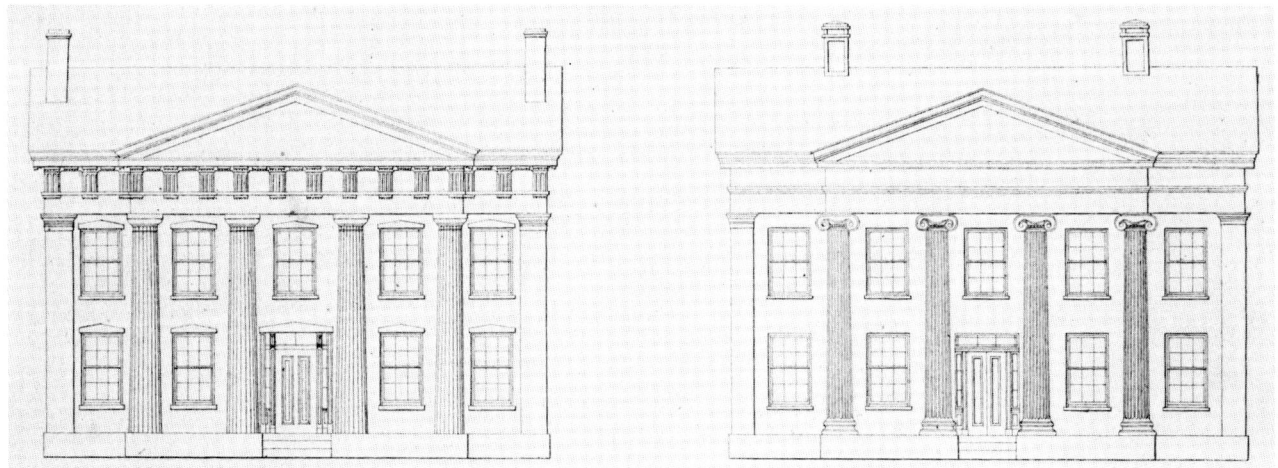

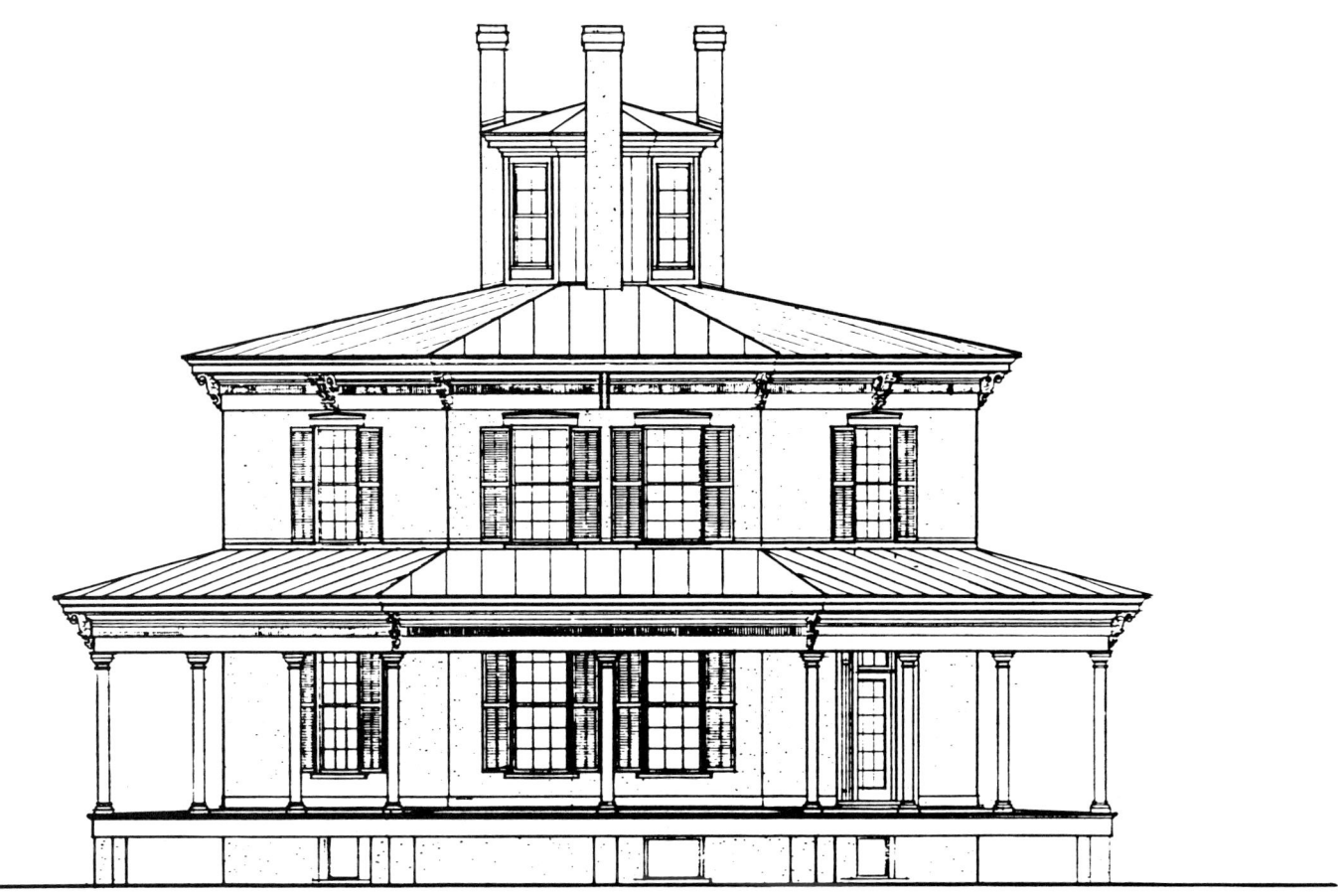

FRONT [WEST] ELEVATION
SCALE : 1/4"=1'0"

8. Benjamin F. Petty house, Clayton, ca. 1860. One of two octagonal dwellings known to have been built in Alabama. (Elevation drawing courtesy Waid, Holmes & Associates, Inc.)

of these fresh ideas about building, arriving in tandem with the advent of mass-produced structural and decorative elements such as jigsaw work and cast iron, the state's architecture began to change. Slowly, almost imperceptibly at first, it began to shift away from both vernacular forms and the prevalent neoclassicism—first in the larger towns, then in the smaller and more out-of-the-way communities. By 1859, Hiram Higgins was advertising in the Limestone County *Democrat* his readiness to furnish "original or copied designs" in "all the styles now in use, such as Grecian, Italian, Gothic, Tudor, Elizabethan, Oriental, and Castilated [*sic*]." He might also have added "octagonal," since it was very likely Higgins who about this time designed for his fellow townsman, General James Lane of Athens, one of the two eight-sided houses known to have been built in antebellum Alabama. (The Lane house is gone, but Alabama's second octagonal domicile, the Petty house at Clayton [8], still stands.)

As eclecticism nudged neoclassicism aside, Alabama builders were simultaneously drawn bit by bit away from folk idiom and into the national architectural mainstream. It would be a process of decades, but the long twilight of locally rooted, locally nourished architectural patterns had begun. The forms and proportions passed down through generations from carpenter to apprentice, the layouts so ingrained by custom and repeated usage as to be taken for granted, would give way more and more—even in small structures—to norms imposed from the outside, to the shifting styles and fashions now abounding on the printed page and ever more easily within reach of the average purse. Advancing technology had rendered unnecessary the folk memory that was at the heart of distinctive vernacular building traditions. In Alabama architecture, this was perhaps the signal event of the late nineteenth century.

Both folkways and regional nuances in architecture grew largely out of common-sense responses to everyday needs. In early nineteenth-century Alabama this was nowhere better illustrated than in building for the climate. It was a climate that further encouraged the expansive, outdoor existence for which southerners of all classes had been noted since colonial days. In fact, the Deep South approach to housebuilding, with an eye to the summer heat instead of the winter cold, was diametrically opposite that found in the Northeast and the upper Midwest. One immediately thinks of the open hall through the middle of humble country dwellings or, in finer houses, of tall floor-length windows and ceilings that could reach heights of eighteen feet or so. And it has become a cliché that the long sultry summers produced the sweeping galleries that were in effect outdoor living rooms. At their grandest, these turned into monumental colonnades or lacy, cast iron verandas, vine-covered and deeply shaded—like those which once lined Mobile's Government Street. [9]

The quest for maximum ventilation forced doors to be ever wider: wide enough in some cases to accommodate as many as three or four leaves, as at the Benjamin Fitzpatrick house* in Elmore County or the Hawthorn house* at Pine Apple. [10] When folded back, these doors allowed hall and veranda to become one single, flowing space. The high, breezy Alabama hallway itself, extending through the house and sometimes crisscrossed midway by another corridor, could reach cavernous proportions. The hall at the Robert Tait house* near Camden was 78 feet long, with a 60-foot transverse corridor. At Ihagee in Russell County, axial hallways extended 50 feet in one direction, 100 in the other, through a sprawling, white, one-story plantation house. Surely among the most unusual solutions to the problem of ventilation was that to be found at Sunnyside, near Talladega. Its raised-cottage form was rare enough in the Appalachian

9. Right, *porch at 154 St. Louis Street, Mobile, recorded by* HABS *in 1934, and* below, *view along Mobile's Government Street during the 1890s. Cast-iron verandas were a happy response, achieved through advancing technology in iron manufacture, to the climatic needs of the Gulf coast. Between 1850 and 1880 such verandas—together with complementary fences, hitching posts, benches, and fountains—proliferated along the residential streets of Alabama's port city. Today, far the greater number have been destroyed.* (HABS: *John J. Carey, delineator; Library of Congress: Detroit Collection.*)

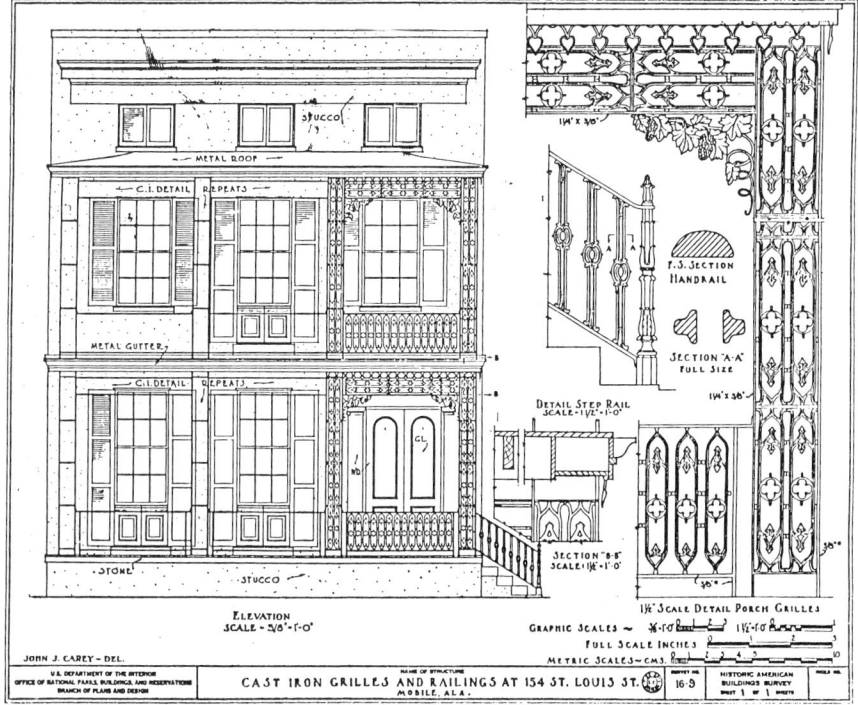

10. Warm-weather windows and doors. Above left: Triple-hung, floor-length windows at Briarwood, now demolished, in Mobile. Note the fixed louvers, which shielded the upper third of the windows from direct sunlight. Hinged louvered blinds also covered the lower portion of the windows, though these had disappeared by the time a HABS crew made this photograph in 1937. Above right: Triple-leaf front door with flanking sash windows at the Joseph Hawthorn house, Pine Apple. When this door and a corresponding one at the rear of the hall were opened, the wide central passage became, in effect, a dogtrot-like breezeway. (HABS: E. W. Russell photo, 1937; HABS: Alex Bush photo, 1937.)

valleys of northeastern Alabama; even more so was a hallway that branched at the rear to create an unusual, loggia-like back hall enclosed winter and summer only by slatted jalousies, in the West Indian manner.

The search for effective ways to cope with the heat also shaped the external form of Alabama houses. It explains the popularity of one-room deep, L- and T-shaped plans, since these permitted maximum outside exposure for each room. It may also account for the H- and U-shaped layouts of residences like Umbria* near Greensboro, Norwood* near Faunsdale, or the Carr house* at Tuskegee. [11] Such arrangements assured that virtually every main room received a cross breeze. And of course a separate kitchen—both as a time-honored concession to warm weather and as a precaution against fire—was standard. Even in the early 1900s when new houses, especially in the towns, no longer displayed any strikingly regional characteristics, the old southern practice of separating the kitchen from the main body of the house had not yet died away entirely. Thus at the 1902 Branch house in Livingston, a narrow open breezeway still isolated the kitchen from the dining room and butler's pantry.

The interplay of climate and custom, isolation and agrarianism, explains much about early Alabama architecture, particularly away from the few towns of any size. It explains why colloquial accents lingered so long in so many buildings. And it offers a clue as to why polite architecture—the high fashion imported from the East—often expressed itself the way it did, producing in more than one remote plantation house an odd mingling of grand scale and crude detail, or

11. *Umbria, Hale County. Its U-shaped plan, forming a rear courtyard, allowed each room to have cross ventilation. Originally, a central hall ran from the front porch to the rear gallery. Umbria burned in 1973. (HABS: J. L. Gatling, Jr., delineator, 1936.)*

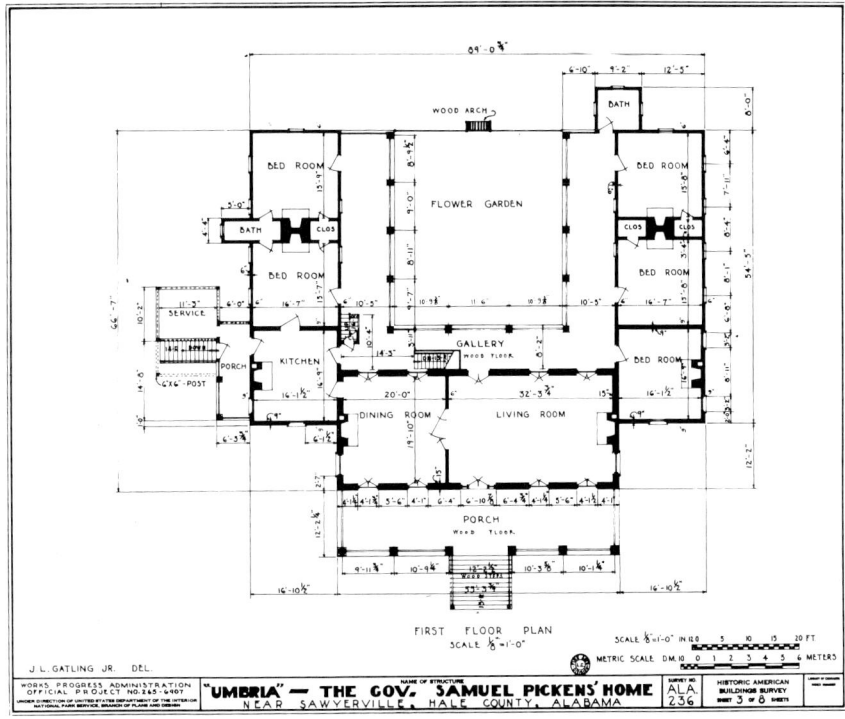

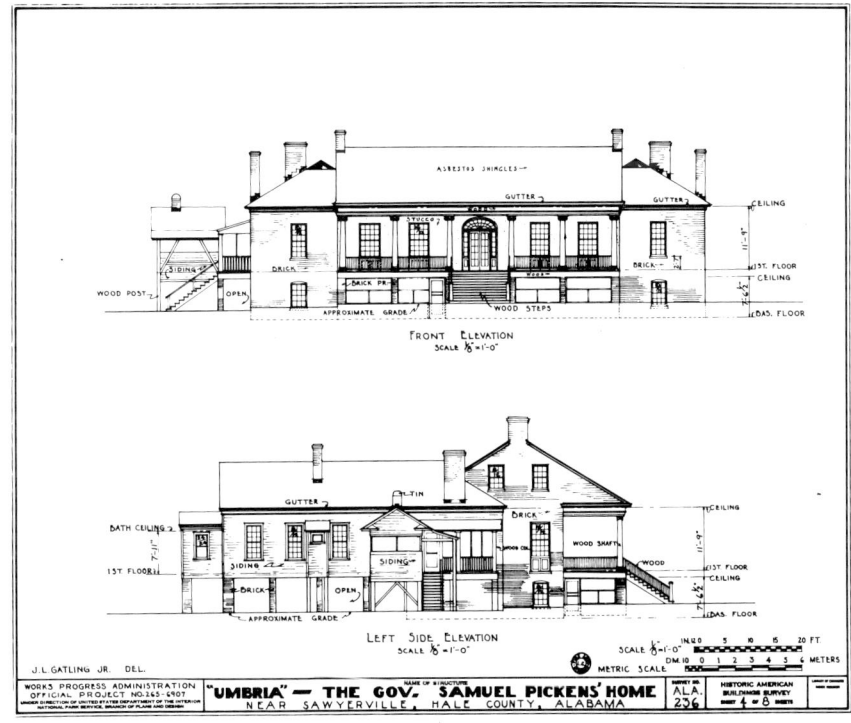

12. *Retardataire paneled overmantel in the Lewis F. Dowdell house, Tuskegee.* (HABS: W. N. Manning photo, 1935.)

features that were curiously old-fashioned like the belated, Georgian-type paneled overmantel in one Tuskegee house of the 1840s. [12]

It also explains why a series of neat categories cannot pretend to comprehend all the variations of early Alabama architecture. Instead, one must constantly balance the relationship between successive waves of fashion and the weight of folk tradition, acknowledging at the same time the role played by shifting economic and social conditions. All became ingredients in the architectural personality of any given locale. The classifications which follow should be considered, then, not as hard-and-fast pigeonholes, but rather as a general roadmap to assist in a more detailed exploration of the terrain. Nor is it pretended that even all folk themes or high-style currents are treated, but only the stronger or more remarkable.

As pointed out earlier, mutations between what are now popularly regarded as distinctive high styles were at least as common as "pure" examples in Alabama. Federal consorted with Greek Revival, which in turn consorted with Gothic Revival or Italianate, and so on. Later, as Victorian pluralism peaked in the 1880s and early 1890s, a single building might display such a hodgepodge of eclectic detail as to defy classification altogether. Here and there occurred glimmerings of those late Victorian subcurrents for which architectural historians of our own day have coined such labels as "stick style" and "shingle style." But these movements, palpable enough at the eastern fountainheads of architectural fashion, never formulated themselves with any real clarity in Alabama.

The architectural picture in the state becomes somewhat less muddled after the end of the century, as national trends themselves shifted back to a more sedate and academically oriented vocabulary, especially for public buildings. About the same time came the experimentalism, on the national scene, of men like Frank Lloyd Wright and others with whom we associate the beginnings of contemporary attitudes in American architecture. These, too, left their imprint in early 1900s Alabama, alongside swansong expressions of dying Victorian taste.

Twentieth-century stylistic developments, however, have here been passed over very lightly. They deserve eventual appraisal in their own right. But more crucial at the moment is a better understanding of the state's earliest architecture, representing a time before the art of building itself passed from an indigenous and largely community-focused activity to one that reflected the knitting together of nation, state, and region. Hence one finds in the following pages what may otherwise seem to be an inordinately heavy accent upon some of the idiosyncratic architectural strains that figured through the Civil War period, and sometimes well beyond. At least one of these, the Tidewater-type cottage, is touched upon as a distinctive genre in Alabama for the first time ever.

The dates given for a particular style apply only to Alabama. Inherited folk forms obviously went back much further in the older states, while fashionable modes such as the Italianate and the Gothic Revival turned up in Alabama only after the usual time lag between their emergence on the East Coast and their advance to the American hinterlands. Always, of course, there was considerable chronological overlap both within a particular place and from region to region, or even from town to town. One locale—more in touch with the outside world, more prosperous, or sometimes simply influenced by the proclivities of a certain builder—turned to a new fashion, while another community clung placidly to an older one. And so it went. Thus, one can never assume that a given style had ended absolutely everywhere by a given date. Nor can it be assumed, conversely, that because a structure exhibits certain physical characteristics and details, it must always date from this or that time period. If this may be generally true, it is also a line of reasoning that can prove deceptive, especially before 1880, and particularly in a rural state. Styles waxed and waned, endured and gave way, and varied in strength from place to place. Whiffs of a departed fashion might remain in a single, out-of-the-way place decades after it had passed from popular favor elsewhere. And always, of course, there was the incalculable factor of human whimsy. With these thoughts in mind, then, let us briefly examine some of the more pronounced drifts of Alabama architecture over the past hundred and fifty years.

Folk Forms

Vernacular or folk architecture might well be called the architecture of habit. It is the simplest, most straightforward way of building, the result of pragmatism and familiarity, of a custom-rooted and ofttimes unconscious preference for certain basic forms and layouts—even on occasion for certain materials and details—that exist independently of passing taste. In the main, it is a salient and underlying *form,* or a pronounced and constant *feature,* that distinguishes one folk building-type from another, as well as from more sophisticated and ambitious architectural ventures. Overlaying such forms and features may be the ornamental trappings of this or that academic style, but stolidly underneath, the primary characteristics remain.

Some scholars prefer to restrict the use of the terms "folk" and "vernacular" to the most rudimentary kinds of buildings: to log or very simple frame habitations; to barns and other utilitarian structures free from any polite refinements. But in early Alabama architecture, certain domestic forms were so clearly regional and folk-rooted, no matter what costume of high style they happened to have temporarily borrowed, that a broader view may be justified.

At the same time, individual examples of a particular form might boast surprising architectural refinement: a classically enframed doorway, a fanlight window, a richly worked cornice, jigsaw-cut brackets, or even a pedimented Greek Revival–style porch. Through such surface detail, such cosmetic dressing, buildings that otherwise might have been run-of-the-mill acquired in their owner's eyes a degree of *chic.* But the form beneath betrayed a more everyday origin, nourished by custom and by need more than by the urge to be fashionable and up-to-date. This is not to say that the overall form, too, was never influenced in its evolution by architecture of a higher order. For instance, Georgian ideas of balance and proportion had clearly worked their influence upon the simple, story-and-a-half cottages transplanted from the Atlantic seaboard to the Tennessee Valley of northern Alabama (see section on the Tidewater-type cottage). Yet whatever fashionable airs a particular folk form might assume, these were incidental to its virtue as a practical and well-tried local building solution.

With the possible exception of the Creole cottage, which some contend was a largely indigenous development of the Gulf Coast, most of the folk house-types appearing in early nineteenth-century Alabama came from the older states along the Atlantic—from Georgia and the Carolinas, Virginia and Maryland—or were introduced from Tennessee and Kentucky to the north. Some of these dwelling-types were concentrated in a single area of the state, or occurred only here and there. Others—notably the basic log or frame "dogtrot" house—were a common feature of the rural landscape almost everywhere. But rising technology eventually spelled the doom of all. By

1860 machine-made materials and advances like the lightweight balloon-type house frame, as well as a growing corpus of easily available alternative designs, were rapidly gaining ascendency in many areas, enticing builder and client alike away from the old vernacular ways. Under such circumstances, latecoming folk forms, like those that might otherwise have been introduced by the German farmers who settled about Cullman during the 1870s and 1880s, made little impact. The rising tide of standardization was too strong.

Counting variations on a few basic themes, Alabama's folk houses might be classified almost endlessly into subtypes. Features normally associated with one type were not infrequently grafted onto the form of another. Thus, while the open hall identifies the basic dogtrot house of rural Alabama, an open hall could also turn up in a Creole cottage. Yet certain fundamental house-types were fairly constant and predictable and were so characteristic of nineteenth-century Alabama as to warrant being singled out. Five of these are discussed below.

The Basic Dogtrot House
(statewide; nineteenth to early twentieth centuries)

As its sobriquet might suggest, the open-passage dogtrot house was the dwelling of the common man in antebellum Alabama. [13, 14] It was not, however, necessarily *limited* to the common man. Numerous antebellum travel accounts attest to the fact that the dogtrot was a familiar sight even in the richest plantation districts—if not as an abode for the planter and his family, then as quarters for his slaves. In some isolated hill districts of northern Alabama, and in the coastal pinelands, the dogtrot house remained the prevalent dwelling stock as late as World War I.

The open-ended central passage—the dogtrot itself—answered superbly as a breeze-swept, yet sheltered and semiprivate outdoor living and working space for the hot summer months. "Various kinds of climbing plants and flowers are trained to cluster about either end of these passages," observed Philip Gosse, an English-born schoolteacher living in the raw new Black Belt planter community of Pleasant Hill in 1838, "and by their wild and luxuriant beauty take away the sordidness which the rude character of the dwellings might otherwise present." The dogtrot formula was also a logical means of enlarging a one-room log cabin. To one side of the original log room or "pen," another was erected. The space between—some ten or twelve feet—was then roofed over and floored to become the breezeway, or dogtrot passage. Countless open-hall houses evolved in just this manner. [15]

13. Dogtrot house near Fatima, Wilcox County, ca. 1910. In southern Alabama round pine logs were frequently used instead of the squared hardwood logs preferred in the northern part of the state. (Geological Survey of Alabama.)

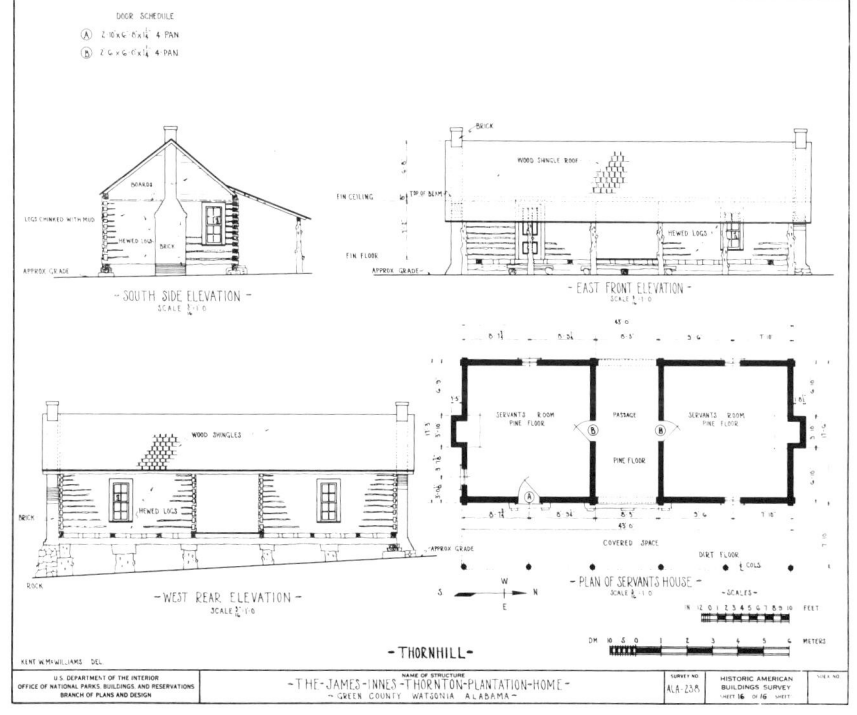

14. Dogtrot servants' quarters, Thornhill, Forkland vicinity. The paneled door and four-over-four sash windows were late-nineteenth-century improvements. (HABS: Kent W. McWilliams, delineator, 1936.)

15. *Members of a rural Alabama family pose before their dogtrot house about 1890. Dwellings of this description, ofttimes neatly whitewashed and with a porch across the front, still dotted the Alabama countryside at the end of the last century. Only a handful remain today. The awkward juncture of the wood-shingled roof directly over the dogtrot passage indicates that this house, like many other dogtrot dwellings, started out as a one-room cabin, to which another log room, separated from the earlier one by an open passage, was eventually added. (Alabama Department of Archives and History.)*

Some theories have placed the origin of the basic dogtrot house on the post-Revolutionary Kentucky and Tennessee frontier, though open-hall log houses were also known as far east as the upper Carolina Piedmont. Without question, it was a dwelling-type widely familiar to the first Anglo-American settlers of Alabama. Normally just a story or a story-and-a-half high, the dogtrot also became, on occasion, a full two-storied structure. Two-story or double dogtrots were, indeed, a badge of affluence on the frontier, sometimes being furnished with sideboards, carpets, and silver plate which the builder had brought from a family home in one of the older states. Probably the best preserved of the few two-story dogtrots standing today in Alabama is the John Looney house near Ashville. [16]

Numbers of log dogtrots were weatherboarded over at an early date, the passage itself often being closed at either end by wide double doors. In fact, the care with which logs were frequently squared and notched at the corners suggests that many dogtrots were intended from the beginning to be "improved" as more permanent residences, if only by being fitted up with glass windows and whitewashed inside and out. Occasionally the dogtrot evolved into a rela-

16. *John Looney house, St. Clair County, ca. 1820. (Author's collection.)*

tively sophisticated dwelling, not only covered over with clapboard, but replete with Federal or Greek Revival-style trim, as for example in the Robert Jenkins house* [17] near Alpine, or the now-ruinous Bird house in Lawrence County, which eventually acquired plaster interior walls, chair-rails, a balustraded stair, and simple Adamesque mantelpieces.

Throughout central and southern Alabama, not just log but frame dogtrot houses were also built. One rare surviving early example is the William Lowndes Yancey house. [18] Originally located on the Yancey plantation near Mount Meigs, this structure was moved to Montgomery's North Hull Street Historic District in 1979. In far southeastern Alabama, gingerbread-trimmed frame dogtrots continued to be erected by homesteading settlers of the Wiregrass region around Geneva even after 1900.

Summary Characteristics

- Normally, two main rooms about 18–20 feet square flanking a wide, open-ended central hall; additions ordinarily took the form of

17. An "improved" dogtrot: the Robert Jenkins house (ca. 1835), Talladega County. Right: *The weatherboarding that sheaths the exterior conceals a pair of story-and-a-half log rooms, originally separated by an open hall. The house probably assumed its present appearance in the 1840s. Countless other "frame" houses evolved in the same way from humble log beginnings. Seldom, however, did they acquire such an extra bit of refinement as the small Tuscan-order portico that fronts the Jenkins house.* Below: *Hallway of the Jenkins house—the former open-ended dogtrot. Note the smooth flush boarding and paneled dado that hide the earlier log walls; also, the wooden bar across the wide double doors at the rear of the hall.* (HABS: *E. W. Russell photos, 1937.*)

18. Frame dogtrot formerly on the William Lowndes Yancey plantation, Montgomery County. (Author's collection.)

a semidetached ell, or of shed rooms to the rear, along with front and back porches.
- Exterior chimneys at each gable end.
- Usually 1 to 1½ stories (if the latter, then an enclosed or "box" stair in one or both main rooms, or more rarely in the passage, leading to the loft space or second story); occasionally two full stories.

The I House with Sheds
(statewide, especially central and southern Alabama; early to middle nineteenth century)

The "I" house, so named by folk architectural specialist Fred Kniffen in the 1930s, was perhaps the most common form of two-story house in English North America. Tall and narrow in profile, it was inevitably two rooms high and one room deep. A gable or more rarely a hipped roof covered the house and, typically, was terminated at one or both ends by a chimney. Among the more distinctive house-types brought to Alabama by settlers from Georgia and the Carolinas was a variant on the basic I form: a variant in which the narrow two-story core is skirted front and rear by one-story shed extensions, or lean-tos.

Distant ancestors can be found in seventeenth-century English vernacular architecture, though British precedent shows the shed extension (likewise called the outshot) always behind, or to the side. In colonial North America, a sophisticated, academicized version of this dwelling-type is the Ludwell-Paradise house at Williamsburg—at first glance a conventional exercise in formal Georgian architecture, but with a giveaway outshot across the rear.

By the time the two-story-with-shed configuration came to Alabama, whatever dim English or colonial antecedents it might have had were long forgotten. The form itself had been altered in the southern back country to suit new conditions and needs, and the rear lean-to had become balanced by a corresponding one at the front. The latter could be a porch, open all the way across; then again, it might be terminated at one or both ends with a small room—sometimes known as the "prophet's chamber" since it provided ready accommodation for the itinerant preacher and other travelers. While generally thought of as a rustic and unpretentious type of habitation (numbers of Alabama examples even had an open dogtrot hall through the middle), the I house with sheds could also attain, from time to time, a surprising degree of stylistic aplomb.

HABS photographers of the 1930s documented several Alabama examples: the Kelly house* near Weaver in Calhoun County; the two Bankhead houses* in Lamar County [19]; the Ferrell house* in Monroe County; the Moses Wheat house* near Opelika, with its especially fine, grained woodwork; and the Bland-Chesnut house* not far from Orrville in Dallas County. Other excellent examples like the Tuck house in Greene County and the Price house near Sulligent have never been formally recorded.

Demonstrating the refinement of which the form was susceptible is the Bland-Chesnut house, with its denticulated entablature as well as the paneled and molded pier-supports of its front porch. [20] The Isaac Wellington Sadler house near Bessemer, fortunately preserved as a house museum, represents a more primitive and far more typical version of the I house with sheds, though it, too, was not without its wainscoted parlor. [21] Still, this parlor opened onto an unenclosed breezeway borrowed from the more humble dogtrot house, an arrangement clearly indicating how even Alabamians of relative affluence oftentimes preferred the familiar and the practical over what was simply the more "elegant."

Summary Characteristics

- End profile composed of a two-story, one-room deep central section with at least one shed-extension front or rear, variously disposed as rooms and/or porches.

19. James Greer Bankhead house—Forest Home—at Sulligent. Built about 1850 for the great-grandfather of actress Tallulah Bankhead. (HABS: Alex Bush photo, 1936.)

20. Bland-Chesnut house, Dallas County, ca. 1840. (HABS: W. N. Manning photo, 1934.)

- End chimneys, often with smaller chimneys serving chambers of lean-to extensions.
- A core plan varying from axial with central hall (or open through-passage) to simpler one- or two-room arrangements.

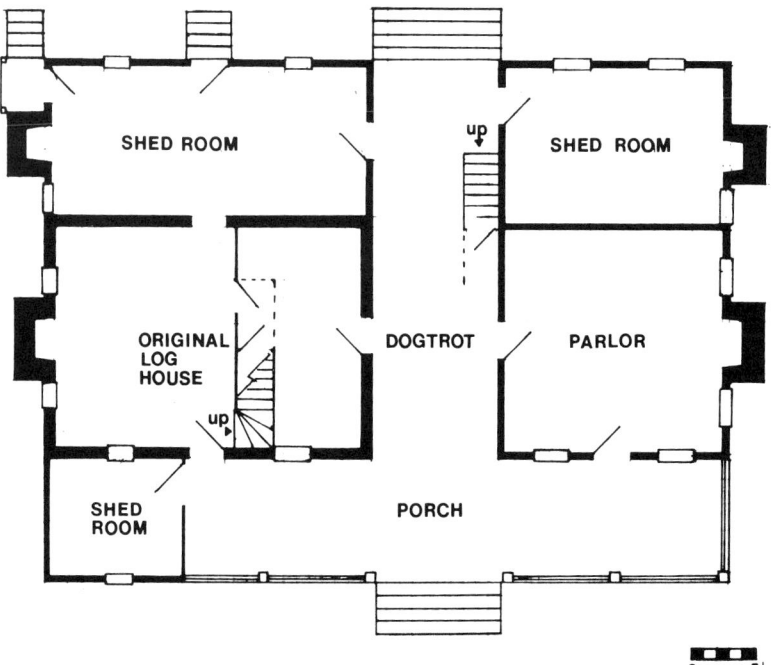

21. Above: *Sadler house, Bessemer vicinity.* Right: *The floorplan of the Sadler house illustrates the casual way in which an "I" house with characteristic shed rooms might develop. Buried inside the house as it stands today is a story-and-a-half log nucleus, denoted in the plan by its thicker walls. To this core was added, about 1840, a corresponding frame section across an open hall borrowed from the dogtrot tradition. Then low shed rooms were built—one at the front and two across the rear. A long, balustraded porch abutting the front shed room completed the familiar profile. (Author's collection.)*

The Tidewater-type Cottage
(Tennessee Valley and central Alabama; early nineteenth century)

Ironically enough, the ancestor of this little-known and largely unappreciated Alabama dwelling-type is one of the most widely admired and imitated of all early American houses: the end-chimneyed, story-and-a-half, gable-roofed cottage of colonial Maryland and Virginia. To the tourist, the form is familiar as that of the tidy frame dwellings which line Duke of Gloucester Street in Williamsburg. Actually, the type goes back much earlier, to such seventeenth-century antecedents as the famous Adam Thoroughgood house (ca. 1650) near Norfolk, and similar dwellings known to have existed elsewhere in the Chesapeake Bay region. These, in turn, derived from contemporary English folk architecture.

Modified by eighteenth-century ideas of symmetry and proportion, the Tidewater-type cottage gradually spread inland to the piedmont region and southward down the Atlantic seaboard. During the 1820s and 1830s, settlers from Virginia and the older southern states along the Atlantic brought the form to Alabama, where the most distinctive examples seem to have occurred in the Tennessee Valley.

Alabama versions of the cottage tend to have a shallower roof-pitch (a general trend in the early nineteenth century) than do their colonial predecessors. Chimneys are also less monumental, and the cabinetwork and other detail, more spartan. But the basic module remains unchanged. And distinguishing the more sophisticated of these houses is the same firm, rational geometry which had become an earmark of antecedents in Virginia and Maryland by the time of the Revolution: a specific set of ratios governing height to width, length to depth, and so on.

Thus the "double square" formula—much used in eighteenth-century Williamsburg—is the controlling figure for such Alabama examples as Bride's Hill* and Albemarle, near Courtland, and the John Johnson house northeast of Leighton. The term *double square* means simply that the elevation of the house is twice as long as it is high, or the groundplan twice as wide as it is deep. Passed on from master craftsman to apprentice for generations, such established proportions gave to the most finished of the Tidewater-type cottages an overriding family resemblance. [22]

Both single-pile (one-room deep) and double-pile (two-room deep) examples were built in Alabama—one instance of the latter being the William Koger house near Florence. Most Tidewater-type cottages employed a center-hall plan, although the hall-and-parlor arrangement (see illustration, page 5), with a respectable lineage that could be traced back to medieval England, was not unknown.

22. *Two Tidewater-type cottages in the Tennessee Valley.* Top: *Bride's Hill, Lawrence County, ca. 1830. Developed according to the double-square formula employed by colonial Virginia house builders, the front elevation of Bride's Hill is almost exactly twice as long as it is high, counting the slope of the roof. Another rare—perhaps unique—feature of this important early Alabama house is the cantilevered chimney pent, the narrow, shed-roofed projection that abuts the left chimney in the drawing (there is another pent to the rear of the right chimney). Such chimney pents were yet another holdover from the colonial tradition. In spite of its significance, Bride's Hill stood abandoned in the mid-1980s.* Bottom: *The John Johnson house near Leighton, another dwelling following the double-square formula—this time in brick. The severe but well-proportioned front, laid in Flemish bond, recalls eighteenth-century precursors such as the famous John Rolfe house in Virginia. Like Bride's Hill, however, the Johnson house has been abandoned—and in recent years stripped by vandals of its paneled wainscoting and mantelpieces. (Author's collection.)*

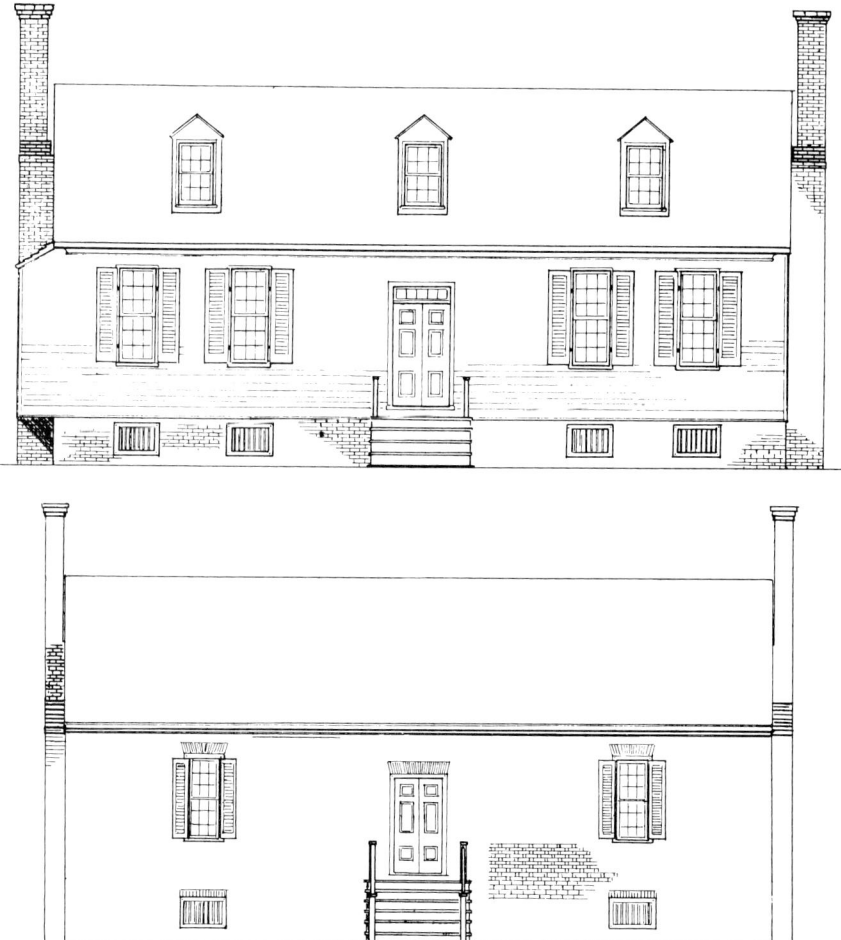

More distantly related to the same Chesapeake-area archetype, via the Carolinas and Georgia, are a number of central Alabama houses such as Cedarwood* near Greensboro, the now much-altered William M. Marks house southeast of Montgomery, and both the Martin-Barnes and Graves-Haigler houses, moved from their original locations to the North Hull Street Historic District, in Montgomery. [23] The long, inset front porch of the Graves-Haigler house represents a characteristic modification of the seminal form in the latitudes south of the Chesapeake.

The superficial impression of a Tidewater-type cottage is also conveyed in the dormered roof and end chimneys of Altwood, a weatherboarded log dogtrot near Faunsdale built in the 1830s by Richard Harrison Adams, a planter from eastern Virginia. But absent in these lower Alabama examples are the taut proportions exhibited by some of their Tennessee Valley cousins.

23. Martin-Barnes house, Montgomery, ca. 1832. A central Alabama dwelling that harkens back to the double-pile story-and-a-half houses of Tidewater Virginia and the southern Atlantic seaboard. To save it from destruction, this house was moved to the North Hull Street Historic District and restored. The porch, designed by restoration architect Nicholas H. Holmes, Jr., is conjectural, based on that which fronted the now-destroyed Chaudron house at Claiborne. (Author's collection.)

Whether modified or as clearly pedigreed as Bride's Hill or the John Johnson house, the story-and-a-half Tidewater-type cottage seems the plausible link in the evolutionary chain between later cottages of similar form—like the 1854 T. A. Fay house* at Prattville—and the little houses of the eighteenth-century Atlantic seaboard. It is a tragedy of popular ill-understanding and scholarly oversight that this vanishing species among Alabama's folk architectural forms has yet to be fully recognized for both its social and architectural implications. One of the best examples, the Hundley house* at Mooresville, was carelessly razed as late as 1968, while at the present time several others stand on the brink of disappearance. [24]

Summary Characteristics

- Strict symmetry in the most academic examples, with a controlling geometry of proportional ratios.
- Longitudinal gable roof, usually pitched between 30 and 45 degrees and buttressed by prominent end chimneys.
- Frequent occurrence of dormer windows.
- Occasional occurrence (extremely rare in Alabama) of the chimney pent: a narrow, shed-roof extension flanking one or both chimneys and serving as an interior closet or pantry.
- Normally, center-hall plan (more rarely, hall-and-parlor arrangement).

24. Mooresville's demolished Hundley house—a bit of colonial Williamsburg transplanted to an early Alabama village. Note (below) the tapered rakeboards above the square garret windows of the gable end. (HABS: Alex Bush photos, 1935.)

The Creole Cottage
(mainly Mobile Bay area and Gulf Coast;
nineteenth to early twentieth centuries)

Tradition has long rooted the so-called Creole cottage in the vernacular French colonial architecture of the Gulf Coast. [25, 26] The term may in reality be more picturesque than precise, since the origin of this domestic form is by no means so clear-cut. Some see in it a mixture of architectural influences from various parts of France's far-flung colonial empire: from the West Indian islands the front porch or *galerie*; from Canada the high, gabled roof sweeping down over the porch and sheltering beneath its steep slope an attic story or *grenier*. The simplest and most forthright examples of the Creole cottage also exhibited such French colonial characteristics as a passageless interior layout, composed of two or more side-by-side rooms served by a central chimney and opening directly onto the *galerie*. But theories about the exclusively French origins of the Creole cottage fail to explain the relationship between this house-type and very similar dwellings in non-Gallic locales as widely dispersed as Key West and Belize. The picture is further clouded by the fact that, although the city of Mobile was founded in 1711, time has effectively erased every architectural vestige of the port's first century of existence—a century that saw French, English, and Spanish overlords successively leave their cultural imprint before the city passed into American hands in 1813.

Whatever its provenance, the Creole cottage underwent considerable refinement during the course of the nineteenth century. Bishop Michael Portier's urbane Mobile residence* of 1834 adopted not only Federal-period trim from American pattern books but also a formal axial hallway. [27] Later Creole-type houses in Mobile, such as the Calef-Staples* residence of the early 1850s, were cloaked in a fashionable if muted overlay of details borrowed from the Greek Revival. [28] Other houses coming afterward were lightly bracketed or even bedecked with gingerbread trim. Yet unexpected holdover features of clearly Gallic origin lingered well into the American period, as with the casement windows used in lieu of good Yankee sash at the Portier and now-destroyed Miguel Eslava* houses.

An unwavering feature of the Creole cottage form remained its full-length gallery, inset beneath the main slope of a prominent gable roof. Double-decker porches treated in the same way, like that of the Thomas Atkinson house* near Tensaw, northeast of Mobile, may be an outgrowth of this formula, although analogous examples can also be found in the Carolinas, from whence Atkinson had come to Alabama.

Because of the tremendous social and economic influence exerted by antebellum Mobile on the upriver cotton country of central Ala-

25. *Creole cottage (demolished) on St. Francis Street, Mobile. (Library of Congress: Frances Benjamin Johnston photo.)*

26. *Worker's house, Mobile. In contrast to larger Creole cottages that might don the latest in cosmetic architectural fashion stood this diminutive house, razed for urban redevelopment during the 1960s. Yet the structure's kinship with more ambitious specimens is evident in the long, high-pitched roof and inset front porch. Actually, with its back-to-back rooms and central chimney, this unpretending house is closer to French colonial archetype than its larger companions. Similar houses can still be seen today in Port-au-Prince and other French-flavored cities of the Caribbean. Note that the rear slope of the roof joins the parallel gable of a small dependency behind the main block, forming a trough that became a catchment for rain water piped into a backyard cistern. This arrangement was called a "butterfly" roof. (HABS: Jack Boucher photo, 1964.)*

27. Portier house, Mobile. A Creole cottage transmuted into a sophisticated essay in waning Federalism. (HABS: G. Chaudron, Jr., delineator, 1934–35.) Bottom right: detail of stair, Portier house, with arrow-motif balusters. (Jack Boucher photo, 1963.)

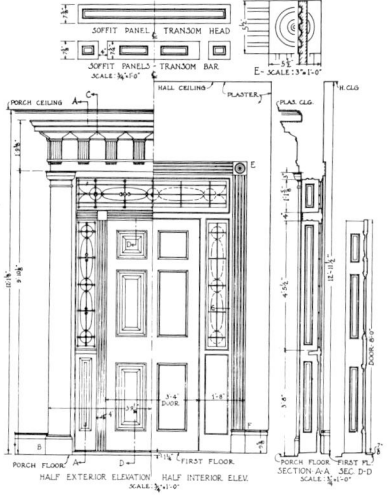
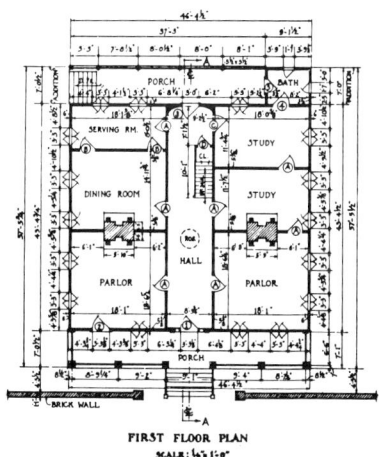

bama, isolated examples of the Creole cottage form occurred as far north as Gainesville on the Tombigbee. Here the Russell-Turrentine house (ca. 1840) closely resembled its Mobile counterparts, even to the segmentally arched dormers it once boasted. Woodlands near Claiborne, built as a country retreat by a Mobile attorney, was a smooth academic rendition of the form, combining both Federal and Greek Revival decorative detail. Inland, however, the Creole cottage form tended to lose the subtle qualities—the pronounced pitch of the roof for one—that usually distinguished it from similar house-types originating on the Atlantic seaboard.

About Mobile Bay, some rural residences adhered tenaciously to the Creole cottage form long after many other options had become available. And throughout the middle and late 1800s, it persisted as a favorite mode for the summer houses erected by Mobile's elite on the high hills along the eastern shore of the bay. We may never know just when and how this dwelling-type became so strongly identified with the Alabama Gulf Coast. Still, there is no question that it emerged as one of the state's most distinctive nineteenth-century expressions of domestic building.

Summary Characteristics

- A tall, prominent, gable roof, normally (but not always) sloping in an unbroken plane from front to back, so as to accommodate a full-length porch inset into the main body of the structure.

28. Calef-Staples house, Mobile. (HABS: E. W. Russell photo, 1937.)

- In more rudimentary examples, one or two main rooms (if the latter, then without a bisecting passage) opening directly onto the porch; a central hall may occur in more formal versions.
- In many smaller, prototypal examples the presence of an inside chimney piercing the ridge of the roof, with back-to-back fireplaces serving a pair of equal-sized rooms.
- As a secondary characteristic, the frequent occurrence of a raised basement.

The Spraddle-Roof House
(statewide, though mainly central and southern Alabama; early to mid-nineteenth century)

The "spraddle-roof house," to borrow a term coined by John Linley of the University of Georgia, describes one more Alabama folk-dwelling form that may be identified by its characteristic profile: a broken gable roof embracing front and rear porches and/or shed rooms. The addition of such lean-to rooms before and behind, covered by a roof pitched out from the main slope, was an obvious way of enlarging any structure. The result is demonstrated by the Dudley Snow house* at Oxford, originally a two-room log dogtrot structure. But the broken-gable profile also appeared full-blown in nineteenth-century Alabama as another of those vernacular mannerisms brought westward from the older South. The roof is normally not quite so steep as that of the typical Creole cottage, which it can strongly resemble, while the Atlantic Coast origins of the spraddle-roof house are further betrayed by a nearly universal preference for prominent outside chimneys at each gable end.

Some of the best examples of the spraddle-roof house occurred in portions of Alabama heavily settled from Georgia or the Carolinas: the Camden and Carlowville areas for instance, and the lower Chattahoochee Valley. In Camden there was the Jeremiah Fail house*—razed in 1983—and in the Chattahoochee area, the Bartlett Smith house*. [29, 30]

A frequently associated characteristic of the spraddle-roof house was the so-called Carolina porch, which carried the flared porch roof well beyond the front edge of the porch itself to rest on freestanding supports that rise directly from ground level. [31] The deck-like sitting area is thus positioned far enough behind the eaves line to be almost perpetually shaded. This arrangement also shields the vulnerable edge of the wooden porch floor against the rain and dampness of the humid southern climate.

From the spraddle-roof form almost certainly evolved another house type that straightened the plane of the roof in a way that made

29. *Jeremiah Fail house, Camden, ca. 1840 (razed 1983). Originally, an open dogtrot-type hall extended from the front to the rear porch. (Library of Congress: Frances Benjamin Johnston photo.)*

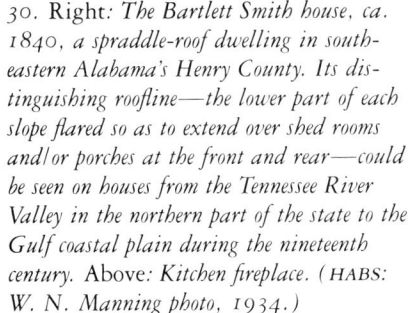

30. Right: *The Bartlett Smith house, ca. 1840, a spraddle-roof dwelling in southeastern Alabama's Henry County. Its distinguishing roofline—the lower part of each slope flared so as to extend over shed rooms and/or porches at the front and rear—could be seen on houses from the Tennessee River Valley in the northern part of the state to the Gulf coastal plain during the nineteenth century.* Above: *Kitchen fireplace. (HABS: W. N. Manning photo, 1934.)*

31. *A spraddle-roof house (demolished) at Perdue Hill. The deck-like "Carolina" porch, set well back behind freestanding supports that carried the overhanging roof, recurred in central and southern Alabama on both small houses such as this and colonnaded mansions like Rosemount and Kirkwood in Greene County. Note the dressed stone chimney—unusual in a state where brick was the normal medium for masonry construction. (HABS: W. N. Manning, 1934.)*

the new mutation a near mirror image of some of the larger and equally formalized Creole cottages. The Joseph E. Patton house* near Coatopa, Sumter County, is one such dwelling, while several other very notable examples may still be seen about the Wilcox County village of Oak Hill, settled in the early nineteenth century by emigrating planters from South Carolina.

Summary Characteristics

- Broken-gable or "spraddled" end profile, with the lower part of each roof slope pitched out over a porch and/or shed rooms; typically, prominent chimneys at one or both gable ends.
- Floorplan ranging from an informal two-room or hall-and-parlor layout to center-hall arrangement.
- Frequently, a "Carolina" porch with freestanding roof supports.

The High Styles

Alabama became a U.S. territory in 1817 and a state two years later, on 14 December 1819. At that time and for some three decades thereafter, the main chord in high-style American architecture was struck by the firmly entrenched spirit of neoclassicism. A romantic reaction, which in Europe had actually been gathering force since before 1800, at last broke the classical thrall and, with the aid of newly available technologies and materials, inaugurated a spree of architectural eclecticism that got seriously underway in the 1850s. The result was, of course, several decades of polyglot building which we lump together today as the "Victorian period"—a time both of creative experimentation and gaucherie, which ended only with a rekindled appreciation for "rational" architecture and, once more, for neoclassicism. This later neoclassicism, however, was of a kind quite distinct from that of half a century before. Simultaneously, new trends emerged in both domestic and commercial design that were harbingers of the architectural functionalism of our own day.

Alabama experienced the ripple effect from all these national shifts of taste. And as we have seen in looking at some of the vernacular forms that prevailed in the state, these ripples could produce an interesting blend of the fashionable and the provincial. From time to time, the impact of new fashion also inspired buildings of genuine urbanity. What follows, then, is a short discussion of each of these currents of new architectural thinking as they made their way into nineteenth- and early twentieth-century Alabama.

Neoclassicism: The Federal and Jeffersonian Phases (ca. 1815 to 1840)

It was in the guise of Federal and Jeffersonian architecture that high-style building came to Alabama. The term "Federal" refers to the blend of contemporary English and Continental influences with holdover Georgian colonial architectural ideas that shaped most stylish American buildings at the beginning of the nineteenth century. The refinements borrowed from the British work of the brothers Robert and James Adam were especially pronounced; hence the descriptive term "Adamesque," which is often used synonymously with the term "Federal." Jeffersonian classicism identifies Thomas Jefferson's own variation on the neoclassical theme, a variation linked chiefly with Virginia and the South.

Both phases owed a great deal to the tenacious influence of the Renaissance Italian architect Andrea Palladio (1508–1580), whose writings Jefferson called his architectural Bible, and whose inspired reinterpretation of ancient Roman forms dominated the English-speaking world in one way or another for the better part of two centuries. At the same time, both Federal and Jeffersonian classicism were animated by that direct and growing archaeological awareness of the ancient world's art and architecture that soon would kindle the spirit of the Greek Revival.

Frontier Alabama of the 1820s and the early 1830s was hardly a congenial setting for the bold, graceful interior spaces—the oval, circular, and octagonal rooms—and the elegant bowfront façades that distinguished some of the great Federal-period houses of Charleston, Richmond, and Savannah. Instead of innovative spatial settings and forceful changes of exterior massing, the style was more modestly articulated through the handling of specific features and details: in the delicately carved sunburst patterns, wire-fine reeding, and attenuated colonettes that appeared on drawing room mantelpieces; in paneled dados and molded chair-rails; in arched Palladian window openings; and in occasional fanlight doorways and spiral stairs. [32–36] Plates from *The American Builder's Companion,* by Asher Benjamin, or *The Young Carpenter's Assistant,* by Owen Biddle, furnished the basic motifs for these elements and others, leaving builder and client to alter them as desired or necessary.

The hilltop Huntsville mansion of Colonel Leroy Pope* is the oldest structure standing today in Alabama that can claim to be a genuine exercise in academic style. Yet despite the urbane note it must have struck in a land of ubiquitous log cabins, the Pope house was conservative of line and already somewhat old-fashioned even when completed around 1815. [37] Like several other Tennessee Valley mansions erected during the next two decades—Belle Mina* near Mooresville, Caledonia near Courtland, Sweetwater* and Woodlawn* near Florence [38]—the Leroy Pope house was just half a step removed in overall form from the stolid pre-Revolutionary mansions of its owner's native Virginia; this, notwithstanding a garnish of Adamesque moldings and architraves, and a richly worked Adamesque cornice.

The George Coalter house*, now Mapleton, at Florence boasts one of the state's preeminent Adamesque interiors, with doors surmounted by carved swags and garlands that recall the New England work of Samuel McIntire. In the wide central hall, an elliptical arch, springing from scrolled consoles, echoes the curvature of the wide fanlights above the front and rear entrances. Once these doorways opened onto narrow, two-tiered pedimented porches, lightly scaled after the manner that was a watchword of Federal taste. [39]

Sometimes two stories, sometimes only one, but almost invariably upheld by either attenuated square supports or equally slender columns of the Tuscan, the Roman Doric, or the Roman Ionic order, such porches were very typical of finer houses in Federal-period Alabama. The long-vanished Allen Glover house in Demopolis boasted

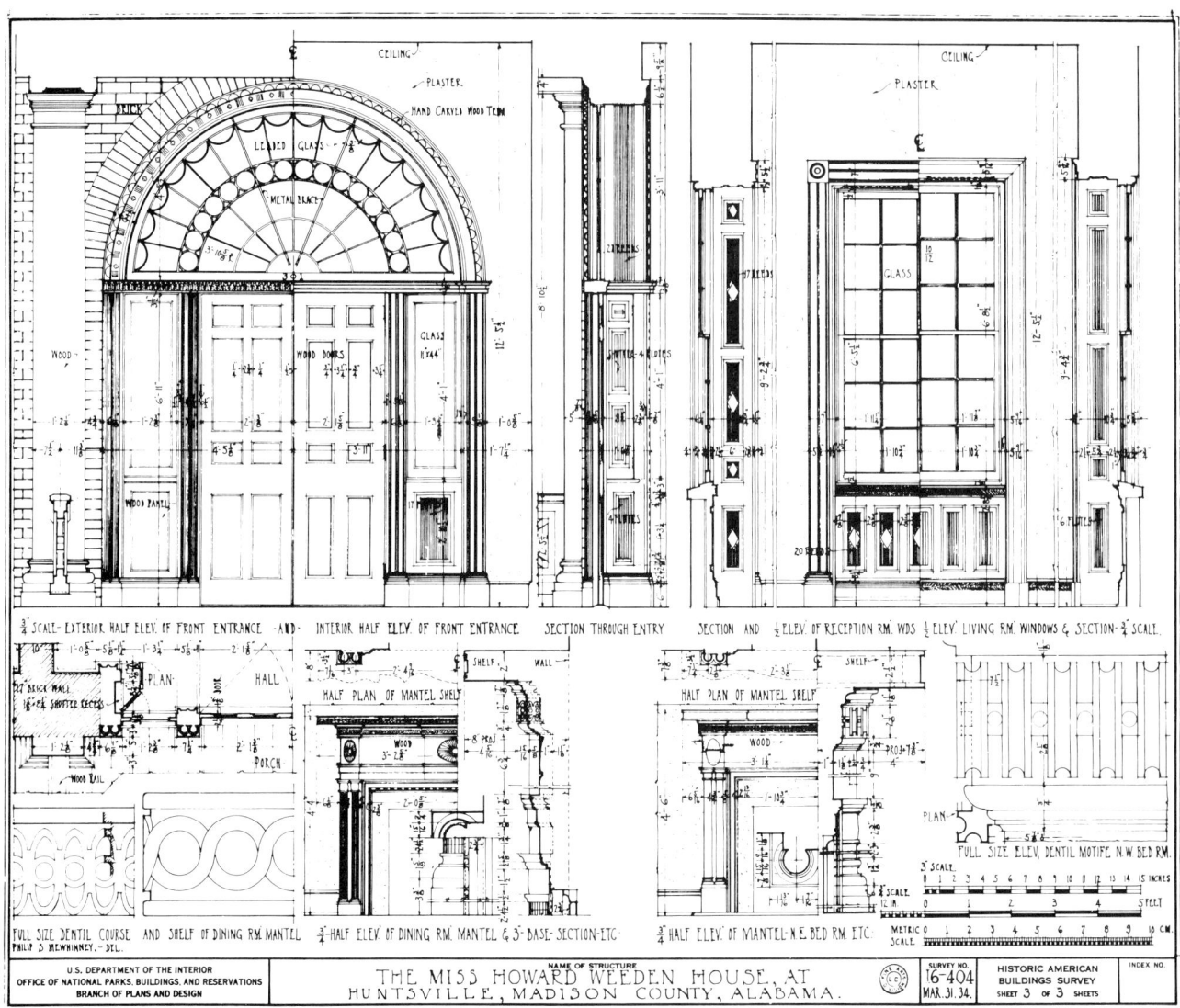

32. *Doorway, window, and mantel details, Weeden house, Huntsville, ca. 1819. (HABS: Philip S. Mewhinney, delineator, 1934.)*

such a porch, and so, probably, did neighboring Bluff Hall before a weightier colonnade of Greek Revival persuasion supplanted the original piazza about 1850. [40] Lamentably few of these light Federal-period porches have survived fully intact. But vintage examples may yet be seen at the 1829 Francis W. Dancy house in Decatur [41], the Judge John Henry house at Centreville, the Robert Savidge Foster house south of Tuscaloosa [42], and the Johnston-Torbert house* in Greensboro.

State Architect William Nichols's handling of the old State Capitol building* at Tuscaloosa, as well as of nearby Christ Church* and the original University of Alabama complex, all now gone, may have owed at least as much to Nichols's English background and training as to American precedent. [43] At the university, Nichols made per-

33. *Above left: James Bennington Irvine house, Florence, ca. 1835. Palladian windows such as that in the pediment of the portico were a favorite Federal-period device in the Florence area. (Duane Phillips photo, 1984.)*

34. *Above right: Interior doorway, John S. Rhea (McEntire) house, Decatur, 1836. The ornamental strapwork on the Ionic pilasters is a type of refinement seldom seen in early Alabama architecture. (Library of Congress: Frances Benjamin Johnston photo.)*

35. *Right: Stairway, Thorn Hill, Talladega vicinity, ca. 1835. (Library of Congress: Frances Benjamin Johnston photo.)*

36. *Stairway, Pope-Alexander-Golson house, Prattville, ca. 1835. (HABS: W. N. Manning photo, 1935.)*

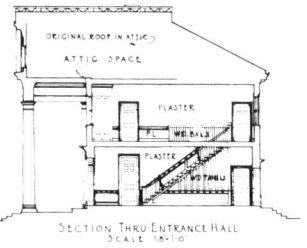

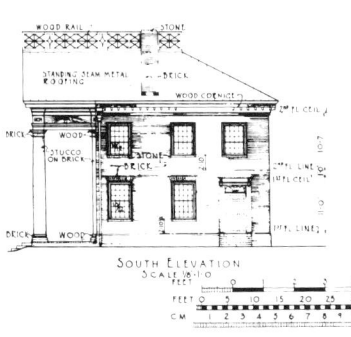

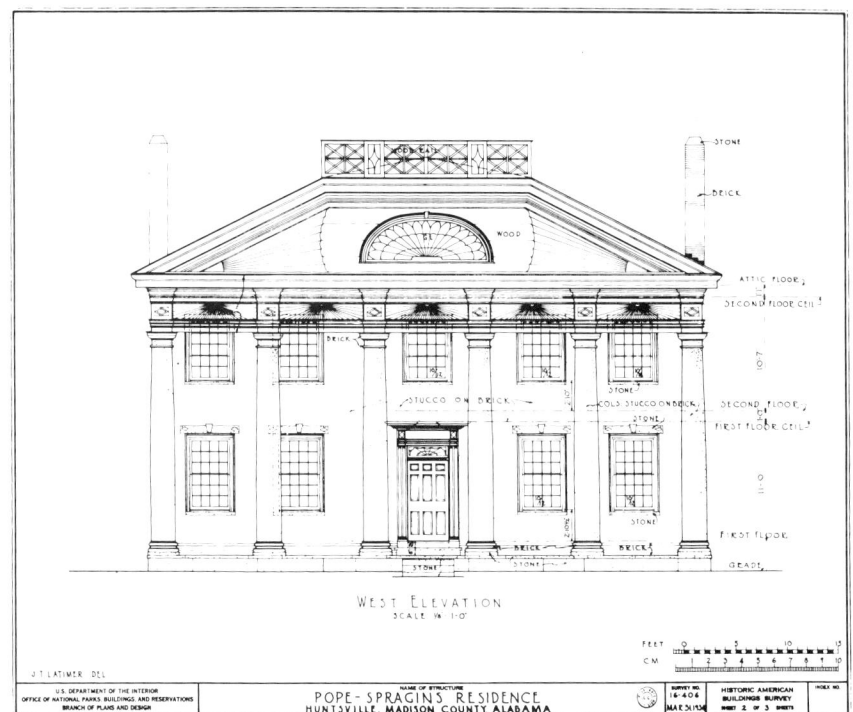

37. *Leroy Pope house, Huntsville, ca. 1815. The conjectural drawing (top right) shows the house as it probably appeared in the beginning. A later colonnade (bottom left and right),* added to the five-bay front, respected the scale and light Adamesque detail of the original structure. The portico's odd, truncated pediment—enriched by reeded sunbursts framing a great elliptical fanlight and topped by a balustraded deck—is unique in the state. *(Conjectural drawing by Harvie Jones, F.A.I.A.; HABS: J. T. Latimer, delineator, 1934.)*

38. Woodlawn, near Florence, ca. 1830. Woodlawn's three-part plan—a main block with lower symmetrical wings to either side—was carried over from mid-eighteenth-century neoclassicism. A further elaboration was the five-part plan, in which the outlying wings were joined to the central block by intervening structural links called "hyphens." Only one five-part house is known to have been built in early Alabama—the now-destroyed Weyanoke in Marengo County. (HABS: W. N. Manning photo, 1934.)

39. Above: Hallway at Mapleton, Florence, ca. 1830. Right: Drawing room at Mapleton. The bas-relief swags and garlands that adorn the friezes above the doors are probably based on designs from the 1827 edition of Asher Benjamin's The American Builder's Companion. *(Duane Phillips photos, 1983.)*

40. *Ca. 1860 view of the Allen Glover house, Demopolis, built about 1830–35. Faintly discernible in the pediment of the light two-tiered portico is a semicircular lunette. (Courtesy Winston Smith.)*

41. *Francis W. Dancy house, Decatur, 1829. (Alabama Historical Commission.)*

haps the earliest use in the state of the colossal neoclassical portico in his 1828 schemes for the Lyceum and the Rotunda. Both structures employed the Roman Ionic order, which abounded in his native Bath. A couple of years later, Nichols's lead was followed by a recently arrived French émigré, Claude Beroujon, when he planned a monumental portico—this time of the Tuscan order—fronting Spring Hill College* at Mobile. [44]

42. *The Robert Savidge Foster plantation house (ca. 1825–30), Tuscaloosa County. The slightly reduced proportions of both the upper windows and the upper tier of Tuscan-order columns on the portico was a typical treatment of the Federal period. (Alabama Historical Commission.)*

Almost beyond question, it was again William Nichols who conceived the heroically scaled peristyle colonnade of the Forks of Cypress plantation house* near Florence. [45] And directly or indirectly, his shadowy figure lay behind the design of other Alabama mansions built not long afterward—particularly around Tuscaloosa. One of these may have been the James Dearing house* [46]; another, the President's House* built between 1839 and 1841 at the Univer-

43. *Old State Capitol, Tuscaloosa, 1828–30. Modeled after the North Carolina statehouse as renovated by the same architect, William Nichols, a few years before, the Tuscaloosa edifice recalled earlier American state capitols such as those of Connecticut and Massachusetts. Yet in the use of an advanced central pavilion with a rusticated basement and a pseudo-Ionic portico, Nichols may also have been thinking of transatlantic precedents like the Guildhall at Bath, which he would have known from his English youth and apprenticeship. Later converted into a school building, the Tuscaloosa capitol burned in 1923. Below: An early twentieth-century photograph of the old House of Representatives' chamber. (HABS: Chip Cooper photocopy, 1978.)*

sity of Alabama. University records speak of one, Michael Barry, as the author of the plans for the President's House; indeed, Nichols had already left Alabama some years before. Still, it is hard not to suspect the latter's sense of architectural aesthetics somehow informing the mansion's conservative Roman Ionic portico, raised above a gracefully arcuated ground floor.

In the Tennessee Valley, the oblique impact of Thomas Jefferson's architectural ideas seems equally apparent. Jefferson's fusion of Palladianism with his acquired love for the Roman temple form is evident

44. *Spring Hill College, Mobile (central section, 1830–31).* The sheer scale of the three-story portico foreshadowed the onrushing Greek Revival, but the detailing—Tuscan order columns, an elliptical lunette piercing the pediment—belonged to an earlier phase of neoclassicism. The pilastered wings to either side were added several years after completion of the main structure. "You may think our colonnaded building an extravagance," wrote one of the Jesuit founders of the school to his superior in France, "but in hot climates galleries are an absolute necessity. Besides, this appearance of elegance and cleanliness was necessary in order to make a favorable impression on people who idolize their children and who place bodily comfort at the head of the list." A similar colonnade also fronted the city hospital, which was erected a couple of years after the college and still stands today. In 1869, the original college building seen here was destroyed by fire. (Courtesy Spring Hill College.)

in the little-known Turner Saunders house* near Town Creek [47], and in the old State Bank building* at Decatur (1834–35) with its odd five-column portico. Most strikingly Jeffersonian of all, there is Belle Mont* near Tuscumbia, a three-part house with a narrow raised central pavilion and a lofty, square entrance salon unique in Alabama. From the standpoint of both form and layout, Belle Mont hints so strongly of the Sage of Monticello that we may wonder if its architect was not a Charlottesville-trained craftsman. [48]

The late 1830s in Alabama brought a decisive shift away from the Federal and Jeffersonian phases of neoclassicism to the more robust Greek Revival. Yet now and again, as evidenced by the fanlight doorway of Camden's temple-type Masonic Hall* erected in 1849, retardataire Adamesque and Palladian features continued to recur, mixed unselfconsciously with elements of the newer style, until the middle of the century.

Summary Characteristics

- Symmetry and a general delicacy of scale and detail, to be discerned especially in doorways, trim, columns, and porches.
- Preference for Roman over Greek orders, with an attenuation of proportions, particularly in mantelpieces and architraves.
- Frequent use of semicircular and elliptical forms, as in fanlight doorways and spiral stairs; also in round, oval, or semicircular windows and vents, as well as arched three-part Palladian or "Venetian" openings.
- Appliqué of rosettes, oval paterae, swags, urns, and garlands on such features as mantelpieces, door and window surrounds, chairrails, etc.

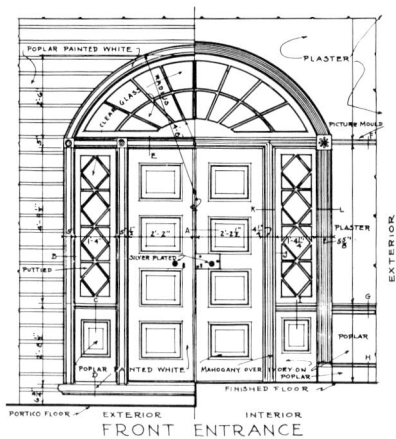

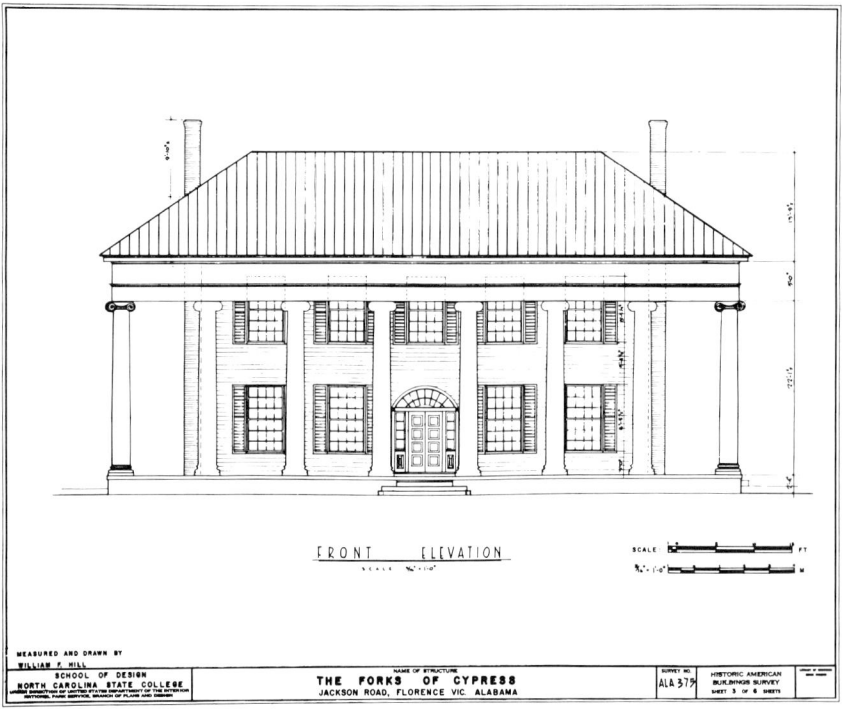

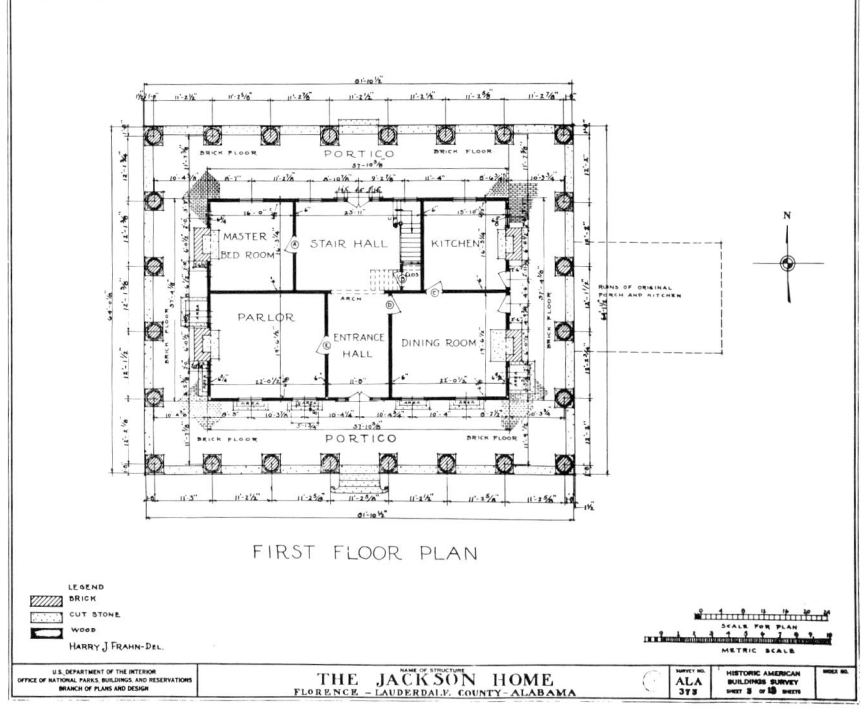

45. *The Forks of Cypress, Florence vicinity, ca. 1830 (William Nichols probably architect). Above and right: The segmentally arched fanlight doorway was a characteristic Nichols element, while the voluptuous Roman Ionic order of the colonnade recalled some of Nichols's work at the University of Alabama. Below: The plan of The Forks, with its separately defined rear stairhall, was also typical of Nichols. The Forks burned in 1965. (HABS: William F. Hill and Harry J. Frahn, delineators, 1935–36 and 1958.)*

46. *James Dearing house, Tuscaloosa, from a ca. 1871 photograph showing the original ornamental wooden parapet and, above, a balustraded deck. (Special Collections, Amelia Gayle Gorgas Library, University of Alabama.)*

47. *Turner Saunders house, Town Creek vicinity, ca. 1830–35. Its Roman Doric portico, with pediment pierced by an arched lunette, was a typical Jeffersonian device. For half a century the great plantation house has waivered uneasily between gentle disrepair and partial restoration. (Duane Phillips photo, 1983.)*

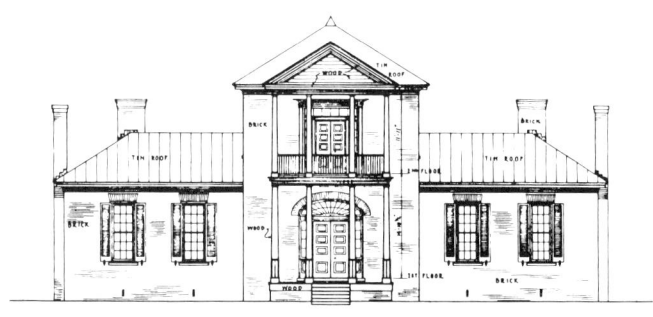

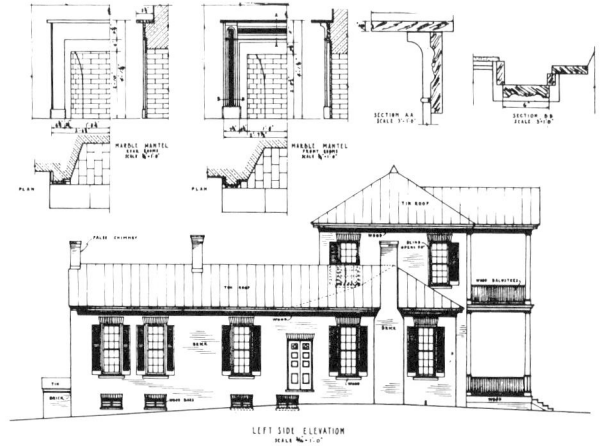
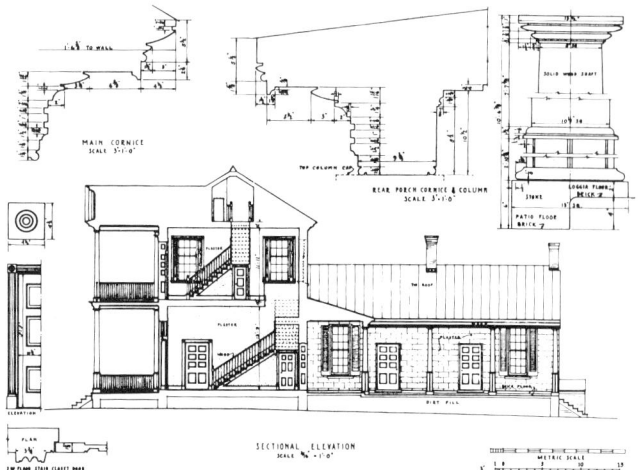

48. Belle Mont, Colbert County, ca. 1828. With its narrow two-story central pavilion and flanking one-story wings embracing a courtyard at the rear, Belle Mont is Alabama's most thoroughgoing Jeffersonian Palladian house. Semiruinous and abandoned in recent years, Belle Mont was donated to the Alabama Historical Commission in 1983 and is now undergoing restoration. Bottom right: Hanging attic stairway at Belle Mont. (HABS: Clive Richardson, delineator, 1937; Alex Bush photo, 1936.)

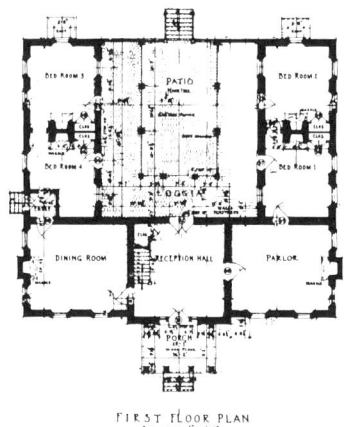

Neoclassicism: The Greek Revival Phase
(mid-1830s to 1860s)

While pre–Greek Revival neoclassicism could display an almost feminine lightness, the Greek Revival itself was heavy, rectilinear, emphatically masculine in scale. The style emerged out of a fervor for things Hellenic that swept the Western world from Czarist Russia to Canada and the United States during the early nineteenth century. Still, it was especially well received in Jacksonian America, where romantic New World democrats regarded themselves as the rightful heirs to the far-off and naïvely understood civilization of Periclean Athens. In the Deep South needless to say, Greek Revival architecture would become indelibly linked with the plantation legend, although the rough-and-tumble, semifrontier society that so eagerly embraced the new fashion could hardly lay claim to the timeless grace with which post–Civil War apologists, and later Hollywood film-makers, sought to imbue it.

In Alabama the Greek Revival style appeared fully matured, at opposite ends of the state, soon after 1835: at Mobile, in such structures as Barton Academy* and the Government Street Presbyterian Church* [49]; and at Huntsville, in George Steele's crisp designs for the Madison County courthouse* [50] as well as the Huntsville Branch of the State Bank*. The Mobile buildings were the joint project of Charles Dakin and James Gallier, fresh from the stimulating architectural atmosphere of Greek Revival New York. George Steele, on the other hand, was a longtime Huntsville resident—self-taught in architectural design so it seems, and no doubt inspired in his schemes for both the courthouse and the bank by a brief eastern sojourn that apparently marked his conversion to the Greek Revival idiom.

The new style spread rapidly, especially in the rich Black Belt counties of central Alabama, where its advent coincided with the first real flush of cotton prosperity. By the late 1840s it held almost unchallenged sway—expressing itself in countless buildings from the conventional pillared house to the country store finished off at the front gable end with a wooden pediment, entablature, and raking cornice.

The monumental colonnade that became so conspicuous a feature of many Alabama dwellings was more than merely an ego-satisfying way through which planter and merchant alike could proclaim their worldly success. It also answered gloriously the need for a broad and lofty "piazza" against the summer sun. But the pedimented temple-form house and the related temple-with-wings dwelling, so widespread throughout the Northeast and Midwest, remained comparatively rare in Alabama. [51] Greensboro counts two examples of

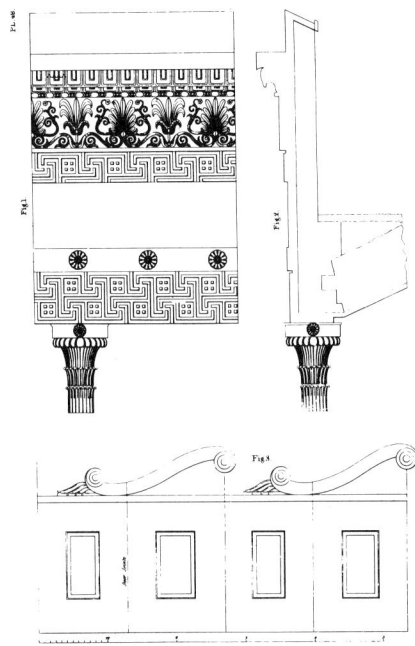

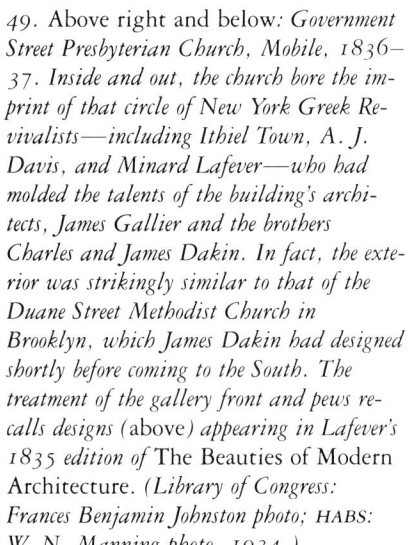

49. *Above right and below: Government Street Presbyterian Church, Mobile, 1836–37. Inside and out, the church bore the imprint of that circle of New York Greek Revivalists—including Ithiel Town, A. J. Davis, and Minard Lafever—who had molded the talents of the building's architects, James Gallier and the brothers Charles and James Dakin. In fact, the exterior was strikingly similar to that of the Duane Street Methodist Church in Brooklyn, which James Dakin had designed shortly before coming to the South. The treatment of the gallery front and pews recalls designs* (above) *appearing in Lafever's 1835 edition of* The Beauties of Modern Architecture. *(Library of Congress: Frances Benjamin Johnston photo;* HABS: *W. N. Manning photo, 1934.)*

the former type, the full-scale temple-front house, in Magnolia Grove* (circa 1840) and the McCrary mansion—built several years later and known as Magnolia Hall*. The temple-with-wings format of both the Kenan house* near Selma and the Northrup-Bateman house* at Wetumpka may have been inspired by Minard Lafever's "Design for a Country Villa," illustrated in *The Modern Builder's Guide* (1833). But the specific treatment is altogether different, and

50. *Madison County Courthouse, Huntsville, 1837–42 (demolished 1913). A temple-type, amphiprostyle structure with Doric porticoes at either end and bold, heavy antae articulating the side walls. Inside, there was a vaulted and coffered courtroom. The lantern topping the dome was based on an ancient prototype used repeatedly by Greek Revivalists: the Choragic Monument of Lysicrates at Athens. (HABS: E. L. Love, delineator, 1935 {based on earlier drawings}.)*

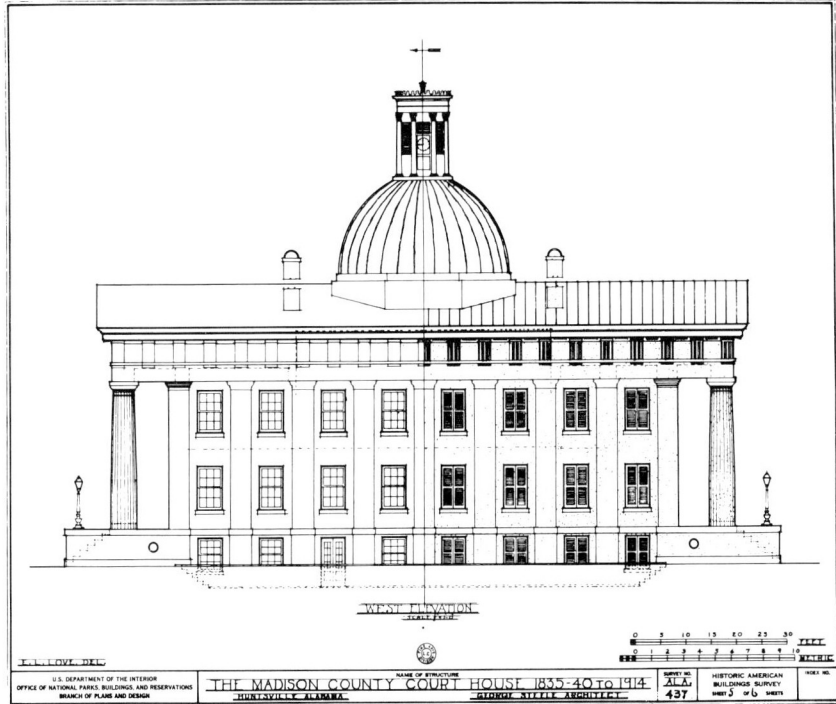

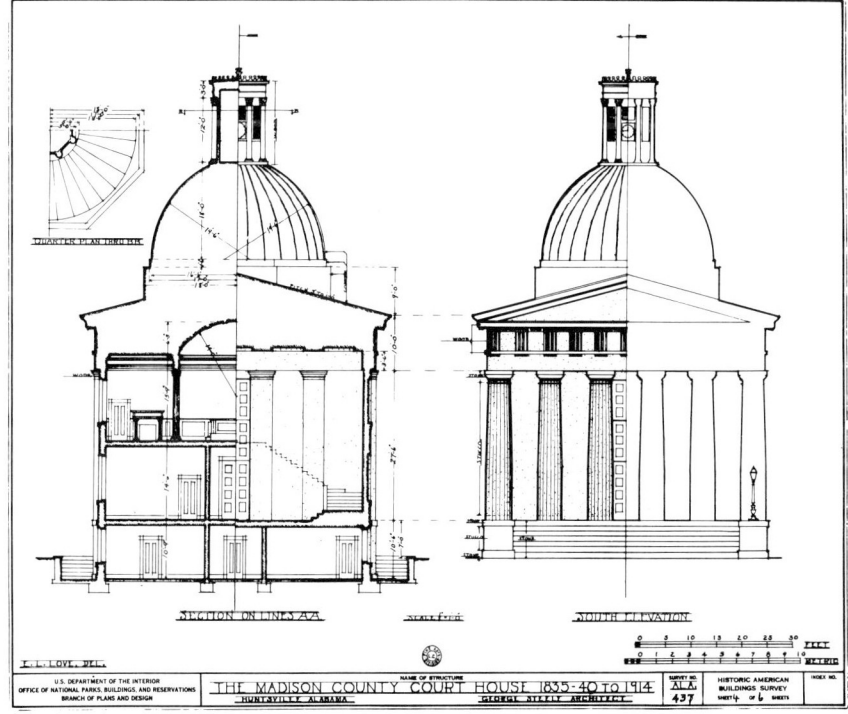

51. Right: *Magnolia Hall, Greensboro, ca. 1855. The Ionic porticoes front and rear are echoed institutionally a few miles away in the amphiprostyle Perry County courthouse (1855–56), at Marion. Both Magnolia Hall and the courthouse were designed by the same architect-builder, the Massachusetts-born Benjamin F. Parsons. In Alabama domestic building, however, such full-width temple-type fronts were as infrequent as the temple-with-wings arrangement of the Kenan house,* below, *near Selma. From the same Palladian tradition that had inspired Thomas Jefferson, Greek Revivalists borrowed the latter form, though cloaking it—as at the Kenan house—with heavier detail than an earlier phase of neoclassicism would have normally admitted.* Opposite: *Quite possibly a plate from Minard Lafever's* The Modern Builder's Guide *provided the starting point for the design of the Kenan house. (Library of Congress: Frances Benjamin Johnston photos.)*

for Lafever's square piers the Alabama structures substitute fluted Doric pillars.

Far more common throughout the state than such domesticated temples was either a pedimented central portico projecting from a broad-bodied, gabled main block, as with the Beaty-Mason house* in Athens [52], or else a wide hipped roof, sans pediment of any kind, that swept down over a colonnade running the length of the front and sometimes wrapping around one or both sides of the building. However, the encircling or peripteral colonnades so common in Louisiana were all but unknown in Alabama.

If a standard Greek order was utilized it was normally Doric, less often Ionic, and only toward the end of the Greek Revival era, Corinthian. Glennville* in Russell County is one of the best developed of these hipped roof, colonnaded houses, with full Doric regalia and matching neoclassical doorways at both balcony and main-floor levels. [53] At Thornhill* near Forkland the Ionic order is employed; and so, too, at neighboring Rosemount*, where the hipped roof rises to a plump colonnaded rooftop observatory that must surely rank as one of the most ample anywhere in nineteenth-century America. [54] In most cases, however, square pier supports sufficed to carry the sloping roof of the piazza, as at Tuscaloosa's Battle-Friedman* and Collier houses*, or at Arlington* in old Elyton (now swallowed up by modern Birmingham). [55]

Application of the hipped-roof-with-colonnade formula at a reduced scale produced appealing one-story domiciles like Georgia Cottage* and the Benjamin F. Marshall house* in Mobile. [56] About

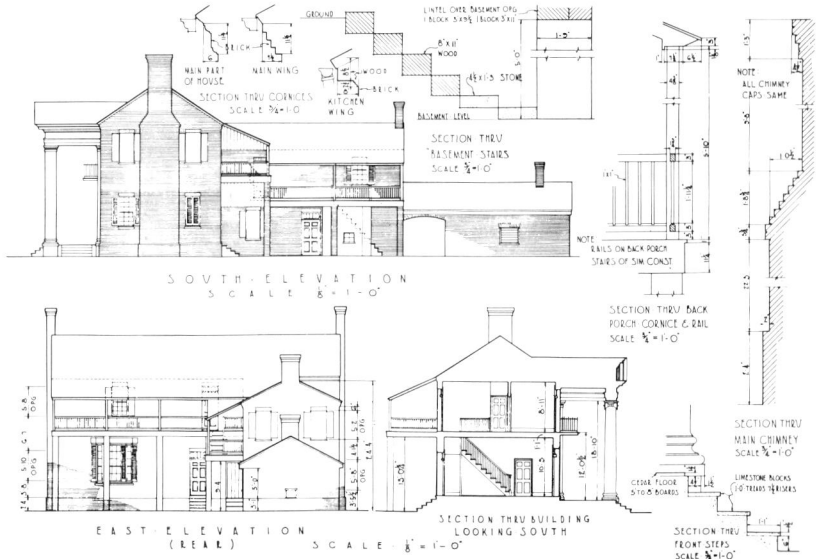

52. *Above and top right: Beaty-Mason house, Athens. The basic format of the façade, a central portico projecting from a three- or five-bay front, was commonplace in both one- and two-story versions throughout Alabama. Not so, however, the portico treatment itself: two rotund Ionic columns paired with heavy square outer piers. In reality, the entire front represents the 1845 overhauling of an earlier structure. Hiram Higgins was probably the architect for the renovation. Compare the Beaty-Mason house façade with Higgins's design for the East Alabama Masonic Female Institute at Talladega (illustration 63). (Library of Congress: Frances Benjamin Johnston photo; HABS: Samuel H. Pope, Jr., delineator, 1934.)*

53. *Glennville Plantation, Russell County, 1842–44. (HABS: W. N. Manning photo, 1935.)*

Auburn and Tuskegee in east central Alabama, and around Eufaula in the far southeastern corner of the state, the same formula became a favorite for both town and country dwellings. The Kidd-Halliday-Cary house* at Auburn, a raised-cottage version where square pillars rise directly from ground level, and the Bray-Barron house at Eufaula, are two particularly good examples. [57]

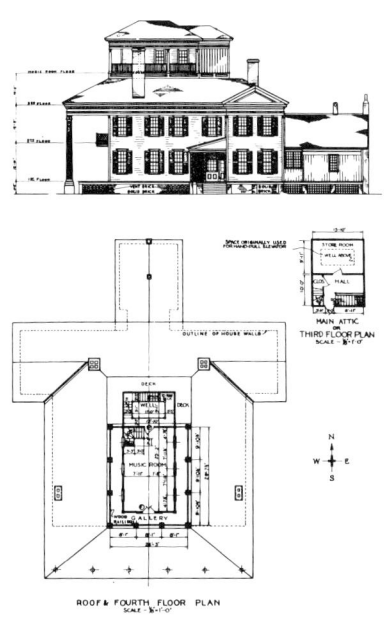

54. *Rosemount, Greene County, ca. 1840. (Library of Congress: Frances Benjamin Johnston photo;* HABS: *A. Brandt, delineator.)*

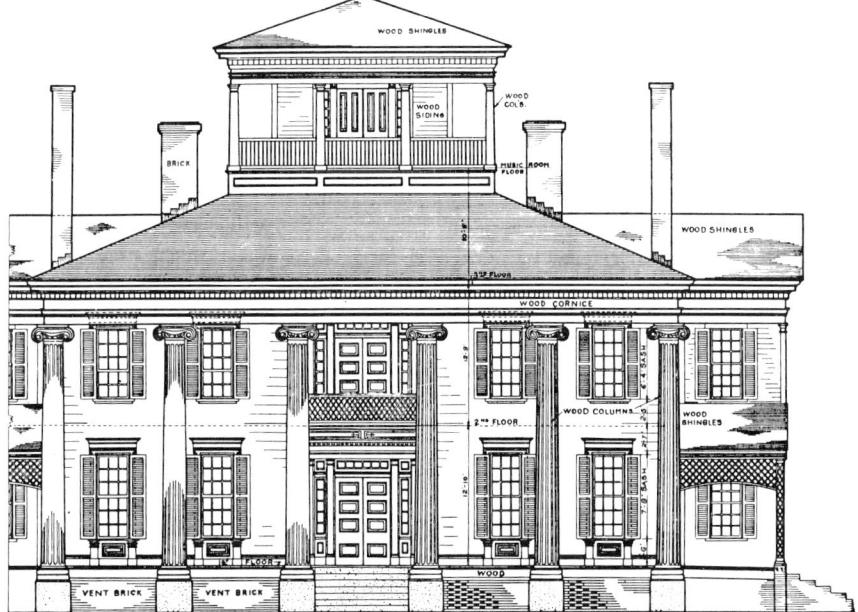

If the colossal portico was usually the order of the day for larger, two-story Greek Revival houses in Alabama, there were some notable exceptions. In Mobile the gallery was often remanded to the rear, and allegiance to the Greek Revival proclaimed only by a shouldered architrave about the door—as at the Dargan-Waring house*. [58] Architect George Steele chose a diminutive yet highly formal in antis

55. The colonnade of the Governor Henry W. Collier house (ca. 1835–40) at Tuscaloosa exemplifies the kind of implacable dignity that could be achieved through the substitution of tapered and molded piers for a conventional Grecian order. Both the paneled faces of the piers and the second-floor balcony, suspended between the two innermost pillars and railed with a wheatsheaf balustrade, are typical Tuscaloosa features of the period. Note, too, the smooth-plastered façade. (HABS: Alex Bush photo, 1935.)

56. Georgia Cottage, Mobile, 1840. (HABS: Jack Boucher photo, 1963.)

Doric entrance porch for his own country house, Oak Place*, near Huntsville. [59] Similarly, at Elm Bluff below Selma and Barton Hall* near Cherokee, small-scale Doric porches were in each case grafted onto a two-story, hipped-roof body behind. Barton Hall's restrained and impeccably detailed porch turns out to be but the prelude for a lofty hallway built around a soaring double stair. [60]

Through the 1840s and 1850s plain, robust pediments, along with piers, pilasters, and entablatures, were applied alike to houses, rustic law and medical offices, banks, courthouses, churches, academies, and even fire halls. [61–64] They lent an air of sober refinement to otherwise stark country meetinghouses like the Baptist church* at Orion in Pike County and the Ebenezer Presbyterian Church at Clinton, or the Summerfield Methodist Church* near Selma. [65] Ultimately, they transformed what might otherwise have been lackluster utilitarian structures into small monuments of taste.

57. *Kidd-Halliday-Cary house, Auburn, ca. 1848. Plain untapered piers complemented by equally plain bold trim were peculiar characteristics of the Greek Revival in the Auburn area.* Below: *Corkscrew stair between ground floor and raised first floor, Kidd-Halliday-Cary house.* (HABS: J. L. Irving, delineator, 1935.)

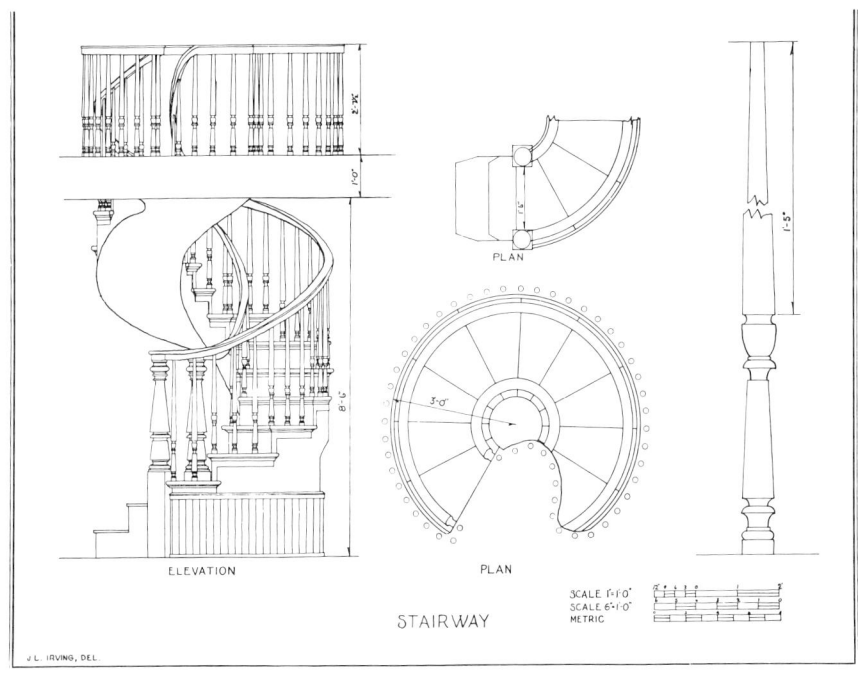

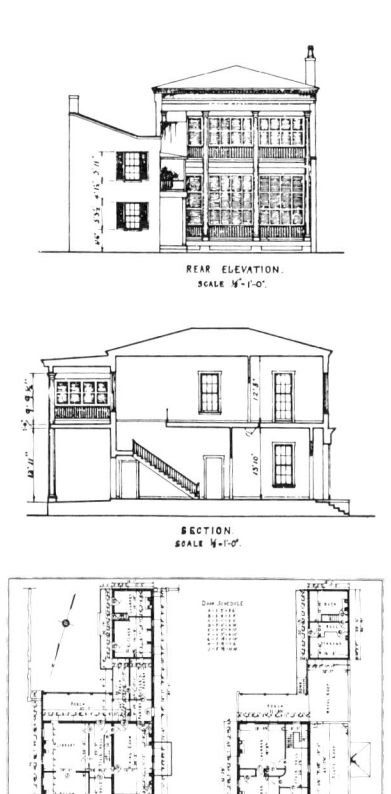

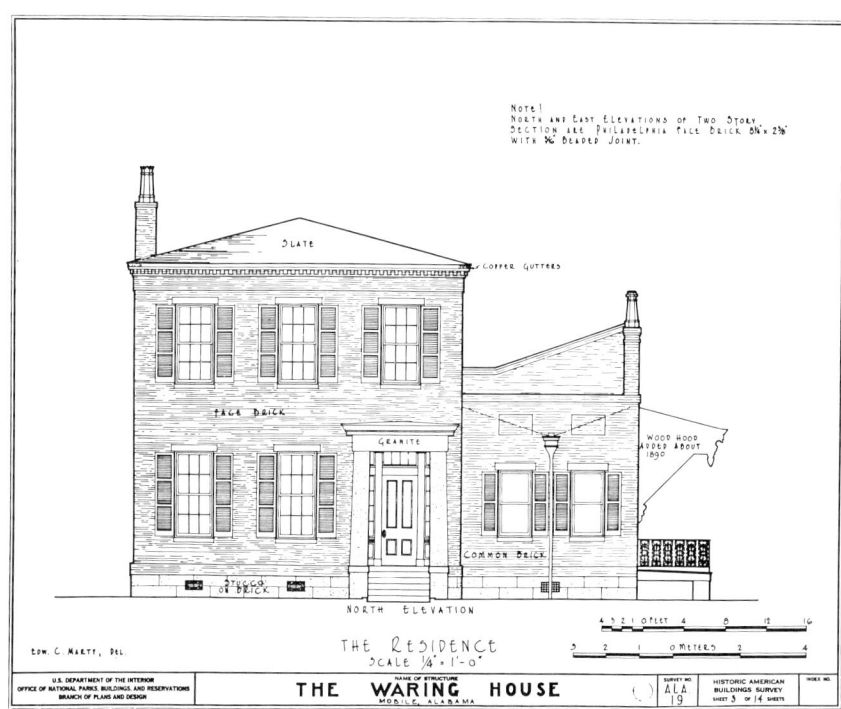
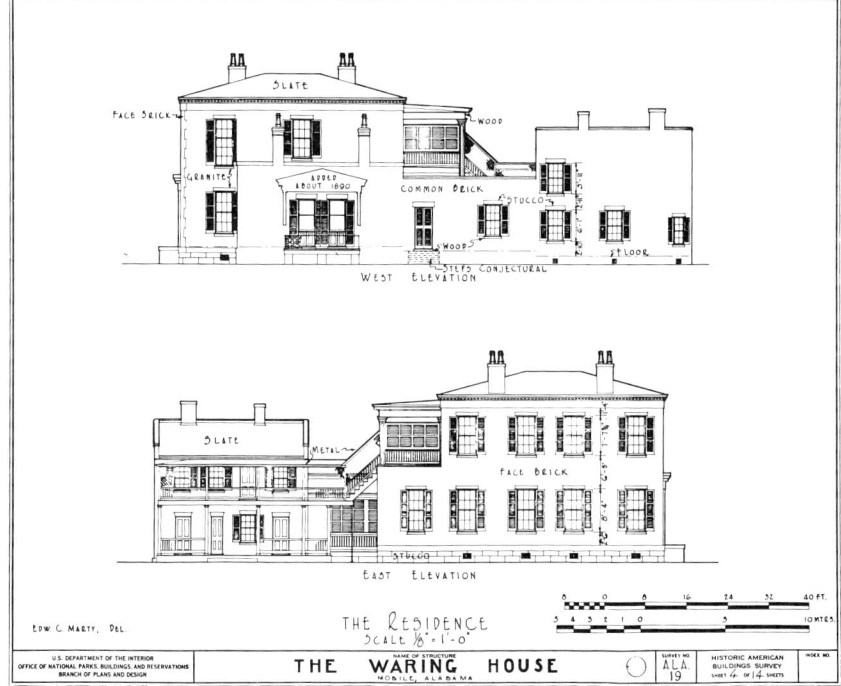

58. *Dargan-Waring house, Mobile, 1846. (HABS: Edward C. Martt, delineator, 1935.)*

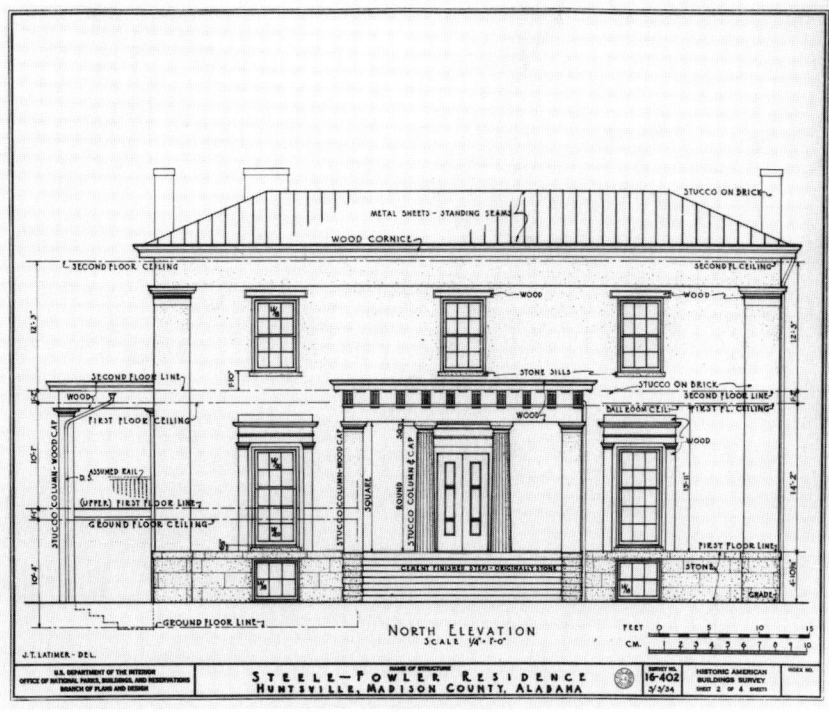

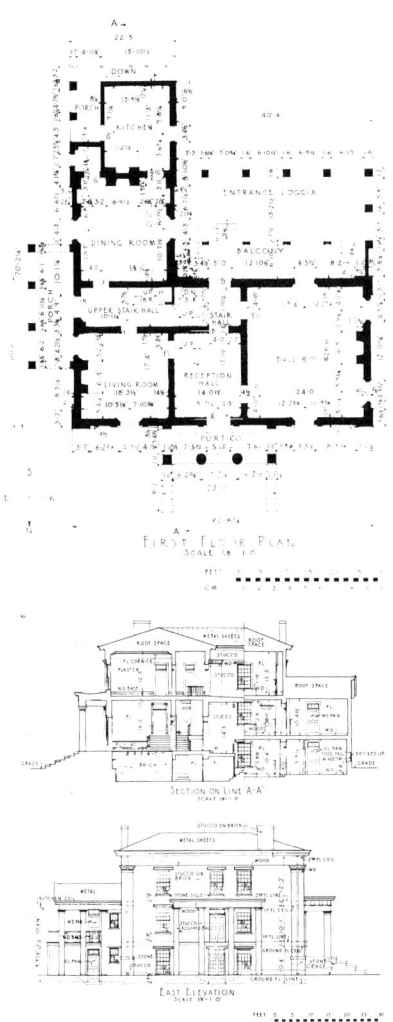

59. *Oak Place, Huntsville, 1840–44. Behind an austere Doric façade, owner-architect Steele concealed a novel split-level room arrangement devised to isolate entertainment areas from family quarters and to make judicious use of volumetric space without sacrificing formal dignity.* (HABS: *J. T. Latimer, delineator, 1934.*)

In residential architecture especially, distinct regional or local twists could often be detected. There were, for example, the low and spreading Greek Revival style houses about Gainesville, Boligee, and Eutaw in western Alabama—dwellings whose elongated façades seem to make them neoclassical precursors of the ranch-style suburban houses of the 1950s. [66] The aesthetic possibilities of a forthright colloquialism are epitomized by Oakleigh*, which stood in rural seclusion near Mobile when finished around 1838. It is difficult to imagine such a house anywhere but along the Gulf Coast. Here, amid semitropical live oaks, the Grecian spirit was adapted to the raised-cottage format of coastal tradition and to the T-shaped layout popular in antebellum Mobile—producing a residence of striking beauty and conceptual originality. [67]

Stephen D. Button's design for the short-lived first Montgomery statehouse, completed in 1847, introduced into central Alabama a lush rendition of the Greek Revival that made use of the several variations on the Corinthian order. [68] In the case of the state capitol building, this was Minard Lafever's own composite design based, as he put it, on "antique specimens." A domestic counterpart to the capitol's ornate, hexastyle portico was that which Button incorporated into his plans for the circa 1848 Montgomery residence of William Knox, one of the building commissioners for the statehouse. [69] The Knox mansion was followed in the 1850s by others of a

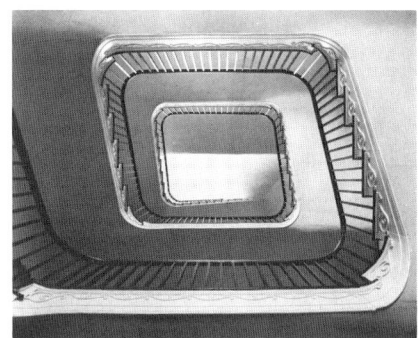

60. Barton Hall, Cherokee vicinity, ca. 1847–49. Doric porches at the front and sides are complemented by a stone-paved Doric loggia at the rear. Door surrounds are based on designs from Minard Lafever's Beauties of Modern Architecture. *Above and below right:* Inside, a graceful stairway rises in a series of double flights and bridge-like landings to a railed rooftop observatory. (Duane Phillips photos, 1982.)

61. Above left: *Dr. J. C. Francis medical office, Jacksonville, ca. 1840.* The doorway, with its segmentally arched transom, derives from Plate 29 of Asher Benjamin's Practice of Architecture *(1833). (Author's collection.)*

62. Above right: *Bank, formerly at Gainesville, Sumter County.* Built about 1838, this structure was moved to the grounds of the North River Yacht Club near Tuscaloosa in the 1970s and restored. *(Author's collection.)*

63. Right: *East Alabama Masonic Female Institute, Talladega, 1850–51.* Designed by Hiram Higgins of Athens, this school building was a somewhat elaborated version of another one of his school designs, the Athens Female Institute, erected in the mid-1840s. In 1858 the Talladega school became the State Institute for the Deaf and Blind. A Higgins trademark was the three-part modified Palladian windows flanking a central portico. *(Library of Congress: Frances Benjamin Johnston photo.)*

64. *Washington Fire Engine Company No. 8, Mobile, ca. 1851. The distyle-in-antis arrangement at street level provided for a pedestrian side entrance and two firewagon doors. Upstairs, jib windows opened onto a cantilevered iron balcony—all in all, a winsome application of the Greek Revival to a utilitarian structure. (HABS: T. M. Ellis, delineator, 1934.)*

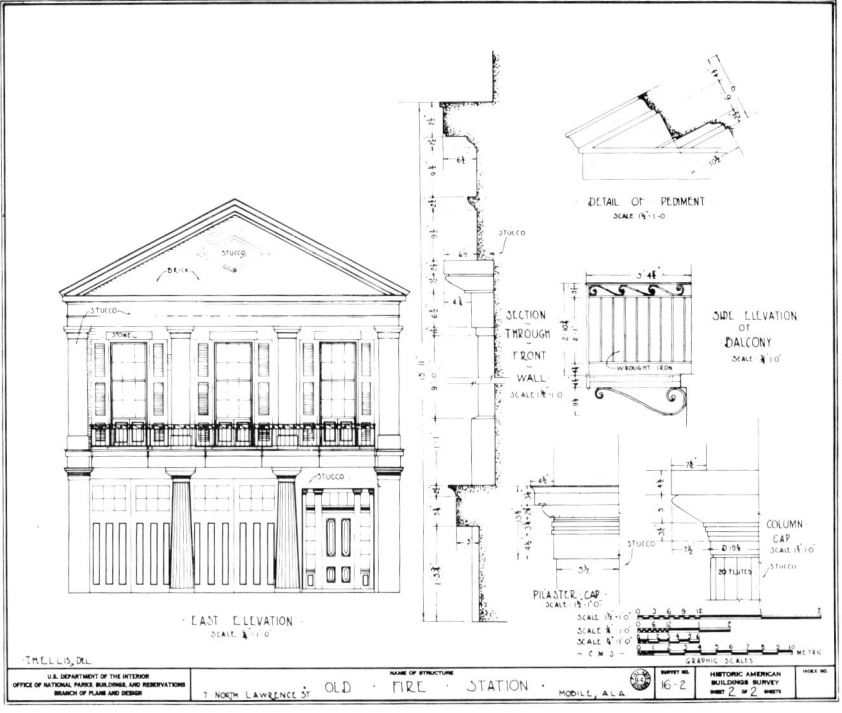

65. *Baptist Church, Orion, 1858. A dignified exercise in country Greek Revival, typical of dozens of other rural Alabama meetinghouses. Two doors were provided—one for the men and one for the women, who sat on opposite sides of the church. Normally, slave members of the congregation sat in designated areas on the main floor or in narrow side and rear galleries. (HABS: W. N. Manning photo, 1935.)*

similar ilk: the Gerald*, Murphy*, and Pollard* houses in Montgomery; the Edward Watts house* (now called Sturdivant Hall) in Selma; and in Tuscaloosa, the opulent residence of William Cochrane*. {70, 71} Montgomery County's 1854 courthouse, with double, iron-railed stairs curving up to a raised portico of the Tower of the Winds order, likewise belonged to the same strain. {72}

Increasingly during this last decade of the antebellum period, such structures took on the ever more florid ornamentation and the freedom from Grecian rubrics of proportion that had begun to gain national favor with Thomas U. Walter's neo-Renaissance scheme for the enlargement of the U.S. Capitol in Washington. The suffusion of the pristine Greek Revival of the 1830s with newer ideas that admitted a more fluid and picturesque approach is vividly evident in the irregular massing and non-axial layout of Gaineswood* at Demopolis, as enhanced and expanded by its owner-architect, General Nathan Bryan Whitfield, during the 1850s. Still, Whitfield stuck consistently to a neoclassical vocabulary of *detail,* producing, in the end, a series of elaborate suites paralleled by few houses anywhere in the South. {73}

This mixing of classical and nonclassical impulses, so noticeable in the years just before the Civil War, resulted in a curious hybrid strain of architecture that might be dubbed "bracketed Greek Revival." Retaining the monumental colonnade of the Greek Revival's heyday,

66. Right: "Ranch-style" Greek Revival: Adustin Hall, Gainesville, 1844. Below: Double parlors at Adustin Hall. Such forthright, pleasingly proportioned interiors are a legacy of the Greek Revival in Alabama. The door facing, with its fretted cornerblocks and raked lintel, is yet another example of Asher Benjamin's pervasive influence upon buildings throughout the state at this period. (Don Fleming, exterior photo, 1983; Duane Phillips, parlor photo, 1983.)

this new departure then substituted for conventional Grecian elements such features as turned eaves brackets and jigsaw-cut porch railings. Frequently, builders altered the treatment and proportions of the columns themselves, or glibly replaced them outright with octagonal supports or other equally nonclassical members. At times, the massing itself of a structure was shifted about so as to make for a

67. *Oakleigh, Mobile. The detailing of its lightly proportioned portico and side galleries mirrors mainstream Greek Revival taste of the late 1830s and 1840s, but the raised brick ground floor was in the tradition of the Gulf Coast. (HABS: Jack Boucher photo, 1963.)*

68. *Old State Capitol, Montgomery, 1846–47 (burned 1849). From an original watercolor by the architect, Stephen D. Button. The present Capitol building, erected on the same site in 1850–51, incorporates portions of the foundation of this earlier statehouse. (Alabama Department of Archives and History: John Scott photocopy.)*

69. William Knox house, Montgomery, ca. 1848. The first of several central Alabama houses distinguished by a colossal hexastyle portico employing one of the variants on the Corinthian order. Here, the order was actually one devised and published by Minard Lafever. The same order was used for the porticoes of both the 1847 and 1851 state capitol buildings. (From Art Work of Montgomery and Vicinity, 1894.)

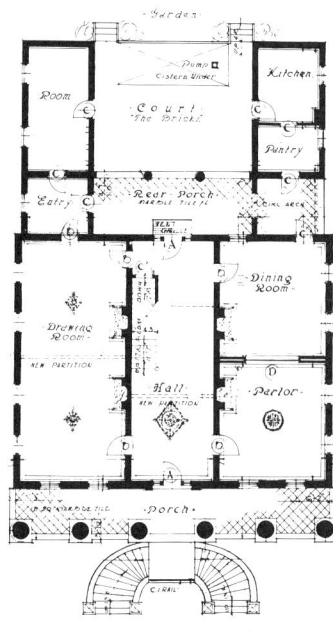

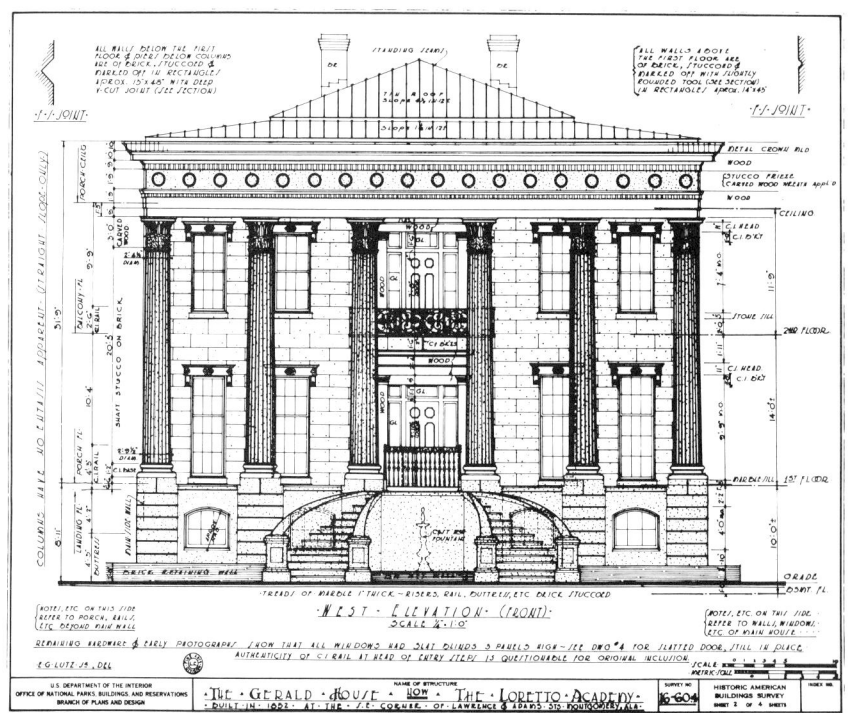

70. Above and right: *Gerald house, Montgomery, ca. 1858 (razed 1964). Right: Drawing room of Sturdivant Hall, Selma, ca. 1856. Sturdivant Hall's interior finish, as seen in this 1930s photo, mirrored the growing taste for opulence that characterized the 1850s.* (HABS: C. O. Lutz, Jr., delineator, 1934; Library of Congress: Frances Benjamin Johnston photo.)

71. William Cochrane house, Tuscaloosa, ca. 1855 (demolished 1964). (Library of Congress: Frances Benjamin Johnston photo.)

72. Montgomery County Courthouse, Montgomery, 1854. Over the next several years, the raised portico and curving steps were imitated on a smaller scale in other central Alabama courthouses at Hayneville, Tuskegee, Dadeville, Greenville, and Opelika. (Alabama Department of Archives and History: John Scott photography.)

73. *Gaineswood, Demopolis, ca. 1842–60. Slowly, Alabama's finest neoclassical house evolved from a log dogtrot nucleus (later the logs themselves were removed) into a complex arrangement of formal spaces reflecting in their layout the growing preference for picturesque asymmetry. Opposite: Gaineswood interiors.* (HABS: *Clarice Payne, delineator, 1936; Duane Phillips photos, 1983.*)

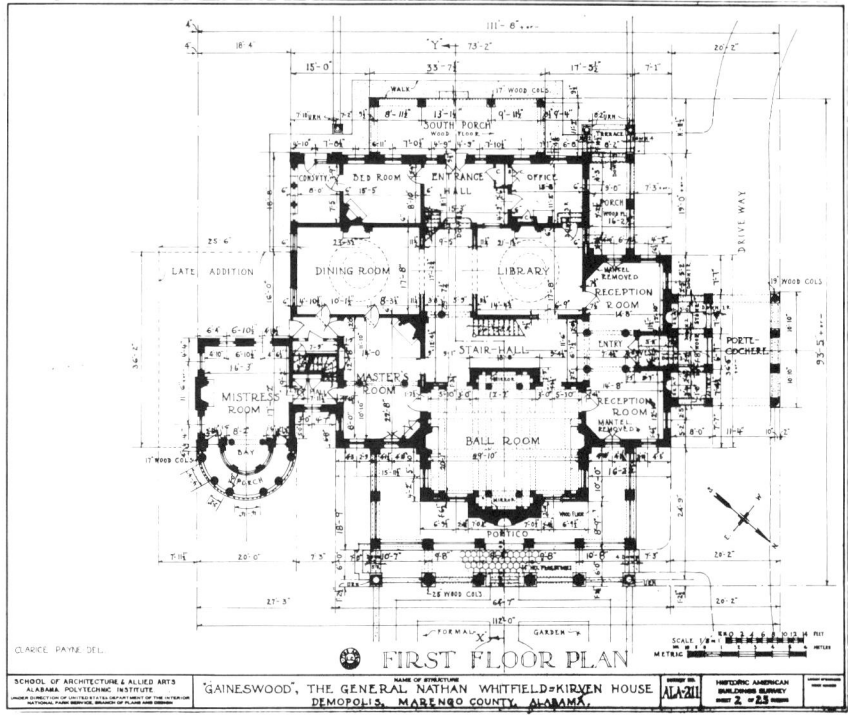

Neoclassicism: Greek Revival

74. "Bracketed Greek Revival": Felix Tait house, Camden vicinity, 1860. Beneath the wide eaves, scroll-sawn brackets have replaced classical denticulation. The doorway retains a typical Greek Revival shouldered architrave, but the columns are octagon-shaped, and the overall massing of the house itself is irregular and deliberately asymmetrical. The gingerbread-like bannisters of porch and balcony were likewise an innovation of the 1850s. (Library of Congress: Frances Benjamin Johnston photo.)

brashly asymmetrical impression, as with Alexander J. Bragg's design for the Tait-Starr house* (1860) near Camden. [74] Yet the rule continued to be one of fundamental symmetry—a rule that Bragg faithfully observed in his treatment of the Wilcox County courthouse* of 1858–59, and in the residence* he probably planned for his brother, Judge John Bragg of Mobile, about 1855. Other instances of this late antebellum fusion of stylistic influences include Kirkwood* in Eutaw; the J. H. Y. Webb house* and the Southern University Chancellor's residence*, both at Greensboro; the Wash Smith house in Selma; Tuskegee's Varner-Alexander house*; and the Gideon Coates house near Gadsden. Finally, there is the eccentric Drish house* in Tuscaloosa, where an Italian-villa tower with tall arched windows neatly halves a bracketed Ionic portico. [75]

Despite a progressive drift away from the clear-cut Hellenic vision of the late 1830s and early 1840s, neoclassicism proved a hardy survivor in out-of-the-way corners of Alabama. Thus, at Gainesville, the primly pedimented and pilastered Methodist church of 1872 mirrors in miniature the older and larger Presbyterian church built not far away, over three decades earlier. In fact, the neoclassical spirit never flickered out completely in post–Civil War Alabama and, transformed, would vigorously reemerge at century's end.

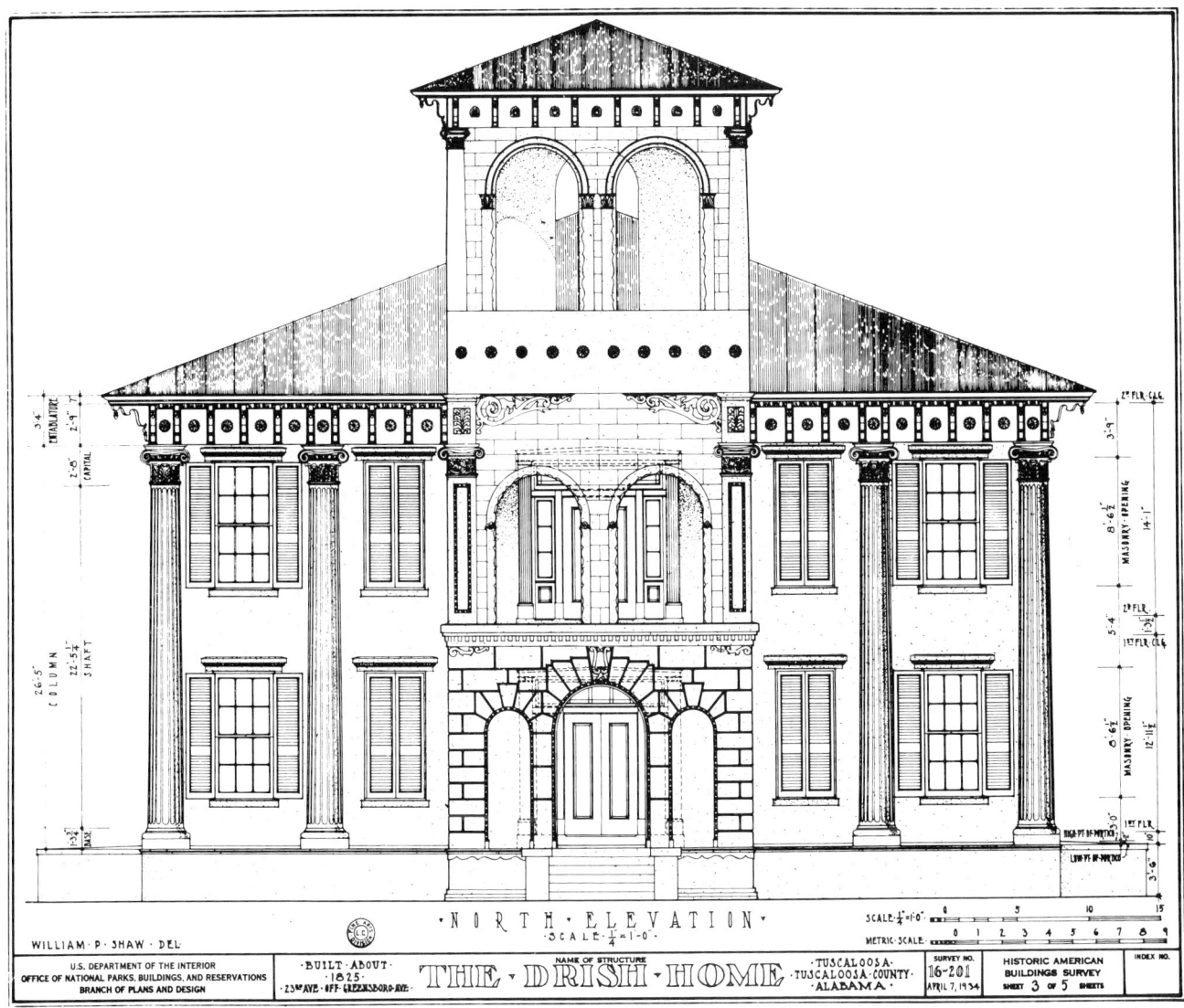

75. *Drish house, Tuscaloosa. Italianate superimposed upon Greek Revival. (HABS: William P. Shaw, delineator, 1934.)*

Summary Characteristics

- Symmetry and balance both of plan and elevation (the side-hall plan simply being half of a symmetrical unit).
- Rectilinearity of line and a general heaviness of scale (for example, square-headed door and window openings and rectangular transoms, as opposed to the fanlights and Palladian windows of the Federal period).
- Low-pitched or even flat rooflines and the use of wide, heavy entablatures; gable ends are often treated as triangular pediments.
- Engaged antae or pier-like pilasters articulating wall surfaces.
- Bold, heavy interior trim; use of applied Grecian-based ornament such as acanthus leaf, palmette, egg-and-dart molding.

The Gothic Revival
(principally 1840s to 1870s)

Not to be confused with its offspring, the High Victorian Gothic of the post–Civil War era, the Gothic Revival was perhaps the most self-consciously literary of all the nineteenth century's attempts to evoke through architecture the distant in time and place—whether ancient Greece, sunny Italy, or medieval England. It was, of course, a romantic rediscovery of the English Middle Ages through such agencies as the immensely popular novels of Sir Walter Scott, coupled with a general reaction against eighteenth-century rationalism, that spurred the Gothic Revival in both Great Britain and America.

As early as the 1820s a vague and whimsical Gothic consciousness was proclaimed in Alabama by the pointed doors and windows of a handful of buildings like the Masonic lodges at Huntsville and Athens, and the First Presbyterian Church in Tuscumbia—structures that were otherwise classically detailed and proportioned. [76] There was also the 1822 Protestant Union Church at Mobile, boasting not only pointed-arch openings but also wooden battlements and a pinnacled belltower fashioned of sawn pine lumber. [77] Churches built during the mid-1840s—First Presbyterian, Montgomery; the first St. Stephen's Church, Eutaw; and the original Church of the Nativity in Huntsville—were gothicized through similar devices. [78] Still, these affectations did nothing more than mask traditional meetinghouse forms with naïve and superficial Gothic detail.

It was as a vehicle of the Anglo-Catholic trend—the "ecclesiological movement"—within the Protestant Episcopal church that the Gothic Revival finally achieved maturity in Alabama during the last decade before the Civil War. This is attested by a dozen or so Episcopal churches erected in the state between 1850 and 1861. Although based on the questionable assumption that Gothic architecture was the only truly "Christian" setting for divine worship, these structures attained a veracity of form and design that sets them apart and makes them believably medieval in mood if not in materials. Collectively, they rank as one of the state's finest nineteenth-century architectural achievements.

Three of the churches—Trinity, Mobile; St. John's, Montgomery*; and Nativity, Huntsville—were designed by the nationally renowned partnership of Frank Wills and Henry Dudley, who, along with Richard Upjohn, became virtually the arbiters of Ecclesiological Gothic throughout North America. All three churches are built of brick, each with a corner tower capped by a soaring spire. Two of the churches, Trinity at Mobile and Nativity in Huntsville, carry the ideal Ecclesiological interior to its logical conclusion in having narrow, aisled naves, dimly lit by clerestory windows. [79]

76. *Masonic Hall, Athens, 1826 (razed 1968). This building was patterned after an even earlier Masonic lodge at Huntsville, built in 1823 and demolished in 1918. (HABS: Samuel H. Pope, Jr., delineator, 1934.)*

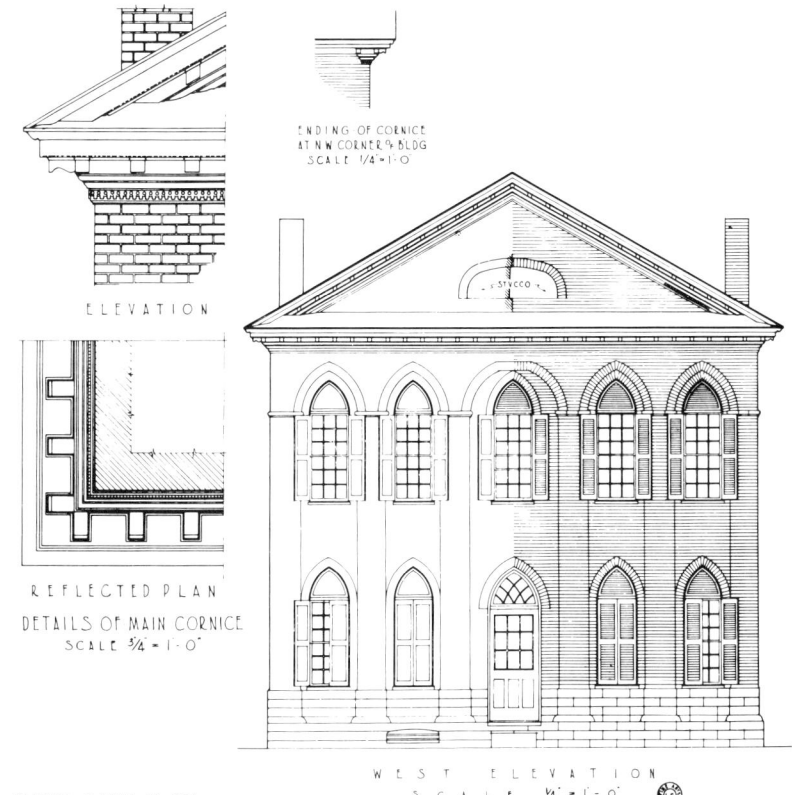

77. Right: *Protestant Union Church, Mobile (from "Plan and View of the City of Mobile," James M. Goodwin and C. Haire, 1824). (Library of Congress: Allen Goldstein photocopy.)*

78. Far right: *First Presbyterian Church, Montgomery, 1846–47. The stiff, boxey proportions of the traditional American meetinghouse are still evident beneath the thin Gothic veneer. (Author's collection.)*

79. *Church of the Nativity, Huntsville, 1857–59. Opposite: Nave. The handsome timbered ceiling was fashioned of native oak at a local steam mill. (Duane Phillips photo, 1983; Victor Haagen photo, 1963.)*

The other Alabama churches composing this group were small wooden buildings that followed closely Richard Upjohn's precepts for an economical, yet dignified and distinctly Episcopal house of worship. Upjohn, in fact, may himself have designed the best known of these little churches, St. Andrew's* at Prairieville. [80] Additional examples like St. Luke's, Cahaba*; St. John's, Forkland*; and St. Luke's, Jacksonville, show the influence of Upjohn's widely circulated *Rural Architecture* (1852), which presented two basic plans for inexpensive frame houses of worship—Upjohn favored board-and-batten construction—of appropriate Gothic demeanor. [81, 82] Even four decades later, country chapels such as the 1892 Grace Church at Mount Meigs bespoke the persistence of the Upjohnian spirit in the rural Episcopal churches of Alabama.

Other denominations avoided the ecclesiological militancy of the

80. *St. Andrew's Church, Prairieville, 1853–54. (John Scott photo, 1963.)*

Episcopalians, although Presbyterian churches at Wetumpka, Mobile, and Huntsville did turn to a mild Gothic of a somewhat less scrupulous nature. The Wetumpka church,* dating from 1856–57, was almost certainly inspired by the design for "A Gothic Church" which Samuel Sloan included in *The Model Architect*. [83] The Jackson Street Presbyterian Church in Mobile and the First Presbyterian Church of Huntsville—the latter designed in 1859 by Adolphus Heiman of Nashville—were both larger but also more ungainly than the Wetumpka church: conventional Protestant "preaching boxes" with a Gothic veneer.

Mid-century Gothic enthusiasm in Alabama also produced a handful of "castellated" school buildings variously bedecked with battlements, buttresses, turrets, and other paraphernalia presumed to impart an air of cloistered academic respectability. George Steele prepared the plans for the Huntsville Female Seminary; those for Wesleyan University at Florence and Southern University* at Greensboro were drawn by Adolphus Heiman. [84] In 1854 John Stewart of Philadelphia was commissioned to devise a suitably medieval-looking design for the Tuskegee Female College. And twelve years later, state university officials at Tuscaloosa settled upon a castellated plan submitted by Alexander Jackson Davis for Woods Hall, which rose on the ashes of the original university buildings destroyed during the

81. St. Luke's Church, Dallas County, 1852–53. Formerly at Cahaba, this building was moved to Martin's Station in 1878. St. Luke's is the only one of Alabama's mid-nineteenth-century Gothic Revival churches for which HABS *recording teams prepared a full set of measured drawings. The church remains today much as it did when the photo at right was made in 1934. (*HABS: *W. N. Manning photo, 1934; Helen M. Tigner and James L. Murphy, Jr., delineators, 1936.)*

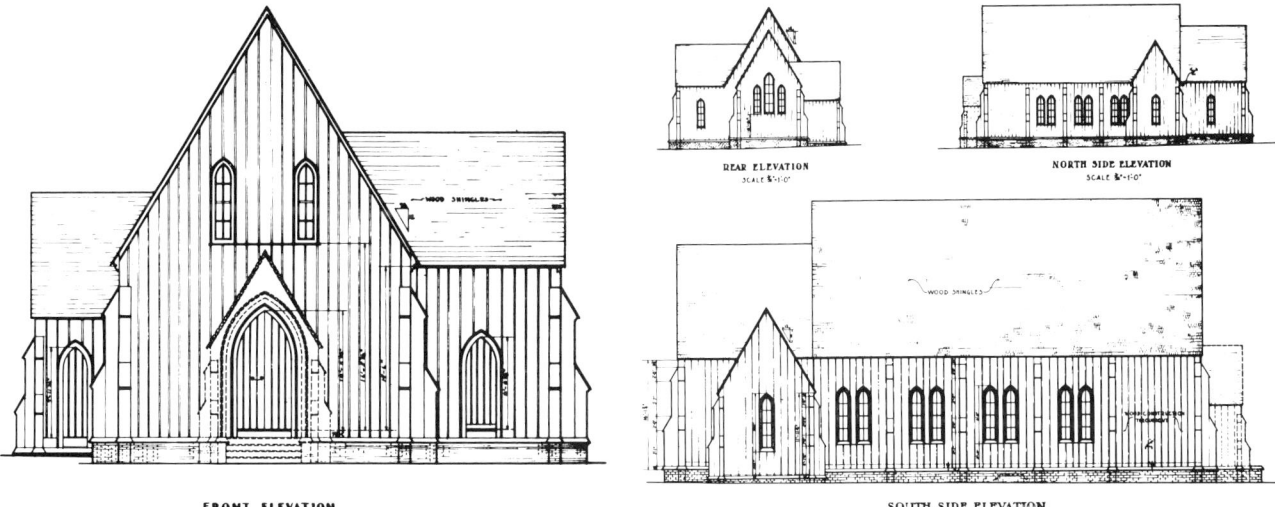

Civil War. Actually, the design was the same that Davis had conceived in the 1840s for the Virginia Military Institute. This scheme was subsequently modified by two University of Alabama faculty members who themselves had former VMI connections: Colonel James T. Murfee, the supervising architect for Woods Hall, and Captain John F. Gibbs. In a long, brick structure that is still a major campus landmark, lanky battlemented corner turrets commingled with unlikely tiers of rear cast-iron galleries.

Within the domestic sphere Gothic Revival taste made relatively little headway in Alabama. Those few genuinely Gothic Revival

82. Right: *Comparison of this plate from* Upjohn's Rural Architecture *with the 1856 St. Luke's Church, Jacksonville (below) suggests the fidelity with which some small Episcopal congregations followed the architect's published plans for economical yet "churchly" buildings of inexpensive board-and-batten construction. The Jacksonville church is virtually a mirror image of the Upjohn design but for the fact that the sacristy, which in Upjohn's drawings is placed on the side of the chancel opposite the tower, here shares the same elevation. (Duane Phillips photo, 1983.)*

Gothic Revival

83. *First Presbyterian Church, Wetumpka, 1856–57, and* (below left) *the possible source of its basic design—Samuel Sloan's scheme for "A Gothic Church," from* The Model Architect. *Sloan's specifications called for a masonry structure, but the builder of the Alabama church opted for a simpler board-and-batten version. Its interior* (below right) *still remained unmistakably neoclassical. (*HABS: *W. N. Manning photos, 1935.)*

84. *Main building of Southern University (forerunner of Birmingham-Southern College), Greensboro, 1857–59. Architect Adolphus Heiman here reinterpreted in brick much the same design he had previously developed in stone at the University of Nashville: a rectangular main block dominated by a square pinnacled and crenellated tower. During the late 1960s the building was used as a private school (Southern Academy) until the structure was devastated by a tornado in May 1973. That same month the ruins were leveled by clean-up crews. (HABS: W. N. Manning photo, 1934.)*

85. *Murray Forbes Smith house, Mobile, completed 1851. Mock battlements, a Tudor-arched wooden porch, and windows bedecked with hoodmolds were novel accretions thinly disguising a typical center-hall domestic "box." Smith was a cotton broker whose daughter, Alva, grew up here to become a grande dame of Gilded Age society—first as Mrs. William K. Vanderbilt, then as Mrs. O. H. P. Belmont, of New York and Newport. (Courtesy Historic Mobile Preservation Society.)*

houses that were built have until recently been ignored, with the result that the 1982 demolition of the state's last great urban Gothic Revival residence—Mobile's long-abused Goldsby mansion*— provoked scarcely a murmur from the preservation establishment. Until 1930 Mobile could also count the Murray Forbes Smith house,

86. *Wemyss house, Greensboro vicinity, ca. 1855 (demolished). (Library of Congress: Frances Benjamin Johnston photo.)*

with a porch distinguished by flattened Tudoresque arches and a roofline that fairly bristled with cardboard-like crenellations. [85]

Inland and northward were other notable Gothic-style houses, all now gone: Forest Hill at Demopolis—a romantic essay in clustered chimneypots and bargeboard-trimmed gables—as well as the Wemyss house near Greensboro, the Buck house at Tuscaloosa, and Highland, Governor Lewis Parson's 1854 Gothic brick house at Talladega. [86, 87] In fact, a clustering of Gothic Revival dwellings about Talladega and nearby Oxford, in the Appalachian foothills of northeastern Alabama, may well be attributed to the Victorian notion that the style was especially fitted for a broken, mountainous landscape.

Hardly more than a score of good examples of residential Gothic Revival stand today in Alabama. Waldwick* at Gallion and Ashe

87. Highland, Talladega, 1854. This ca. 1875 photo shows the house before its original one-story porch was replaced by an exuberant two-tiered gallery about 1880. From the middle of the rooftop deck sprouted an octagonal turret. Highland was razed in the 1960s. (Courtesy Mrs. Edwin Jewell.)

88. Waldwick, Hale County, ca. 1840 (renovated in Gothic Revival style ca. 1852). (HABS: W. N. Manning photo, 1935.)

Cottage in Demopolis—both dating in their present form from the 1850s—are two of the oldest and best preserved: pleasant, bay-windowed houses with gables playfully highlighted by curvilinear bargeboard trim. [88] Boxwood, a Talladega house of the same vintage, takes its latticed porches and Gothic wall dormers straight from the Hudson Valley designs of Alexander Jackson Davis. But it was Davis's friend and colleague, A. J. Downing, who, through works like *Cottage Residences* and *The Architecture of Country Houses*, became the chief purveyor of a cheerful household Gothic mode to a mass American audience. Spring Villa* and the Edwards house, both in Lee

89. Right: *Buell house, Greenville (1874);* below: *Marshall house, Selma (ca. 1875). (Author's collection.)*

County, are Downing-inspired, although the festive porch of the latter, with its frivolous and lacey ogival arches, carries the ideal of Gothic picturesqueness a little far.

Scattered about the state at Selma, Clayton, Greenville, Troy, Tuskegee, Huntsville, and Tuscaloosa are other isolated instances of domestic Gothic Revival, generally dating from the 1860s and 1870s.[89] Most of these manage to achieve a Gothic effect with little or no specific Gothic detail, relying instead upon steep, accentuated cross-gables, clustered chimneys, and ornamental porches that suggest rather than seriously imitate. Indeed, their light-hearted Gothic mannerisms could place the majority of these houses as easily in that more general class of picturesque dwelling that the nineteenth century knew simply as the *cottage orné,* a genre touched on later.

Summary Characteristics

- Prominent, often steeply pitched and bargeboard-trimmed, gables and cross gables.
- Especially in the "ecclesiological" churches of the 1850s, a tendency toward asymmetrical massing; secular versions of the Gothic Revival in Alabama tended to remain symmetrical in their disposition.
- Frequent preference for board-and-batten sheathing in frame construction, so as to lend a vertical accent and also to express honesty of construction.
- Pointed or triangular-headed windows, sometimes filled with tracery.
- Cosmetic application of pinnacles, battlements, and buttresses to walls, rooflines, and towers.

The Italianate
(1850s to 1880s)

Appearing in Alabama around 1850, the Italianate style was another facet of that same broad, European-based romantic movement that included the contemporary Gothic Revival. Italian architecture—whether the spreading, towered farmhouses of Tuscany or the urban palazzi of Renaissance Rome—exerted a strong pull on the nineteenth-century artistic imagination, as concepts of what was acceptable in architectural design broadened to include more and more of the exotic and the faraway.

With its connotations of a warm and sunny landscape, the "Italian style"—so the architectural pattern books dubbed it—was touted as being peculiarly suited to the South. The broad overhanging eaves were regarded as being readymade for the southern climate, as were the expansive verandas developed in Americanized versions of the Italian villa. Needless to say, such verandas also responded nicely to the long-standing southern custom of porch-sitting. No doubt another factor in the appeal of the Italianate was the freedom of arrangement its fluid volumes allowed. Little wonder, then, that the style was more prevalent in antebellum Alabama than is generally realized, or than nostalgic notions about the Greek Revival would care to admit.

Italian-inspired architecture first made its way, via the British Isles, into East Coast domestic designs during the late 1830s. Modified according to American taste, the style was eventually disseminated far and wide through books like A. J. Downing's *The Architecture of Country Houses* and Samuel Sloan's *The Model Architect,* both of which appeared in the early 1850s. Sloan made an especially strong impact on the South, catering from his Philadelphia office to an elite southern clientele that included planters, cotton brokers, and professional men. In fact, Sloan can probably claim credit for first introducing an Italian flavor into Alabama domestic architecture through his circa 1851 design for the Montgomery residence of Joseph S. Winter. Plans for the Winter house, along with a perspective view, were published in *The Model Architect*. [90] During the decade that followed, dozens of other buildings in Alabama's capital city, ranging from cottages and suburban mansions to commercial structures, were either remodeled or erected from the ground up in the Italianate manner. One of these was the so-called White House of the Confederacy*—the residence that in 1861 would briefly become the Confederate executive mansion. [91] Indeed, to a visiting newspaper correspondent that year, it seemed as if Montgomery were a town consisting almost entirely of houses built "in the style of the Italian villa, surrounded by expensive and carefully kept gardens."

Italianate elements could also be adapted to the most constricted of urban settings, as witnessed by the tall, bracketed, closely built houses that began to appear in Mobile during the same period. [92] But the distinctive qualities of the Italianate style continued to be most memorably displayed in the expansive designs conceived for garden-surrounded rural or suburban mansions. Some of these were symmetrical in disposition, presenting an axial façade even though side elevations might be randomly broken out with low wings and bay windows. Others were boldly irregular compositions, frequently dominated by an offset tower—an arrangement deemed particularly appropriate for broken terrain.

To the symmetrical class of villas belonged Montgomery's destroyed Garrett-Hatchett house,* very likely designed either by Samuel Sloan himself or John Stewart, his sometime architectural partner. [93] Stewart has definitely been documented as the architect of another of Alabama's symmetrical villas, the Robert Jemison house* (1860–62) in Tuscaloosa. [94] Crowned by a glazed observatory and girdled by arched wooden porches, the stuccoed brick mansion not only represented the height of 1860s fashion but also incorporated such novelties as a private gas plant and some of the state's earliest indoor plumbing.

Of the same general type are Dean Hall and Homewood (now called Kendall Manor) at Eufaula, as well as two Jacksonville

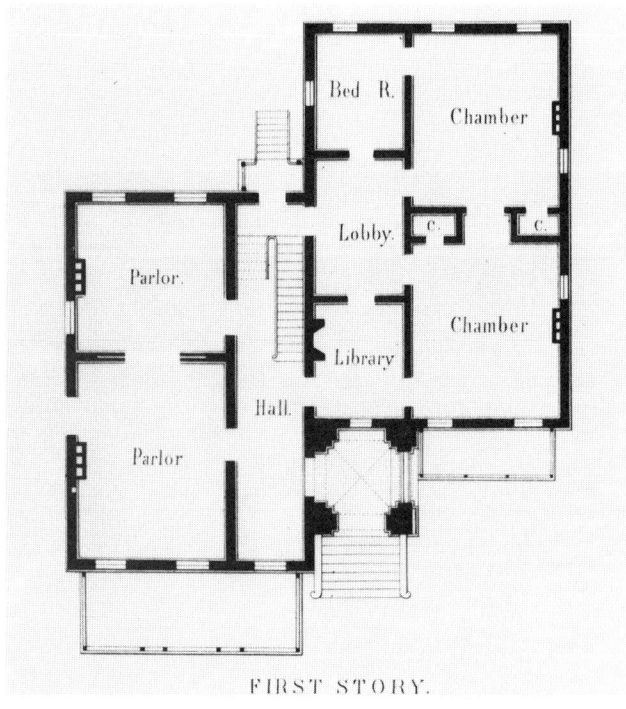

90. *Perspective rendering from* The Model Architect *of "A Southern House" designed by Samuel Sloan "in the Italian style." Sloan noted in the accompanying text that the design was "similar in most of its features" to plans he had prepared for the residence of Joseph S. Winter in Montgomery. Above right: An old photo of the long-destroyed Winter house confirms the truth of Sloan's statement. With only slight modification, the interior layout, too, seems to have accorded with Sloan's published plan* (right) *and marked a radical break from the strict symmetry of still-prevalent neoclassicism. (Perspective drawing and plan courtesy Mr. and Mrs. Robert Thorington; photo Alabama Department of Archives and History {John Scott photocopy}.)*

91. Confederate White House, Montgomery. A sober hip-roofed, Federal-style house built about 1835 and "Italianized" during the 1850s. (HABS: Walter L. Harrison and Merriam A. Delanay, delineators, 1935.)

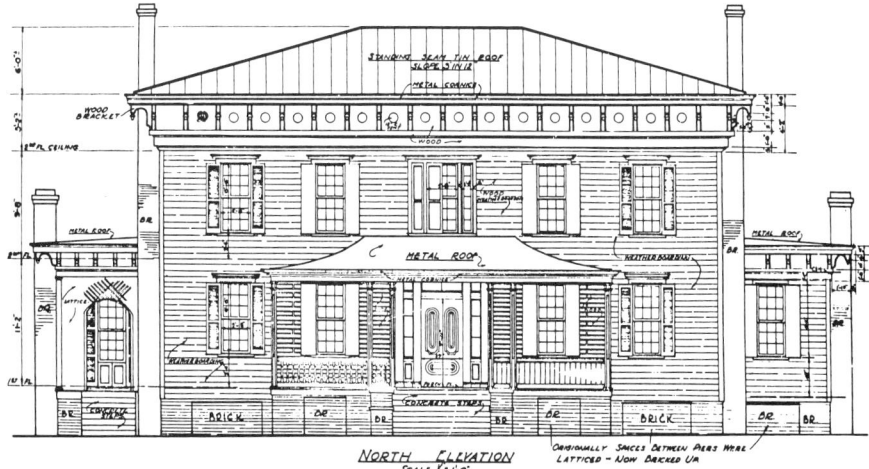

92. Frederick V. Cluis house, Mobile, 1857. (Roy Thigpen photo, 1974.)

93. *Garrett-Hatchett house, Montgomery, 1860.* (HABS: P. F. Hudson and E. O. Lutz, Jr., delineators, 1935.)

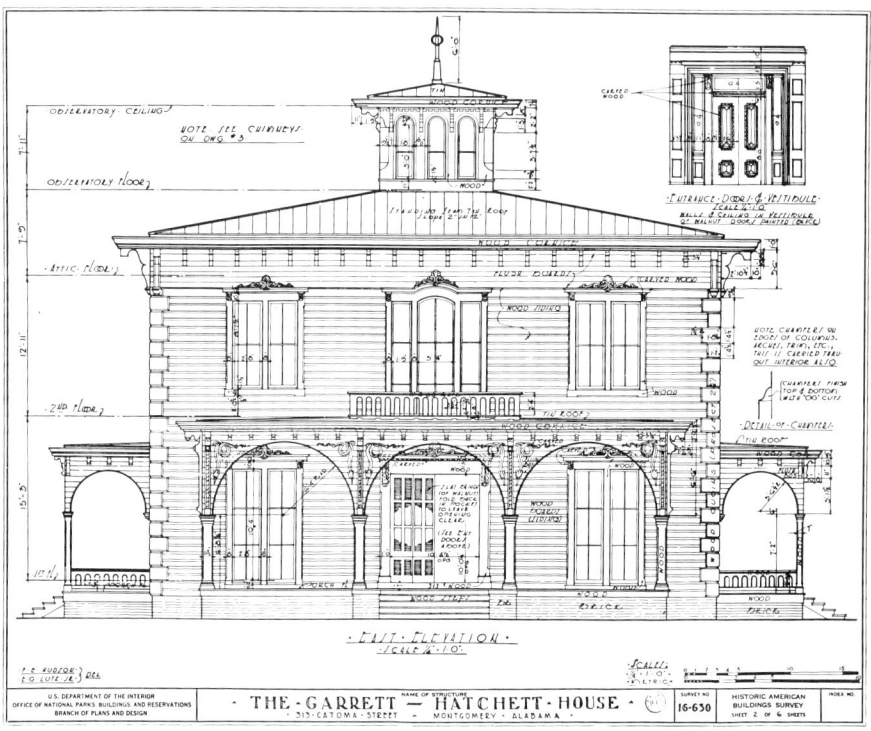

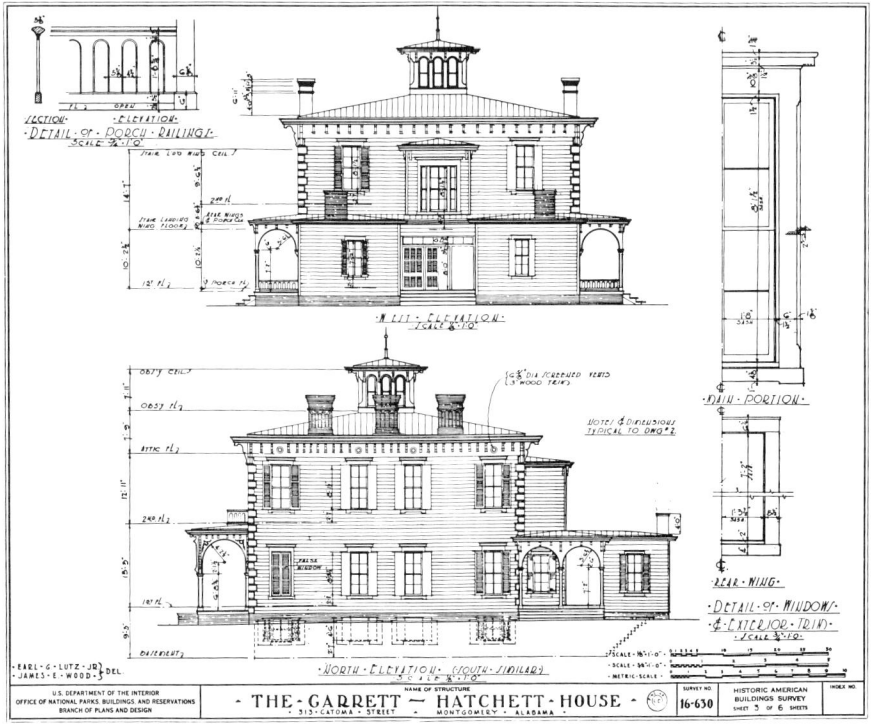

94. Jemison house, Tuscaloosa, 1860–62. (From City of Tuskaloosa, 1887.)

houses—Ten Oaks and The Magnolias*. Each of the Jacksonville structures, however, substitutes a central three-story entrance tower with hooded balcony for the ornate rooftop belvederes that distinguish their Tuscaloosa and Eufaula counterparts. Here again, the Sloan influence is evident, for both houses are obviously based on Design 6, a scheme for a "Villa in the Italian style," from *The Model Architect*. [95] Nor was Italianate symmetry reserved merely for larger dwellings. The 1874 Leckey house* at Leighton embodies essentially the same design concept translated to a charming cottage scale. [96]

Mobile's Ketchum house* of 1861, now the episcopal residence for the Roman Catholic Diocese of Mobile, is likewise symmetrically composed. But in feeling, the structure occupies a class by itself—somewhere between a cold, self-contained little urban palazzo and a hospitable, spreading country mansion. Its rather stiff outward formality is agreeably relieved by a lacey, cast-iron veranda that sweeps around two sides. [97]

A number of fine asymmetrically designed villas were also erected in Alabama during the years just before the Civil War. Most are gone today: the Gideon Nelson house at Greensboro [98], the Battle house in Tuscaloosa, Huntsville's Abingdon Place, and in Montgomery the Thomas Hill Watts mansion in addition to Samuel Sloan's Winter house. Happily, however, one of those still standing is Kenworthy Hall* near Marion, built between 1858 and 1861. Its architect was either Richard Upjohn or his son and partner, Richard M. Upjohn—the provenance is not altogether clear. At any rate, the great brick-and-brownstone dwelling is quite extraordinary, ranking among

95. *Symmetrical villas. Top left: Homewood (now Kendall Manor) at Eufaula, 1874. Top right: Ten Oaks, Jacksonville, ca. 1855. Compare the Jacksonville house with the plate above from Sloan's* Model Architect, *showing a "Villa in the Italian Style." Bottom right: Side view and latticed wellhouse at Ten Oaks. In 1864 this house served as headquarters for Confederate General P. G. T. Beauregard. (Courtesy Eufaula Heritage Association; Duane Phillips photos, 1983.)*

those houses directly traceable to the elder Upjohn's scheme for the 1845 Edward King mansion at Newport. Kenworthy Hall long ago lost its original porch. Still, its massing and composition unmistakably reveal its lineage. {99}

For the moment at least, the abandoned and mutilated Seibels house* in Montgomery, another early exercise in romantic Italianate asymmetry, is also standing. [100] It, too, may be the work of either Sloan or Stewart, though this cannot be proven. Certainly, however, the house's organic room arrangement was remarkably advanced for 1850s Alabama. Cresting in popularity as a domestic mode between 1850 and 1875, the Italianate impulse had not altogether spent itself even by the late 1880s, when another Montgomery residence, the Tyson-Maner house, was built with a belated Tuscan tower and retardataire eaves-bracketing.

96. *Leckey house, Leighton, 1874. (Duane Phillips photo, 1983.)*

97. *Dr. George Ketchum house, Mobile, ca. 1860. Charles T. Lernier appears to have been the architect of the Ketchum house, although he may have taken his cue from a design appearing in Samuel Sloan's* Homestead Architecture. *(Library of Congress: Arthur Rothstein photo, 1937.)*

98. *Gideon Nelson house, Greensboro, ca. 1860 (razed ca. 1890). (Courtesy Mrs. Robert Cantrell.)*

In Sloan's design for the state mental hospital at Tuscaloosa (1853–61), stylistic considerations were obviously secondary to the hospital's pioneer implementation of the so-called Kirkbride Plan, which called for semi-autonomous wards aimed at achieving a more effective and humane treatment of the mentally ill. Nevertheless, Sloan invoked a Tuscan flavor in the building's wide bracketed eaves, in pairs of arched windows, and in shallow overhanging gables. [101]

Meantime, the Italianate style was put to further civic and institutional use during the 1850s in structures as varied as Mobile's Phoenix Fire Station* on the one hand and its City Hall* on the other, the latter combining municipal offices above with a sprawling and noisy markethouse below. [102] There was also the East Alabama Male College, forerunner of Auburn University, which was built to a design by Stephen D. Button [103]; likewise, the Union Female College in Eufaula, and the Prattville Male and Female Academy. As a medium for public architecture, the Italianate style would persist after the Civil War in the 1870 Autauga County courthouse at Prattville and its contemporary, the Pickens County courthouse at Car-

99. *Kenworthy Hall, Marion vicinity, 1858–61, as seen* (right) *in an old watercolor, possibly the architect's original rendering, and* (below) *as recorded by* HABS *in 1934. By that time, the house had lost its original porch. The branched main stair* (below right) *is one of three fine stairways in the house. (Original watercolor in possession of Mrs. Robert Fry {Lewis Kennedy photocopy};* HABS: *W. N. Manning photos, 1934.)*

100. Right: *Seibels house, Montgomery, 1850s. Shorn of its octagonal rooftop observatory and arcuated porch, the Seibels house stood derelict in the mid-1980s.* Above: *Stairhall of Seibels house.* (HABS: W. N. Manning photo, 1934.)

rollton, along with similar courthouses that once existed in Birmingham, Talladega, and Cullman.

The 1860 Memphis and Charleston railroad depot in Huntsville capitulated to the rising tide of Italianate influence in commercial and industrial architecture by adopting bracketed eaves and louvered roundels, and by dressing its windows and doors with segmentally arched lintels.

From the early 1850s on, in fact, Italianate ornamental devices in the form of brackets and decorative lintels of cast iron or terra cotta were increasingly incorporated into Alabama commercial façades. Notable examples are the 1856 Central Bank of Alabama in Montgomery—yet another Stephen D. Button design—and the slightly later Eastern Bank of Alabama* at Eufaula. [104]

In the guise of a Renaissance palazzo, the Daniels, Elgin and Company building* was erected near the Mobile waterfront around 1860 as one of the state's first full-scale iron-front edifices. [105] Cast by the D. D. Badger firm to designs prepared by J. H. Giles, the metal components for the four-story façade were shipped prefabricated from New York. Not far away, the sober, granite-faced U.S. Custom House designed by Ammi B. Young represented Alabama's most monumental application ever of those principles that had governed the formal urban architecture of the Italian Renaissance. [106] Its scale and ponderous dignity placed the custom house alongside the best eastern examples of Young's work. This, however, did not save the structure from the wrecker's ball when it was toppled in 1963 to make way for a skyscraper bank.

101. *Samuel Sloan's scheme for the Alabama State Hospital for the Insane (now Bryce Hospital), Tuscaloosa. The scheme cloaked an innovative layout in Italianate dress. The cast-iron covered balcony fronting the main pavilion was later replaced by a colonnade. Plan and elevation from Thomas Kirkbride's* On the Construction, Organization, and General Arrangements of Hospitals for the Insane *(Philadelphia, 1854). (Courtesy Bryce Hospital Library {Chip Cooper photocopy}.)*

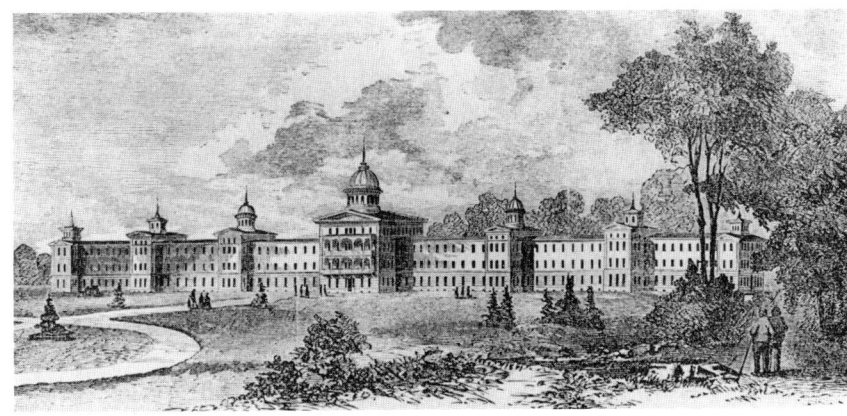

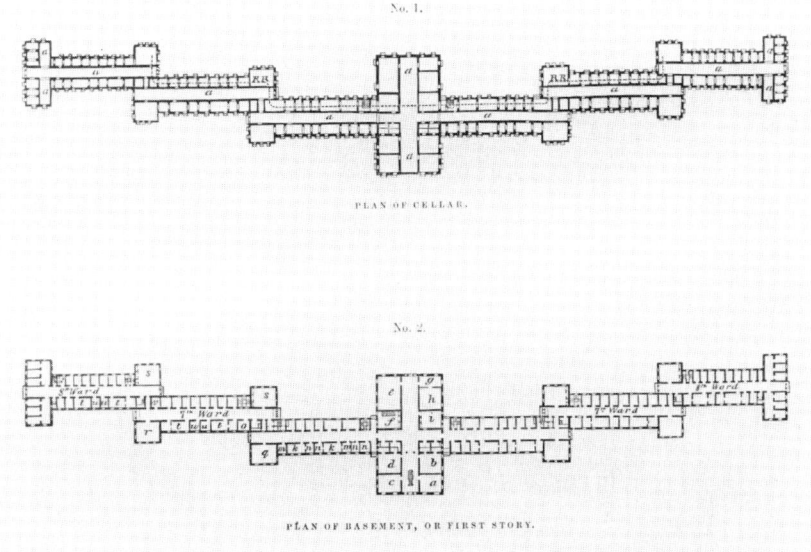

As we have seen in the "bracketed Greek Revival" forms of the 1850s, aspects of the Italianate style melded nicely with the florid qualities of late antebellum neoclassicism. The style formed a logical bridge, in fact, between rationalism and romanticism. Indeed, from more than one point of view the Italianate was a bridge style in Alabama, prevailing as it did during the state's transition from a slave-based economy to a nominally free labor system, and from near-unalloyed agrarianism to an agrarianism that at least admitted a slowly widening industrial base. Eventually, the style's distinctive elements were suffused in the general hodgepodge of post–Civil War eclecticism, but not until it had left its mark on a broader sweep of mid-century Alabama building types than any other single movement save the Greek Revival.

102. *City Hall and Southern Market, Mobile, 1856–57.* Right: *Detail of belfry.* (From Ballou's Pictorial Drawing-Room Companion, *June 27, 1857;* HABS: *Jack Boucher photo, 1963.*)

103. *East Alabama Male College, Auburn, 1856–58.* (Courtesy Auburn University Archives.)

104. *Central Bank of Alabama (later Klein & Son Jewelers), Montgomery, 1856. The lower floor of the building has been remodeled.* (Author's collection.)

105. Daniels, Elgin and Company, Mobile. (HABS: Roy Thigpen photo, 1966.)

Summary Characteristics

- In those designs based on the prototype of the Italian country villa, a general relaxation of the neoclassical ideal of perfect balance and symmetry (even axially planned houses frequently have irregular lateral extensions); on the other hand, symmetry is preserved in those buildings, usually public or commercial, based on the prototype of the urban Renaissance palace.
- Preference for low-pitched roofs, often combining shallow hipped and gable forms.
- Occurrence of wide bracketed cornices or eaves.

106. *Ammi B. Young's original elevation drawings for the U.S. Custom House, Mobile. In the final scheme the urbane continental flavor of the initial design was somewhat diluted by the substitution of stock guillotine sash for the mullioned windows proposed by Young. (National Archives.)*

- In villa-based designs, a frequent feature is a tower or rooftop cupola.
- Slender, round or segmentally arched openings (though not as common in Alabama examples as in the East), with windows oftentimes grouped as pairs or triplets.
- Preference for lightly scaled one-story porches of wood or cast iron, sometimes arcuated, in villa-based designs; also such appendages as balconies or bay windows.
- In domestic structures especially, variance in size and shape of rooms, even when an essentially axial interior arrangement occurs.

The "Cottage Orné"
(1850s through 1870s)

Along with those dwellings that can broadly be labeled as Gothic Revival or Italianate, the eclectic groundswell of the 1850s produced other houses in Alabama that cannot be disposed of by linking them, however tenuously, with some fancied associational style. Insofar as they borrowed "Gothic" windows or "Italian" brackets or even neoclassical details, such features were incidental to an overall effect that owed clear-cut allegiance to none of these modes. Generically, such domiciles might be grouped together as a collective expression of the "cottage orné" impulse, to borrow a designation often used in nineteenth-century architectural circles.

The term *cottage orné* as employed by Victorians could refer to any small or medium-sized house rustically situated in a rural or semi-rural setting, and ornamented so as to convey a picturesque effect. Thus, domiciles feigning to be vaguely "Gothic" or "Italian" many times might just as easily have fallen into the broader category of the cottage orné, along with others whose romantic yearnings went no further than a pleasantly trellised porch or a bit of scalloped fascia. Certainly in Alabama, the immediate sources were much the same: the publications of Downing and Sloan, plus lesser-known manuals like Cleavelend and Backus's *Village and Farm Cottage* (1852) or Gervase Wheeler's *Homes for the People* (1855). Popular household periodicals such as *Godey's Lady's Book* also carried influential designs. That these might be capriciously labeled as "alpine" or "oriental" or "Anglo-French" was beside the point. The objective, quite simply, was to suggest a mood: one of civilized, quasi-agrarian domesticity, as rural-minded Alabamians were pleased to note.

Accordingly, Chantilly at Greensboro follows no particular style, although it vaguely recalls the "semi-oriental cottage" pictured in A. J. Downing's 1841 *Treatise on Landscape Gardening.* Rather, pedimented wings flank a gallery sporting machine-sawn "oriental" arches. {107} In the same manner, trellis-work and scroll-sawn gingerbread were used to enliven the porches of otherwise unpretending residences. On the Norfleet Harris plantation near Faunsdale, a trellised gallery and a balconied "Italian" tower flanked by unlikely wall dormers became the means for animating the façade of the bland wooden house behind. The lightly springing porch supports and wide eaves of Montebrier (circa 1860) at Brierfield call to mind some of the cottage designs to be seen in Downing's *The Architecture of Country Houses.* {108} In and about Eufaula, Marion, Greensboro, Tuscaloosa, and the suburbs of Mobile could once be seen other houses likewise ornamented and sited so as to effuse the spirit of the cottage orné. {109} Such dwellings, by their very nature, invited that unabashed mixing and matching of architectural components

107. *Chantilly, Greensboro. (Courtesy Mrs. Frank Spain.)*

108. Above: *Montebrier, Brierfield, ca. 1850. The frankly exposed wooden structural members of this ornamented country cottage foretold developments later in the century. (Courtesy Dr. Mike Mahan.)*

109. Right: *Dargan-Ledyard house, Mobile, ca. 1850. (Lee Pake Collection {courtesy James W. Parker}.)*

that became the norm, for many smaller houses especially, during the 1880s and 1890s.

Summary Characteristics

- Generally modest or medium-sized in scale, with a rustic or semi-rustic setting; in Alabama, wood is the normal medium of construction.
- "Picturesqueness" without reference to any particular historical style, although specific details may be borrowed.

- Trellis-work, fancy scrollsaw work, or lightweight post supports characteristically used for porches; balconies and eaves trim may also be employed from time to time.

Romanesque Revival
(late 1850s through 1870s)

Introduced to America by way of such buildings as Richard Upjohn's Church of the Pilgrims (1844–46) in Brooklyn and James Renwick's Smithsonian Institution (1849–55) in Washington, the Romanesque Revival style—in those days people usually called it the "Norman" or "Lombard" mode—drew inspiration from the heavy, round-arched architecture of pre-Gothic Europe. It was not a style well calculated to domestic needs, but as an institutional form it had gained a respectable following by the time of the Civil War. Church builders were especially fond of the Romanesque Revival, since it provided an alternative both to the Gothic Revival and to an overworked neoclassicism. Indeed, in Alabama it seems to have been used for few if any other types of buildings.

While Victorian art critics might indulge in erudite hairsplitting over which elements of an avowedly Romanesque structure properly belonged to the "Italian," "German," "French," or "English" schools, such distinctions blurred in Alabama. Instead, the important thing was simply a display of one or more highly generalized features: rounded openings frequently emphasized (as about a main doorway) by a deeply molded embrasure; likewise, a dripped corbel cornice used in combination with wheel or round-arched windows and sometimes crenellation. Buttresses could also form part of the composition. And where there was a tower or pair of towers, these might be topped by concave or straight-sided conical spires. Irregularity of massing and outline was regarded as an advantage of the style, though most Alabama examples were considerably less venturesome.

St. Peter's Catholic Church, Montgomery, dating from 1857, is the oldest Romanesque Revival structure standing today in Alabama. In 1881 it acquired a twin-towered façade which—while not unsympathetic to the style of the building—considerably altered its original appearance. But architecturally more enticing, and still little changed outside, is the slightly later Temple Beth-Or (now the Catoma Street Church of Christ) a few blocks away. [110] The temple was one of only two Jewish houses of worship in Alabama when completed in 1862. Its references to Romanesque, or perhaps in this case "Byzantine," antiquity are unmistakable in the crisp drip corbeling which runs beneath the cornice, in the round-arched doorway, and in the wheel windows of varying sizes that puncture the main el-

110. *Temple Beth-Or (now Catoma Street Church of Christ), Montgomery, 1861–62. The designer of the temple seems to have been a youthful Montgomerian named Pelham J. Anderson, whom a local paper praised as "an Architect of great diversity of ideas— not the disciple of any particular order or style, but one who seems to be proficient in all alike." (Author's collection.)*

evation. Yet these elements are mixed in a way that is brash, naïve, and thoroughly American.

The design of Temple Beth-Or is a paradigm of symmetry. But Tuskegee's First Methodist Church as well as the Roman Catholic Church of the Visitation in Huntsville, begun in 1860 and 1861 respectively, were conceived as asymmetrical compositions. [111] The Church of the Visitation has a front of dressed stone, anchored at either side by two curiously stunted polygonal towers. A pair of unequal towers—one slightly peaked and the other stubbily pinnacled—also marks the front of the Tuskegee church. These towers, too, are oddly disproportionate in relation with the broad nave and round-arched window between. The church's aspect, in fact, lends credence to the local tradition that the intervention of the Civil War forced the congregation to modify its grandiose original plan.

The Presbyterian congregations at Jacksonville and Talladega likewise started Romanesque Revival-style buildings on the eve of the

111. *First Methodist Church, Tuskegee, 1860–72. The low arcaded porch is a twentieth-century addition. (Author's collection.)*

Civil War. [112] These designs, however, focused on a central bell-tower pierced at ground level by an arched doorway. Anticipating Mobile's similar but larger St. Francis Street Baptist Church of 1873, the Talladega church was handsomely finished off by a tall and slender broached spire soaring from a sturdy, three-staged brick base. [113] Of the same general type, but with scaled-down spires, were Huntsville's Reconstruction-era First Methodist Church and Mobile's State Street A. M. E. Church—begun in the late sixties by one of the oldest and largest black congregations in the city. [114]

112. *First Presbyterian Church, Jacksonville, 1859–65. (HABS: T. S. Christopher, delineator, 1935.)*

Elsewhere in Alabama, the axial tower was left spireless altogether. Crenellations capped the belfry of the old First Presbyterian Church, Selma, after it was remodeled in the Romanesque Revival manner in 1868. A decade later Presbyterians at Marion picked up on the same motif in their smaller look-alike building. [115] And at the First

Romanesque Revival

114. *State Street A. M. E. Church, Mobile. (Courtesy Historic Mobile Preservation Society.)*

113. *Old view of First Presbyterian Church, Talladega, 1861–68. (Author's collection.)*

Methodist Church of Oxford (1872–75), a handsome triple-arched belfry was surmounted by a small copper-covered dome.

With the shift of stylistic winds in the 1880s toward High Victorian Gothic as the pervading ecclesiastical genre in Alabama, enthusiasm for the Romanesque Revival quietly faded. Still, unwittingly, the style had managed to foreshadow those buildings of a few years later that would emulate the peculiar stripe of Romanesque influence found in the works of H. H. Richardson, whose influence would in time also make its way to the Deep South.

Summary Characteristics

- General sense of massiveness, sometimes reinforced by use of buttresses; variously symmetrical or asymmetrical façade, with tendency toward the symmetrical in Alabama architecture.
- Emphatically round-arched openings, sometimes set deeply into the wall, normally occurring in concert with features like drip corbeling, round windows, etc.
- Where towers are employed, these may on occasion (but rarely in Alabama) be used as unequal pairs—differing from each other in both scale and detail.

115. *First Presbyterian Church, Marion, 1878. (Author's collection.)*

High Victorian Gothic
(1860s through early 1900s)

After the Civil War the forthright and restrained Gothic revivalism of a previous generation became increasingly diluted by that looseness of form and fascination for detail that marked the full blossoming of the Victorian architectural temperament. The writings of John Ruskin incalculably influenced this transformation. His books *The Seven Lamps of Architecture* and *The Stones of Venice* pointed the way toward a sort of pictorial Gothic that borrowed from several traditions—Italian, French, and German as well as English—to create an idiom that was flexible of line and free in its use of contrasting textures, materials, and colors. Implicit in such an approach, of course, was an almost boundless latitude of design. The predictable result was a mixing of vaguely Gothic forms and features with such outpourings of Victorian technology as metal roof-cresting and fussily decorative wooden entrance porches—nurturing an effect quite different from the relatively sober Gothic Revival of the 1850s.

High Victorian Gothic was also more secular in spirit than its forerunner. Perhaps its earliest glimmering in Alabama was the Venetian Gothic loggia of Selma's Hotel Albert, begun in 1860 by a group of entrepreneurs who flaunted the building as an imitation of the Palace of the Doges. Nevertheless, as in the case of the Romanesque Revival, the style most vividly imprinted itself on the state's religious architecture. The picturesquely massed façade of the Eufaula First Presbyterian Church (1869) [116], overtopped by a saddle-roofed belltower that once sprouted ornate metal cresting, foretold the even more flamboyant High Victorian Gothic churches of the 1880s and 1890s: Birmingham's First Presbyterian Church and St. Paul's Cathedral for example [117, 118]; and in Anniston, the Parker Memorial Baptist Church.[119]

Between 1882 and 1885 Grace Episcopal Church was also built in Anniston, according to plans devised by Richard M. Upjohn. [120] While tending heavily toward that freedom of composition universally characteristic of the High Victorian Gothic mode, Upjohn's scheme for Grace Church was still controlled by that liturgical restraint that the same architect had exercised a decade earlier in his design for St. Paul's Church, Selma (1871–75).

Wood, brick, and sometimes stone provided the materials through which small-town congregations like the Presbyterians of Union Springs and the Methodists of Livingston followed their city brethren in raising churches that donned this end-of-the-century Gothic apparel. [121] The momentum maintained even after 1900 by the High Victorian Gothic style is attested by the impressively towered

116. First Presbyterian Church, Eufaula, 1869. The architect is unknown, but in character the church recalls some of the eastern work of Frederick C. Withers and E. T. Potter. Indeed, the latter is credited with at least two Alabama buildings. The polychromatic slate roof and metal cresting, which placed the First Presbyterian Church squarely in the mainstream of typical High Victorian Gothic design, unfortunately no longer exist. (Courtesy First Presbyterian Church {Earl Roberts photocopy}.)

First Baptist Church of Selma, completed in 1904 and originally capped by a jaunty array of spirelets worthy of some Disney fantasy. [122]

Perhaps Alabama's most thoroughly committed secular application of the style came about as a result of the 1880s expansion of the state university complex at Tuscaloosa. In patterned brick, slate, and terra cotta, with an added sprinkling of metal decorative components, the five-building cluster dominated by Clark Hall represented an enthusiastic if provincial response to John Ruskin's call for architectural

117. Above left: *First Presbyterian Church, Birmingham, 1887–88. (Author's collection.)*

118. Above middle: *St. Paul's Cathedral, Birmingham, 1891–93. (Department of Archives and Manuscripts, Birmingham Public Library {Jo Roy photocopy}.)*

119. Above right: *Parker Memorial Baptist Church, Anniston. Gone is the long taut nave of the earlier, Anglican Gothic Revivalists. Instead, a Gothic skin is casually stretched over a broad-bodied structure built to accommodate both a large "auditorium" for worship and the equally important Sunday school meeting rooms. Constructed of quarry-faced stone, with a slate-covered spire, Parker Memorial was declared the finest Baptist church in Alabama when completed in 1889. (From* Scenes in Alabama, *1895 {Jo Roy photocopy}.)*

120. Right: *Grace Episcopal Church, Anniston. When the nave was extended during the 1950s, the ornate stickwork porch and tall chimney were removed. (Courtesy Judge William C. Bibb.)*

pictorialism. [123] In a similar vein were the designs for the Powell and Paul Hayne schools, built about the same time in Birmingham.

But Alabamians showed little inclination to adopt High Victorian Gothic for home and hearth. Among the few remaining examples are the companion Baldwin houses in Montgomery [124], as well as the William Weaver house in Selma—the cautious demeanor of the Selma residence actually looking back toward an earlier and more

High Victorian Gothic

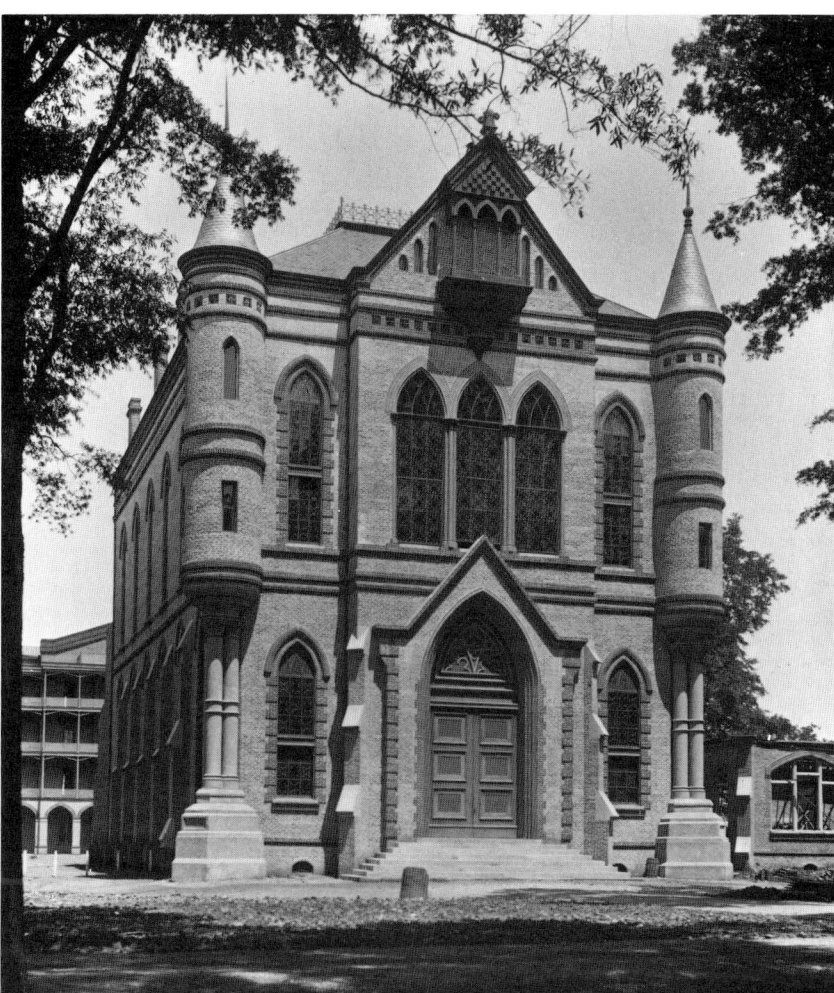

121. Top: *First Methodist Church, Livingston, 1892. (Don Fleming photo, 1983.)*

122. Above: *First Baptist Church, Selma, 1900–1904. A belated embodiment of High Victorian Gothic principles, with a flamboyant landmark tower. (From* Art Work of Central Alabama, *1907 {Jo Roy photocopy}.)*

123. Right: *Clark Hall, University of Alabama, shortly after its completion in 1885. Rising to the right are the unfinished walls of Garland Hall—one of four other buildings that completed the ensemble of which Clark Hall was the center. (Geological Survey of Alabama.)*

straightforward phase of pseudo-Gothicism. But these houses, like the Second Empire-style dwellings that were their Alabama contemporaries, comprised on the whole a negligible group. This is particularly true when compared to the ubiquitous Queen Anne–style dwelling that came to the fore in the late 1880s and arrested the attention of Alabama homebuilders for the last dozen years of the nineteenth century.

Summary Characteristics

- Loose, romantically asymmetrical massing and form, most notably expressed in complex rooflines and the irregular application of such features as towers, turrets, and emphatic gables.
- Use of variegated textures and colors in facing materials, particularly so as to accentuate window and door openings, stringcourses,

124. One of the twin Baldwin houses (ca. 1885) in Montgomery: a rare instance in Alabama of High Victorian Gothic translated into a domestic design. (Author's collection.)

and the like. Pointed openings themselves are very often segmentally arched.
- In institutional buildings especially, the embellishment of belfries, towers, and roof ridges with wood, stone, or terra cotta, as well as serrated cast-iron cresting.
- Occurrence of highly decorative wooden porches and trim, often of a kind that emphasizes exposed structural members and cross-bracing as ornamental motifs.

Second Empire
(1870s to early 1890s)

Taking its cue from architectural trends in the France of Napoleon III, the Second Empire style appeared on the American East Coast about 1855. Its affected historical character was that of the French

125. Top: LeGrand Building (later Imperial Hotel), Montgomery. (Courtesy James W. Parker.)

126. Above: Bullock County courthouse, Union Springs. (Author's collection.)

Renaissance, although in the polyglot architectural atmosphere of late nineteenth-century America, Gallic mannerisms were as apt as any other to become hopelessly intermingled with a rash of superfluous influences. Thanks, however, to the style's most striking feature, the mansard roof, the Second Empire is readily identified.

Montgomery's 1871 LeGrand Building was among the first structures in Alabama to affect the mansard style. [125] The Montgomery City Hall, finished the same year, also boasted a mansard-capped central section, though in general this edifice represented an uncertain and rather coarse mélange of stylistic influences. About the same time, the commissioners of Bullock County approved the construction of a courthouse at Union Springs whose dominant feature was a pair of mansarded corner pavilions framing a recessed entry. [126] Over the next several decades, the Second Empire mode asserted itself in a fair number of other civic, commercial, and institutional buildings around the state, at Selma, Eufaula, Mobile, and in the newly established city of Birmingham.

One of the most ambitious of these ventures was Birmingham's Morris Building (1888–89), the work of a French-born architect named Edouard Sidel. [127] Roughly contemporary with the Morris Building were the Judson Female Institute at Marion and its near look-alike, the Southern Female University in Florence. Designed by Fenton L. Rousseau of Birmingham, both structures echoed—no matter how dimly and distantly—the format established by the celebrated prototype of all Second Empire buildings, the New Louvre in Paris. This format consisted of a convex-roofed main block, with subordinate wings linking accentuated end pavilions. [128]

Like some of the other nineteenth-century eclectic styles, the Second Empire made only a minor impact upon Alabama domestic architecture. Where it did occur, it was usually in amalgamated fashion, with a spray of all-purpose jigsaw or spoolwork about porches and eaves. (More correctly, diminutive renditions of the classical columnar orders popular during the Renaissance should have been used.) To be sure, such freedom of choice was part of the spirit of the times, fully sanctioned in popular house-pattern books like *Bicknell's Village Builder* and a host of others. Scattered examples of the few Second Empire–style houses still standing in Alabama include the William Moseley house in Decatur, Thimbleton at Florence, and the Wiley-Trotman house in Troy. [129] By eastern standards these structures, like most of their commercial and institutional counterparts, were curiously belated, since, for all intents and purposes, the Second Empire style had already passed from the national repertory even before most of the Alabama buildings were begun.

127. *Morris Building, Birmingham. (Department of Archives and Manuscripts, Birmingham Public Library.)*

128. *Judson Female Institute, Marion, 1889. (From Saffold Berney's* Handbook of Alabama, *1892 {Jo Roy photocopy}.)*

Summary Characteristics

- A mansard roof, sometimes convex or concave in form, usually flat-topped and trimmed with cast-iron cresting (or sculpture in more monumental edifices).
- Ornate dormers—round-arched, pedimented, or circular—and similar decorative treatment, including frequent use of pediments and sculpted lintels for all openings.
- Heavy projecting cornices, with brackets.

129. Captain William Moseley house, Decatur, ca. 1885. A provincial rendition of the Second Empire, with a stickwork Eastlake-type porch that would have belonged more properly on a Queen Anne-style residence. (Author's collection.)

- In larger buildings, an advanced center with complementary end pavilions; also, a vigorous articulation of advancing and receding planes.

Queen Anne
(1880s to early 1900s)

Among the glibly confected American architectural movements of the late nineteenth century, the Queen Anne is probably the most deceptively named of all. Theoretically, it was this country's response to the "Old English" or "Queen Anne" revival spawned in Great Britain around 1860. The parent movement had begun as a nostalgic rediscovery of vernacular British domestic architecture of the late seventeenth and early eighteenth centuries—an architecture that retained a highly irregular, medieval character while borrowing rudimentary neoclassical details from England's late-blooming Renaissance.

But in the main, Queen Anne as developed on this side of the Atlantic bore little resemblance to its English cousin—save for occasional cosmopolitan structures in places like Boston, Newport, and Chicago. No doubt this was partly intentional: a nationalistic urge to develop an authentically American vocabulary, especially after the Centennial celebration of 1876. Yet it was also the old story of fainter and ever more distorted echoes of a germinal style, farther and farther from the style's point of origin. Ultimately, the term *Queen Anne* itself came to be a catchall phrase for creative eclecticism at its zenith. Promulgated through the *American Architect and Building News* and other national journals of the builder's profession, the corner towers and piled-up rooflines, the rambling wooden porches and stained glass windows, the half-timbered gables and tall ornamented chimneys typical of the American Queen Anne movement would, in time of course, become practically synonymous with the word *Victorian*.

As it happened, the crest of the Queen Anne tide coincided with the boom years of the late 1880s and early 1890s in Alabama. Thus the Queen Anne style determined the residential physiognomy of hopeful new industrial towns like Anniston and Birmingham, Bridgeport, New Decatur, Fort Payne, Bessemer, and Sheffield. Even the workers' villages that crowded near the railroads and the new mills were apt to have their traces of Queen Anne shingles and spoolwork. Several of Anniston's industrial barons, drawing heavily upon architectural talent from Atlanta ninety miles to the east, erected a pleasant scattering of residences in shingle, brick, and the abundant native stone which still, today, perfectly summarizes the finer qualities of the Queen Anne idiom. [130] Meanwhile, exuberant Queen Anne–style houses were rising along the streets of older communities like Mobile and Montgomery, Selma, Huntsville, Florence, Eufaula, Greensboro, and Talladega. [131] The popularity of the Queen Anne is attested by the fact that nearly a century later, in the 1980s, at least one reasonably good example of the style could be located in almost any sizable Alabama town.

Among dozens of specific structures across the state that might be mentioned are Anniston's Noble and Crowan cottages, along with the Nininger, McCaa, and McKleroy houses; in Mobile, the Tacon-Gordon house* [132]; the Kennedy-Sims house in Montgomery; the Whitcher house at Bridgeport; the Wood-Spahn house in Troy; the Mellon house at Oxford; the Nathan house in Sheffield; the Bradford house on Birmingham's Highland Avenue; the Purefoy and Ragsdale houses in Talladega; the Borton-Chenault and Jervis houses in Decatur; and the Booker T. Washington house—The Oaks*—at Tuskegee. Both the Marshall-Atchison house in Orrville and the Dr. H. W. Stephenson house at Oakman in Walker County represent the type of small-scale Queen Anne dwelling that flourished in country towns and rural areas: peak-roofed, with an inevitable porch, and often naïvely turreted. [133]

130. The Queen Anne in Anniston: (above) *A. R. Nininger house, ca. 1888;* (above right) *Noble guest cottage, ca. 1886. (Author's collection.)*

Large or small, rural or urban, all these houses share a fundamentally pan-American quality that would have been unthinkable during the antebellum period. As good as vanished—except perhaps for inordinately spacious porches and a generous use of louvered blinds—are the nuances of region and locale. Collectively, such dwellings signified that the standardization of domestic design was almost complete. Thanks to mass production and railroads and taste-making popular magazines, specific plan ideas along with modish items such as the fish-scale shingles and spindle friezes that delighted the Victorian eye were now available almost everywhere—to an up-and-coming middle class as well as to the local economic and social elite.

Writings of the day praised the Queen Anne's "home-like" qualities: the feeling of domestic well-being supposedly induced by interiors richly paneled in dark wood, with beamed ceilings and cozy windowseats, tiled fireplaces, and snug chimney corners known as "inglenooks." Some of Alabama's Queen Anne houses clung to a conservative, hall-centered, and compartmentalized interior arrangement. But in others such as Decatur's Borton-Chenault house, the floorplan opened fluidly out from a central "living hall," dominated by an ornate fireplace and a grandly ceremonial oaken staircase. [134] It was this free-flowing and functional spatial concept that was the Queen Anne's most portentous contribution to American domestic architecture, the concept that has come to be the norm for domestic design today.

131. Right: Queen Anne houses along South Perry Street, Montgomery, about 1895. The porch at far left is that of the Kennedy-Sims house (above), which still stands substantially unaltered today. (Library of Congress: Detroit Collection; author's collection.)

Because of its ability to convey an opulent yet intimate "home-away-from-home" atmosphere, the Queen Anne style also became a favorite medium for hotel architecture. In fact, the Anniston Inn (1883–85) was possibly the first expression, either domestic or non-domestic, of the Queen Anne style anywhere in Alabama. Other hostelries followed suit: Gadsden's Bellevue and Printup hotels (circa 1888), the Fruithurst Inn (1895) near Heflin, and The Tavern (1888) at Decatur—the last a particularly flavorful rendition of "Old English" half-timbering, overtopped by mountainous gables, clustered chimneys, and a bell-roofed observatory. [135]

From the Queen Anne mode evolved that unique mutation, the "shingle style," which smoothed out the angularity and eliminated the fussy extraneous features of the standard American Queen Anne house—stretching over the exterior a skin of dark-stained wood shingles that played against other surfaces of brick or rough native stone to achieve an altogether more plastic effect. In Alabama, however, the shingle-style variant on the Queen Anne never really became a clearly separate movement, although sculpting the character of a few turn-of-the-century residences like the now destroyed Walker Percy house in Birmingham.

Summary Characteristics

- Highly irregular elevations, roof silhouettes, and massing.
- Frequent occurrence of corner towers, sometimes square, but more

132. *Tacon-Gordon house, Mobile, 1899–1901. (HABS: Jack Boucher photos, 1974.)*

133. *Country Queen Anne:* (above right) *Dr. H. W. Stephenson house at Oakman, Walker County, 1888;* (above) *Marshall-Atchison house at Orrville, Dallas County, 1896. (Author's collection.)*

134. Right: *"Living hall" of the Borton-Chenault house, Decatur, ca. 1905. (Duane Phillips photo, 1983.)*

135. *The Tavern, Decatur, as depicted in* The American Architect and Building News, *January 14, 1888.*

often round or octagonal, with bulbous or conical roofs; also gable-end porches and balconies.
- Tall, ornamentally ribbed or paneled chimneys.
- Large wrap-around porches with elaborate, frequently lathe-turned and gouged, woodwork (in later examples, circa 1895–1905, quieter neoclassical details began to supplant more flamboyant ornamentation).
- Variegated treatment of outside wall surfaces, mixing shingled sheathing with clapboard and sometimes brick or fieldstone.
- Open interior plans that convey a sense of spatial flow from one area to another; often in larger houses unfolding from a ceremonial stairhall with a fireplace area (inglenook) and a broad, ornate stair with landings.
- Abundant use of stained and leaded glass, as well as paneling, beams, spool friezes, tilework, etc.

Richardsonian Romanesque
(1880s to early 1900s)

The term *Richardsonian Romanesque* refers to the highly individualistic, Romanesque-based idiom devised by a single late nineteenth-century architectural giant, Henry Hobson Richardson of

Boston. Widely imitated especially in the years immediately following Richardson's death in 1886, the style can be recognized by its general ponderousness; its preference for massive pyramidal roofs, peaked towers, and turrets; and its almost universal use of the low, round Syrian arch for porches or major openings. In more ambitious examples, walls are normally sheathed in rough-hewn ashlar, at least at the base. Bands of closely spaced arched or trabeated ribbon windows likewise demarcate the upper stories. Though few of Richardson's imitators handled the disposition of these features as brilliantly as the master himself, the impression of most Richardsonian Romanesque buildings is one of time-defying solidity.

Birmingham's Union Depot, a brick and stone edifice built in the mid-1880s, displayed its indebtedness to the Richardsonian idiom in walls that were battered and rock-faced at the base, in a peaked roof, and in a rhythmic repetition of emphatically arched openings. The depot was quickly followed by a pair of other Birmingham structures of the same caste: the new Jefferson County courthouse and the Federal Building. The courthouse was topped by an unlikely neo-Baroque belfry. But the Federal post office and courthouse—signaled from afar by its massive, campanile-like tower rising from a ground floor of banded masonry—was thoroughly Richardsonian in manner. [136] Over the next several years, courthouses in Bay Minette, Brewton, Prattville, Tuskegee, and other county towns obligingly echoed in miniature the stolid image of Birmingham's Federal building as the Richardsonian style became, for a time, a favored medium for institutional, civic, and, to some degree, commercial building. [137]

Architect B. B. Smith drew from several possible sources, not the least being the neo-French Renaissance designs of Richard Morris Hunt, when he conceived the plan for Union Station in Montgomery—Alabama's largest railroad depot when finished in 1898. But the low, spreading Syrian arch about the main door can hardly have been other than Richardsonian in derivation, despite a surrounding spray of terra cotta fleur-de-lis. The same could be said for the banded voussoirs and the emphatically horizontal ribbon windows at the third-floor level. [138]

Several of the best examples of the Richardsonian Romanesque style in Alabama were churches. First Methodist, Birmingham, was built in 1890–91 according to plans prepared by the Akron, Ohio, firm of Weary and Kramer—specialists in those broad-bodied auditorium churches, with their rank upon rank of curving pews, preferred by evangelical Victorians. [139] Harrod and Andry of New Orleans, on the other hand, designed for the Roman Catholics of Mobile the equally Richardsonian Sacred Heart Chapel (1894–95) at the Convent and Academy of the Visitation. In Anniston, the

136. *U.S. Post Office and Federal Courthouse, Birmingham, 1889–90. (Department of Archives and Manuscripts, Birmingham Public Library {Jo Roy photocopy}.)*

137. *Macon County courthouse, Tuskegee, 1905. (Author's collection.)*

Church of St. Michael and All Angels was the work of the New York architect William Halsey Wood. [140] The impassive outer simplicity of St. Michael's contrasts with its sumptuous chancel, dominated by an alabaster altar and roofed over by an elaborate system of sturdy hammerbeam trusses such as Richardson himself had used so successfully in his landmark Trinity Church, Boston. Wood reputedly had in mind ancient Welsh precedent when he designed St. Michael's, but the low nave with its round-arched windows also

138. Above right: *Union Station, Montgomery*, 1898–99 *(adaptively renovated and restored 1982–83)*. Above left. *Main doorway. (Author's collection.)*

139. *First Methodist Church, Birmingham. (From* Scenes in Alabama, 1895 *{Jo Roy photocopy, 1983}.)*

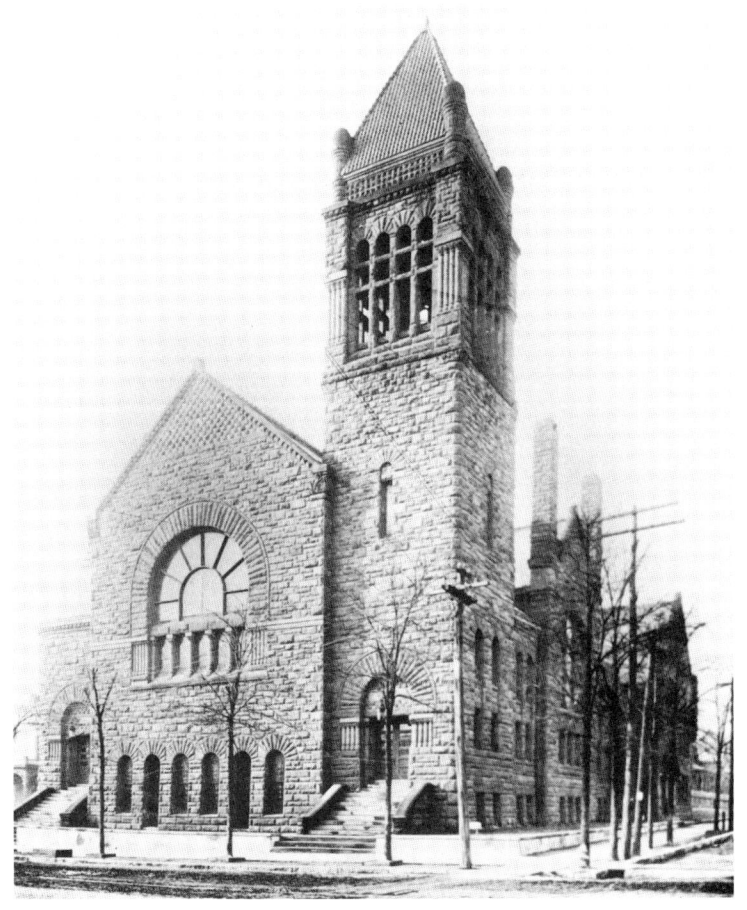

140. St. Michael's and All Angels Episcopal Church, Anniston, 1888–90. Below: Chancel and nave. (Duane Phillips photos, 1983.)

141. Schiffman Building, Huntsville. A mid-nineteenth-century commercial structure given a Richardsonian Romanesque façade in 1895 (George W. Thompson, architect). (Linda Bayer photo {courtesy City of Huntsville Department of Planning}.)

markedly recalls H. H. Richardson's design of a few years earlier for Emmanuel Church, Pittsburgh.

Commercial structures like the Steiner Bank in Birmingham, the Cheshire-Webb Building in Demopolis, and the Schiffman Building in Huntsville likewise adopted some of the robust and craggy features of the Richardsonian Romanesque. [141] As a domestic vogue, however, Richardsonian qualities lent themselves more to urban rowhouse requirements than to the open, expansive living habits of most Alabamians. Anniston's Duncan T. Parker house (1889) was one

142. Duncan T. Parker house, Anniston. (Author's collection.)

of the few residences in the state that exuded the strong yet reticent and almost withdrawn air which Richardson imparted to some of his East Coast domestic designs. [142] Mobile's demolished Quill house on Government Street was another.

Altogether, then, the Richardsonian style in Alabama was an eminently public mode—more so, perhaps, than any of the other seemingly inexhaustible architectural idioms of the late Victorian age. It was pushed aside by the new, yet old, fascination for neoclassicism. And even as the finishing touches were applied to such belated Richardsonian buildings as the 1905 Macon County courthouse in Tuskegee, the style had become passé among the state's architectural vanguard.

Summary Characteristics

- General massiveness and weightiness of scale.
- Prominent, and especially pyramidal, roof silhouettes.
- Frequent use of wall dormers, in combination with square or round, conically topped turrets.
- Rock-faced exterior walls.
- Use of a low Syrian arch for portals and other major openings.
- Bands of upper-story arched or trabeated ribbon windows, especially in institutional and commercial structures.

The Colonial Revival
(mid-1890s to ca. 1915)

Even before the Civil War, intellectual Boston was becoming conscious of its colonial architectural roots. And by the late 1860s, the city had produced a handful of buildings harking back to eighteenth-century Georgian neoclassicism. The Centennial celebration of 1876 encouraged a broader interest in American colonial architecture. But outside the Northeast, the movement toward a revival of colonial architectural forms—or what were wistfully thought to be "colonial"—did not get under way till after 1890. Then, spearheaded by the prestigious eastern firm of McKim, Mead, and White, the Colonial Revival came to the fore as a coherent national movement.

The term *colonial* itself could refer to any number of picturesque embodiments of both colonial and post-colonial architectural forms, since all—up to and including buildings from the Greek Revival period—were naïvely lumped together. These might range from gambrel-roofed "Dutch Colonial" cottages to pillared mansions. [143] Usually the objective was some vague evocation of "quaintness" rather than the scrupulous replication of, say, a Georgian or Federal

143. *The gambrel-roofed "Dutch Colonial" David Grayson house, Huntsville, 1901. (Author's collection.)*

period house. Architectural styles as we think of them today were, in any case, little understood by the average architect, much less by his client. Hence the unsettling elements oftimes encountered in Colonial Revival structures: Victorian stained glass peeping from behind neoclassical colonnades; pediments and modillions of an exaggerated scale; and a cavalier looseness of composition that had little to do with historical prototype.

It was the neoclassical aspect of the Colonial Revival that captured the fancy of most Alabamians, since white pillars could readily be identified with the state's own, increasingly romanticized antebellum past.

Intimations of the new vogue had appeared as early as 1892 in Birmingham's H. H. Sinnige house. [144] But not until four years later did the Colonial Revival surface with unmistakable clarity in Alabama when The Pines, at Anniston, was completed for the Edward Tyler family. The architect of this foursquare, hipped-roof, neo-Georgian residence was probably Walter T. Downing of Atlanta. Soon afterward came the columned Thigpen house in Montgomery, and still others of a similar ilk. [145] The Colonial Revival was in full swing. And from the late 1890s until World War I, dozens of white-pillared houses mushroomed across the state.

The flamboyant Corinthian colonnades of the Eli Shorter mansion in Eufaula and the J. D. Holman residence at Ozark typify the kind of pompous overstatement toward which some of these dwellings tended. [146] Other houses—William Lott's Mobile residence and the Lathrop house in Birmingham are two examples—adopted neoclassical "colonial" features of a less exuberant stripe. [147] But still others persisted in displaying a startling mix of ostensibly colonial features with residual Queen Anne traits. At the 1906 H. W. Sweet house in Bessemer, a peaked corner tower was brazenly sandwiched between a pair of Ionic-order "colonial" porticoes.

The image of what properly comprised a "colonial style" house—even a neoclassical one—remained nebulous in the public mind throughout this period. Actually, despite repeated obeisance to early American precedent in both the architectural and popular literature of the time, more than a little was owed to the larger stream of *beaux arts* neoclassicism that formed a parallel and overlapping current with the Colonial Revival.

Insofar as they earnestly attempted to mimic early American precedent in architecture, most Alabama ventures of the time seem to have attempted to make up in bluster what they lacked in command. Yet a few managed to be urbane and persuasive. In Birmingham, architect Thomas U. Walter III designed a house of pleasing scale and convincing detail in the red-brick and white-porticoed domicile he conceived for Robert Jemison IV. [148] Two equally accomplished es-

144. *H. H. Sinnige house, Birmingham. In 1892 the local press hailed the newly completed Sinnige house as Birmingham's first example of the ascendant trend toward the "colonial style." A white-painted exterior and a neoclassical porch did indeed provide contrast to the russet hues and gingerbread trim that then prevailed in domestic architecture. Yet in overall form the Sinnige house remained faithful to the still-dominant Queen Anne style and underscored the naïve understanding most architects then had of authentic early American architecture. (Birmingham Public Library {Jo Roy photocopy}.)*

145. *Thigpen house, Montgomery, ca. 1898. (Author's collection.)*

says were the U.S. Post Office buildings at Tuscaloosa and Eufaula, both elegant evocations of Federal-period neoclassicism attuned to twentieth-century requirements. [149] In fact, the Tuscaloosa facility may have taken its stylistic cue from William Nichols's old state capitol building (see illustration 43) which, at that time, still stood at the far end of the same street, as it had since the late 1820s. Certainly, there are striking similarities.

Buildings like the Tuscaloosa Post Office signified a trend in the Colonial Revival, as time went on, toward a more knowing if not

146. "Colonial Residence for J. D. Holman, Esquire"—so reads the caption on the original plans (right) *for this 1912 Ozark house, designed by Montgomery architect Frank Galliher. In a good-natured reference to his humble beginnings as a mule trader, Holman had the likeness of a mule emblazoned on the tile face of one of the mantelpieces in his new mansion. (Author's collection; plan courtesy of Jack Mizell.)*

purely imitative use of early American guises—a trend leading eventually to the skillfully concocted "period" houses (see below) of the 1920s, and a more adept handling everywhere of rediscovered neoclassicism.

147. William Lott house, Mobile, 1906. (HABS: Jack Boucher photo, 1974.)

148. Robert Jemison IV house, ca. 1905. A romantic evocation of plantation days in the New South steel city of Birmingham. (From Art Work of Birmingham, *1907.)*

Summary Characteristics

- Use of forms purportedly inspired by early American architecture, with a strong preference in Alabama for neoclassicism, as opposed to the "Cape Cod" and "Dutch Colonial" modes more common in the eastern states.
- Renewed emphasis upon ordered formality and symmetry, though

149. *U.S. Post Office and Federal Courthouse, Tuscaloosa, 1909–10. (Author's collection.)*

with a generous residual admixture of Queen Anne and other eclectic Victorian influences in both massing and detail.
- On larger houses, frequent use of the classical colonnade, with a partiality for the more elaborate Ionic and Corinthian orders, plus a free and often exaggerated handling of scale and detail.

The *Beaux Arts* Influence: Neo-Renaissance Ideals and the "New" Neoclassicism

The Colonial Revival paralleled, complemented, and to no small degree was influenced by the general return to neoclassicism that began during the 1890s—a return that some architectural historians have termed "the American Renaissance." This rebirth was eloquently proclaimed at the Chicago World's Fair in 1893. More modestly, southerners greeted it a few years later in a handful of buildings that formed the centerpiece of the Atlanta Cotton States and International Exposition (an influence, incidentally, that historians of southern architecture have been slow to discover).

Proponents of this resurrected neoclassicism were guided by the

150. *Mobile County courthouse, 1885. The Ionic portico recalled the old county building which this structure replaced, but the statuary-studded roofline was more attuned to the bourgeois neo-Renaissance taste of architect Rudolph Benz's native Stuttgart. (Courtesy James W. Parker.)*

lofty architectural principles of the renowned Ecole des Beaux-Arts in Paris, which by 1890 counted some of the foremost practicing American architects—figures such as Richard Morris Hunt, Charles Follen McKim, and Stanford White—among its graduates. Looking to Italian or French Renaissance and Baroque models, the Ecole grounded its approach in centuries-old classical attitudes toward design: attitudes that placed a premium on rational order and composition. As a design alternative to what more and more people now felt was the overly rambunctious spirit of the 1870s and 1880s, this latest ideology from abroad found ready acceptance in standard architectural periodicals, and quickly spread nationwide.

Rudolph Benz's porticoed and highly sculptural design for the mid-1880s Mobile County courthouse anticipated by a full decade the reemergence of neoclassicism in Alabama's public architecture, although Benz may have as much been deferring to the columned façade of the old courthouse as making an avant-garde statement of *beaux arts* classicism. [150] Paying similar homage to an older building, neoclassicism set the tone for the 1894 renovation and enlargement of the Montgomery County courthouse. By 1900, newly built neoclassical county buildings at Opelika, Lafayette, and Anniston foretold the style in which more than a score of other Alabama courthouses would be erected over the next twenty years or so.

As a completely orthodox rendering of *beaux arts* classicism in civic architecture, however, few buildings in the state matched the 1904 Carnegie Library at Montgomery, with its textbook façade of interplaying arches and coupled columns—a recurrent *beaux arts* theme. [151] Architects for the Montgomery structure were the New York firm of York and Sawyer. The building's family resemblance to a host of other Carnegie libraries throughout the country was a virtue in the eyes of one early critic, prompting him to note approvingly that the edifice would "be known at a glance" as "a seemly and well-behaved Carnegie Library."

Unsurprisingly, the federal post offices and court buildings whose plans came from the Washington office of the U.S. Supervising Architect likewise mirrored *beaux arts* thinking. These included handsome buildings at Selma, Anniston, Gadsden, Florence, and Mobile, among others. The tiled-roof form of the Italian Renaissance palazzo—a strong subcurrent of the *beaux arts* movement—was evident in several of these. The U.S. Post Office and Courthouse at Mobile (1914–16) was particularly fine, with a gracefully arched Florentine loggia flanked by pedimented aediculae. [152]

A few affluent Alabamians like John M. Caldwell of Birmingham and Mobile cotton broker David R. Burgess commissioned opulent homes in the same Mediterranean Renaissance manner, as filtered through the lens of *beaux arts* classicism. [153] And in the spirit of

151. *Carnegie Library, Montgomery. (John Scott photo, 1955.)*

some Renaissance patron of the arts, Burgess even engaged the talents of a local artist named Thil Wilbergand to enrich the hallway of his Government Street mansion with a mural depicting scenes along Mobile Bay.

In its later stages especially, the "new" neoclassicism nourished by the American disciples of the Ecole des Beaux-Arts tended to become more subdued and less obviously Renaissance-oriented. Overwrought detail gradually gave way to a stricter reign of calm façades like those found in the schemes for Smith, Comer, and Morgan halls—buildings that were part of the University of Alabama's early twentieth-century campus expansion program. [154] In these structures, quiet ranges of engaged columns are carried across the façade above a podium-like ground floor, which is matched by a raised attic story.

152. *U.S. Post Office and Courthouse, Mobile (razed 1968). (HABS: Roy Thigpen photo, 1966.)*

The general character of these structures suggests that they were more than a little influenced by Charles Follen McKim's acclaimed design of a few years earlier for the new Columbia University campus in New York.

Frank Lockwood's plans for the 1906–12 enlargement of the Alabama State Capitol sought to harmonize new construction with the historic Greek Revival nucleus of the building. [155] But in its thoughtful, compositional approach and its attempt to provide for balancing wings that would perfectly complement without mimicking or overwhelming the original structure, the Lockwood plan was just as clearly a statement of *beaux arts* principles as were the new university buildings. To what degree this can be laid to the fact that McKim himself was called in for consultation on the capitol project may never be known.

Throughout Alabama during the early decades of this century, scores of other building enterprises were inspired by reinvigorated neoclassicism; to cite a few: the Southside Baptist Church (1911) in Birmingham, the 1915 Opera House at Dothan, and the marble-faced Jasper First Methodist Church of 1916. The low, saucer-like dome which dominates the interior of the Jasper church was a favorite *beaux arts* device for enhancing the ceremonial atmosphere of large, enclosed spaces. William C. Weston incorporated the same feature into his design for Birmingham's Temple Emanu-El (1913), an edifice mixing Roman and Byzantine elements much in the spirit—if hardly on the scale—of McKim, Mead, and White's much-acclaimed Madison Square Presbyterian Church of 1906 in New York. [156]

153. Top left and right: David R. Burgess house, Mobile, 1907 (George B. Rogers, architect). Above left and right: Drawing room and servant bellbox, Burgess house. (HABS: Jack Boucher photo, 1974.)

Looking to an ever greater clarity of form, neoclassicism in early twentieth-century Alabama continued to refine itself—inspiring, after World War I, such structures as the Birmingham Public Library (1925), the Federal Building, and the now-demolished Temple Theater. Though less and less resembling those turn-of-the-century *beaux arts* buildings that had heralded its birth, this later neoclassicism remained a significant force in Alabama civic and institutional architecture on through the 1920s and well beyond.

154. Smith Hall at the University of Alabama, Tuscaloosa, as it neared completion in 1910. Below: Atrium. (Courtesy Geological Survey of Alabama.)

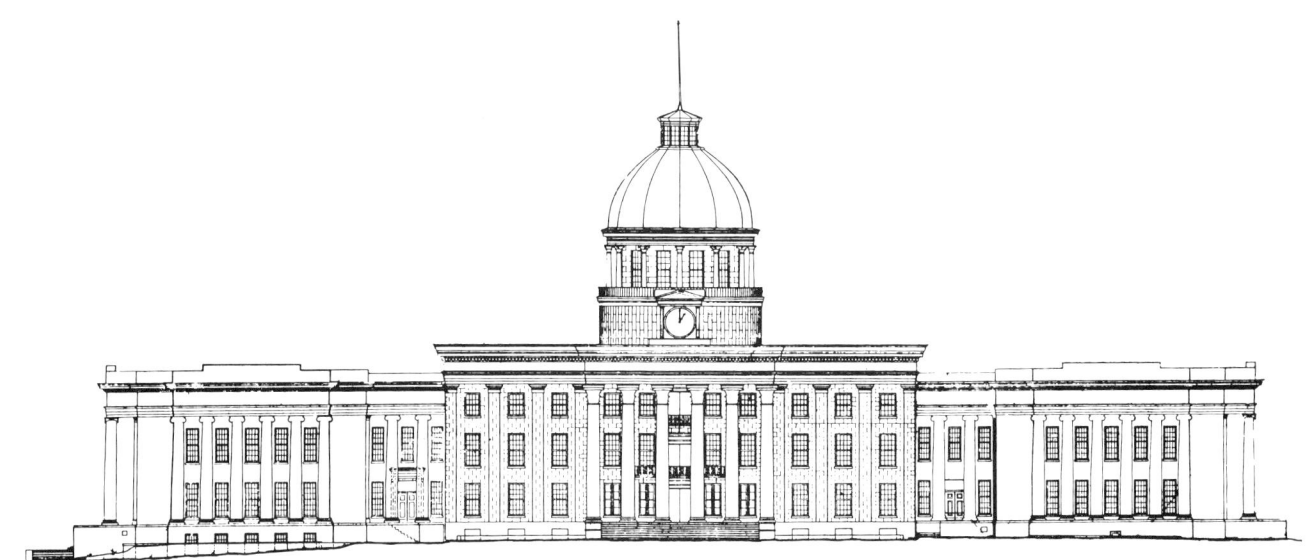

155. *Alabama State Capitol, Montgomery, showing the two-story neoclassical wings added between 1906 and 1912 to the 1851 core of the building. (Courtesy Nicholas H. Holmes, Jr., F.A.I.A., and the Alabama Historical Commission.)*

156. *Temple Emanu-El, Birmingham. (Department of Archives and Manuscripts, Birmingham Public Library {O. V. Hunt Collection; Jo Roy photocopy}.)*

Summary Characteristics

- In most cases, a symmetrical and highly formal, compositional treatment of both ground plan and major elevations.
- Use of a classically based decorative vocabulary derived, in the earlier phases of the style, almost exclusively from Renaissance sources; in later stages, often referring more directly to sources from classical antiquity.

- In public and large institutional buildings a fondness for monumental interior spaces, frequently employing an open rotunda or barrel-vaulted arcade, colonnades, and shallow interior domes (sometimes composed of stained glass).

Arts and Crafts Philosophy and the "Craftsman" Style (ca. 1900 to 1920s)

The resurgence of neoclassicism in one form or another, along with the slowly waning enthusiasm for the Queen Anne style, were but part of the architectural scene in turn-of-the-century Alabama. Soon after 1900 another strain appeared that was distinct from any of these, although its earliest sources could be found in that same English aesthetic impulse, the so-called Arts and Crafts movement, that had given rise to the Queen Anne.

The Arts and Crafts movement was a worldwide phenomenon in some respects, and its influence upon architecture was only one facet of a whole attitude toward arts and design that also encompassed furnishings, interior decor, and landscape. This attitude stressed directness and simplicity, an honest expression of materials and the uniting of practical, everyday craftsmanship with solid and flexible design. Building arrangements should be in harmony with setting and closely tailored to the needs and means of the client.

In such self-proclaimed aspirations the movement sounded at times like a restatement of A. J. Downing and other mid-Victorian romantics whose influence upon Alabama architecture we have already seen. Indeed, philosophically there was a certain kinship, although Arts and Crafts architecture at its best shunned affected historicisms. Rather, it strove to break free entirely from overt imitation of the past, at the same time acknowledging itself to be part of an architectural continuum that could respect and put to use the "good and true" elements of any craft tradition—whether European, American, or Japanese.

Frank Lloyd Wright owed not a little to Arts and Crafts ideas as, in the Chicago suburbs of the 1890s, he worked toward the development of the long, low "prairie" house that would bring him international notice in the early 1900s. More explicitly in the Arts and Crafts vein was the work of Wright's California contemporaries, Bernard Maybeck and the brothers Charles Sumner and Henry Mather Greene, who were evolving a residence type that would be popularized across the country as the "California bungalow."

The *Ladies' Homes Journal, House Beautiful,* and—for the professional—the *Architectural Record* all exposed Alabamians to the new order: to Arts and Crafts philosophy in general and to the distinctive work of creative American architects in the Arts and Crafts vein. Perhaps the most influential publication of all, however, was *The Craftsman* magazine, started in 1901 by Gustav Stickley—not an architect, but a leading proponent of Arts and Crafts ideology. Through *The Craftsman*, Stickley hoped to spread the movement's views about building design and furniture making far and wide. He succeeded to such an extent that today the name of his magazine has become virtually synonymous with a whole genre of building that flourished mainly between 1900 and 1920.

One can still trace the influence of this "Craftsman" style throughout Alabama, with Birmingham having an especially large concentration of such buildings. The city's mushroom growth as the steel-producing "Pittsburgh of the South" during the early 1900s attracted numbers of architects who enthusiastically took up the Craftsman banner. And today, dozens of houses are yet to be seen in older Birmingham suburbs—the South Highlands, Forest Park, Graymont, Mountain Terrace, West End, Norwood, East Lake—which owe their seminal design concept to Arts and Crafts ideas as refracted through Stickley's magazine.

The Arts and Crafts philosophy espoused by *The Craftsman* clearly encouraged enormous flexibility in approaching a specific design problem. But almost always, even if a building was two or three stories high and the site itself restricted, there was an emphatic horizontality, as if to anchor the structure to the land. Deep porches enshadowed by wide eaves glided casually into open pergolas or rock-rimmed terraces. Wooden structural members were accentuated. And sometimes half-timbered gables gave more conservative specimens a slightly snobbish, mock-Tudor air. On every hand there was a relish about displaying the innate qualities of building materials, whether wood, fieldstone (which abounded about hilly Birmingham), tile work, or dark-stained shingles. Interior layouts were as fluid and open as the outside treatment of such buildings would suggest. Fussy Queen Anne spoolwork and bric-a-brac were replaced by clean, uncluttered living areas with smoothly beamed walls and ceilings, built-in bookcases, and brick or stone-faced fireplace openings—all bold, rectilinear, and straightforward.

Yet it was not a domestic design but the 1903 Birmingham Country Club, planned by the local firm of Miller and Martin, that may first have heralded the Craftsman style in Alabama. [157] Over the next two decades, dwellings like the G. J. Robertson, Leonard T. Beecher, and Frank Nelson houses in Birmingham, the McQueen house in Tuscaloosa, and The Pines at Greensboro all revealed Craftsman ideals at home in comfortable upper and upper middle-class circumstances. [158, 159, 160]

But the movement's most lasting legacy to Alabama was the ubiq-

157. *Birmingham Country Club (later Highland Golf and Country Club)*, 1903. Below: *Plan of first floor from* The Architectural Record, *July* 1911. *(Department of Archives and Manuscripts, Birmingham Public Library {Jo Roy photocopy}.)*

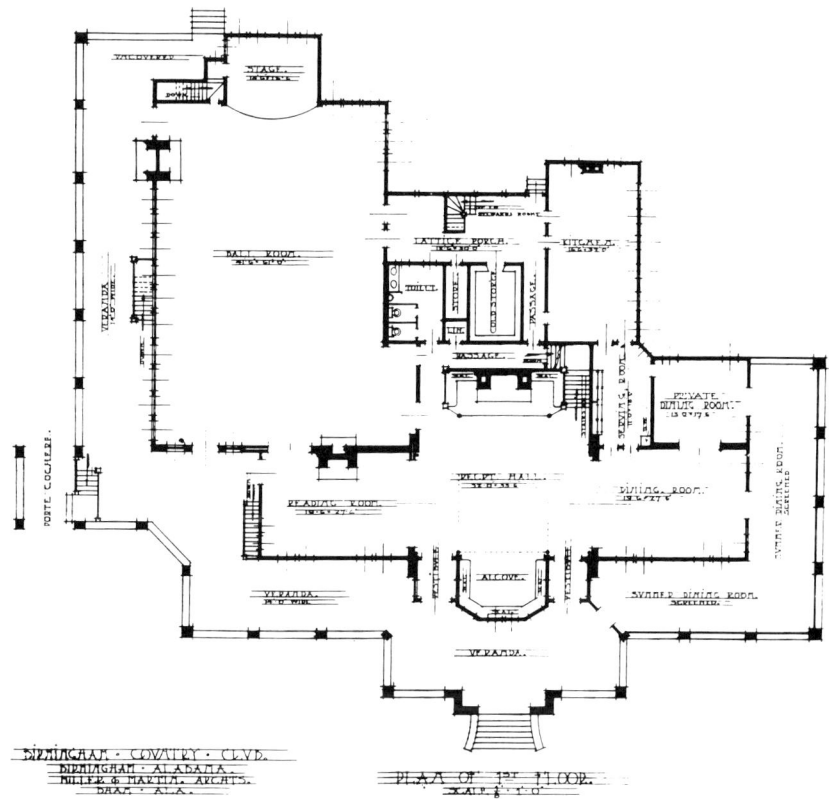

uitous middle-class bungalow—a sort of developer's version of the grander prototype designs originating on the West Coast and widely publicized by *The Craftsman*. In planned residential communities like Corey (now Fairfield), laid out in 1910, the bungalow became the predominant domestic mode. [161, 162] The simple functionalism of Craftsman design philosophy lent itself readily to mass-housing

158. *G. J. Robertson house, Birmingham, 1911 (William Leslie Welton, architect). (Department of Archives and Manuscripts, Birmingham Public Library { Jo Roy photocopy}.)*

159. *Living room and floorplan of Leonard T. Beecher house, Birmingham, 1909. (From* The American Architect, *May 24, 1916 { Jo Roy photocopy}.)*

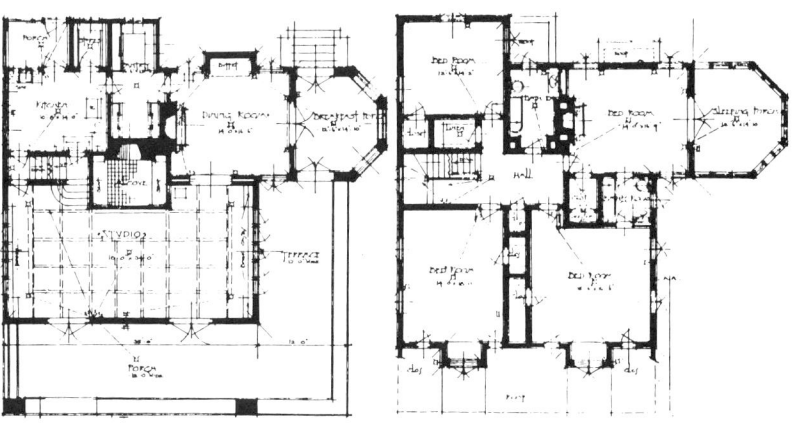

160. *McQueen house, Tuscaloosa, 1915.* *(Author's collection.)*

needs. And for this reason its subtle influence is evident even in the pages of the *Progressive Farmer,* which during these years spread plans and pictures of comfortable yet inexpensive homes to vast areas of the rural South; likewise, in some of the "mail-order" house plans retailed by Montgomery Ward and the Sears company until the 1920s.

If the Craftsman architectural ideal lost ground, particularly among upper-crust Alabamians, to the "period" house after World War I, its contribution to middle-class housing needs was irrefutable. Moreover, its implicit philosophy helped both client and architect to approach the design process in general with far more open minds. Thus the movement may be treated as a legitimate ancestor of the flexible and open-ended arrangements that have come to be taken for granted in today's domestic architecture.

Summary Characteristics

- Informal, practical arrangements and, in smaller houses particularly, asymmetrical elevations.
- Massive, spreading rooflines, usually low-pitched and with broad overhanging eaves (in smaller bungalows, a single broad gable with a subordinate gable extending to cover the porch is a frequent feature).
- Porches often extending into open decks or terraces; a pergola-like open roof is a favorite device.
- Accentuation of building materials (wood, fieldstone, shingles, brick, and sometimes even logs.)

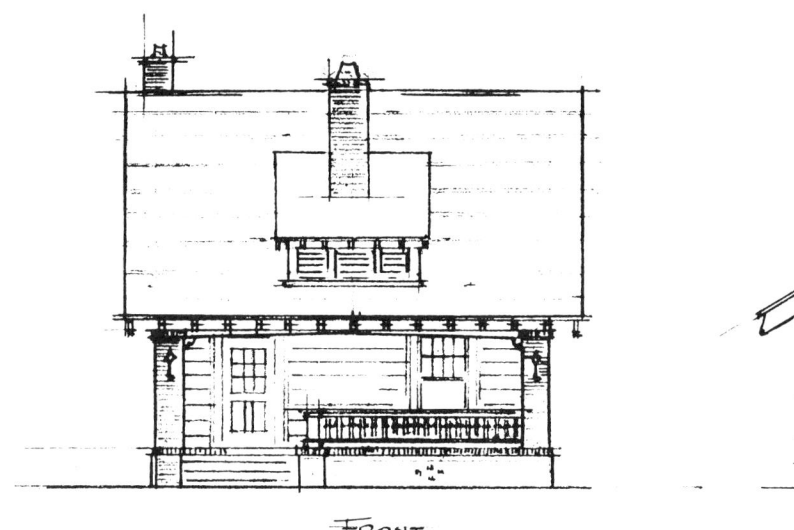
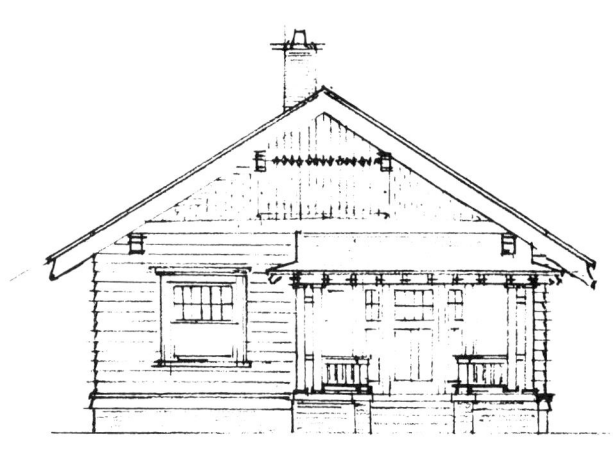
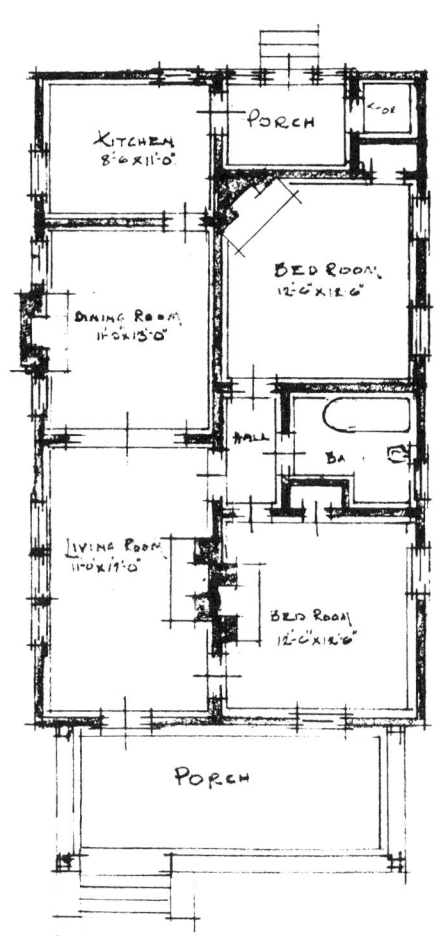
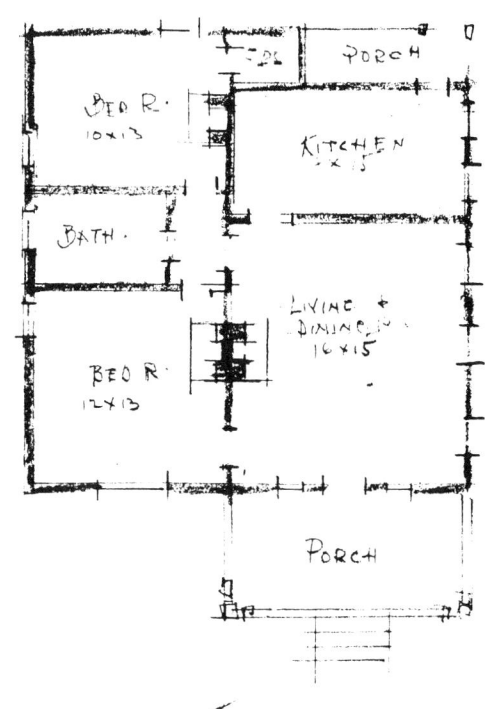

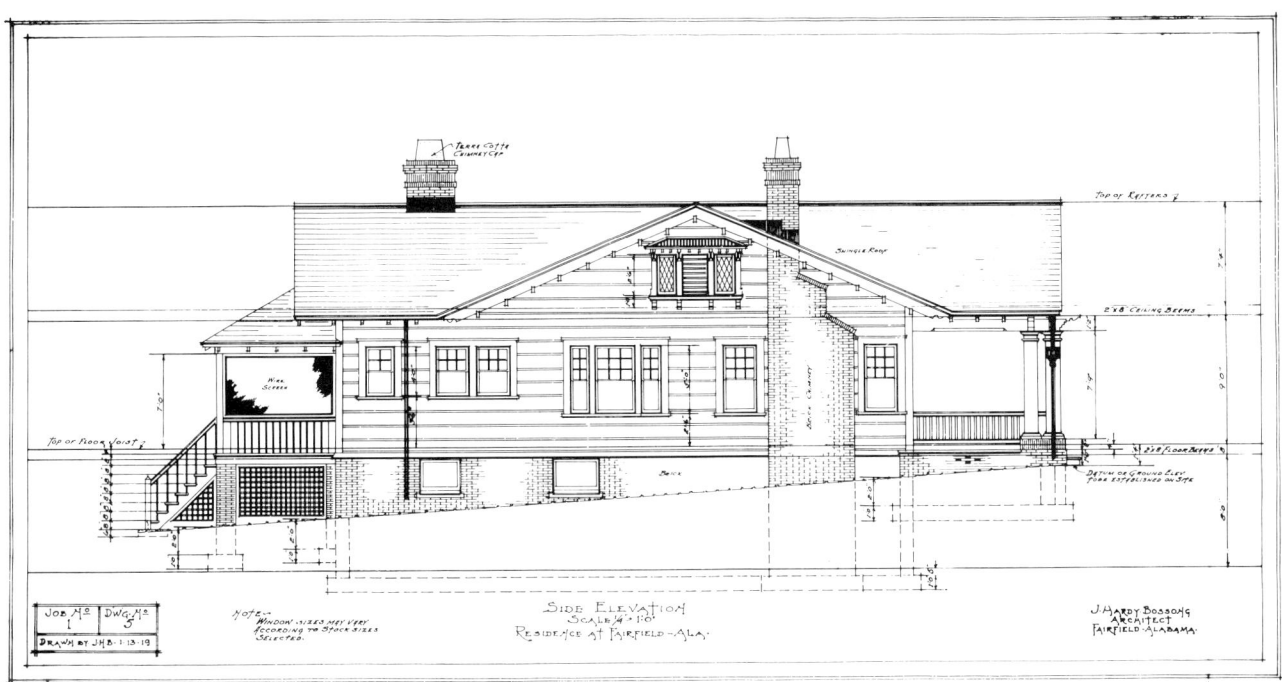

162. Fairfield bungalow, 1919, designed by J. Hardy Bossong. (Department of Archives and Manuscripts, Birmingham Public Library.)

161. Opposite: Model bungalows designed by Birmingham architect William T. Warren in 1910 for the planned industrial community of Corey (now Fairfield). Such middle-class houses became a ubiquitous legacy of the Craftsman movement to Alabama architecture. (Department of Archives and Manuscripts, Birmingham Public Library.)

- Casual, open interiors, frequently highlighted by simple and bold, natural wood trim; frequency of built-in elements such as shelves, bookcases, and windowseats.

The Mission Style
(ca. 1905–1920)

About 1905, Atlanta architect P. Thornton Marye designed a railroad station that helped break new stylistic ground in Alabama. Tiled and arcaded, with curvilinear parapets, a ribbed dome, and a lightly sculptured front, the Gulf, Mobile, and Ohio passenger terminal at Mobile was among the very first structures in the state to draw design inspiration from the Hispanic presence in early North America. [163] More than a decade before, the California Building at the 1893 Chicago World's Fair had called attention to the efforts of a handful of West Coast architects to develop a genre that was both functional and frankly of its own day, and yet redolent of the West's Spanish heritage. Not until after 1900, however, did the so-called Mission style—propagated by glowing magazine articles and an awakened curiosity about American colonial architecture of all sorts—really call itself to the attention of eastern architects and clients as yet another alternative building mode.

With roots deeply embedded in the Latin cultural traditions—both Spanish and French—of the Gulf Coast, Mobile was the logical

163. Gulf, Mobile, and Ohio passenger terminal, Mobile, 1907. (HABS: Jack Boucher photo, 1974.)

place for an early blossoming of the Mission style in Alabama. And even before the GM&O Station was finished, local architect George B. Rogers had drawn up renovation plans for the Government Street Methodist Church that made a still more forceful allusion to Spanish American precedent. In fact, the dramatically sculptured doorway of the church was unabashedly Catholic Baroque in feeling—a strange choice for a Protestant congregation—and anticipated in its explicit archaeological demeanor the Spanish Colonial vogue of the 1920s. [164]

Elsewhere in the state, too, the Mission style soon gained a foothold. The 1909 Otto Marx mansion on Highland Avenue in Birmingham was regarded as a significant enough example of Mission influence in the Deep South to make the pages of *The Architectural Record*. [165] So was its nearby contemporary, the Highlands Methodist Church, another Alabama commission for P. Thornton Marye. There were even Mission overtones in Marye's baroque-flavored design for Birmingham's Terminal Station—as if the architect were reluctant to abandon altogether the Spanish feeling with which he had imbued both the GM&O Station at Mobile and his railroading masterpiece—the 1905 Terminal Station in Atlanta. Indeed, the Mission style continued to enjoy popularity for several years as an architectural medium for new railroad facilities in Alabama. A particularly nice example is the 1917 L&N station at Bridgeport. Meanwhile, the style made domestic inroads here and there in residences like the Judge Samuel Brewer house in Tuskegee and the Perrin P. Hunter house at Jasper. [166, 167]

From Mission style architecture it was but a short step to the full-blown Spanish Colonial mode. But the Mission format maintained its distinctiveness in being less bound by considerations of historical be-

164. Pseudo-Spanish baroque doorway of Government Street Methodist Church, Mobile. (HABS: Jack Boucher photo, 1974.)

lievability. This unfettered attitude toward architectural precedent—alluding to an historical genre but seldom imitating outright—was one of the characteristics that the Mission style shared with the simultaneously popular Craftsman style. And possibly this is one of the reasons that both lost ground among post–World War I Alabamians who, like other Americans, began to look to an architecture that was more fantasy-fulfilling, an architecture at once more exotic and more directly evocative.

165. *Otto Marx house, Birmingham, 1909. (From* The Architectural Record, *July 1911 {Jo Roy photocopy}.)*

166. *Judge Samuel Brewer house, Tuskegee, 1909. (Author's collection.)*

167. *Perrin P. Hunter house, Jasper, ca. 1910. (Author's collection.)*

Summary Characteristics

- Arcaded porches, the arches themselves usually being semicircular or segmental in shape.
- Low-pitched tile roofs, normally hipped in form and often abutting curvilinear parapets.
- Plastered or stuccoed walls, usually in tones of buff, yellow, or white.
- Occasional use of neo-Spanish Baroque sculptural ornament on larger, and especially institutional, buildings.
- Sometimes, in larger structures, the occurrence of balconies, as well as towers capped by pyramidal tiled roofs.

The Early Skyscraper Era
(ca. 1890 to 1920s)

The advent of buildings that rose first six, then ten, and finally more than twenty stories was, of course, a technological achievement rather than a shift in taste. But the visual changes that resulted—the outward expression of a steel skeletal-support system, the vertical bands of wide windows, a flat roof usually defined by a ponderous neoclassical cornice—eventually led to coinage of the term *Commercial style* as a means of summarizing the basic traits associated with the skyscraper.

Buildings of six floors or more already commanded the New York and Philadelphia skylines by the late 1870s. But during the following decade, burgeoning Chicago became the focus for skyscraper development. From there, the fascination for height began to spread nationwide.

In 1889 Alabama saw its first pair of skyscrapers—if they could really be called that—with the completion of Birmingham's Caldwell Hotel and Montgomery's Moses Building. [168] Both structures were diminutive and already old-fashioned by Chicago or New York standards, disguising their six-story height with conventional eclectic architectural garb. But for Alabamians, most of whom had never seen an edifice taller than three or four stories, the two buildings were awesome.

A dozen years passed before the first true Commercial style skyscraper appeared in the state. This was the ten-story Woodward Building in Birmingham. [169] True to form, the Woodward was clean-lined and rectilinear, with plain, rhythmically spaced piers encasing a steel frame that rose between generous expanses of glass to the obligatory overblown cornice. William C. Weston was the architect; Ino Griffiths and Son of Chicago, the contractors. The Wood-

168. *Moses Building, Montgomery. (Alabama Department of Archives and History {John Scott photocopy}.)*

169. *Woodward Building, Birmingham, 1901. (Birmingham Public Library {Jo Roy photocopy}.)*

170. *Jefferson County Savings Bank (now John Hand Building), Birmingham. (Courtesy Warren, Knight & Davis, Architects.)*

ward Building sparked a rash of enthusiastic skyscraper construction in Alabama's largest city, culminating in 1913 with the 20-story Jefferson County Savings Bank. [170] Not to be wholly outdone, Mobile and Montgomery imitated Birmingham's passion for height by putting up skyscrapers of their own: the Van Antwerp Building (1907) in Mobile, and in Montgomery the 12-story Bell Building, finished a year later at a cost of half a million dollars. [171] The sky-

171. Van Antwerp Building, 1906–1907. In this early postcard view, Mobile's first skyscraper soars incongruously above the low, pre–Civil War brick commercial structures that still established the scale of the harbor-side business district in the early 1900s. (Lee Pake Collection {courtesy James W. Parker}.)

172. Empire Building, Birmingham, 1909–10. (Department of Archives and Manuscripts, Birmingham Public Library {Jo Roy photocopy}.)

scraper had become the municipal status symbol for pre–World War I America, much as would the civic-center complex during the 1960s.

Nothing in the design of Alabama's early skyscrapers set them apart from hundreds of others being built throughout the country at the same time. Still, in 1911 *The Architectural Record* did praise the "Florentine treatment" setting off the upper two stories of Bir-

173. *Birmingham skyscrapers of the 1920s. Left: Alabama Power Company Building, 1925, topped by a gilded statue of the goddess Electra. Right: Watts Building, 1927. (Courtesy Alabama Power Company; Department of Archives and Manuscripts, Birmingham Public Library {O. V. Hunt Collection; Jo Roy photocopy}.)*

mingham's new Empire Building as something of a stylistic "refreshment." [172]

References to historical styles were subdued, if not discarded altogether, in the skyscrapers of the 1920s designed by the Birmingham firm of Warren, Knight, and Davis. The Watts and Alabama Power Company buildings and, in Mobile, the Merchants National Bank broke away from the static cornice-topped roofline of earlier decades to achieve a dramatic silhouette through setbacks and

174. Thomas Jefferson Hotel, Birmingham, 1925. (Department of Archives and Manuscripts, Birmingham Public Library { Jo Roy photocopy}.)

175. First National Bank (Timmerman Building), Andalusia, 1920–21. Frank Lockwood, architect. (Author's collection.)

angular profiles. External ornamentation likewise tended toward those spare, abstract surface patterns—zigzags, chevrons, and the like—by which architects of the 1920s sought to capture the apotheosized spirit of "the modern age." [173]

The skyscraper also became a prestigious format for the luxury city hotel, though hotel exteriors failed to adopt the modernistic veneer that became the rule for multistoried office buildings in the 1920s. There was the new Exchange Hotel in Montgomery, which in 1906 replaced its venerable antebellum predecessor; likewise, the new Battle House at Mobile, opened in 1908 with a rooftop garden and an elegant domed lobby. In Birmingham, the Tutwiler and the Molton rose a few years later, to be followed in the 1920s by the Bankhead and the Thomas Jefferson. [174]

The mystique of the skyscraper soaring above a town center can be gauged by the fact that Tuscaloosa, Anniston, Huntsville, and even little Andalusia—none of which could claim a population greater than 15,000 or 20,000—erected their own scaled-down versions of the big-city office or hotel tower between 1920 and 1930. [175] The onset of the Depression ended the first era of skyscraper-building in Alabama. And only in the 1960s would it be resumed at a pace comparable to that of the first three decades of the century.

Summary Characteristics

- The outward, functional expression of structure in vertically thrusting piers that denote the steel skeletal frame, with linear bands of windows between.
- In pre-1920s skyscrapers, an invariable reference to historical guises in outer decorative treatment. This ordinarily followed neoclassical lines as, for example, a columnar treatment of the entire building: visually dividing the whole into "base" (the first two or three floors), "capital" (the cornice-capped topmost floors), and "shaft" (the intervening stories).
- Tendency in the 1920s to abandon historical guise altogether in favor of a modernistic posture, emphasizing a break with the past through abstract and dynamic design.

The Twentieth-Century Academic Revivals and "Period" Architecture
(ca. 1910 to 1930s)

It was inevitable that a better understanding of past architectural styles should lead to a more sophisticated rendering of them. And as the average architect gained a firmer command of the Georgian idiom, or colonial Spanish architecture, or Tudor or French provincial, this is precisely what happened. Likewise, the cavalier mingling and reshaping of architectural elements that had occurred in the earlier phases of the Colonial Revival gradually became—as we have already seen—a studied and rather knowing paraphrase of this or that particular facet of colonial building. Whatever the historical style alluded to, mere picturesqueness gave way to clever academic replication, yet a replication that was clearly adaptive. Repertories for the design of public and institutional buildings expanded to include direct evocations of stately Georgian or English Gothic, beside which most earlier attempts to recall the spirit of these styles paled.

At the national level, a looming figure like architect Ralph Adams Cram might present (to the dismay of *beaux arts* classicists) brilliant philosophical justifications for a new yet timeless modern Gothic that would, as Cram put it, take up where the parent style had left off four centuries earlier. But to the average person, sheer delight for the eye and satisfaction for the soul were reasons enough to erect a believable yet functional "period" building.

The whole movement toward period architecture was helped along enormously during the 1920s by the paradoxical yearning among Americans for streamlined modernity on the one hand and, on the other, for a fanciful escape to the reassuring forms of the past. Hence, Alabamians of the 1920s could build frankly contemporary skyscrapers like Birmingham's Watts Building, and, at the same time just a few blocks away, revel in the eclectic fantasy that was the crimson and gold lobby of the Alabama Theater. Thus might a prosperous Birmingham businessman commute from his tenth-floor office to a convincingly Elizabethan "manor house" or tile-roofed "hacienda" in the swank new suburb of Mountain Brook.

Boston, Philadelphia, New York, and Chicago were beginning to see chaste pseudo-Georgian and pseudo–English Gothic structures even before 1900. In 1910, with the completion of John Jefferson Flowers Hall at Huntingdon College, this same well-bred historicism gained a respectable foothold in Alabama. [176] After reading an article about the Collegiate Gothic style then sweeping eastern campuses, one of Huntingdon's building commissioners proposed that a similar architectural format be adopted for the college's new Montgomery campus. The proposal was accepted, and H. Langford Warren and F. Patterson Smith of Boston were retained to design Flowers Hall in conjunction with local architects B. B. Smith and Weatherly Carter. Montgomerians were assured that the building's simulated patina of antiquity would "compare favorably with the old Gothic buildings of Oxford and Cambridge, England." If the claim was a bit outrageous, it is nonetheless certain that Flowers Hall

176. *John Jefferson Flowers Hall, Huntingdon College, Montgomery. (John Scott photo, 1968.)*

pointed the way stylistically for other Alabama academic institutions, such as Woodlawn High School (1922) in Birmingham, Sidney Lanier High (1929) in Montgomery, and state normal schools at Jacksonville and Florence, which carried the Collegiate Gothic theme into the 1930s.

Ralph Adams Cram himself furnished plans for a Montgomery church begun the same year, 1910, that Flowers Hall was dedicated. This was the Episcopal Church of the Ascension, Alabama's only example of Cram's work and a reposeful essay in the English Gothic spirit of which Cram was acknowledged master. [177] Construction stalled, and Ascension was not finished until 1927, when the last block was placed in the stone tower above the crossing of the nave. In the meantime, a similar neo-Gothic vocabulary had become the

177. Episcopal Church of the Ascension (1910–27), Montgomery (right and opposite). In June of 1984, the interior of this exquisite parish church designed by Ralph Adams Cram was heavily damaged by fire. (Courtesy Seay and Seay, Architects; John Scott photo, 1970.)

chosen style for a number of other Alabama churches—most notably perhaps, Birmingham's Independent Presbyterian Church of 1925–26, designed by Warren, Knight, and Davis.

Still other institutional structures such as Munger Memorial and Stockham halls at Birmingham-Southern College, and even business houses like Jemison and Company of Birmingham, turned to a dignified pseudo-Georgian vocabulary. [178] More festive and playful, and of course equally derivative, was the little Renaissance palazzo in glazed terra cotta and marble that Birmingham architect D. O. Whilldin produced during the same decade for the city's Club Florentine. [179]

But it was in the affluent suburbs of the 1920s—Mobile's historic

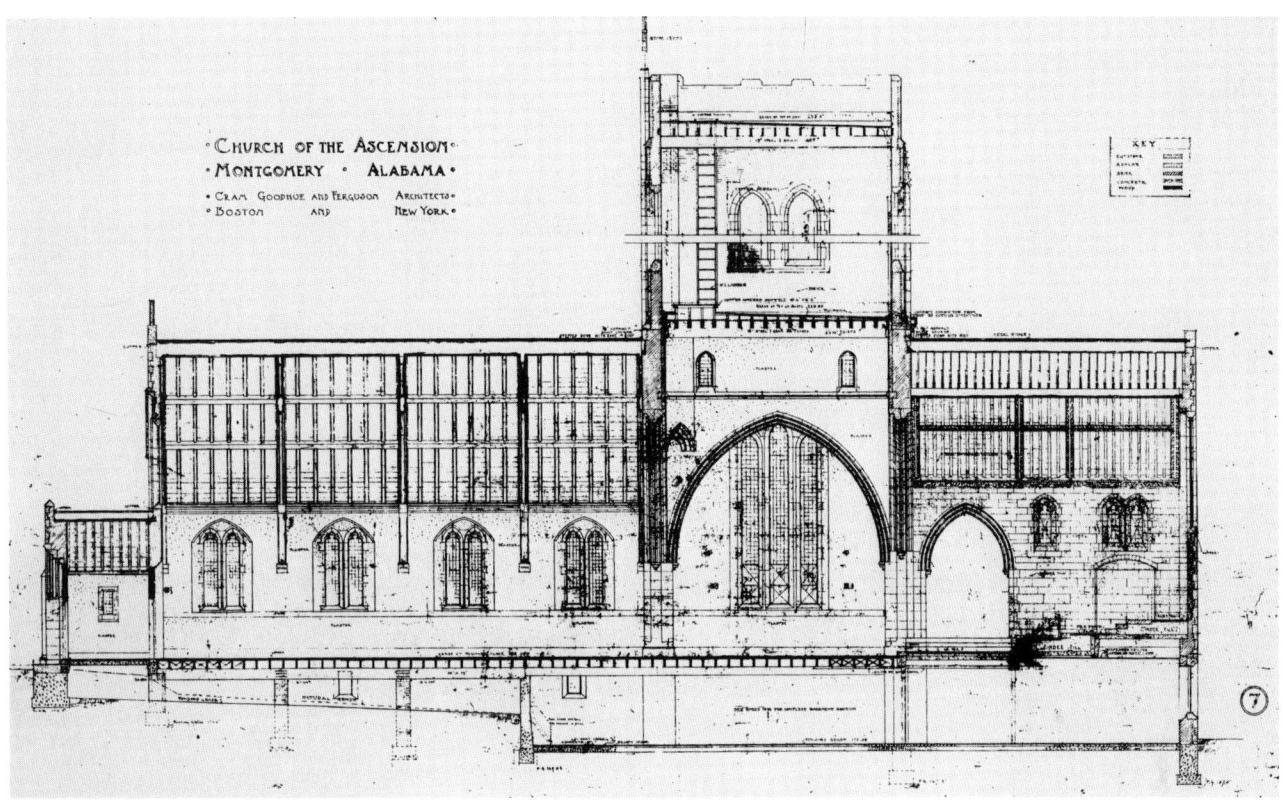

Spring Hill, Cloverdale in Montgomery, The Highlands in Tuscaloosa, Redmont Park and Mountain Brook in Birmingham—and along the fashionable thoroughfares of smaller towns, that this resuscitation of past and distant genres reached its zenith in the period house. And to the period house might be added the period country club and, at least in the case of Mountain Brook, a period Old English shopping village. Expensive residences ensconced in manicured lawns postured now as Tudor country places, now as Norman chateaux (complete with towered dovecotes), now as Spanish haciendas with grilled windows and wooden balconies; or masqueraded as "southern colonial" mansions with a good deal more finesse than would have been the case two decades earlier. [180, 181, 182] Cape Cod cottages and little houses made to look exotically Old Spanish through touches of pastel stucco and red tile brought the same period ideal within reach of more modest incomes.

Yet in plan and site orientation, these dwellings were wholeheartedly twentieth century. Breakfast nooks and large informal living rooms, garages and cabineted kitchens, French doors opening onto a terrace or a sequestered patio, all bespoke half a century of quiet domestic revolution. At the same time, the most magnificent of the pe-

178. Munger Memorial Hall, Birmingham-Southern College, 1927–28. (Philip Shirley photo {courtesy Birmingham-Southern College}.)

179. Club Florentine, Birmingham, ca. 1925. (Author's collection.)

180. *Dr. Marcus Skinner house, Selma, 1928. Frank Lockwood of Montgomery was the architect. Starting before World War I with house designs that reflected the more conservative and Anglo-oriented aspects of the Arts and Crafts ideal, Lockwood moved steadily toward a full-blown Tudor-inspired academicism during the 1920s. (Author's collection.)*

181. *Above,* G. B. McCormick house *and above right,* Erswell house, *Birmingham—period dwellings of the 1920s. (From* Southern Architecture Illustrated, *1931.)*

182. *Herbert Tutwiler house, Birmingham, 1925. The "Mount Vernon" portico was a favorite feature of period houses built in the American colonial manner. (Author's collection.)*

183. Hassinger house, Birmingham, 1929. (Author's collection.)

riod residences, such as the great Tudor-style Swann and Hassinger mansions in Redmont Park, rivaled in splendor their European prototypes. [183] And one would have been hard put to find an early American counterpart equal in scale and urbanity to the spreading "southern colonial" establishment that New York architect Aymar Embury II designed in the late 1920s to house the Mountain Brook Club. [184] It was a vision of the past, improved and perfected.

184. *Mountain Brook Club, Birmingham. Architect Aymar Embury's intention was to create the effect "of a big country house that just grew from the ground in response to the needs of its owner. . . ." Overlooking the rolling golf course was what Embury dubbed "a long wide piazza with the Southern Tall columns," flanked by open terraces used for outdoor dining and dancing. Here we see the club shortly after it opened in 1930. (Courtesy Mountain Brook Club.)*

The Depression momentarily halted both the development of posh suburbs dotted with period houses and the construction of costly churches and schools after some idealized vision of Gothic or Georgian or other historical prototypes. But in Alabama it by no means extinguished the love for architectural revivalism itself—for reincarnating something of the past in what is built for the present. The impulse was still alive and well three decades later. Proof enough was Samford University's multimillion-dollar Birmingham campus [185], all of a piece in Georgian red brick, not to mention the costly church complexes of spired Georgian Colonial design, like First Methodist, Sylacauga, or Hunter Street Baptist in Birmingham, erected during the church-building boom of the 1950s. In fact, looking back from the vantage point of the 1980s, one could conclude that academic revivalism and the impulse toward period architecture had never really ended.

185. Harwell Goodwin Davis Library, Samford University, Birmingham, 1956. (Lew Arnold photo, 1983 {courtesy Samford University}.)

Summary Characteristics

- Use of reasonably accurate "costuming" in terms of proportion and massing, detail and materials, to refer to a specific historical period, at the same time treating spatial arrangements in a highly functional manner.
- Consideration of site-orientation and landscaping in the same plastic, functional, terms applied to the building itself.

Epilogue

More than half a century's worth of architectural innovation and experimentation has come and gone in Alabama since 1930. Toward the end of the Depression era, there was the Resettlement Administration's hopeful experiment in low-cost housing with the rammed-earth dwellings built at Mount Olive near Gardendale. [186] A little later, Frank Lloyd Wright introduced his Usonian concept to Alabama via the Rosenbaum house at Florence. [187] Here, as in similar houses that he had already designed, Wright sought to achieve a reasonably priced domicile that would be architecturally distinctive while incorporating all the conveniences of new building technology and new concepts of spatial planning.

The 1940s saw the arrival of those stark, linear buildings in chromium, concrete, and glass that owed their allegiance to the Bauhaus movement and to the strivings in the world of architecture toward a pan-cultural, international style. Alabama-born architect Paul Rudolph began his career as a Bauhaus disciple but soon broke away to develop his own *parti,* characterized by architectural historian Frederick Koeper as "a collision of forms and interlocking spaces." During the 1960s Rudolph gave to his native state the organic, dramatically unfolding interiors of both the John Wallace house in Athens—designed for a friend of his youth—and the widely acclaimed Tuskegee Institute chapel. [188]

By and large, however, the state's architecture maintained a conservative cast. In their private inclinations, if not always in the public image they wished to project through ambitious new civic centers, sprawling industrial parks, and gleaming office towers, most Alabamians retained an extraordinary affection for traditional forms—for buildings that somehow evoked the past. From time to time this affection reached extravagant proportions. Thus, both a Mississippi River plantation mansion, Houmas House, and Stratford Hall, the Virginia birthplace of Robert E. Lee, inspired costly Alabama imitations during the 1960s and 1970s. Closer at hand, the Gorgas house in Tuscaloosa—evolved from a plain little university refectory building into one of the most photogenic residences in the state—has fired the imagination of countless homebuilders and even the architects of new banks, who have copied with varying degrees of success its twin curving stairs and raised portico. [189] Another famous Alabama house, the Forks of Cypress, provided the design for the new quarters of a Florence bank in 1983, though in detail the building fell disappointingly short of the faithful exterior replica it purported to be.

The unfortunate pastiches that have often resulted from well-meaning efforts to paraphrase the past do not invalidate the desire for architecture to suggest cultural continuity; yes, and regional identity

186. *Rammed-earth house at Mount Olive Estates, near Gardendale, designed in 1936 by Resettlement Administration architect Thomas Hibben. (From* The Birmingham News, *13 Sept. 1941.)*

as well. The paradox symbolized during the 1920s by the modernistic skyscraper on the one hand and the period house on the other still remained, and was broadened during the 1970s and 1980s to include, throughout Alabama, a wave of popular interest in restoring old buildings. That the paradox existed in the first place was perhaps not so much indicative of stylistic confusion or conflict as of a profound truth: that buildings and building tastes mirror in a very fundamental way, and far more than we may be aware, the paradoxes within human nature itself, the paradox that is the human condition, whether in classical Greece or nineteenth- and twentieth-century Alabama. [190] Even as jet travel and interstates, rapidly changing social mores and speech patterns, knit Alabamians ever closer to other Americans, an appreciative rebirth of regional values in architec-

187. Sidney Rosenbaum house, Florence, 1939. (Duane Phillips photo, 1983; plan reprinted from Frank Lloyd Wright's Usonian Houses *by John Sergeant through courtesy of Watson Guptill Publications, New York.)*

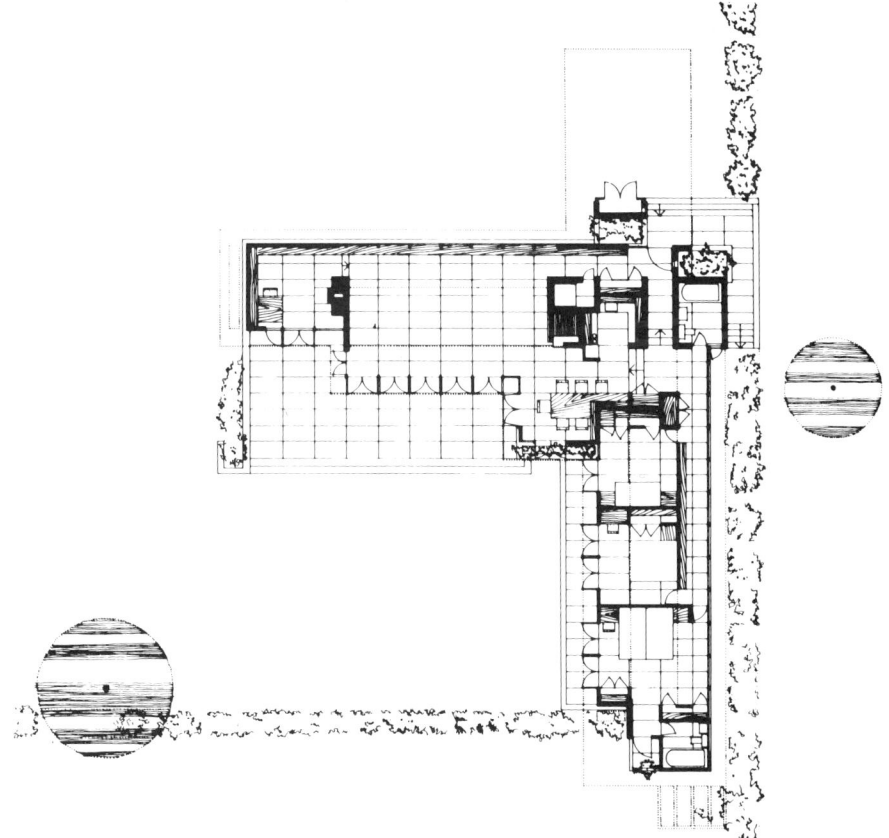

188. *Chapel, Tuskegee Institute, 1969. (Ezra Stoller photos, from* Architectural Record, *November 1969.)*

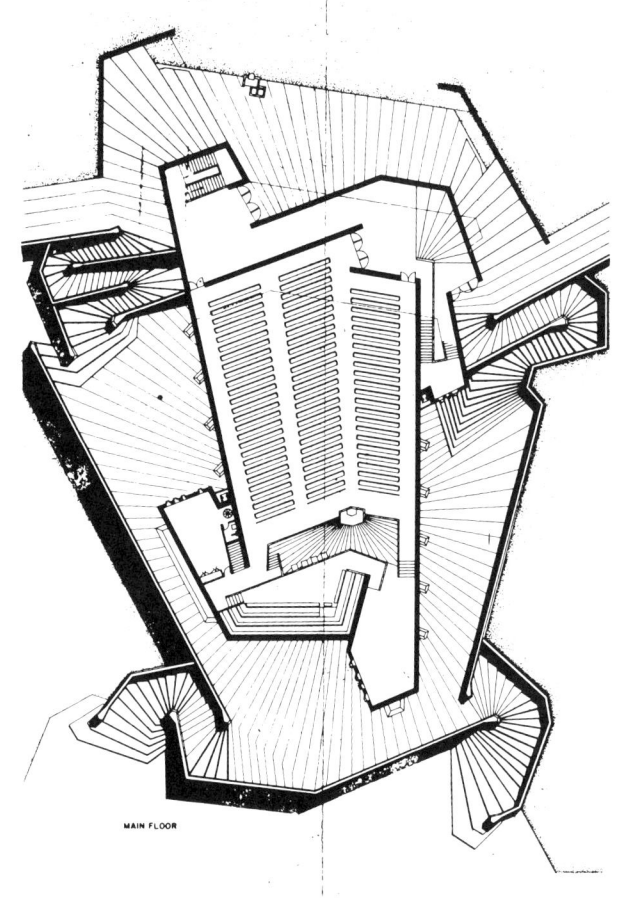

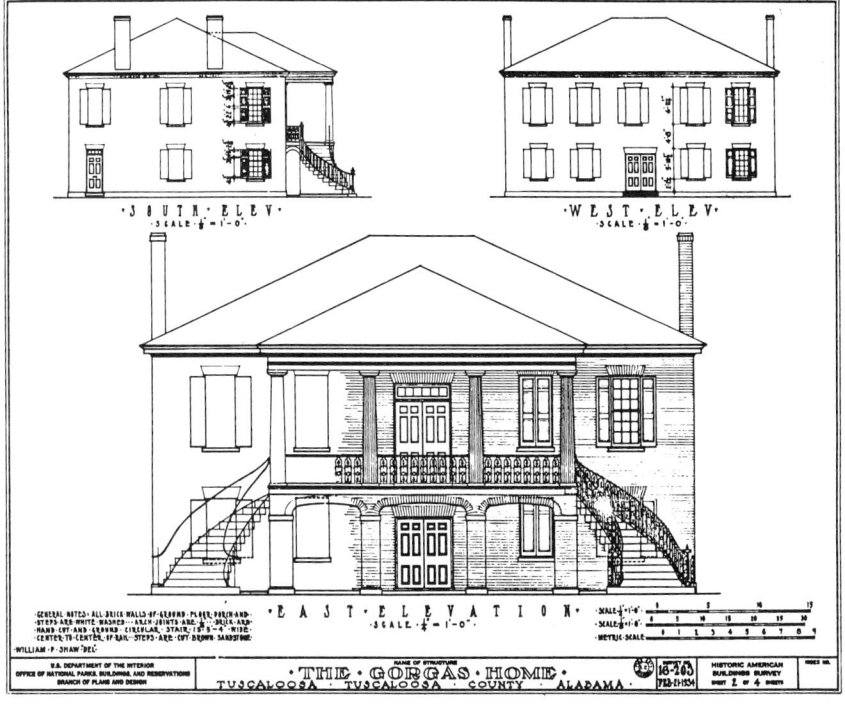

189. *Persistent traditionalism.* Above: *The Home Bank, Guntersville (1978)—one of several post–World War II Alabama buildings that have sought to evoke the flavor of Tuscaloosa's much-admired Gorgas house (right), sole surviving edifice from the original 1830 state university complex. (Courtesy The Home Bank, Guntersville;* HABS: *William P. Shaw, delineator, 1934.)*

190. *Mulberry Medical Plaza (1984), Montgomery, designed by the firm of Watson, Watson, and Rutland. The sudden sprouting of so-called post-modern structural complexes such as this one, with its slightly tongue-in-cheek reference to an array of past architectural styles, was probably the most striking single development in Alabama architecture during the early 1980s. (Robert Fouts photo {courtesy of Watson, Watson, and Rutland, AIA].)*

ture—largely as a side effect of the historic preservation movement—signaled once again that architecture must look both inward and outward to fulfill its highest social purpose; must answer the human need for identity with place and for the comforting symbols of tradition even while broadening our horizons to limitless future possibilities.

Part Two The HABS Catalog

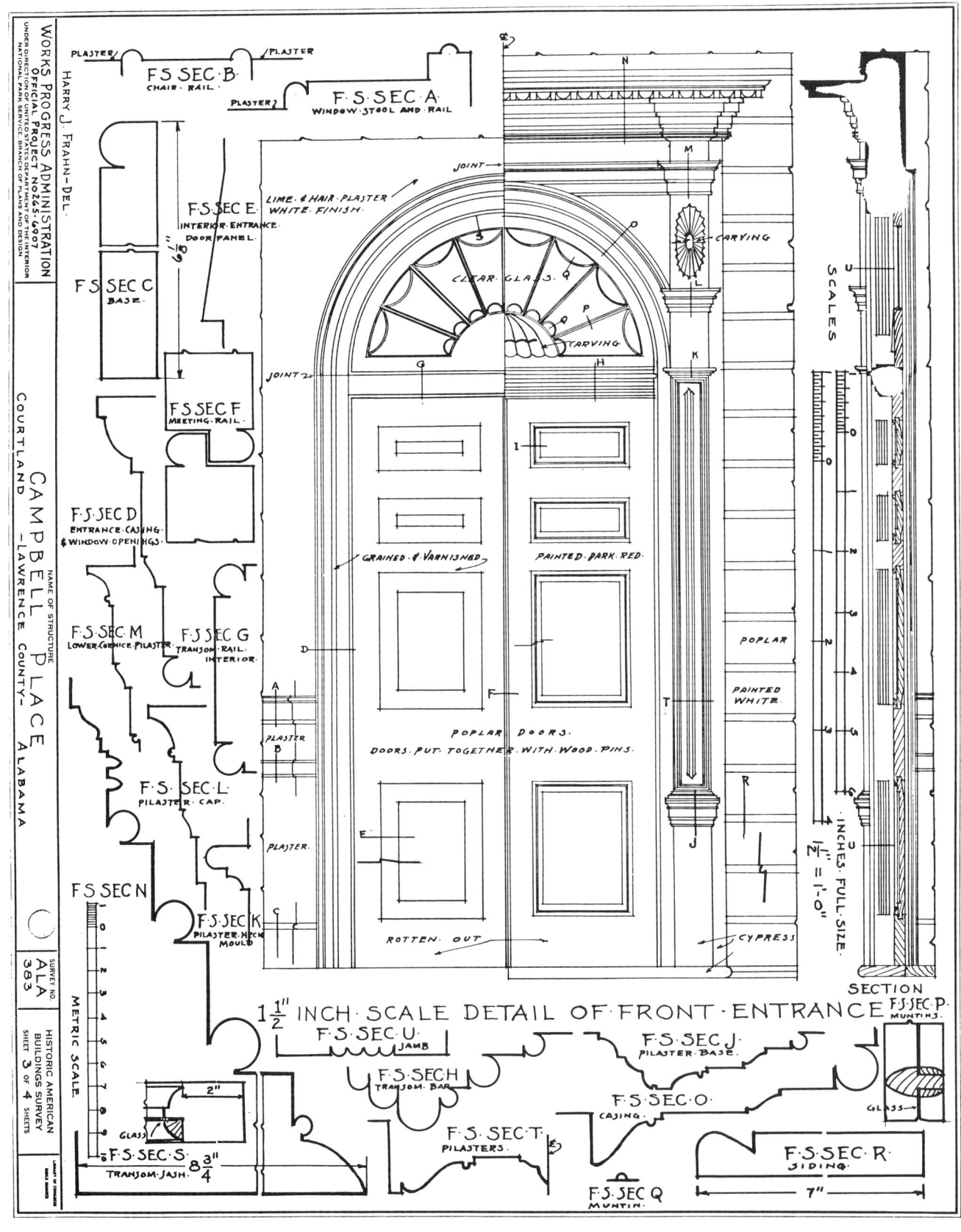

HABS Recording in Alabama

More than 720 structures and structural complexes scattered throughout Alabama are currently represented in the Historic American Buildings Survey collection. These holdings consist of some 900 measured drawings, over 6,000 photographs, and approximately 900 pages of historical and architectural data. The Alabama collection is, in fact, one of the largest for any of the states, and—with the exception of Virginia—the most extensive single collection by far relating to the Southeast.

Since initial recording efforts began in 1934, fire, storm, and neglect have taken their toll among the buildings documented. But man himself has been the chief destroyer. Today, forty percent of the Alabama structures represented in the HABS collection are gone (as against a comparatively modest eighteen percent of those recorded in neighboring Georgia). Of nearly 200 structures documented in the city of Mobile since 1934, around 140 have now disappeared—a singularly high attrition rate but one in which some other localities are not far behind. Dozens of additional Alabama buildings investigated by HABS during the early years of its existence have since been damaged by heedless and inept alteration—at times occurring, sadly, under the guise of "restoration."

To be sure, the recent growth of popular interest in saving old buildings has sparked the rescue of some HABS structures that had fallen upon evil days. Happy examples are the Huntsville mansion of George Steele, one of the state's foremost early builders, as well as Selma's King-Welch house, the Donnell house—Pleasant Hill—in Athens, Orange Vale near Talladega, and the McMillan house near Orrville. One edifice, the picturesque Gliddon house in Mobile, with its unusual West Indian character, was even deemed important enough to be reconstructed in 1980 on the basis of HABS drawings prepared forty-four years earlier.

Yet the destruction continues. Several HABS-recorded buildings disappeared while fieldwork for this catalog was underway: Deer's Store at Claiborne, both the McQueen and Seaman-Airey houses at Wetumpka, and the Mardis-Batchelor house at Mardisville in Talladega County. After the manuscript had gone to press, the notable, raised-cottage Kaster house in Camden was bulldozed by a local bank over the protests of the Alabama Historical Commission and numbers of concerned citizens. And during the summer of 1982, Mobile's Goldsby house, a major Gothic Revival landmark in the state, was likewise pulled down after sustaining roof damage from Hurricane Frederick. That same summer, the abandoned Moses Wheat house in Lee County, with its rich complement of grained and stippled interior woodwork, was burned by vandals. At this writing, other structures stand on the brink of disappearance barring some last-minute turn of fortune: Sweetwater—the Governor Robert Patton house near

Doorway of the demolished Westwood Wallace James House (ca. 1825), Courtland, Lawrence County, as drawn by HABS delineator Harry J. Frahn in 1937.

Florence; the Seale-Mosley house near Union Springs; Bride's Hill near Courtland; and in Wilcox County both the Bethea and Sellers houses. The plight of these buildings underscores only too well the fact that the HABS archives for Alabama form an invaluable chronicle of an architectural legacy steadily being eroded away. (Appendix A gives a county-by-county numerical breakdown of the current status of HABS structures, insofar as this could be determined in 1984–85.)

Some six thousand buildings erected before 1860 were estimated still to be standing in Alabama when the nationwide HABS recording program began half a century ago. The time was the Great Depression, and the project was conceived not only as a means through which to build a centralized archives of early American architecture similar to those already existing in Europe, but also as a way of providing much-needed jobs for out-of-work professionals. So it was that in November of 1933 the Historic American Buildings Survey came into being as a cooperative venture between the National Park Service, the American Institute of Architects (the AIA), and the Library of Congress. A joint circular issued through the Department of the Interior a few weeks later spelled out the Survey's dual objectives: to establish a ten-week unemployment relief project for architects and architectural draftsmen (at this point, the number of personnel was limited to a thousand), and, by tapping these skills, to document significant early "architectural specimens" so that they "should not pass into unrecorded oblivion." Fundamental criteria and work standards were to be devised by a small administrative staff within the Park Service itself.

To implement the program as quickly as possible, the organizational structure of the AIA, with its national network of seventy-one chapters, was adopted. The statewide area encompassed by the seventeen-year-old Alabama chapter was designated as HABS District Number 16. And at the recommendation of one of the founding members, Dean Frederick Child Biggin of the Alabama Polytechnic Institute (now Auburn University), Professor E. Walter Burkhardt was named District Officer to oversee the Alabama survey effort.

A native of Leipzig, Burkhardt had come to the United States with his American-born mother in 1908, at the death of his German father. After earning architectural degrees at Washington State University and Columbia, Burkhardt joined the Alabama Polytechnic Institute faculty in 1929. He quickly recognized the merit of the early buildings in the area, at a time when most people paid them scant mind. And from the very outset of his teaching career in Alabama he asked each fourth-year architectural student to select, measure, and draw what he described as a building "of the ante-bellum type," in fulfillment of graduate requirements. This demonstrated interest in the state's nineteenth-century architecture made Burkhardt a logical choice to spearhead the first systematic study of the subject.

To assist him in drawing up a preliminary list of candidate structures for investigation, Burkhardt, in turn, named a three-man state advisory committee of fellow architects. They were William T. Warren of Birmingham, George B. Rogers of Mobile, and Edgar L. Love of Huntsville. Warren, a partner in the well-known firm of Warren, Knight, and Davis, was also a member of the AIA's national committee for the preservation of historic monuments.

Selection criteria for the buildings to be examined went well beyond monumental architecture. "The project," Burkhardt later recalled, "was intended to record not merely structures of unusual architectural merit, but also types of typical buildings from the beginning of settlement in Alabama up to 1860," the official national cutoff date at that time. Anticipating a later generation's interest in folk architecture, Burkhardt called for the documentation of a "cross-section of pioneer structures." If the actual survey failed to be as comprehensive in this regard as it should have been, certainly the incipient awareness was there.

In January 1934 federal funds were allotted for the Survey, and work actually began. Auburn was the state headquarters, since the university campus there provided office space. But branch offices were also set up in Birmingham, where the federal relief rolls indicated the greatest concentration of unemployed architects and draftsmen, as well as in Montgomery and Mobile. A "squad leader" headed up each branch office, coordinating activities within the office itself and dispatching the newly organized recording teams to town and countryside. In Birmingham the squad leader was Philip S. Mewhinney; in Montgomery, Earl Guthrie Lutz, Jr.; and in Mobile, Fred W. Clarke, later to be succeeded by Edward C. Marty. For Mewhinney's accomplishments, Burkhardt reserved special praise. "The best drafting work of the whole project was done under his direction," Burkhardt would later note, "although he was greatly handicapped at times by some of the talent assigned him."

That portion of the state from Tuscaloosa northward fell under the domain of the Birmingham office, while the Montgomery and Mobile units, together with HABS headquarters at Auburn, covered central and southern Alabama. Initially, a single Auburn-based photographer, Alex Bush, worked statewide. In just over three months' time, HABS personnel completed twenty-four sets of measured drawings, supplemented by several hundred photographs. An index card listing of historic structures was also started, and the first data sheets for some of the buildings compiled. But at the end of April federal funding, which had been channeled through the Civil Works Administration, expired. Ironically, more architects and draftsmen than ever had by now joined the ranks of the unemployed.

At Professor Burkhardt's request, the state government assumed partial sponsorship of the program, adding its resources to money from Washington that soon became available again through the Federal Emergency Relief Administration. For its part, the university continued to provide working space, while at the same time contributing the services of Walter Burkhardt. Through this felicitous combination of support from state, nation, and academia, the program moved forward on an even larger scale than before. Three other branch offices were established—at Gadsden, Huntsville, and Sheffield. And when its activity peaked during late 1935 and early 1936, the Survey was employing forty-four people, including the ten percent of its personnel not required to actually be on the relief rolls. Among these were two additional photographers, W. N. Manning and E. W. Russell.

While fieldwork proceeded, Burkhardt's architectural students continued to turn out scaled, watercolor renderings of historic buildings, usually in or about Auburn. Typically, such a drawing consisted of a façade elevation, with small corner insets of the floorplan and noteworthy details—the balustrade of a stair or a detail from a Doric entablature. Often, the renderings were wonderfully fanciful, with romantic flourishes like moss-draped oaks, crinolined belles, and horse-drawn barouches. Most of these pictures were eventually lost, but a few survive today in the Auburn University Archives.

On 1 July 1935, after several months of joint state and federal funding, the Historic American Buildings Survey reverted to full federal sponsorship under the Works Progress Administration—the WPA. And so it remained during the two years of steady recording activity that followed. In retrospect, it is remarkable that so much was accomplished beneath the umbrella of a shifting, temporary bureaucracy. The total quantity of material assembled—over 5,000 photographs and 750 sheets of measured drawings—would prove a lasting tribute to the commitment of Professor Burkhardt.

Some of the drawings display exquisite attention to detail, reflecting an era when architectural draftsmanship still stressed artistic quality as well as utilitarian function. The number of sheets prepared for each structure varied from a single page to as many as twenty-four for Gaineswood at Demopolis. Ideally, documentation for all the more important buildings should have taken the form of both measured drawings and photos. But the time-consuming process of first sketching, then meticulously measuring, and finally preparing to scale a full set of floorplans, elevations, cross-sections, structural details, and sometimes landscape arrangements clearly made this impossible. So Burkhardt and his associates established an informal priority list of the more significant or more immediately endangered structures upon which to concentrate their energies. For the rest, photographic coverage had to suffice, although the photographers themselves were not specialists in architectural recording. If the cal-

Miss Octavia Atkinson and her "smart bucket," Bullock County, 1935. Occasionally HABS photographers moved beyond strict architectural recording to capture such novel folk scenes as this. (HABS: W. N. Manning photo, 1935.)

iber of these early photos is often disappointing by today's standards, at least a record was made—one which may now be the best we have for many destroyed buildings.

Quite apart from their architectural interest, many of the pictures afford a poignant if unintentional glimpse of the Depression years—a glimpse at times reminiscent of the famous Walker Evans photographs commissioned about the same time by the Farm Security Administration. Buildings are dilapidated; rooms are meagerly furnished, and the evidence of rural Deep South poverty is all too evident. Now and again, homely details of everyday life appear: a commercial wall calendar bearing a photograph of President Roosevelt; a family snapshot; or a humble personal memento on the mantelpiece. A turbaned old black woman leans heavily on a cane in front of her log home on a Butler County plantation. In contrast a portly, bespectacled white matron and a pretty, well-dressed young woman take their ease on a columned Eutaw veranda. Some of the subjects had little or nothing to do with architecture, but were simply included for their folk flavor. There is the "smart bucket" devised by Miss Octavia Atkinson to hoist spring water up a hundred-foot slope to her log house atop Chunnennuggee Ridge in Bullock County. And among a batch of pictures taken at Dixons Mills in Marengo County is one showing a homemade, wooden-wheeled vehicle wryly labeled a "Hoover Wagon."

Written information—historical data and architectural descriptions—received only cursory attention when compared with photographic coverage and measured drawings. The important thing, after all, was to quickly record the physical appearance of the buildings. This left little time for documentary investigation of the history of a structure, and in most cases heavy reliance was placed upon word-of-mouth tradition. Thus the pages of historical data compiled during these early years of the Survey must be regarded with a healthy skepticism. Written architectural analysis likewise tends to be superficial or nonexistent.

Despite its weaknesses, the HABS effort in Depression-era Alabama touched upon numerous facets of the state's early and mid-nineteenth century material culture. At a time when Alabama history was perceived through a veil of Old South nostalgia, white-columned houses inevitably took center stage, notwithstanding a consciously broad-based approach to the survey. It should be no surprise, then, that those locales most redolent of pre–Civil War plantation culture were given particular attention: the old cotton-producing counties of the Black Belt and the Tennessee Valley, planter communities like Greensboro and Eutaw, and the great antebellum cotton-shipping port of Mobile.

In Mobile, dozens upon dozens of photographs were made of tall, cast-iron bedecked houses and raised Creole cottages; likewise, of old commercial buildings near the waterfront and neoclassical mansions in the outlying suburbs. Measured drawings of the privy that served the Dargan-Waring house on Government Street furnish a rare glimpse of urban antebellum sanitary arrangements. Nor did documentary efforts in Mobile fail to include hitching posts and street lamps, or an ornate mid-nineteenth century mounting block. A special survey of the city's decorative ironwork (see Appendix B) recorded the lacy details of balustrades, trellis work, fences, and gates—a goodly portion of which would eventually end up as scrap metal.

Around the state the Survey included churches, schools, courthouses, Masonic lodges, country stores, and diminutive law offices facing onto sleepy town squares. Covered bridges were not forgotten, nor water-powered mills. And photographs of the abandoned Chewacla Lime Works near Opelika foretold the later recording projects of the Historic American Engineering Record. Pictures were also made of the curious grave shelters standing in some rural and small-town Alabama cemeteries. Folk dwelling-types like the ubiquitous open-passage log houses, hundreds of which still dotted the state during the 1930s, were seriously regarded for the first time. Also documented were the characteristic dependencies that clustered about mansion and cabin alike in pre–Civil War Alabama: kitchens and servants' quarters, wellhouses, laundries, corncribs, smokehouses, barns, stables, privies, cotton presses, gazebos, and even walled family cemeteries. And while the neoclassical theme was constantly stressed, the Survey also ventured into such previously ignored realms of architectural style as the Gothic Revival and the Italianate, though many of the best examples were roundly and inexplicably passed over. The 1860 cutoff date itself was stretched, unknowingly perhaps, to include buildings like the tiny 1870s medical office of Dr. A. L. Moorman at Bexar in Marion County, and the Presbyterian Church built at Camden a decade later.

Through most of its three-and-a-half-year existence, the 1930s Survey effort received fortuitous statewide newspaper coverage. This began soon after recording activity itself got underway, when the *Birmingham News,* Alabama's leading daily, requested that Professor Burkhardt prepare a series of articles on early Alabama architecture for its Sunday magazine. Illustrated with HABS photographs, these were to be based on concurrent fieldwork. Burkhardt responded willingly, and the first of twelve articles initially scheduled appeared in June of 1934. These highlighted a succession of topics from characteristic stairway treatments to early Alabama school buildings or the architecture of a particular community. Readers of the *News* reacted so favorably that the editors decided to continue the series.

Feeling the press of other duties, however, Burkhardt at this point turned the responsibility over to his wife, Varian. It was a task she took on with enthusiasm, despite the demands of a household and children.

In order to gather material for the stories, especially the human interest details that would appeal to a general readership, Varian Carpenter Burkhardt often accompanied the HABS photographers on distant recording assignments. She interviewed those who lived in the old houses—descendants of planters, plain folk, and slaves. She pored through faded letters and diaries and tramped about old cemeteries, pulling bits and pieces of information together. Forty-five years later she would recall those "wonderful days" in the midst of national hard times: jostling along back roads that were alternately choked in dust or hub-deep in mud; putting up at country hotels where the night wind brought a shower of acorns clattering down on a tin roof and where a steaming breakfast could be had next morning for a quarter; arriving one purple twilight at the front steps of Rosemount, deep in the Black Belt—unannounced except for a swirl of baying hounds. There, the HABS crew was taken in for the night by the chatelaine of the great old house, Amelia Walton Legare. And that evening, all sat down to a rural repast in the faded elegance of the shadowy dining room. Yet Varian Burkhardt's most vivid memory of the night at Rosemount was not the meal itself, nor the conversation, but rather the pearly white mussel shells from the nearby Tombigbee River which served as ashtrays; and, more poignantly, how the leftovers quickly vanished—spirited away to "the quarters" to be devoured by the children of the plantation tenants.

Telephones were few and far between in rural Alabama of the 1930s. Most of the time recording teams just "appeared," as they did at Rosemount. Yet never, Mrs. Burkhardt could also recall, were they treated discourteously. Returning to Auburn after each field trip, she would sit down at her breakfast-room table to type up another round of stories for the Birmingham paper under the pen name of "Varian Feare." The Burkhardt articles eventually numbered fifty-eight, and they continued at intervals for more than two years.

But by early 1937, HABS activity in Alabama was winding down, as more and more of its personnel found regular employment in the private sector. Thus, when Professor Burkhardt was notified from Washington that sponsorship of the Survey would return to the state at the beginning of July, it was decided to terminate the program. The accumulated records—measured drawings, photographs, negatives, and data pages—were packed off to the Library of Congress for editing and permanent deposit; but not before the Birmingham Public Library and the Auburn history department had each purchased several hundred prints made from HABS negatives. Those acquired by the Birmingham Library remain there today. In Auburn, many of the prints were subsequently turned over to the university archives, now housed at the Ralph Brown Draughon Library.

In a 1941 publication commemorating the twenty-fifth anniversary of the founding of the Alabama chapter of the AIA, Professor Burkhardt briefly traced the origin and achievements of the HABS program in Alabama. That same year a national catalog itemizing the records accumulated during the seven years of coast-to-coast HABS activity was published by the National Park Service. The catalog enumerated over five hundred structures and structural groups documented for Alabama.

Still, the published listing was incomplete. Many buildings for which photographs existed were not mentioned because the editors considered the pictures—if not the buildings themselves—to be of marginal quality. One also suspects that an editorial prejudice was operating against anything that looked too suspiciously "Victorian." These "discards" became part of a separate, supplementary file. Included among them, strangely, were the only HABS views of such notable landmarks as St. Andrew's Church, Prairieville—a foremost Gothic Revival structure in the state—as well as Carlisle Hall near Marion, an Italianate mansion designed by Richard Upjohn. Some of these discarded photographs have assumed unforeseen importance as a record of structures since damaged or destroyed. For instance, Carlisle Hall was later heavily vandalized. And photographs of another structure consigned to the discard group, Rocky Hill near Courtland, include unique interior views of a mansion destroyed in 1960.

A few states continued to support HABS recording projects for a time after activity ceased in Alabama. But the entire documentation program, nationwide, became an early casualty of World War II. The records themselves were trundled off to a hiding place safely away from Washington for the war's duration. Afterward they were returned to the Library of Congress where, for more than ten years, the Survey existed only as one of the collections within the Division of Prints and Photographs.

Yet there were those who recognized the need for an ongoing architectural recording program, especially in a rapidly changing and urbanizing culture. Nothing was done during the 1940s and the early 1950s. But in 1957, HABS was reactivated—although upon a basis substantially different from that upon which it had existed in the 1930s. Summer field teams, composed of qualified university students under the guidance of a professional in the field of architecture or architectural history, would thenceforth carry the work forward. This arrangement continues to the present. At the same time, it is local initiative and largely local material support that now determines those geographical areas where recording projects occur.

Documentary standards are likewise more stringent than they were in the thirties. Carefully executed measured drawings are complemented by high-quality photographs, preferably the work of a specialist in architectural photography. Similarly, accompanying data sheets are based on careful documentary research.

Since the 1957 reactivation of HABS, full-fledged recording projects in Alabama have occurred only at Mobile. In 1963 and again in 1966, projects were initiated there to document significant architecture threatened by urban redevelopment and the construction of Interstate Highway 10 through the oldest part of the city. At the same time, the historic Middle Bay Lighthouse in Mobile Bay was measured and drawn. Further photographic recording in 1974 focused upon buildings in the city's Oakleigh Garden Historic District.

Given this longtime commitment to the HABS program, it was appropriate that Mobile should have been the place where, on June 12, 1983, a small exhibit opened to mark HABS' fiftieth year of existence. Organized under the auspices of the Alabama Chapter of the American Institute of Architects, the exhibit was one of several mounted throughout the country to celebrate the founding of HABS. Mobile architect Nicholas H. Holmes, Jr., son of another Mobile architect who had worked as part of one of the original HABS teams, spearheaded the development of the exhibit, which consisted of selected HABS drawings of early Alabama buildings.

Needless to say, the massive recording effort of the 1930s remains unmatched in sheer volume. Walter Burkhardt died in 1977, Mrs. Burkhardt in 1984. But both lived to see the republication of their 1934–37 series of *Birmingham News* articles in book form, as a project of the Alabama Historical Commission. Edited by Commission staff member Cathy Donelson, *Alabama Ante-Bellum Architecture: A Scrapbook View from the 1930s* appeared in 1976, a year after the Historical Commission had presented Dr. and Mrs. Burkhardt with a Distinguished Service Award for their pioneering work.

Still, on the whole, Alabama preservationists have been slow to recognize the value of a thoroughgoing architectural recording program. Awareness of the need to thoroughly *document* a building of high significance, and not simply to "identify" and superficially photograph it, has failed to grow apace with public interest in historic preservation. This is no doubt partly because documentation, as a scholarly undertaking, lacks the broad, activist appeal of actual restoration work. Moreover, selecting exactly *which* buildings to record, among many, and how best to record them, requires not just enthusiasm and good intentions, but broad architectural knowledge and an informed historical perspective.

The result is an odd situation. First-rate structures never documented by HABS—especially those dating from the late nineteenth and early twentieth centuries—may be listed on the National Register of Historic Places. Yet adequate pictorial analysis, not to speak of comprehensive measured drawings, may be lacking entirely. A well-preserved, nineteenth-century rural residential community like Gainesville in Sumter County—overlooked by the HABS teams of the 1930s—is today widely recognized for the invaluable historical resource it represents. Nonetheless, Gainesville remains virtually undocumented according to accepted standards of architectural recording. The same may be said for such endangered groups of early buildings in the state as the Tidewater-type cottages of the Tennessee Valley. Even "oldest houses" are not immune from this neglect, as witnessed by the fate of the Hampton house a few miles north of Huntsville. Long recognized as possibly the oldest dwelling left in one of the earliest-settled regions of the state, the Hampton house may have dated from as early as 1812. Yet the house remained undocumented either through analytical photographs or measured drawings. And so things stood in 1982, when the local fire department deliberately burned the empty and rotting structure at its owner's request. Similarly, even listing on the National Register failed to dissuade the owners of the likewise unrecorded McGehee-Stringfellow house near Greensboro from bulldozing the structure, despite the fact that the house was one of the oldest brick dwellings in west Alabama, with a singularly elaborate Federal-period cornice. The Queen Anne mansions that once stood on Highland Avenue in Birmingham or South Perry Street in Montgomery were obviously in a different category—both more recent and more predictable as a house type. Yet they, too, have now passed into that "unrecorded oblivion" foreseen by the men who organized the first HABS efforts in 1933.

Surprisingly, the same neglect has sometimes extended to landmarks clearly within the revered "big house" tradition of plantation days, such as the Kimbrough house at Old Erie in Hale County, or Elm Bluff on the Alabama River below Selma. Both these once-elegant structures awaited documentation in the early 1980s, despite their imminent destruction. Actually, it was already too late. In 1976 the lush interior trim of the Kimbrough was cannibalized by a nationally noted restoration architect in search of decorative components. And by 1980, Elm Bluff in Dallas County languished as a vine-clad, Greek Revival brick shell on the lands of the Miller Lumber Company.

Architectural documentation must be an ordered and broad-visioned, if selective, process: one requiring discernment and awareness. It demands not the parochial attitude of the aesthete or of the collector, but rather the archaeologist's sense of how material culture, be it pottery shards or a ruined building, may contribute to human knowledge. The efforts of HABS in Alabama have clearly pointed in this direction. But the task remains unfinished. At its best, then, this catalog should serve not only as an introduction to a rich collection of existing material, but also as a stimulus to continue such documentation, lest unique evidence that could deepen understanding of the state's cultural development be erased forever.

How to Use the HABS Alabama Catalog

A master guide to the entire Historic American Buildings Survey collection was published in 1983, replacing the 1941 general catalog and its 1959 supplement. But the need for more detailed information, especially architectural and historical data, than permitted by a highly abbreviated national format has also prompted the publication of a series of annotated state and area guides to the HABS collection. The Alabama catalog is one of the latest in this series, which was initiated in 1963. Ideally, each of these volumes should serve both as an in-depth guide to that portion of the HABS collection dealing with the locale in question, and as a general introduction to the locale's early architecture. Collectively, the volumes are intended to convey a panoramic sense of the remarkable diversity to be found in early American architecture.

The following catalog listing for Alabama describes all structures within the state for which some record exists in the HABS collection. In each instance, a brief standard architectural description and, wherever possible, an historical note, is followed by an itemization of the types of records—photos, measured drawings, and written data—available for the structure.

Every effort has been made to assure that the background information on individual buildings is accurate and relatively up to date. In fact, a good deal of historical data, some of it quite recently come to light, is here published for the first time. Nevertheless, errors are inevitable, particularly when opportunity for primary historical research on each structure has been limited. HABS therefore welcomes the assistance of those who consult the catalog in correcting or updating the published information. Correspondence should be addressed to the Historic American Buildings Survey, National Park Service, Department of the Interior, Washington, D.C. 20240.

Preparation of the Alabama catalog entailed revisiting each of the several hundred sites hitherto documented by HABS, with particular attention being given to those buildings recorded prior to World War II. One objective was to pinpoint the precise location of all buildings, something frequently neglected in the early days of the Survey. This proved to be a relatively simple matter in towns and cities. But in the country, it often meant endless inquiry and could lead down miles of backroads, across fields, through cattle gaps, over fences, and along overgrown creek banks. It was an exercise that sparked admiration for the intrepid HABS "explorers" of the 1930s.

A second objective was simply to ascertain the fate of the buildings—whether altered or restored, abandoned or destroyed. All too often the search ended with the discovery that a structure was gone or had fallen into hopeless disrepair. In one instance, a house had been torn down only the week before; in another, the ashes were still warm from the fire that had just destroyed the building.

During the course of field visits, new historical information was gathered wherever possible; and always there was an architectural reassessment, if the building still stood. On more than one occasion the physical examination of a building called into question the traditionally accepted date of erection. Many times, too, it was discovered that not one but several epochs of construction and renovation had to be reckoned with, as a structure changed and grew over perhaps a century and a half of existence. When feasible, each building's date of construction, as well as the date of major renovations, is reflected in the corresponding catalog entry. Most such dates must be estimated. Rarely did time permit a search of county or municipal archives—an examination of deeds and tax assessments for example—to authenticate a structure's supposed origin. To do so for hundreds of widely scattered buildings obviously could prove the task of a lifetime. Fortunately, in several cases the primary research of others was generously made available. Yet most HABS-recorded structures still demand adequate deed searches and historical investigation.

An informal byproduct of catalog-related fieldwork was the identification of worthy structures as yet undocumented by HABS. Perhaps someday these too can be properly recorded. Fieldworkers often used their own cameras, notebooks, and measuring tapes to compile rough notes on particularly outstanding non-HABS buildings, or buildings that were endangered.

Entries in the Alabama catalog are grouped by county, then by community or vicinity within each county. Under these subheadings, structures are arranged in alphabetical order, usually by their *historic* name. Other commonly used names are cross-referenced. With regard to domestic architecture, the historic name ordinarily means that of the person or family for whom a house was built, or a person or family significantly associated with the house. Where two or three families have been importantly linked to a residence in the past, the name may be hyphenated, as for example, the "Oates-Danzey House." Antebellum Alabamians often applied romantic names to their houses—Rosemount, Youpon, Sweetwater, Orange Vale, and so forth. Such names are used whenever appropriate, though not ordinarily when they are of recent origin (an exceptional case is Sturdivant Hall, in Selma, and others now widely recognized under a later name as house museums). Where virtually nothing is known about the origin of a structure, it may be listed merely as a "house" or "commercial building," following by its specific address.

Outlined below is the general format employed for each catalog entry:

- *historic name* (if known), followed by cross-referenced names
- *HABS file number* for the structure (e.g., AL-850)
- *address or exact location*

- *summary architectural description* (including construction material, overall shape or dimensions, number of stories, important interior and exterior elements, etc.)

- *date or estimated date of construction*

- *builder or architect and/or contractor* (when known or reasonably suspicioned)

- *original owner* (if known, and not previously mentioned in connection with the historic name of the structure; brief biographical notes and the names of other prominent owners may also be included)

- *major later alterations and additions*

- *significant historical information*

- *quantity and date of HABS measured drawings, photos, photocopies, and data pages on deposit*

If a building is open to the public, this is indicated immediately following the address, at the beginning of the entry. And, if a building is individually listed on the National Register of Historic Places (as opposed to being included within the boundaries of a National Register Historic District), this is indicated by the letters NR. If a structure, by virtue of its nationwide historical or architectural importance, has been designated a National Historic Landmark by the Secretary of the Interior, this is shown by the letters NHL.

In addition to the HABS material, the Library of Congress has custody of two related photographic collections: the Frances Benjamin Johnston Collection and the Robert Tebbs Collection. Where Alabama structures recorded by HABS are represented by additional photos in either of these collections, the standard catalog entry is followed by the designation "FBJ" or "Tebbs," and the appropriate Library of Congress serial number or numbers.

Below is a list of abbreviations, symbols, and terms used in the catalog:

AL-331	Historic American Buildings Survey number. All structures recorded by HABS are assigned such a number, which serves to facilitate processing. They should always be used when inquiring about a specific structure or when ordering reproductions of photographs, drawings, or data pages.
C.	century
ca.	circa
Co.	County, e.g., "Co. Rd. 45"

data pages	Written historical and/or architectural data that sometimes form part of the HABS documentation for a structure. In a few instances, data pages but no photos or measured drawings may occur.
ext.	exterior
FBJ	Refers to the Frances Benjamin Johnston Collection of architectural photographs, Library of Congress.
HAER	Historic American Engineering Record: a parallel documentary program to HABS for the recording of structures of technological significance.
int.	interior
NAER	National Architectural and Engineering Record, the unit within the National Park Service that administers both HABS and HAER.
n.d.	no date ascertainable
NR	National Register of Historic Places; the nation's official listing of properties of historical, architectural, archaeological, and cultural significance.
NHL	National Historic Landmark; refers to a building that has been assessed by the Secretary of the Interior as possessing *national* significance. Properties so designated are automatically listed on the National Register of Historic Places.
photos	HABS negatives are normally 5″ × 7″ although some may be slightly smaller (4″ × 5″) or larger (8″ × 10″). The catalog entry for each structure includes the number of exterior and interior photos, together with the dates when they were made.
photocopies	HABS records sometimes include copies of old views, plans, or other documents related to a building. The date of the item is given whenever known.
sheets	Refers to the sheets of measured drawings available for study and reproduction. These sheets are a standard size, 15 ½″ × 20″ inside border lines. The number of sheets in a set and the kinds of drawings (plans, elevations, sections, etc.) are listed, together with their date. Prints of measured drawings are reproduced at actual size.
Tebbs	Refers to the Robert Tebbs Collection of architectural photographs.

A County-by-County Listing

Stairway of the Irwin-McAllister house (destroyed), Shorterville, Henry County.

AUTAUGA COUNTY

Mulberry Vicinity

Ivy Creek Methodist Church (AL-724), 0.1 mi. N of Ala. 14, approx. 0.3 mi. W of Ivy Creek Bridge; 8.5 mi. W of Autaugaville. Frame with clapboarding, rectangular with pedimented temple-type façade, modified distyle in antis Doric portico, square belfry; open interior plan with 2 aisles, simple Greek Revival style trim, raised pulpit platform enclosed by gothicized wooden Communion rail, slave gallery at rear. Built 1854; materials and possibly plans furnished by the Hon. John Steele, local planter and state legislator. 2 ext. photos (1934), 1 int. photo (1934).

Prattville

Coe-Swift-Fay House (Thomas Avery Fay House) (AL-653), 403 Washington St. (SE corner Washington and First sts.). Frame with clapboarding, rectangular (5-bay front) with ell, 1½ stories, gable roof, 4 exterior end chimneys (main block), pedimented entrance porch with square columns; center-hall plan, ell originally separated from main block by open passage. Built ca. 1845 for George Coe; porch later extended full width of front. 3 ext. photos (1935), 1 int. photo (1935).

Fay, Thomas Avery, House. *See* Coe-Swift-Fay House (AL-653), 403 Washington St.

Golson, John B., House. *See* Pope-Alexander-Golson House (AL-654), 815 Shadow Ln.

Pope-Alexander-Golson House (John B. Golson House, Pope-Golson House) (AL-654), 815 Shadow Ln. Frame with clapboarding, rectangular (5-bay front), 2½ stories, hipped roof with dormers and monitor, 4 exterior end chimneys, 1-story pedimented tetrastyle portico (with modillioned cornice repeated in main cornice, dormers, and monitor), fanlight doorway, sides and rear encircled by 1-story shed porch; center-hall plan, continuous spiral stairway to third floor. Probably built 1830s; reputedly located on Alabama River plantation of Dr. Edgar A. Pope, near Washington Ferry, and moved to present site ca. 1860. 4 ext. photos (1935), 10 int. photos (1935).

Pope-Golson House. *See* Pope-Alexander-Golson House (AL-654), 815 Shadow Ln.

Pratt, Daniel, Factory Complex (AL-685), S bank of Autauga Creek, just W of spillway and Bridge St. Mid- to late-19th-C. industrial complex consisting of large brick structures ranged along creek. Earliest extant buildings are old *Daniel Pratt Cotton Gin Factory* (L-shaped, 3 stories, combination hipped-and-gable roof surmounted by square wooden belfry) forming easternmost part of complex; also *Sash, Door, and Blind Factory* and *Machine Shop* (rectangular, 3 stories with gable roof terminating in stepped parapets), which form single long range to W of gin factory. Other structures in original complex included saw and gristmill, cotton textile factory, and foundry. Complex initially developed ca. 1839–52 by Daniel

Pratt. Cotton Gin Factory, succeeding earlier structure, built 1854; Sash, Door, and Blind Factory and Machine Shop shortly afterward; subsequent extensive additions. As nucleus of industrial village of Prattville, founded in 1839, the Pratt factories were Alabama's most important antebellum industrial complex. 2 ext. photocopies of mid-19th-C. engravings (n.d.). *See also* HAER (AL-5).

Pratt, Daniel, House (AL-686), W bank of Autauga Creek, approx. 200' NW of original Pratt factory complex. Main block frame with clapboarding, rectangular (5-bay front), 2½ stories, gable roof, full-height pedimented entrance portico composed of 2 pairs of Doric columns flanking doorway, unusual scrolled triglyphs of cornice adapted from Asher Benjamin; center-hall plan. Also semidetached frame rectangular 1-story wing at corner, linking main house and brick dependency (rectangular, 2 stories, stepped parapet at each gable end); other appurtenances included carriage house and hillside wine cellar, balustraded terrace across front; lawn enclosed by cast-iron fence. House and possibly dependencies built 1841–42; Pratt, who had previously built several dwellings in the Milledgeville, Ga., area, was presumably his own architect. Renovated late 19th C., including leaded glass doorway and flanking semielliptical bays, balustraded terrace, other alterations; demolished Sept. 1961. Born in Temple, N.H., Pratt (1799–1873) was one of South's pioneer industrialists, founder of Prattville, early philanthropist, and patron of the arts. Residence complex formerly included private art gallery (frame, razed in late 1850s) and family cemetery. 12 ext. photos (1934–35, including dependencies), 4 int. photos (1935).

Smith, McQueen, Stables (AL-669), McQueen Smith Farm, NW of intersection of Cobbs Ford Rd. and Co. 75. Frame with clapboarding, rectangular (5-bay front), hipped roof surmounted by louvered cupola, modillioned cornice, pedimented central bay with Palladian window flanked by fluted Ionic pilasters, 1-story shed with columnar supports across front; central passage with stalls to each side. Built 1895–96 as part of estate complex for noted planter and sportsman McQueen Smith; burned ca. 1935. Training racetrack originally located nearby. 1 ext. photo (1934), 2 int. photos (1934).

Prattville Vicinity

Buena Vista (Montgomery-Jones House, Stewart House) (AL-695), N side of Co. 4 (Reynolds Mill Rd.), approx. 0.9 mi. E of junction with Washington Ferry Rd., 3 mi. SE of Prattville. Frame with clapboarding, rectangular (5-bay front), 2½ stories, gable roof with pedimented gable ends pierced by semielliptical lunettes, 4 interior end chimneys, full-height tetrastyle Ionic portico across front (physical evidence suggests originally central 2-tiered portico), semielliptical fanlight doorways above and below; center-hall plan, continuous spiral stairway to third floor, Federal period woodwork, unusually fine decorative plaster cornices and chandelier medallions. Built ca. 1835–40, reputedly for William Montgomery; renovated ca. 1916 for Patrick Henry Stewart, including addition of portico and interior changes. 4 ext. photos (1935), 19 int. photos (1935). NR.

Montgomery-Jones House. *See* Buena Vista (AL-695).

Pope-Golson House. *Under Prattville, see* Pope-Alexander-Golson House (AL-654), 815 Shadow Ln.

Stewart House. *See* Buena Vista (AL-695).

BALDWIN COUNTY

Gulf Shores Vicinity

Fort Morgan (AL-101), on Mobile Point overlooking E passage to Mobile Bay from Gulf of Mexico, W end of Ala. 180 (Fort Morgan Parkway), approx. 22 mi. W of junction with U.S. 59 in Gulf Shores. State historical site and museum. Regular pentagonal fortification with quadrilateral bastions at each corner, main work (enceinte): brick, approx. 110 yds. including bastions on each side, continuous vaulted casemates, outer drymoat and glacis pierced by vaulted entrance tunnel, rusticated neoclassical-style main gateway with flat-arched portal flanked by Tuscan pilasters carrying full entablature; brick, 10-sided "citadel" or inner defensive barracks originally located in middle of parade ground. Built 1819–34 according to plans devised in 1817 by French-born military engineer Simone Bernard; heavily damaged during Civil War and citadel subsequently razed. Reinforced concrete gun emplacements installed 1895–98, also adjacent frame barracks, officers' homes, hospital, and other structures built as part of Spanish-American War training base; acquired by State of Alabama in 1927 and partially restored in 1930s; reactivated as coastal artillery training post and naval base during World War II; placed under administration of Alabama Historical Commission in 1977. Primary fortification at mouth of Mobile Bay and one of major works in 19th-C. U.S. coastal defense system. Seized by state militia during Civil War; besieged and recaptured by U.S. forces 5–23 Aug. 1864. 2 photocopies of original plans (1817, including plan, sections). NHL.

Point Clear

Battle House (Gunnison House) (AL-120), at Great Point Clear overlooking Mobile Bay on W side of U.S. 98 (Ala. 42), approx. 1.2 mi. N of junction with Co. 32. Frame with clapboarding (flush boarding on front), 50' (8-bay front) X 34' including 9'-deep porch, 2 stories, gable roof, front overhang forming 2-tiered porch with stationary wooden awning at upper level, and additional ground-level shed-roof porch (now removed) across front and S side, 1-story porch across back, outside stairs front and rear; 4 end-to-end rooms on each floor. Built ca. 1850 as summer home for John A. M. Battle of Mobile; ground-level porch probably later; altered 20th C. including ca. 1940 interior renovation for dormitory use. Confederate hospital 1863–65; later, noted gaming house and dancing pavilion. 3 ext. photos (1934); 2 data pages (1936).

Stockton

Kitchen-McMillan House (House) (AL-118), E side of Co. 21, approx. 0.1 mi. N of intersection with Ala. 59 in Stockton. Originally frame rectangular 1-story house consisting of 4 rooms clustered about central chimney, porch across front with shed room at one end, detached dining room and kitchen off rear. Later greatly altered and enlarged, covered with board and batten. Extant dependencies include old commissary building, blacksmith shop, slave quarters. Built ca. 1844 for Col. William Kitchen (1805–66), founder of Stockton community (1839) and sawmill owner, planter, entrepreneur. 2 ext. photos (1934).

Tensaw Vicinity

Atkinson, Thomas, House (AL-116), E side Ala. 59, approx. 0.9 mi. NE of Pine Creek Bridge, 1.0 mi. SW of junction with Co. 80 at Tensaw. Frame (heart pine) with clapboarding, rectangular (5-bay front), 2½ stories, gable roof with front slope extending over full-length 2-tiered balustraded porch, 2 pairs of exterior end chimneys, small hipped-roof porch at rear; center-hall plan, paneled dado, parlor mantel probably based on Plate 51 of Asher Benjamin's *Practical House Carpenter* (1830). Built ca. 1840. 2 ext. photos (1934), 1 int. photo (1934).

House (Tunstall House, Woolf House) (AL-115), W side Ala. 59, approx. 1.0 mi. SW of junction with Co. 80 at Tensaw. Frame with clapboarding, rectangular (5-bay front), 1 story, gable roof extending over full-length porch, 2 exterior end chimneys; center-hall plan. Reputedly built early 19th C.; renovated late 19th C., including turned porch supports and scroll-cut balustrade. 1 ext. photo (1934).

BARBOUR COUNTY

Eufaula

Baptist Church (St. Luke A.M.E. Church) (AL-590), 234 S. Van Buren St. (NW corner Van Buren and Union sts.). Frame with clapboarding (façade has novelty siding, with flush siding inside portico), approx. 45′4″ × 70′5″, 1 story, gable roof, temple-type façade (distyle in antis Doric portico with flanking windows framed by eared architraves), 2 entrances with window originally between, square pilastered belfry topped by raked parapet with acroteria, frieze at front and sides enriched with guttae; open interior plan with 2 aisles, originally pulpit at front (E end) with galleries at sides and rear. Dedicated 23 May 1841 as the Eufaula Baptist Church. Following completion of new church in 1869, building housed black Baptist congregation until 1877, when it became St. Luke A.M.E. Church. Changes from original structure include installation of art glass windows, reorientation of interior with pulpit and choir loft at W end, small gallery across E end; mid-20th-C. educational addition at rear. 3 ext. photos (1935), 2 int. photos (1935).

Cato, Lewis Llewellyn, House (AL-554), 823 W. Barbour St. Frame with clapboarding (façade has novelty siding), main block 74′4″ (5-bay front) × 54′6″ plus flanking set-back wings (14′1″ × 24′4″) forming overall T-shape, 1 story, truncated hipped roof extending over continuous balustraded porch at front and sides (bracketed subordinate gable over 3 middle bays), large 3-bay hipped-roof belvedere with peristyle balustraded gallery, originally raised central porch at rear; modified center-hall plan with back-hall dining room, grandly scaled interior with 14′ ceilings. Built 1859 under supervision of contractor with labor of Cato's slaves. Rear wing added 1880s; minor interior changes in late 19th C., including Queen Anne style living room mantel; further changes in 1930s. Cato (1823–68) was a prominent lawyer, legislator, and secessionist leader. 3 ext. photos (1935), 7 int. photos (1935). NR.

Cowan-Ramser House (AL-519), 441 E. Barbour St. (SW corner Barbour St. and Forsyth Ave.). Frame with clapboarding (façade has novelty siding), approx. 40′6″ (5-bay front) × 38′0″ overall, 2 stories, hipped roof extending over tetrastyle Doric portico, 2 pairs of interior end chimneys, doorway adapted from Plate 28 of Asher Benjamin's *Practice of Architecture* (1838); center-hall plan, double parlor to E, mantels possibly from Asher Benjamin. Built ca. 1840 for Dr. William L. Cowan; 2-story rear addition and abutting 2-tiered porch added late 19th C. 5 ext. photos (1935), 5 int. photos (1935).

East Alabama National Bank. *See* Eastern Bank of Alabama (AL-592).

Eastern Bank of Alabama (East Alabama National Bank, McNab Bank Building) (AL-592), 201 Broad St. (SE corner Broad and Randolph sts.). Brick covered with stucco and scored to simulate ashlar, 26′3″ (3-bay front) × 79′0″, 2 stories, flat roof concealed by cast-iron modillioned cornice with acanthus-leaf consoles, trabeated Corinthian order cast-iron front, recessed double-leaf glazed doorway with flanking casements, segmentally arched French windows at second floor opening onto long balcony with grillework balustrade, double flight of ornate cast-iron steps at front and side, cast-iron basement grilles; interior has large banking room at front with ribbed plaster ceiling and iron vault, bisecting stairhall to rear with offices beyond (original mantelpieces and woodwork). Built ca. 1859 as Eastern Bank of Alabama; later operated as John McNab Bank (ca. 1865–91). Second-floor modifications in 20th C.; renovated and restored in 1965. Notable example of mid-19th-C. commercial architecture. 8 ext. photos (1935), 9 int. photos (1935). NR.

Hart-Milton House (AL-591), 211 Eufaula Ave. Frame with clapboarding, main block approx. 48′6″ (5-bay front) × 34′2″ plus porch and ell, 1 story, hipped roof, full-length balustraded Doric porch, denticulated entablature, recessed doorway; center-hall plan, sliding doors between 2 front rooms on N side, simple plaster ceiling centerpieces and Greek Revival style woodwork, basement room at rear possibly early dining room or kitchen. Reputedly built ca. 1843 for John Hart, one of town founders. 3 ext. photos (1935), 13 int. photos (1935). NR.

Irwinton Inn. *See* The Tavern (AL-516), 105 Riverside Dr.

McDonald-Smartt House (AL-517), 315 N. Randolph St. Frame with clapboarding raised on brick piers with open work between, 53′8″ (5-bay front) × 37′10″ plus porch and parallel rear wings, 1½ stories, gable roof with dormers at front, 2 interior end chimneys, continuous balustraded porch at front and formerly along N side, double flight of entrance steps, parallel rear wings; modified center-hall plan, back-hall dining room at rear. Unusual frame bathhouse with adjacent well shelter (demolished) formerly at rear. Front portion of house built ca. 1839 for Alexander McDonald as simple raised cottage with gable roof, 2 interior end chimneys, and small central entrance portico flanked by 12-over-12 sash windows. House extensively altered in middle and late 19th C. including rear additions, larger porch with double steps, raising of roof-pitch and installation of dormers, Victorian period doorway, floor-length windows; side porches removed and other modifications made during 1950s. 4 ext. photos (1935, including 1 photo of bathhouse and well shelter), 5 int. photos (1935); 2 data pages (1937).

McNab Bank Building. *See* Eastern Bank of Alabama (AL-592), 201 Broad St.

Mashburn House. *See* The Tavern (AL-516), 105 Riverside Dr.

Pease Tavern. *See* The Tavern (AL-516), 105 Riverside Dr.

St. Luke A.M.E. Church. *See* Baptist Church (AL-590), 234 S. Van Buren St.

Tavern, The (Irwinton Inn, Mashburn House, Pease Tavern) (AL-516), 105 Riverside Dr. (E side Riverside Dr. opposite intersection with Broad St.). Frame with clapboarding, approx. 50'6" (5-bay front) X 28'0" plus ell 20'3" X 32'0", 2 stories, gable roof extending over full-length 2-tiered hexastyle porch with Tuscan order superimposed over square piers, 2 exterior end chimneys, formerly exterior stairway to second floor; originally 3 end-to-end rooms across front, simple Federal style woodwork, matched board interior walls. Built ca. 1837 as inn for Edward Williams; subsequently deeded to daughter and converted to residence. Renovated 1870s, including installation of new doorways and sashing; 2-tiered porch replaced by square columns ca. 1940; adaptively renovated and restored 1966–67 for Cowikee Mills Foundation, including reconstruction of porch; N end chimney also removed, as well as partition and enclosed stairway between N rooms. 3 ext. photos (1935), 3 int. photos (1935); 2 data pages (1937). NR.

Wellborn, Dr. Levi Thomas, House (AL-520), originally located at 134 Livingston St. (W side of Livingston, approx. 330' N of intersection with Broad St.); moved to N side of Broad St. opposite intersection with Riverside Dr. Open to public. Frame with clapboarding, 48'0" (5-bay front) X 32'6", 2 stories, hipped roof, 2 interior chimneys, 3-bay pedimented tetrastyle portico with freestanding stuccoed brick columns, balcony at upper level, corner pilasters, full entablature enriched with guttae, 3-bay 2-tiered shed porch at rear with scroll-cut balustrade at upper level. Built ca. 1839; original rear porch apparently replaced in late 19th C. by 2-tiered porch; 1-story late-19th-C. wing on E side. Given to City of Eufaula in 1971 and moved to present location in 1972; later additions torn away, original chimneys removed, and stuccoed brick columns replaced by replicas made of cast-iron tubing coated with plaster. Said to be Eufaula's first example of Greek Revival style domestic architecture. Wellborn died in 1841 from wounds received during Creek Indian War. 5 ext. photos (1935), 4 int. photos (1935). NR.

BULLOCK COUNTY

Chunnennuggee Ridge.

See *Union Springs Vicinity.*

High Ridge and Vicinity

Berry, Mastin, House (E. B. Braswell House) (AL-595), S side of Co. 14 just E of junction with Co. 7 in High Ridge community; approx. 3.8 mi. S of Co. 14 intersection with U.S. 82 at Hector community. Frame with clapboarding (façade flush boarding), approx. 42'5" (5-bay front) x 43'9" including porch, 1 story, hipped roof extending over full-length porch supported by 4 square columns; porch has unusual paneled wainscoting; center-hall plan, paneled dado with flush board walls above. Built mid-19th C.; later rear additions. 3 ext. photos (1935), 2 int. photos (1935).

Braswell, E. B., House. *See* Mastin Berry House (AL-595), Co. 14.

Hough-Roughton House (AL-561), S side of Co. 14, approx. 1.5 mi. E of intersection with Co. 15 at Hooks Crossroads; 4.4 mi. E of High Ridge, in former Mascot community. Frame with clapboarding, rectangular (5-bay front) with long ell, 2 stories (ell 1 story), hipped roof, 2 exterior end chimneys, shed porch across front; center-hall plan (possibly open hall as built), enclosed stairway, flush board interior walls. Built ca. 1845 probably for John Baugh Hough (1802–72), who emigrated in 1834 from Newberry, S.C.; porch renovated late 19th C. including addition of jigsaw trim, first-floor front sashing also replaced by larger 2-over-2 windows; ell razed late 1930s; house burned in 1940. 2 ext. photos (1935), 2 int. photos (1935).

Peachburg and Vicinity.

See *Union Springs Vicinity.*

Union Springs

Foster House. *See* Laurel Hill (AL-599), 201 Kennon St.

Laurel Hill (Foster House) (AL-599), 201 Kennon St. (W side Kennon St. just S of juncture with Conecuh Ave.). Frame with clapboarding (façade has novelty siding), approx. 52'5" (3-bay front) x 49'3" including portico, 2 stories, shallow hipped roof extending over full-length portico of unusual design composed of 4 square columns supporting series of 3 ogee arches surmounted by classic entablature; doorway flanked by broad jib windows, three-quarter-length balcony with lattice balustrade at second-floor level; center-hall plan with notable stair, simple Greek Revival style woodwork. Kitchen and wellhouse at rear. Built 1852–56 for Dr. Sterling Johnston Foster, who came to Union Springs from Greene County, Ga. Semidetached brick kitchen and privy added to SW corner ca. 1890; demioctagonal 2-story bathroom bay added to N side 1912–13, small rectangular S side addition 1940; kitchen and wellhouse razed ca. 1950. Called Laurel Hill from ca. 1912. 8 ext. photos (1935, including 1 photo of kitchen and wellhouse), 6 int. photos (1935).

Union Springs Vicinity

Atkinson, Octavia, House. *See* Cunningham-Atkinson House (AL-539), relocated to Wilson Rd., Mobile.

Cunningham-Atkinson House (Octavia Atkinson House) (AL-539), originally located on N side of Co. 40 (Peachburg Rd.), approx. 0.5 mi. E of Southern Railroad crossing in former Peachburg community, which is approx. 5.1 mi. NE of Peachburg Rd. intersection with U.S. 82 in Union Springs; relocated in Mobile on N side of Wilson Rd., approx. 0.2 mi. W of intersection with Dawes Rd. Log partially covered with clapboard resting on cedar-piling foundation, originally double pen (each pen 1 bay), approx. 50'0" x 25'0" overall with open passage between, 1 story, gable roof, 2 exterior end chimneys; open hall or dogtrot (later enclosed) with single room on each side, original Federal style pine mantels. Built mid-19th C. for Col. C. J. L. Cunningham; later purchased by Saul Atkinson. Kitchen wing added at left rear late 19th C. House dismantled, moved to Mobile, and reconstructed in 1973 for Dr. Raymond Self; modifications included new foundation (cedar pilings reused as walkway), replacement of limestone chinking with cement, new brick chimneys (original brick used on inside fireplace), heightening of doors; late-19th-C. kitchen wing removed and replaced by wing at right rear. 1 ext. photo (1935), 2 int. photos (1935).

"*Smart Bucket,*" device to bring water from spring at foot of ridge back of house; consisting of pulley-drawn bucket on wooden track, water channeled into bucket by trough leading from spring. Built and named ca. 1915 by Miss Octavia Atkinson, occupant of house during early 20th C.; destroyed. 2 photos (1935).

Evergreen Bower (Col. Luther Walker House, Walker-Adams House) (AL-598), approx. 0.1 mi. NW of Co. 40 (Peachburg Rd.) junction with Co. 109, facing SE; 8.4 mi. NE of Co. 40 (Peachburg Rd.) intersection with U.S. 82 (Conecuh Ave.) in Union Springs. Frame with clapboarding above high basement, 54'5" (3-bay front) X 30'11" plus large gabled dining wing at center rear, 2 stories (wing 1½ stories), shallow hipped roof covering main block, bracketed cornice, 2 interior end chimneys, 1-story cast-iron porch across front with tall floor-length triple windows flanking recessed doorway; center-hall plan with cross hall at rear containing stairway, Italianate style. Built ca. 1858 for Walker (1822–88) at cost of $17,000; Charles Stuart, contractor. Rear wing demolished ca. 1950, back porch built and main block partially renovated, mantels removed, and hardwood floors installed. Finest of extant plantation houses along Chunnenuggee Ridge NE of Union Springs. House later called Mulberry. 2 ext. photos (1935), 9 int. photos (1935).

Frazer, Sen. Thomas Sidney, House. *See* Walker-Frazer House (AL-538), Co. 40.

Seale-Mosley House (AL-546), approx. 100 yds. SE of point where Peachburg Rd. (Co. 40) crosses Southern Railroad in former community of Peachburg; approx. 5.6 mi. NE of Peachburg Rd. intersection with U.S. 82 in Union Springs. Frame with clapboarding (façade has novelty siding), basically square (5-bay front), 1 story, shallow hipped roof extending over full-length porch supported by 6 heavy square columns with molded capitals and bases, floor-length windows, loggia at rear; center-hall plan, folding doors between hall and flanking drawing rooms, ceilings approx. 15' high. Built ca. 1855 for Arnold Seale (1795–1871), construction engineer for Mobile and Girard Railroad during 1850s and for whom town of Seale in neighboring Russell Co. is named. House moved from undetermined original site in early 20th C.; abandoned and ruinous in 1979. Notable as regional type of Greek Revival cottage and one of few surviving antebellum plantation houses along Chunnennuggee Ridge. 4 ext. photos (1935), 5 int. photos (1935).

Walker, Col. Luther, House. *See* Evergreen Bower (AL-598), Co. 40 junction with Co. 109.

Walker-Adams House. *See* Evergreen Bower (AL-598), Co. 40 junction with Co. 109.

Walker-Frazer House (Sen. Thomas Sidney Frazer House) (AL-538), N side of Co. 40 (Peachburg Rd.) 0.1 mi. E of junction with Co. 49; approx. 3.3 mi. NE of Peachburg Rd. junction with Conecuh Ave. (U.S. 82) in Union Springs. Frame with clapboarding (façade has novelty siding), main block approx. 52'6" (5-bay front) X 52'3" including porch, 1 story, truncated hipped roof extending over full-length balustraded porch supported by coupled square columns resting on high brick pedestal bases, porte cochère attached to W side of porch; modified center-hall plan. Built ca. 1875 for Merritt Warren Walker (1834–87); reconditioned ca. 1920 (including reconstruction of porch and addition of porte cochère) as summer home of State Sen. Thomas Sidney Frazer, lawyer, planter, horticulturalist, and livestock breeder. 2 ext. photos (1935), 3 int. photos (1935).

BUTLER COUNTY

Greenville

Beeland, Leroy, House. *See* Dunklin-Beeland-Kendrick House (AL-693), 504 Fort Dale Rd.

Beeland-Stanley House. *See* Henry-Beeland-Stanley House (AL-692), 218 E. Commerce St.

Burnett-Dunklin-Smith House (Dunklin-Smith House, Waller House) (AL-691), SE corner Commerce and Pine sts. Brick with stucco scored to simulate ashlar, rectangular (5-bay front) with frame ell, 2 stories (ell 1 story), gable roof, 4 exterior end chimneys, overhang of roof forms full-height tetrastyle portico across front, with attenuated columns and balcony enclosed by unusual lattice balustrade; lattice sunscreens at each end of porch, belt courses above both first and second floor; center-hall plan. Built ca. 1835 for William Burnett (1794–1856). Extensively renovated later by daughter and son-in-law Daniel G. and Susan (Burnett) Dunklin, including addition of stucco, lattice sunscreens, ell; original cedar floor of portico replaced by red tile early 20th C.; demolished 1968 to make way for bank. 4 ext. photos (1935), 5 int. photos (1935).

Dunklin-Beeland House (AL-688), 111 Herbert St. (SW corner Herbert and Oglesby sts.). Frame with clapboarding (flush siding beneath portico), basically rectangular (3-bay front) with 1-bay side wings, 1 story, hipped roof, 5 exterior end chimneys, narrow hexastyle Doric portico with denticulated cornice and flanking balustraded decks, engaged fluted colonnettes framing main doorway, broken denticulated pediments above flanking windows; center-hall plan. Built ca. 1860 for Maj. James Hilliard Dunklin (1834–77); wings added, porch altered, and other renovations ca. 1910. 2 ext. photos (1935).

Dunklin-Beeland-Kendrick House (Leroy Beeland House) (AL-693), 504 Fort Dale Rd. (E side Fort Dale Rd., approx. 0.5 mi. N of intersection with Commerce St.). Frame with clapboarding (flush siding beneath portico), rectangular (3-bay front) with ell, 2 stories, truncated hipped roof extending over full-height tetrastyle portico with attenuated Corinthian columns, denticulated cornice, balcony resting on scrolled consoles and enclosed by lattice balustrade; center-hall plan, marbleized wainscoting. Built ca. 1850 for William A. J. Dunklin; 1920s renovation included addition of wings, leaded glass doorway, replacement of door onto balcony with window. 2 ext. photos (1935).

Dunklin-Smith House. *See* Burnett-Dunklin-Smith House (AL-691), Commerce and Pine sts.

Gravehouse, Pine Crest Cemetery (now Magnolia Cemetery) (AL-689A), S side of W Commerce St., immediately W of intersection with Dohrmeier St. Brick, rectangular (3 bays wide, 4 bays long), all 4 elevations arcuated, hipped roof with bracketed cornice. Encloses burial plot containing 4 marble obelisk-type markers. Built ca. 1870 over J. T. Perry family lot; razed to coping in April 1955. 1 photo (1935).

Henry-Beeland-Stanley House (Beeland-Stanley House) (AL-692), 218 E. Commerce St. (SW corner Commerce and Pine sts.). Frame with clapboarding, main block basically rectangular (5-bay front), 2 stories, truncated hipped roof extending over full-height tetrastyle Corinthian portico with denticulated cornice and full-length balcony, leaded-glass doorway; center-hall plan, Eastlake style interior woodwork. Built ca. 1850 for Judge John Kelly Henry (1814–86); enlarged and altered ca. 1900 including present portico, doorway, much interior woodwork; also extensive additions to rear. 4 ext. photos (1935), 4 int. photos (1935).

Waller House. *See* Burnett-Dunklin-Smith House (AL-691), Commerce and Pine sts.

Greenville Vicinity

Crenshaw, Nolan, House. *Under Manningham Vicinity, see* Judge Anderson Crenshaw House (AL-690B).

Crenshaw, Will, House. *Under Manningham Vicinity, see* Walter Henry Crenshaw House (AL-690).

Gravehouses, Fort Dale Cemetery (AL-689B), W side of Ala. 185, 3.7 mi. N of junction with I-10. Rectangular shelters over family burial plots, each shelter consisting of a gable roof (originally covered with wooden shakes) resting on wooden supports and open at sides. Usually enclosed by picket fence or scroll-cut wooden railing. Erected late 19th C.; only 1 gravehouse extant by 1970s. 1 photo (1935).

Hartley, Joseph, House. *See* The Palings (AL-694), Co. 58.

Palings, The (Joseph Hartley House, Stagecoach Inn) (AL-694), Fort Dale community, on N side of Co. 58, approx. 0.4 mi. W of junction with Ala. 185 and 0.6 mi. E of Sterling Lake. Frame with clapboarding (flush siding on porch), rectangular, 2½ stories, gable roof extending over 2-tiered porch with chamfered supports, 2 exterior end chimneys, enclosed stair on porch; later board-and-batten kitchen ell. Built ca. 1825 for Hartley, who emigrated from Putnam County, Ga. and kept a tavern here; burned 11 July 1953. Called The Palings from early 19th C. because of fence enclosing yard. 2 ext. photos (1935), 2 int. photos (1935).

Stagecoach Inn. *See* The Palings (AL-694), Co. 58.

Womack, T. Augustus ("Gus"), House. *See Ridgeville Vicinity.*

Womack-Crenshaw House. *See Ridgeville Vicinity.*

Manningham Vicinity

Crenshaw, Judge Anderson, House (Nolan Crenshaw House) (AL-690B), S side of Co. 54, approx. 0.5 mi. NW of junction with Co. 19 (W of Manningham community). Frame with clapboarding, rectangular (5-bay front), 2 stories, gable roof, 4 exterior end chimneys, 2-tiered pedimented tetrastyle central portico with Tuscan colonnettes below and Ionic above; center-hall plan, simple Federal style woodwork including dado with marbleized baseboards and false graining; plaster ceiling medallions employing grapeleaf design. Built 1838–40; John Fitch and Telford Forsyth, builders; later alterations include replacement of sashing, addition of 1-story ell and back porch in 1960. Crenshaw (1783–1847), born in South Carolina, was a prominent juror and planter for whom neighboring Crenshaw County was named. Still owned by descendants in 1980s. 1 ext. photocopy (n.d.).
Law Office, NW of house near entrance to lane. Frame, rectangular (2-bay front), 1 story, gable roof; 2-room plan with double entrance. Built ca. 1835 close to public road; ruinous in 1978. 1 ext. photocopy (n.d.).

Crenshaw, Walter Henry, House and Plantation Complex (Will Crenshaw Plantation) (AL-690), N side of Co. 54, approx. 0.5 mi. NW of junction with Co. 19 (W of Manningham community). Antebellum plantation complex including main house and dependencies, earlier dwelling, slave house, barn, and corncribs.
Main House. Frame with clapboarding on raised brick foundation, rectangular (5-bay front with inset 3-bay porch), 1½ stories, gable roof (slightly broken front and rear), 4 exterior end chimneys, full-length rear porch linking adjacent dependencies; center-hall plan, paneled dado with graining, marbleized baseboards and mantels; dining room originally in basement; frame smokehouse to N (rear). Built 1853. 5 ext. photos (1935), 4 int. photos (1935).
Earlier House. Frame with clapboarding on wood pilings, rectangular (2 bays at front), 1 story, gable roof (broken at rear to extend over shed room), door in gable end. Built 1840 (possibly as open-hall house) for Walter Henry Crenshaw; became dependency when 1853 dwelling completed. Half of structure removed to rear of new house as kitchen (later moved again, to serve as storage house); remaining section used as overseer's quarters, afterward for storage. 1 ext. photo (1935).
Slave House. Double-pen log cabin (square-notch construction), rectangular, gable roof, stone and brick exterior end chimney, 2 rooms with separate doors. Probably built early 19th C., demolished. 1 ext. photo (1935).
Barn and Corncribs. Log and frame complex of buildings, gabled roofs covered by wooden shakes; barn and 3 small cribs surrounded by split-rail fence. Probably built mid-19th C. 2 ext. photos (1935).

Gravehouse (AL-689C), exact location unknown (possibly in Shiloh Church cemetery, E side of Co. 54, approx. 0.2 mi. S of junction with Co. 42, E of Manningham). Rectangular open shelter, consisting of 4 chamfered posts supporting shake-covered gable roof; enclosed by picket fence. Probably mid-19th C.; destroyed. 1 photo (1935).

Ridgeville Vicinity

Womack, T. Augustus ("Gus"), House (AL-690C), N side of Co. 54, approx. 2.7 mi. W of junction with Co. 19 between Manningham community to E and Ridgeville to W. Frame with clapboarding, rectangular (5-bay front) with rear lean-to, 1 story, gable roof, 2 exterior end chimneys, shed porch across front; center-hall plan, ceilings 18' high. Built ca. 1850 for son of Jacob Lewis Womack (see Womack-Crenshaw House, AL-690A). 1 ext. photo (1935).

Womack-Crenshaw House (AL-690A), N side of Co. 54, approx. 2.2 mi. W of junction with Co. 19, between Manningham community to E and Ridgeville to W. Frame with clapboarding (flush siding beneath portico), rectangular (5-bay front), 2½ stories, gable roof, 4 exterior end chimneys; overhang of roof forms full-height hexastyle portico with paneled square columns resting on brick piers, full-length balcony with wheatsheaf balustrade, shed pantry wing between W chimneys, full-length 1-story shed porch across rear; center-hall plan, paneled dado, plaster chandelier medallions. Semidetached frame rectangular 1-story dependency at NW rear. Built ca. 1850 for Jacob Lewis Womack; burned Feb. 1973. 8 ext. photos (1935), 8 int. photos (1935).

CALHOUN COUNTY

Alexandria

Green-Woodruff House (AL-468), N side of Alexandria-Jacksonville Rd., approx. 0.9 mi. E of intersection with U.S. 431; 0.1 mi. E of crossroads in village of Alexandria. Frame with clapboarding, main block 54'4" (3-bay front) × 32'0" plus ell (33'6" × 24'0"), 2-story main block with 1-story shed extension and ell, gable roof, 4 exterior end chimneys, central projecting pedimented distyle in antis Ionic portico with upper porch, flanking 3-part windows; center-hall plan, notable grained wainscoting and stippled mantelpiece in SE front room. Built mid-19th C. for Jacob Green; kitchen wing added to W side of ell in late 19th C. Still occupied by descendants of builder in 1979. 5 ext. photos (1935), 6 int. photos (1935).

Anniston Vicinity

Water Mill. *Under Jacksonville Vicinity, see* Aderholdt's Mill (AL-421).

Jacksonville

Arnold-Rowan House. *See* Snow-Arnold-Rowan House (AL-450), 201 Murphy St.

Crow Building. *See* Old Tavern (AL-416), NE corner of public square.

Daugette, Dr. C. W., House. *See* The Magnolias (AL-415), 601 N. Pelham Rd.

First Presbyterian Church (Presbyterian Church) (AL-419), NE corner E. Clinton and N. Chinabee sts. Brick, 42'0" (3-bay front) × 57'7" with projecting center (tower) bay and semioctagonal apse, 1 story, gable roof, pilastered front and sidewalls, 4-stage tower with arched doorway at base and polygonal spire with hand-carved cedar finial, flanking arched windows with louvered roundels; open plan, 2 aisles, original pews with low partition dividing middle block, gallery at rear over narthex. Built 1858–65; woodwork crafted by Gillan Southers, ruling elder of congregation, ca. 1865; church renovated and restored 1951; new spire added. Design for building possibly adapted from Samuel Sloan's *Model Architect*. Early example of Romanesque Revival in state. Incomplete structure used as hospital for both Union and Confederate wounded during Civil War. 7 sheets (1935, including plans, elevations, sections, details); 3 ext. photos (1935), 4 int. photos (1935); 2 data pages (1937).

Greenleaf, W. I., House. *See* Williams-Greenleaf House (AL-417), Pelham Rd.

Greenleaf's Store. *See* Old Tavern (AL-416), NE corner of public square.

Hoke House (AL-481), originally located at NE corner of N. Pelham Rd. (Ala. 21) and Clinton St. on N side of square. Frame with clapboarding, 2 stories, basically L-shaped structure with gabled 2-bay corner section adjoined on N by slightly lower 5-bay section facing N. Pelham Rd.; full-length 1-story shed porch across W (Pelham Rd.) elevation. Built mid-19th C. probably for John D. Hoke (1803–73), early Jacksonville merchant from Lincolnton, N.C.; subsequent additions and alterations. Moved N between 1910 and 1928 to make way for service station; demolished 1950s. Used variously as store, hotel, and residence. 1 ext. photo (1935, also showing old Masonic Hall in distance N of building).

McCampbell-Martin House (Thomas Martin House) (AL-480), E side of N. Pelham Rd. (Ala. 21), opposite and just S of intersection with Ala. 204 on site of present Martin Hall, Jacksonville State University campus; approx. 0.8 mi. N of public square. Frame with clapboarding, rectangular (3-bay front), 2 stories, shallow hipped roof, central pedimented tetrastyle Ionic portico, large upper balcony with bracketed supports and lattice balustrade, projecting 1-story semioctagonal wing at rear; center-hall plan. Built ca. 1860 possibly for James McCampbell; burned 1964 and Martin Hall (1966) erected on site. 1 ext. photo (1935), 2 int. photos (1935).

Magnolias, The (Dr. C. W. Daugette House, Walker-Daugette House) (AL-415), 601 N. Pelham Rd. (Ala. 21); NE corner N. Pelham Rd. and E. Washington St., approx. 0.5 mi. N of public square. Brick, 56'4" (3-bay front) × 46'2" with advanced center bay breaking into tower, 2 stories (tower 3 stories), shallow hipped roof with wide bracketed cornice, 2 interior chimneys, 1-story bracketed porch across front with slender octagonal supports carrying shallow Tudoresque arches with paneled soffits; hooded window at second-floor middle bay, originally 1-story loggia at rear with abutting service chambers and projecting porte cochère; center-hall plan with vestibule leading into foyer flanked by drawing rooms, wide stairhall at rear. 2 gabled brick 2-story dependencies at rear ("commissary" on N, kitchen and servants' quarters on S). Built ca. 1850–55 for Judge Thomas A. Walker (1811–88), state legislator and early railroad magnate (president of Selma and Rome Railroad 1858–64). Minor early-20th-C. changes included enclosure of rear loggia and construction of second-floor sleeping porch; main house and S dependency heavily damaged by 6 March 1944 tornado (dependency rebuilt as 1-story hipped roof structure). Modified Italianate design (possibly adapted from Samuel Sloan's *Model Architect,* 1852); architecturally similar to nearby Ten Oaks (Crook-Rowan House) on S. Pelham Rd. Residence 1903–42 of Dr. Clarence W. Daugette (1899–1942), president of Jacksonville State Normal School (later Jacksonville State University). 5 ext. photos (1935, including 2 photos of dependencies), 8 int. photos (1935); 2 data pages (1937).

Martin, Thomas, House. *See* McCampbell-Martin House (AL-480), N. Pelham Rd.

Nisbet-Weaver House (Weaver House) (AL-420), 420 E. Ladiga St. (N side of Ladiga St., approx. 0.3 mi. E of public square, on Reservoir Hill facing W). Frame with clapboarding, approx. 44'3" (5-bay front) × 32'0" as originally built, 2 stories with 1-story shed extension across rear, 2 exterior end chimneys (main block), formerly 2 exterior end chimneys on shed extension; hexastyle portico across front composed of slender square columns with wider middle bay carrying large upper balcony; center-hall plan, some simple Federal style woodwork. Built ca. 1838 for Dr. John Nisbet; colonnade probably later; glazed doors replaced original front doors in early 20th C. House extensively renovated 1942–43 (rear shed removed and entire back rebuilt as 2-story addition, new brick foundation, wooden porch floor replaced by poured concrete, partition removed between front hall and N room, plus other interior changes including construction of second stairway at rear). 2 ext. photos (1935), 4 int. photos (1935).

Presbyterian Church. *See* First Presbyterian Church (AL-419), E. Clinton and N. Chinabee sts.

Snow-Arnold-Rowan House (Arnold-Rowan House) (AL-450), 201 Murphy St. (SW corner Murphy and Drayton sts.). Frame with clapboarding, rectangular (3-bay front) with ell, 2 stories, gable roof, 2 exterior end chimneys (main block), 1 exterior chimney (ell), central 2-tiered pedimented tetrastyle portico with square columns capped by modified Ionic style capitals; center-hall plan, 3 stairways, full basement (kitchen beneath ell). Built 1850s for Fielding Snow, local tanner and brother of builder of Dudley Snow House (AL-465) in nearby Oxford; minor changes include partial enclosure of rear porch along S side of ell. 4 ext. photos (1935), 4 int. photos (1935).

Tavern, Old (Crow Building, Greenleaf's Store) (AL-416), NE corner of public square on S side of E. Clinton St. ("Crow Corner"), facing W. Brick (W and N elevations Flemish bond), main block 46'3" (6-bay front) × 27'0" plus shed extension at rear and ell, 2 stories, gable roof with notable molded brick

Old Tavern, Jacksonville (1838).

cornice, 2 interior end chimneys (main block), 1 exterior end chimney (ell), originally twin doorways with semicircular transoms; 2 large rooms on first floor of main block with dining room at rear, several small bedrooms on second floor, Federal style interior woodwork. Detached frame rectangular 1-story dependency at rear (demolished after 1935). Built 1838 for Aaron Haynes as "house of entertainment"; Thomas J. Crutchfield, master-builder. Lower story extensively altered ca. 1930, including elimination of original door and window openings; additional first-floor alterations ca. 1955–60 (although second floor largely intact in 1979); shed extension also rebuilt at undetermined date. One of earliest extant commercial structures in northeastern Alabama. 4 sheets (1935, including plans, elevations, sections, details); 1 ext. photocopy (n.d., showing relatively unaltered façade), 3 ext. photos (1935), 6 int. photos (1935); 2 data pages (1937).

Walker-Daugette House. *See* The Magnolias (AL-415), 601 N. Pelham Rd.

Weaver House. *See* Nisbet-Weaver House (AL-420), 420 E. Ladiga St.

Williams-Greenleaf House (W. I. Greenleaf House) (AL-417), w side of Pelham Rd. just S of intersection with Alexandria Rd., approx. 0.7 mi. S of public square. Brick, rectangular (5-bay front) with large 1-story central rear wing, 2 stories, hipped roof with bracketed cornice, 2 pairs of exterior end chimneys, central projecting distyle in antis Ionic portico surmounted by paneled parapet, large balcony at second floor; center-hall plan terminating in large dining room occupying rear wing, paneled dado with chair-rail. Brick rectangular 2-story smokehouse at SW rear. Completed 1852 for Col. Thomas Richard ("Dick") Williams, builder of Aderholdt's Mill (AL-421); Thomas J. Crutchfield, contractor (son-in-law of Williams). Open balustraded decks added to each side of portico early 20th C.; house badly deteriorated in 1979. 4 ext. photos (1935), 6 int. photos (1935).

Woods-Crook-Tredaway House (AL-418), 517 N. Pelham Rd. (Ala. 21); SE corner of N. Pelham Rd. and E. Washington St., approx. 0.4 mi. N of public square. Frame with clapboarding, approx. 48'10" (3-bay front) X 20'4" plus long ell, 2 stories, gable roof with bracketed cornice, 2 exterior end chimneys (main block), 1 interior chimney (wing), central pedimented tetrastyle Ionic portico with bracketed cornice and scroll-cut pendant, large bracketed balcony over doorway, portico flanked by 2-part windows, full-height L-shaped porch at rear with slender square columns; center-hall plan. Built ca. 1860 for Alexander Woods, teacher and county official; Elbert Green Morris, contractor. Late-19th-C. kitchen addition at end of ell, rear porch enclosed ca. 1940, aluminum siding added 1977. Stylistic mixture of Greek Revival and Italianate elements. 1 ext. photo (1935), 3 int. photos (1935).

Jacksonville Vicinity

Aderholdt's Mill (Water Mill) (AL-421), S side of Aderholdt's Mill Rd., approx. 0.5 mi. E of junction with Ala. 21, which is 2.4 mi. S of public square in Jacksonville; on N branch of Little Tallasseehatchee Creek. Private museum. Brick on blue granite foundation, approx. 49'8" (5-bay E and W elevations) X 36'6", 2½ stories (set into side of hill with entrances on 2 levels), gable roof, molded brick cornice, wooden waterwheel originally at S end of building (replaced by water turbine after 1935), unusual 12-panel half-doors in E and W elevations; open interior plan with much early mill machinery, unusual corner fireplace on second floor with diagonal flue leading to chimney at ridge of N gable. Built ca. 1835–40 for Col. Thomas Richard ("Dick") Williams; Thomas J. Crutchfield, contractor (son-in-law of Williams). Wheel replaced by horizontal turbine in 1930s. Mill-powered cotton gin as well as sawmill, gristmill, and sorghum mill (building also housed cabinet shop). Known as Aderholdt's Mill since ca. 1921. 5 ext. photos (1935), 2 int. photos (1935).

Oxford

Snow, Dudley, House (AL-465), 704 Snow St.; S side of Snow St., approx. 0.2 mi. E of U.S. 431 at Quintard Mall, on knoll approx. 300' E of Snow Branch. Frame with clapboarding (center portion log), approx. 49'6" (5-bay front) X 43'2", 1½ stories, broken gable roof, 2 pairs of exterior end chimneys; center-hall plan (originally open dogtrot) with wide double doors at each end, flush-board walls, paneled dado in hallway. Nucleus is 2-room log house with open passage or dogtrot between, built ca. 1832; shed rooms added to front and rear, hall enclosed, and entire structure clapboarded ca. 1833–40; small rectangular 1-bay wing added to SE corner (probably in mid-19th C.). Altered 1962–70 including removal of double-leaf front doorway, rear chimneys, and stack of NE chimney, as well as some original sashing and clapboarding, some interior changes. Oldest known extant structure in Calhoun County. From Roane Co., Tenn., Snow was founder of Oxford. 3 ext. photos (1935), 5 int. photos (1935).

Wheat House, S of main house. Frame with clapboarding on high brick foundation, rectangular (1-bay front), gable roof cantilevered over single doorway; probably built mid-19th C.; demolished. 1 ext. photo (1935).

Oxford Vicinity

Boiling Spring (Caver-Christian House, Freeman-Caver-Christian House) (AL-470), E side of Upper Friendship Rd., approx. 0.3 mi. S of intersection with U.S. 78, which is 0.1 mi. S of I-20 overpass, and 2.4 mi. E of U.S. 78 intersection with U.S. 431 at Oxford; 0.2 mi. N of Choccolocco Creek. Originally frame with clapboarding, approx. 52'0" (5-bay front) X 20'4" plus ell (approx. 40'0" [including flanking porches] × 46'6"), 2 stories (ell 1 story), gable roof with ell covered by broken gable, 2 exterior end chimneys, central 1-story pedimented portico with slender square supports; center-hall plan. Built mid-19th C. for planter Thomas J. Caver (1802–72); brick veneer added ca. 1950, rear porches enclosed. 5 ext. photos (1935, including 1 photo of natural spring near house), 8 int. photos (1935).

Slave House, S of main dwelling. Log (half-dovetail notching) and frame (board-and-batten), rectangular double-pen dwelling with open dogtrot, 1 story, gable roof, 2 exterior end chimneys. One-bay log portion possibly built as early as 1832; later enlarged by frame portion and intervening passage; demolished. 1 ext. photo (1935).

Kitchen, N of main house. Brick, rectangular (2-bay front), 1 story over high basement, gable roof, 1 exterior end chimney; 1 room. Built ca. 1840–45; demolished. 1 ext. photo (1935).

Store, SE of main house. Brick, rectangular (3-bay front), 1 story, gable roof. Built mid-19th C.; demolished. 1 ext. photo (1935).

Borders-Blackman House
(AL-471), SE side of old DeArmanville-Choccolocco Rd., approx. 0.6 mi. SW of Harmony Baptist Cemetery; approx. 2.3 mi. NE of intersection with U.S. 78 at DeArmanville (about 5 mi. E of U.S. 78 intersection with U.S. 431 at Oxford). Frame with clapboarding, approx. 48'0" (5-bay front) × 30'3" overall, 2 stories with 1-story shed extension across rear, gable roof, 2 pairs exterior end chimneys, central 1-story gabled porch; center-hall plan, very notable Federal style mantelpieces. Built ca. 1840–42 for John Borders, planter from Franklin Co., Ga.; tradition asserts that construction was supervised by 2 slave craftsmen, Lev and Griff, who built other houses in Choccolocco Valley. Renovated 1952–64 including removal of original sashing, NE rear chimney, construction of closed porch off rear of breezeway and kitchen; house covered with vinyl siding in fall 1978. 2 ext. photos (1935), 7 int. photos (1935).

Kitchen, linked to N side of house by 24' covered way. Brick, approx. 34'6" × 18'0", 1 story over deep basement, gable roof with stepped end parapets, 2 exterior end chimneys, corbeled brick cornice; 2-room plan with large walk-in fireplace (9'3" wide × 5'4" high × 3'8" deep) in N room. Built ca. 1840; parapets removed ca. 1940, covered way enclosed after 1952, and shed extension built off rear. 2 ext. photos (1935), 2 int. photos (1935).

Smokehouse, to rear (E) of house. Brick, square, 1 story, 1 bay, pyramidal roof with wood finial, open diaperwork ventilators at top of walls, covered way (partially enclosed with brick wall) off S side of smokehouse linking it with other dependencies and sheltering brick-lined cistern. Built ca. 1840; demolished in 1950s. 1 ext. photo (1935).

Caver-Christian House. *See* Boiling Spring (AL-470), Upper Friendship Rd.

Freeman-Caver-Christian House. *See* Boiling Spring (AL-470), Upper Friendship Rd.

Weaver and Vicinity

Glover, Dr. Wylie, House (Lenlock) (AL-466), E side of Weaver Rd., 0.2 mi. N of junction with Ala. 21 at Lenlock Shopping Center, just N of Lenlock Dr.; 2.1 mi. N of Ala. 21 junction with U.S. 431; approx. 0.2 mi. S of bridge over Cane Creek. Frame with clapboarding, rectangular (3-bay front), 2 stories with 1-story rear shed extension, gable roof, 2 pairs of exterior end chimneys, central pedimented 2-column portico with square columns capped by modified Ionic capitals, balcony at upper level, flanking 3-part windows; center-hall plan, interior walls originally composed of matched boarding scored and marbleized, paneled wainscoting in SW front room, mantels have primitive fluted Ionic pilasters. Built ca. 1852; board-and-batten 1-story ell added late 19th C. Renovated after 1941, including removal of later ell, installation of pseudo-Federal style woodwork in hall and NW front room, replacement of original stair balusters with turned balusters, removal of chimneys from shed extension; reconditioned 1979 as administrative offices and community center for senior citizens' housing development built on surrounding acreage. 4 ext. photos (1935), 7 int. photos (1935).

Kelly House (AL-467), on knoll W side of Peaceburg Rd., approx. 0.8 mi. NE of junction with Russell Dr. in Weaver; 1.4 mi. SW of junction with Alexander Rd. between Weaver and Jacksonville. Frame with clapboarding on irregular ashlar piers, rectangular (54'4" across with 3 bays below, 6 bays above), 2 stories with 1-story shed extensions front and rear, gable roof, 2 exterior end chimneys (stuccoed and scored to simulate ashlar), shed-roof porch flanked by 1-bay end rooms, brick nogging insulation; 14'-wide open center passage, simple Federal style woodwork, unusual birdseye maple graining on plasterwork beneath chair-rail. Built ca. 1835–40, possibly for Simon Kelly; second floor and shed extensions removed ca. 1940; framework only still standing in early 1980s. 1 ext. photo (1935), 2 int. photos (1935).

Lenlock. *See* Dr. Wylie Glover House (AL-466), Weaver Rd.

Weaver, D. F., House. *See* Weaver-Rowe House (AL-464), Weaver Rd.

Weaver-Rowe House (AL-464), 0.1 mi. W of Weaver Rd., approx. 3.1 mi. N of junction with Ala. 21 at Lenlock; between Cave Creek (0.1 mi. N) and Cane Creek (0.6 mi. S). Frame with clapboarding, rectangular (3-bay front) with long ell, 2 stories with 1-story rear shed extension, hipped roof, bracketed cornice, central pedimented tetrastyle portico consisting of outer piers paired with fluted inner columns (both topped by modified Ionic capitals); center-hall plan. Frame rectangular 1-story dependency at rear. Built ca. 1865 for Mrs. Lucinda Weaver (mother of subsequent owner, D. F. Weaver); demolished ca. 1970 when farm became part of Terra Firma, agricultural vocational center for Anniston public school system. Stylistic mixture of Greek Revival and Italianate elements as applied to traditional house-form. 4 ext. photos (1935), 4 int. photos (1935).

White Plains

Cobb, Tom, House. *See* Cook-Johnson House (AL-469).

Cook-Johnson House (Tom Cobb House) (AL-469), exact location undetermined. Frame with clapboarding (façade flush boarding), rectangular (4-bay front), 2 stories with 1-story shed extension across rear, gable roof broken at front to extend over 2-tiered full-length porch, 2 exterior end chimneys, stair to second floor at end of porch; probably 2-room plan. Built early 19th C. for Thomas Cook, Choccolocco Valley settler from Abbeville District, S.C.; destroyed. 1 ext. photo (1935), 1 int. photo (1935).

CHAMBERS COUNTY

Lafayette

Andrews-Allen House (AL-553), W side of S. Lafayette St. (U.S. 431) between Court Dr. and 2nd Ave. SW. Frame with clapboarding (façade scored to simulate rustication), basically square (3-bay front), 2 stories, full-length tetrastyle portico with false entablature carried on square piers, recessed doorway with modified classical architrave flanked by 3-part windows (later replaced by double windows), full-length balcony above; center-hall plan, mixture of Federal and Greek Revival style woodwork. Built ca. 1845–50, possibly for Mark Andrews; demolished ca. 1970 by adjacent First Baptist Church to make way for parking area. 5 ext. photos (1935), 4 int. photos (1935).

Goodman, Benjamin L., House (A. A. Tatum House) (AL-535), 226 N. Lafayette St.; E side of Lafayette St. (U.S. 431), approx. 0.4 mi. N of courthouse square. Frame with clapboarding, 40'0" (3-bay front) × 21'6" plus ell, 2 stories (ell 1 story), gable roof with pedimented gable ends, 2 exterior end chimneys, central pedimented portico originally supported by 2 pairs of slender fluted Ionic columns with 2 corresponding wall pilasters, denticulated cornice with tympanum pierced by lunette, balcony over main doorway; center-hall plan, Federal period interior woodwork. Built ca. 1840–45; columns replaced by square supports in early 20th C. (also rear additions); entire portico removed and doorways replaced by picture-glass ca. 1945. 6 ext. photos (1935), 5 int. photos (1935).

McLemore House. *See* McNamee-Kinsey-McLemore House (AL-530), 342 N. Lafayette St.

McNamee-Kinsey-McLemore House (McLemore House) (AL-530), 342 N. Lafayette St.; E side Lafayette St. (U.S. 431), approx. 120' S of intersection with 2nd Ave., NE, and 0.2 mi. N of courthouse square. Brick reinforced with iron and covered with stucco, rectangular (3-bay front), 1 story above raised basement, shallow hipped roof extending over full-length portico with heavy square columns rising from ground level and carrying raised balustraded porch, subordinate pediment over middle bay of portico; center-hall plan, Greek Revival style interior woodwork, basement dining room. Built ca. 1850 for Thomas McNamee; demolished ca. 1951. Home 1878–1951 of J. J. McLemore family. 5 ext. photos (1935), 7 int. photos (1935).

Tatum, A. A., House. *See* Benjamin L. Goodman House (AL-535), 226 N. Lafayette St.

Oak Bowery

Bullard House. *See* Dowdell-Mathews-Bullard House (AL-506), U.S. 431.

Dowdell-Mathews-Bullard House (Bullard House) (AL-506), W side of U.S. 431, approx. 0.2 mi. N of Chambers-Lee county line and junction of Chambers Co. 1 W; 0.3 mi. S of U.S. 431 intersection with Gold Hill Rd. at Oak Bowery. Frame with clapboarding, originally 52'4" (5-bay front) X 20'0" plus ell 20' X 20', 2 stories, hipped roof, 2 exterior chimneys (main block), 1 exterior end chimney (ell), 3-bay pedimented tetrastyle portico with unusual fluted square columns and paneled entablature, balcony over main doorway enclosed by latticed balustrade; center-hall plan, paneled dado. Built ca. 1850 for planter James Dowdell. Early 2-story shed addition at rear creating overall rectangular form; burned ca. 1950. Boyhood home of World War I hero Gen. Robert Lee Bullard. Dowdell family cemetery S of house site. 3 sheets (1934, including plans, elevations, section, details); 2 ext. photos (1934); 2 data pages (1936).

CLARKE COUNTY

Coffeeville

Figures-York House (Vickers-Chapman House) (AL-110), E side of Ala. 69, approx. 0.1 mi. N of junction with U.S. 84 (Ala. 12) and 0.6 mi. due E of Tombigbee River. Frame with clapboarding, approx. 54'0" (5-bay front) X 60'6" including 11'-deep portico, 2 stories, hipped roof extending over hexastyle modified Doric portico with full-length balcony, denticulated cornice, 2 pairs of interior end chimneys; center-hall plan, jib windows onto portico. Built ca. 1856–60 for John W. Figures, merchant, cotton gin owner, and postmaster of Coffeeville; rear portion collapsed and house ruinous 1978; demolished 1984. 2 ext. photos (1934).

Vickers-Chapman House. *See* Figures-York House (AL-110), Ala. 69.

Suggsville

Wilson, Albert J., House (AL-109), W side of Co. 35, approx. 4.5 mi. S of intersection with U.S. 84 (Ala. 12); about 10 mi. SE of Grove Hill. Frame with clapboarding, rectangular, 2 stories with 1-story shed-roof extension across rear, gable roof, 4 ashlar exterior end chimneys, broad kick-off extending over full-length 2-tiered porch, triple windows flanking main doorway; center-hall plan. Built ca. 1840; reduced to 1 story and otherwise extensively altered ca. 1948. 1 ext. photo (1934).

CLEBURNE COUNTY

Edwardsville

Cleburne County Courthouse, Old (AL-775), approx. 180′ s of U.S. 78 and approx. 7.3 mi. E of junction with Ala. 46 at Heflin; approx. 0.3 mi. W of Town Creek bridge. Brick, 60′4″ X 40′3″ (5 bays each elevation), 2 stories, hipped roof, brick watertable and belt course, segmentally arched openings with projecting voussoirs; originally T-shaped hall on first floor, large courtroom and antechambers on second floor. Built ca. 1867 as courthouse for newly organized county. Interior extensively renovated and original plan altered for use as school ca. 1900; burned ca. 1965. 13 sheets (1963, including plot plans, elevations, sections, details).

COLBERT COUNTY

Allsboro Vicinity

Big Bear Creek Covered Bridge (AL-361A), on Co. 7 where it crosses Big Bear Creek, approx. 0.1 mi. SE of junction with Co. 1, which is approx. 0.5 mi. N of confluence of Big Bear and Cripple Deer creeks; about 3 mi. N of Allsboro community and 8 mi. SW of Cherokee. Frame (Town lattice truss secured with pegs) resting on ashlar abutments, board-and-batten sheathing, gable roof. Built ca. 1860; underpinned with concrete caissons in early 20th C.; demolished ca. 1940. 3 ext. photos (1936, including 1 view S from bridge), 1 int. photo (1936).

Cripple Deer Creek Covered Bridge (AL-361), on Co. 1 where it crosses Cripple Deer Creek, approx. 2.2 mi. SW of junction with Co. 7; about 2 mi. N of Allsboro community and 9 mi. SW of Cherokee. Frame (Town lattice truss secured with pegs) resting on ashlar abutments, vertical board sheathing (clapboarding at each end), gable roof, wooden causeway from S end of bridge. Built ca. 1860; demolished and replaced 1936 with steel and concrete bridge built by WPA. 5 ext. photos (1936), 1 int. photo (1936).

Brick Vicinity

Old Brick Presbyterian Church. *See Leighton Vicinity.*

Cherokee Vicinity

Barton Hall (Cunningham Plantation) (AL-337), S side of Old Memphis Rd., 1.0 mi. E of Buzzard Roost Creek and 0.7 mi. S of U.S. 72; approx. 1.3 mi. due E of Natchez Trace Pkwy. or 1.9 mi. W of U.S. 72 intersection with Main St. at Cherokee. Frame with clapboarding on ashlar foundation, 64′2″ (5-bay front) X 44′0″ with symmetrical parallel rear wings (20′0″ X 36′4″), 2 stories (wings 1 story), hipped roof with balustraded deck, 4 interior end chimneys (main block), 1-story tetrastyle Doric entrance portico on ashlar stylobate with balustraded deck, similar pedimented distyle Doric porticoes on E and W sides, Doric loggia at rear with ashlar-paved forecourt, full Doric entablature with triglyphs and metopes repeated in frieze of porticoes and rooftop deck; center-hall plan, outstanding stairway rising from each end of main hall in series of double reverse flights connected by bridgelike flying landings, woodwork probably adapted from Minard Lafever's *Beauties of Modern Architecture*. Built ca. 1847–49 for Armistead Barton, who died before its completion; occupied by widow until 1884. Restored 1942–47. Enclosed cupola originally surmounting roof destroyed by storm ca. 1900 and replaced by balustrade during restoration. 12 sheets (1937, including plans, elevations, section, details); 7 ext. photos (1935–36), 18 int. photos (1935–36); 2 data pages (1937). NHL.

Kitchen and Servants' Quarters (SW dependency). Brick, 40′4″ (4-bay front) X 20′0″, 1 story, gable roof, shed porch with 8 brick pier-supports. 1 sheet (1937, including plan, elevation); 1 ext. photo (1935), 1 int. photo (1935).

Smokehouse, approx. 0.5 mi. NW of house on Chisca Rd. (originally part of neighboring William Dickson plantation complex). Frame with clapboarding on high brick base, hipped roof. 1 ext. photo (1936).

Slave House, approx. 0.3 mi. W of house. Frame with clapboarding, rectangular, gable roof, single brick-and-stone exterior end chimney. Probably one of original row of slave cabins. 1 ext. photo (1936, W end and chimney only).

Mounting Block and Hitching Posts, in front of house. Granite; hitching posts obelisk in shape, mounting block has steps to narrow platform. 2 photos (1935–36). *See also* FBJ (J7-ALA-1041 through 1049).

Buzzard Roost Covered Bridge (AL-361B), Old Memphis Rd. (Gaines Trace Rd.) at crossing of Buzzard Roost Creek, approx. 0.2 mi. E of Natchez Trace Pkwy. and 0.5 mi. S of U.S. 72 overpass. Frame (Town lattice truss secured with pegs) resting on ashlar abutments, 94' span, board-and-batten sheathing, gable roof. Built ca. 1860; underpinned with concrete caissons in early 20th C.; burned by arsonists in 1972. 1 ext. photo (1936), 1 int. photo (1936).

Colbert, George, House (AL-4), overlooking W bank of Tennessee River 0.1 mi. NW of Natchez Trace Parkway at W end of river bridge (site included in Natchez Trace National Park); approx. 6.0 mi. N of Cherokee. Frame with clapboarding, rectangular (3 bays downstairs, 2 upstairs), 2 stories with 1-story lean-to across rear, 2 exterior end chimneys at E end, shed porch at front; single large downstairs room plus lean-to. Begun ca. 1801 for Colbert, a Chickasaw chieftain, by U.S. soldiers according to provision of 1801 treaty (Colbert himself finished house prior to 1806); burned 1929. Possibly first frame house in northern Alabama. Colbert operated Tennessee River ferry on Natchez Trace. 1 ext. photocopy (n.d.); 1 int. photocopy of mantel (n.d.).

Cunningham Plantation. *See* Barton Hall (AL-337), Old Memphis Rd.

Goodloe, John Calvin, House (AL-310), approx. 0.3 mi. N of old U.S. 72 facing W at end of farm lane (entrance to lane approx. 3.0 mi. E of junction of U.S. 72 with Co. 15 at Cherokee); 0.2 mi. due E of Mulberry Creek. Frame with clapboarding on stuccoed and scored brick foundation, rectangular (5-bay front), 2½ stories over full basement, gable roof with bracketed cornice, full-height pedimented entrance portico composed of 2 pairs of fluted Ionic columns, recessed doorway with balcony above enclosed by cast-iron balustrade, house partially encircled by unusual brick-paved drymoat with ashlar retaining wall topped by cast-iron railing (space served to light basement windows), low 2-story lean-to and porch across rear; center-hall plan, curved stairway, decorative plasterwork. Built ca. 1855 incorporating earlier log house at rear; stairway reputedly built by skilled black craftsman whose name is unknown; demolished 1964. First owner, J. Calvin Goodloe (1817–95), was large cotton planter, prominent Union sympathizer during Civil War. 9 ext. photos (1935), 12 int. photos (1935).

Kitchen, SE of house. Brick, rectangular, 1 story, gable roof, 1 exterior end chimney, porch. 1 ext. photo (1935), 1 int. photo (1935).

Leighton

Leckey, Hugh C., House (AL-863), SW corner of intersection Ala. 20 and Co. 48 (County Line or Byler Rd.) in Leighton. Frame with clapboarding, approx. 48'5" (3-bay front) × 36'5" plus rear cross hall and wing, 1 story, truncated hipped roof (main block) with balustraded deck, 2 interior chimneys, arcuated entrance porch with pediment, flanking double-arched windows, bracketed cornice; center-hall plan with open porch originally connecting main block with gabled 2-room kitchen and dining wing at rear. Built 1872–73 for Leckey, an Irish-born merchant; rear porch replaced by 2-tiered octagonal room ca. 1915; restored 1978–79, including reconstruction of rooftop deck. Notable example of Italianate stylistic elements applied to smaller dwelling. 2 ext. photos (1978).

Leighton Vicinity

Oaks, The (Abraham Ricks House) (AL-362), facing N on W side of Ricks Lane, approx. 0.4 mi. S of junction with Ala. 157; approx. 0.7 mi. due N of Polk Branch. Built in 2 sections (designated as Old House and New House) with connecting 1-story hyphen forming overall H-shaped plan. Front section (New House): frame with clapboarding, rectangular main block (5-bay front), 2 stories on raised basement, gable roof with subordinate gable over middle bay of façade (originally surmounted by stepped wooden parapet), 2 exterior end chimneys, 1-story entrance porch with balustraded deck; center-hall plan. Old House: frame with clapboarding over log construction, rectangular, 1½ stories, gable roof, 2 exterior end chimneys, full-length rear porch; 2-room plan with enclosed stairway between. Semidetached log kitchen (rectangular, gable roof, stone exterior end chimney) to W of New House. Rear section (Old House) said to predate 1825; New House and hyphen built ca. 1835; Thomas Dial, master-builder. Renovated and restored 1966–70. 4 ext. photos (1935), 6 int. photos (1935); 2 data pages (1937). NR.

Slave Quarters. Log (half-dovetail notching), rectangular (1 bay), 1 story, gable roof, 1 exterior end chimney. Antebellum; later board-and-batten side addition; demolished. Known as Mammy Rose's Cabin. 1 ext. photo (1935).

Smokehouse. Log (half-dovetail notching) covered with clapboarding, rectangular (1 bay), 1 story, gable roof. Antebellum; demolished. 1 ext. photo (1935).

Old Brick Presbyterian Church (AL-382), S side of Mt. Pleasant Rd., approx. 0.2 mi. E of junction with Ala. 48 and 5.7 mi. N of Ala. 48 intersection with Ala. 20 at Leighton; 0.1 mi. due S of McKiernan Creek. Brick, rectangular (3-bay front), gable roof, simple pilastered exterior; open plan, 2 aisles, rear slave gallery (now enclosed) formerly reached by outside stair, original slip pews with central divider separating men from women. Built 1828 as Mount Pleasant Cumberland Presbyterian Meeting House, reputedly identical to nearby and long-destroyed Mount Pleasant Baptist Church. Extensive alterations ca. 1900 including installation of art glass windows, new roof, interior changes. One of oldest extant churches in Alabama. Congregation merged with Presbyterian Church USA ca. 1906 and name changed officially to Old Brick Presbyterian Church. 1 ext. photo (1935).

Vinson, Drury, House (AL-381), E side Colbert Co. 63 (Sockwell Lane), approx. 0.3 mi. S of intersection with Ala. 20; 2.1 mi. W of junction of Ala. 20 and Co. 48 at Leighton. Frame with clapboarding, rectangular (5-bay front) with ell, 2 stories (ell 1 story), gable roof, 2 exterior end chimneys, 1-story shed porch across front (probably replacing original 1-story entrance porch with deck), denticulated cornice with fascia board sawn to simulate dentilwork; center-hall plan, notable interior woodwork including Federal period mantels, chair-rails, and stair trim. Latticed wellhouse (square, with roof of wooden shakes). Built ca. 1835. Vinson (1788–1862) was a planter and a member of the colony of North Carolinians who settled in Leighton area. Altered ca. 1900 (including probable replacement of porch); demolished 1972. 2 ext. photos (1935, including wellhouse), 3 int. photos (1935).

Sheffield

Barner House. *See* Winter-Barner House (AL-323), 2708 Tenth Ave.

Winston, Anthony, House (AL-316A), approx. 30′ SE of intersection of Eighth St. and Fourteenth Ave. (facing S and situated partially within present Eighth St. right-of-way); approx. 300′ NE of Winston Cemetery, just outside northern city limits of Tuscumbia. Brick (Flemish bond façade), approx. 50′ (5-bay front) X 22′ plus ell (approx. 20′ X 20′), 2 stories (ell 1 story), gable roof, 2 exterior end chimneys (main block), originally 1-story entrance porch with balustraded deck; center-hall plan. Built ca. 1825 as plantation residence of Winston, father of first native-born Alabama governor. Makeshift shed porch replaced original ca. 1900; house demolished ca. 1936 when 8th St. extended. Also called Andrew Jackson House because Winston purchased property from Jackson. Later home of a Mr. Elliott, admirer of Jackson, who burned candles in windows each year on 8 January in commemoration of Jackson's victory at New Orleans. 2 ext. photos (1934).

Winter-Barner House (Barner House) (AL-323), 2708 Tenth Ave., at SE corner Twenty-eighth St. Log covered with clapboarding on stone piers, rectangular (3-bay front) with lean-to across rear, 1½ stories, gable roof, 2 exterior end chimneys, full-length shed porch on front; center-hall plan (evidence of original open passage or dogtrot). Built ca. 1830. One-time home of Benjamin Ricks Winter, later of John W. Barner, whose York's Bluff plantation became site of city of Sheffield in late 19th C. Extensively altered ca. 1950 including rear ell, dormers, and asbestos siding, and subdivided into apartments. 2 ext. photos (1934), 1 int. photo (1934).

Sheffield Vicinity

House (AL-862), S side of Co. 40 (River Rd.), 0.1 mi. W of intersection with Co. 83 (Old Bainbridge Rd.); 1.2 mi. due W of McKiernan Creek Bridge. Frame with clapboarding, 48'7" (5-bay front) x 20'5", 1½ stories, gable roof with 3 dormers front and rear; center-hall plan, simple Federal period mantelpieces, chair-rail, and stair. Built ca. 1830, possibly for D. Greenly; dormers partially removed, badly deteriorated in 1981; demolished June 1985. Rare occurrence in Alabama of single-pile Tidewater-type cottage originating in Chesapeake Bay region. 1 ext. photo (1978).

Spring Valley Vicinity

Belle Mont (Belmont, Henry P. Thornton Plantation) (AL-388), on high knoll approx. 0.4 mi. due W of U.S. 43 at intersection with Co. 52 (Cook Lane); approx. 3.5 mi. S of U.S. 43 intersection with U.S. 72. House museum. Brick (Flemish bond), 3-part composition (76'2" x 65'5" overall) with 2-story 1-bay center pavilion flanked by symmetrical 1-story 2-bay wings, hipped roof over main pavilion with projecting 2-tiered pedimented portico, fanlight doorway, wings extend to rear to form brick-paved court enclosed on 3 sides by U-shaped porch, walls stuccoed and scored to simulate ashlar; modified Palladian interior plan, with center section consisting of large square entrance hall and single room above containing hanging stair to attic, 3 large rooms in each wing, exceptionally fine Federal period interior including splayed paneled reveals and black marble mantels. Dependencies include log slave quarters, barn, frame (board-and-batten) privy. Built ca. 1828 for Dr. Alexander W. Mitchell; sold ca. 1833 to Isaac Winston. Form and layout suggest direct influence of Thomas Jefferson's architectural ideas and possibly hand of Monticello-trained craftsmen. House heavily vandalized 1965–83; donated to the Alabama Historical Commission in 1983 for restoration. Important example of Palladian/Jeffersonian neoclassicism in Alabama and one of few extant structures of this type in lower South. 13 sheets (1937, including plans, elevations, section, details); 31 ext. photos (1935–37, including dependencies), 13 int. photos (1935–37). NR.

Tuscumbia

Abernathy House. See Houston-Abernathy-Minor House (AL-355), 204 N. Main St.

Aycock House (AL-350), 205 W. Jefferson St. Log (later covered with brick veneer), rectangular (6 irregular bays), 1 story, gable roof (2 interior chimneys), brick-paved shed porch extending length of W elevation (original front); 4 end-to-end rooms. Built early to mid-19th C. Formerly dependency (kitchen and servants' quarters) of 2-story frame John Henry Aycock house, which stood to W and was burned during Civil War; dependency subsequently renovated as Aycock family residence. Structure reoriented toward Jefferson St. and porch added to E side in late 19th C.; W porch removed after 1935. 7 ext. photos (1934–37), 3 int. photos (1937).

Bell-Prout-Edwards House (Edwards House) (AL-354), NE corner Dickson and E Second sts. Brick (fragmentary Flemish bond at SW corner), rectangular (5-bay front, originally 3-bay), 2 stories, hipped roof, S exterior end chimney, later N interior end chimney, segmentally arched windows; center-hall plan (originally side hall). Built before 1828 for Abram Bell; originally rectangular 3-bay structure with gable roof and 1-story ell at SE rear; extensively altered and enlarged 1905–10 including extension of N side by 2 bays, replacement of original roof, sashing, and doors, construction of 2-tiered veranda along W and S sides, rear additions; veranda later removed. Abram Bell was uncle of John Bell of Tennessee, prominent southern statesman and 1860 presidential candidate. 2 ext. photos (1934), 1 int. photo (1934).

Carriage Factory. See Young's Carriage Shop (AL-315), Main and E. Fourth sts.

Carroll-Johnson House (G. W. Carroll House) (AL-322), 801 E. North Commons (N end of Mulberry St. at end of private drive). Frame with clapboarding, L-shaped (5-bay S and W fronts), 2 stories, hipped roof with denticulated cornice, 3 interior end chimneys, 2-tiered pedimented entrance porticoes on S and W; center-hall plan with side hall and secondary stair, some grained interior woodwork. Built 1835–37 for George W. Carroll, from Maryland; William Smoot, masterbuilder (?). Remodeled late 19th C., including replacement of first-floor sashing on front with floor-length Victorian windows, addition of balustraded wooden deck to either side of S portico. Original boxwood planting and cedar-lined entrance lane. One of best-preserved early-19th-C. complexes in area. 3 ext. photos (1935), 7 int. photos (1935); 1 data page (1936).

Office. Frame with clapboarding, rectangular (1 bay), 1 story, gable roof, 1 exterior end chimney; antebellum. 1 ext. photo (1935). *Smokehouse.* Brick, rectangular (1 bay), 1 story, gable roof projecting to cover brick-paved porch, 1 interior end chimney; antebellum. 1 ext. photo (1935). *Kitchen* (semidetached at rear of house). Frame, rectangular (1 bay), 1 story, gable roof; probably mid-19th C. 1 ext. photo (1935).

Christian-Lindsay House (Gov. Robert Lindsay House, Tennessee Valley Country Club) (AL-312), approx. 0.2 mi. N of U.S. 72 (0.6 mi. W of Woodmont Dr. intersection) on grounds of Tennessee Valley Country Club. Brick (Flemish bond) on ashlar foundation, rectangular (4-bay front below, 3 bays above), 2 stories over basement, hipped roof, 2 exterior end chimneys, originally 2-tiered pedimented entrance portico, entablature and pediment embellished with triglyphs, double entrances below with single entrance onto upper gallery of portico; 2-room plan, paneled dado and Adamesque mantels, basement kitchen. Built ca. 1825–30 possibly for John T. and Archibald S. Christian from Virginia. Later 2-story addition across rear; clubhouse since 1920s. Home in late 19th C. of Robert Burns Lindsay, governor of Alabama (1870–72). 5 ext. photos (1934–37), 9 int. photos (1934–37). NR.

Kitchen. Brick, rectangular (3 bays), 1 story, gable roof, 1 exterior end chimney. Antebellum, demolished. 1 ext. photo (1937), 2 int. photos (1934–37).

Colored Barber's House. *See* House (AL-351), 306 W. Fifth St.

Commercial Buildings (Morgan House) (AL-321), 107 and 109 E. Fifth St.

107 E. Fifth St. (Morgan House). Brick (façade Flemish bond), approx. 30′ (4-bay front) × 50′, 2½ stories with basement, gable roof, alternating window and door bays across lower story, side-hall plan (first floor) with straight-run stair. Built ca. 1820–25; extensive alterations both inside and out after 1935, including application of pebble stucco to exterior. Possibly oldest commercial structure in Tuscumbia and one of earliest extant commercial buildings in Alabama. Occupied by Sarah Morgan before 1880. 2 ext. photos (1934–35), 3 int. photos (1935). *109 E. Fifth St.* (E side of No. 107). Frame with clapboarding, approx. 20′ (3-bay front) × 40′ (including rear shed room), 1 story, gable roof, 1 exterior end chimney. Built ca. 1830; later municipal water office; demolished 1973. 1 ext. photo (1934).

Commercial Row (AL-360), N side of Fifth St. between Main and Water sts. Brick, approx. 165′ (21-bay front) × 55′, 2 stories, shed roof concealed by paneled brick parapet; pilastered S (front) and E elevations; divided for commercial purposes into 7 3-bay units. Built ca. 1832–35 at the Fifth St. terminus of the Tuscumbia, Courtland, and Decatur railroads; extensive alterations to interior and store fronts. Possibly oldest surviving commercial range in Alabama. E (corner) section occupied by the *North Alabamian,* early Tuscumbia newspaper edited by Capt. Arthur Keller, father of Helen Keller. 2 ext. photos (1934–35), 1 int. photo (1935).

Coons-Steele-Armistead House (Edward Goodloe House) (AL-356), 406 N. Main St. Brick, rectangular (3-bay front) with ell, 1½ stories over raised basement, gable roof with dormers, 2 exterior end chimneys, full-length raised porch; side-hall plan. Built ca. 1820 reputedly for J. W. Coons; sold to John Anthony and Martha Bacon (Winston) Steele in 1852; later porch and rear additions. Notable and rare example in northern Alabama of raised dwelling. 2 ext. photos (1934), 3 int. photos (1935); 1 data page (1936).

Edwards House. *See* Bell-Prout-Edwards House (AL-354), Dickson and E. Second sts.

First Methodist Church, Old (AL-313), NE corner Dickson and E. Seventh sts. Brick, originally rectangular (approx. 40′ × 70′) with gable roof, 2 tiers of windows and probably 2 identical front entrances; open interior plan with U-shaped gallery. Built 1826–27; Edward Stegar, master-mason; and Nelson Anderson, carpenter. Extensively altered ca. 1890, including addition of diagonally set entrance tower at NW corner, extensive changes in fenestration and gutting of interior; sold to City of Tuscumbia ca. 1920 for municipal purposes and subsequently reduced to 1 story; demolished 1960. 2 ext. photos (1934).

First Presbyterian Church (AL-314), SE corner Broad and

Fourth sts. Brick (façade Flemish bond), 46′2″ (3-bay front) x 57′9″, 1 story, gable roof, 2-stage belfry with octagonal domed cupola topped by iron weathervane, pedimented façade with modillioned cornice and oval-shaped panel in tympanum, tall pointed central door, pointed windows (originally filled with double-hung sash covered by louvered blinds); open plan, U-shaped gallery with 2 tiers of Tuscan style colonnettes supporting coved ceiling, pulpit area and flanking doors enframed by large triple-lancet architrave. Built 1827–28; pipe organ installed in gallery in 1849; extensive interior renovations in 1888 (including removal of original pulpit and pews); art glass windows installed 1904; rear annex replaced original small Session room wing at rear 1923–24; exterior cleaned and repainted 1972. Unusual example in Alabama of "Georgian Gothick" combining Federal period neoclassical form and detail with pointed windows. 9 sheets (1935, including plans, elevations, sections, details); 4 ext. photos (1934–35), 4 int. photos (1934–35); 2 data pages (1936).

Goodloe, Edward, House. *See* Coons-Steele-Armistead House (AL-356), 406 N. Main St.

Grissom House. *See* Stonecroft (AL-319), 608 E. Fifth St.

House (Colored Barber's House) (AL-351), 306 W. Fifth St. Frame with clapboarding, rectangular (2-bay front), 1 story, gable roof, 1 exterior end chimney, shed porch, probably 1 room. Built ca. 1830; demolished. Reputedly home of popular black barber, Willis, who had large white clientele. 1 ext. photo (1935).

House (John Johnson House) (AL-357), W side of Broad St. in middle of block, approx. 70′ S of Third St. intersection and immediately NE of St. John's Episcopal Church. Brick, approx. 40′ (5 bays first floor, 4 bays above) x 20′ with ell approx. 30′ x 20′, 2 stories (ell 1½ stories), gable roof, 2 exterior end chimneys (main block); 2-room plan. Built ca. 1830; later owned by Cloud, Garmon, and Johnson families; demolished ca. 1940. 2 ext. photos (1934), 1 int. photo (1934).

Houston-Abernathy-Minor House (Minor House) (AL-355), 204 N. Main St. Brick (façade Flemish bond) with partial frame construction at rear, rectangular (3-bay front), 1½ stories over raised basement, gable roof broken at rear to cover extension, 2 exterior end chimneys, high brick stoop with ashlar treads and platform; side-hall plan, basement dining room with herringbone pattern brick floor, 1-room wing on side with porch across front and end elevation, frame shed addition. Built ca. 1825; side wing added ca. 1870; damaged by fire 1974. Notable example of small Federal style cottage. Earliest known owner Nathan Houston; home 1855 to 1895 of Dr. Robert T. Abernathy, physician and editor of *Tuscumbia Constitution*. First house in Tuscumbia with bathroom and electricity. 2 ext. photos (1934), 3 int. photos (1934); 1 data page (1936).

Dependency, forming detached ell at N rear. Brick and frame, rectangular (5 irregular bays), 1 story, gable roof with brick-paved shed porch along S side, 4 end-to-end rooms housing kitchen, laundry, servant room, and smokehouse. 1 ext. photo (1935), 1 int. photo (1935).

Ivy Green (Helen Keller House) (AL-317), 300 W. North Commons (NW corner Keller Lane). Historic house museum. Frame with beaded clapboarding, rectangular (5-bay front), 1½ stories, gable roof, 2 pairs of exterior end chimneys with frame pent between E pair of chimneys, wooden entrance porch; center-hall plan. Early boxwood garden. Built ca. 1820 for David and Mary Fairfax (Moore) Keller from Virginia, grandparents of Helen Keller; later side additions and 3-bay shed porch at front. Acquired and restored by City of Tuscumbia for house museum in 1954 (lean-to on W side removed, porch replaced by smaller covered stoop simulating original); interior heavily damaged by fire on 8 April 1972, including destruction of original stairway; restored with modifications 1972–73. Helen Keller lived here as a child and remembered Ivy Green as her "Rose and Honeysuckle Home"; setting for play and movie *The Miracle Worker*. 2 ext. photos (1934), 1 int. photo (1934); 3 data pages (1937).

Plantation Office. Frame with clapboarding, rectangular (2 bay), gable roof with 1 exterior end chimney; 1-room plan. Built ca. 1870, probably as estate office. "Bridal suite" occupied by Capt. Arthur H. Keller and his second wife, née Kate Adams, and was birthplace of their daughter Helen Keller on 27 June 1880. 1 ext. photo (1934).

Kitchen. Board and batten, rectangular (2 bays), 1 story, gable roof, central chimney. Probably mid-19th C. 1 ext. photo (1935), 3 int. photos (1934–35). *See also* Tebbs (T3-ALA-441245 through 441247).

Johnson, John, House. *See* House (AL-357), Broad St.

Jones-Winston-Rand House (Carl Rand House) (AL-352), 501 E. Third St. (NE corner E. Third and High sts.). Frame with beaded clapboarding, rectangular (5-bay front), 1½ stories over basement, gable roof with dormers on rear slope, 2 exterior end chimneys, modillioned cornice; flanking subordinate gabled 2-bay wings with exterior end chimneys and (originally) inset twin porches across front; center-hall plan, notable Federal period woodwork and Adamesque mantels, basement kitchen and dining area. Built ca. 1832 for Samuel Jones; later owned by Isaac Winston of Belle Mont (AL-388); acquired ca. 1890 by Henry Rand, who added porticoes and enclosed porches of flanking wings. Severely altered 1976 including removal of much original woodwork and louvered blinds. 4 ext. photos (1937), 5 int. photos (1937), 2 photos of antebellum tool collection (1937).

Keller, Helen, House. *See* Ivy Green (AL-317), 300 W. North Commons.

Lindsay, Gov. Robert, House. *See* Christian-Lindsay House (AL-312), U.S. 72.

Locust Hill (John Daniel Rather House) (AL-318), 209 S. Cave St. (E side of Cave St. occupying E portion of block between Sixth and Seventh sts.). Brick (W and S sides Flemish bond), rectangular (5-bay front) with ell, 2 stories, gable roof with brick dentil course, 2 exterior end chimneys (main block) and 1 exteri-

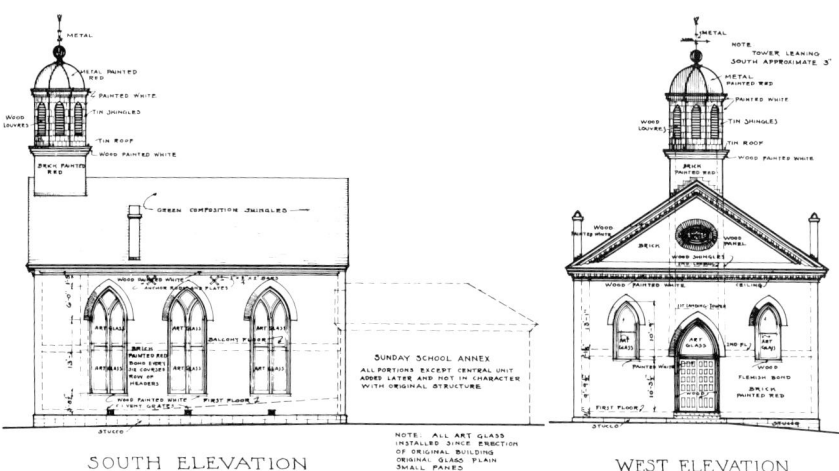

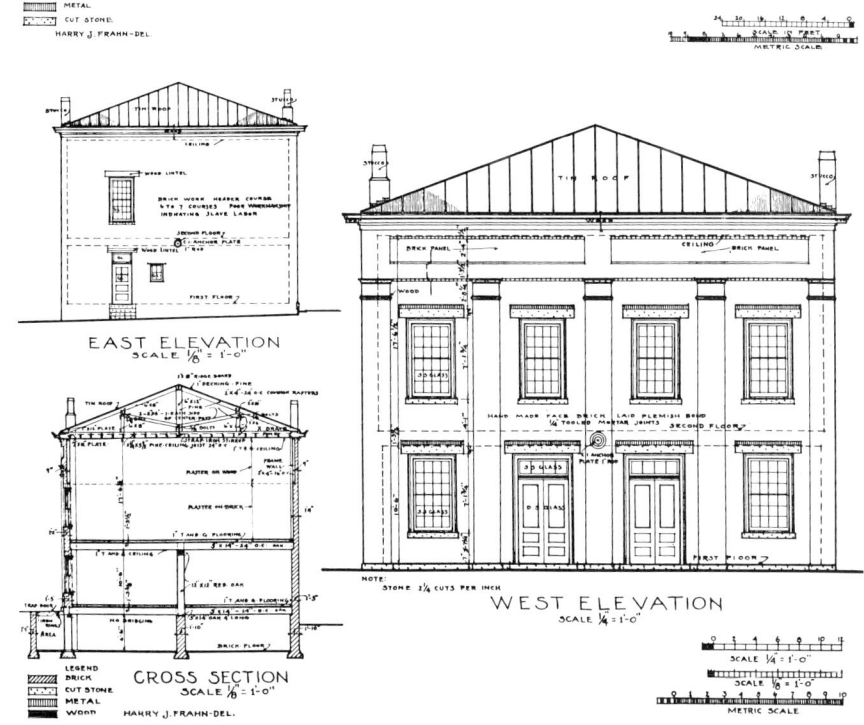

Top: First Presbyterian Church, Tuscumbia (1827–28).
Above: Young's Carriage Shop, Tuscumbia (ca. 1835, demolished 1968).

or end chimney (ell), formerly 3-bay 1-story porch with balustraded deck; center-hall plan, enclosed stair. Built 1823 for William Hooe and Catherine (Washington) Winter, from Prince William County, Virginia; mantels executed by local craftsman Andrew Braden. Headquarters of Gen. Florence N. Cornyn (U.S. Army) in 1863; acquired by Capt. John Taylor Rather in Dec. 1865 and repaired as residence; renovated during 19th C. including replacement of original sash and construction of Eastlake style porch along W (front) and N side and 1-story service wing at SE rear; additional brick, 2-story ell and single-story room built onto NE rear ca. 1900. Notable gardens. Home of Mary Wallace Kirk (1890–1978), author and artist. 2 ext. photos (1934), 1 int. photo (1934). NR.

Minor House. *See* Houston-Abernathy-Minor House (AL-355), 204 N. Main St.

Morgan House. *See* Commercial Building (AL-321), 107 E. Fifth St.

Rand, Dr. R. A., House. *See* Violet Hall (AL-353), 404 W. North Commons.

Rather, John Daniel, House. *See* Locust Hill (AL-318), 209 S. Cave St.

Stine House. *See* Young-Stine House (AL-349), 407 W. Second St.

Stonecroft (Grissom House) (AL-319), 608 E. Fifth St. (SW corner E. Fifth and Lafayette sts.). Frame with clapboarding on ashlar foundation, rectangular (5-bay front) with wing on W side, 2 stories over basement (wing 1 story), gable roof, 2 exterior end chimneys on main block and 1 exterior end chimney on wing, 2-tiered pedimented entrance porticoes with turned colonnettes on N (front) and S sides; center-hall plan. W wing connected at right angle to semi-detached dependency at SW rear. Built ca. 1830 supposedly for James W. Rhea, early Tuscumbia innkeeper. Present doors probably late 19th C.; vacant 1916–43; subsequent renovations include removal of original porticoes and other exterior and interior modifications, demolition of rear dependency and construction in 1967 of new wing, aluminum siding applied in 1972. 2 ext. photos (1934), 4 int. photos (1934–36).

Tennessee Valley Country Club. *See* Christian-Lindsay House (AL-312), U.S. 72.

Violet Hall (Dr. R. A. Rand House) (AL-353), 404 W. North Commons. Frame with clapboarding (rear portion incorporates log construction), rectangular (5-bay front), 2 stories with saltbox-like 1½-story extension across rear, gable roof, originally 4 exterior end chimneys, 1-story entrance porch with balustraded deck; center-hall plan. Built ca. 1825–30; owned in mid-19th C. by Archibald S. Christian. Original porch replaced in late 19th C. by porch with elaborate scroll-cut trim; house reduced to 1½ stories after 1953 fire, covered with asbestos siding. 2 ext. photos (1935), 3 int. photos (1935); 1 data page (1936).

Winston, William, House (AL-316), North Commons (W of Broad St.). Brick (Flemish bond) with ashlar trim, approx. 55′ (5-bay front) × 40′, 2 stories, truncated hipped roof originally terminating in balustraded deck, 4 interior end chimneys, small 1-story tetrastyle porticoes at front, rear, and E side, granite sills and bull's-eye lintels; center-hall plan, continuous spiral stairway from first floor to attic. Begun ca. 1835 for Clark T. Barton, Tuscumbia merchant; acquired and completed by William and Judith Winston ca. 1840. Rooftop deck destroyed and house damaged by tornado on 22 Nov. 1874; reconditioned in 1950, after long abandonment, as part of Deshler High School complex. 2 ext. photos (1934).

Young's Carriage Shop (Carriage Factory) (AL-315), SE corner Main and E. Fourth sts. Brick on ashlar foundation, 44′4″ (4-bay front) × 60′5″, 2 stories with basement, hipped roof, W and N elevations articulated by piered pilasters with astragal molding and caps carrying paneled brick frieze; open plan. Built ca. 1835 for Isaac E. Young, carriage-maker from Washington, D.C. Used as opera house and post office ca. 1880–97; 1897–1967 housed Helen Keller Library; demolished 1968 to make way for bank. 4 sheets (1935, including plans, elevations, section, details); 3 ext. photos (1934–35); 2 data pages (1936).

Young-Stine House (Stine House) (AL-349), 407 W. Second St. Frame with clapboarding, rectangular (2-bay front) with 2-bay wing on W side, 2 stories (wing 1 story), gable roof, 1 exterior end chimney (main block), gabled entrance porch; side-

hall plan; stair risers, parlor mantel, and interior doors formerly grained. Built 1835 for Isaac E. Young, Tuscumbia carriage-maker; William Smoot (brother-in-law of Young), builder. Rear addition made between 1852 and 1871 (removed 1933); renovated ca. 1945, including replacement of clapboarding and insertion of additional window bay on front, construction of 2-story rear addition and 1-story E wing. 3 ext. photos (1934–35), 3 int. photos (1935); 3 data pages (1937).
Smokehouse. Brick, square (1 bay), 1 story, hipped roof. Built between 1852 and 1864; demolished. 1 ext. photo (1935).

Tuscumbia Vicinity

Belmont (AL-388). *Under Spring Valley Vicinity, see* Belle Mont.

Goodloe, Col. John Calvin, House (AL-310). *See Cherokee Vicinity.*

Thornton, Henry P., House (AL-388). *Under Spring Valley Vicinity, see* Belle Mont.

Vinson, Drury, House (AL-381). *See Leighton Vicinity.*

Winston, Anthony, House (AL-316A). *See Sheffield.*

CRENSHAW COUNTY

Rutledge

Gravehouses (AL-689-D), Rutledge cemetery, N side of Ala. 10, approx. 0.4 mi. W of U.S. 331 intersection (just E of Rutledge Primitive Baptist Church). Roofed-over wooden shelters enclosed by fence of wooden palings; slender chamfered supports carry roof, with scalloped fascia beneath eaves. Built late 19th C.; destroyed ca. 1955. Construction of such shelters or gravehouses over family burial plots or individual graves was a popular practice in rural Alabama during late 19th and early 20th C. 2 photos (1935).

DALLAS COUNTY

Cahaba

Barker-Kirkpatrick House (Kirkpatrick House) (AL-727), N end of Oak St. (W side), just N of Seventh North St. intersection on original Cahaba plat. Brick, rectangular (5-bay front), 2 stories, full-height tetrastyle portico with second-floor porch and balustraded roof deck, similar 1-bay distyle portico at rear, roof concealed by paneled brick parapet and surmounted by tall octagonal cupola with arched windows and pyramidal roof terminating in urn-like finial, deeply recessed main doorway; center-hall plan, lavish plasterwork in parlor with triple frieze-band employing palmette, anthemion, and grapeleaf motifs enriched by egg-and-dart moldings. Frame 1-story service rooms at each rear corner, also brick 2-story dependency to SW rear. Built 1857 for "Shoestring" Barker; burned ca. 1935 (dependency survives in altered condition as private residence). Eclectic mixture of Greek Revival and post–Greek Revival elements. Model stockfarm in early 1900s under ownership of Clifton Kirkpatrick. 3 ext. photos (1934), 3 int. photos (1934).

Bell House. *See* Fambro-Troy House (AL-731), First North and Oak sts.

Crocheron-Mathews House (AL-728), E end of Second North St. (N side) on original plat of Cahaba (W bank of Cahaba River at point of confluence with Alabama River). Brick, 5-bay E front, 2 stories, hipped roof, full-height pedimented distyle Ionic entrance portico with balcony on E façade, 5-column veranda along N side (overlooking river) with unplastered Doric columns carrying full-length upper porch; probably center-hall plan. Built ca. 1850 for Henry Crocheron, a merchant from New York; destroyed ca. 1900. Home of Col. Thomas Mathews in April 1865 when Union and Confederate commanders met here to discuss prisoner exchange at end of Civil War. 1 ext. photocopy (ca. 1890), 1 photo of ruins (1934, columns of N veranda only).

Duke, Captain, House. *See* House (AL-729), near Alabama River.

Evans, Grace, House. *See* House (AL-729), near Alabama River.

Fambro-Troy House (Bell House) (AL-731), SE corner First North and Oak sts. on original plat of Cahaba. Frame with clapboarding, rectangular (5-bay front) with ell along Oak St. and offset rear service wing, 1 story on high brick piers (partially enclosed as raised basement), gable roof, 1-bay gabled entrance porches on N (front) and W sides; center-hall plan. Artesian well at SW rear. Built ca. 1845 for Judge William W. Fambro; later home of Col. Daniel Troy; ruinous in 1975. 2 ext. photos (1934), 1 int. photo (1934), 1 photo of well (1934).

First State Capitol Marker (AL-725), in middle of unmarked road (formerly Capitol Ave. at Vine St. on original Cahaba plat). Rough-hewn granite monument approx. 3'6" wide × 7'0" high on concrete base. Erected 1919 by Alabama Centennial Commission to commemorate Cahaba ("Cahawba") as first state capital 1818–26. SW of marker stood brick rectangular (approx. 58' × 43') 2-story statehouse from 1820 until its collapse on 26 March 1833. 1 photo (1934).

Gayle, Col. Rees D., House (AL-732), SE corner of Oak and First South sts. on original plat of Cahaba. Frame with clapboarding, rectangular (4 irregular bays across front), 2 stories, gable roof, central chimney, 2-tiered shed porch with stairway to second floor; probably 2-room plan. Built ca. 1835; destroyed ca. 1940. 1 ext. photo (1934).

House (Captain Duke House, Grace Evans House) (AL-729), near Alabama River, possibly at E end of Third South St. (N side) on original Cahaba plat; exact location undetermined. Frame with clapboarding, probably rectangular (6 bays first floor, 4 bays second floor), 2 stories, gable roof, central chimney, 2-tiered gabled porch with lattice balustrade upstairs and lattice sunscreens below, double entrance; probably 2-room plan. Built early 19th C.; destroyed by flood ca. 1940. 1 ext. photo (1934).

Kirkpatrick House. *See* Barker-Kirkpatrick House (AL-727), Oak St.

Methodist Church (AL-726), E side of Walnut St. between Second South and Third South sts. on original Cahaba plat. Brick, 40'1" × 60'1", gable roof with pedimented front pierced by louvered lunette, recessed 3-bay porch with modified Doric pillars sheltering double entrance doors, 3-stage tower with octagonal cupola, brick dentil course; open interior plan, 2 aisles, simple Greek Revival style interior woodwork including notable pulpit with flanking lampstands, pulpit area enclosed by Communion rail terminating in scrolled volutes, slave gallery at rear. Built 1849–50; burned 1954. 6 sheets (1936, including plans, elevations, section, details); 1 ext. photo (1934), 2 int. photos (1934); 2 data pages (1936).

St. Luke's Episcopal Church (AL-734). *See Martin Vicinity.*

Martin Vicinity

St. Luke's Episcopal Church (AL-734), W side Co. 21, approx. 0.8 mi. N of junction with Ala. 22; 0.2 mi. N of L&N Railroad crossing at Martin community, formerly Martins Station, approx. 3 mi. W of Orrville; originally located in Cahaba, at SE corner of Pine and First North sts. on original plat. Frame with board and batten, nave (27'2" × 58'2") and chancel (19'3" × 17'8" deep) with square vestry chamber on S side of chancel and baptistry off nave to N, originally tower and spire at NW corner, also projecting entrance porch, steeply pitched roof, wooden buttresses, lancet windows with double lancets along side walls of nave; open plan with center aisle, triple lancet window above altar, slave gallery at rear. Completed 1854; plan adapted from Richard Upjohn's *Rural Architecture*. Building modified 1878 (including removal of tower, gallery, and stained glass windows) when moved to Martins Station; badly deteriorated in 1983. One of more

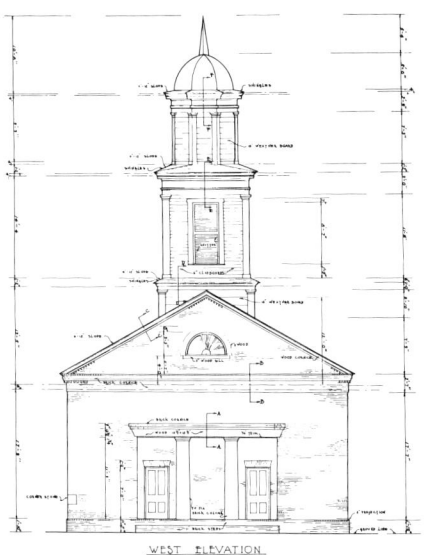
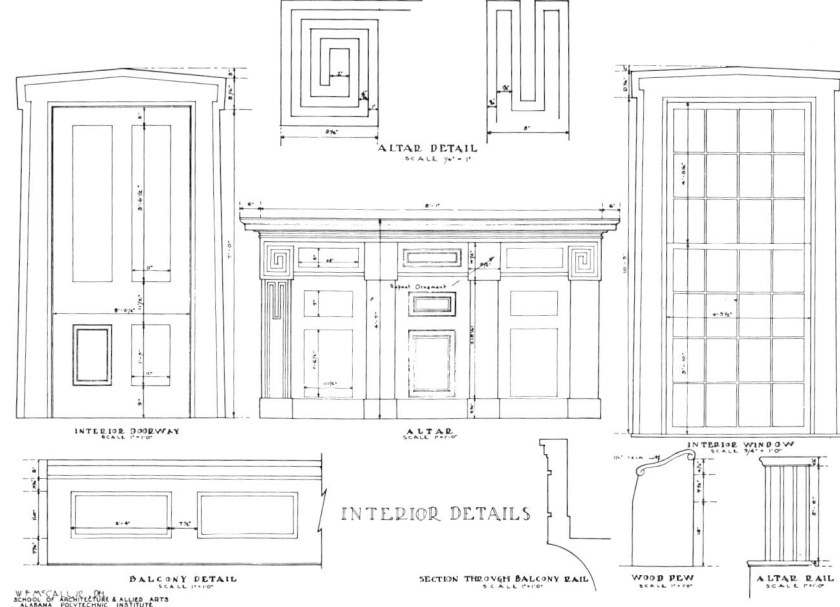

Methodist Church, Cahaba (1849–50, burned 1954).

elaborate board-and-batten Gothic Revival churches built in Alabama during 1850s. 6 sheets (1936, including plan, elevations, sections, details); 2 ext. photos (1934), 2 int. photos (1934); 5 data pages (1936). NR.

Martins Station.

See Martin Vicinity.

Orrville

Craig-Wilson House (AL-738), N side of Co. 2, approx. 0.1 mi. SE of intersection with Ala. 22 at Orrville. Frame with clapboarding, rectangular (5-bay front) with slightly offset ell, 1½ stories, gable roof with pedimented dormers, 4 exterior end chimneys, Victorian style porch across front; center-hall plan. Frame rectangular smokehouse at NE rear. Built ca. 1845; porch ca. 1900. 1 ext. photo (1934).

Dunaway, Ben Ellis, House. *See Orrville Male Academy* (AL-737), Ala. 22.

Kelly-Bland-Ward House (AL-755). *See Orrville Vicinity.*

Milhous-Albritton House (Mill-Albritton House) (AL-736), S side of Ala. 22, approx. 0.5 mi. W of intersection with Co. 33 at Orrville. Frame with clapboarding, rectangular (5-bay front), 2 stories, gable roof extending over full-height hexastyle portico with freestanding octagonal columns on brick piers sheltering balustraded deck-type porch and small balcony over main doorway, 4 exterior end chimneys, French doors onto portico; center-hall plan. Built ca. 1860. 1 ext. photo (1934).

Mill-Albritton House. *See Milhous-Albritton House* (AL-736), Ala. 22.

Orrville Male Academy (Ben Ellis Dunaway House) (AL-737), approx. 0.1 mi. S of Ala. 22 on S side of paved road 0.2 mi. W of intersection with Co. 33. Frame with clapboarding, rectangular (5-bay front) with shed extension at rear, 2 stories, gable roof, full-height pedimented 3-bay tetrastyle portico composed of 2 fluted Ionic columns set between paneled antae, balcony over doorway, denticulated cornice; center-hall plan. Built 1850 as boys' academy; Willis H. Green, contractor. Converted to residential use in 1880 by Benjamin F. Ellis; rear addition and interior renovations in 1923; aluminum siding added. 2 ext. photos (1934), 1 int. photo (1934).

Smith-Sutton House (AL-735), S side of Ala. 22, approx. 0.4 mi. W of intersection with Co. 33 at Orrville. Frame with clapboarding, rectangular (5-bay front), 2 stories, gable roof with pedimented gable ends, 2 interior chimneys, full-height pedimented entrance portico composed of 2 paneled rectangular columns, balcony at upper level; center-hall plan, enclosed stairway. Built ca. 1850. 1 ext. photo (1934).

Orrville Vicinity

Bland-Chesnut House (AL-749), approx. 0.2 mi. due E of confluence of Bogue Chitto and Tatum creeks; 1.0 mi. W of Co. 11/Co. 170 intersection on N side of unpaved Co. 170, approx. 1.0 mi. N of junction with Ala. 22, just W of Orrville. Frame with clapboarding, rectangular (5 bays below, 4 bays above), 2 stories with 1-story shed extension across rear, gable roof, 2 pairs of exterior end chimneys, 1-story balustraded shed porch across front with paneled rectangular columns and full entablature, denticulated cornice with molded cornice return; hall-and-parlor plan with enclosed stair between rooms. Built ca. 1840, possibly for Ezra Bland. 20th-C. addition at E rear. Good example of refined I house with sheds. 3 ext. photos (1934), 2 int. photos (1934).

Cochran House. *See* Cochran-Crumpton House (AL-750), Co. 21.

Cochran-Crumpton House (Cochran House, McCreary House, Crumptonia) (AL-750), S side of Co. 21, approx. 6.7 mi. S of intersection with Ala. 22, in Crumpton community (approx. 7 mi. SW of Orrville). Frame with clapboarding, rectangular (5-bay front) with small hipped-roof wing on W side, 2 stories (wing 1 story), gable roof with pedimented gable ends, 2 interior chimneys, full-height pedimented 3-bay tetrastyle portico with paneled square columns and large upstairs balcony with turned balusters, corner pilasters, 1-story shed porch across rear; center-hall plan. Frame rectangular barn SW of house. Built ca. 1855 for Claudius M. Cochran; interior renovations in 1920, including installation of Colonial Revival style wainscoting, ceiling beams, and mantelpieces in SW parlor. 3 ext. photos (1934), 1 int. photo (1934).

Crumptonia. *See* Cochran-Crumpton House (AL-750), Co. 21.

Kelly-Bland-Ward House (AL-755), W side of unmarked dirt road, approx. 0.6 mi. S of junction with Co. 2 near Whites Bluff community; approx. 5.6 mi. SE of junction of Co. 2 and Ala. 22 at Orrville. Frame with clapboarding, rectangular (5-bay front), 2 stories, gable roof, 4 exterior end chimneys, full-height pedimented distyle Doric entrance portico projecting over 1-story shed porch across front with Doric colonnettes resting on brick piers (upstairs balcony inset into porch beneath center portico), also 1-story porches along N side and across rear; center-hall plan. Frame rectangular kitchen dependency connected to rear porch by covered way. Built ca. 1855; demolished 1945. 2 ext. photos (1934), 1 int. photo (1934), 1 photo of kitchen fireplace (1934).

McCreary House. *See* Cochran-Crumpton House (AL-750), Co. 21.

McMillan, Lewis, House (AL-752), S side of Co. 31 overlooking Alabama River at Pinebelt community; approx. 3 mi. E of confluence of Bogue Chitto Creek with Alabama River. Frame with clapboarding, rectangular (5-bay front), 2 stories, gable roof with pedimented gable ends, 4 interior end chimneys, full-height pedimented 3-bay tetrastyle portico on N front with paneled square columns and large balcony with ornate turned balusters, similar full-length hexastyle portico on S (river) front, full entablature; center-hall plan. Built 1858; restored 1978–79 after long period of abandonment. 2 ext. photos (1934).

Molett Houses (AL-753), S side of unmarked dirt road, approx. 7.7 mi. SE of intersection of Co. 33 and Co. 31 E of Pinebelt community; approx. 0.4 mi. due N of Alabama River in Molette's Bend about 13 mi. SE of Orrville. Two separate structures, both frame with clapboarding. Older structure: rectangular (irregular bays), 2 stories, gable roof, 2 exterior end chimneys, shed front porch with chamfered posts and connecting balustrade across S; rear shed extension with loggia between; center-hall plan. Later structure situated at right angle to earlier one: rectangular (5-bay front), 1 story, gable roof extending over full-length balustraded porch with bracketed eaves; center-hall plan. Ruinous greenhouse at side. First structure built ca. 1835 as plantation residence for William Page Molett, who emigrated in 1817 from Beaufort District, S.C., to Dallas County. Second structure (ca. 1860) reputedly built partially with materials salvaged from burned home erected nearby in 1840s by Molett's son, John Ulmer Molett. Second dwelling moved 0.2 mi. S and extensively altered in 1975 as retirement house. Older structure one of earliest frame dwellings in central Alabama. 2 ext. photos (1934, one of each structure).

Moseley-Seale House (Seale House) (AL-751), on W side of Co. 083, approx. 0.3 mi. S of Co. 33 at Tasso community; 3.1 mi. SE of junction of Co. 33 and Co. 31 at Five Points community, or about 9 mi. S/SE of Orrville. Frame with clapboarding, rectangular (5-bay front), 2 stories, gable roof, 4 exterior end chimneys, full-height pedimented tetrastyle entrance portico with paneled square columns and large balcony with turned balusters, corner pilasters; center-hall plan, marbleized mantel in parlor. Built 1857 for Lewis B. Moseley. Chimney tops destroyed by 1974 tornado; restored 1974–75, including kitchen addition at rear. 1 ext. photo (1934), 2 int. photos (1934).

Seale House. *See* Moseley-Seale House (AL-751), unmarked road off Co. 33.

Selma

Blake, Samuel R., House (Harvey L. McKee House) (AL-701), 911 Mabry St. Brick, rectangular (3-bay front) with ell, 1 story, shallow gable roof with cross-gable above middle bay and widely overhanging eaves, small latticed entrance porch, segmentally arched doors and windows; center-hall plan. Built ca. 1860; later rear additions. One of earliest extant Victorian style structures in Selma. 2 ext. photos (1934), 3 int. photos (1934–35). *See also* FBJ (J7-ALA-1207).

Burns-Bell House (AL-707), 412 Lauderdale St. Frame with clapboarding, main block rectangular (3-bay front) with rear wing, 2 stories, gable roof, tall pedimented entrance portico composed of slender paired wooden columns flanking main doorway, balcony above, portico flanked by 1-story projecting bays each surmounted by balustraded deck with cantilevered canopied roof, bracketed cornice; center-hall plan. Built ca. 1860–65; extensive rear additions. 1 ext. photo (1934).

Byrd-Pitts House (L. B. Pitts House) (AL-708), 504 Broad St. Frame, rectangular (3-bay front with 2-bay setback) plus offset rear wing, 2 stories (wing 1 story), hipped roof breaking into shallow 3-bay pediment over full-height hexastyle portico composed of attenuated paneled square columns, balcony above doorway at reentrant angle of setback façade, flanking triple windows, bracketed cornice; center-hall plan. Built ca. 1870 for Judge William McKendree Byrd (1819–74), associate justice of State Supreme Court; demolished 1958. 2 ext. photos (1934–35, 1 photo defective).

Dawson-Vaughan House (AL-711), 704 Tremont St. (NE corner Tremont and Third sts.). Frame with shiplap siding, approx. 55′ (5-bay front) × 45′ plus shed addition across rear, 2 stories, hipped roof breaking into shallow gable over front middle bay, ornate full-length 1-story porch with mansard roof and iron cresting enclosing second-floor deck, heavily carved double-leaf doorway with etched glass transom; center-hall plan, curving stairway (also rear service stair), acanthus-leaf plaster medallions, marble mantels. Reputedly built ca. 1842 for Col. John Marks with materials from Cahaba; extensively altered in Victorian style ca. 1865–70 for Nathaniel H. R. Dawson (1829–95), lawyer, Confederate officer, and U.S. Commissioner of Education under Pres. Grover Cleveland. Demolished 1960; front door incorporated into new house built on same site. Mrs. Dawson (née Elodie Todd) was half sister of Mary Todd Lincoln. 2 ext. photos (1934), 9 int. photos (1934–35).

First Christian Church Property. *See* House (AL-710), 207 Franklin St.

Franklin, H. F., House. *See* House (AL-704), 819 Jeff Davis Ave.

House (C. Jones House) (AL-706), 433 Lauderdale Ave. Frame with clapboarding, rectangular (3-bay front) with ell, 1 story, gable roof, 2 interior end chimneys (main block), 3-bay porch across front composed of coupled Doric colonnettes; center-hall plan. Built ca. 1860; porch probably ca. 1900; demolished 1962. 2 ext. photos (1934).

House (Dr. Kirkpatrick House) (AL-709), 601 Washington St. (NW corner Washington St. and Furniss Ave.). Raised cottage, brick with stucco, L-shaped (3-bay E front, 4-bay S front), 1 story over full ground floor, shallow hipped roof, balustraded porch raised on brick piers across E and S fronts with lattice-enclosed stairway from ground level at N end, bracketed cornice; center-hall plan (E to W). Built ca. 1860; later rear additions resulting in overall rectangular shape, W end bay of S porch enclosed. 2 ext. photos (1934–35), 1 int. photo (1935).

House (First Christian Church Property) (AL-710), 207 Franklin St. Frame with clapboarding, rectangular (5-bay front), 2 stories, hipped roof, full-height pedimented 3-bay tetrastyle Doric portico with full-length balcony; center-hall plan. Built ca. 1855; demolished ca. 1960. 1 ext. photo (1934).

House (H. F. Franklin House) (AL-704), 819 Jeff Davis Ave. (NW corner Jeff Davis Ave. and Nance St., which is an extension of Church St.). Frame with clapboarding (board-and-batten rear addition), 2 stories, main block basically narrow rectangle (5-bay front) with advanced 1-bay pedimented center pavilion, also irregularly shaped rear wings, 2 stories, gable roof, 1-story porch across front with trellis supports, bracketed and denticulated cornice, projecting semioctagonal 1-story end bays surmounted by balustraded porches; center hall with flanking parlors. Built ca. 1860 (portion of rear believed to be early 19th C.); demolished 1960. One of earliest Victorian style dwellings in Selma. 2 ext. photos (1934), 3 int. photos (1934).

Jones, C., House. *See* House (AL-706), 433 Lauderdale Ave.

King-Welch House (AL-703), 607 Union St. (NW corner Union St. and Furniss Ave.). Frame with clapboarding, square (5-bay front) with narrow 1-story service wing on N side, 2 stories, truncated hipped roof terminating in monitor, full-height 3-bay tetrastyle Doric portico with full-length balcony, corner pilasters; center-hall plan. Frame rectangular 1-story kitchen dependency to N linked to service wing by short latticed covered way. Built 1853 for William B. King. Used as hospital for Union wounded after Battle of Selma (2 April 1865). 1 ext. photo (1934). *See also* FBJ (J7-ALA-1208 through 1211).

Kirkpatrick, Dr., House. *See* House (AL-709), 601 Washington St.

Mabry-Jones House (AL-705), 629 Tremont St. (SW corner Tremont and McLeod sts.). Brick, rectangular (3-bay front) with large 2-bay recessed side wing, gable roof, temple-type façade with pedimented tetrastyle Doric portico, 3-bay balcony at upper level with Chippendale balustrade, 1-story cast-iron porch on wing, main block pilastered; side-hall plan. Lawn enclosed by mid-19th-C. fence with stuccoed brick piers and wooden palings; notable gardens. Built 1849 for Dr. Albert Gallatin Mabry; side wing later; 20th-C. rear additions. Mabry (1810–74) was instrumental in establishment of state mental hospital and organization of state medical association (1849). Later home of Lt. Catesby ap R. Jones (1821–77), commander of Confederate ironclad *Virginia* (formerly the *Merrimac*) in renowned battle with *Monitor* on 9 March 1862, and afterward commandant of Confederate naval gun foundry and ordnance works at Selma. 1 ext. photo (1934), 4 int. photos (1934–35). *See also* FBJ (J7-ALA-1184).

McKee, Harvey L., House. *See* Blake, Samuel R., House (AL-701), 911 Mabry St.

Marks-Plattenburg House (Plattenburg House) (AL-702), 1009 N. Lapsley St. (NW corner Lapsley St. and Jeff Davis Ave.). Brick, rectangular (5-bay S front, 3-bay E front) with ell at NW rear, 2 stories, shallow hipped roof, full-height pedimented tetrastyle Doric portico with upper balconies on both S and E fronts (S portico pedimented), 3-bay shed porch at rear (W) flanked by 1-story brick service rooms, denticulated cornice; center-hall plan with side hall to E portico. Built 1860 for Col. John Marks; demolished 1960. Four of columns subsequently incorporated into portico of Shiloh Baptist Church, Sardis (S of Selma). 5 ext. photos (1934–35), 3 int. photos 1934–35). *See also* FBJ (J7-ALA-1185 and 1186).

Morgan, Sen. John T., House. *See* Wetmore-Morgan-Agee House (AL-712), 719 Tremont St.

Morgan-Agee House. *See* Wetmore-Morgan-Agee House (AL-712), 719 Tremont St.

Pitts, L. B., House. *See* Byrd-Pitts House (AL-708), 504 Broad St.

Plattenburg House. *See* Marks-Plattenburg House (AL-702), 1009 N. Lapsley St.

St. James Hotel (AL-713), 1200 Water Ave. (SE corner Water Ave. and Washington St.). Brick with stucco scored to simulate ashlar, main block basically rectangular with large rectangular rear wing, 3 stories (wing 1 story over cellars set into slope toward river), gable roof with stepped parapets at each end, 4 interior end chimneys, ornate 2-tiered cast-iron gallery along front (N) and W side; first floor used for commercial purposes with double-leaf doors opening onto sidewalk, second floor bisected by longitudinal hall with center stairhall. Reputedly built ca. 1837 as Brantley Hotel; renovated and enlarged 1848 as Planters Hotel, 1860 as Troupe House; later warehouse; most of ironwork stripped after 1937. 9 ext. photos (1937), 2 int. photos (1937); also 2 views of adjacent commercial buildings from across Alabama River (1937).

Sturdivant Hall (Watts-Parkman-Gillman House) (AL-700), 713 Mabry St. House museum. Brick covered with stucco; rectangular (5-bay front), 2 stories, shallow hipped roof with square 2-bay cupola, giant order hexastyle Corinthian portico sheltering full-length upper balcony enclosed by ornate cast-iron balustrade, recessed doorway with flanking engaged Corinthian colonnettes, 3-bay modified Doric loggia at rear with upper gallery reached by outside stairway, full entablature with denticulated cornice, cast-iron porch on S side and cantilevered cast-iron balcony on corresponding S side of house; modified center-hall plan with side hall, double drawing room with columnar screen and sliding doors, ornamental plaster frieze with laurel wreath motif and other classical elements, ornamental centerpieces, marble mantels; main hall formerly embellished with trompe l'oeil fresco painting; door surrounds recall designs in Samuel Sloan's *Model Architect* (1852); corkscrew stairway to rooftop observatory. Dependencies facing courtyard at rear include kitchen, servants' quarters, and smokehouse. Built ca. 1853–55 for Edward T. Watts; construction supervised by Thomas Helm Lee, Selma master builder. Fresco work probably added in 1870s. House acquired 1957 by City of Selma through bequest from Robert D. Sturdivant; subsequently renovated and named Sturdivant Hall. Post-1957 changes included installation of gray and white marble floor in hallway (Earl Hart Miller of Natchez, consultant). One of Alabama's most sophisticated expressions of Greek Revival domestic architecture. 5 ext. photos (1934), 4 int. photos (1934), 1 photo of smokehouse (1935). NR. *See also* FBJ (J7-ALA-1166 through 1177).

Watts-Parkman-Gillman House. *See* Sturdivant Hall (AL-700), 713 Mabry St.

Wetmore-Morgan-Agee House (Morgan-Agee House, Sen. John T. Morgan House) (AL-712), 719 Tremont St. Open to public. Frame with clapboarding, rectangular (3 bays first floor, 5 bays second floor) with central rear wing, gable roof breaking into steeply pedimented cross-gable above middle bay of porch, 2-tiered porch across front with paneled square piers and wheatsheaf balustrade at upper level, projecting entrance bay with flanking floor-length windows; center-hall plan, slightly curved reverse-flight stair with landing. Frame rectangular servant house at rear, later renovated as garage. Built 1859 for Thomas Badger Wetmore; later additions flanking rear wing; acquired 1972 by Alabama Historical Commission for partial restoration and adaptive use. Wetmore was a lawyer and the Confederate provost marshal of Selma during Civil War. Home in late 19th C. of John T. Morgan (1824–1907), Confederate general, later U.S. senator instrumental in American commitment to Panama Canal project. 2 ext. photos (1935), 2 int. photos (1934), 1 ext. photo of dependency (1935). NR.

Selma Vicinity

Harrison-Hunter-Harper House (Dr. Harper House, The Oaks) (AL-754), approx. 0.2 mi. NW of junction of Ala. 219 (Land Line Rd.) and Co. 344, at end of private lane. Frame with clapboarding, rectangular (5-bay front), 2½ stories, gable roof with pedimented (board-and-batten) gable ends, 4 interior end chimneys, full-height hexastyle portico across front with paneled square columns and full-length balcony enclosed by wheatsheaf balustrade, portico carries entablature with denticulated cornice, 1-story shed porch across rear; center-hall plan. Semidetached frame rectangular 1-story wing at SW rear. Built ca. 1850 for Dr. Kirkland Harrison. 2 ext. photos (1934), 4 int. photos (1934).

Kenan House (AL-739), W side of Co. 37 (Summerfield Rd.), approx. 2.0 mi. N of intersection with U.S. 80. Frame with clapboarding, temple-with-wings composition with 2-story (3-bay) central pavilion flanked by 1-story (2-bay) symmetrical wings, full-height pedimented tetrastyle Doric portico with full-length balcony; transverse entrance hall with parlor behind, main doorway and interior woodwork probably adapted from Asher Benjamin; frame dependencies. Built ca. 1840, possibly for Dr. Algernon Jeffries.

Overall design may derive in part from Minard Lafever's *Modern Builder's Guide* (1833 edition). Acquired 1854 by Mrs. Mary Rand Kenan and still owned by descendants in 1978. N side addition 1900, rear additions 1936, aluminum siding applied 1969. 4 ext. photos (1934–36), 6 int. photos (1934–36).

Smokehouse, W of house. Frame, rectangular (1 bay), gable roof. Built mid-19th C. 1 ext. photo (1936), 1 int. photo (1936).

See also FBJ (J7-ALA-1179 through 1183).

Summerfield

Bank Building (AL-757), E side of Main St., one block N of College St. intersection. Brick, rectangular (3-bay front, 4 irregular bays along side), gable roof with raked parapet at each end, corbeled brick cornice with brick dentil course. Built 1843; drastically altered ca. 1955 for residential use (including removal of brick gable ends and cornice, gutting of interior). 1 ext. photo (1934).

Blacksmith Shop (AL-763), NE corner Centenary and Main sts. Brick, rectangular (3-bay front), 1 story, shallow hipped roof, sawtooth brick cornice, large double door at center, flanking oblong windows with horizontally hung batten shutters. Built ca. 1850 for a Mr. Johnston who invented an improved plow. Possibly a stable originally; later abandoned and destroyed ca. 1950 through neglect. 1 ext. photo (1936).

Boys' Methodist College. *See* Centenary Institute, Boys' Dormitory (AL-746); *see also* various other listings under Centenary Institute.

Centenary Institute, Boys' Dormitory (AL-746), NE corner Centenary and Main sts. Brick (Flemish bond), rectangular (6-bay front), 2 stories, gable roof, pedimented gable ends with lunettes. Built ca. 1842; abandoned and finally demolished 1948. 1 ext. photo (1934), 1 int. photo (1934).

Centenary Institute, Dr. Hudson Building (AL-742), E side of College St. about 2 blocks SE of intersection with Main St. Frame with clapboarding, rectangular (5-bay front), 1½ stories, gable roof with pedimented gable ends, 4 interior end chimneys, small cantilevered roof over entrance stoop, porch across rear; center-hall plan. Built ca. 1855; burned 1965. 2 ext. photos (1934), 1 int. photo (1934).

Centenary Institute, Dr. Jackson Building (AL-743), SE of intersection of Main and College sts. Frame with clapboarding, rectangular (6 irregular bays), 1 story, gable roof, shed porch across front, lean-to at rear; asymmetrically placed center passage (possibly open originally). Probably built early 19th C.; original and subsequent use unknown; destroyed. 1 ext. photo (1934), 1 int. photo (n.d.).

Centenary Institute, Main Building (AL-741), SE of intersection of Main and College sts. Brick with stucco scored to simulate ashlar, overall dimensions approx. 150′ (13-bay front) × 46′ plus slightly later setback wing on N side (approx. 50′ × 38′ with 5-bay front), 2 stories, gable roof with raked end parapets, large octagonal cupola with dome, recessed Doric portico with full-length upper gallery, flanking 3-bay gabled end pavilions. Built ca. 1842–43 to house Methodist educational institution chartered in 1841; after closing of school in 1886, housed Methodist Orphans' Home of Alabama Conference from 1890 to 1911; eventually abandoned and burned in summer of 1935. 2 ext. photos (1934).

Centenary Institute, Music Building (AL-740), N side of former circular drive in front of Main Building (1 of 2 identical structures situated to N and S of drive). Frame with shiplap siding, 31′0″ (3-bay front) × 51′6″, 1 story, hipped roof extending over balustraded porch with 4 paneled square columns, arched central doorway and windows, bracketed cornice; 1-room plan. Built ca. 1860–65; companion structure (destroyed before 1934) was Fine Arts Building; demolished 1938. 5 sheets (1936, including plot plan, plan, elevations, details); 3 ext. photos (1934).

Childers-Tate House (AL-730), S side of Centenary St., approx. 0.4 mi. W of intersection with Co. 37. Frame with clapboarding, rectangular (5-bay front), 2 stories, gable roof, 2 exterior end chimneys, full-length shed extension across front (N) with end rooms flanking 3-bay porch; open center passage on first floor. Built ca. 1825–30 for George Childers (1792–1853) from Washington County, Ga.; passage later enclosed, early 20th-C. addition to W side; covered with asbestos siding ca. 1950. Childers was original trustee of Centenary Institute. 1 ext. photo (1934).

Dr. Hudson Building, Summerfield College. *See* Centenary Institute, Dr. Hudson Building (AL-742), College St.

Dr. Jackson Building, Summerfield College. *See* Centenary Institute, Dr. Jackson Building (AL-743), Main and College sts.

King House. *See* Mitchell-King House (AL-758), Centenary St.

Main Building, Summerfield College. *See* Centenary Institute, Main Building (AL-741), Main and College sts.

Methodist Church (AL-748), E side of College St., one block E of Main St. Frame with clapboarding, 41'0" (3-bay front) X 61'4" (5 bays deep), gable roof with pedimented façade, battered 2-stage louvered belfry, middle (entrance) bay divided into 2 single-leaf doors; open interior plan, 2 aisles with center block of pews divided down middle. Built 1844–45 for Methodist Episcopal congregation. 1 ext. photo (1934).

Mitchell-King House (King House) (AL-758), N side Centenary St., approx. 0.2 mi. W of Co. 37 intersection. Frame with clapboarding on high brick piers, main block rectangular flanked by offset advanced (1-bay) gabled end pavilions forming forecourt, 3-bay balustraded porch (with pedimented middle bay) across front of main block, porch enclosed by louvered shutters; center-hall plan. Built ca. 1845 for Archelus Hughes Mitchell; burned 1936. Mitchell (1807–1903) was Methodist minister and first president of Centenary Institute. 1 ext. photo (1934).

Moore-Hudson House (Hudson House) (AL-744), W side of Co. 37, 1 block N of intersection with College St. Frame with clapboarding, rectangular (5-bay front) with parallel rear wings, 1 story, hipped roof, 4 interior end chimneys, pedimented tetrastyle Doric entrance portico; center-hall plan. Built ca. 1845 for Dr. Clement Billingslea Moore; original court between wings at rear later enclosed as addition to house. 1 ext. photo (1934).

Music Building, Summerfield College. *See* Centenary Institute, Music Building (AL-740).

Sturdivant-Moore-Hartley House (AL-745), SW corner Centenary and Main sts. Frame with clapboarding, rectangular (5-bay front) with long (5-bay) ell, 2 stories, gable roof, 2 exterior end chimneys (main block), 1 interior chimney (ell), 2-tiered pedimented Tuscan entrance portico with louvered lunette in tympanum, fanlight doorways above and below, modillioned cornice, L-shaped shed extension and later offset dependency at rear, small porch on side; center-hall plan with side passage and secondary stair in ell, unplastered main hall, paneled dado in parlor. Also old wellhouse. Built ca. 1838 for Robert Sturdivant (1789–1856), who came to Dallas County from Hancock County, Ga. Inner colonnettes of portico removed after 1934. Rare survival in Dallas County of Federal style dwelling. 5 ext. photos (1934–36), 2 int. photos (1934–36), 1 photo of wellhouse (1936).

Summerfield College. *See* various listings under Centenary Institute.

Swift-Moore-Cottingham House (AL-747), N side Persimmon St., half a block from intersection with Centenary St. Frame with clapboarding, rectangular (5-bay front) with ell, 2 stories (ell 1 story), hipped roof, 2 exterior end chimneys (main block), 1 exterior end chimney (ell), full-height pedimented tetrastyle entrance portico composed of 2 pairs of paneled square columns with upper balcony, L-shaped shed porch at rear; center-hall plan, notable Greek Revival style interior woodwork, decorative plaster. Semidetached frame dependency off ell; also brick dependency at rear. Built ca. 1850 for Wiley Pope Swift (1812–59), former mayor of Selma. 3 ext. photos (1934), 3 int. photos (1934).

ELMORE COUNTY

Elmore Vicinity

Fitzpatrick, Gov. Benjamin, House. *See* Oak Grove (AL-697), between Elmore and Coosada community.

Oak Grove (Gov. Benjamin Fitzpatrick House) (AL-697), between Elmore and Coosada community, approx. 1.5 mi. NE of Mortar Creek; E side of unmarked dirt road approx. 0.5 mi. S of Ala. 14 at point 1.1 mi. E of Ala. 14 intersection with Ala. 143 at Elmore. Frame with clapboarding, rectangular (6-bay front), 2 stories, gable roof, 4 exterior end chimneys, encircled by 1-story shed porch raised on brick piers, notable Palladian style doorway; center-hall plan, paneled dado and "country Federal" style woodwork throughout, unusual 4-leaf folding doorway at rear of main hall. Built ca. 1835 for Benjamin Fitzpatrick (1802–69), governor of Alabama (1841–45), adjoining Huntingdon, the plantation home of his father-in-law, Gen. John Archer Elmore; burned 1975. 3 ext. photos (1935), 14 int. photos (1935).

Robinson Springs

Methodist Church (Robinson Springs United Methodist Church) (AL-682), E side Ala. 143, approx. 0.1 mi. S of intersection with Ala. 14 just N of Millbrook. Frame with clapboarding, 40'3" X 60'2", 1 story, gable roof, temple-type façade with distyle in antis Doric portico sheltering twin entrances with flanking lateral doors to gallery, 2-stage belfry with pyramidal roof; auditorium style interior with 2 aisles and 3 blocks of slip pews, rear slave gallery supported by Tuscan colonnettes, Eastlake style late 19th-C. Communion rail enclosing pulpit dais, twin doors at rear. Built 1845 for Methodist Protestant congregation organized in 1828 by the Rev. Peyton Dandridge Bibb, brother of first two governors of Alabama; original window sashes replaced by translucent glass and educational building added to rear ca. 1940. Very similar in appearance to later Ivy Creek Methodist Church (AL-724) in neighboring Autauga County. 3 ext. photos (1935), 4 int. photos (1935). NR.

"Methodist Parsonage" (AL-698), E side of Ala. 143, approx. 0.2 mi. S of intersection with Ala. 14, just N of Millbrook; immediately S of Robinson Springs Methodist Church. Frame with clapboarding, 52'6" (5-bay front) X 30'6" plus ell on N side, 1 story on brick piers, hipped roof, central 4-bay pedimented porch; center-hall plan with chimney at rear of hall. Built ca. 1850, possibly for Toddy Robinson or member of Gayle family; heavily altered, including removal of interior woodwork and original partitions, 20th-C. hardwood flooring, addition of metal wood-grain siding and 7'6" extension ell (1978). Tradition asserts that historian Albert Pickett wrote portion of his *History of Alabama* (1852) here while visiting the nearby mineral springs. No documentary evidence that house served as Methodist parsonage. 2 ext. photos (1935).

Wetumpka

Airey, J. Bruce, House. *See* Seaman-Airey House (AL-659), 1202 W. Tuskeena St.

Baptist Church. *See* First Baptist Church (AL-657), 205 W. Bridge St.

Bateman, Florence Golson, House. *See* Northrup-Bateman House (AL-660), 311 Government St.

Bates-Jesse House. *See* Northrup-Bateman House (AL-660), 311 Government St.

Bradford-Stowe House (AL-664), 401 W. Main St. (NW corner W. Main and Tallassee sts.). Frame with clapboarding, approx. 32' (3-bay first story, 2-bay second story) X 28', 2 stories with 1-story rear shed extension, gable roof, 2 exterior end chimneys, originally small central entrance porch with open deck at upper level, semidetached rectangular 1-story gabled 2-room kitchen wing at NW rear; basically 2-room plan with smaller shed rooms flanking hall at rear, enclosed stair to second floor. History of structure obscure: reputedly built in early 19th C. as Indian trading post; later home of merchant James Bradford. Small porch replaced by full-length 1-story porch in late 19th C.; renovated 1943, including rear addition and demolition of early NW kitchen wing. Possibly one of oldest extant structures in Coosa-Tallapoosa river basin. 2 ext. photos (1934–35), 1 int. photo (1935).

Cantelou, Lamar, House. *See* House (AL-663), 207 W. Tuskeena St.

First Baptist Church (Baptist Church) (AL-657), 205 W. Bridge St. (Ala. 14), s side of W. Bridge St., approx. 0.1 mi. w of Coosa River Bridge. Brick, 43′2″ × 72′3″, 2 stories (auditorium above ground-floor meeting rooms), gable roof with pedimented front, 2-stage tower with octagonal belfry and cupola, central ground-floor doorway with single window, all windows originally pointed and inset into blind Gothic arch, main floor reached by twin stairways from vestibule to narthex; auditorium plan with 2 aisles. Building dedicated 11 July 1852; extensively renovated in 1909, including replacement of pointed windows with round-topped art glass memorial windows, auditorium embellished with fluted Corinthian pilasters and modillioned cornice, new pews installed, basement renovated ca. 1910; educational annex built at rear in 1929. Used as chapel since completion of new edifice in 1966. 2 ext. photos (1935), 5 int. photos (1935).

First Methodist Church (Methodist Church) (AL-655), 306 W. Tuskeena St. (NE corner Tuskeena and Broad sts.). Brick, approx. 50′0″ × 80′0″ (5 bays long), 2 stories (auditorium above ground-floor meeting rooms), gable roof with bracketed cornice and pedimented front, 3-stage pilastered tower, broad paneled pilasters at front and sides, originally 2 ground-floor entrances; main floor reached by twin stairways rising from vestibule to narthex; open plan with center aisle, evidence that interior walls were once embellished with trompe l'oeil decoration, including painted pilasters and cornice. Built 1853–54 under supervision of Tilman Leak. Extensively renovated 1909 including elimination of twin entrances and construction of central doorway enframed by small pedimented portico, new stairs to narthex, replastering of auditorium and addition of Roman Doric pilasters carrying denticulated cornice, replacement of clear-glass sashing and louvered blinds with art glass memorial windows, new pulpit, curved pews, and organ, also educational annex at rear; chancel area again refurbished 1972. 2 ext. photos (1935), 4 int. photos (1935). NR.

First Presbyterian Church (Presbyterian Church) (AL-656), NW corner of W. Bridge and N. Bridge sts., just NW of Coosa River bridges. Frame (board and batten) with slate roof, approx. 37′6″ (3-bay front) × 60′0″, 1 story, gable roof, projecting buttressed central tower with broached spire (originally 3-stage tower with pinnacles), recessed entrance set into blind Gothic arch at base of tower; open interior plan with center aisle, original slip-pews and pulpit furnishings, narrow slave gallery at rear, pulpit dais bearing paneled pulpit and flanking lampstands framed by tall pedimented classical architrave with pair of Doric pilasters, original brass chandelier. Building dedicated 13 June 1857; Mr. Alley, contractor. Third stage of tower replaced by octagonal broached spire ca. 1890; Pilcher organ installed to N of pulpit in 1906; E wing added 1947; W wing added 1957, interior also renovated including extension of pulpit dais and placement of organ and choir behind pulpit. 2 ext. photos (1935), 8 int. photos (1935); 2 data pages (1937).

Fitzpatrick, Kelly, House. *See* Trimble-Fitzpatrick House (AL-658), Autauga St.

House (Lamar Cantelou House) (AL-663), 207 W. Tuskeena St. Frame with clapboarding, main block approx. 36′0″ (5-bay front) × 36′0″ plus ell, 1½ stories, gable roof extending over inset full-length balustraded porch with 4 square columns, central chimney, double-leaf doorway with transom; small center entrance vestibule with single large room to either side, smaller rooms and ell (w side) at rear. Probably built mid-19th C.; purchased by merchant Lamar Cantelou in 1869. Subsequent changes included replacement of original sashing, completion of unfinished attic and installation of present stair, also additions at rear; further renovated 1973–74, including addition of E wing and rear carport, removal of central chimney. Birthplace of artist Kelly Fitzpatrick (1888–1953). 2 ext. photos (1935), 1 int. photo (1935).

McQueen-McCullers House. *See* Tavern (AL-662), Broad and W. Bridge sts.

Methodist Church. *See* First Methodist Church (AL-655), 306 W. Tuskeena St.

Northrup-Bateman House (Bates-Jesse House, Florence Golson Bateman House) (AL-660), 311 Government St. (sw corner Government and Tallassee sts.). Frame with clapboarding (façade flush siding), pedimented "temple with wings" composed of 2-story 3-bay main block (26′ × 43′) with flanking 1-story gabled wings (15′ × 28′), tetrastyle Doric portico carrying full-length upper balcony with wheatsheaf balustrade, each wing originally fronted by secondary Doric porch; side-hall plan, mantels and woodwork probably adapted from Asher Benjamin. Built 1846 for Elisha Milton Cain as present to daughter and son-in-law, Mr. and Mrs. John Northrup. Wings extensively altered in early 20th C., including enclosure of porches and addition of second story with casements; partially restored during 1936–38 renovation, although porches not reconstructed. Wetumpka's outstanding example of Greek Revival style domestic architecture. 5 ext. photos (1934–35), 5 int. photos (1935).

Presbyterian Church. *See* First Presbyterian Church (AL-656), W. Bridge and N. Bridge sts.

Seaman-Airey House (J. Bruce Airey House) (AL-659), 1202 W. Tuskeena St. (NW corner Tuskeena and Opotheohola sts.). Frame with clapboarding, approx. 42'6" (3-bay front) X 32'6" plus ell (approx. 16'0" X 27'0"), 1 story, hipped roof, 2 interior chimneys, heavy pedimented 3-bay tetrastyle portico with 4 square columns; center-hall plan. Built ca. 1857 for George Seaman; front door replaced late 19th C. and extensive later additions including concrete foundation; gutted by fire in June 1978 and subsequently razed. 3 ext. photos (1935), 6 int. photos (1935).

Smoot, E. L., House (AL-661), 705 Mansion St. (W side Mansion St., approx. 0.2 mi. NE of intersection with Company St.). Frame with clapboarding, rectangular (5-bay front), 1½ stories, gable roof, 2 square interior chimneys, central pedimented Tuscan portico with coupled columns linked by wood balustrade, flanking 12-over-12 windows, outside stairway on rear porch; center-hall plan, carved mantels, molded chair-rail. Built mid-19th C.; later ell and N side addition; demolished ca. 1947 to make way for new dwelling built closer to Mansion St. 5 ext. photos (1935), 5 int. photos (1935).

Tavern (McQueen-McCullers House) (AL-662), NW corner Broad and W. Bridge sts., facing E. Frame with clapboarding, rectangular, 2 stories, gable roof, central chimney, inset 1-story 2-thirds length porch at front with 4 square columns, partially enclosed stair to upper floor at N end of porch, eared architrave enframing asymmetrically placed main door; unusual plan, consisting of 2 rooms with chimney between on first floor plus smaller third room at N end of porch, 4 rooms grouped around central hall on second floor. Built mid-19th C. reputedly as stagecoach inn and tavern; later converted to residence; demolished spring 1979. Rare example in Alabama antebellum architecture of plan arranged around single central chimney. 2 ext. photos (1935), 2 int. photos (1935).

Trimble-Fitzpatrick House (Kelly Fitzpatrick House) (AL-658), W side of Autauga St. opposite intersection with W. Tuskeena St. Frame with clapboarding, rectangular (5-bay front) with ell, 2 stories, hipped roof with shed at rear, 2 exterior end chimneys (main block), tall central pedimented portico with 2 heavy square columns carrying upstairs porch, double-leaf doors with semielliptical fanlights above and below, modillioned cornice with denticulation; center-hall plan with enclosed stair, semielliptical transom over rear hall door, both Federal period and later Greek Revival style interior woodwork. Built ca. 1840 probably for Benjamin Trimble (ca. 1810–76), merchant and banker; some sources say Col. Howell Rose was the builder. Later interior changes; demolished ca. 1955. Residence and studio ca. 1900–53 of Alabama painter Kelly Fitzpatrick (1888–1953). 3 ext. photos (1934–35), 5 int. photos (1934–35); 2 data pages (1936).

Wetumpka Vicinity

Brannon, Peter, House. *See* Sugarberry Hill (AL-665), lane off Harrogate Springs Rd.

Bullard, John, House. *See* Sugarberry Hill (AL-665), lane off Harrogate Springs Rd.

Henderson Place. *See* Sugarberry Hill (AL-665), lane off Harrogate Springs Rd.

Owen, Marie Bankhead, House. *See* Sugarberry Hill (AL-665), lane off Harrogate Springs Rd.

Sugarberry Hill (Peter Brannon House, John Bullard House, Henderson Place, Marie Bankhead Owen House) (AL-665), at end of private lane, approx. 0.3 mi. S of Harrogate Springs Rd. (old U.S. 231) and 0.2 mi. E of Harrogate Springs Rd. intersection with U.S. 231, S of Wetumpka. Frame with clapboarding, rectangular (5-bay front), 2 stories, gable roof, 2 exterior end chimneys (main block), 2-tiered shed porch across front with scroll-cut balustrade and turned posts; center-hall plan (originally open passage), simple Federal period woodwork, interior walls sheathed with flush boarding. Built ca. 1823 for John Bullard from North Carolina as 2-story open-hall structure, possibly with 1-story shed extension at rear; improved and enlarged ca. 1850 for later owner W. T. Hatchett, secretary of the Central Plank Rd. from Wetumpka to Winterboro in Talladega County; other alterations and enlargements in late 19th C., including further rear additions, 2-over-2 sashing, present gingerbread style front porch. Home of Peter A. Brannon and later of Mrs. Marie Bankhead Owen, directors successively of State Department of Archives and History. 1 ext. photo (1934), 7 int. photos (1934); 2 data pages (1936).

FAYETTE COUNTY

Fayette Vicinity

Hollingsworth Mill. *See* McCaleb's Mill (AL-390), on Mill Creek.

McCaleb's Mill (Hollingsworth Mill) (AL-390), on Mill Creek, approx. 0.2 mi. SE of Co. 53 at point 0.7 mi. NE of intersection with Co. 49 in New River community, which is 1.5 mi. SE of Hubbertville; approx. 6 mi. NE of U.S. 43 intersection with Ala. 102 between Fayette and Winfield. Complex consisting of mill, cotton gin, and smithy. Motive power was steel overshot wheel 25' in diameter, originally turned by current from wooden millrace. Small rectangular frame 1-story structure with gable roof housing mill machinery; open gabled shed just downstream sheltering forge; gin house once adjacent. Mill established at site in mid-19th C. by David Thornton; property acquired in 1897 by John Tyler McCaleb, who may have rebuilt mill. Metal overshot wheel (replacing 2 wooden wheels) installed in 1906 (hauled by oxen from railroad station at Bazemore, assembled by Jim Allred); frame millhouse replaced by cinderblock structure ca. 1970; operation ceased in 1978; wheel and blacksmith shop ruinous. 3 ext. photos (1936, including 1 of forge), 1 int. photo of millhouse (1936).

GREENE COUNTY

Boligee Vicinity

Bethsalem Presbyterian Church (AL-282), on hill SE of Co. 1, approx. 1.1 mi. S of intersection with U.S. 11 at southern edge of Boligee. Frame with clapboarding, approx. 24'6" (1-bay front, 3 bays deep) X 44'4", 1 story, gable roof, recessed porch framed by segmental arch, fish-scale shingles in pediment; open interior plan with plain slip pews. Built ca. 1870 with materials from earlier and larger edifice; subsequent modifications include enclosed porch added ca. 1900, concrete floor; restored 1946. Congregation organized 1835; services discontinued 1917. 1 ext. photo (1935), 1 int. photo (1935); 1 data page (1936).

Boligee Hill. *See* Myrtle Hall (AL-209), lane off Co. 34.

Hill of Howth (McKee-Gould House) (AL-208), on high knoll at southern edge of Boligee, approx. 0.5 mi. S of U.S. 11 intersection with Co. 19 and 0.4 mi. W of Co. 19, approx. 700 yds. S of Alabama Power Co. transformer. Squared logs (half-dovetail construction) partially covered with clapboards, rectangular (7-bay front) with ell, 1½ stories, gable roof broken to extend over full-length porch with chamfered posts, 2 exterior end chimneys (main block); center-hall plan, interior walls consist of whitewashed logs and flush beaded boarding. Dependencies include late 19th-C. well shelter and barn. Built ca. 1816 as double-pen loghouse with open hall or dogtrot for Col. John McKee (1771–1833), U.S. agent to Choctaw and Cherokee Indians; enlarged and partially covered with clapboarding, hall enclosed ca. 1835 for William Procter Gould, planter and adopted son of Col. McKee; demolished 1954 and materials utilized in constructing Spencer D. Bayer House, approx. 1 mi. E of Eutaw on N side of Ala. 14. 4 ext. photos (1934–35, including 2 photos of well shelter and barn), 5 int. photos (1934–35); 2 data pages (1936).

McKee-Gould House. *See* Hill of Howth (AL-208), near U.S. 11 intersection with Co. 19.

Myrtle Hall (Boligee Hill) (AL-209), on high hill, approx. 0.7 mi. SE of U.S. 11 (entrance lane on S side of Co. 34, approx. 0.7 mi. S of intersection with U.S. 11); 1.5 mi. NE of Boligee. Frame with clapboarding on raised brick basement, approx. 52′1″ (5-bay front) X 42′0″, 1½ stories over full ground floor, gable roof (broken at rear) with dormers, 2 pairs of exterior end chimneys, raised central tetrastyle Doric portico at front (S elevation), 3-bay porch at rear with flanking shed rooms, heavily paneled double-leaf doorways front and rear; center-hall plan, notable interior woodwork, brick-paved ground floor. Completed 1840 for Dr. John David Means from Fairfield District, S.C.; first called Boligee Hill; known as Myrtle Hall since ca. 1870. Home during post–Civil War period of Charles Hays (1834–79), prominent Alabama "scalawag" Republican and Reconstruction leader. 6 ext. photos (1934, 1936), 9 int. photos (1935–36); 1 data page (1936). NR.

Weston (AL-272), on hill approx. 0.2 mi. SE of U.S. 11; entrance lane on S side of U.S. 11, approx. 0.8 mi. S of U.S. 11 intersection with Co. 19 in Boligee. Frame with clapboarding, rectangular (5-bay front), 2 stories, gable roof, 2 pairs of interior end chimneys, central pedimented distyle portico with paneled square columns, 3-part window above doorway enframed by classical architrave, shed porch across rear; center-hall plan. Built ca. 1843 for family named Friend; acquired by Ulysses T. McLemore in 1860. Subsequent changes include late 19th-C. semidetached kitchen addition, 2-story sleeping porch on W side (early 20th C.); demolished ca. 1960 and some of materials used to construct Fellowship Hall at Boligee Presbyterian Church. 2 ext. photos (1936), 3 int. photos (1936).

Schoolhouse. Frame with clapboarding, rectangular (1-bay front), 1 story, gable roof, 1 exterior end chimney, small gabled porch. Probably built mid-19th C.; demolished. 1 ext. photo (1936).

Smokehouse. Squared log (square-notch construction), rectangular with single door in gable end, 1 story, gable roof. Probably built mid-19th C.; demolished. 1 ext. photo (1936).

Clinton

Masonic Hall (AL-229), SE corner of Ala. 14 intersection with Ala. 39. Frame with clapboarding, rectangular, 2 stories, gable roof, pedimented front with corner pilasters, narrow recessed entry at gable end with 2 large windows above; open plan (store on first floor, Masonic hall on second), marbleized Greek Revival style pulpit at N end of Masonic room flanked by square pillars supporting pointed arch. Built ca. 1857 for George Washington Lodge No. 24; demolished ca. 1940. 2 ext. photos (1934–35), 2 int. photos (1935); 1 data page (1936).

Eutaw

Alexander-Webb House (Webb-Alexander House) (AL-245), 309 Main St. Frame with clapboarding (façade plastered), approx. 42′0″ (5-bay front) X 19′9″ plus portico and rear ell, 2 stories (ell 1 story), gable roof extending over full-width portico with 4 square piers, balcony over doorway; latticed sidelights and transom; center-hall plan. Moved to site in mid-1840s from old Erie for Dr. Abram Franklin Alexander, and renovated (including addition of colonnade and remodeling of façade); ell replaced by rear addition ca. 1950. 2 ext. photos (1934–35), 2 int. photos (1935); 1 data page (1936).

Anthony, David Rinehart, House (Winn or Wynne House) (AL-244), 307 Wilson Ave. (SW corner Wilson Ave. and Main St.). Frame with clapboarding (façade flush boarding), approx. 42′9″ (3-bay front) X 39′6″ including porch, 2½ stories, gable roof extending over full-length tetrastyle portico with octagonal columns, balcony with wheatsheaf balustrade above doorway, 2 interior chimneys, gable ends trimmed with scalloped bargeboards. Completed 1860 by local architect-constructor as own family residence; 1-story service wing added to S side ca. 1884; demolished

1984. D. R. Anthony (1808–71) came from North Carolina to build now-destroyed Rose Hill (William M. High House) near Forkland; also built First Presbyterian Church (AL-252). 3 ext. photos (1934–35), 1 int. photo (1935); 1 data page (1936). NR.

Banks House. *See* Shawver-Coleman-Banks House (AL-246), Springfield Ave. and Pickens St.

Braune House-Studio. *Under* Mesopotamia Academy (AL-243), *see* Music Building.

Clark-Malone House. *See* Meriwether-Clark-Malone House (AL-240), 243 Wilson Ave.

Dunlap House. *See* Wilson-Herndon-Dunlap House (AL-270), 237 Wilson Ave.

Eutaw Female Academy (A. W. Smith House) (AL-251), 220 Main St. (NE of Main St. and Wilson Ave. intersection just E of old Mesopotamia Academy building, on Miles College campus). Frame with clapboarding (portico flush boarding), rectangular (5-bay front), 2 stories, gable roof, 2 pairs of exterior end chimneys, 3-bay pedimented tetrastyle Doric portico with full-length cantilevered balcony, secondary entrances flanking main doorway; center-hall plan. Dependencies include wellhouse, servant house, corncrib. Built ca. 1840; converted to residence (ca. 1895), including Victorian style interior woodwork; demolished 1972. 9 ext. photos (1935, including 3 photos of dependencies), 2 int. photos (1935); 1 data page (1936). *See also* FBJ (J7-ALA-1222 through 1224).

First Presbyterian Church (AL-252), NW corner Main St. and Wilson Ave. Frame with clapboarding, approx. 42'8" (3-bay front) X 70'0", 2 stories, gable roof, pedimented façade, all 4 elevations articulated by pilastrade, tall central double-leaf door enframed by eared architrave, 2-stage pilastered belfry topped by slender octagonal spire and weathervane; meeting and Sunday school rooms on first floor with second-floor auditorium reached by stairs from narthex, 2 aisles with original slip pews (divider removed from central block), slave gallery at rear, pulpit dais backed by architrave. Built 1851; David R. Anthony, contractor. Late-19th-C. changes included installation of pipe organ and choir loft at front of auditorium, pressed tin ceiling; auditorium reconditioned and partially restored 1959, adjacent educational building and connecting covered way built 1970. 4 ext. photos (1935), 6 int. photos (1935, including original basement meeting room); 1 data page (1936). NR. *See also* FBJ (J7-ALA-1218); Tebbs (T3-ALA-339179).

Greene County Courthouse and Probate Office (AL-218), courthouse square (bounded by Main and Boligee sts., Prairie and Monroe aves.). Brick covered with stucco and scored to simulate ashlar, approx. 47'4" X 68'0" plus entrance vestibule (approx. 25'11" X 10'4") on W front, 5-bay N and S elevations, 2 stories, shallow hipped roof with wide bracketed cornice, upper story articulated by pilasters, small central cantilevered balconies with cast-iron balustrade on each elevation; first floor has center hall with cross hall, large courtroom on second floor reached by stairs in vestibule. Built 1868–69 to replace courthouse destroyed by fire; George M. Figh, contractor. Nearly identical to earlier structure erected 1839–40 under supervision of John V. Crossland; subsequent interior modifications include poured concrete first floor, extensive alteration of courtroom after 1936 entailing removal of original seats and semicircular balustrade enclosing judge's bench. 4 ext. photos (1936), 4 int. photos (1936); 2 data pages (1936). NR.

Probate Office. NW corner of courthouse square, brick, rectangular (3-bay front), originally 1 story, gable roof with stepped parapet at each end, 2 interior end chimneys, pilastered elevations, heavy cast-iron shutters; 2-room plan, original marble floor. Built 1856 as one of 2 ancillary structures to courthouse (Grand Jury Building dating from 1842 stands on NE corner of square); extensively altered in 1938, including addition of second story, application of stucco over original brick walls, gutting of interior. 2 ext. photos (1936).

Kirksey, Dr. H. A., House. *See* Kirkwood (AL-210), Mesopotamia St. and Kirkwood Dr.

Kirkwood (Dr. H. A. Kirksey House) (AL-210), NE of intersection of Mesopotamia St. (Ala. 14) and Kirkwood Dr., approx. 0.6 mi. NW of courthouse square. Frame with clapboarding (flush boarding on S and W façades), approx. 62'4" (5-bay front) X 47'10" overall, also ell at NW rear, 2 stories (ell 1 story), hipped roof extending over L-shaped 8-column Ionic portico with cantilevered balcony along front (S) and W elevations, wide bracketed cornice with low parapet, roof terminating in glazed monitor originally forming base for large belvedere with Ionic peristyle and bracketed cornice; center-hall plan, flashed glass sidelights and transom, ornate marble mantels, Greek Revival style woodwork. Begun late 1850s for Foster M. Kirksey, planter and merchant; David R. Anthony possibly contractor. Cast-iron railing for balcony never installed and interior finish simplified because of Civil War; belvedere and parapet removed late 19th C. Reconditioned and restored 1973–79, including reconstruction of belvedere, installation of cast-iron balcony railing and decorative interior plaster cornices; Edward Vason Jones, supervising architect. 3 ext. photos (1934–35), 5 int. photos (1934–35); 2 data pages (1936). NR. *See also* FBJ (J7-ALA-1216 and 1217).

Law Office. *See* William P. Webb Law Office (AL-273), Main St.

Meriwether-Clark-Malone House (Clark-Malone House) (AL-240), 243 Wilson Ave. Frame with clapboarding (façade flush boarding), 46′7″ (5-bay front) X 46′6″ overall, 2½ stories, high gable roof extending over full-length portico with 6 square piers, balcony above doorway, 2 interior chimneys; center-hall plan, flush board dado in SW room. Built 1856 for Dr. Willis Meriwether with materials from earlier structure or structures (possibly Joseph Meriwether House in nearby Springfield community); later changes include back porch and other rear additions, removal of chimneys and interior partition between hall and NW room. 2 ext. photos (1934–35), 2 int. photos (1935); 1 data page (1936). NR.

Mesopotamia Academy (Eutaw Female College, Mesopotamia Female Seminary) (AL-243), NE corner Main St. and Wilson Ave.; originally located approx. 1 mi. W on Mesopotamia St. (Ala. 14). Frame with clapboarding (façade flush boarding), approx. 75′6″ (7-bay front) X 51′3″ originally, 2 stories, hipped roof extending over full-length 5-column Ionic portico with unusually wide intercolumniation, exterior possibly rusticated originally; asymmetrical center-hall plan. Built ca. 1845 as Mesopotamia Academy (became Mesopotamia Female Seminary in 1853); David R. Anthony probably contractor. Moved to present site 1889 to house Eutaw Female College (narrow addition subsequently built at rear); elementary school 1892–1910; extensively altered 1944 for apartment use, including asbestos siding, fenestrational changes, gutting of interior. Dormitory for Miles College, Eutaw Campus, since 1972. 4 ext. photos (1934–35), 2 int. photos (1934–35); 1 data page (1936).
Music Building (Braune House-Studio). Formerly to rear of academy building (originally located at NE corner Wilson Ave. and Boligee St.). Frame with clapboarding, rectangular (narrow 3-bay front), 1 story, gable roof, pedimented porch with 2 octagonal columns. Built 1860–63 for Gustave or Charles H. Braune (occupied by latter ca. 1862 as residence and music studio); moved late 19th C. to site at rear of Eutaw Female College and wing added to E side; moved again 1968 to 151 Kirkwood Dr. and restored as private residence. 1 ext. photo (1936).
See also FBJ (J7-ALA-1212 and 1213); Tebbs (T3-ALA-339182).

Perkins-Spencer House (AL-241), N side Spencer St. (facing E) between Prairie and Wilson aves. Frame with clapboarding (façade flush boarding) on high brick basement, rectangular (5-bay front), 2½ stories, gable roof extending over full-length raised tetrastyle portico composed of freestanding Ionic columns on square brick bases, balcony over main doorway, 4 exterior end chimneys, shed room and porch on S side; center-hall plan. Frame 1-story servant house at rear. Built ca. 1855 for William Perkins (1808–68), merchant; later additions at rear. 4 ext. photos (1934–35, including 1 photo of servant house), 2 int. photos (1935); 1 data page (1936). NR.

Reese-Lucius House (AL-242), 242 Wilson Ave. Frame with clapboarding, approx. 48′6″ (5-bay front) X 43′2″ overall, 2½ stories, gable roof extending over full-length tetrastyle Ionic portico, balcony with scroll-cut balustrade above main doorway, 2 pairs exterior end chimneys, smaller 1-story porches with octagonal supports at rear and S side; center-hall plan, double parlor on N side. Built ca. 1855 for Edwin Reese, carriage maker; minor alterations in 20th C. 3 ext. photos (1935–36), 2 int. photos (1935); 1 data page (1936). NR.

Shawver-Coleman-Banks House (Banks House) (AL-246), SE corner Springfield Ave. and Pickens St.

Frame with clapboarding (façade stuccoed), approx. 47′10″ (5-bay front) x 34′3″, 2½ stories, gable roof extending over full-length tetrastyle Ionic portico, 3-bay balcony at upper level, 2 pairs of exterior end chimneys; center-hall plan, spiral stairway, double parlor on N. Built between 1847 and 1853 by George W. Shawver, local brickmason and contractor, apparently as family residence. Kitchen wing at NE rear and other rear additions prior to 1909, subsequent installation of masonry porch floor, interior alterations including oak strip flooring, addition of carport at rear. 9 sheets (n.d., including site plan, plans, elevations, section, details, dependencies); 2 ext. photos (1934), 5 int. photos (1935); 1 data page (1936). NR.

Smokehouse. One of 2 original dependencies (also kitchen-washhouse) at SE rear of house. Brick, approx. 16′ x 16′, 1 story with single doorway, pyramidal roof, open brickwork at top of walls to afford ventilation. 1 ext. photo (1935).
See also Tebbs (T3-ALA-339180).

Smith, A. W., House. See Eutaw Female Academy (AL-251), 220 Main St.

Webb, William P., Law Office (Law Office) (AL-273), N side of Main St., approx. 50′ E of intersection with Prairie Ave., facing courthouse square. Frame with clapboarding (façade flush boarding), rectangular (narrow 4-bay front), 1 story, gable roof, pedimented façade divided by pilasters into 2 units of 2 bays each; 4-room plan. Built ca. 1848; moved 1970 to new site on Ala. 14 (Greensboro Hwy.) E of Eutaw and subsequently destroyed by fire. Eutaw City Hall occupies part of original site. 1 ext. photo (1936), 1 int. photo (1936).

Webb-Alexander House. See Alexander-Webb House (AL-245), 309 Main St.

White-McGiffert House (AL-269), N side Mesopotamia St., opposite intersection with Eutaw St. Frame with clapboarding, rectangular (7-bay front) with small 1-story rear wing, 2½ stories, gable roof extending over 2-tiered porch with square columns, 2 pairs of exterior end chimneys, central doorway with flanking subordinate doorways occupying middle bay to each side; center-hall plan, continuous stairway to third floor, notable woodwork throughout. Rare 19th-C. picket fence at front. Built ca. 1833 for Asa White. Demioctagonal glazed sunroom added to E end of porch in late 19th C. (subsequently removed); rear wing (probably later addition) removed after 1936 and replaced by lean-to addition; carport added to E side. Georgia-born Asa White (1783–1861) owned site on which Eutaw was established in 1838. House is first of larger Eutaw residences. 5 ext. photos (1936, including picket fence), 4 int. photos (1936). NR.

Office. SW of house in front yard. Frame with clapboarding, rectangular, 1 story, 1 exterior end chimney. Built early to mid-19th C.; demolished. 1 ext. photo (1936, damaged).

Wilson-Herndon-Dunlap House (Dunlap House) (AL-270), 237 Wilson Ave. Frame with clapboarding raised on brick piers, rectangular (5-bay front) with semidetached ell at NW rear, 1½ stories, gable roof, 2 pairs exterior end chimneys (main block), 3-bay pedimented tetrastyle Doric portico, 3-part windows in each gable end; center-hall plan. Landscaped yard, mid-19th-C. picket fence across front with gate design from Plate 33 of Asher Benjamin's *Practical House Carpenter* (1830), circular gravel walkway to portico. Dependencies include brick kitchen and smokehouse, frame servants' house. Built ca. 1845 for Catlin Wilson, merchant, born in New York; minor later additions. 4 ext. photos (1936, including 2 photos of fence and rear dependencies), 3 int. photos (1936). NR.

Winn or Wynne House. See David Rinehart Anthony House (AL-244), 307 Wilson Ave.

Forkland

Brewer House. See Mrs. Ann Lewis House (AL-258), Co. 4.

Episcopal Church. See St. John's Episcopal Church (AL-255), Co. 4.

Glover, Miss Virginia, House (AL-253), NW corner of intersection of Co. 19 and Co. 4, approx. 0.2 mi. S of Co. 4 intersection with U.S. 43. Frame (board and batten) on raised brick basement, rectangular (approx. 47′2″ x 33′0″) plus ell (approx. 16′0″ x 19′0″), 1½ stories, steeply pitched gable roof with widely overhanging eaves, raised inset porch at SE corner extending across three-quarters of façade and supported by rough freestanding cedar posts, shed porch across E gable end; irregular plan with small semienclosed entrance hall at W end of porch containing stairway to upper floor. Detached log kitchen at end of ell. Built mid-19th C. reputedly for Williamson Allen Glover; saloon said to have once occupied basement; detached kitchen demolished ca. 1940. Vernacular expression of picturesque Gothic cottage. 4 ext. photos (1936, including kitchen), 3 int. photos (1936).

Glover, William, House. *See* Inn (AL-259), Co. 19 at junction with Co. 4.

Inn (William Glover House) (AL-259), S side of Co. 19 opposite junction with Co. 4; approx. 0.2 mi. S of Co. 4 intersection with U.S. 43. Frame with clapboarding, rectangular (5-bay front), 1½ stories, gable roof, 2 pairs of exterior end chimneys, recessed 3-bay front porch with square wooden supports and flanking shed rooms; center-hall plan, simple reverse flight stair with landing. Built probably mid-19th C.; reputedly stagecoach stop and sometime home of Glover. 4 ext. photos (1935), 7 int. photos (1935). *See also* FBJ (J7-ALA-1214 and 1215).

Lambuth Memorial Methodist Church. *See* Methodist Church (AL-256), Co. 19.

Levy-Glover Store (Store) (AL-254), NE corner of intersection of Co. 19 and Co. 4, approx. 0.2 mi. S of Co. 4 intersection with U.S. 43. Frame (board and batten), rectangular (3-bay front), 1 story, gable roof projecting over front porch with false front and bracketed cornice, paneled doorway with flanking display windows; open plan with original fixtures including counters, bracketed shelves. Built 1877 for merchant J. L. Levy; N. B. Cassey of Forkland, master-builder. Later owned by Cato Glover; demolished ca. 1960. 3 ext. photos (1935), 2 int. photos (1935).

Lewis, Mrs. Ann, House (Brewer House, Parker House) (AL-258), W side Co. 4, approx. 0.3 mi. NW of intersection with U.S. 43. Frame with clapboarding, rectangular (5-bay front) with ell, 1½ stories, gable roof, central gabled porch with 4 square columns, L-shaped porch at rear; center-hall plan; semidetached kitchen wing at S side. Built mid-19th C. for Mrs. Lewis. Home (1971–) of Greene County's first black sheriff, Thomas Gilmore. 3 ext. photos (1936), 1 int. photo (1936).

Methodist Church (Lambuth Memorial Methodist Church) (AL-256), N side of Co. 19, approx. 0.1 mi. SE of junction with Co. 4; approx. 0.2 mi. S of U.S. 43, immediately E of old Methodist cemetery. Frame with clapboarding, rectangular (2-bay front), gable roof, pedimented façade, twin doors; open interior plan with original benches, simple Greek Revival style pulpit. Built ca. 1850 as successor to nearby Ebenezer Church (founded 1823); tongue-and-groove ceiling and other modifications (ca. 1900). Renamed Lambuth Memorial Church 1954; dismantled and reconstructed 1968–69 at Blue Lake United Methodist Assembly near Andalusia. 2 ext. photos (1935), 2 int. photos (1935).

Methodist Parsonage, Old (AL-256-A), E side of Co. 4, approx. 0.1 mi. S of intersection with U.S. 43, which is just N of Episcopal cemetery. Squared logs (square-notch construction) later covered with clapboards, rectangular (3-bay front), 1½ stories, gable roof extending over full-length porch, formerly 2 exterior end chimneys; center-hall plan (possibly open hall or dogtrot originally). Built early 19th C.; demolished ca. 1965. Used as school at one time. 2 ext. photos (1935), 2 int. photos (1935).

Parker House. *See* Mrs. Ann Lewis House (AL-258), Co. 4.

St. John's Episcopal Church (Episcopal Church, formerly St. John's-in-the-Prairies) (AL-255), E side of Co. 4, approx. 0.1 mi. S of intersection with U.S. 43. Frame (board and batten), approx. 22′2″ × 50′6″ plus entrance porches at front (W) and S side, vestryroom at N side of chancel, steeply pitched broken gable roof, 4-bay nave with chancel, lancet windows, cusped doorways at front and S side; open plan with center aisle, triple lancet above altar, original pews, chancel furnishings, stained glass windows, brass lamps. First erected 1860–61 as second building for rural parish of St. John's-in-the-Prairies on E side of Warrior River in present Hale County (E side of Co. 35, approx. 3.0 mi. N of intersection with Co. 16). Dismantled and reconstructed at Forkland ca. 1878 as St. John's, Forkland; memorial stained glass windows date from that time. Architectural design based on Richard Upjohn's scheme for a "Wooden Chapel," published in *Upjohn's Rural Architecture* (1852). 2 ext. photos (1935), 2 int. photos (1935).

Store. *See* Levy-Glover Store (AL-254), Co. 19 and Co. 4.

Forkland Vicinity

Fair Hill. *See* Perrin-Willis House (AL-280), Co. 19.

Glen Alpine (McAlpine House) (AL-281), 1.7 mi. N of Watsonia community on high knoll at E side of unmarked road intersecting Co. 19 at Watsonia; approx. 4.1 mi. NW of Forkland on Co. 19. Frame with clapboarding, rectangular (5-bay front), 2 stories, gable roof, 2 pairs of exterior end chimneys, originally 2-tiered pedimented portico, heavily paneled double-leaf doors above and below. Built ca. 1840 for William McAlpine, Georgia-born planter. Portico removed before 1934; demolished ca. 1935. 1 ext. photo (1934).

Perrin-Willis House (Fair Hill) (AL-280), approx. 0.8 mi. N of Co. 19; (entrance lane on N side of Co. 19, approx. 3.0 mi. SE of intersection with Co. 9 at Five Points and 6.3 mi. NW of Forkland). Frame with clapboarding raised on brick piers, basically H-shaped with 5-bay inset front porch flanked by 1-bay end pavilions extending to rear as parallel wings, 1½ stories, gable roof with pedimented subordinate cross-gables at each end, 4 interior chimneys, U-shaped gallery at rear overlooking service court; center-hall plan, Late Greek Revival style woodwork. Probably built ca. 1850–60 for Dr. George Perrin family; burned ca. 1965. Unusually large raised-cottage style dwelling. Later named Fair Hill after former William H. Bullock plantation to W, when it became the home in early 20th C. of local writer Virginia Bullock Willis. 2 ext. photos (1934), 1 int. photo (1934).

Rosemount (AL-212), between Co. 19 and U.S. 43, approx. 0.2 mi. N of Co. 19; (entrance lane on N side of Co. 19, approx. 7.4 mi. SE of intersection with Co. 9 at Five Points and approx. 2.1 mi. NW of intersection with Co. 4 at Forkland); just W of Strawberry Hill (AL-271). Frame with clapboarding (façade flush boarding), T-shaped with 5-bay central pavilion (approx. 60'4" across front X 59'2" deep) and narrow (1-bay) projecting wings at rear, 2 stories, hipped roof (with rear subordinate cross-gables) surmounted by large hipped-roof belvedere, denticulated cornice, roof extends over full-length hexastyle Ionic portico with freestanding fluted columns, balcony over main doorway, belvedere partially encircled by balustraded Tuscan colonnade; center-hall plan with flanking parlors and large cross hall to rear, formal dining room beyond, Greek Revival and some Federal period woodwork, formerly hand-pulled elevator from third-floor attic space to belvedere. Built ca. 1835–40 for planter Williamson Allen Glover. Elements from earlier structure incorporated; board-and-batten kitchen wing added to rear in late 19th C. (moved from earlier site and attached to house). Outstanding example in state of Greek Revival architecture. 14 sheets (1934–35, including plot plan, plans, elevations, details); 9 ext. photos (1934–35), 7 int. photos (1934–35); 2 data pages (1936). NR.

Dependency ("slave kitchen"), NW of main house. Frame with clapboarding, approx. 32'3" (2-bay front) X 28'2" overall, 2 stories, gable roof extending over 2-tiered porch, central chimney, exterior stair; 2-room plan. Built mid-19th C. probably as servants' quarters; burned 1934. 1 sheet (1934–35, including plans, elevations, section); 1 ext. photo (1934, also showing in foreground frame wellhouse and water tower).

Schoolhouse, NE of main house. Frame with clapboarding, approx. 17'11" (1-bay front) X 15'0", 1 story, gable roof, 1 exterior end chimney; 1 room. Built mid-19th C.; destroyed. 1 sheet (1934–35, including plan, elevations); 1 ext. photo (1934).

Tool Houses, 2 adjacent structures NW of house. Log (square-notch construction), rectangular, 1 story, gable roofs covered with wooden shakes. Built early to mid-19th C.; destroyed. 1 ext. photo (1934).

See also FBJ (J7-ALA-1219 through 1221).

Strawberry Hill (AL-271), between Co. 19 and U.S. 43, approx. 0.3 mi. N of Co. 19 and 0.3 mi. E of U.S. 43 (present entrance lane on U.S. 43, approx. 1.6 mi. NW of intersection with Co. 4 at Forkland; 2.1 mi. SW of Zion Creek Bridge). Frame with clapboarding (façade flush boarding), rectangular (5-bay front) with central rear wings, 1½ stories, gable roof with dormers extending over full-length 4-bay porch supported by octagonal colonnettes, 2 interior end chimneys; center-hall plan with cross hall at rear, heavy Greek Revival style woodwork. Built mid-19th C. for Mrs. Justina Gennerick Walton (widow of William Walton) probably on site of earlier house. Original rear wing reputedly replaced during 1880s. Renovated early 1970s, including application of masonite siding, removal of rear wing, and construction of new rear addition, enclosure of W end of cross hall to form library; Sprott Long of Birmingham, renovation architect. 4 ext. photos (1936), 5 int. photos (1936); 3 data pages (1937).

Slave House. Double-pen log house (square-notch construction), 1 story, gable roof, exterior end chimney; open dogtrot. Possibly built early 19th C.; demolished. 1 ext. photo (1936), 1 int. photo (1936).

See also FBJ (J7-ALA-1225).

Thornhill (AL-238), on high knoll, approx. 0.1 mi. N of Co. 19 just E of junction with unmarked road at Watsonia (entrance lane on N side of Co. 19, approx. 4.2 mi. NW of intersection with Co. 4 at Forkland). Frame with clapboarding, original main block approx. 54'5" (5-bay front) X 58'10" including portico, 2 stories, hipped roof slightly broken at front to extend over full-length hexastyle Ionic portico, balcony with wheatsheaf balustrade above main doorway, 2 pairs of interior end chimneys; center-hall plan, curving stairway, sliding doors between parlor and dining room, silver-plated hardware, many original furnishings. Several dependencies (see below). Built ca. 1835–40 for James Innes Thornton from Fredericksburg, Va., as seat of 2,600-acre plantation. Portico and present façade possibly result of mid-19th-C. renovation; 2-story shed addition and 1-story ell added to rear ca. 1900. One of few plantation houses still owned by original family in 1978. 11 sheets (1936, including plot plans, plans, elevations, details); 5 ext. photos (1934, 1936), 16 int. photos (1934–36, including 3 photos of memorabilia); 2 data pages (1936).

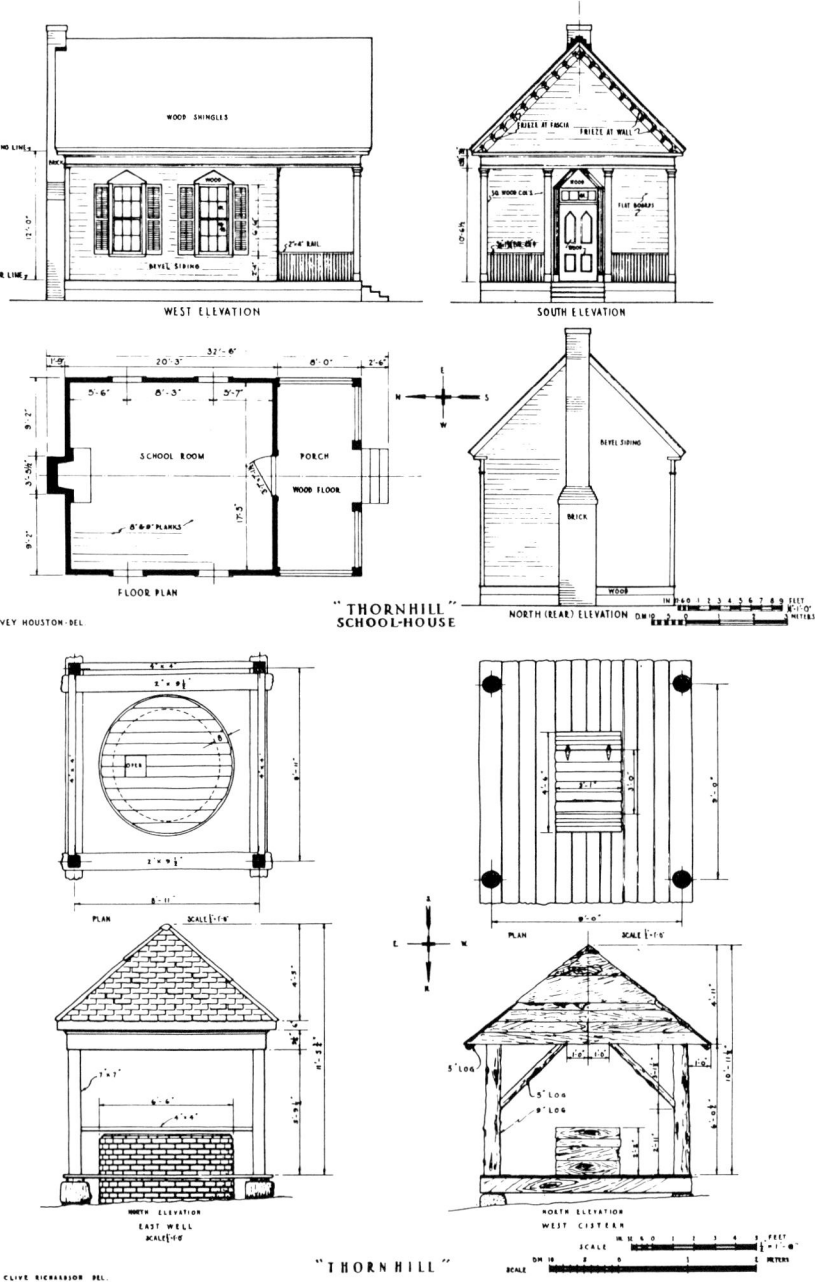

Schoolhouse, approx. 175' SW of main house. Frame with clapboarding, approx. 21'9" (1-bay front) X 28'3", 1 story, steeply pitched gable roof, 1 exterior end chimney at rear, balustraded porch at gable end with cusped

Schoolhouse and well shelters at Thornhill plantation, Forkland vicinity (ca. 1835 and later).

bargeboard; 1 room. Built mid-19th C. 2 sheets (1936, including plan, elevations, details); 2 ext. photos (1934–36).

Well Shelters, to rear of main house. East Well: pyramidal-roof shelter with frame supports over brick well casing. West Cistern: pyramidal-roof shelter with log supports on wooden platform enclosing frame well casing. Built probably mid-to-late 19th C. 1 sheet (1936, including plans, elevations); 2 photos (1934).

Housekeeper's Cabin, N of main house along lane to barn. Squared logs, approx. 18′11″ (1-bay front) X 19′10″, 1 story, gable roof, 1 exterior end chimney. Possibly built early 19th C. 1 sheet (1936, including plan, elevations, detail); 1 ext. photo (1934), 1 int. photo (1934).

Servants' House, N of main house along lane to barn. Double-pen log structure (square-notch construction), approx. 43′0″ X 17′6″, 1 story, gable roof, 2 exterior end chimneys (originally mud and stick), shed porch across front; open-hall or dogtrot plan. 1 sheet (1936, including plan, elevations); 2 ext. photos (1934), 1 ext. photocopy (n.d.).

Miscellaneous. 5 miscellaneous photos (1934, 1936) including drawing of general layout of dependencies, stable and barn interiors, plantation bell, old washpot; 1 photo (1934) of Thornton family genealogical chart.

See also FBJ (J7-ALA-1226 through 1230).

Watsonia

See Forkland Vicinity.

HALE COUNTY

Akron Vicinity

Tanglewood (AL-177), 0.5 mi. E of Co. 21 approx. 3.0 mi. S of intersection with Ala. 60, E of Akron. Frame with clapboarding, rectangular (3-bay front), 1½ stories, gable roof, 2 pairs of exterior end chimneys, originally central pedimented distyle portico with square wooden piers; center-hall plan. Built 1859 for Page Harris as center of 480-acre plantation. Altered ca. 1900–20, including addition of kitchen wing at rear, extension of front porch by 1 bay to either side of original pediment, and construction of dormer windows on front slope of roof. Maintained by University of Alabama since 1949 as natural, botanical, and wildlife sanctuary. 1 sheet (1978, including plans, elevations). NR.

Gallion Vicinity

Spencer House. *See* Waldwick (AL-260), lane off Ala. 69.

Waldwick (Spencer House) (AL-260), W side of Ala. 69 at end of private lane, approx. 1.8 mi. S of junction with U.S. 80; approx. 2 mi. SW of Prairieville. Frame (both vertical sheathing and clapboarding), basically H-shaped, 1½ stories, gabled central section with monitor along ridge, cross-gabled end-pavilions with bay windows flanking trellis-work porch, central second-floor chamber with balcony projecting over middle bay of porch, pointed latticed windows in gable above, cusped bargeboards; center-hall plan with formal rooms to either side, naïve "gothicized" woodwork, unusual ogee arch framing parlor alcove. Kitchen connected to rear of house by covered way. Central section built ca. 1840 as simple rectangular 1½-story cottage for Robert Sinclair Gracey. Remodeled during early 1850s for Mr. and Mrs. Minor Winn Gracey (possibly based on design for "Waldwic Cottage" by William H. Ranlett, in *The Architect,* vol. 2, 1851); kitchen razed after 1935; minor interior alterations 1978. Rare example in Alabama of Gothic Revival style domestic architecture. 4 ext. photos (1935), 4 int. photos (1935).

Slave House, one of 2 identical dependencies to rear (W) of main dwelling. Frame (board and batten), rectangular (2-bay front), 1½ stories, steeply pitched gable roof with scalloped bargeboards, central chimney; 2-room plan. Built mid-19th C. 2 ext. photos (1935).

Slave House, SW of main dwelling. Frame (board and batten), rectangular (1-bay front), 1 story, gable roof, 1 exterior end chimney. Built mid-19th C. 1 ext. photo (1935).

Greensboro

Carson, Dr., House. *See* Gov. Thomas Seay House and Law Offices (AL-234), area of E. Main and Whelan sts.

Derrick House. *See* Drake-Northrup House (AL-250), 603 E. Main St.

Drake-Northrup House (Derrick House) (AL-250), 603 E. Main St. (s side of Main St. just E of Northrup St.). Frame with clapboarding (flush boarding on portico and in each gable end), approx. 52′10″ (5-bay front) X 40′0″, 1½ stories, steeply pitched gable roof with pedimented gable ends, 4 interior end chimneys, 4-bay tetrastyle portico with high triangular pediment carried on short heavy octagonal columns; center-hall plan, unusual eclectic woodwork with denticulated architraves, mantels with freestanding octagonal colonnettes. Built ca. 1855 for Dr. Gaston Drake; subsequent changes include inset rear wing and replacement sashing in gables (probably late 19th C.), also Victorian period stairway. Architectural oddity reflecting naïve eclecticism. 4 ext. photos (1936), 7 int. photos (1936).

Dependency, SW of house abutting Northrup St. Frame with clapboarding on raised brick basement, rectangular with smaller set-back addition at N end, 1 story, gable roof, 1 exterior end chimney, full-length porch along W side overlooking street. Probably built mid-19th C. as kitchen and servants' house; demolished 1970. 1 ext. photo (1936).

Erwin, Cadwallader, House. *See* Glencairn (AL-266), Tuscaloosa St.

Gayle-Hobson-Tunstall House (AL-232), 1801 W. Main St. (S side of Main St. W of Demopolis St.). Brick (Flemish bond N and E sides), formerly rectangular (3-bay N front) altered to L-shape in early 20th C., 2 stories, originally gable roof, 1-story pedimented porch on W; side-hall plan. Outbuildings include notable kitchen-smokehouse (brick, rectangular, 2 stories, gable roof, 1 exterior end chimney, 2-room plan), also brick bathhouse and privy. Dwelling and kitchen-smokehouse reputedly built ca. 1828 for John Gayle, later governor of Alabama. Bathhouse erected after 1834 for subsequent owner Matthew Hobson; 1-story Victorian style porch added to front in late 19th C.; house drastically altered ca. 1900–30, including replacement of original gable roof with hip, construction of bungalow-type 1-story porch across front and E side, extensions on W side and at rear. Believed to be birthplace of Amelia Gayle Gorgas; also of Col. Edwin Hobson, CSA, head of Tredegar Ironworks, Richmond, Va., during Civil War. Still occupied by Hobson descendants in 1978. 4 ext. photos (1934–35, including kitchen-smokehouse), 5 int. photos (1935); 1 data page (1936).

Gayle-Locke House. *See* House (AL-278), College St.

Glencairn (Cadwallader Erwin House) (AL-266), facing N on W side of Tuscaloosa St. S of Erwin Dr. (original entrance to grounds on South St., opposite intersection with Church St.). Frame with clapboarding, main block approx. 53′0″ (5-bay front) X 35′0″ with slightly inset ell (approx. 20′0″ X 22′6″), 2 stories, main block hipped roof (gable on ell), 4 exterior end chimneys, central 2-tiered pedimented tetrastyle Tuscan portico with wheatsheaf balustrade at upper level, deeply recessed doorways (upper and lower porches) with heavily paneled reveals enframed by ornate Greek Revival style architrave having Doric frieze carried by paneled pilasters with applied palmette motif; center-hall plan with cross hall and secondary stair between main block and rear wing, plaster cornices and chandelier medallions, black marble mantels, many of the original furnishings. Built 1837 for Col. John Erwin, lawyer, state legislator, and benefactor of Southern University (AL-221); subsequent changes include kitchen addition (ca. 1900) off ell and enclosure of rear porch after 1935. Still owned and occupied by descendants of first owner. 4 ext. photos (1935–36), 7 int. photos (1936); 2 data pages (1936). NR.

Slave House. Frame with clapboarding, rectangular (1 bay), 1 story, gable roof, 1 interior end chimney. Built mid-19th C. 1 ext. photo (1935).

See also FBJ (J7-ALA-1111 and 1112).

Greenwood. *See* Col. Sydenham Moore House (AL-235), 2201 Main St.

Hannah, Dr. Robert C., House (AL-275), NE corner Church and South sts. Frame with clapboarding, built in 2 sections; N section: 3-bay front, 2 stories, gable roof broken to extend over 2-tiered porch; S section: 5-bay front, 1 story, gable roof broken to extend over full-length porch, shed rooms across rear. One-story S section probably built ca. 1825–30; 2-story N section added before 1850; demolished. 1 ext. photo (1936), 3 int. photos (1936).

Hobson House. *See* Magnolia Grove (AL-219), 1002 Hobson St.

House (Gayle-Locke House) (AL-278), N side of College St. (University Ave.) between Second and Third sts. Frame with clapboarding on high brick piers, 1 story, rectangular 5-bay main block with full-length porch flanked by advanced 2-bay pedimented wings, gable roof broken at rear to extend over shed rooms; center-hall plan, notable Federal period mantelpieces. Built early 19th C.; razed late 1930s. Sometime home of Mr. and Mrs. James Whitehead Locke, son-in-law and daughter of Gov. John Gayle. 5 ext. photos (1936), 2 int. photos (1936). *See also* FBJ (J7-ALA-1115 through 1118).

Jackson-Locke House (AL-287), W side of Demopolis St. between State and Cedar sts. Frame with clapboarding, rectangular (5-bay front), 2 stories, also raised 1-story ell over full brick basement, gable roof, 2 exterior end chimneys (main block), 1 exterior end chimney (ell), central pedimented 2-tiered tetrastyle Tuscan portico; center-hall plan, unusual stair arrangement divided at landing. Built ca. 1835, probably for Dr. Reuben H. Jackson; ell added mid-19th C.; demolished 1951. Federal style mantelpiece from parlor installed in Gwaltney McCollum house built on same site. 2 ext. photos (1935), 3 int. photos (1935).

Japonica Path (Knight House, Norris-Smaw House, Smaw House, Miss Virginia Withers House) (AL-220), 512 Main St. (N side of Main St. at end of semicircular private drive). Frame with clapboarding on raised brick basement, rectangular (5 bays below, 6 bays above) with ell at NW rear, 2 stories over ground floor, hipped roof, 2 exterior end chimneys (main block), 1 exterior end chimney (ell), 1-story central pedimented portico with 2 heavy square piers; center-hall plan (first floor), good Federal period woodwork. Built ca. 1845 for Calvin Norris; NE 1-story addition soon afterward. Kitchen wing added at NE rear 1898; restored with subsequent minor additions ca. 1950; landscaped grounds adorned with giant camellias (japonicas). 1 ext. photo (1934), 4 int. photos (1935–36); 1 data page (1936).

Johnston-Torbert House (Judge W. E. Torbert House) (AL-286), 1101 South St. (S side of South St. just E of intersection with Whelan St.). Brick (façade Flemish bond), rectangular (5 bays below, 6 bays above) with inset ell, 2 stories, gable roof, 2 exterior end chimneys, 1 interior end chimney (ell), 1-story central tetrastyle Tuscan portico; center-hall plan, Federal period woodwork including mantelpieces, chair-rails, grained cupboards in dining room. Built ca. 1835 for Thomas M. Johnston (1802–69), planter; believed to incorporate brick structure erected ca. 1828 for Thomas B. Childress. One-story frame extension added to ell ca. 1908; second addition in 1957 on W side of ell. 1860 census lists Johnston as third-largest slaveholder in Alabama with 539 slaves. 5 ext. photos (1936, including 1 photo of wellhouse), 7 int. photos (1936).

Knight House. *See* Japonica Path (AL-220), 512 Main St.

McCrary-Otts House. *See* Magnolia Hall (AL-265), 805 Otts St.

Magnolia Grove (Hobson House) (AL-219), 1002 Hobson St. (facing W end of Main St. at end of private drive). House museum. Brick (façade stuccoed), approx. 53′7″ (5-bay front) × 54′2″ including portico, 2 stories, modified temple-type façade with pedimented hexastyle Tuscan portico, balcony with wheatsheaf balustrade over main doorway, jib windows to either side of door, tall shed-roof porch across rear with slender freestanding cast-iron colonnettes; center-hall plan, curving stairway, black marble Greek Revival style mantels. House set amid large landscaped grounds with a number of early dependencies to rear. Built ca. 1842 for Col. Isaac Croom of North Carolina, planter and a founder of the University of the South at Sewanee, Tenn.; plan reputedly provided and construction supervised by Dr. John Drish of Tuscaloosa. Rear porch probably added mid-to-late 19th C.; later frame additions at rear. Birthplace of Admiral Richmond Pearson Hobson, Spanish-American War hero. 8 sheets (1936, including plot plan, plans, elevation, details); 5 ext. photos (1934, 1936), 7 int. photos (1934); 6 data pages (1936). NR.
Cook House, NW rear at right angle to mansion. Brick, approx. 36′4″ (4-bay front) × 18′2″, 1 story over raised basement containing wine cellar, gable roof extending over full-length porch resting on 4 brick pillars, 1 interior end chimney; basically 2-room plan. Probably built ca. 1838; renovated as apartment in mid-20th C. 1 sheet (1936, including plans, elevations); 1 ext. photo (1934).
Servants' House, SW of mansion. Frame, rectangular (1-bay front), 1-story gable roof, 1 exterior end chimney; 1 room. Built mid-19th C.; one of 2 similar houses. 1 ext. photo (1934). NR.

See also FBJ (J7-ALA-1119 through 1122).

Magnolia Hall (McCrary-Otts House, J. W. Otts House) (AL-265), 805 Otts St. (S of Main St. at end of Otts St.). Frame with clapboarding (N and S elevations have novelty siding), approx. 54'6" (5 bays wide) x 61'6", 2 stories, temple-type structure with identical pedimented hexastyle Ionic porticoes both front and rear, denticulated cornice, front and rear doorways framed by classical architrave with slender in-antis Ionic colonnettes, cast-iron balcony above, 1-story demioctagonal bay on W side, rectangular 1-story service wing on E side; center-hall plan, notable interior woodwork, chandelier medallions, colored-glass transoms above interior doors. Dependencies include frame servants' house, smokehouse, and icehouse. Built ca. 1855 for David F. McCrary; B. F. Parsons, architect; E service wing (renovated late 19th C.) said to incorporate part of ca. 1828 Murphy house on same site. Kitchen at SW rear adjoining S portico; restored 1970 including removal of kitchen wing to E of house. Notable example of late Greek Revival domestic architecture. 8 sheets (1936, including plot plan, plans, elevations, section, details); 11 ext. photos (1935–36, including 3 photos of dependencies), 10 int. photos (1936); 1 data page (1936). *See also* FBJ (J7-ALA-1123 and 1124).

Methodist Hospital. *See* Southern University, Chancellor's House (AL-277).

Moore, Col. Sydenham, House (Greenwood, W. C. Pickens House, E. G. Rothenberg House) (AL-235), 2201 Main St. Frame with clapboarding (façade flush boarding with dado), rectangular (5-bay front), 2 stories, gable roof (pedimented at each end) extending over full-height tetrastyle Ionic portico, paneled double-leaf doors, cast-iron balcony above main doorway; center-hall plan. Built 1856 incorporating materials from Greenwood, early plantation home of Gov. Israel Pickens on the prairies just S of Greensboro. First owner, lawyer and Confederate officer Sydenham Moore (1817–62), died from wounds received at Battle of Seven Pines. 1 ext. photo (1934). *See also* FBJ (J7-ALA-1125).

Norris-Smaw House. *See* Japonica Path (AL-220), 512 Main St.

Otts, J. W., House. *See* Magnolia Hall (AL-265), 805 Otts St.

Otts, Lee, House. *See* Shackelford-McCrary-Otts House (AL-274), 901 Centreville St.

Pickens, W. C., House. *See* Col. Sydenham Moore House (AL-235), 2201 Main St.

Rothenberg, E. G., House. *See* Col. Sydenham Moore House (AL-235), 2201 Main St.

Seay, Gov. Thomas, House and Law Offices (Dr. Carson House, J. A. Vaughn House) (AL-234), area of E. Main and Whelan sts.
House, SW corner Main and Whelan sts. (W and across Whelan St. from Hale County courthouse). Frame with clapboarding (N façade has rabbeted clapboarding on porch), irregular rectangle, 2 stories, hipped roof, asymmetrical 4-bay N façade with demioctagonal 1-story bay, paneled corner pilasters carrying full entablature, ornate 1-story cast-iron veranda along N and E elevations opposite courthouse; center-hall plan. Two-room dependency at SW rear. Built ca. 1860 for a Mr. Kennedy; purchased and renovated by Gov. Thomas Seay ca. 1875; again renovated and reoriented toward E (1920–26) when service station erected on former front lawn; demolished ca. 1965. Home ca. 1875–96 of Gov. Seay. 4 ext. photos (1934–36), 3 int. photos (1935–36); 1 data page (1936).
Early Law Office, E side Whelan St. just N of intersection with Main St. Frame with clapboarding (façade has rabbeted clapboarding), approx. 24'4" (3-bay front) x 37'11" including porch, 1 story, gable roof, central chimney, pedimented porch with 4 slender square columns; single large room across front with 2 doors flanking central window, 2 smaller rooms directly behind. Built ca. 1855; originally located at NE corner Main and Whelan sts.; moved approx. 30' N after 1925 and turned toward Whelan St. to make way for service station. 1 ext. photo (1935).
Later Law Office, 1105 Main St. (S side of Main St., approx. 35 yds. W of intersection with Whelan St.). Brick, approx. 25'2" (3-bay front) x 42'1", 1 story, gable roof (hipped at rear) concealed by false-front façade with metal cornice, segmentally arched doors and windows with hood molds; single large room at front with two smaller rooms directly behind. Built ca. 1870. Housed law offices of Gov. Seay, sometime

offices of DeGraffenreid and Evins, James J. Garrett, and A. M. Tunstall. Hale County Public Library since 1925. 1 ext. photo (1935).

Shackelford-McCrary-Otts House (Lee Otts House) (AL-274), 901 Centreville St. (E side of Centreville St. just S of Hale County courthouse). Frame with clapboarding, rectangular (5-bay front), 2 stories with 1-story extension across rear, shallow hipped roof, 4 exterior end chimneys, full-height tetrastyle portico, full entablature; center-hall plan with reverse stair from rear of hallway. Dependencies include small brick semidetached milk house at SE rear and kitchen-servant house (see below). Built mid-19th C. for merchant J. W. McCrary, incorporating earlier 1-story structure erected for Robert D. Shackelford; late 19th-C. additions at rear. 2 ext. photos (1935), 1 int. photo (1935); 2 data pages (1936).

Kitchen-Servant House, at NE rear of main house. Frame with clapboarding, rectangular (2-bay front), 2 stories, gable roof, central chimney; 2-room plan. Probably built mid-19th C.; demolished. 1 ext. photo (1935), 1 int. photo (1935).

Smaw House. *See* Japonica Path (AL-220), 512 Main St.

Southern University (AL-221), S side of College St. (University Ave.) just E of Armory St. Brick, basically rectangular (11-bay front) with advanced 3-bay center pavilion and tower, large rear wing, 2 stories, buttressed and battlemented 3-stage entrance tower pierced by blind Gothic arch enframing Tudor doorway with large pointed window above, buttressed walls terminating in crocketed finials, crenellated parapets, corner turrets, Tudoresque porches at E and W ends of main block; broad center hall with bisecting lateral hallway, auditorium at rear with gallery and apsidal end, paneled wainscoting throughout. Erected 1857–59 under auspices of Methodist Episcopal Church, South, as main building of college chartered in 1856; Adolphus Heiman of Nashville, architect; Mullins and Hall of Selma, contractors. Interior renovated ca. 1880, including installation of Eastlake style woodwork; refurbished as private academy in 1960s; partially destroyed by tornado in May 1973, and ruins subsequently demolished. Outstanding example in state of castellated style widely used in mid-19th-C. academic architecture. Forerunner of Birmingham-Southern College. Occupied by Southern University 1859–1918. 4 ext. photos (1934–36), 11 int. photos (1935–36); 2 data pages (1936).

Southern University, Chancellor's House (Methodist Hospital) (AL-277), S side of College St. just W of Armory St. Brick, approx. 58'0" x 34'4", 2 stories, shallow hipped roof, similar façades front (N) and rear with recessed asymmetrical 3-bay portico composed of heavy paneled square columns abutted by 1-story demioctagonal bay window; center-hall plan, double parlors to E. Built ca. 1859–60; Adolphus Heiman probably architect. One-story frame kitchen wing added to rear ca. 1900; rear portico enclosed (ca. 1950) and 1-story cinderblock rear wing added 1952–54 when converted into nursing home. Became Greensboro's first hospital in 1918. 6 ext. photos (1934, 1936), 6 int. photos (1936).

Tinker House. *See Greensboro Vicinity.*

Torbert, Judge W. E., House. *See* Johnston-Torbert House (AL-286), 1101 South St.

Tunstall House. *See* Gayle-Hobson-Tunstall House (AL-232), 1801 W. Main St.

Vaughn, J. A., House. *See* Gov. Thomas Seay House and Law Offices (AL-234), area of E. Main and Whelan sts.

Webb, J. H. Y., House (AL-289), 520 Main St. (at end of private drive on N side of Main St.). Frame with clapboarding (façade has novelty siding), basically rectangular (5-bay front) with offset at NE rear, 2 stories, hipped roof with bracketed cornice extending over full-height hexastyle portico composed of paneled brick piers with unusual denticulated capitals, ornate cast-iron balustrade, cantilevered balcony above main doorway; center-hall plan with side hall. Built 1855 for Col. Lucius Quintus Cincinnatus deYampert as gift to daughter and son-in-law, Mr. and Mrs. Webb. Minor rear additions late 19th to early 20th C. 4 ext. photos (1935–36), 6 int. photos (1936); 2 data pages (1936).

Slave House, to rear (N) of dwelling. Frame with clapboarding, rectangular (4-bay front), 1 story, gable roof, central chimney; 2-room plan. Built ca. 1855; demolished. 1 ext. photo (1935), 1 int. photo (1935).

Carriage House, NE of dwelling.

Frame with clapboarding, rectangular, 1 story, gable roof, double elliptically arched doorways. Built mid-19th C.; ruinous in 1978. 1 ext. photo (1936). *Smokehouse,* W of dwelling. Frame with clapboarding on high brick base, square, pyramidal roof, 2 doors in base. Built mid-19th C.; ruinous in 1978. 1 ext. photo (1935).

Withers, Miss Virginia, House. *See* Japonica Path (AL-220), 512 Main St.

Greensboro Vicinity

Cedarwood (AL-843). *See Moundville Vicinity.*

Tinker House (columns only) (AL-220A), from house located approx. 8 mi. S of Greensboro, exact site undetermined. Fluted shafts (approx. 2'6" diameter) of 4 wooden columns, possibly of Ionic order. Salvaged from portico of 2-story plantation residence built ca. 1850 possibly for Robert Tinker; demolished ca. 1930. Columns taken to grounds of Japonica Path (AL-220) in Greensboro; subsequently disintegrated. 3 photos (1936); 1 data page (1940).

Moundville Vicinity

Cedarwood (AL-843), originally located on S side of Ala. 14, approx. 3 mi. W of Greensboro; moved to new location just S of Woodland (AL-279) on E side of Ala. 69, approx. 0.2 mi. N of junction with Ala. 60 at Havana community; approx. 6 mi. S of Moundville.

Frame with clapboarding, rectangular (5-bay front) with laterally projecting wings, 1½ stories, gable roof, 2 exterior end chimneys; center-hall plan, simple Federal style interior. Built early 19th C. for Joseph Blodgett Stickney; moved to present site for restoration in 1974. 6 sheets (1974, including plans, elevations, details).

Woodland (J. W. Whatley House) (AL-279), E side of Ala. 69, approx. 0.3 mi. N of junction with Ala. 60 at Havana community; approx. 6 mi. S of Moundville. Frame with clapboarding, main block 53'0" (5 bays below, 6 above) × 21'0" plus slightly inset ell (approx. 19'0" × 27'0"), 2 stories, gable roof, 2 exterior end chimneys (main block), 1 exterior end chimney (ell), central 1-story pedimented tetrastyle Tuscan portico, double-leaf paneled doorway, L-shaped gallery at rear; center-hall plan with cross hall between main block and ell, Federal period woodwork. Dependencies include well shelter. Built ca. 1828–32 for planter William Kennon; gabled board-and-batten 1-story addition at end of ell (ca. 1870); replaced by frame kitchen wing in 1960s. Reputedly stage stop on old Huntsville-Mobile stagecoach road, which ran a short distance N of house. 4 ext. photos (1936, including well shelter), 2 int. photos (1936). NR.

Newbern

Baptist Church and Masonic Hall (AL-237), W side of Ala. 61, approx. 0.3 mi. N of Southern Railroad crossing; approx. 0.6 mi. S of Ala. 61 intersection with Co. 16.

Frame with clapboarding (façade flush boarding), approx. 32'10" (2-bay front) × 51'8" including portico, 2 stories, gable roof, temple-type front with pedimented tetrastyle Tuscan portico (outer bays have wider intercolumniation), corner pilasters, outside rear stairway to upper floor; open interior plan (first floor), large Masonic room with 2 antechambers (second floor). Built 1849 for joint use of Baptist congregation and local Masons; church meeting room (first floor) renovated late 19th C. including installation of dark wainscoting, Victorian style pulpit, pulpit chairs, and pews; frosted glass sashing installed and Sunday school addition built at NW rear ca. 1955. 2 ext. photos (1936), 1 int. photo (1936); 1 data page (1936).

Presbyterian Church (AL-288), E side of Ala. 61 just N of Southern Railroad crossing; approx. 0.8 mi. S of Ala. 61 intersection with Co. 16. Frame with clapboarding (façade flush boarding), approx. 34'4" (2-bay front) × 60'5" including portico, 1 story, gable roof, temple-type front with unusual 3-column pedimented Tuscan portico; open interior plan. Built 1848; subsequent renovations include dark wainscoting, curved Victorian style pews, 2-over-2 sashing with frosted glass. Slaves originally sat on benches flanking pulpit. 3 ext. photos (1935–36), 1 int. photo (1936); 2 data pages (1937).

Walthalia. *See* Walthall House (AL-215), Ala. 61.

Walthall House (Walthalia) (AL-215), E side of Ala. 61, approx. 0.1 mi. N of Southern Railroad crossing; approx. 0.7 mi. S of Ala. 61 intersection with Co. 16. Frame with clapboarding (façade rabbeted clapboarding), approx. 54′6″ (5-bay front) x 41′6″ plus porch and central rear wing, 1 story, hipped roof, half-hipped porch with pedimented central bay across front, 2 interior chimneys (main block), pilastered lateral walls carrying full entablature; center-hall plan, ceilings 15′ high, simple Greek Revival style woodwork, rear wing separated from main house by open porch. Built 1854–56 for Mrs. Margaret Hill Walthall, widow of planter Robert K. Walthall, on her removal to village from nearby family plantation, White Cross; said to have been erected by itinerant craftsman from Mississippi who built several homes in area. Original porch replaced ca. 1920, rear wing extended (ca. 1900) and replaced entirely in 1939; wing added to SE rear in 1955. Still occupied by Walthall family in 1978. 3 ext. photos (1935), 3 int. photos (1935); 2 data pages (1936).

Smokehouse. Frame with clapboarding on low brick piers, rectangular, gable roof, single doorway in gable end. Built mid-19th C.; demolished. 1 ext. photo (1935).

Prairieville

St. Andrew's Episcopal Church (AL-291), N side of U.S. 80, approx. 0.5 mi. W of junction with Ala. 69. Frame (board and batten) with buttresses, nave (approx. 42′0″ x 24′6″) and chancel (20′6″ x 15′6″) plus galilee porch (11′0″ x 11′0″) at SW corner and vestry (6′0″ x 9′0″) on N side of chancel, steeply pitched gable roof with carved bargeboards and single triangular latticed dormer on N slope of roof to light interior gallery, lancet windows, main gable originally capped by flêche or bellcote; open plan with center aisle, collar-braced trusses,

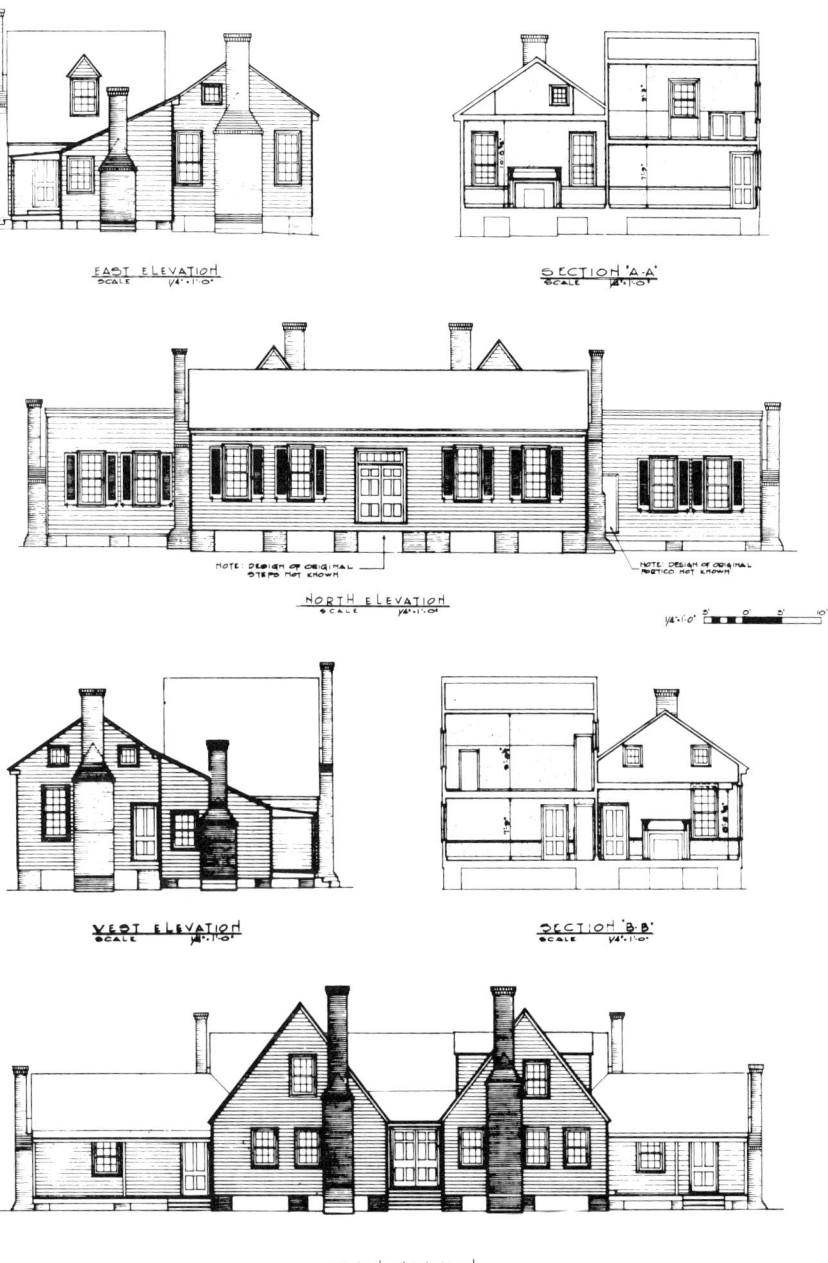

Cedarwood, Moundville vicinity (ca. 1825).

rear gallery (interior virtually unchanged, including original altar rail and chancel furnishings, pews, Jardine organ, stained glass). Adjoining cemetery contains Victorian period tombstones. Built 1853–54, possibly from design furnished by Richard Upjohn; Peter Lee and Joe Glasgow (slaves of parishioner, Capt. Henry A. Tayloe), master-carpenters. Interior woodwork reputedly stained with mixture brewed from stems of tobacco plant; subsequent changes include bracing of interior with steel tie rods, asbestos tile roof replacing wooden shakes. Outstanding example of board-and-batten Gothic Revival chapel embodying ideas set forth in *Upjohn's Rural Architecture* (1852). 4 ext. photos (1936), 4 int. photos (1936). NHL.

Sawyerville

Pickens, Samuel, House. *See* Umbria (AL-236), Ala. 14.

Umbria (Samuel Pickens House) (AL-236), approx. 200 yds. S of Ala. 14 at end of private lane just E of junction with Co. 17, which is 0.4 mi. W of junction with Co. 35; approx. 7.5 mi. W of Greensboro. Raised cottage, frame and brick, main block approx. 55'4" (5-bay front) x 40'6" (including porches) with identical offset flanking wings (approx. 17'0" x 52'0") extending to rear, 1½ stories over ground floor, gable roof extending over full-length raised balustraded porch with Ionic colonnettes, semielliptical fanlight doorway flanked by jib windows, raised U-shaped rear gallery supported by Tuscan colonnettes overlooking service court; originally center-hall plan, notable Federal style interior woodwork. Built ca. 1829–30 for Col. Pickens, from Mecklenburg County, N.C.; wings added 1850; minor subsequent changes including small frame additions to wings, elimination of partition between center hall and W room (parlor) of main block, replacement of original double-leaf front door with glazed French doors; destroyed by fire in 1973. 8 sheets (1936, including plot plan, plans, elevations, details); 15 ext. photos (1934–36), 9 int. photos (1934–36); 1 data page (n.d.).

Schoolhouse, approx. 150' S and rear of main dwelling. Frame with clapboarding, rectangular (3-bay front), 1 story, gable roof, 1 exterior end chimney, small shed porch at front. Probably contemporary with main dwelling; moved 1973 to North River Yacht Club (Watermelon Rd., Tuscaloosa) and restored as part of historic-building complex. 2 ext. photos (1935–36), 2 int. photos (1935–36).

Wellhouse, approx. 150' NW of dwelling house, frame (vertical sheathing), rectangular, small shed covered by gable roof extending over well at S end. Probably built mid-19th C. 1 ext. photo (1935).

See also FBJ (J7-ALA-1126).

HENRY COUNTY

Abbeville

Oates-Danzey House (AL-523), NE corner W. Washington and Trawick sts., approx. 0.2 mi. W of courthouse square. Frame with clapboarding, rectangular (3-bay front) composed of parallel front and rear sections, 1 story, 2 parallel gable roofs front and rear, front section has 2 interior chimneys, full-length front porch with square columns; center-hall plan, interior walls finished with flush boarding. Built ca. 1870 for Gen. William Calvin Oates (1835–1910), Confederate officer, lawyer, and governor of Alabama 1894–96. Moved back from original site ca. 1954, demolished early 1960s except for rear portion (moved to W side of Trawick St. opposite entrance to municipal cemetery; still extant in 1979). 2 ext. photos (1934), 4 int. photos (1934).

Columbia (Houston County) Vicinity

Dunwoody, S. M., House, *See* House (AL-579), Ala. 95.

House (S. M. Dunwoody House) (AL-579), W side of Ala. 95 (Abbeville Hwy.), approx. 1.8 mi. N of Ala. 95 intersection with Ala. 52 in Columbia (approx. 0.7 mi. N of Houston County line in Henry County); 1.0 mi. S of Baker Creek Bridge. Frame with clapboarding, rectangular (5-bay front) with ell at SW rear, 1 story, gable roof, 2 interior chimneys, central 3-bay gabled porch with crude box supports, wide double-leaf door with flanking sidelights; center-hall plan. Built ca. 1870 possibly for Alford family; owned in 1930s by Dunwoody; destroyed by arson 1978. Plain frame plantation house typical of lower Chattahoochee Valley during late 19th C. 2 ext. photos (1934), 1 int. photo (1934).

Haleburg Vicinity

Fluker, "Col." Baldwin M., House (AL-566), W side of Co. 71 (Abbie Ridge Rd.), approx. 1.8 mi. S of junction with Co. 28 at Barnes community NE of Haleburg. Frame with clapboarding, rectangular (3-bay front) with ell, 1 story, gable roof broken to extend over full-length porch at front and shed rooms to rear, 2 exterior end chimneys; center-hall plan. Built ca. 1840; burned ca. 1939. Fluker (1809–77) was a planter born in Georgia. 2 ext. photos (1934).

Smith, Barlett, House (AL-544), E side of Co. 97 (River Rd.) between Haleburg and Shorterville in former community of Smithville, approx. 0.8 mi. N of junction with Co. 71 (Abbie Ridge Rd.) E of Haleburg. Frame with clapboarding (façade flush siding), rectangular (6-bay front) plus long semidetached rear wing, 1 story, gable roof broken to extend over full-length porch with chamfered posts at front and shed rooms at rear, formerly 2 pairs of exterior end chimneys; 2-room plan with separate entrances, interior walls finished with flush boarding, simple Federal period interior woodwork. Evidence of wing at NE corner. Outbuildings include frame barn, shop, and smokehouse. Built early 19th C.; rear wing later; unoccupied and badly deteriorated in 1979; outbuildings demolished. One of oldest frame dwellings in southeast Alabama, and good example of once-characteristic house-type in area. Smith (1792–1843) was a planter born in North Carolina. 5 ext. photos (1934, including 3 photos of outbuildings), 6 int. photos (1934).

Shorterville and Vicinity

Chittey House (AL-575), W side of Co. 97 (River Rd.), approx. 5.1 mi. SE of junction with Ala. 10 at Shorterville. Frame with clapboarding, rectangular (5-bay front), with semidetached rear wing, 2 stories, gable roof, originally 2 exterior end chimneys, 1-story 3-bay shed porch across front supported by 4 square columns, rectangular 1-story gabled semidetached wing at rear; center-hall plan. Built ca. 1840–50, possibly for Howell Chittey; dwelling reputedly incorporated materials salvaged from barge wrecked in nearby Chattahoochee River. Destroyed by fire ca. 1960. 2 ext. photos (1934), 2 int. photos (1934).

Fluker, Col. B. M., House (AL-566). *See Haleburg Vicinity.*

Irwin-McAllister House (AL-524), N side of Ala. 10 (Fort Gaines Hwy.), approx. 0.9 mi. E of junction with Co. 97 (River Rd.) and Co. 65 in Shorterville, on knoll overlooking Chattahoochee bottomlands to SW. Frame with clapboarding, rectangular (7 bays below, 5 bays above) plus ell, 2 stories with 1-story rear shed extension and ell, gable roof (2 exterior end chimneys), distyle pedimented 2-tiered porch with wheatsheaf balustrade at upper level, wide double-leaf doors upstairs and down, secondary entrances in middle bay to each side of porch; center-hall plan, notable Federal period interior woodwork, closed stringer stairway (rare in Alabama) with graining underneath, paneled dado and chimney breasts. Built early 19th C. for Gen. William Irwin (1794–1860), state senator and commander of state militia during Creek War of 1836–37. House restored 1946–60; destroyed by fire 21 Dec. 1960. Graves of Gen. Irwin and two nieces lie E of house. Good example of Federal elements applied to basic vernacular form. 2 ext. photos (1934), 5 int. photos (1934).

Smith, Barlett, House (AL-544). *See Haleburg Vicinity.*

Smithville.

See Haleburg Vicinity.

HOUSTON COUNTY

Columbia

McGriff, T. P., House. *See* Taylor-McGriff House (AL-565), Washington St.

Taylor-McGriff House (T. P. McGriff House) (AL-565), W side of Washington St. just N of intersection with South St., facing E toward former courthouse square; approx. 0.1 mi. S of Washington St. intersection with U.S. 84 (Church St.). Frame with clapboarding (façade flush siding), rectangular (5-bay front) with ell, 1 story, gable roof extending over full-length porch with unusual trellislike supports, long windows, 2 exterior end chimneys; center-hall plan. Probably built ca. 1850 and subsequently renovated; razed ca. 1946. Home in mid-19th C. of John Burt Taylor, Massachusetts-born lawyer, state superintendent of education (1856), and executive secretary for Gov. John Gill Shorter. 2 ext. photos (1934), 1 int. photo (1934).

Teague-Riegel House (AL-567), SE corner South and Washington sts., facing N toward former courthouse square; approx. 0.2 mi. S of Washington St. intersection with U.S. 84 (Church St.). Frame with clapboarding, rectangular (5-bay front) with ell, 1½ stories, gable roof extending over full-length porch with 4 rectangular columns, 2 exterior end chimneys; center-hall plan. Built mid-19th C.; demolished ca. 1950. 2 ext. photos (1934).

Gordon and Vicinity

Bowdon, Charles, House. *See* Britt-Williams-Bowdon House (AL-568), Ala. 95.

Bowdon, Samuel, House (AL-580), S of Ala. 95 on E side of Greenwood St.; approx. 1.0 mi. N of Greenwood St. intersection with U.S. 84. Frame with clapboarding, rectangular (5-bay front), 2 stories, shallow hipped roof, 2 interior chimneys, shed porch across front and W side; center-hall plan; rectangular 1-story gabled semi-detached kitchen at SW rear corner. Built mid-19th C. possibly for North Carolinian Arthur J. Bowdon (1809–51), father of later owner Samuel Bowdon (1835–1917). Original porch railing and posts replaced in late 19th C.; razed 1960s. Also known popularly as Sam Bowdon Hotel because it was one of several houses in the community that took in drummers and other transients arriving by riverboat. 1 ext. photo (1934).

Britt-Williams-Bowdon House (Charles Bowdon House) (AL-568), S of Ala. 95 on W side of Greenwood St.; approx. 1.0 mi. N of Greenwood St. intersection with U.S. 84. Frame with clapboarding, approx. 46'0" (5-bay front) × 31'9", 1 story, gable roof, 2 exterior end chimneys, central 3-bay gabled porch with latticed balustrade; center-hall plan with single large room to either side, inset rear porch with shed rooms at each end. Built mid-19th C.; altered 1947, including rebuilding of E chimney, fenestrational changes, construction of concrete porch on E side and enclosure of rear porch, center hall also widened and other interior changes; front porch enclosed 1966. 1 ext. photo (1934).

House (Nunnley-Bowdon House) (AL-569), N side of Ala. 95, approx. 0.6 mi. NW of Mill Creek and 0.7 mi. SE of junction with Greenwood St. (old road to Greenwood, Fla.) at Gordon. Frame with clapboarding on high brick piers, rectangular (5-bay front) with ell, 1 story (half-story above unfinished), steep gable roof, 2 small interior chimneys, central gabled porch; center-hall plan. Built mid-19th C. reputedly for Lewis Bowdon, never completed; demolished ca. 1965 and brick house built on site. Surrounding plantation later owned by kinsman Samuel Bowdon (1835–1917) and house used as residence for Bowdon's overseer John J. Neely (1856–1944); possibly sometime residence of Dr. W. E. Nunnley, early area physician. 2 ext. photos (1934), 1 int. photo (1934).

Nunnley-Bowdon House. *See* House (AL-569), Ala. 95.

JEFFERSON COUNTY

Birmingham

Arlington (Mudd-Munger House) (AL-424), 331 Cotton Ave. SW. House museum. Frame with clapboarding (flush boarding on façade), 50'4" (5-bay front) X 39'3", 2 stories, hipped roof, 4 exterior end chimneys, hexastyle portico across front composed of paneled wooden piers, main door derived from Plate 28 of Asher Benjamin's *Practical House Carpenter*; center-hall plan. Built mid-19th C. for Judge William S. Mudd. Dependencies date from late 19th C. House extensively renovated ca. 1902, including replacement of small balcony over main doorway with full-length upper gallery, construction of pedimented rear portico (replacing smaller 1-story porch), installation of Colonial Revival mantelpieces and removal of partition between 2 S first-floor rooms to form single large drawing room; also development of formal gardens. Purchased by City of Birmingham as historic house museum in 1953. Originally called The Grove. Mudd (1816–84) was lawyer, legislator, circuit judge, one of founders of Birmingham. 13 ext. photos (1937, including gardens and dependencies), 10 int. photos (1937); 2 data pages (1937). NR.

Smith House. *See* Walker-Smith House (AL-425), 300 Center St.

Walker-Smith House (AL-425), 300 Center St. in old Elyton, S of intersection of Center St. and Division Ct. (between First St. SW and Center Pl.). Frame with clapboarding, rectangular (5-bay front) with ell, 2 stories (ell 1 story), hipped roof, 4 exterior end chimneys, tetrastyle portico across front with attenuated square columns, balcony over doorway; center-hall plan; also latticed wellhouse S of residence. Built in 1848 as 1-story dwelling; second story and present portico added ca. 1900, also interior renovations; demolished 1964. First owner, William Augustus Walker, Sr., was an early Elyton merchant. 4 ext. photos (1937), 5 int. photos (1937), 1 photo of wellhouse (1937); 2 data pages (1937).

Worthington, Benjamin Pinckney, House (AL-426), W side of Sixth Ave. S. (Ave. F) opposite intersection with Thirty-first St. (address in 1928: 3033 Sixth Ave. S.). Frame with clapboarding (flush boarding on façade), rectangular (5-bay front), 2 stories, truncated hipped roof formerly surmounted by balustraded deck, 4 exterior end chimneys, hexastyle portico across front composed of paneled wooden piers, balcony with scroll-cut balustrade above doorway; center-hall plan. Built 1858 as plantation residence; later engulfed by growth of Birmingham and demolished in 1953. 6 ext. photos (1937), 6 int. photos (1937).

LAMAR COUNTY

Crews

Bankhead, George, House. *See* Bankhead-Crews House (AL-397), Old Military Rd.

Bankhead-Crews House (George Bankhead House) (AL-397), facing E on high knoll, W side of Old Military Rd., approx. 0.1 mi. S of intersection with U.S. 278 at Crews; approx. 3.3 mi. E of U.S. 278 intersection with Ala. 17 in Sulligent. Frame with clapboarding, rectangular (3-bay front), 2 stories, gable roof, 2 exterior end chimneys, full-length 1-story porch; open hall with partially enclosed stairway to upper floor. Built for Bankhead in early 19th C.; demolished 1953. Operated as stagecoach inn. Bankhead, from Union District, S.C., settled in Marion (now Lamar) County in 1818 and was progenitor of Bankhead political dynasty: grandfather of Sen. John Hollis Bankhead, great-grandfather of Speaker of the House William Brockman Bankhead, great-great-grandfather of actress Tallulah Bankhead. 1 ext. photo (1936), 2 int. photos (1936).

Sulligent

Bankhead, James Greer, House (Forest Home) (AL-391), on hill approx. 0.1 mi. S of U.S. 278 facing NW (entrance lane at Bankhead Cir.), approx. 0.7 mi. E of U.S. 278 intersection with Ala. 17 in Sulligent; formerly situated on old Wolf Rd. (now part of private drive in front of house). Frame with clapboarding, approx. 46'4" (7 bays first story, 5 bays second story) x 37'6" overall, 2 stories with 1-story rear shed extension, gable roof, originally 2 pairs of exterior end chimneys, 5-bay balustraded porch across front; open hall through first floor with single room to either side and smaller shed rooms behind, simple paneled dado in NE room. Log dining room and kitchen once to rear of house (burned late 19th C.). Built ca. 1850; open hall enclosed and ell added late 19th C.; ell and SW chimney destroyed in 1933 cyclone; subsequent minor alterations and additions. Birthplace of Sen. John Hollis Bankhead (1842–1920), initiator of federal highway legislation; also father of Speaker of the House William Brockman Bankhead (1874–1940) and grandfather of actress Tallulah Bankhead. Farm known in early days as Forest Home. 4 ext. photos (1936, including 1 of well), 3 int. photos (1936). NR.

LAUDERDALE COUNTY

Center Star Vicinity

Taylor-Cunningham Houses (Cunningham Houses) (AL-377), N side of Bellevue Rd., 0.3 mi. W of junction with Houstontown Rd. and 1.7 mi. S of intersection of Houstontown Rd. with U.S. 43/72; approx. 1.2 mi. E of Center Star. Two dwellings, log and frame respectively, forming part of 19th-C. plantation complex. Owned by same family from 1820 to 1970.
First House. Log (square-notch construction), double-pen dwelling (W pen 3 bays, E pen 2 bays) with open passage or dogtrot and rear ell separated from main block by breezeway, gable roof, originally 2 exterior end chimneys; 2 large rooms flanking open passage, ladder-like stair in W room; also double-pen log barn and well with wooden casing. Built ca. 1820; barn and well destroyed. 7 ext. photos (1935–36), 1 int. photo (1936), 1 photo each of barn and well (1936).
Second House. Frame with clapboarding, rectangular (3-bay front) with ell, 2 stories (ell 1 story), gable roof, 2 exterior end chimneys, 2-tiered pedimented entrance porch with flanking triple windows, modillioned cornice; center-hall plan, retardataire "country Federal" interior woodwork. Built ca. 1850 for Benjamin Taylor. Severely altered in 1975, including removal of original chimneys, enclosure of upper porch, application of aluminum siding. 2 ext. photos (1936), 3 int. photos (1936); 1 data page (1936).

Florence

Ashcraft House. *See* James Bennington Irvine House (AL-358), 461 N. Pine St.

Coalter-McFarland House (Mapleton, McFarland House) (AL-376), 420 S. Pine St. (house oriented N to S between Limestone and Reeder sts.). Frame with clapboarding, rectangular (identical 5-bay N and S façades), 2½ stories, gable roof, 2 exterior and 2 interior end chimneys, originally 2-tiered pedimented tetrastyle N and S entrance porticoes (Tuscan colonnettes on S, square colonnettes on N), elliptical fanlight doorways, Palladian window at E gable end; center-hall plan, excellent Federal period interior detail (including Adamesque architraves with molded cornices and applied urns, swags, and grapeleaf motifs) probably derived in part from Asher Benjamin's *American Builder's Companion* (1st ed. 1806), paneled dado, elliptical arch in hallway with bead molding and raised keystone, paneled folding doors between double parlors. Brick 1-story semidetached kitchen wing on W side. Built ca. 1830 for Dr. George Coalter, lawyer and planter from Kentucky. Roof replaced late 19th C. (including application of brackets at gable ends), porch extended by addition of flanking 1-story bays. House renovated ca. 1945, including replacement of 2-tiered porches with piered pedimented porticoes, addition of low brick office on E wing and remodeling of original kitchen wing. Named Mapleton at that time. 2

ext. photos (1934), 2 int. photos (1934). NR.

Courtview (Foster-O'Neal-Rogers House, Rogers Hall) (AL-329), N end of Court St. on University of North Alabama campus. Brick, 62'7" (5-bay front) x 52' overall, 2 stories over high ground floor, truncated hipped roof with deck, 4 interior end chimneys, full-height tetrastyle entrance portico composed of 2 pairs of large fluted Ionic columns flanking deeply recessed main doorway, balcony above with cast-iron balustrade, cast-iron balustraded decks to either side of portico with tall French doors, full entablature with denticulated cornice (originally bracketed), cast-iron lintels and column bases; center-hall plan formerly with side stairhall, decorative plasterwork and marble mantels. Built ca. 1855 for George Washington Foster; Adolphus Heiman of Nashville possibly architect. Renovated ca. 1900 and 1922, including addition of rear solarium, replacement of original wooden deck floors with concrete base, removal of cornice brackets, addition of metal roof cresting; also removal of original stairway and construction of divided stair in main hallway. Home from 1900 to 1922 of Gov. Emmet O'Neal. 17 sheets (1934–35, including plot plan, plans, elevations, details); 10 ext. photos (1934–35), 1 ext. photocopy (ca. 1890), 22 int. photos (1935); 3 data pages (1936). NR.

First Presbyterian Church (AL-328), S side of E. Mobile St. between Seminary St. and Wood Ave. Brick (façade Flemish bond), originally rectangular (2-bay front, 7 bays deep) with 2 tiers of 12-over-16 sash windows, gable roof, pedimented façade with Palladian window in tympanum, large frame 3-stage domed cupola with arched belfry openings and metal weathervane, double entrance doors surmounted by blind fan transoms, façade has molded brick watertable and belt course; open interior plan with U-shaped gallery. Built ca. 1824. Greatly altered 1898–99, including removal of cupola, extensive changes to façade and construction of corner towers, installation of art glass windows, removal of side galleries, and placement of choir loft behind pulpit. Rear addition 1910; roof burned 1930, followed by further renovations. Possibly first brick church erected in Alabama. 1 ext. photo (1934), 1 ext. photocopy (n.d.) showing church before alterations; 2 data pages (1936).

Hawkins-Sample House (Miss Mattie Sample House) (AL-326), 219 Hermitage Dr. Frame with clapboarding over log, rectangular (5-bay front) with ell, 1½ stories, gable roof, 2 exterior end chimneys (main block), 1 exterior end chimney (ell); center-hall plan. Nucleus is log cabin (2 S bays) built ca. 1829; covered with clapboarding and enlarged 1844 for Wiley T. Hawkins by addition of central hall, 2 N bays, and long ell. Heavily damaged by fire Feb. 1976 and subsequently demolished. 2 ext. photos (1934), 3 int. photos (1934–35); 1 data page (1936).

Irvine, James Bennington, House (Ashcraft House) (AL-358), 461 N. Pine St. Brick (façade Flemish bond), rectangular (5-bay front), 1½ stories over full basement, gable roof with stepped parapet at each end, 2 pairs of interior end chimneys, subordinate cross-gable, pedimented 4-bay tetrastyle portico with fluted Ionic colonnettes, Palladian window in tympanum, Palladian windows also at each gable end and at rear; center-hall plan with elliptical archway in hall resting on scrolled consoles, unusual paneled transoms, basement kitchen and service area. Frame rectangular servants' house and brick smokehouse at rear. Built ca. 1832; raised full-length gable porch added to rear (ca. 1900). Notable local example of Federal style architecture. 2 ext. photos (1934), 5 int. photos (1935), 1 ext. photo of outbuildings (1935); 1 data page (1936).

Irvine Place. *See* Simpson-Irvine House (AL-332), 459 N. Court St.

Lambeth House. *See* Pope's Tavern (AL-334), 203 Hermitage Dr.

McFarland House. *See* Coalter-McFarland House (AL-376), 420 S. Pine St.

Mapleton. *See* Coalter-McFarland House (AL-376), 420 S. Pine St.

Patton, Gov. Robert, House. *See* Sweetwater (AL-333), near Sweetwater Ave. and Florence Blvd.

Patton-Perry House (Perry House) (AL-359), SW corner N. Pine and Tuscaloosa sts. Brick, basically rectangular (4-bay front with 3-bay setback) plus long ell, 2 stories (ell 1 story), hipped roof, bracketed cornice, 1-story porches at front and sides. S portion built ca. 1830, probably as 3-bay gabled main block with side-hall plan and large rear extension terminating in stepped parapet; extensively altered and enlarged ca. 1875 with 1-bay N addition and ell (incorporating original detached brick kitchen); also construction of porches and alteration of roof to hipped form, plus interior changes including new stairway; front porch replaced ca. 1920; house demolished ca. 1955. Possibly residence of Robert Patton (later governor) ca. 1830–35. 2 ext. photos (1934), 4 int. photos (1935); 2 data pages (1936).

Perry House. *See* Patton-Perry House (AL-359), SW corner N. Pine and Tuscaloosa sts.

Pope's Tavern (Lambeth House) (AL-334), 203 Hermitage Dr. (NW corner Hermitage Dr. and N. Seminary St.). Museum. Brick, rectangular (7-bay front) with parallel rear wings, 1½ stories, gable roof with frame overhang forming full-length porch, corbeled cornice with unusual double brick dentil course; center-hall plan with tavern room to N, single large room upstairs. Built ca. 1820. Later frame lean-to addition and porch at rear; pent-roof dormers also added late 19th C.; acquired 1973 by City of Florence and subsequently restored as museum. 3 ext. photos (1934–35), 3 int. photos (1935); 1 data page (1936). *See also* FBJ (J7-ALA-1062), Tebbs (T3-ALA-441250 and 441251).

Rogers Hall. *See* Courtview (AL-329), N end of Court St.

Sample, Miss Mattie, House. *See* Hawkins-Sample House (AL-326), 219 Hermitage Dr.

Simpson-Irvine House (Irvine Place) (AL-332), 459 N. Court St. Brick (façade Flemish bond) with ashlar trim, rectangular (5-bay front), 2 stories over full basement, truncated hipped roof, 4 interior end chimneys, originally small 1-story entrance porch on E front and 1-story ground-level brick-paved shed porch across rear, granite bull's-eye lintels; center-hall plan with side stairhall on N, wide paneled double doors between S parlors, unusual paneled overdoors, notable Greek Revival style black marble mantels, also basement kitchen and service area. Built 1843 for John Simpson, merchant born in Ulster, on site of earlier frame house. Acquired 1853 by James Bennington Irvine, who built small semi-detached brick rectangular 1-story law office on N side; original entrance porch replaced late 19th C. by bracketed Victorian porch. Renovated and restored 1946–47, including replacement of E and W porches by full-height 3-bay tetrastyle porticoes with square columns, demolition of law office and other N additions and replacement by 1-story kitchen-service area; Dudley E. Jones of Memphis, Tenn., architect. 2 ext. photos (1934), 2 ext. photos (1977), 4 int. photos (1934–35), 2 int. photos (1977); 1 data page (1936), 6 data pages (1977).

Simpson, John, House (AL-330), 112 S. Pine St. Frame with clapboarding, approx. 25' (3-bay front) x 30', 2 stories over basement, gable roof, 1 pair of exterior end chimneys; side-hall plan. Built ca. 1825. Late 19th-C. 1-story porch across front (replaced by 2-story porch ca. 1925), also 1-story gable addition at rear; demolished ca. 1950. 2 ext. photos (1934); 2 data pages (1936).

Sweetwater (Gov. Robert Patton House) (AL-333), approx. 0.2 mi. SE of intersection of Sweetwater Ave. and Florence Blvd. (U.S. 43/72) at end of long private lane; 0.1 mi. due N of Sweetwater Creek. Brick (façade Flemish bond), rectangular (5-bay front), 2 stories over basement, hipped roof, 4 interior end chimneys, 1-story entrance portico with balustraded deck (deck probably late 19th C.), small pedimented porch on S side, 1-story shed porch across rear, modillioned cornice; center-hall plan with side hall and secondary stair, notable original Greek Revival style marble mantels in double drawing rooms. Dependencies include brick L-shaped 1-story kitchen and servants' quarters, frame barn with vertical sheathing. Approach to house is boxwood-bordered heart-shaped drive with marble fountain in center. Begun 1828 for Gen. John Brahan (1774–1834), completed 1835 for son-in-law Robert Miller Patton; reconditioned 1920s, including addition of frame-and-brick kitchen wing at NE rear; again unoccupied and deteriorated 1983. Patton was post–Civil War governor of Alabama (1865–68). 3 ext. photos (1934–35), 5 int. photos (1934–35), 2 ext. photos of dependencies (1935); 2 photocopies of genealogical data on Patton family (1935). NR.

Florence Vicinity

Forks of Cypress, The (AL-375), on knoll 0.2 mi. N of Jackson Rd. and 0.4 mi. E of Jackson Ford Bridge over Big Cypress Creek; approx. 1.5 mi. NW of Jackson Rd. intersection with Cox Creek Pkwy. (Ala. 133). Frame with beaded clapboarding plus ashlar and stuccoed-brick colonnade, rectangular (overall dimensions 82'1" x 64'1", including colonnade which encloses frame nucleus 57′10″ × 37′5″), 5-bay front, 2 stories, hipped roof, 4 exterior end chimneys, segmentally arched fanlight doorway, house surrounded by monumental colonnade composed of 24 Ionic columns on brick-and-ashlar stylobate; center-hall plan with wide rear stairhall, notable Federal style interior woodwork. Complex also includes saddlebag-type log house, frame smokehouse, privy, and cemetery (see below). House built ca. 1830 for James Jackson; probably designed by William Nichols; struck by lightning and burned 6 June 1966; ruins extant. Only example in Alabama of dwelling with peristyle colonnade and unique in America in such use of Ionic order. Jackson (1782–1840), born in Ulster, was a planter and nationally known horsebreeder of early 19th C.; private racetrack once located NE of house. 24 sheets (1935–36, including plot plan, plans, elevations, sections, details), 6 sheets (1958, including plans, elevations, details); 3 ext. photos (1934–35), 12 int. photos (1934–35); 2 data pages (1936).

Log House, NE of main house. Saddle-notch construction, 45′8″ × 20′2″ consisting of 2 pens (1 bay each) with rubblestone chimney between, 1½ stories, gable roof; 2 rooms. Believed to have been built ca. 1818 or earlier; 20th-C. additions and siding. Rare example in Alabama of saddlebag-type log house. Jackson's first residence; later servants' quarters. ¾ sheet (1935–36, including plans, elevations); 6 ext. photos (1935–36), 2 int. photos (1935).

Privy, NE of house. Frame with clapboarding on stone footing, 8′0″ (1 bay) × 6′0″, gable roof, louvered vents at each end; "four-seater." Built probably mid-19th C.; destroyed. ¼ sheet (1935–36, including plan, elevations); 1 ext. photo (1935).

Smokehouse, NE of house. Frame with beaded clapboarding on rubblestone foundation, 18′6″ (1 bay) × 18′6″, gable roof. Probably built early 19th C. 1 sheet (1935–36, including plan, elevations, section, details); 1 ext. photo (1935).

Plantation Cemetery, on knoll 0.3 mi. E of house. Ashlar wall enclosing rectangular plot entered over stone stile at NW corner; 19th- and early 20th-C. granite markers including several Greek Revival style monuments. Graves data from ca. 1819. ⅔ sheet (1935–36, ashlar wall and stile only); 2 photos (1935).

Sorghum Trough. Hewn from large poplar log, 16′0″ × 2′10″ × 3′1″ in size. Used as receptacle for syrup extracted from sorghum plant. Probably early 19th C.; destroyed. ⅓ sheet (1935–36).

See also FBJ (J7-ALA-1052 through 1061).

Hood, James, House. See Woodlawn (AL-331), Co. 14 and Ala. 20.

Sweetwater. *See Florence.*

Woodlawn (James Hood House) (AL-331), approx. 0.2 mi. directly SW of intersection of Co. 14 and Ala. 20 (Savannah Hwy.) at end of private lane; approx. 0.5 mi. due W of Cypress Creek. Brick (façade Flemish bond), main block rectangular (5-bay front) with flanking symmetrical 1-bay wings and rear ell, 2 stories (wings and ell 1 story), gable roof, single exterior chimney at each gable end of main block and flanking wings, large fanlight doorway approached by granite steps, 1-story shed porch across rear; center-hall plan, notable Federal period interior including Adamesque mantels, paneled reveals; outstanding formal boxwood garden at front. Built ca. 1825 for Hood, a planter and merchant born in Ulster; renovated and restored 1929, including addition of low second story to ell. Formerly called Woodland. 4 ext. photos (1934–36), 12 int. photos (1934–36); 2 data pages (1937). See also FBJ (J7-ALA-1050 and 1051).

Rogersville

Cunningham Houses. *Under Center Star Vicinity, see* Taylor-Cunningham Houses (AL-377).

Weaver, Adam, House (AL-374), W side of Weaver Branch immediately S of Old U.S. 72, approx. 0.5 mi. W of intersection with Lambs Ferry Rd. in Rogersville. Double-pen log house (half dovetail-notch construction) later covered with clapboarding, rectangular (3-bay front) with ell, 1½ stories, gable roof, 2 massive ashlar (limestone) exterior end chimneys; open central passage or dogtrot, ladder-like stair to raised attic, paneled chimney breasts. Built 1838; later covered with clapboarding and frame ell added; demolished 1936. Good example of yeoman log dwelling. 9 ext. photos (1935–36), 3 int. photos (1935–36); 1 data page (1936).

LAWRENCE COUNTY

Courtland

James, Westwood Wallace, House (Campbell House) (AL-383), S side of Tennessee St., approx. 210' W of intersection with Alabama St. at public square, immediately N of Southern Railroad tracks. Frame with beaded clapboarding, main block 30'4" (5-bay front) X 20'3", also 3-bay W wing, 1½ stories, gable roof, 2 exterior end chimneys (main block) and 1 exterior end chimney (wing), notable Adamesque fanlight doorway enframed by architrave with applied sunbursts and heavily molded cornice with bead-and-reel fillet; unusual occurrence in Alabama of hall-and-parlor plan. Carriage house at SW rear. Built ca. 1825; W wing later; demolished ca. 1940. James (1795–1866) was a Virginia-born cabinetmaker. Good example of small Federal period dwelling. 4 sheets (1937, including plan, elevations, section, details); 3 ext. photos (1935), 1 int. photo (1935). See also FBJ (J7-ALA-1063 and 1064).

Courtland Vicinity

Bride's Hill (Pointer House, Sunnybrook) (AL-865), S side of Co. 43 (Lock "A" Rd.), approx. 1.5 mi. NE of junction with Alt. U.S. 72 (Ala. 20) at Wheeler community, approx. 3.5 mi. E of Courtland. Frame with clapboarding, 54'8" (5-bay front) X 20'2", 1½ stories over basement, gable roof with dormers, 2 exterior end chimneys with single shed-roof pent on each gable end, small pedimented entrance porch; center-hall plan. Built ca. 1830, probably for Mrs. Elizabeth Dandridge; Daniel Wade possibly master-builder. Rear lean-to added later. Rare occurrence in Alabama of chimney pents characteristic of early Virginia and Maryland domestic architecture. Renamed Sunnybrook in early 20th C. 1 ext. photo (1978).

Pointer House. See Bride's Hill (AL-865), Co. 43.

Sunnybrook. See Bride's Hill (AL-865), Co. 43.

Wheeler, Gen. Joseph, House (also known as Home Sweet Home, formerly called Pond Spring) (AL-347), S side of Alt. U.S. 72 (Ala. 20), approx. 3.7 mi. E of junction with Co. 29 (Jackson St.) in Courtland. Nucleus of large working plantation including dwelling, log outbuildings, extensive gardens, and family cemetery; home 1869–1906 of Gen. Joseph ("Fightin' Joe") Wheeler, noted military figure of Civil and Spanish-American wars, lawyer, planter, congressman. Residence actually 2 dwellings, West Wing and East Wing, linked by breezeway. Both structures frame with clapboarding, rectangular (5-bay front), 2 stories, gable roof; center-hall plan. Old House has 2-tiered pedimented central porch, simple Federal period sidelights, transoms; New House has 1-story porch across front, 2-tiered porch at rear; original furnishings. Old House built ca. 1830; New House built 1884 under supervision of Mrs. Joseph Wheeler. Outbuildings included dogtrot log house (ca. 1818) which was first dwelling; also log barn, smokehouse, icehouse. Complex evolved ca. 1818–90 as home first of Hickman family, then Sherrod and Wheeler families. Notable as ensemble of 19th-C. structures; also for historical associations. 1 sheet, plan of overall complex (1935), 7 sheets, West Wing (1935, including plans, elevations, details), 2 sheets, East Wing (1935, plans only), 1 sheet, log house (1935, including plan, elevations); 5 ext. photos, West Wing, and 4 ext. photos, East Wing (1934–35), 4 int. photos, West Wing, and 9 int. photos, East Wing (1934–35), also 4 ext. photos of dependencies (1935, including log house, barn, smokehouse, icehouse), 6 photos of grounds and family cemetery (1934–35); 6 data pages (1936). See also FBJ (J7-ALA-1065 through 1068).

Moulton

Lawrence County Courthouse (AL-310), Courthouse Square (block bounded by Court, Lawrence, Market, and Main sts.). Brick, 54'0" X 54'0" (5 bays on each side), 2 stories, hipped roof surmounted by 3-stage tower with spired belfry and weathervane, 4 interior end chimneys, bays articulated by pilasters with molded caps and bases carrying full entablature; central stairhall surrounded on 3 sides by county offices, large second-floor courtroom with gallery. Built 1859–60 to replace courthouse burned on 18 March 1859; Gen. Hiram H. Higgins, architect. 1-story brick vault wing added to E side 1904; renovated ca. 1900 including replacement of original 9-over-9 sashing; demolished 1935 for new courthouse. 13 sheets (1935, including plot plan, plans, elevations, sections, details); 2 ext. photos (1934), 1 ext. photocopy (ca. 1904),

7 int. photos (1935); 2 data pages (1936).

Town Creek Vicinity

Rocky Hill (James Edmonds Saunders House) (AL-311), approx. 0.1 mi. N of Alt. U.S. 72 (Ala. 20), 2.5 mi. E of junction with Ala. 101 in Town Creek, midway between Town Creek and Courtland. Brick with stucco scored to simulate ashlar, rectangular (5-bay N and S fronts) with flanking symmetrical wings, 2 stories (wings 1 story) over raised basement, hipped roof surmounted by ornate arcuated cupola with finial, 2 interior end chimneys, bracketed cornice, N and S fronts have identical 1-story raised tetrastyle Doric porticoes with balustraded deck, each wing has projecting arcuated bay window on N front and 2-bay Tuscan porch on S; center-hall plan, very elaborate interior, including curved stairway, ornate elliptical archway between drawing rooms, decorative plaster cornices and chandelier medallions, marble mantels. Dependencies include 5-story crenelated octagonal tower linked to W side of house by high brick wall with Tudor-arched gate; also kitchen and servants' quarters (brick, rectangular, 4 bays, 1½ stories, 2 exterior end chimneys). Built ca. 1858–61 on site of earlier dwelling; interior woodwork and tower attributed to Welsh-born itinerant craftsman Hugh Jones. Abandoned after 1935; ruins demolished 1961. Unusually eclectic mixture of neoclassical and picturesque elements in single complex. First owner, Saunders (1806–96), was state legislator, planter, cotton merchant, noted political figure in 19th-C. Alabama. 3 ext. photos (1935), 5 int. photos (1935); 2 data pages (1936).

Saunders-Goode-Hall House (Hall House) (AL-324), at end of farm lane 0.8 mi. E of Ala. 101, approx. 3.0 mi. N of junction with

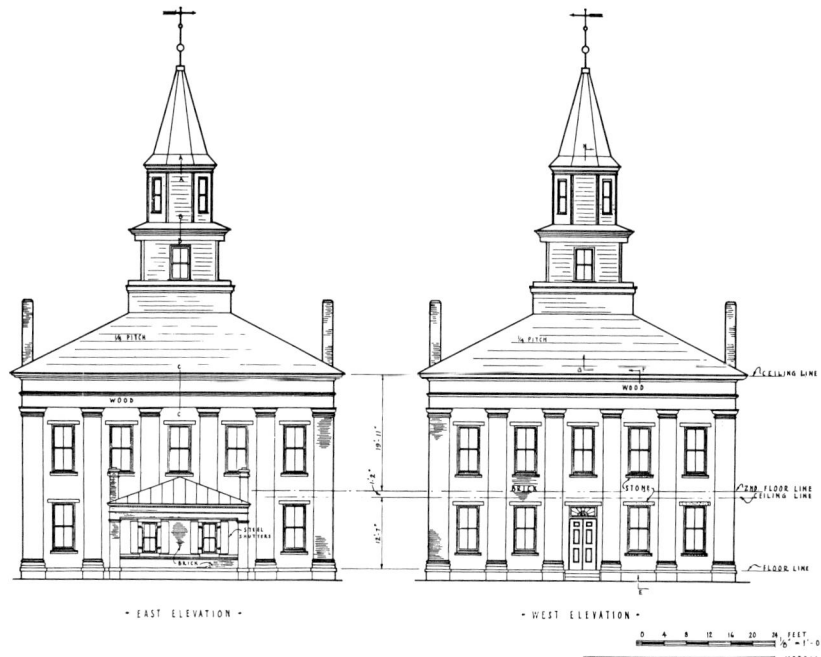
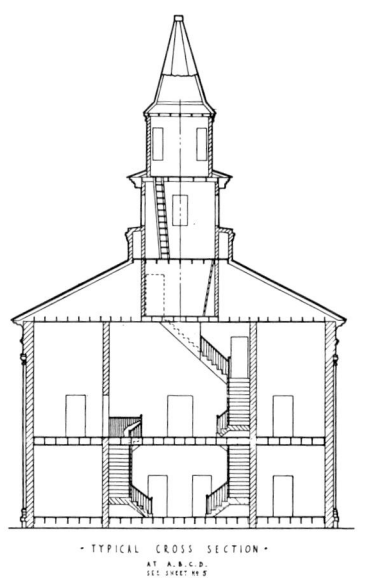
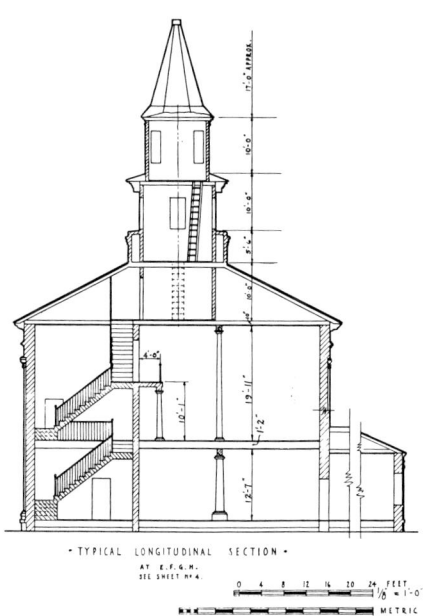

Lawrence County Courthouse, Moulton (1859–60, demolished 1935).

Alt. U.S. 72 (Ala. 20) at Town Creek. Brick (Flemish bond), 3-part composition, rectangular (3-bay) central block with flanking (2-bay) wings, 2 stories over raised basement with 1½-story wings and parapeted end chimneys, central pavilion fronted by pedimented tetrastyle Roman Doric portico with semielliptical lunette in tympanum; wings are pedimented and have brick pilasters with molded caps and bases, paneled doorway framed by geometrical sidelights and transom, with flanking engaged fluted colonnettes carrying molded entablature (treatment echoed in pilasters and entablature of adjacent windows); unusual H-shaped interior arrangement with 1-room-deep center section (side-hall plan) between 2-room-deep wings. Two log dependencies (destroyed). Built ca. 1830–35 for the Rev. Turner Saunders, planter and Methodist minister from Brunswick County, Va. Outstanding expression in Alabama of Jeffersonian classicism exhibiting Palladian influence. 19 ext. photos (1935–37, including dependencies), 15 int. photos (1935–37); 2 data pages (1937). NR. *See also* FBJ (J7-ALA-1069 through 1077).

Wheeler.

See Courtland Vicinity.

LEE COUNTY

Auburn

Drake-Samford House (AL-503), 449 N. Gay St. (SW corner N. Gay St. and E. Drake Ave.). Frame with clapboarding (façade flush boarding), basically square (3-bay front), 2 stories, hipped roof extending over full-length balustraded tetrastyle portico with heavy square piers carrying upper-level gallery, wide double-leaf Greek Revival style doorways above and below; center-hall plan, spiral stairway. Built mid-19th C.; demolished spring 1978. Residence after 1857 of Dr. John Hodges Drake, native of Nash County, N.C.; later home of daughter Caroline, wife of Gov. William James Samford. 1 ext. photo (1934), 1 int. photo (1934).

Halliday-Cary House. *See* Kidd-Halliday-Cary House (AL-540), 360 N. College St.

House (Meadows House) (AL-582), 342 N. College St. Frame with clapboarding (façade stuccoed), 52'6" (5-bay front) × 27'6" including portico, 1 story, hipped roof extending over full-length tetrastyle portico composed of heavy square piers, wide double-leaf door flanked by floor-length windows, originally 2 interior end chimneys; center-hall plan. Built mid-19th C.; late 19th-C. rear shed additions; sides and rear covered with asbestos siding, original front door replaced by glazed doors, window sashes on portico replaced by smaller metal sashes. 3 ext. photos (1935), 5 int. photos (1935).

Jones Hotel. *See* McElhaney House (AL-550), 135 N. College St.

Kidd-Halliday-Cary House (Halliday-Cary House) (AL-540), 360 N. College St. Raised cottage, frame with clapboarding (façade flush siding) on brick basement, 48'0" (3-bay front) × 53'2", 1 story over ground floor, originally hipped roof (now truncated) extending over full-length tetrastyle portico composed of heavy stuccoed brick piers rising directly from ground level and carrying raised balustraded porch (latticed beneath) reached by central stairway, wide double-leaf doorway with flanking floor-length windows, smaller 2-column portico at rear with raised porch reached by double stairway; center-hall plan with unusual freestanding corkscrew stair with turned balusters between basement and main floor (said to have been constructed by itinerant French cabinetmaker). Built ca. 1848 for James W. Kidd; renovated ca. 1900–10, including alteration of roofline and addition of two cross-gables on each slope to accommodate second story, construction of rear wing and enclosure of rear portico as sleeping porch; reconditioned and partially restored in 1953, including removal of later rear wing and cross-gables. 6 sheets (1935, including plans, elevations, section, details); 3 ext. photos (1934), 6 int. photos (1934); 2 data pages (1936). *See also* FBJ (J7-ALA-1001 through 1003).

McElhaney Hotel. *See* McElhaney House (AL-550), 135 N. College St.

McElhaney House (Jones Hotel, McElhaney Hotel) (AL-550), 135 N. College St. (W side College between

Glenn Ave. and Magnolia St.). Frame with clapboarding (façade flush siding), rectangular (5-bay front), 2 stories, hipped roof extending over full-length tetrastyle portico composed of slender fluted columns, full-length balcony at upper level, bracketed cornice, doors and windows enframed by fluted pilasters with abbreviated architrave; center-hall plan, heavy Greek Revival style interior woodwork. Built ca. 1860, apparently as residence and hostelry for F. G. McElhaney (1826–1904), born in Pennsylvania, dentist, planter, and hotelkeeper; various additions and alterations at rear (late 19th and early 20th C.); demolished 1960 to make way for Auburn University Baptist Student Center. 4 ext. photos (1934–35), 10 int. photos (1935).

Meadows House. *See* House (AL-582), 342 N. College St.

Perry-Cauthen House (AL-551), 283 E. Drake Ave. (N side of E. Drake Ave. just W of intersection with N. Ross St. and 0.2 mi. E of Drake Ave. intersection with N. Gay St.). Raised cottage, frame with clapboarding (façade stuccoed) on brick basement, rectangular (3-bay front), 1 story over ground floor, hipped roof extending over full-length tetrastyle portico composed of square columns resting on high brick piers, raised balustraded porch reached by central stairway, bracketed cornice, wide double-leaf door flanked by jib-windows, pedimented and eared architraves; center-hall plan, late Greek Revival style woodwork, molded chair-rail. Built ca. 1855–60 for Simeon Perry, early civil engineer; Mr. Shelton, of building firm of Shelton and Williams, reputed contractor; destroyed by tornado in 1953. 2 ext. photos (1934–35), 6 int. photos (1934–35).

Auburn Vicinity

Frazer-Brown House (Noble Hall) (AL-502), W side of Shelton Mill Rd. (Co. 35), 1.6 mi. NE of junction with N. College St. in Auburn. Rubblestone covered with stucco (outer walls 22" thick), 53'6" (3-bay front) X 55'10" overall, 2 stories, shallow hipped roof extending over full-length tetrastyle porticoes front and rear (modified Doric order at front, piers at rear) resting on pedestal bases, upper balconies enclosed by wheatsheaf balustrade, floor-length windows with unusual split louvered blinds; center-hall plan, "hanging" reverse-flight stair, Greek Revival trim. Original dependencies include kitchen and smokehouse (stuccoed rubblestone). Built ca. 1852–54 for Addison Frazer (1809–1873) as seat of 2,000-acre plantation; Henry Foster, builder. Reconditioned 1932–41, including rebuilding of original wooden columns in stuccoed brick, partial brick reconstruction of N end of kitchen. Rare occurrence in 19th-C. Alabama of ashlar domestic construction. 3 sheets (1934, including plans, elevations, section, details); 4 ext. photos (1934, including 1 photo of kitchen and smokehouse, 1 photo of meat-salting trough hewn from poplar log); 4 data pages (1936).

Moore-Whatley House (AL-501), S side of Moore's Mill Rd. (Co. 12), approx. 0.3 mi. SE of I-85 intersection; on crest of hill approx. 0.3 mi. NW of Co. 12 bridge over Chewacla Creek. Frame with clapboarding (façade stuccoed) on brick piers, main block 44'10" (3-bay front) X 48'4" plus semidetached dining wing at center rear across open porch, 1 story, hipped roof extending over full-length balustraded tetrastyle portico supported by square columns with molded capitals, paneled dado across façade (characteristic of houses in area); center-hall plan. Built mid-19th C. (rear wing possibly later) for Austin Osborne Moore, planter and owner of mill that stood nearby on W bank of Chewacla Creek just N of Moore's Mill Rd. Bridge; house demolished ca. 1960. 3 sheets (1934, including plan, elevations, section, details); 2 ext. photos (1934); 2 data pages (1936).

Noble Hall. *See* Frazer-Brown House (AL-502), Shelton Mill Rd.

Chewacla.

See Opelika Vicinity.

Gold Hill

Ellington House. *See* Gold Hill (AL-581), Oak Bowery Rd.

Gold Hill (Ellington House) (AL-581), facing NW toward Oak Bowery Rd. just W of intersection with Ala. 147 in Gold Hill community (approx. 3.3 mi. NW of Ala. 147 intersection with U.S. 280 W of Opelika); 0.5 mi. N of Little Loblockee Creek. Frame with clapboarding (façade rabbeted), 50'3" (5-bay front) X 40'8", 2 stories, hipped roof extending over full-length tetrastyle Doric portico, 3-bay balcony above doorway, hood-mold window surrounds, 2 pairs of exterior end chimneys; center-hall plan, spiral stairway, both Federal and late Greek Revival style woodwork, interior walls partially finished with flush boarding. Built ca. 1850, reputedly for Edmund S. Harris, as home for daughter and son-in-law; parallel board-and-batten gabled 1-story rear wings added late 19th C.; reconditioned ca. 1949, including partial removal of E rear wing and enclosure of rear shed porch; notable log and frame dependencies. 6 ext. photos (1935), 9 int. photos (1935).

Loachapoka

Baptist Church (AL-512), N side of Stage Rd. (Ala. 14) just E of junction with Waverly Rd. (Co. 11). Frame with clapboarding (façade flush boarding), 40'3" (2-bay front) X 60'3" overall, 1 story, gable roof, pedimented tetrastyle portico composed of slender square columns with molded caps and bases, tall 2-stage square belfry, twin doorways; open interior plan with 2 aisles. Built ca. 1859, William Ellis, contractor; demolished ca. 1970 to make way for new structure. Virtually identical to nearby Loachapoka Methodist Church erected shortly afterward by same builder (heavily damaged by fire in June 1977 and subsequently demolished). 2 sheets (1934, including plan, elevations, section, details); 2 ext. photos (1934); 2 data pages (1936).

Loachapoka Vicinity

Hammack House (AL-513), 0.3 mi. W of Co. 11 (Waverly Rd.) on S side of unmarked dirt road intersecting Co. 11, approx. 1.1 mi. N of junction with Ala. 14 at Loachapoka. Frame with clapboarding (façade flush siding), approx. 40'6" (3-bay front) X 40'7", 2 stories, hipped roof extending over balustraded tetrastyle portico with slender square columns, twin single-leaf doorways flanked by 3-part windows, 2 pairs of exterior end chimneys; unusual interior arrangement with no central hallway, 4 rooms on each floor (upstairs front isolated from upstairs rear by lateral partition, separate stairways). Built ca. 1850, possibly as school; William Ellis probably contractor; dilapidated in 1934 (reduced to 1 story ca. 1940); deteriorated in 1979. 3 sheets (1934, including plans, elevations, section, details); 2 ext. photos (1934); 2 data pages (1936).

Mount Jefferson.

See Opelika Vicinity.

Notasulga Vicinity

LeSueur's Mill (AL-537), on SE bank of Ropes Creek (northern tributary of Saugahatchee Creek), due N of Notasulga (between Notasulga and Roxana community); 100 yds. E of unmarked dirt road at point approx. 4.1 mi. N of road's juncture with Ala. 81, which is approx. 1.7 mi. N of Ala. 81 intersection with Ala. 14 at Notasulga. Frame with clapboarding on wood pilings, small rectangular 1-story structure with gabled roof covered by wooden shakes; adjacent wooden waterwheel and sluice. Built 1912–13 by Howard Grady LeSueur on earlier mill site; both mill dam and mill wheel rebuilt in 1920s after former washed away and latter rotted; mill abandoned in late 1930s as population in area dwindled; subsequently collapsed (remains of ashlar dam still extant). 2 ext. photos (1934).

Opelika Vicinity

Chewacla Lime Works (AL-509), E side of Co. 63 (Limekiln Rd.), approx. 0.9 mi. S of junction with Ala. 169 at Spring Villa community. Mid-19th-C. industrial complex covering several acres and consisting of large quarry, remains of limekilns, commissary building, quarters for convict labor, and stables. *Kilns*: ashlar rubble construction, truncated conical shape. *Commissary*: ashlar rubble (approx. 80' X 28'), 1 story, hipped roof, segmentally arched openings. *Laborers' Quarters*: ashlar-rubble ground floor with log superstructure, cruciform shape, hipped roof. *Stables*: ashlar rubble construction with frame gable ends and lean-to, rectangular, 1 story with loft. Complex developed after 1853 as Chewacla Lime Company (Charles T. Pollard, president; Avery T. Clapp, superintendent). Only ruins of commissary and 1 kiln extant in 1979; abandoned quarry now lake. 1 photo of quarry (1937), 1 ext. photo of kiln (1937), 2 ext. photos, 1 int. photo of commissary (1937), 2 ext. photos, 1 int. photo of laborers' quarters (1937), 1 ext. photo of stable (1937).

Moffitt's Mill (AL-507), at falls of Little Uchee Creek (E bank) just S of

Co. 12 bridge over creek; 0.8 mi. W of Co. 12 intersection with Co. 79 at Meadows Mill community about 16 mi. SE of Opelika. Frame with clapboarding on ashlar foundation, 46′2″ × 36′3″, 2 stories, gable roof, 2 low batten doors on N elevation, turbine-powered mill with millrace at W end of building; open interior plan, heavy chamfered posts supporting upper floor. Built 1839–40 for Capt. Henry Moffitt, a Georgian who purchased the tract following Creek Indian removal in 1836; formerly site of Wetumpka Council House of Lower Creek nation. Converted to cotton gin in early 20th C. and open lean-to shed subsequently built across N elevation; destroyed except for traces of foundation and dam. 1 sheet (1934, including plan, elevations, section, details); 1 ext. photo (1934), 2 int. photos (1934); 2 data pages (1936).

Mount Jefferson Methodist Church (AL-505), 0.4 mi. NE of U.S. 431 on E side of unmarked dirt road entering U.S. 431 approx. 0.2 mi. N of intersection of Co. 67 (Cusseta Rd.) and U.S. 431; N of Opelika in old Mount Jefferson community. Brick, rectangular (2-bay front, 3 bays long), 1 story, steeply pitched roof with frame gable ends, 2 entrance doors. Built ca. 1845–50 for Methodist Protestant congregation founded by the Rev. Eppes Tucker (see Wheat-Tucker-Fincher House, AL-878); roof probably rebuilt with greater pitch in late 19th C.; ruinous in 1935 and subsequently destroyed. 1 ext. photo (1935).

Spring Villa (AL-508), facing W on S side of Co. 36 (Spring Villa Rd.), approx. 1.5 mi. E of junction with Ala. 169 and 0.1 mi. W of Little Uchee Creek Bridge. Frame with clapboarding, approx. 52′4″ (3-bay front) × 20′6″, 1½ stories, steeply pitched gable roof with 3 subordinate cross-gables over bays of upper story, 2 exterior end chimneys, wide eaves with cusped bargeboard trim, possibly 1-story porch across front originally, small decorative balconies (formerly with latticed balustrade) at each of upper windows; center-hall plan, unusual partially enclosed corkscrew stairway with arched statuary niche. Built mid-19th C. (date variously given between 1851 and 1872) for W. Penn C. Yonge (1823–78); design possibly adapted from A. J. Downing. Seat of estate that included artificial lake and private racetrack. Acquired 1927 by City of Opelika and renovated 1934 by Civil Works Administration as clubhouse, including construction of central rear wing replicating style of front portion. Architecturally very similar to John C. Edwards house in Opelika. Locale of 1876 Centennial celebration, at which time house received its present name. 3 sheets (1934, including plans, elevations, section, details); 2 ext. photos (1934), 2 int. photos (1934); 3 data pages (1936). NR.

Tucker-Fincher House. *See* Wheat-Tucker-Fincher House (AL-878), unmarked road off U.S. 431.

Wheat-Tucker-Fincher House (Tucker-Fincher House) (AL-878), 0.4 mi. NE of U.S. 431 on W side of unmarked dirt road entering U.S. 431, approx. 0.2 mi. N of Co. 67 (Cusseta Rd.) intersection with U.S. 431; N of Opelika in old Mount Jefferson community. Frame with clapboarding, 50′2″ (5-bay front) × 35′1″, 2 stories with 1-story rear shed extension, gable roof, 2 exterior end chimneys, originally central 2-tiered pedimented portico; center-hall plan, notable interior with rare closed stringer stairway, Federal period woodwork including marbleized dados and mantelpieces, grained doors. Built ca. 1840 for Moses Wheat; later home of son-in-law, the Rev. Eppes Tucker, founder and pastor of nearby Mount Jefferson Methodist Church (AL-505); shed across rear later extended and central 2-tiered porch replaced by full-length double porch; long rectangular 1-story gabled semi-detached wing also added at SW corner of house (dismantled after 1935). House burned by vandals in 1982. 5 ext. photos (1935, including 1 photo of late-19th-C. service wing), 6 int. photos (1935).

LIMESTONE COUNTY

Athens

Beaty-Mason House (J. G. and Mary Mason House) (AL-306), 211 S. Beaty St. (NE corner S. Beaty and Green sts.). Brick (façade stuccoed), main block 55'0" (3-bay front) × 23'1" with low ell (18'4" × 35'2") at NE rear, 2 stories, gable roof, 2 exterior end chimneys (main block), full-height pedimented tetrastyle entrance portico composed of 2 Ionic columns flanked by 2 antae, balcony over doorway, triple windows to either side, 2-tiered L-shaped porch at rear; center-hall plan. Semidetached brick 1-story kitchen separated from ell by segmentally arched passage. Built 1826 for Robert Beaty. Façade remodeled 1845 in Greek Revival style for Beaty's son-in-law, Capt. John Mason: Hiram H. Higgins, architect for renovation; again renovated 1960 (including removal of original stairway) as official residence for Athens College president. 7½ sheets (1934, including plot plan, plans, elevations, section, details); 2 ext. photos (1934), 5 int. photos (1934); 2 data pages (1936).

Slave Quarters, SE (rear) of house. Log (V-notch construction) partially covered with clapboard, 29'10" (2-bay front) × 18'1" plus porch and lean-to addition, gable roof, central chimney. Built ca. 1826; renovated 1960. Rare example in Alabama of saddlebag style log house. ½ sheet (1934, including plan, elevations, section).

Wellhouse, NE (rear) of house. Latticed, rectangular, gable roof. Demolished. 1 ext. photo (1934).

Office (unrecorded), moved to rear from front lawn. Frame, octagonal with pyramidal roof and finial, arched doorway and windows. Mid-19th C.

See also FBJ (J7-ALA-1084 through 1087).

Cedars, The (AL-368), N side of E. Pryor St., approx. 0.3 mi. W of intersection with U.S. 31 (approx. 0.5 mi. W of Swan Creek). Frame with clapboarding, rectangular (3-bay front) with ell, 2 stories, gable-and-hipped roof, main block has 2 exterior end chimneys, full-height pedimented tetrastyle portico composed of 2 pairs of square columns supporting upper gallery, flanking triple windows; center-hall plan. Built ca. 1846 for James Henry Malone; demolished late 1940s. 4 ext. photos (1935, partially defective), 6 int. photos (1935).

Coman Hall. *See* Jones-Coman-Westmoreland House (AL-338), 517 S. Clinton St.

Donnell, "Father" Robert, House. *See* Pleasant Hill (AL-338), 601 S. Clinton St.

Founders Hall, Athens College (AL-301), E side Beaty St., between Pryor and Bryan sts. Brick, 102'5" (7-bay front) × 52'6", 2 stories, unusual tetrastyle-in-antis Ionic portico (originally pedimented) with full-length balcony enclosed by picket-balustrade, portico flanked by large triple windows above and below, full entablature, molded brick watertable, corners pilastered; H-shaped interior plan (central block contains central assembly rooms upstairs and down with through hallways to either side), Greek Revival interior trim. Built ca. 1843–45 as Athens Female College of the Tennessee Methodist Conference; Hiram H. Higgins, architect; James M. Brundidge, master mason; Ira E. Hobbs, woodwork. Roof altered to mansard style ca. 1890; subsequent additions to S side and rear. 10 sheets (1934, including plans, elevations, section, details); 1 ext. photo (1934), 1 int. photo (1934); 2 data pages (1936).

Houston, Gov. George S., House (AL-341), 101 Houston St. (NW corner S. Houston and W. Market sts.). Frame with clapboarding over log construction, rectangular (6-bay front) with ell, 2 stories, gable roof, main block has 2 exterior end chimneys, modillioned cornice, full-height pedimented tetrastyle entrance portico composed of 2 pairs of square columns supporting gallery at second floor, double entrances above and below, originally 2-tiered porch on ell; 2 room plan (without hall), paneled dado, Adamesque mantels. Latticed wellhouse. Nucleus of structure is early-19th-C. log house reputedly built for Micajah Thomas; covered with clapboarding and embellished by Federal period detail ca. 1835. Home from 1845 to 1879 of George Smith Houston, governor of Alabama 1874–78. 3 ext. photos (1934–35, including wellhouse), 3 int. photos (1934–35); 2 data pages (1937).

Jones-Coman-Westmoreland House (Coman Hall, Westmoreland House) (AL-338), 517 S. Clinton St. Brick, approx. 64' (5-bay front) × 55', 2 stories over raised basement, hipped roof with cupola, bracketed cornice, full-height tetrastyle portico across front with square wooden columns, recessed 2-story corner porch at NE rear (now partially enclosed); center-hall plan with side stairhall. Largely built 1859–61 for Dr. Haywood Jones and completed ca. 1865 for Joshua P. Coman; Alex Price Hamilton, master-builder. Present portico added, back porch partially enclosed, and interior modifications ca. 1920; cupola removed ca. 1950. 5 ext. photos (1935), 5 int. photos (1935); 2 data pages (1937).

Mason, J. G. and Mary, House. *See* Beaty-Mason House (AL-306), 211 S. Beaty St.

Masonic Hall (AL-305), NE corner Monroe and E. Hobbs sts. Brick (base stuccoed and scored), 38′6″ (6 bays) X 38′7″ (6 bays), 2 stories, gable roof, 4 lateral chimneys, W (front) and S elevations have blind pointed arches with slightly wider truncated middle entrance bay, pointed doors and windows (louvered at top with flanking louvered blinds), modillioned cornice with elliptical lunette in tympanum of W elevation; center-hall plan (first floor) with side stairhall, large meeting room occupying N two-thirds of second floor. Built 1826–27. Used as Masonic lodge until 1912; subsequently converted to residence, with addition of 1-story brick porch across S side; demolished 1968. Rare occurrence in Alabama architecture of naïvely Gothicized Federal-period structure. 4 sheets (1934, including plans, elevations, section, details); 1 ext. photo (1934); 2 data pages (1936).

Pettus House. *See* Sloss-Pettus House (AL-340), NE corner N. Beaty and Hobbs sts.

Pleasant Hill ("Father" Robert Donnell House) (AL-367), 601 S. Clinton St. (on grounds of Athens Middle School). Frame with clapboarding, rectangular (3-bay front) with central rear wing, 2 stories, gable roof, main block has 2 exterior end chimneys, full-height pedimented tetrastyle portico composed of 2 pairs of square columns, balcony over doorway, flanking triple windows; center-hall plan with rear cross hall, front and rear stairways, simple Greek Revival style woodwork. Built ca. 1845; additions and modifications to rear wing early 20th C.; house restored 1976–82. First owner, Donnell (1784–1855), was prominent Cumberland Presbyterian preacher. House later became part of State Secondary Agricultural School complex (1889–1936). 3 ext. photos (1935), 5 int. photos (1935). NR.

Pryor House (Frances Snow Pryor House) (AL-304), 405 N. Jefferson St. (NW corner N. Jefferson and Pryor sts.). Frame with clapboarding, 52′11″ (3-bay front) X 44′6″ plus long board-and-batten ell at NW rear, 2 stories (ell 1 story), hipped roof surmounted by cupola, arcuated 6-bay portico with full-length balcony enclosed by cast-iron balustrade, small cast-iron side porch with deck on S, 2-tiered porch at rear, bracketed cornice; center-hall plan with double parlors to S, enclosed stairway. Built ca. 1836 for James K. Murrah. Extensively altered to Italianate style ca. 1868 for Sen. Luke Pryor, who lived here from 1854 to 1900; interior subdivided into apartments ca. 1950. Adamesque mantel from house later installed in NW parlor of Jones-Coman-Westmoreland house (AL-338) at 517 S. Clinton St. 5 sheets (1934, including plans, elevations, details); 2 ext. photos (1934), 1 int. photo (1934); 2 data pages (1936).

Law Office, in yard to S of house. Frame with clapboarding, 18′0″ (1-bay front) X 18′3″, 1 story, gable roof, exterior chimney at rear, elaborate cast-iron porch with anthemion cresting; 1-room plan. Probably built mid-19th C. for Luke Pryor. 1 sheet (1934, including elevations, details); 1 ext. photo (1934).

Richardson, William, House (AL-370), 401 S. Clinton St. (SE corner Clinton and South sts.). Brick (earliest portion of façade Flemish bond), rectangular (5-bay front) with ell, 2 stories, gable roof, main block has 2 interior end chimneys, tetrastyle 3-bay portico composed of paneled wooden piers, semicircular transom over door, L-shaped porch at rear; center-hall plan (evolved from original side-hall arrangement). Built ca. 1835 as 3-bay-front house. Enlarged ca. 1844, including addition of 2 N bays and portico; ell extended and further alterations made in late 19th C., including enlargement of lower front windows and installation of present stair. 3 ext. photos (1935), 3 int. photos (1935).

Sloss-Pettus House (Pettus House) (AL-340), NE corner N. Beaty and Hobbs sts. Frame with clapboarding, rectangular (5-bay front) with ell, 2 stories (ell 1 story), hipped roof, 2 interior chimneys, full-height 3-bay tetrastyle portico with paneled piers, balcony above doorway enclosed by decorative iron balustrade and resting on wrought-iron scrolled brackets; center-hall plan with sliding doors between principal rooms. Built ca. 1855 for James Withers Sloss; interior altered for apartments by Athens College in 1960, including removal of all woodwork except stair. Sloss (1820–90) was an Athens merchant and prominent 19th-C. railroad promoter and industrialist; he built Sloss-Sheffield Furnace (NHL) at Birmingham and was instrumental in the establishment of that city. 4 ext. photos (1935), 1 int. photo (1935).

Vasser House. *See* Vining-Wood-Vasser House (AL-379), 301 E. Washington St.

Vining-Wood-Vasser House (Vasser House) (AL-379), 301 E. Washington St. (NE corner E. Washington and S. Beaty sts.). Brick, rectangular (5-bay front) with center rear wing, 2 stories over basement, gable roof, main block has 2 interior end chimneys, full-height pedimented tetrastyle entrance portico with denticulated cornice, fanlight doorway, unusual splayed stucco lintels, quarter lunettes in each gable end, 2-tiered porches along both sides of rear wing; center-hall plan, originally basement dining room. Brick rectangular kitchen at rear. Built ca. 1825 for Thomas Vining; Hiram H. Higgins, architect. Acquired 1846 by Richard W. Vasser (1800–1865); later changes include frame addition at rear and renovation of interior (with replacement of original stair). 2 ext. photos (1934), 2 int. photos (1934).

Walker, Judge William Harrison, House (AL-371), 309 E. Clinton St. Frame with clapboarding, rectangular (3-bay front) with ell, 2 stories (ell 1 story), gable roof, main block has 2 exterior end chimneys, full-height pedimented tetrastyle entrance portico composed of 2 pairs of square columns supporting gallery at second floor, flanking triple windows; center-hall plan. Built 1849; early 20th-C. additions at rear; restored late 1970s. 3 ext. photos (1935), 8 int. photos (1935).

Westmoreland House. *See* Jones-Coman-Westmoreland House (AL-338), 517 S. Clinton St.

Athens Vicinity

Cotton Hill (Jack Rowe House) (AL-343), at end of long private lane 0.3 mi. N of Brown's Ferry Rd., approx. 3.3 mi. E of intersection with U.S. 31 (Bee Line Hwy.) at Tanner community. Brick (façade Flemish bond), rectangular (5-bay front) with traces of low frame ell at W rear, 2 stories over full basement, gable roof, 2 interior end chimneys, probably 2-tiered pedimented entrance porch originally, arched transoms above upper and lower doorways, molded brick water table; center-hall plan. Built ca. 1830 for Luke Matthews, planter from Sussex County, Va.; attributed to William Parham, early area craftsman (although he may be responsible for woodwork only). Porch and ell removed ca. 1930; later addition of rear wing and dormers. 2 ext. photos (1935), 2 int. photos (1935); 2 data pages (1937).

Rowe, Jack, House. *See* Cotton Hill (AL-343), lane off Brown's Ferry Rd.

Belle Mina

Belle Mina (Gov. Thomas Bibb House) (AL-303), W side of Co. 71, approx. 1.2 mi. N of intersection with Ala. 20 at Mooresville, or 0.7 mi. S of Southern Railroad crossing at Belle Mina; 0.6 mi. due E of Piney Creek. Brick (Flemish bond), 60'0" (5-bay front) × 60'0" including portico, also semidetached ground-level 3-room service wing (72'6" × 26'0") on E side, 2 stories (service wing 1 story), hipped roof originally surmounted by balustraded deck, 4 exterior end chimneys, full-height hexastyle Tuscan portico across front with brick-paved stylobate, fanlight doorway with triple window above, small pedimented entrance portico at rear, covered passage along N front of service wing; center-hall plan with side hall and secondary stair, exceptionally fine Federal period woodwork including spiral stairway, Adamesque mantels, paneled reveals. Built ca. 1826–35 for Thomas Bibb (1783–1839), planter, lawyer, and second governor of Alabama. House and grounds formerly surrounded by 5' brick wall (razed during Civil War); rooftop deck destroyed and other damage in tornado of 16 July 1875. Renovated 1941, including installation of wall paneling in SE first-floor room: E. B. Van Keuren of Birmingham, architect; again renovated 1967, including construction of kitchen wing and carport, installation of raised paneling above chair-rail in main hallway, other minor interior modifications. Name also spelled "Belmina" in 19th century. One of earliest and most sophisticated of Alabama's plantation mansions. 7 sheets (1934, including plot plan, plans, elevations, section, details); 3 ext. photos (1934), 4 int. photos (1934, including 2 photos of original kitchen fireplace and bake oven); 2 data pages (1936). NR. *See also* FBJ (J7-ALA-1078 through 1083).

Mooresville

Hundley House. *See* Minor-Hundley House (AL-369), Market St.

Minor-Hundley House (Hundley House) (AL-369), W side of Market St., approx. 350′ S of intersection with Ala. 20. Brick (façade Flemish bond), rectangular (4 irregular bays), 1½ stories, steeply pitched gable roof with slightly splayed eaves, dormer windows, 2 interior end chimneys, corbeled brick cornice with brick dentil course, small shed roof entrance porch with lattice railing enframing doorway; asymmetrically placed center hall with enclosed stairway. Herringbone pattern brick walk and paling fence at front. Built ca. 1825, possibly for Dr. William Tompkins Minor (1791–1854) from Louisa County, Va.; later (probably mid-19th C.) frame shed-roof addition across rear, with flanking dependencies; demolished 1968. Unusually good example in Alabama of Tidewater-type cottage, antecedents of which occur in 17th- and 18th-C. architecture of Tidewater Virginia, Maryland, and North Carolina. 2 ext. photos (1935), 2 int. photos (1935).

Peebles-Zeitler-McCrary House (Henry Zeitler House) (AL-302), W side of High St., between Piney and Lauderdale sts. Frame with clapboarding, rectangular (5-bay front) with ell, 2 stories, gable roof, main block has 2 exterior end chimneys, 3-bay 1-story shed porch across front; center-hall plan, mantelpiece in SE room (parlor) from now-destroyed Kimbell House near Mooresville. Log and frame dependencies, picket fence enclosing yard. Reputedly built ca. 1826; remodeled ca. 1840 for Robert and Sophia (Withers) Peebles from Northampton County, N.C. Ell added mid-19th C.; porches ca. 1895; kitchen wing and baths 1917; further renovations and additions 1972–75. Also schoolhouse built to N of house in 1854; moved and attached to rear of house in 1860s. 2 ext. photos (1934), 4 int. photos (1935, including 1 photo of artifacts from antiques collection of Henry Zeitler, then owner and noted antiquarian).

Tavern (AL-308), E side of High St., approx. 195′ S of intersection with Ala. 20. Frame with clapboarding, 24′2″ (2 irregular bays) x 16′5″, 2 stories, gable roof with wooden shakes, 1 exterior end chimney, 1-story shed porch across front (originally with chamfered posts), board-and-batten door, exterior stair to upper floor on E side, sawtooth trim on eaves of porch and roof, small postal window next to door; interior first floor has 1 large room with 2 smaller rooms at E end, upstairs has narrow rear passage with 2 chambers. Built ca. 1825, probably for Griffin Lampkin, as tavern and stagecoach inn. Subsequent additions include frame wing on E side (now removed) and lean-to across rear; much exterior clapboarding replaced. Rare survival in Alabama of very early hostelry. 2 sheets (1934, including plot plan, plans, elevations, section, details); 2 ext. photos (1934), 2 int. photos (1934); 2 data pages (1936).

Zeitler, Henry, House. *See* Peebles-Zeitler-McCrary House (AL-302), High St.

LOWNDES COUNTY

Benton

Masonic Hall (AL-756), SE corner 2nd and Church sts. Brick, rectangular (5-bay front), 2 stories, hipped roof, brick corner pilasters, simple Greek Revival style interior trim. Built ca. 1855, first floor used as school, Masonic chamber upstairs; demolished late 1930s. 1 ext. photo (1934), 1 int. photo (1934).

Burkville Vicinity

Stone-McCarty-Robinson House (AL-652), S side of Co. 40, 0.7 mi. E of junction with Co. 54 in Manack community, which is approx. 1.3 mi. S of Alabama River. Frame with clapboarding, rectangular (5-bay front), 2 stories, truncated hipped roof, hexastyle Doric portico, full entablature carried around house (paired brackets across front), balcony above doorway with scroll-cut balustrade; center-hall plan, modified Greek Revival style interior woodwork (probably adapted from Minard Lafever). Built 1853 for Warren T. Stone; refurbished 1973, including addition of rear utility wing and construction of balustraded rooftop deck. One of 3 extant Greek Revival style structures built by Stone family in area, including Stone-Young House (AL-650), in nearby Montgomery County, and Burkville United Methodist Church. 1 ext. photo (1935), 3 int. photos (1935).

Stone-Young House (AL-650). *Under Montgomery Vicinity (Montgomery County), see* Stone-Young House (AL-650).

Lowndesboro

Boxwood. *See* President's House, Lowndesboro Female Institute (AL-677), Ala. 97.

Cottage, The. *See* Lewis-Hall-James House (AL-670), Ala. 97.

Episcopal Church. *See* St. Paul's Episcopal Church (AL-674), Ala. 97.

Hagood House. *See* Thomas-Hagood House (AL-678), Ala. 97.

Howard House. *See* Lewis-Cilley-Howard House (AL-679), Ala. 97.

James, E. L., House. *See* Lewis-Hall-James House (AL-670), Ala. 97.

Lewis, Francis, House (Old Homestead) (AL-671), W side of Ala. 97 (Co. 29), approx. 0.5 mi. N of junction with U.S. 80. Frame with clapboarding, rectangular (5-bay front) with offset rear wing, 2 stories over basement (wing 1 story), hipped roof, 2 exterior end chimneys, 1 interior chimney, originally central 2-tiered pedimented portico, notable segmentally arched fanlight enframed by architrave with keystone and applied modified bead-and-reel motif; center-hall plan. Built ca. 1825–30; original portico replaced before 1889 by 2-tiered porch across front and S side with scroll-cut balustrade and trim; 1947 renovations included removal of Victorian porch and construction of pedimented porticoes at front and side, also interior changes and wing on N side. Lewis (1768–1837) was father of U.S. Sen. Dixon Hall Lewis (1802–48). 3 ext. photos (1934).

Lewis-Cilley-Howard House (Howard House) (AL-679), E side Ala. 97 (Co. 29) 0.1 mi. N of intersection with U.S. 80. Frame with clapboarding, rectangular (5-bay front) with lean-to and ell, 1½ stories (ell 1 story), gable roof, 2 exterior end chimneys, full-height shed porch across front (E) and N side. Built ca. 1840 for U.S. Sen. Dixon Hall Lewis; porch and rear addition ca. 1900. Lewis sold this house to Dr. Phillip Cilley from New England, retaining the Lewis-Hall-James House (AL-670) as his own residence. 2 ext. photos (1934–35).

Lewis-Hall-James House (The Cottage, E. L. James House) (AL-670), E side of Ala. 97 (Co. 29), approx. 0.5 mi. N of intersection with U.S. 80 and just S of St. Paul's Episcopal Church. Frame with clapboarding, basically rectangular (3-bay front) with flanking offsets at rear, 1½ stories, gable roof with dormers, exterior end chimneys, rear slope of roof extends beyond lateral walls of main block to form unusual half-gable or "flounder" roof over rear offsets, front slope of roof broken to extend over full-length deck-type porch with freestanding roof supports; originally 2 doors opened into single large room across front which could be divided by folding partition (arrangement later modified to form center-hall plan, double entrances removed). Built ca. 1835 for Sen. Dixon Hall Lewis (1802–48). Subsequent changes include addition of rear ell, enlargement of N dormer, scroll-cut porch balustrade. Unusual variation on small vernacular dwelling of early 19th-C. Alabama. 3 ext. photos (1935), 4 int. photos (1935).

Meadows-Powell House (Mockingbird Place) (AL-681), E side of Ala. 97 (Co. 29), 1.2 mi. N of intersection with U.S. 80 (immediately N of Presbyterian Church). Frame with clapboarding, rectangular (5-bay front, 2 bays deep), 1 story over half basement, hipped roof, 2 interior chimneys, pedimented tetrastyle central portico with square columns; center-hall plan, basement (enclosed only on N side) contains brick-paved dining room and kitchen. Built ca. 1850; 5' brick wall formerly enclosed front lawn. 2 ext. photos (1934–35), 3 int. photos (1935, including basement).

Methodist Church (Negro Methodist Church) (AL-651), approx. 0.1 mi. E of Ala. 97 (Co. 29), 1.3 mi. N of intersection with U.S. 80. Frame with clapboarding, rectangular (2-bay front composed of 2 identical doorways with 2 windows above), gable roof, pedimented portico with 4 slender square columns; 3-stage cupola with octagonal belfry capped by copper-plated ogee-roofed dome; open plan, 2 aisles with 3 blocks of slip pews, slave gallery at rear. Built ca. 1833 through efforts of wealthy planter Maj. William Robinson (1799–1882); cupola brought from first Alabama statehouse (built 1825, destroyed 1833) at Cahaba. Church taken over by black congregation (St. James C.M.E. Church) when new edifice built; pulpit alcove added to rear; abandoned in 1983. One of oldest extant churches in Black Belt of Alabama. 2 ext. photos (1934–35), 2 int. photos (1935).

Mockingbird Place. *See* Meadows-Powell House (AL-681), Ala. 97.

Negro Methodist Church. *See* Methodist Church (AL-651), Ala. 97.

Old Homestead. *See* Francis Lewis House (AL-671), Ala. 97.

Presbyterian Church (AL-687), E side Ala. 97 (Co. 29), approx. 1.1 mi. N of intersection with U.S. 80. Frame with clapboarding, rectangular (3-bay front composed of 3 identical doorways), gable roof, pedimented tetrastyle Doric portico with square louvered belfry surmounted by broached spire, triple-hung sash windows; open plan with central aisle, slip pews, mid-19th-C. bronze-and-glass chandelier. Built 1856 as second building for congregation established in 1816 as New Harmony Presbyterian Church; attributed to itinerant English-born builder "Mr. Nunley" who built other structures in area. Portico and spire damaged by tornado 1974, restored 1975. 3 ext. photos (1935), 1 int. photo (1935). *See also* Tebbs (T3-ALA-339190).

President's House, Lowndesboro Female Institute (Boxwood, Reese House) (AL-677), W side Ala. 97 (Co. 29), approx. 0.7 mi. N of junction with U.S. 80. Frame with clapboarding, L-shaped (5-bay E and N fronts), 2 stories, hipped-and-gable roof, modillioned cornice, identical pedimented 2-tiered tetrastyle entrance porticoes on E and N fronts (Tuscan order superimposed upon Doric, lunettes in tympanums), upper and lower fanlight doorways; center-hall plan with side hall, paneled dado, Adamesque mantels, decorative plasterwork including medallions and egg-and-dart moldings. Built ca. 1840–45; refurbished 1969. Notable example in central Alabama of retardataire Federal style dwelling. 3 ext. photos (1934–35), 7 int. photos (1934–35).

Reese House. *See* President's House, Lowndesboro Female Institute (AL-677), Ala. 97.

Rosewood. *See Lowndesboro Vicinity.*

St. Paul's Episcopal Church (Episcopal Church) (AL-674), E side of Ala. 97 (Co. 29), approx. 0.6 mi. N of junction with U.S. 80. Frame (board and batten) with wooden buttresses, nave and chancel with corner tower and projecting entrance porch, vestry chamber off N side of chancel, steeply pitched slate-covered roof, lancet windows, broached spire; open plan with center aisle, slave gallery at rear, batten doors, scissor-truss roof, triple lancets with original stained glass above altar, brass rood screen. Built 1857; adapted from Richard Upjohn's *Rural Architecture*. Rood screen added, E end refurbished, and nave windows stenciled late 19th C. Building formerly painted red, hence locally called "the red church." Well-preserved and outstanding example of Gothic Revival style in Alabama. 2 ext. photos (1934–35), 7 int. photos (1934–35).

Thomas-Hagood House (Hagood House, Meadowlawn) (AL-678), E side of Ala. 97 (Co. 29), approx. 0.7 mi. N of junction with U.S. 80. Frame with clapboarding, square (5 bays wide, 5 bays deep) with rear ell, 2 stories (ell 1 story), hipped roof extending over full-height Doric colonnade across front (W) and S side with scroll-cut balustrade, bracketed cornice, identical doorways on W and S fronts with cast-iron balconies above; center-hall plan with side hall, ornate plaster medallions and cornices, marble mantels. Two brick dependencies (slave quarters and smokehouse). Built 1853 for "Squire" George Thomas (1797–1867); attributed to itinerant builder "Mr. Nunley." Good example of eclectic mixture of Greek Revival and early Victorian stylistic elements. 7 ext. photos (1934–35, including dependencies), 11 int. photos (1934–35). *See also* Tebbs (T3-ALA-339188 and 339189).

Tyson, Archibald, House (AL-672), E side Ala. 97 (Co. 29), approx. 0.3 mi. N of junction with U.S. 80. Frame with clapboarding, L-shaped (5-bay W front, 6-bay S front), 2 stories, hipped roof extending over full-height hexastyle Doric portico across W front with subordinate pediment over 3 middle bays, pedimented tetrastyle Doric portico on S front, 2-tiered porch with paneled square columns formerly at rear; center-hall plan. Built ca. 1850; attributed to itinerant builder "Mr. Nunley." One-story E wing added late 19th C.; renovated 1965, including application of aluminum siding. 6 ext. photos (1934–35), 9 int. photos (1934–35). *See also* FBJ (J7-ALA-1005 through 1008); Tebbs (T3-ALA-339186 and 339187).

Williams-Bragg House (AL-673), W side of Ala. 97 (Co. 29) approx. 0.1 mi. N of junction with U.S. 80. Frame with clapboarding, rectangular (3-bay front), 1½ stories over raised basement, gable roof, 2 interior chimneys, pedimented tetrastyle entrance portico with square columns. Built 1843. Single-flight wooden steps to portico replaced by double flight with wrought-iron balustrade 1956–57; destroyed by fire in May 1957. 3 ext. photos (1934–35), 4 int. photos (1934–35).

Wooten-Meadows House. *Under Lowndesboro Vicinity, see* Rosewood (AL-680).

Lowndesboro Vicinity

Dicksonia. *See* Turner-Dickson House (AL-676), Ala. 90.

Rosewood (Wooten-Meadows House) (AL-680), N of Lowndesboro and approx. 0.5 mi. E of Ala. 97 (Co. 29) on unmarked lane 0.5 mi. due N of Dry Creek Bridge; 2.8 mi. N of Ala. 97 intersection with U.S. 80. Raised cottage, frame with clapboarding on stuccoed brick basement, square (5-bay front), 1 story over ground floor, truncated hipped roof with glazed monitor, raised porch reached by twin flights of curving steps over arcuated ground-level entrance, 3-bay loggia at rear; center-hall plan. Built ca. 1854–55 by "Col. Harrison and slaves" according to specifications of owner, Dr. Hardy Vickers Wooten. 5 ext. photos (1934–35), 3 int. photos (1934–35).

Turner-Dickson House (Dicksonia) (AL-676), S of Lowndesboro on W side Ala. 90 (Co. 29), approx. 0.6 mi. S of junction with U.S. 80. Frame (heart pine) with clapboarding, rectangular (5-bay front), 2 stories, hipped roof extending over full-height Doric portico across front (E) and S side with scroll-cut balustrade, cast-iron balcony above door, bracketed cornice; center-hall plan; boxwood garden to front and side. Built or remodeled ca. 1850 for Wiley Turner; attributed to itinerant builder "Mr. Nunley." Large rear addition after 1902; burned 1939 and reconstructed 1939–40 in concrete and steel, utilizing farm labor; again destroyed by fire in 1964. 7 ext. photos (1934–35), 5 int. photos (1934–35); 2 data pages (1936). *See also* FBJ (J7-ALA-1004).

Wooten-Meadows House. *See* Rosewood (AL-680), lane off Ala. 97.

MACON COUNTY

Tuskegee

Callaway House. *See* Hunter-Callaway House (AL-559), 811 N. Maple St.

Carr, W. B., House. *See* House (AL-536), 301 Maple St.

Cobb House. *See* Foster-Cobb-Laslie House (AL-541), 504 S. Main St.

Dowdell, Rev. Lewis Flournoy, House (Thornton House) (AL-585), 1.0 mi. SE of town square on NE side of U.S. 29 (Ala. 15). Frame with clapboarding, rectangular (5-bay front) with 2-room ell at SE rear, 2 stories (ell 1 story), hipped roof, 2 exterior end chimneys, full-height hexastyle portico across front with slender square wooden columns and full-length balcony, upper portion of portico screened by segmentally arched latticework between columns; center-hall plan, ell dining room has retardataire paneled overmantel (rare in Alabama). Built mid-19th C.; later service wing and garage addition to rear. 4 ext. photos (1935), 4 int. photos (1935).

Foster-Cobb-Laslie House (Cobb House) (AL-541), 504 S. Main St. Frame with clapboarding, 50′4″ (3-bay front) × 20′6″ with large rear wing (31′9″ × 39′10″), 2 stories, hipped roof extending over tetrastyle Ionic portico with full-length balcony enclosed by wheatsheaf motif in balustrade; center-hall plan. Semidetached frame kitchen at end of ell. Built ca. 1860; builder reputedly a Mr. Daniel. Later home of Col. Wilbur Foster; minor 20th-C. alterations. 6 sheets (1935, including plans, elevations, section, details); 2 ext. photos (1934), 3 int. photos (1934); 2 data pages (1936). See also FBJ (J7-ALA-1010 and 1011).

Grey Columns. See Varner-Alexander House (AL-875), Ala. 126.

Harris-Wadsworth House (AL-533), 615 N. Main St. (W side of Main, just S of Water St. intersection). Frame with clapboarding, rectangular (5-bay front), 2 stories with 1-story shed extension at rear, gable roof, 4 exterior end chimneys stuccoed and scored to simulate ashlar, roof overhang forms full-height hexastyle portico across front with square wooden columns; center-hall plan, severely plain interior. Built 1855 for W. K. Harris, probate judge of Macon County. 3 ext. photos (1934–35), 5 int. photos (1934–35).

House (W. B. Carr House, Martin House) (AL-536), 301 Maple St. (SE corner Maple and E. Massey sts.). Frame with clapboarding, U-shaped (6-bay front) with parallel wings forming court at rear, 1 story, gable roof with cross-gables at each end, recessed 4-bay front porch with wheatsheaf balustrade, pointed windows in gabled end bays of façade, U-shaped rear porch around central court; from each end of front porch 2 elliptically arched doorways screened by louvers lead to parallel open passages through main block of house to rear porch or gallery; interior has chair-rail and simple Federal period woodwork. Built 1843; moved forward (W) in late 19th C. to make way for expansion of Alabama Conference Female College. Highly unusual floorplan, possibly unique in Alabama. 5 ext. photos (1936), 6 int. photos (1936, including passages and mantelpieces).

Hunter-Callaway House (Callaway House) (AL-559), 811 N. Maple St. (N end of Maple St. facing S, above Water St. intersection). Frame with clapboarding, rectangular (3-bay front), 1 story, hipped roof, pedimented tetrastyle Doric entrance portico with fluted columns and pilasters; center-hall plan. Built ca. 1842 for Dr. J. W. Hunter, Tuskegee physician; bay window addition to W side early 20th C., numerous rear additions. 2 ext. photos (1934–35), 5 int. photos (1935).

Johnston-Abercrombie-Lamar House (Lamar House, Dr. Vason House) (AL-532), 1.0 mi. SE of town square on SW side of U.S. 29 (Ala. 15). Frame with clapboarding, rectangular (5-bay front) with ell, 2 stories (ell 1 story), hipped roof, 2 exterior end chimneys, full-height hexastyle portico across front with square wooden columns and full-length balcony; center-hall plan. Built ca. 1850, reputedly for Burr Johnston; later rear additions. 3 ext. photos (1935), 5 int. photos (1935).

Lamar House. See Johnston-Abercrombie-Lamar House (AL-532), U.S. 29.

Martin House. See House (AL-536), 301 Maple St.

Tate-Thompson House (G. C. Thompson House) (AL-542), 302 N. Main St. (NE corner Main and Lee sts.). Frame with clapboarding, 47'5" (5-bay front) x 65'7" (5 bays deep) including front and rear porticoes, 2 stories, truncated hipped roof, 4 interior end chimneys, bracketed cornice with octagonal ventilator openings in frieze-band, modified hexastyle Corinthian portico at front with cast-iron balcony bearing lyre motif, similar portico with octagonal columns at rear, 1-story arcuated side porches with scroll-cut trim, quoined corners; center-hall plan with cross hall, curving stairway with statuary niche, elaborate woodwork, and decorative plaster. Built ca. 1855–60, reputedly on site of first frame house in Tuskegee, erected by Peter Coffee Harris; later 1-story rear additions. Most elaborate of Tuskegee's antebellum frame dwellings; notable example of stylistically transitional house combining late Greek Revival and Italianate elements. Pres. William McKinley spoke from portico on visit to Tuskegee and Tuskegee Institute in 1898. Dismantled 1983 for reconstruction at Carrollton, Georgia. 3 sheets (1934, including plans, elevations, section, details); 5 ext. photos (1934–35), 11 int. photos (1934–35); 2 data pages (1936). NR. See also FBJ (J7-ALA-1015 and 1016).

Thompson, G. C., House. See Tate-Thompson House (AL-542), 302 N. Main St.

Thornton House. See Rev. Lewis Flournoy Dowdell House (AL-585), U.S. 29.

Tuskegee Institute, Band Cottage. See Tuskegee Institute, Foundry and Blacksmith Shop (AL-868).

Tuskegee Institute, Carver Museum (Old Laundry) (AL-62), on campus, approx. 500' N of Ala. 126 (Old Montgomery Hwy.). Brick, rectangular (6 bays of trisectional sash windows across front, with pair of entrances), 1 story with basement, hip-on-hip roof pierced by semicircular louvered vents, central projecting 5-bay entrance porch (arcuated and pilastered) with pediment spanning center bays, flanking half-hipped entrance bays; basically open interior plan originally. Built 1915; 1938–41 converted to museum and laboratory under supervision of Dr. George Washington Carver; interior heavily damaged by fire in 1947 and subsequently reconditioned. Acquired by National Park Service in 1974 as part of Tuskegee Institute National Historic Site. 11 sheets (1978, including site plan, plan, elevations).

Tuskegee Institute, Foundry and Blacksmith Shop (Band Cottage) (AL-868), on campus. Brick, 1 story, main block 7 bays long with lateral 4-bay subordinate wing, shallow gabled roof, corbeled brick cornice, segmentally arched windows. Early 20th C. 5 sheets (1978, including plans, elevations).

Tuskegee Institute, The Oaks (Booker T. Washington House) (AL-877), S side of Ala. 26 (Old Montgomery Hwy.) on campus. Brick, irregularly shaped, 2½ stories, steeply pitched hipped roof broken by projecting subordinate gables, gable ends imbricated, tall ribbed chimneys with corbeled caps, segmentally arched windows, 1-story porch across front with turned balusters and colonnettes, porte cochère extension on E side; irregular interior plan developed around axial front stairhall, tongue-and-groove paneled wainscoting, Queen Anne period detailing. Built 1899 as residence for Booker T. Washington, founder and president of Tuskegee Institute; Robert R. Taylor, architect. Most of materials manufactured locally and installed by students as part of vocational training. House occupied by Washington until his death in 1915, by his wife until her death in 1925. Converted 1950s to administrative offices for institute. Acquired by National Park Service in 1974 as part of Tuskegee Institute National Historic Site. 11 sheets (1978, including site plan, plans, elevations, section).

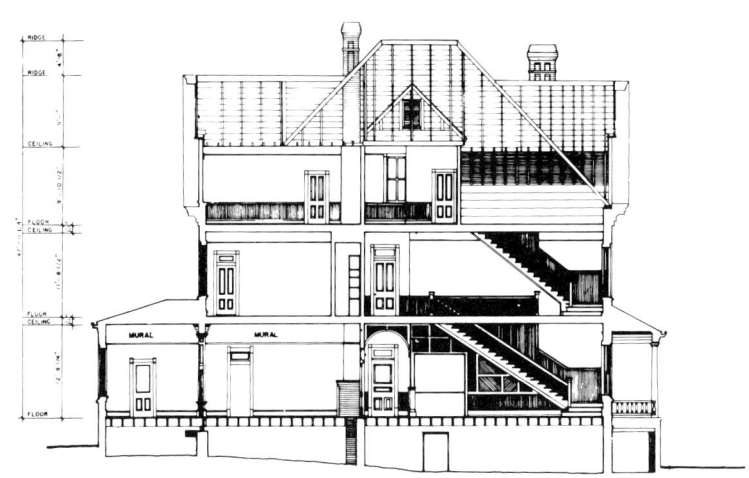

The Oaks (Booker T. Washington House), Tuskegee (1899).

Tuskegee Institute, Old Laundry. See Tuskegee Institute, Carver Museum (AL-62).

Tuskegee Institute, Booker T. Washington House. See Tuskegee Institute, The Oaks (AL-877).

Varner-Alexander House (Grey Columns) (AL-875), S side of Ala.

126 (Old Montgomery Hwy.) approx. 0.4 mi. W of junction with N. Main St. Open to public. Brick with buff-colored stucco scored to simulate ashlar, overall dimensions 75'6" (7 bays) x 75'6" (7 bays) including colonnade, main block T-shaped with projecting 5-bay front pavilion forming stem of T encased by U-shaped colonnade of modified Doric order, 2 stories, shallow hipped roof surmounted by large octagonal belvedere, wide bracketed eaves, ornate cast-iron balcony above recessed main door, also cast-iron sills, lintels, ventilator grilles; center-hall plan, double stairway ascending from front and rear halls to common landing. Built 1854–57 for William Varner; design reflects possible influence of Philadelphia architect John Stewart (of Sloan and Stewart), who designed Alabama Conference Female College at Tuskegee in 1854. House altered in 1920s following fire, including kitchen wing addition, bathrooms; additional minor alterations during 1950s. Acquired by National Park Service in 1975 as reception center and headquarters for Tuskegee Institute National Historic Site. One of largest and most elaborate of state's late antebellum period mansions. 3 sheets (1934, including plans, elevations, section, details), 15 sheets (1978, including site plan, plans, elevations, details); 7 ext. photos (1934), 5 int. photos (1934); 2 data pages (1936). NR. *See also* FBJ (J7-ALA-1017 through 1020).

Vason, Dr., House. *See* Johnston-Abercrombie-Lamar House (AL-532), U.S. 29.

Tuskegee Vicinity

Alexander-Hurt-Whatley House (Judge W. H. Hurt House) (AL-560), S side of Co. 10 (Old Columbus Hwy.), 0.3 mi. E of junction with Ala. 15, which is approx. 2 mi. SE of Tuskegee town square. Raised cottage, brick covered with stucco, overall dimensions 57'5" (5-bay front) x 66'2", 1 story over low ground floor, hipped roof, 4 interior end chimneys, full-length raised porches front and rear with front porch carried by massive hexastyle modified Doric colonnade rising directly from ground level, tall jib windows (4' x 8') opening onto front veranda; center-hall plan. Dependencies include frame octagonal plantation office, 1 brick and frame slave house, wagon shed. Built ca. 1855 for Judge Lewis Alexander; Victorian modifications late 19th C., including Eastlake style front door and hall screen. 11 sheets (1935, including plot plan, plans, elevations, section, details, dependencies); 3 ext. photos (1934–35), 5 int. photos (1935); 2 data pages (1937). *See also* FBJ (J7-ALA-1012 through 1014).

Cox House. *See* Stagecoach Inn (AL-534), Co. 26.

Frame Plantation House. *See* Stagecoach Inn (AL-534), Co. 26.

Hurt, Judge W. H., House. *See* Alexander-Hurt-Whatley House (AL-560), Co. 10.

Lamar House. *Under Tuskegee, see* Johnston-Abercrombie-Lamar House (AL-532).

Stagecoach Inn (Cox House, Frame Plantation House) (AL-534), S side of Co. 26, approx. 1.3 mi. E of junction with Co. 10, which is approx. 3.5 mi. SE of Tuskegee town square. Frame with clapboarding, rectangular (5-bay front), 2 stories (1 story at rear), unusual gable roof with rear slope breaking into gambrel across back of building, 2 exterior end chimneys, 1-story central entrance porch; center-hall plan, simple Federal period woodwork, chair-rail. Built ca. 1830. Altered after 1935 with removal of original chimneys and replacement of rear gambrel slope by ordinary shed roof; ruinous in early 1980s. Significant as one of oldest frame structures in area. 2 ext. photos (1935), 3 int. photos (1934–35).

MADISON COUNTY

Huntsville and Vicinity

Bank Building. *See* Huntsville Branch, State Bank of Alabama (AL-405), Jefferson St. and Fountain Row.

Beirne House. *See* Bibb-Bradley-Beirne House (AL-403), 303 Williams St.

Bibb-Bradley-Beirne House (Beirne House, Bibb-Newman House) (AL-403), 303 Williams St. Brick with stone trim, 65′1″ (5-bay front) × 57′0″ plus portico and service wings, 2 stories, gable roof with pedimented gable-ends, 4 interior end chimneys, pilastered façade with full-height 3-bay pedimented tetrastyle Ionic portico, full entablature, shed porch and low 2-story wing at rear; center-hall plan. Semidetached offset rear service wing: 50′11″ (5 bays) × 20′3″, 1 story over raised basement. Early history of house obscure. Built ca. 1835 on site of earlier house for ex-governor Thomas Bibb; afterward home of Bibb's daughter, Mrs. James Bradley. Refurbished ca. 1920, including raising floor level of service wing. Commandeered as headquarters of Gen. William T. Sherman during 1864 Federal occupation of Huntsville, when owned by George P. Beirne. 5 sheets (1934, including plans, elevations, section, details); 2 ext. photos (1934), 6 int. photos (1934); 2 data pages (1936). *See also* FBJ (J7-ALA-1088).

Bibb-Newman House. *See* Bibb-Bradley-Beirne House (AL-403), 303 Williams St.

Boswell, C. S., House. *See* McClung-Watkins House (AL-478), 415 McClung St.

Brandon-Read-Burritt House (Burritt House) (AL-474), 303 Eustis St. (S side of Eustis St. between Greene and Lincoln sts.). Frame with beaded clapboarding over logs, approx. 55′ (5-bay front) × 22′ with long frame-and-brick ell, 2 stories, gable roof, 2 exterior end chimneys (main block), gable roof, formerly small pedimented tetrastyle Tuscan entrance porch, notable doorway with semicircular transom enframed by fluted and molded architrave, door with raised reeded panels; center-hall plan, good Federal period woodwork including stair embellished with unusual wood sunburst motif beneath molded stringer. Main block 2-story log house covered with clapboard and remodeled ca. 1820 for Thomas Brandon, clerk of Madison County Court; brick ell extension added ca. 1835 for Col. John Read from Bedford County, Va.; small entrance porch later replaced by full-length shed porch with turned colonnettes, also new sashing and frame rear additions; demolished ca. 1949. 5 ext. photos (1935), 5 int. photos (1935); 2 data pages (1936).

Burritt House. *See* Brandon-Read-Burritt House (AL-474), 303 Eustis St.

Cabaniss House. *See* Roach-Cabaniss House (AL-431), 603 Randolph St.

Chase, Henry, House. *See* McDowell-LeVert-Chase House (AL-409), 517 Adams St.

Clarke-Fackler House (Pynchon House) (AL-430), 518 Adams St. Brick, 57′11″ (5-bay front) × 41′7″ plus long ell, 2½ stories over basement (ell 1½ stories over ground floor due to rear slope of lot), 2 pairs of end chimneys, 1-story tetrastyle Ionic entrance portico, rear has deeply recessed porch in middle bay with secondary stair (porch breaks into wooden deck along ell); center-hall plan. Low 2-story service wing abutting ell, shed porch on S side. Built ca. 1835–40 for Mrs. William Clarke; renovated ca. 1860 for John J. Fackler, including Victorian mantelpieces and trompe l'oeil decoration (now covered) in parlor. 4 sheets (1934, including plans, elevations, section, details); 6 ext. photos (1934), 2 int. photos (1934); 3 data pages (1936).

Clay, J. Withers, House. *See* Steward's House, Huntsville Female Seminary (AL-408), 513 Eustis St.

Cox-White House (Thomas W. White House) (AL-475), 461 Eustis St. Brick, rectangular (3-bay front) with rear ell and large L-shaped wing on E side, 2 stories (E wing 1 story), gable roof, single pair of exterior end chimneys (main block); side-hall plan. Built ca. 1836 for George Cox, Jr. Altered and enlarged including E wing ca. 1844 for White; shed porch added late 19th C. across front and along E side. 2 ext. photos (1935), 5 int. photos (1935).

Kitchen and Slave Quarters, W of house set into sloping side of hill. Brick, rectangular (irregularly spaced bays), 2 stories, gable roof, 2 interior end chimneys, 2-tiered porch along E side with brick piers. Built ca. 1844. 1 ext. photo (1935).

Dilworth, W. P., House. *See* Oaklawn (AL-411), 2709 Meridian Pike.

Fearn-Garth House (AL-414), 517 Franklin St. Brick, main block basically rectangular, 58'6" (5-bay front) x 49'0", 2 stories, shallow truncated hipped roof with glazed monitor, pilastered façade, small 1-story Doric entrance portico, 3-bay loggia at NE rear corner with brick piers carrying upper gallery, 1-bay wing (21'3" wide) on N side with triglyph-and-metope frieze; center-hall plan. Two-story brick dependency attached to wing at rear; also brick smokehouse. Built ca. 1820 as 3-bay house with side-hall plan. Renovated and enlarged to present aspect in 1849 by addition of S bays, remodeling of N wing, application of Grecian detail: George Steel, architect for renovation; further interior changes in late 19th C., with installation of Victorian period stairhall in NE corner of main block. Originally home of Dr. Thomas Fearn (1789–1863), prominent local physician; owned by descendants until 1964. 9 sheets (1935, including plans, elevations, details); 4 ext. photos (1934–35), 7 int. photos (1935), 1 ext. photo of smokehouse (1935); 3 data pages (1936).

First National Bank. *See* Huntsville Branch, State Bank of Alabama (AL-405), Jefferson St. and Fountain Row.

Greenlawn (Otey House) (AL-476), E side of U.S. 431 (Memorial Pkwy., Meridian Pike), 0.5 mi. N of intersection with Countess Rd. Frame with clapboarding, rectangular (5-bay front), 2-story main block (1 story across rear), gable roof with 3 parallel gables over rear, 2 exterior end chimneys (main block), full-height 3-bay pedimented tetrastyle portico with cement columns of rudimentary Doric order; center-hall plan, partially enclosed stair rising from rear hallway. Built ca. 1850 for William Madison Otey. Later rear additions; present portico and 1-story wing on N side added early 20th C. Originally extensive formal gardens. 4 ext. photos (1935), 5 int. photos (1935). NR.
Dependencies, rear of dwelling. Log slave house (rectangular, gable roof) and smokehouse (square, pyramidal roof). Probably built early 19th C. as part of dwelling complex that preceded ca. 1850 house; destroyed. 1 general photo (1935).

Hamlet House. *See* William Windham House (AL-413), 413 E. Holmes St.

Horton-McCracken House (McCracken House) (AL-410), W side of Meridian Pike, approx. 0.5 mi. N of intersection with U.S. 72. Frame with clapboarding, rectangular (5-bay front), 2 stories, gable roof with 3 parallel rear gables, 2 exterior end chimneys (main block), full-height 3-bay pedimented tetrastyle Doric portico with stuccoed brick columns; center-hall plan. Built 1843–44 for Rhoda Horton; demolished ca. 1950. Formerly extensive landscaped grounds, including lagoon. 3 ext. photos (1934–35), 2 int. photos (1935); 3 data pages (1936).

House (Mastin House) (AL-436), E side of Meridian Pike, approx. 0.25 mi. S of Chase Rd. on site of later Wilkenson Dr. NE. Brick, rectangular (5-bay front), 2 stories, gable roof, 2 exterior end chimneys, small pedimented entrance porch with 2 slender Ionic colonnettes, shed-roof extension at S rear abutting 2-tiered porch across back of house; center-hall plan. Semi-detached rectangular 1-story gabled kitchen at NE corner off rear porch. Built ca. 1835. Shed porch later added across S side, also modifications at rear; demolished ca. 1950. 4 ext. photos (1934–35), 3 int. photos (1934–35).
Slave Quarters. Log (half-dovetail notching), rectangular (3 irregular bays), 1 story, gable roof, 2 exterior end chimneys; 2-room plan. Built early 19th C.; demolished. 1 ext. photo (1935).

Huntsville Branch, State Bank of Alabama (First National Bank) (AL-405), NW corner Jefferson St. and Fountain Row (W side of Courthouse Sq. on bluff overlooking Big Spring Park). Stuccoed brick (with ashlar façade and trim) resting on flagstone terrace, 49'10" (3-bay front) x 77'0" including portico, temple-type structure with full-height hexastyle Ionic portico of limestone across front, full-width flight of limestone steps, tall central paneled doorway with flanking smaller doors, copper-covered roof; foyer with flanking antechambers (added 1899) opens into large central banking room with vault and offices at rear, cashiers' counter with engaged Ionic colonnettes originally across back of room, second floor (designed as living quarters for cashier) has center-hall plan. Large semi-detached service wing (6 bays long), linked to main building by 2-tiered Tuscan-style porch along W side overlooking courtyard; wing has basement cells where slaves were impounded for owner's debt. Entire complex enclosed by cast-iron fence with limestone piers. Built 1835–40 at cost of $76,000; George Steele, architect. Side doors and upper windows of façade added ca. 1900–1910 (also balcony, removed ca. 1940); interior remodeled in 1950 (including removal of Ionic-style cashiers' screen); rear wing altered several times although retaining essential lines. Small cupola from demolished 1914 courthouse added ca. 1965. One of state's most sophisticated Greek Revival style buildings and among oldest commercial structures in Alabama still in use. 5 sheets (1934, including plot plan, plans, elevations, section, details, service wing); 6 ext. photos (1934), 3 int. photos (1934); 4 data pages (1936). NR. *See also* CSAS (J7-ALA-1089).

Lewis-Clay-Anderson House. *See* Steward's House, Huntsville Female Seminary (AL-408), 513 Eustis St.

McClung-Watkins House (C. S. Boswell House) (AL-478), 416 McClung St. Brick, rectangular (5-bay W front) with ell to S and service wing on E, 2 stories (E wing 1 story), shallow hipped roof, ornate 2-tiered early Victorian style porch along N and W sides surmounted by paneled wooden parapet, French doors opening onto W porch; center-hall plan, etched glass in sidelights and transom of main doorway, decorative plasterwork, marble mantels from John Jacob Astor House. Also terraced formal gardens on W side. Built ca. 1838 for Col. James W. McClung. Extensively altered mid-19th C. for James L. Watkins, including porch, interior embellishment, addition of gardens; rear porte cochère added ca. 1972. McClung, from Knox County, Tenn., was early Huntsville lawyer. 5 ext. photos (1935), 7 int. photos (1935).

McCracken House. *See* Horton-McCracken House (AL-410), Meridian Pike.

McDowell-LeVert-Chase House (Henry Chase House) (AL-409), 517 Adams St. Brick, rectangular (3-bay front with 2-bay setback), 2 stories, truncated hipped roof originally surmounted by balustraded deck and extending over asymmetrical 2-tiered recessed porch; center-hall plan; rectangular 2-story gabled dependency at rear. Built 1848–50 for William McDowell, cotton merchant; remodeled ca. 1925 in Colonial Revival style, including replacement of original porch with full-height portico composed of slender paired Roman Doric columns, removal of original interior stair. Headquarters April 1862 of Gen. Ormsby M. Mitchel, during first Federal occupation of Huntsville. 2 ext. photos (1934), 3 int. photos (1935); 2 data pages (1936).

Madison County Courthouse, Old (AL-437), Courthouse Sq., bounded by Randolph, Eustis, Madison, and Franklin sts. Brick and granite, amphiprostyle temple-type structure, 54'0" (5-bay N and S fronts) X 140'0", 2 stories over partially subterranean basement, pedimented hexastyle Doric porticoes at either end with S portico screening distyle in antis entrance bay, full Doric entablature with triglyphs and metopes, pilastered side walls, large central dome resting on octagonal drum with tall lantern derived from Choragic Monument of Lysicrates, brick-paved drymoat along each side giving access to basement offices; center-hall plan on first floor, large central courtroom on second floor (also brick-paved basement containing grand jury room, vault, additional county offices). Built 1837–42 as second county courthouse; George Steele, architect. Demolished 1913. Outstanding example in state of Greek Revival style in local governmental architecture. 6 sheets (1935, redrawn from sheets prepared in 1913 by C. K. Colley, architect, of Nashville, Tenn., including plans, elevations, section, details); 3 ext. photos (n.d.).

Mastin House. *See* House (AL-436), Meridian Pike.

Morgan-Neal House (Neal House) (AL-412), 558 Franklin St. Brick, rectangular (3-bay front) with flanking symmetrical advanced 2-bay wings, main block 2 stories plus tower room, wings 1 story, principal roof concealed by wooden parapet above bracketed cornice, side wings gabled, pilastered façade with asymmetrical tower, deeply recessed doorway in middle bay; irregular plan, both Adamesque mantels and mid-19th-C. woodwork. Semidetached brick kitchen and dependencies at rear. Nucleus of structure is house built ca. 1822 for Calvin Morgan. Main block renovated ca. 1855 for George W. Neal in Italianate style, including addition of third-floor tower room with arched window above S bay; again renovated in 1965 with addition of iron balcony over main door, painting of exterior, carport and service wing at rear incorporating old kitchen. Childhood home of Gen. John Hunt Morgan (1826–64), noted Confederate cavalryman. 2 ext. photos (1934), 5 int. photos (1934–35), 1 ext. photo of kitchen (1935); 2 data pages (1937).

Neal, George W., House. *See* Morgan-Neal House (AL-412), 558 Franklin St.

Oaklawn (W. P. Dilworth House, John Robinson House) (AL-411), 2709 Meridian Pike, between Mastin Lake Rd. on N and Max Luther Dr. on S (approx. 0.2 mi. S of U.S. 72 overpass). Brick, 59'8" (5-bay front) × 46'9" with flanking, slightly advanced 2-bay wings (22'5" × 19'4" each) having corner offsets at rear (12'4" × 10'3"), 2 stories (wings 1 story), gable roof with pedimented gable ends, 4 interior end chimneys, full-height 3-bay pedimented tetrastyle Doric portico on brick stylobate with stone coping; center-hall plan, decorative plaster ceiling in hallway and SE parlor. Detached brick kitchen originally off middle rear. Built ca. 1845 for John Robinson, planter; restored ca. 1920. Neighboring Forest Field, built by Robinson's brother and burned during Civil War, was reputedly very similar in design. 8 sheets (1935, including plans, elevations, section, details); 4 ext. photos (1934–35, including 1 photo of garden), 6 int. photos (1934–35); 3 data pages (1936). NR.
Smokehouse, W (rear) of main house. Brick, rectangular (single entrance with door above), 2 stories, gable roof. Built mid-19th C.; flanking frame sheds added ca. 1920 for garage and storage. 1 ext. photo (1935).

Oak Place (Steele-Fowler House) (AL-402), 808 Maysville Rd. (SE of intersection with Stevens Ave.). Brick with stucco on ashlar foundation, 62'7" (3-bay front) × 30'5" with ell (22'5" × 39'10"), 2 stories over raised basement, shallow hipped roof, 2 interior end chimneys (main block), 1 interior end chimney (ell), projecting 1-story distyle in antis Doric entrance portico approached by broad flight of (formerly) ashlar steps, originally tall paneled sliding entrance doors on metal tracks, corner pilasters, raised tetrastyle portico on E side with 4 square piers, deep brick-paved loggia at rear occupying re-entrant angle and sheltering raised arcuated latticework porch; center-hall plan with side hall, unusual split-level arrangement behind symmetrical façade, basement "banqueting hall" occupying E side and ell; once surrounded by formal mid-19th-C. gardens. Built ca. 1840–44 as his own residence by George Steele. Dependencies demolished ca. 1940; acquired by East Huntsville Baptist Church in 1960, with subsequent interior alterations; adaptively renovated and restored 1980 under direction of Harvie P. Jones, AIA. Steele (1798–1855), born in Bedford County, Va., was Huntsville's leading architect and was responsible for many of the city's principal structures. 3½ sheets (1934, including plans, elevations, section, icehouse, and slave quarters); 4 ext. photos (1934–35), 6 int. photos (1934); 5 data pages (1936). NR.

Dependencies. Slave quarters: brick with stucco, 43'2" × 17'5", 1 story, gable roof, porch across front. Icehouse: brick with stucco, 14'7" × 9', 2 stories, pyramidal roof, single entrance bay with louvered window above and adjacent enclosed stair, structure encircled by shed-roof porch. Built ca. 1840–44; slave quarters partially remodeled as garage in early 20th C. ½ sheet (1934, including plans, elevations); 1 general ext. photo (1934).

Otey House. *See* Greenlawn (AL-476), U.S. 431.

Perkins-Winston-Orgain House (AL-473), 401 Lincoln St. Brick, approx. 50' (3-bay front) × 20' plus rear ell and wing on N side, 2 stories (N wing 1 story), gable roof, 1 exterior end chimney (main block), 1-story 3-bay Victorian entrance porch, elliptical fanlight over doorway with paneled reveal, triple windows utilized on façade; center-hall plan, Federal period woodwork. Built ca. 1815 for Col. Peter Perkins from Virginia; N side wing probably mid-19th C. (extended to rear after 1900); other rear additions include brick extension to ell incorporating old dependency. One of oldest extant brick dwellings in Alabama. Home 1819 to 1842 of Arthur Francis Hopkins, member of State Constitutional Convention of 1819. 3 ext. photos (1935), 3 int. photos (1935).

Pope, Col. Leroy, House (AL-406), 407 Echols St., on Echols Hill. Brick (façade stuccoed), 54'7" (5-bay front) × 46'7" including portico, 2 stories, originally hipped roof (later altered by addition of portico) with modillioned cornice, 3 interior end chimneys, full-height hexastyle Tuscan portico across front with unique truncated pediment surmounted by balustraded deck, tympanum bears large elliptical fanlight flanked by reeded sunburst motif which is repeated in frieze below, notable Federal period doorway with sunburst transom and heavily molded cornice; center-hall plan with side hall to carriage entrance, some Adamesque trim. Built 1814 for Pope (1765–1844), founder of Huntsville. Portico added later by George Steele; subsequent additions and alterations include 3-bay 2-story N wing (ca. 1920), 2-tiered porch across rear, replacement of most original sashing, installation of arched sliding doors between side hall and parlor, and other interior changes. Possibly oldest brick house in Alabama. May have been called Poplar Grove by Pope. 3 sheets (1934, including plans, elevations, section, details); 6 ext. photos (1934), 6 int. photos (1934); 2 data pages (1936).

Dependencies, N and E of house. 2 brick, 1-story, rectangular structures (kitchen and slave quarters) with gable roofs. Built early 19th C. 1 general ext. photo (1934). *See also* FBJ (J7-ALA-1090 through 1093).

Pynchon House. *See* Clarke-Fackler House (AL-430), 518 Adams St.

Roach-Cabaniss House (Cabaniss House) (AL-431), 603 Randolph St. Brick, 29′3″ (3-bay front) × 37′1″ plus 3-bay ground-level side wing (36′6″ × 30′4″), 2 stories over basement (wing 1 story), gable roof, small entrance porch with slender paneled piers and wheatsheaf balustrade; side-hall plan with front and rear stairway, dining room and kitchen in basement. Frame dependency at rear, also lattice wellhouse and brick dairy. Reputedly built 1832 for John C. Roach; George Steele, architect. Wellhouse and dairy demolished 1952. Acquired 1843 by Septimus D. Cabaniss and still occupied by descendants in

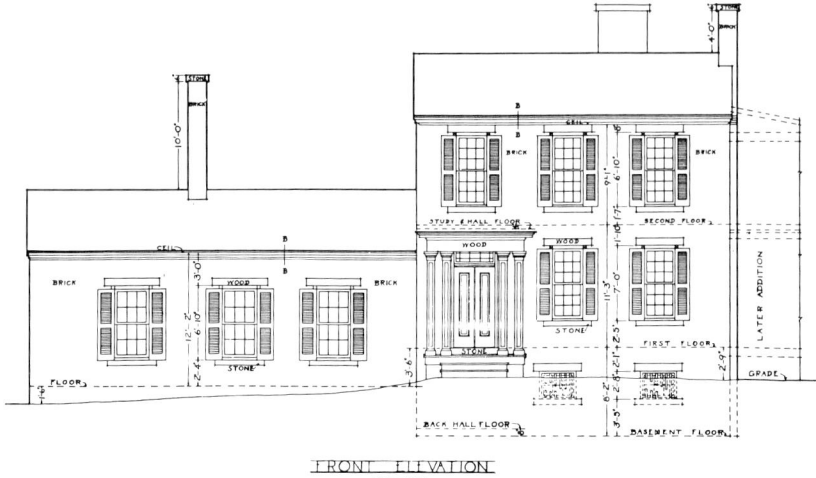

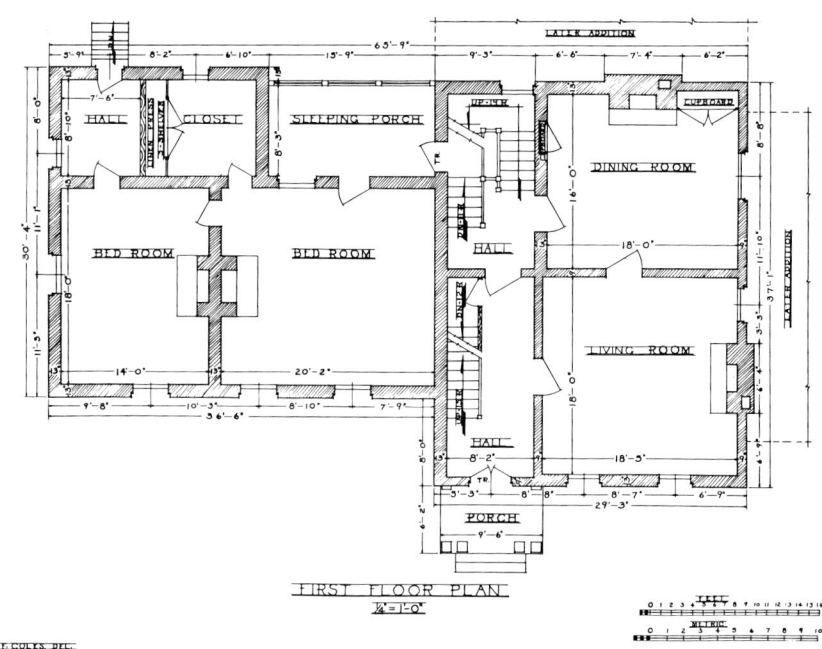

Roach-Cabaniss House, Huntsville (1832).

1978; later porch on E side, frame additions at rear. One of earliest extant dwellings designed by Steele; plan reveals architect's characteristic utilization of several floor levels to separate living, sleeping, and service areas. 11 sheets (1935, including plans, elevations, details, dependencies); 2 ext. photos (1934–35), 4 int. photos (1935); 2 data pages (1936).

Robinson, John, House. *See* Oaklawn (AL-411), 2709 Meridian Pike.

Robinson-Dilworth House. *See* Oaklawn (AL-411), 2709 Meridian Pike.

Steele-Fowler House. *See* Oak Place (AL-402), 808 Maysville Rd.

Steward's House, Huntsville Female Seminary (J. Withers Clay House, Lewis-Clay-Anderson House) (AL-408), 513 Eustis St. Brick, rectangular (3-bay front), 2 stories, gable roof, 2 pairs of exterior end chimneys, 1-story entrance porch with paired Ionic colonnettes, fanlight doorway; side-hall plan. Built ca. 1830–35 as steward's house for Huntsville Female Seminary, which stood immediately to rear; George Steele, architect. 1-story set-back wing added to W side of house ca. 1938. Home 1870–99 of J. Withers Clay, editor of *Huntsville Democrat*. 2 ext. photos (1934); 2 int. photos (1934); 2 data pages (1936).
Dependency, NW rear. Brick, rectangular, 2 stories, gable roof, 3-bay loggia with brick piers on E side. Built ca. 1839 after house acquired as residence by John H. Lewis; demolished ca. 1938. 2 ext. photos (1934).

Wade, David, House (AL-477), N side of Bob Wade Lane, 1.7 mi. W of intersection with U.S. 431. Brick, rectangular (5-bay front) with extension at middle rear, 2 stories over full basement, roof composed of parallel gables concealed at front by oversized false wooden entablature, full-height hexastyle portico (brick-paved) with 6 unplastered brick columns of rudimentary Doric order rising from ground level, deeply recessed doorway in antis; center-hall plan. Built ca. 1840; demolished late 1940s. 5 ext. photos (1935), 4 int. photos (1935).
Kitchen and Dining Room, N (rear) of house. Brick, rectangular (4-bay front), 1 story, gable roof, 2 exterior end chimneys, porch across front; 2-room plan. Built as adjunct of dwelling; demolished. 1 ext. photo (1935).
Smokehouse, NW (rear) of house. Brick, square (1 bay), 2 stories, gable roof. Built as adjunct of main house; adaptively restored as studio. 1 ext. photo (1935).
Carriage House. Frame with clapboarding, rectangular (large central double door), 1 story with loft. Built mid-to-late 19th C.; demolished. 1 ext. photo (1935).
See also FBJ (J7-ALA-1094 through 1096).

Weeden House (AL-404), 300 Gates St. (NE corner Gates and Greene sts.). House museum. Brick (façade Flemish bond), 57′4″ (5-bay front) × 21′1″ plus ell (approx. 20′ × 20′), 2 stories, gable roof, 2 exterior end chimneys (main block), 1 exterior end chimney (ell), outstanding fanlight doorway with leaded glass and richly detailed archivolt, elaborate cornice enriched with modillions and "i"-dentils; center-hall plan, notable interior woodwork including spiral stairway, Adamesque mantels, paneled reveals. Rectangular 2-story dependency at rear. Built ca. 1819 for Henry C. Bradford. Entrance porch with deck added ca. 1850; kitchen wing built off SE corner of ell in late 19th C.; 20th-C. frame additions; dependency razed ca. 1940 and garage built on site; restored 1976–80 by City of Huntsville, including removal of mid-19th-C. entrance porch and 20th-C. rear additions: Harvie P. Jones, AIA, architect in charge of restoration. Home 1824–29 of John McKinley, afterward U.S. Supreme Court justice; also birthplace and home of Miss Howard Weeden (1847–1905), poet-artist of post–Civil War southern romantic school. 3 sheets (1934); 2 ext. photos (1934), 8 int. photos (1934); 3 data pages (1936).

White, Thomas W., House. *See* Cox-White House (AL-475), 461 Eustis St.

Windham, William, House (Hamlet House) (AL-413), 413 E. Holmes St. Brick, rectangular (5-bay front) with ell, 1 story, originally gable roof, 1 exterior and 1 interior end chimney (main block), small pedimented entrance porch; center-hall plan. Built ca. 1830; later renovations include alteration of roof to hipped configuration (before 1935), installation of Eastlake style front door and mantelpieces, elongation of windows. Windham was early Huntsville blacksmith; house still owned by Windham descendants in 1978. 3 ext. photos (1935, including later frame servant house at rear of ell), 4 int. photos (1935).

New Market

Five Oaks (W. L. Laxon House) (AL-407), E side of Winchester Pike, 0.2 mi. S of intersection with Co. 87 (Hurricane Rd.). Brick, rectangular (3-bay front) with ell, 2 stories, hipped roof, 2 interior chimneys (main block), 1 interior end chimney (ell), 2-story pedimented entrance porch with scroll-cut balustrade at upper level, flanking triple windows; center-hall plan. Built ca. 1860; rear 1-story frame addition late 19th C.; rear porch enclosed ca. 1960. 6 ext. photos (1934–35), 4 int. photos (1935).

Smokehouse, E (rear) of house. Brick, rectangular (single door), gable roof, lozenge-shaped ventilators. Built ca. 1860. 1 ext. photo (1935).

MARENGO COUNTY

Dayton

Jones, Leroy King, House. *See* Magnolia Grove (AL-153), Ala. 25.

Magnolia Grove (Leroy King Jones House) (AL-153), E side of Ala. 25 just N of junction with Co. 44 E; approx. 8.5 mi. S of Ala. 25 intersection with U.S. 80 at Faunsdale. Frame with clapboarding, rectangular (5-bay front) with ell, 2 stories with 1-story shed across rear (ell also 1 story), gable roof, 2 pairs exterior end chimneys, central distyle pedimented portico with paneled wooden piers, balcony above main door; center-hall plan. Dependencies included frame tenant house and smokehouse, log barn. Built ca. 1845, possibly for Dr. Sidney J. Harris (may have incorporated earlier log dwelling); demolished 1972–73. 10 ext. photos (1936, including 5 photos of dependencies), 6 int. photos (1936).

Methodist Church (AL-149), E side of Ala. 25, approx. 0.1 mi. S of junction with Co. 44 and 8.6 mi. S of Ala. 25 intersection with U.S. 80 at Faunsdale. Frame with clapboarding (façade stuccoed) over brick ground floor, approx. 40′ (2-bay front) x 54′ (4 bays deep), slate-covered gable roof, raised pedimented tetrastyle portico of modified Doric order (columns approx. 3′ in diameter, without entasis; each rests on brick pier 3′6″ square and 14′ high), branching wooden stair with turned balustrade originally ascended to tall doors in each outer bay of portico; interior has open plan with 2 aisles, mahogany-trimmed slip pews probably adapted from Asher Benjamin, semicircular pulpit dais enclosed by kneeling rail, pulpit backed by blind classical architrave, large mid-19th-C. cut-glass chandelier suspended from ceiling, single large brick-paved assembly room occupies ground floor. Built 1849–50; B. F. Parsons possibly architect; J. T. Terrell, contractor. Portico originally topped by large belfry (removed early 20th C.); wooden steps replaced by concrete flight in 1955. Outstanding example in state of rural antebellum religious architecture. 8 ext. photos (1936), 7 int. photos (1936, including memorial plaque to early benefactors).

Walton-Bruce House (Bruce House) (AL-140), E side of Ala. 25, approx. 0.1 mi. N of junction with Co. 44 and 8.4 mi. S of Ala. 25 intersection with U.S. 80 at Faunsdale. Frame with clapboarding, main block was irregular rectangle with massive T-shaped rear wing, 2 stories, shallow hipped roof with projecting subordinate gables and wide bracketed eaves, asymmetrical 3-bay façade with 3-story central tower in reentrant angle, projecting bay window at front, house partially surrounded by 1-story porches with bracketed supports and scroll-cut balustrade; center-hall plan, very elaborate interior including ornate raised plaster cornices and centerpieces, branched stairway at rear of main hall, freestanding corkscrew stair from upper hall to tower room; lawn enclosed by picket fence with scroll-cut gate swung between square piers capped by finials. Reputedly completed 1863 for John T. Walton, planter; tradition has attributed plan to Thomas Helm Lee of Selma, although he

died in 1850s. Restored 1961 (original fence removed at time); destroyed by fire on 24 Feb. 1963. A foremost example in state of Italianate design, reflecting influence of Samuel Sloan. 5 ext. photos (1935).
Dependency (possibly kitchen and servants' quarters), to rear of house. Frame with clapboarding, T-shaped (2-bay front), 1 story, gable roof with wide bracketed eaves. Contemporary with house; survived 1963 fire. 1 ext. photo (1935).

Demopolis

Bluff Hall (Lyon-Smith House) (AL-213), 407 N. Commissioners Ave. House Museum. Brick (façade stuccoed and scored to simulate ashlar), approx. 50′ (5-bay front) X 35′ plus ell approx. 19′ X 46′, 2½ stories, combination gable and hipped roof, 3 interior end chimneys (main block), full-height hexastyle portico at front composed of heavy stuccoed brick piers carrying full entablature and linked by wrought-iron balustrade, upper and lower semielliptical fanlight doorways (balcony at second-floor level), 2-tiered louvered gallery at rear (along N side of ell); center-hall plan with side hall to secondary S entrance, notable Federal period interior trim with later neoclassical modifications, folding doors set into deep paneled reveal between side hall and ell dining room directly behind, unusual stair with hanging flight from landing to upper hall. Main block of house believed to have been completed in 1832 for Francis Strother Lyon, state senator and U.S. and Confederate congressman. House originally may have had 2-tiered central pedimented portico; present portico and perhaps ell also added in mid-19th C.; double parlors redecorated in 1874, including installation of columnar screen; dwelling converted into apartments early 20th C.; porte cochère replaced small porch on S side in early 20th C. Acquired 1967 by Marengo County Historical Society and restored as house museum; porte cochère removed. Confederate Pres. Jefferson Davis entertained here in Oct. 1863. 6 ext. photos (1934–36), 7 int. photos (1935); 3 data pages (1936). NR.
Gate and Fence, N side of house (originally located at front). Picket fence with ornate scroll-cut gate swung between finial-topped paneled piers. Erected 1883; later moved to side of house; removed in 1940s. 2 photos (1936).
Carriage House. Brick, rectangular, 2 stories, gable roof.
Smokehouse. Brick, square, 1 story, pyramidal roof. Both dependencies situated at right angle to ell on N side. Built early-to-mid 19th C.; razed ca. 1937 and brick used to erect small residence adjoining house on S (now used as museum headquarters). 2 ext. photos (1934–35).
Privy. Frame, rectangular, gable roof cantilevered over doorway, louvered vent in gable end. Probably built mid-19th C.; demolished. 1 ext. photo (1935).
See also FBJ (J7-ALA-1231 through 1239).

Gaineswood (AL-211), 805 S. Cedar St.; E side Cedar St. (U.S. 43), approx. 0.3 mi. N of intersection with U.S. 80. House museum. Unique and nationally significant Greek Revival style mansion. Brick covered with stucco and lightly scored (also some frame construction), irregular rectangle (approx. 112′0″ X 93′5″ overall including E wing, porte cochère, and porticoes), 2 stories (E wing 1 story), complex roof design concealed by false entablature and parapets, principal (N) façade 7 bays wide with advanced 3-bay pavilion breaking into rounded center bay (with statuary niche) and enclosed by freestanding piers, pedimented tetrastyle Doric portico projecting into enclosed forecourt from ambulatory formed by piers, Doric porte cochère on W side, small portico at rear, single-story E wing (mistress's bedroom) terminating in rounded bay with Doric style colonnade, main block surmounted by circular open observatory with turned balustrade; lavish interior with highly unusual spatial arrangement, formal entrance through porte cochère into foyer flanked by reception rooms and opening into E-W hall (library, dining room, and ancillary rooms to S, ballroom to N, master's and mistress's sleeping apartments beyond), elaborate use throughout formal rooms of Greek Revival decorative details employing Corinthian and Ionic orders, applied palmette and acanthus motifs, palmette-studded domed ceilings with lantern in library and dining room, coffered ceiling in ballroom. Landscaped grounds formerly included gate and porter's lodge, artificial lake and balustraded terraces, classic style gazebo, Grecian statuary, and dependencies. House evolved ca. 1842–60 from earlier structure on site, as center of 480-acre estate; Gen. Nathan Bryan Whitfield (1799–1868), owner and architect. Frame bath and kitchen addition to E wing and minor modifications during late 19th and early 20th C. Purchased by State of Alabama 1966 and restored 1971–75 as house museum (under direction of Luther Hill, AIA, and Jack Stell, Alabama Historical Commission), including removal of later additions. Called Marlmont until 1856. 23 sheets (1936, including plot plan, plans, elevations, section, details); 1 ext. photocopy of John Sartain engraving (ca. 1860); 26 ext. photos (1934–36), 32 int. photos (1934–36); 4 data pages (1936). NHL.

Gate and Porter's Lodge, originally located N of house on the Uniontown Rd. (old U.S. 80), now Pettus St. Gateway composed of 2 pairs stuccoed brick piers (approx. 4′ × 4′) carrying wooden entablature capped by finials, rinceaux bearing palmette above central carriageway, cast-iron carriage gates with flanking pedestrian gates. Adjacent porter's lodge stuccoed brick, approx. 13′10″ (1-bay front) × 25′11″, 1 story, gable roof, central chimney, small entrance porch in gable end; 2-room plan. Built mid-19th C. Gates moved to present location W of house on Cedar St. (U.S. 43) in early 20th C.; porter's lodge razed 1958 to make way for Demopolis High School. ½ sheet (1936, including plan, elevations); 2 ext. photocopies (ca. 1910); 2 ext. photos (1935).

Gazebo (pavilion), NE of mansion. Masonry base with frame superstructure, approx. 8′4″ in diameter, round open structure with Corinthian columns and denticulated cornice (based on the Choragic Monument of Lysicrates); formerly overlooking artificial lake. Built mid-19th C.; restored 1971–75. 1 sheet (1936, including plan, elevation, section); 2 ext. photos (1936, one photo damaged).

Slave House, SE of mansion. Frame with clapboarding, approx. 36′4″ (2-bay front) × 20′4″, 1 story, gable roof extending over full-length porch, central chimney; 2-room plan. Built mid-19th C.; restored 1971–75. ½ sheet (1936, including plan, elevation, fireplace detail); 1 ext. photo (1935), 1 int. photo (1935).

See also FBJ (J7-ALA-1240 through 1249); Tebbs (T3-ALA-538212 through 538225).

Glover Mausoleum (AL-212A), in Riverside Cemetery, approx. 50 yds. E of bluff overlooking Tombigbee River (cemetery entrance at Decatur and Griffin sts.). Brick covered with stucco and scored to simulate ashlar, 29′2″ × 29′1″ × 14′3″ (to top of cornice), raked parapet concealing shallow slate roof capped by stone finial and cross, brick-paved ambulatory enclosing sepulchre (17′2″ × 17′0″) containing 3 tiers of vaults, 4 bays on each façade articulated by slender cast-iron Tuscan colonnettes resting on masonry plinths; lot and mausoleum enclosed by ornate cast-iron fence with gothicized gate on E side. Built 1840s by Mrs. Mary Ann Diven Glover, widow of Allen Glover, as family mausoleum; possibly designed by Nathan Bryan Whitfield. Cast-iron fence erected 1858 (most of fence removed after 1935). 4 sheets (1934–35, including plot plan, plan, elevations, section, fence details); 12 ext. photos (1934–36, mausoleum and fence).

Lyon Hall (AL-239), 102 S. Main Ave. (facing N toward Franklin St. on W side of S. Main Ave.). Frame with clapboarding (façade stuccoed), rectangular (5-bay front), 2 stories, shallow hipped roof terminating in glazed monitor surmounted by cast-iron balustrade, 4 interior end chimneys, full-height hexastyle portico across front composed of stucco-on-brick piers carrying 2-tiered porch enclosed with cast-iron balustrade, smaller 2-tiered porch on E side, 3-bay lattice-enclosed double loggia at rear; center-hall plan. Built 1853 for George Gaines Lyon (1821–96), nephew of Francis Strother Lyon of Bluff Hall. Subsequent additions at rear and W side; upper tier of E porch removed before 1934. 4 ext. photos (1934–35), 2 int. photos (1935); 2 data pages (1936).

Dixons Mills Vicinity

Wright-Pearson House (AL-145), in Marengo community, on N side of Co. 6, approx. 0.6 mi. NE of intersection with Ala. 10 and approx. 1.3 mi. W of Ala. 10 intersection with U.S. 43 at Dixons Mills. Frame (board and batten), rectangular (3-bay front), 1 story, hipped roof terminating in glazed monitor, 4 exterior end chimneys, shed porch across front with trellis supports, scalloped fascia trimming eaves of porch, main roof, and monitor; center-hall plan, board-and-batten interior, colored glass sidelights and transom. Dependencies included milk house, smokehouse to NW, and barn to E. Built ca. 1870 possibly for Sarah Wright. Stair in front hall reversed and other changes after 1905, also rear additions; demolished 1950–51 to make way for new house on same site. 5 ext. photos (1935, including 2 photos of dependencies), 1 int. photo (1935).

Faunsdale Vicinity

Cedar Grove (AL-200), S side of unpaved old Uniontown road, approx. 1.4 mi. E by SE of intersection with Church St. in Faunsdale; approx. 0.8 mi. due S of U.S. 80 and approx. 1.3 mi. E of U.S. 80 intersection with Ala. 25 at Faunsdale. Frame with clapboarding, rectangular (5-bay front) with low rear wing (N) and semidetached service rooms (S), 2 stories, hipped roof (main block), continuous porch across front and along each side (slightly advanced 2-tiered center bay with flanking 1-story extensions), denticulated cornice; center-hall plan with broad cross hall at rear, heavy Greek Revival style interior woodwork, elaborate plaster moldings and chandelier medallions; original parlor suite and many other original furnishings. Dependencies include frame servants' house, smokehouse, and wood house. Built ca. 1855 (low wing at NW rear possibly earlier) for Charles and Margaret (Jemison) Walker, who came to Marengo County in 1852 from Pulaski County, Ga. Subsequent changes include extensive renovation of porch in early 20th C. with new flooring, ceiling, boxing-in of original columns. 11 ext. photos (1936, including 3 photos of dependencies), 21 int. photos (1936).

Norwood (AL-261), in grove S of Co. 54, approx. 2.6 mi. W of junction with Ala. 25 just S of Faunsdale; 1.7 mi. W of old St. Michael's Episcopal Church Cemetery. Frame with clapboarding, approx. 90′8″ across front (5-bay façade) including slightly advanced 1-bay end pavilions, parallel rear

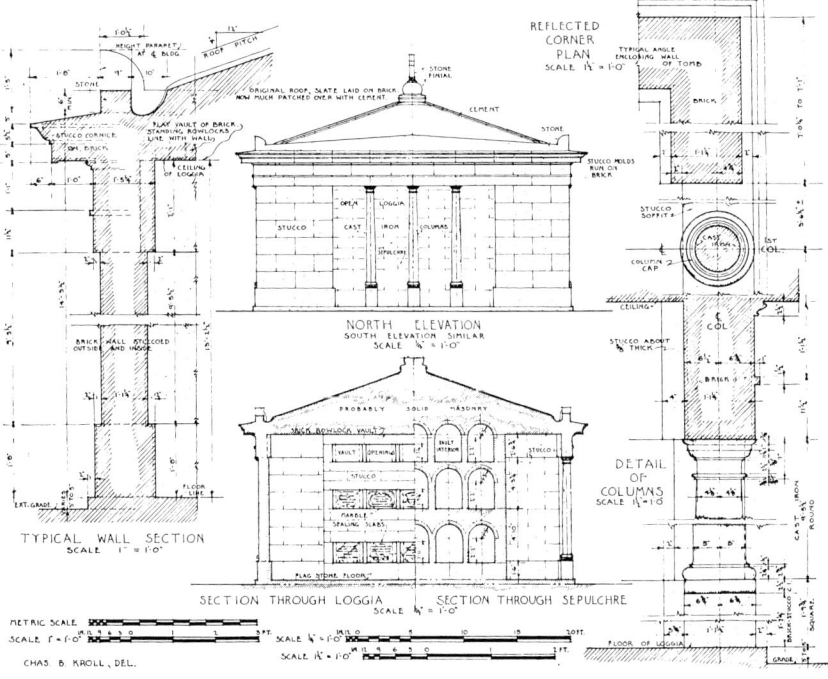

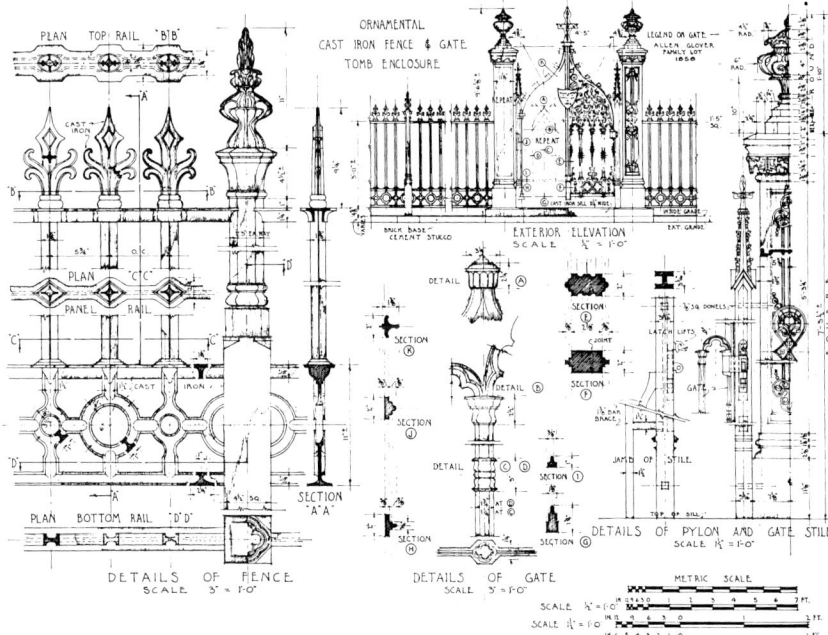

Glover Mausoleum, Riverside Cemetery, Demopolis (1840 and later).

"Hoover Wagon." Mule-drawn home-made cart apparently built by tenant on Pearson place (1 photo, 1935).

wings (embracing service court) to form overall U-shaped structure, 1 story (raised approx. 7′ on brick piers with latticework between), shallow gable roof with subordinate pedimented cross-gable on each end pavilion, central pedimented tetrastyle portico with paired square columns, U-shaped porch at rear partially enclosed by latticework, raised passage to kitchen on E; center-hall plan (main block) with 2 lateral rooms to each side, heavy Greek Revival style woodwork. Dependencies included frame rectangular 2-room structure at SW rear (ruinous in 1978). Built ca. 1845–50 for David Minge (grandson of Benjamin Harrison, signer of Declaration of Independence), who came to Marengo County in 1833 from Charles City County, Va. Disassembled and moved to Texas after 1935; subsequent fate unknown. Good example of elaborated raised-cottage style. 2 ext. photos (1935), 2 int. photos (1935).

Jefferson Vicinity

Evergreen (W. G. Allen House) (AL-142), N side of Ala. 28, approx. 4.0 mi. W of Chickasawbogue Creek Bridge; 2.3 mi. E of junction with Co. 21 at Jefferson. Frame with clapboarding, approx. 52′4″ (5-bay front) × 48′10″ overall, 2 stories, shallow hipped roof, 2 interior chimneys, full-length 2-tiered hexastyle portico across front with superimposed Doric colonnettes (wheatsheaf balustrade at upper level), 3-bay pedimented tetrastyle Tuscan portico at rear, 1-story 3-bay pedimented portico on W side; offset 1-story kitchen wing at NW rear; center-hall plan with rear stairhall, simple Greek Revival style interior woodwork. Dependencies include 2 frame barns (destroyed). Built ca. 1846–48 for Col. and Mrs. James Richard Bryan II. Kitchen wing added late 19th C. (removed ca. 1938); all original porches (front, rear, W side) removed in 1966 and front porch replaced by full-height portico with slender square columns, balcony above doorway. 3 ext. photos (1935, including barns), 5 int. photos (1935).

Grant, Basil, House (Charles Brasfield Grant House) (AL-144), in Pin Hook community on S side of Ala. 28, approx. 3.3 mi. W of Chickasawbogue Creek bridge; approx. 3.0 mi. E of Ala. 28 intersection with Co. 21 at Jefferson. Frame with clapboarding, approx. 50′0″ (5-bay front) × 20′4″ plus shed rooms and porch across rear (also ell), 2 stories (ell 1 story), gable roof, 4 exterior end chimneys, originally central 2-tiered gabled porch, shed porch across rear; center-hall plan, original random-width flooring, beaded board ceiling, batten doors. Built ca. 1840 as plantation dwelling. Porch extended and renovated in early 20th C.; entire porch replaced by central pedimented portico 1958; rear chimneys removed, aluminum siding added 1973; various additions and modifications at rear. 4 ext. photos (1935), 2 int. photos (1935).

Smokehouse, SE of house. Log (saddle-notch), rectangular, gable roof with wooden shakes cantilevered over single door in gable end. 1 ext. photo (1935).

Store, facing road to NW front of house. Frame (board and batten), rectangular, 1 story, gable roof, 1 exterior end chimney at rear. Built mid-19th C.; demolished. 1 ext. photo (1935, E side and rear only).

Linden

Marengo County Courthouse, Old (AL-143), SW corner Cahaba Ave. (Ala. 28) and Mobile St., approx. 0.1 mi. W of Ala. 28 intersection with U.S. 43 (Main St.). Brick (façade stuccoed and lightly scored to simulate ashlar), approx. 44′3″ (5-bay front) × 64′4″, 2 stories, temple-type façade with distyle in antis Doric portico, wooden steps flanking entrance porch ascend to upper gallery before courtroom; bisecting cross halls (first floor), courtroom upstairs with antechambers to rear. Built ca. 1850 to replace courthouse burned in 1848; Erastus Bardwell, builder; became Baptist church ca. 1902; American Legion Hall and VFW Lodge 1948–78, when acquired by municipality for restoration. 20th-C. modifications include replacement of original brick floor with scored concrete pavement, removal of wooden gallery balustrade, sealing of middle entrance to old courtroom. 6 ext. photos (1935), 3 int. photos (1935).

MARION COUNTY

Bexar

Apothecary, Old. *See* Dr. A. L. Moorman Office (AL-389), Co. 13.

Moorman, Dr. A. L., Office (Old Apothecary) (AL-389), approx. 500' E of Co. 13 facing S on unmarked dirt road 0.6 mi. S of Co. 13 intersection with U.S. 78 and 0.1 mi. N of old U.S. 78; about 10 mi. W of Hamilton. Frame with clapboarding (façade flush boarding), rectangular (3-bay front), 1 story, gable roof with wooden shingles, façade at gable end embellished by applied wooden ornamentation, scroll-cut fascia; 2 rooms (front to back). Built between 1873 and 1875 for Achilles Lucien Moorman (1843–1922), ex-Confederate officer, physician, and graduate of the Kentucky School of Medicine; front room used as office, back room initially as lodging for Dr. Moorman. Structure moved to Booneville, Miss., ca. 1975 and restored. Stylistically similar to nearby M. D. L. Spearman House (later Dr. Moorman residence), built ca. 1870 and ruinous in 1980. 2 ext. photos (1936), 2 int. photos (1936).

MOBILE COUNTY

Chastang

Chastang, Zeno, House (AL-187), 0.7 mi. E of U.S. 43 on bluff overlooking Mobile River at old Chastang Landing, approx. 11 mi. N of junction with I-65. Frame with rough clapboarding raised on wood pilings, rectangular (irregular 5-bay front), 1½ stories, high gable roof covered with wooden shakes extending over porches front and rear (shed rooms at each end of rear gallery), 2 interior end chimneys; broad central passage with heavy batten doors at either end, rough board interior partitions. Built ca. 1850 for Chastang; demolished 1960s. Reputed to have been constructed as river landing warehouse. Chastang also operated a wood yard for use of riverboats. 4 ext. photos (1937), 1 int. photo (1937).

Citronelle

Pullman Hotel (Pullman House, Jones House) (AL-163), 104 Center St. Frame with clapboarding (rear is log covered with clapboarding), basically T-shaped with off-center 3-bay front (approx. 25' X 30') projecting from older rectangular rear portion (approx. 65' X 25'), 1 story, high gable roof with front cross-gable, continuous balustraded gallery along front and S side, main doorway flanked by projecting bays, gallery also at rear. Log portion built ca. 1820 as dwelling for Simms family. Enlarged for use as hotel (ca. 1853) with extensions to either side and construction of front block as lobby and office; subsequent minor changes; demolished 1960 to make way for funeral home. 7 ext. photos (1937), 1 int. photo (1937); 2 data pages (1937).

Dauphin Island

Fort Gaines (AL-102), Pelican Point at eastern tip of Dauphin Island, overlooking W passage to Mobile Bay from Gulf of Mexico; E end of Bienville Blvd., 2.3 mi. E of intersection with LeMoyne Dr. State monument and museum. Five-sided fortification with quadrilateral bastions at each corner, main work (enceinte): brick, approx. 500' (W or landward elevation) X 317' (N and S elevations) X 290' (easterly elevations) including bastions, average height of walls approx. 22'6", outer drymoat and glacis, inner earthen ramparts, gate with rusticated surround and vaulted entrance tunnel on W side, vaulted casemates in each bastion; officers' quarters, barracks, and ancillary structures grouped around parade ground. Foundation work begun 1819–21; subsequently suspended. Construction of actual works initiated 1856 according to plans developed by U.S. Army Chief Engineer J. G. Totten; completed by Confederate government ca. 1861. Civil War damage repaired and fort improved ca. 1865–75; reinforced concrete gun emplacements installed 1895–1901; following long abandonment, acquired and partially restored by County of Mobile; opened 1956 as museum. With Fort Morgan (AL-101) it protected mouth of Mobile Bay. Seized during Civil War by state militia; besieged and recaptured by U.S. forces 3–8 Aug.

1864. 1 photocopy of plans (1858); 3 ext. photocopies (1928, 1934), 12 int. photos (1934, including parade ground, casemates, barracks, bake oven, smithy); 3 data pages (1936).

Dawes

Vogtner Farm (AL-188), at end of private lane, approx. 0.4 mi. N of Jeff Hamilton Rd., 0.2 mi. W of intersection with Dawes Rd.; approx. 0.2 mi. due S of Miller Creek. Originally log (saddle-notch construction) with rough clapboards nailed over cracks, foundation of wood pilings, 43'0" (3-bay front) X 25'3" including shed addition across rear, 1½ stories, gable roof covered with shakes, 2 clay-and-cattail exterior end chimneys encased by rough boards, gallery (7'5" wide) across front with wooden supports connected by single rail, open shed attached to S end of house, batten shutters over windows; open central passage with single large room to either side and shed rooms behind, closed stringer stair in passage. Built ca. 1854 by George Vogtner, Sr., a Bavarian immigrant who purchased 150-acre tract from Mobile and Ohio Railroad. Later frame additions at rear; passage enclosed 1930s; chimneys rebuilt in native sandstone 1940s. Rare surviving example of yeoman farmhouse in coastal pinelands. 5 ext. photos (1937), 2 int. photos (1937).
  Smokehouse. Log (saddle-notch construction), square with gable roof forming overhang above doorway. Demolished. 1 ext. photo (1937).

Mobile*

Anderson, Decatur C., House (AL-52), 251 N. Conception St. (NW corner Conception and State sts.). Frame with clapboarding (galleries plastered), approx. 30' (3-bay front) X 50' with offset brick wing to rear, 2 stories, gable roof, 2-tiered pedimented portico with denticulated cornice and wheatsheaf balustrade, 2-tiered loggia on S side (Tuscan order below, Ionic above, wheatsheaf balustrade at upper level), jib windows on galleries; side-hall plan, Federal period woodwork. Built 1835–36; demolished. 7 ext. photos (1937), 7 int. photos (1937); 2 data pages (1937).

Ashland (Augusta Evans Wilson House) (AL-68), equidistant between Spring Hill Ave. and Old Shell Rd., S end of Lanier Ave. (formerly private lane to house), approx. 750' S of intersection with Spring Hill Ave. in Ashland Place subdivision. Elaborated version of raised cottage, frame with clapboarding on high brick basement, main block approx. 50' (5-bay front) X 80' with flanking 4-bay wings (each approx. 40' wide X 25' deep), 1 story over full ground floor, longitudinal gable with identical porticoes front and rear carrying raised balustraded gallery and composed of 6 slender fluted Doric columns rising directly from ground level to heavy pediment, double stairway to portico, wings also galleried front and rear; center-hall plan (main block), service area in basement. Built 1844 for Lorenzo M. Wilson, prominent Maryland-born merchant, as seat of 40-acre suburban estate; extensive surrounding azalea gardens; renovated 1907 for George Fearn, Jr.; destroyed by fire on 15 March 1926, and ruins subsequently razed. Home 1868–91 of Augusta Evans Wilson, popular 19th-C. romantic novelist; at Ashland Mrs. Wilson wrote *At the Mercy of Tiberius* and *Infelice.* 4 photos of ruins (1937), 1 ext. photocopy (1893); 2 data pages (1937).

Augustine-Ottenstein House. *See* Thomas S. James Double House (AL-27), 207–209 N. Jackson St.

Ayers House (Private School, Madame Paul Robert House) (AL-49), 57 S. Hamilton St. (E side Hamilton between Conti and Government sts.). Frame with clapboarding, 36'6" (4-bay front) X 46'7", 1½ stories, gable roof over full-length balustraded porch; 2 front rooms with pair of smaller rooms behind, shed rooms flanking rear gallery. Built 1831 by Andrew Ayers, carpenter from Belfast, as his own dwelling. Private school opened in house by Ayers descendant in 1871 (partition between 2 front rooms on N side removed following year); demolished before 1960. Excellent and very early example of typical small Mobile cottage. 5 sheets (1935, including plans, elevations, section, details); 2 ext. photos (1935), 2 int. photos (1935); 2 data pages (1936). *See also* FBJ (J7-ALA-1340).

Azalea Grove (John C. Dawson House, McKeon House, Palmetto Hall) (AL-54), 55 S. McGregor Ave. (Spring Hill). Raised cottage, frame with clapboarding on high brick basement, rectangular (6-bay front), 1 story over full ground floor, hipped roof, full-length raised hexastyle gallery composed of slender fluted Doric columns superimposed on short columnar-type bases at

---

*For listing of Mobile structures by street address, see Appendix C.

ground level, loggia-like rear gallery partially enclosed beneath with jalousies; center-hall plan on ground floor, modified French colonial plan above with 3 rooms across front, 3 directly behind (center rooms connected by paneled sliding doors), Greek Revival interior trim. Built ca. 1850 for John C. Dawson. Renovated 1919–22, including addition of divided stair rising from ground level to front gallery and of interior stair in NE corner of lower hall; dismantled in 1963 and reconstructed in elaborated version of original house, utilizing same materials. 10 ext. photos (1937), 11 int. photos (1937); 2 data pages (1937).

Barker, P. D., House. *See* House (AL-21D), 109 St. Anthony St.

Barnewall-Mitchell House. *See* Joshua Kennedy House (AL-800), 607 Government St.

Barton Academy (AL-32), 504 Government St. (between Cedar and Lawrence sts.). Brick with stucco scored to simulate ashlar, approx. 136′ (17-bay façade including 3-bay advanced end pavilions) × 71′5″, 2 stories above ground floor, shallow hipped roof concealed by low parapet, pedimented hexastyle Ionic portico, pilastered end pavilions, lanterned dome resting on wooden drum encircled by Ionic colonnade; center-hall plan with transverse halls. Built 1835–37; James Gallier and Charles Dakin, architects. Iron balcony added to portico before 1885; extensive late-19th and early 20th-C. alterations. Exterior restored 1969–70, interior adaptively renovated. Barton Academy became Alabama's first free public school in 1852 and continued as such until 1965 when taken over by Board of School Commissioners. Federal hospital during Civil War period. One of state's most notable early institutional buildings. 6 sheets (1936–37, including plans without interior partitions, also elevations, sections, details, ironwork); 15 ext. photos (1934–36), 3 int. photos (1935–36, details only); 3 data pages (1936). NR.

Entrance Gate and Fence. Gate composed of 4 paneled piers (11′4″ high) with caps, bases, applied palmette motif, topped by fleur-de-lis finials; arched wrought-iron gate; fence with spiked palings, each section anchored to iron posts simulating classical fasces. Fence arrived from New York in March 1837 aboard S.S. *Lewis Cass.* 5 photos (1935–37).

See also Tebbs (T3-ALA-434082).

Bates-Henderson House (Dr. Henderson House) (AL-22A), 12 N. Jackson St. Brick with stucco scored to simulate ashlar, 26′10″ (3-bay front) × 51′2″, 2 stories, shallow hipped roof concealed by parapet at front and sides, doorway with battered architrave, floor-length windows opening onto ground-level deck enclosed by iron railing at front and along 2 side bays of house, full-length second story iron balcony with cast-iron brackets; side-hall plan. Built mid-19th C., probably for James F. Bates; altered ca. 1940, including removal of exterior blinds and conversion of first-floor middle bay from window to door; deck railing removed ca. 1950 and reused at 21 S. McGregor Ave. 1 ext. photo (1934).

Batre-Bernheimer-Saad House (Batre-Saad House, Bernheimer House) (AL-801), 155 Monroe St. Brick, approx. 25′6″ (3-bay front) × 39′0″ with low stuccoed-and-scored offset wing at E side, 2 stories, gable roof, double end chimneys with curtain walls, brick dentil course, cast-iron gallery with deck and curved cast-iron steps; side-hall plan. Cast-iron fence. Built in 1856 for Charles and Mary Batre. Acquired in 1873 by Leah Bernheimer, who added cast-iron gallery and fence with gate bearing nameplate. 1 ext. photo originally filed as AL-9M (1936, steps only), 2 ext. photos (1963); 1 data page (1963).

Batre-Hamilton House (W. M. Broun House) (AL-58), 320 Avalon St. (Spring Hill). Raised cottage, stucco-over-frame on brick basement, square (5-bay front), 1 story over full ground floor, shallow hipped roof, encircling balustraded gallery with chamfered posts resting on brick piers; center-hall plan. Mid-19th-C. formal garden. Built ca. 1830 for Paul Batre. Acquired 1852 by attorney Thomas A. Hamilton as summer residence; rear gallery later partially enclosed; demolished ca. 1955 for subdivision. 4 ext. photos (1937); 2 data pages (1937). *See also* FBJ (J7-ALA-1280).

Batre-Saad House. *See* Batre-Bernheimer-Saad House (AL-801), 155 Monroe St.

Battle-Ross House (William H. Ross House) (AL-9V), 602 Government St. (NW corner Government and Warren sts.). Pressed brick, rectangular (3-bay front) with 2-story semioctagonal bays flanking 2-tiered cast-iron gallery, shallow hipped roof originally surmounted by cupola, alternating brackets and applied garland motif beneath eaves, cast-iron window grilles; center-hall plan; Italianate detail. Built in 1850s for John Battle. Purchased 1878 by William H. Ross; later housed Knights of Columbus; demolished 1969. Very similar architecturally to James Battle house on opposite (NE) corner of Government and Warren sts. Iron gate and fence placed in front of house in 1878; moved in 1920s to 456 S. Conception St., in 1963 to 3333 Riviere du Chin Rd. 1 ext. photo (1936, façade detail only); 1 ext. photocopy (n.d.). *Under* Gates and Fences, *see also* 456 S. Conception St. (AL-8CX).

Beal-Gaillard House (S. P. Gaillard House) (AL-107), 111 Myrtlewood Ln. (Spring Hill). Frame with clapboarding (gallery plastered) on high brick piers with latticework between, 51′2″ (5-bay front) × 45′2″ overall, 1½ stories, gable roof, full-length balustraded gallery with chamfered posts, continuous jalousies screening upper portion of gallery, unusually wide doorway with paneled double-leaf doors of heart cypress enframed by sidelights and transom, flanking floor-length windows; center-hall plan, Greek Revival interior trim, original locks. Built 1836–37 as country home for Gustavus Beal, wholesale grocer. In late 19th C. dining room enlarged and north rear (kitchen) wing added, summer house built; south rear wing added and north wing enlarged ca. 1920; rear porch enclosed 1969. Outstanding example of Creole cottage. 6 ext. photos (1937). *See also* FBJ (J7-ALA-1299 and 1300).

Beck House. *See* Goelet-Randlette-Beck House (AL-855), 1005 Augusta St.

Beehive Church. *See* Franklin Street Methodist Episcopal Church (AL-26), SW corner Franklin and St. Michael sts.

Bernheimer House (originally AL-9M). *See* Batre-Bernheimer-Saad House (AL-801), 155 Monroe St.

Bestor, Daniel Perrin, Jr., House (AL-9X), 208 Government St. (NE corner Government and S. Joachim sts.). Brick, irregularly shaped with projecting bays, 2½ stories, cast-iron galleries including unusual entrance porch reproducing Eastlake motifs in metal, cast-iron window grilles and lintels, leaded-glass sidelights and transom; side-hall plan. Brick carriage house and brick-paved courtyard to rear. Built 1882; demolished. Original owner, Daniel Perrin Bestor, Jr. (1840–1911), was noted local attorney, son of eminent Alabama Baptist divine, mayor of Mobile 1877, chairman of the board of trustees of the Alabama Medical College. 2 ext. photos (1936).

Bishop's Residence. *See* William H. Ketchum House (AL-9U), 400 Government St.

Bloodgood's Row (AL-818), 306, 308, 310 Monroe St. Brick with stucco scored to simulate ashlar, approx. 60′ (9-bay façade divided into 3 units of 3 bays each) × 42′ plus ell at no. 306, 3 stories above raised basement, contiguous cast-iron galleries (2 bays before each unit) resting on slender cast-iron posts; side-hall plan in each unit. Built as row house development ca. 1836 for John Bloodgood. Cast-iron galleries added later; nos. 306 and 308 demolished in Feb. 1941; no. 310 demolished in 1971 to make way for Municipal Auditorium. 1 ext. photo originally filed as AL-9CA8 (1936, galleries only); 2 ext. photos (1963, no. 310 only); 1 data page (1963). *See also* FBJ (J7-ALA-1271 and 1272).

Bowers, Lloyd, Double House (Huger-Douglas Double House) (AL-60), 109, 111 S. Conception St. Brick, 47′3″ (6-bay front) × 39′6″ plus centrally placed rear wing, 2 stories, gable roof, 2 pairs of double end chimneys with curtain wall, full-length cast-iron gallery and deck; side-hall plan in each unit. Cast-iron fence. Built ca. 1857 (cast-iron gallery possibly later); deck covered and screened in 20th C. 5 sheets (1976, including plans, elevations); 10 ext. photos (1937, including details of cast iron); 2 data pages (1937).

Bragg, Judge John, House. *See* Bragg-Mitchell House (AL-30), 1906 Spring Hill Ave.

Bragg-Mitchell House (Judge John Bragg House) (AL-30), 1906 Spring Hill Ave. (in old Summerville). Frame with clapboarding, basically T-shaped plus rear wings with stem of T projecting forward to form 3-bay center block with flanking 1-bay extensions, 2 stories, hipped roof with bracketed cornice extending over U-shaped colonnade enclosing main pavilion and composed of 16 slender fluted columns with polygonal bases and caps, small cast-iron balcony at upper level, 2-tiered L-shaped gallery in rear; elaborated side-hall plan, curved stairway, double parlors separated by triple archway, marble mantels, eared architraves. Built ca. 1855 for Bragg, brother of Confederate General Braxton Bragg; Alexander J. Bragg, brother of first owner, probably architect. Eclectic combination of Greek Revival and Italianate elements; notable landscaping and azalea gardens. 6 ext. photos (1934–35), 7 int. photos (1934–35); 2 data pages (1936). NR. *Servants' Quarters,* behind main structure. Frame with clapboarding, rectangular with lean-to rear addition, 3-bay front with 2 additional entrance bays on first floor, 2 stories, hipped roof, 2 interior end chimneys, full-length gallery with small room at one end. Possibly built prior to present dwelling as part of earlier residential complex. 1 ext. photo (1935), 5 int. photos (1935). *See also* FBJ (J7-ALA-1273 through 1277).

Briarwood (Judge Kiah B. Sewall House) (AL-69), approx. 1,000′ N by NW of intersection of Dauphin Way and Mobile St.; approx. 150′ E of Gulf, Mobile and Ohio Railroad right-of-way. Raised cottage, frame with clapboarding, rectangular (3-bay front) with large offset L-shaped rear wing, 1 story over partially enclosed brick basement, temple-type pedimented 4-column Doric portico on raised brick piers, principal entrance at W side sheltered by smaller raised Doric porch, jalousied rear gallery; lateral hall bisecting main block, Greek Revival style interior trim. Built 1839 as country home for jurist Sewall, born in Maine. Demolished 1953 to make way for University Military School. 14 ext. photos (1936–37), 10 int. photos (1937, including detail of pegs used in construction); 2 data pages (1937). *See also* FBJ (J7-ALA-1278 and 1279).

Brisk and Jacobson Store. *See* Daniels, Elgin and Company (AL-790), 51 Dauphin St.

Brooks House. *See* House (AL-7B), 108-110 N. Conception St.

Broun, W. M., House. *See* Batre-Hamilton House (AL-58), 320 Avalon St. (Spring Hill).

Brown, Milton S., House (AL-78), 108 S. Conception St. Brick with stucco deeply scored and marbleized to simulate rustication, rectangular (3-bay front) with slightly recessed side wing, 2 stories plus raised attic, gable roof concealed by low brick parapet above molded cornice, ornate full-length cast-iron gallery with canopy roof, recessed entrance, frieze ("eyebrow") windows covered by cast-iron grilles above second story; side-hall plan. Built ca. 1855; demolished before 1960. Milton S. Brown was president of the Mobile and Ohio Railroad, opened in 1852. 2 ext. photos (1936).

Bunker, Robert S., House (Moreland House) (AL-802), originally at 157 Monroe St., reconstructed at 201 S. Warren St. Brick, approx. 23′ (2-bay front) × 44′ with semidetached service wing at right angle to main block, 2 stories, shallow hipped roof, 2-tiered cast-iron gallery with cresting said to have come from France; double window at both levels; side-hall plan, double parlors with elliptical archway between. Built 1858–59; dismantled 1968 to make way for I-10 tunnels; rebuilt at new location with several modifications, including elimination of original rear wing. 1 ext. photo originally filed as AL-9L (1936, gallery), 3 ext. photos (1963), 3 int. photos (1963); 1 data page (1963).

Bunker-DuMont House (DuMont House, Annie B. Noble House) (AL-28), 157 Church St. Brick, rectangular (2-bay front) with ell, 2 stories, shallow hipped roof, 2-tiered cast-iron gallery; side-hall plan. Brick kitchen and servants' quarters to rear. Nucleus of house reputedly built for Alexander Purdy ca. 1845. Acquired in 1860 by Robert S. Bunker and extensively renovated, gallery added; later bequeathed to Bunker's daughter, Mrs. Alphonse DuMont; demolished. Similar to Robert S. Bunker House (AL-802). 8 ext. photos (1934–36), 9 int. photos (1936); 2 data pages (1936).

Burgess-Maschmeyer House (AL-847), 1209 Government St. Buff-colored brick, basically rectangular main block (5-bay front) with slightly advanced central pavilion, 2 stories plus raised attic, tile-covered hipped roof with widely overhanging eaves resting on paired brackets alternating with frieze windows, neoclassical 1-story porch across front and partially along sides (breaking into porte cochère on E), large Palladian window opening onto balustraded deck above main doorway; center-hall plan with very elaborate interiors, including neo-Georgian stairhall containing frescoes of Bay Shell Rd. painted and signed by Thil Wilbergand (1907); 16th-C. Italian Renaissance reception room, Louis XVI salon, Tudor style library, neo-Classic style dining room with wall paintings on canvas backing of putti and garlands. Built 1907 for David R. Burgess, cotton broker; George B. Rogers, architect; interiors by William F. Behrens & Co., Cincinnati. House is outstanding example of Renaissance Revival style in Mobile residential architecture;

first-floor interiors in largely original condition with rugs and draperies especially designed for house. 10 ext. photos (1974), 8 int. photos (1974).

Bush-Mohr House (Dr. Charles H. Mohr House) (AL-9J), 254 St. Anthony St. Brick, rectangular (3-bay front) with offset wing, 2 stories, bracketed cornice topped by stuccoed brick parapet, 2-tiered cast-iron gallery with attenuated post-supports, cast-iron lintels embellished with scallop-shell detail resting on acanthus-leaf scrolls; side-hall plan, ornate interiors. Cast-iron fence. Built 1868–69 for J. G. and Thomas Bush, cotton factors. 4 ext. photos (1936, emphasizing ironwork). See also FBJ (J7-ALA-1332).

Butt-Kling House (Kling House) (AL-820), 254 N. Jackson St. Brick, 27'0" (2-bay asymmetrical front with semioctagonal bay) × 74'7" including offset ell, 2 stories, shallow hipped roof with bracketed cornice, hooded cast-iron porch, quoined corners, window grilles; side-hall plan, original chandeliers and interior fittings. Cast-iron fence along sidewalk; wrought-iron fence between carriageway and SW corner of house. Built 1861 for Cary W. Butt, Jr., commission merchant and son of early Mobile builder; later residence of Augustus Kling, German immigrant and owner of Home Industry Foundry. Notable local example of Italianate style. 2 photos originally filed as AL-7WG and AL-9R (1936, ironwork details only).

Calef-Staples House (Staples House) (AL-51), 1614 Old Shell Rd. Frame with clapboarding, 46'4" (6-bay front) × 44'2" plus later ell (28'3" × 14'0"), 1½ stories, gable roof extending over full-length balustraded gallery, 3 dormers on each slope, 4 exterior end chimneys; center-hall plan, enclosed hall stairway. Built 1851–52 for John F. Calef, commission merchant; ca. 1925 modifications included partial replacement of stairway and addition of plaster arch in hallway, original detached kitchen moved and joined to house as rear ell. Outstanding example of Creole cottage. 4 sheets (1966, including site plan, plans, elevations, section); 11 ext. photos (1937), 12 int. photos (1937); 2 data pages (1937), 7 data pages (1966, 1972). See also FBJ (J7-ALA-1343).

Calvert-Webster House (AL-55), 265 N. Conception St. (SW corner N. Conception and Congress sts.). Frame with clapboarding, rectangular (3-bay front), 2½ stories on raised basement, 1-story ell, broken gable roof extending over full-length 2-tiered gallery (superimposed Tuscan order with wheatsheaf balustrade at upper level), Victorian period door with semicircular transom possibly replacing original fanlight; side-hall plan, spiral stairway with unusual sunburst-motif brackets beneath each tread. Built ca. 1836 for William Calvert; George E. Redwood (?), masterbuilder. Demolished ca. 1965 and some of material incorporated into new residence at 4111 Crossway Dr., Spring Hill. Very similar to Thomas Price (Heustis) House at SW corner of St. Anthony and St. Joseph sts., which was razed in 1935 for federal courthouse building. 6 ext. photos (1937), 15 int. photos (1937); 2 data pages (1937).

Carolina Hall (William A. Dawson House, Perdue House) (AL-10), 76 S. McGregor Ave. (Spring Hill). Frame with clapboarding (galleries plastered), 60'5" × 78'11" overall, T-shaped with projecting 3-bay center pavilion and flanking 2-bay wings, 2 stories over raised basement, pedimented 2-tiered tetrastyle Corinthian porticoes front and rear with similar 2-bay side galleries, bracketed and denticulated cornice; side-hall plan, very elaborate interior with ornamental plaster cornices and ceilings, woodwork continuing Corinthian motif, marble mantels, paneled overdoors. Built ca. 1845 for William Alfred Dawson, cotton factor born in Charleston. Interior additions and modifications in 1883; further modified ca. 1917, George B. Rogers, architect-in-charge. 6 sheets (1934, including plans, elevations, sections, details); 2 ext. photos (1934), 6 int. photos (1934); 3 data pages (1936). NR.

Playhouse, SW of main house. Frame with vertical tongue-and-groove siding, rectangular (3-bay front), gable roof with bracketed eaves. Built late 19th C.; moved to new site on grounds in 1972 and restored as guest house and studio. 1 ext. photo (1934).
See also FBJ (J7-ALA-1288 through 1295).

Carriage Block, Government St. See Street Furnishings (AL-36).

Cast-iron work. See Ironwork.

Cathedral of the Immaculate Conception (AL-35), W side Claiborne St. between Dauphin and Conti sts., occupying entire block. Brick with granite foundation and trim, approx. 102' × 162' overall with projecting corner towers and laterally projecting bays at east end, full entablature with denticulated cornice surmounted by paneled parapet; granite hexastyle pedimented Roman Doric portico (approx. 70' X 20') screening distyle in antis entrance bay, flanking 3-stage towers topped by octagonal cupolae and crosses; modified basilica plan with semicircular apse, 3 aisles, barrel-vaulted nave with double row of Corinthian columns, walls and ceiling adorned with stenciling and applied classical ornament, stained glass from Franz Meyer Co., Munich. Notable cast-iron fence surrounding cathedral premises. Nave and apse of cathedral built 1835–49; consecrated 1850; Claude Beroujon, supervising architect. Cast-iron fence, ca. 1860; portico 1890; twin towers 1895. Built largely through efforts of the Rev. Michael Portier (1795–1859), first bishop of the Diocese of Mobile; designated minor basilica by Pope John XXIII on 10 May 1962. 16 ext. photos (1936), 19 int. photos (1936); 4 data pages (1936). *See also* FBJ (J7-ALA-1281).

Chamberlain and Rapier Double House (Girard Double House) (AL-12), 56, 58 S. Conception St. Brick, 53'6" (7-bay front) X 34'5" plus rear wings, 2 stories, gable roof, elliptically arched carriageway between 2 units of 3 bays each, deeply recessed twin entrances with battered architraves, identical cast-iron galleries with balustraded deck; side-hall plan, double parlors in each unit. Twin rectangular, 2-story, gabled dependencies (no. 56 connected to main block before 1878; no. 58, before 1915). Built 1852 for Henry Chamberlain and Charles W. Rapier, law partners; galleries removed ca. 1950 and section of balustrade placed flush against façade as decorative element; wings razed. Only remaining example in Mobile of double house with bisecting arched carriageway. ½ sheet (1934, elevation and details only); 6 ext. photos (1934–35), 4 int. photos (1935); 3 data pages (1936). *See also* FBJ (J7-ALA-1301 and 1302).

Chandler, Daniel, House. *See* McGill Institute (AL-77), 252 Government St.

Christ Episcopal Church (AL-31), 114 St. Emanuel St. (NW corner Church and St. Emanuel sts.). Brick with stucco scored to simulate ashlar, 64'1" X 106'0" excluding later rear additions (43' from cornice), temple-type façade with pedimented distyle in antis Doric portico originally surmounted by 5-stage tower, pilastered front and side elevations, full Doric entablature; open plan, formerly U-shaped gallery and Palladian style chancel recess with elliptical arch springing from Corinthian columns in antis. Cornerstone laid 1835, completed 1838–40; Charles and James Dakin (?), Cary Butt, architects; James Barnes, builder. Chapter House added 1887, J. H. Hutchisson, architect; church damaged by 1906 hurricane, which destroyed tower and wrecked interior; subsequent interior alterations. Oldest Episcopal church in Alabama. 6 sheets (1936–37); 22 ext. photos (1934–36, including 8 photos of wrought-iron fence and street lamp), 1 ext. photocopy (ca. 1840); 5 int. photos (1936), 1 photocopy (n.d.) of interior before 1906; 2 data pages (1937).

Church Street Block Study (Delamier House, Hamilton-Gaillard House, Frederick P. Ravesies House) (AL-803), S side Church St. (Nos. 401, 403, 405, 407) between Franklin and Hamilton sts. Four dwellings: *Frederick P. Ravesies House,* 401 Church St. Brick with stucco scored to simulate ashlar, 30'3" (3-bay front) X 49'6" plus ell and offset E wing, gable roof fronted by raked parapet, double end chimneys, recessed doorway with battered architrave, 2-tiered L-shaped rear gallery; side-hall plan. Built 1860 for cotton broker and son of French refugee, Frederic Ravesies, president of Vine and Olive Colony at Demopolis. Renovated and restored (including removal of 20th-C. gallery) in 1969. *Delamier House,* 403 Church St. Brick, rectangular (3-bay front) with ell, gable roof, double end chimneys, cast-iron gallery with deck and floor-length windows; side-hall plan. Built ca. 1860 for J. Delamier; demolished 1960s for urban renewal. *House,* 405 Church St. Frame with clapboarding, irregular square (5-bay front with stepped-back entrance bay), hipped roof with cross-gables, 2-tiered balustraded gallery with turned colonnettes on square pedestals; irregular side-hall plan. Built ca. 1890; demolished 1960s for urban renewal. *Hamilton-Gaillard House,* 407 Church St. Brick, rectangular (3-bay front) with offset ell, gable roof, double end chimneys, 2-tiered cast-iron gallery with floor-length windows; side-hall plan. Built 1859 for Thomas A. Hamilton, Mobile attorney who was instrumental in dredging of ship channel in Mobile Bay; James Hill and James Robertson, contractors. Acquired by urban renewal authorities and sold in 1967 for resto-

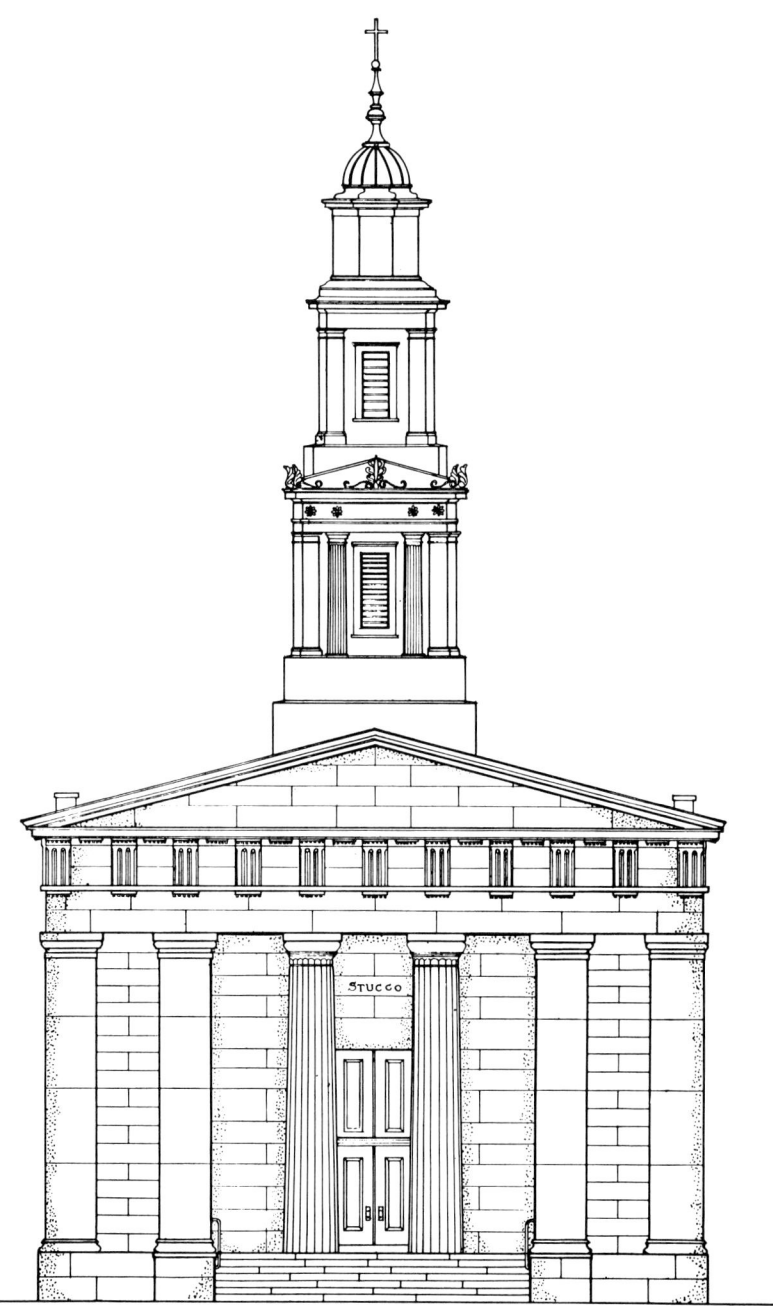

FRONT ~ EAST ~ ELEVATION
~ SCALE: 1/8"= 1'-0" ~

Christ Episcopal Church, Mobile (1835–40, belfry destroyed 1906).

ration. 1 ext. photo of Hamilton-Gaillard House originally filed as AL-9BA4 (1936), 3 ext. photos (1963, general view).

Church Street Cemetery Ironwork (Old Mobile Cemetery Ironwork) (AL-845), Church St. between Bayou St. and Washington Ave. (entrance on S. Scott St. S of Government St.). Examples of wrought-iron and cast-iron fences enclosing private burial plots. Ironwork ranges in date from ca. 1835 to 1890; partially destroyed. Plots include those of Gen. Edmund Pendleton Gaines, Don Miguel Eslava, Thaddeus Sanford, and other early Mobilians. Earliest burial 1819; acquired by city as municipal burying ground 1820; closed to interment in 1899. 1 sheet filed under AL-7F (1934, cast-iron burial plot enclosure); 4 photos originally filed as AL-7, AL-8 series (1934, part of general ironwork survey). *See also* Magnolia Cemetery Ironwork (AL-844).

City Hall and Southern Market (Southern Market) (AL-5), 111 S. Royal St. (E side Royal extending through block to Water St., between Church and Government sts.). Brick with stucco scored to simulate ashlar, irregular complex consisting originally of 3 2-story buildings; main building (approx. 119' x 114') has 9-bay façade with projecting pedimented end pavilions, arcaded first story with simulated voussoirs and keystones, quoined corners, wide bracketed eaves, octagonal wooden cupola; crenellated walls pierced by triple archways with wire grille transoms link central building to flanking structures (each with 3-bay pedimented front, bracketed cornice); larger S flanker (approx. 30' x 275') has 46-bay elevation along Church St. bisected by driveway into inner courtyard; Italianate detail throughout. Built 1856–57 as combination city hall and municipal marketplace (the "Southern Market" of two projected markets); Richard H. Redwood, B. F. Scattergood, George W. Gregory, chief contractors; woven wire grilles in arches manufactured by New York Wire Railing Co. Upper floor of central building housed municipal offices, market area occupied first story and flanking structures (upper floor of S flanker also housed armory and militia company rooms); open market sheds at rear. Fire station (facing Water St.) constructed behind main building in 1925; north flanker demolished 1966 and reconstructed along original lines. Restored following extensive damage from Hurricane Frederick in 1979; Nicholas H. Holmes, Jr., FAIA, restoration architect. Entire complex now houses Mobile City Hall. Nationally important example of early civic complex. 15 sheets (1934, including plot plan, plans, elevations, section, details); 15 ext. photos (1934–35), 7 ext. photos (1963), 4 int. photos (1935); 3 data pages (1936); 1 data page (1963). NHL. *See also* FBJ (J7-ALA-1341 and 1342).

City Hospital (AL-13), 850 St. Anthony St. (N side St. Anthony, between Broad and Jefferson sts.). Brick with stucco (façade scored to simulate ashlar), original dimensions 183′8″ × 65′10″ overall, 5-bay center pavilion with flanking 5-bay wings, 2 stories over full ground floor, low longitudinal gable roof breaking into broad crossgable above center pavilion, full-height Tuscan colonnade across front with advanced pedimented central pavilion, continuous balustraded galleries at main and second-floor levels, fanlight doorway, corresponding elliptical lunette in tympanum; center-hall plan with bisecting transverse hall. Forecourt enclosed by low masonry wall. Built 1833–36 as municipal hospital (later under care of Roman Catholic Sisters of Charity 1853–1959); William George, architect; John H. Collins, contractor. Building extended 1 bay at each end 1907–8, rear wings also added 1912, 1917, and 1926; interior renovated 1972–74 for county use. Outstanding example in state of early institutional architecture. Functioned as hospital until 1966. 5 sheets (1934, including plans, elevations, section, details); 8 ext. photos (1934–36), 2 ext. photos (1963), 1 int. photo (1934); 4 data pages (1936, 1963). NR. *See also* Tebbs (T3-ALA-434084).

Clarke House. *See* Smith-Clarke House (AL-15), 161 St. Anthony St. *and* Robinson Twin Houses (AL-807), 157, 159 N. Conception St.

Clitherall House. *See* Hall-Horst House (AL-23), 110 St. Emanuel St.

Cluis-Rubira House (AL-804), 156 St. Anthony St. Brick, approx. 32′0″ (3-bay front) × 52′8″ plus offset W wing extending to rear to form ell, 2 stories, hipped roof, wide bracketed cornice with paneled soffits, cast-iron gallery (unusual Tudoresque trellis arches) with deck and cast-iron steps, wing has 2-story semioctagonal bay with cast-iron balconies at both levels; side-hall plan, elaborate interior plasterwork, archway between double drawing room. Cast-iron fence. Built 1857 for Frederick V. Cluis, son of Napoleonic refugee; property acquired 1858 by William W. Allen for $12,750. 7 ext. photos (1963), 2 int. photos (1963); 1 data page (1963).

Coley Building. *See* Townsend-Foreman Building (AL-805), 56 St. Francis St.

Commerce Street Stores. *See* Commercial Buildings: Commerce Street (AL-63 series).

Commercial Building (AL-791), 7 N. Commerce St. (SW corner N. Commerce St. and Exchange Alley). Stuccoed brick and cast-iron, L-shaped, 60′6″ (8-bay front) × 102′0″ (11 bays deep), 2 stories, gable roof (concealed by brick parapet), cast-iron post-and-lintel first floor (Commerce St. façade) with folding paneled doors and narrow transoms in each bay, cast-iron arcuated first floor (Exchange Alley façade) with Corinthian detail, segmentally arched second-floor windows surmounted by cast-iron hood molds; interior extensively altered. Portion of structure built ca. 1835. 3 original buildings extensively remodeled ca. 1860 to create 1 structure for Ovid Mazange, who bought property in 1852; demolished 1968 for Water Street Urban Renewal Project. Two of the 3 original buildings erected for Judge Henry Hitchcock, first attorney general of Alabama, chief justice of State Supreme Court, Mobile lawyer, and businessman. Continuously occupied by wholesale and retail grocery and feed companies from early 19th C. until demolition. 1 ext. photo of Exchange Alley front originally filed as AL-64A (1935, detail only), 4 ext. photos (1966), 4 int. photos (1966); 6 data pages (1966, 1972).

Commercial Building, 50, 52 N. Commerce St. *See* McDowell, Withers Company (AL-784).

Commercial Building (AL-67), 67, 69 Government St. (S side Government St. between Royal and Water sts.). Brick with stucco, rectangular (8-bay front divided into 2 4-bay units) with parallel rear wings, 3 stories plus raised attic (wings, 3 stories), shallow gabled roof, trabeated first-story façade with double-leaf glazed doors, modified classic style entablature above third floor with frieze windows; open plan (probably late-19th-C. renovation) at first-floor level, upper floors probably devoted to residential use originally, notable Greek Revival style interior trim on second and third floors, including paneled doors and eared architraves, studded with paterae. Built ca. 1836 (on portion of 18th-C. Fort Condé site) for Judge Henry Hitchcock and Mobile Steam Cotton Press and Building Co.; Charles Dakin, architect. Demolished ca. 1950. Outstanding local example of Greek Revival commercial architecture. 10 ext. photos (1936), 25 int. photos (1936); 2 data pages (1937).

Commercial Building (AL-793), 364 N. Royal St. (NW corner Royal and Lipscomb sts.). Brick with stucco scored to simulate ashlar, rectangular (6-bay front), 2 stories, hipped roof, cast-iron trabeated first floor with double-leaf glazed doors in each bay, cast-iron gallery with deck originally extending over sidewalk; open plan ground floor with cast-iron supports, center-hall plan on upper floor. Built after 1872; demolished ca. 1968. 2 ext. photos (1966), 1 int. photo (1966); 2 data pages (1966).

Commercial Building, 51 S. Royal St. (SE corner Royal and Conti sts). *See* Pollock Building (AL-48).

Commercial Building (AL-792), 7 St. Michael St. (extending through to Planter's Alley). Brick 30′8″ (4-bay front, 3-bay rear facing Planter's Alley) × 84′7″, 2 stories, shallow slate-covered hipped roof concealed by parapet, cast-iron arcuated first-floor front with engaged Corinthian colonnettes, double-leaf glazed doors, arched windows second floor with cast-iron sills and hood molds, brick dentil course N and S façades; open plan. Nucleus of structure built before 1834; heavily altered ca. 1860–70, including extensive changes to both N and S façades; demolished 1968 for Water Street Urban Renewal Project. 1 ext. photo (1935, cast-iron portion of S front only); 2 ext. photos (1966); 7 data pages (1966, 1972).

Commercial Building (AL-795), 3 N. Water St. (NE corner N. Water St. and Exchange Alley). Brick, 23′4″ (3-bay front) × 84′, 2 stories, shallow longitudinal gable roof concealed by bracketed cast-iron cornice, trabeated street-floor front with pair of cast-iron Corinthian colonnettes in antis supporting brick and cast-iron entablature, double-leaf glazed doors in each bay, segmentally arched second-floor windows with ornate cast-iron hood molds. Built ca. 1865; demolished 1969 for Water Street Urban Renewal Project. Small commercial structure typical of Mobile's mid-19th-C. waterfront district. 1 ext. photo (1935, Exchange Alley façade only), 2 ext. photos (1966); 3 data pages (1966, 1972).

Commercial Buildings: Commerce Street (AL-63 series), Commerce St. between Dauphin and St. Anthony sts. Mostly brick, 2 and 3 stories. Built mid-to-late 19th C.; demolished 1960s for urban renewal. Typical storefronts of wholesale district near waterfront. Photos of façade details only.

8 N. Commerce St. (AL-63A). Arcuated street floor (3 bays divided by slender fluted cast-iron colonnettes with lotus capitals), paneled and glazed double doors flanked by 18-light display windows, grilled transoms. 1 ext. photo (1935).

9 N. Commerce St. (AL-63F). Arcuated street floor with rustication (4 bays divided by cast-iron paneled piers with lotus capitals), paneled folding doors, grilled transoms, protective overhang with scrolled cast-iron brackets. 1 ext. photo (1935).

15 N. Commerce St. (AL-63D). Arcuated street floor (series of bays divided by cast-iron chamfered piers), paneled and glazed folding doors, grilled transoms. 1 ext. photo (1935).

16 N. Commerce St. (AL-63G). Trabeated street floor (series of bays divided by cast-iron paneled piers with Corinthian capitals and applied cartouches), cast-iron entablature with egg-and-dart ovolo molding, paneled folding doors, grilled transoms. 1 ext. photo (1935).

104 N. Commerce St. (AL-63J). Series of segmentally arched units separated by brick piers and divided into 3 bays each by cast-iron paneled piers with Corinthian capitals and applied cartouches, paneled folding doors, grilled transoms. 1 ext. photo (1935).

114 N. Commerce St. (AL-63K). Trabeated street floor (series of bays divided by cast-iron piers alternating with Romanesque style pillar with shaft and foliated capital resting on rough-hewn plinth), paneled folding doors, grilled transoms. 1 ext. photo (1935).

117 N. Commerce St. (AL-63L). Arcuated street floor (series of bays divided by cast-iron chamfered piers with molded caps and bases), paneled folding doors, grilled transoms. 1 ext. photo (1935).

150 N. Commerce St. (AL-63M), NE corner Commerce and St. Louis sts. Rusticated façade with paneled double door, grilled transom. 1 ext. photo (1935).

12, 55, 58 S. Commerce St. (AL-63D, AL-63B, AL-63A). Paneled double doors with grilled transoms, some cast-iron elements. 1 photo each (1935).

See also separate listings under Commercial Building, 7 N. Commerce St. (AL-791) *and* McDowell, Withers & Company (AL-784), 50, 52 N. Commerce St.

Commercial Buildings: Dauphin Street (AL-61 series), Dauphin St., principally between Commerce and Water sts. Brick or brick with stucco, 2 and 3 stories. Built mid-to-late 19th C.; demolished 1960s for urban renewal. Photos of typical storefronts (mainly doorways).

2 Dauphin St. (AL-61B). Trabeated entrance in rusticated stucco façade (2 bays divided by slender fluted cast-iron colonnette with lotus capital), paneled and glazed folding doors; grilled transoms. 1 ext. photo (1935).

12 Dauphin St. (AL-61C). Trabeated street floor (3 bays divided by 2 slender cast-iron paneled piers), paneled doors with arched lights; grilled transoms. 1 ext. photo (1935).

56 Dauphin St. (AL-61D). Brick, narrow (approx. 12′ wide) 2-bay façade, 2 stories, gable roof with brick dentil course, shuttered bays at second floor (originally fronted by balcony). Built ca. 1835; lower story remodeled late 19th C. Harness shop ca. 1885; later shop of Benjamin and Marcus Gup, tailors (living quarters upstairs). 1 ext. photo (1935).

715 Dauphin St. (AL-61A), SE corner Dauphin and Scott sts. Brick, rectangular (4-bay front), 2 stories, low hipped roof, brick dentil course, trabeated street floor with slender cast-iron colonnettes, cast-iron balcony with jib windows at upper level. Built ca. 1835 for Emile B. Daniel. Commercial front and balcony late 19th C.; damaged by automobile and demolished 1959; part of balcony used on house located at 2406 Government St. 1 ext. photo (1935).

See also separate listing under Daniels, Elgin and Company (AL-790), 51 Dauphin St.

Commercial Buildings: Government Street (AL-62 series), Government St. between Commerce and St. Emanuel sts. Brick and brick with stucco, 2 to 4 stories. Built early-to-late 19th C.; demolished. Photos of façades and details only.

9 Government St. (AL-62A). Brick (rectangular), 2 stories, gable roof with brick dentil course, covered sidewalk with cast-iron gallery above, double-leaf glazed doors. Built ca. 1840; gallery later. 1 ext. photo (1935).

51–73 Government St. (AL-62G), S side Government St. between Water and Royal sts. Block of brick and brick-with-stucco structures, 2 to 3½ stories, ranging from ca. 1836 (SW corner of Government and Water sts.) to ca. 1885 (SE corner Government and Royal sts.). 1 ext. photo of entire block (1935). See also separate listing under Commercial Building, 67, 69 Government St. (AL-67).

66 Government St. (AL-62F). Brick with stucco, 2 stories, flat roof with brick dentil course and paneled parapet, covered sidewalk with cast-iron gallery above. Built ca. 1840; gallery added later. 1 ext. photo (1935).

110 Government St. (AL-62D). Brick, 2 stories, trabeated street floor with slender fluted cast-iron colonnettes, double-leaf doors (paneled and glazed). Built ca. 1870; demolished. 1 photo of commercial front detail only (1935).

112, 114 Government St. (AL-62E). Brick, 1 story, trabeated (2-bay) doorway, double-leaf doors (paneled and glazed). 1 photo (1935).

See also separate listing under Commercial Building, 67, 69 Government St. (AL-67).

Commercial Buildings: Miscellaneous (AL-66 series). Commercial fronts and façade details of 3 19th-C. structures on Church, Government, and Royal sts. Demolished 1960s for urban renewal. Photos of façade details.

6 Church St. (AL-66A). Stuccoed and scored first floor with arcuated doorway (2 bays separated by slender fluted cast-iron colonnette with lotus capital), paneled double-leaf doors, grilled transoms. 1 photo (1935).

71, 73 Government St. (AL-66D), SE corner Government and Royal

sts. Rusticated first story, entrance bays divided by cast-iron paneled piers, double-leaf paneled and glazed doors, arched side door to stairway. 1 photo of façade detail only (1935).
23 S. Royal St. (AL-66E). Brick, rectangular, 2 stories, cast-iron trabeated first floor, 2-tiered cast-iron gallery. 1 photo (1935).

Commercial Buildings: St. Michael Street (AL-64 series), St. Michael St. between Commerce and Royal sts. Mostly brick and cast iron, generally 2 and 3 stories. Built early 19th to early 20th C.; demolished 1960s for urban renewal. Photos of façades and details only.
10 St. Michael St. (AL-64B). Brick (Flemish bond) with granite trabeated street floor, double-leaf glazed doors. Built ca. 1835; demolished. Excellent example of early 19th-C. commercial front showing Greek Revival influence. 1 photo of façade detail (1935).
56, 58 St. Michael St. (AL-64C). Brick, 5-bay front, 2 stories, trabeated street floor divided into 2 3-bay units with central stair door (slender paneled piers with Ionic caps frame middle bay of each unit), floor-length upper windows, double dogtooth cornice. Built mid-19th C. 1 ext. photo (1935).
57 St. Michael St. (AL-64D). Brick, 4 bays, arcuated first floor with slender cast-iron Corinthian colonnettes, arched upper windows with hood molds and grilles. Built late 19th C. 1 photo (1935).
67 St. Michael St. (AL-64F). Brick, cast-iron trabeated street floor with slender fluted colonnettes bearing lotuslike capital, double-leaf glazed doors in each bay. Built mid-19th C. 1 photo (1935).
74, 76 St. Michael St. (AL-64E). Brick, 7 bays, 2 stories, double dogtooth cornice, trabeated first floor with cast-iron paneled piers. Built mid-19th C. 1 photo (1935).
78 St. Michael St. (AL-64G). Cast-iron trabeated 3-bay front with slender fluted colonnettes, glazed bays. Built ca. 1900. 1 photo (1935, façade detail only).
Alley, s side St. Michael St. (AL-64J, AL-64H, AL-64K), near Royal St. intersection. Details of brick arches and iron grilles (utilitarian commercial structures). Probably built early 19th C. 3 photos (1935).
See also separate listing under Commercial Building, 7 St. Michael St. (AL-792).

Commercial Buildings: Water Street (AL-65 series), N. Water St. between St. Louis and Dauphin sts.; S. Water St. between Dauphin and Government sts. Characteristic commercial façades of Mobile waterfront area dating from 19th and early 20th C., brick, mostly 2 and 3 stories. Demolished 1960s for urban renewal and construction of I-10. Photos of doorways and façade details only.
4, 19 and 21, 55, 106, 108, 110, 112, and 116 N. Water St. (AL-65N, AL-65F, AL-65M, AL-65E, AL-65D, AL-65C, AL-65B, AND AL-65A). Trabeated and arcuated storefronts; some with cast-iron elements, others with granite piers and lintels, glazed double-leaf doors. Built ca. 1835–1900. 8 photos of details only (1935).
4 S. Water St. (AL-65T). Two-bay window opening enframed by cast-iron Corinthian pilasters supporting classical entablature with modillioned cornice, ornamental protective grille. Built ca. 1900 (possibly as doorway). 1 photo (1935).
12 S. Water St. (AL-65G). Cast-iron trabeated street floor with fluted colonnettes and lotus capitals, double-leaf glazed doors with transoms, also service entrance with iron gate. Built late 19th C. 2 photos (1935).
16 S. Water St. (AL-65P). Three-bay trabeated street floor with cast-iron fluted colonnettes bearing lotus capitals; double-leaf glazed doors. Probably late 19th C. 1 photo (1935).
54 S. Water St. (AL-65R). Detail of brick trabeated opening with folding glazed doors; star tie-rods in wall. Probably mid-19th C. 1 photo (1935).
64, 66 S. Water St. (AL-65J, AL-65K, AL-65L), approx. 50′ N of Government St. intersection. Brick with stucco, rectangular (8-bay front) with 2 4-bay units, gable roof with originally 2 segmentally arched dormers; covered sidewalk with cast-iron deck above no. 64; driveway to rear with iron gate. Built ca. 1840; lower floor altered for commercial purposes late 19th C. (including cast-iron trabeated storefront at no. 66). 3 photos (1935).
See also separate listing under Commercial Building, 3 N. Water St. (AL-795).

Conn-Meriwether House (AL-850), 300 Chatham Street (SW corner Chatham and Augusta sts.). Brick, L-shaped with projecting (3-bay) front, 1 story, gable roof in rear breaking into half-hip that extends over front pavilion with full-length gallery embellished by ornate cast-iron supports; side-hall plan, interior much renovated but original fireplaces remain. Built 1869 for Annie Conn. Unusual combination of retardataire Federal features (as seen in parapeted gable ends) with Victorian stylistic elements. 5 ext. photos (1974).

Conti House. *See* Rider House (AL-38), 303 Conti St.

Convent and Academy of the Visitation (Visitation Convent) (AL-73), 2300 Spring Hill Ave. (in old Summerville). Complex formerly composed of 4 main buildings arranged around a central courtyard and connected by a continuous arcaded cloister; also attached stone chapel and ancillary structures. Built between 1854 and 1896, superseding earlier structures destroyed by tornado and fire. Founded in 1832, convent is second oldest establishment of the Visitation Order in the United States. Oldest portion of complex (NE corner of quadrangle) is brick, L-shaped, 2 stories with hipped roof and 2-tiered wooden gallery along N elevation, wooden gallery also superimposed upon inner arcade (S and W elevations) facing courtyard; built 1853–54 with later western extension. *Southeast building* (at SE corner of quadrangle and main entrance to convent) is stuccoed brick, rectangular (9-bay front) with slightly projecting 3-bay pedimented central pavilion, gable roof with cross-gable, façade (E elevation) with arched doorway enframed by paneled pilasters and triangular pediment bearing bas-relief cartouche in tympanum, heavily paneled double-leaf door, brick-paved forecourt; center-hall plan, winding stair, interior woodwork embellished with faux bois graining; built ca. 1864. *South Building* (S side of quadrangle), brick, rectangular (15 bays long), 3½ stories, hipped roof with cross-gable surmounted by wooden 2-stage domed clock tower, 3-tiered cast-iron gallery across S (exterior) elevation; built 1867–70 (cupola added 1888). *School* (W side of quadrangle), brick, rectangular, 3 stories, gable roof; built 1900, closing west side of cloister, demolished 1953 when academy closed, leaving only arcade enclosing W side of cloister. Also surrounding walls and entrance gates. 25 ext. photos (1937, including 1 aerial view, walls and gates, old waterwheel on grounds), 14 int. photos (1937, including dormitories, reception room, notable architectural features); no photographs of chapel.

Cotton Warehouse. *See* Magnolia Cotton Warehouse (AL-74), NE corner Lipscomb and Magnolia sts.

Cox-Deasy House (AL-846), 1115 Palmetto St. Frame with clapboarding, rectangular (3-bay front) with rear wing, 1 story, clipped gable roof, full-length gallery with central entrance flanked by French doors; center-hall plan. Built 1850 as his own residence by George Woodward Cox, English-born master-builder, responsible for Martin Horst House (AL-776) at 407 Conti St. and George Rapelje House at 1005 Government St. Renovated after 1931 fire, including modification of roof line and second story. Erected on land purchased from Oakleigh (AL-47) estate and probably second oldest house in Oakleigh Garden District. 2 ext. photos (1974). NR.

Craft, John, House. *See* Sanford-Staylor House (AL-22), 451, 453 St. Francis St.

Cunningham-Atkinson House (AL-539), Wilson Rd. (moved from Bullock County). *See Union Springs Vicinity,* Bullock County.

Daniels, Elgin and Company (Brisk and Jacobson Store) (AL-790), 51 Dauphin St. (SW corner Dauphin and Water sts.). Brick and stucco with cast-iron façade, irregular rectangle approx. 45′6″ (5-bay front) X 103′11″ (14 lateral bays), 4 stories, low truncated hipped roof, ornate cast-iron N front in Renaissance Revival style (engaged Corinthian colonnettes, arcuated upper stories, modillioned cornice with scrolled consoles), hood molds and cast-iron sills on E (Water St.) side. Built ca. 1860 for Daniels, Elgin and Co., "importers, jobbers and retailers of drygoods." Cast-iron front designed by J. H. Giles, manufactured by D. D. Badger and Co. of New York; later occupied by Brisk and Jacobson Co.; interior extensively altered. Mobile's best surviving example of 19th-C. cast-iron commercial architecture. 3 ext. photos (1966); 6 data pages (1972). NR.

Dargan-Waring House (Waring House) (AL-19), 351 Government St. (SW corner Government and Claiborne sts.). Brick, 31′8″ (3-bay front) X 56′1″ with offset W wing, 2 stories (wing 1 story), hipped roof, denticulated cornice, Greek Revival style door with battered architrave, 2-tiered jalousied porch across rear; side-hall plan, notable Greek Revival interior trim. Semidetached 2-story brick dependency with half-gable roof to rear of side wing. Cast-iron fence, high brick wall enclosing lot. Also unusually complete group of dependencies (see below). Built 1846 for Judge Edmund Spann Dargan (1805–79), chief justice of Alabama Supreme Court 1849–52. Purchased 1851 by Moses Waring; side wing added late 19th C.; demolished ca. 1940. 6 sheets (1935, including site plan, plans, elevations, section, details); 5 ext. photos (1935), 5 int. photos (1935–36).

Gates (cast-iron entrance gate, carriage gate, and side gate). Probably antebellum, now removed. 1 sheet (1935, cast-iron gate only); 3 photos (1936).

Slave Quarters and Stables (now 108 S. Claiborne St.). Brick, T-shaped complex (quarters being stem of T). Slave Quarters: 49′1″ (6-bay front) x 22′2″, 2 stories, hipped roof, 2-tiered gallery (cast-iron supports below, wooden above), 3 end-to-end rooms on each floor. Stables: 60′3″ (3-bay front) x 18′3″, 1 story, shed roof with parapet, elliptically arched bays, open plan with frame partitions separating carriage area, stalls, and feed room. Built ca. 1856; stable portion demolished ca. 1940; quarters acquired by Mobile Housing Authority 1969 and adaptively renovated as offices (curved iron stair added to N end of porch, addition to rear). 2 sheets (1935, including plan, elevations, details); 4 ext. photos (1935, 1936), 2 int. photos (1936).

Privy. Brick with stucco scored to simulate ashlar, approx. 14′6″ (2-bay front) x 7′6″, 1 story, hipped roof, louvered doors; interior divided into 3 separate chambers for men, for women and children, and for slaves (who entered from rear side). Antebellum; demolished ca. 1940. 1 sheet (1935, including plan, elevations, door detail), 1 ext. photo (1936), 1 int. photo (1936).

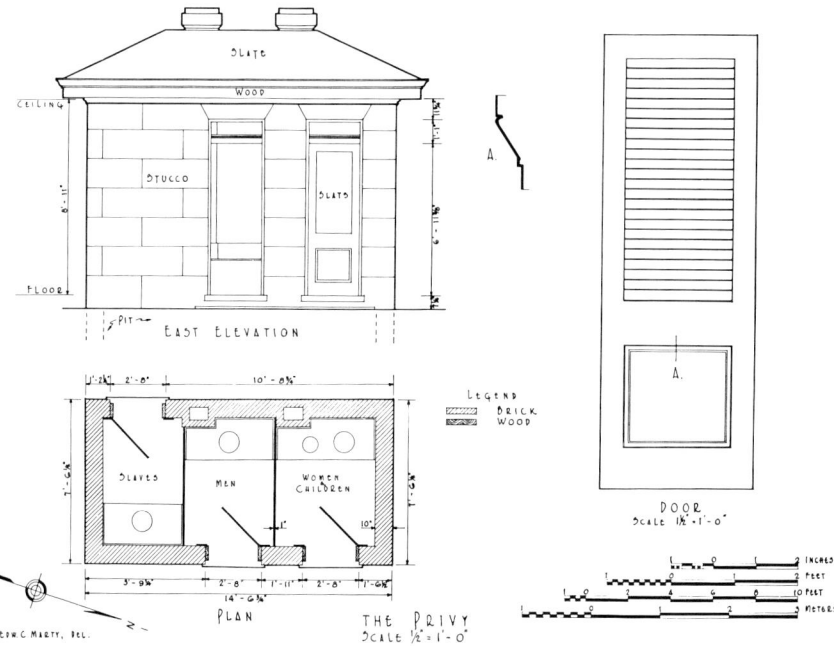

Privy at Dargan-Waring House, Mobile (mid-19th century, demolished ca. 1940).

Waring "Texas" (Garçonniere, The Lodge, Texas House), now 110 S. Claiborne St. Brick with stucco scored to simulate ashlar, irregular rectangle set end-wise to street, approx. 34′ (4-bay front) x 26′, 1 story on raised basement, gable roof with raked parapet, raised wooden gallery along front (S and W side), double wooden stairway, double entrance flanked by floor-length windows; 2 rooms with paneled sliding doors between, cast-iron mantelpieces, Greek Revival trim. Reputedly built during antebellum period for John Nugent. Acquired 1868 by Moses Waring and extensively renovated as bachelors' quarters for sons; restored 1963. 4 sheets (1935, including plans, elevations, section, details), 5 ext. photos (1935, 1936), 4 int. photos (1936).

See also FBJ (J7-ALA-1348 through 1350).

Dauphin Street Stores. *See* Commercial Buildings: Dauphin Street (AL-61 series).

Dawson Creole House. *See* George W. Tarleton House (AL-21), 101 N. Hamilton St.

Dawson, James, House. *See* George W. Tarleton House (AL-21), 101 N. Hamilton St.

Dawson, John C., House. *See* Azalea Grove (AL-54), 55 S. McGregor Ave. (Spring Hill).

Dawson, William A., House. *See* Carolina Hall (AL-10), 76 S. McGregor Ave. (Spring Hill).

Delamier House. *See* Church Street Block Study (AL-803).

Denniston House. *See* Oakleigh (AL-47), 350 Oakleigh Place.

Double House (Durand House) (AL-59), 308–310 Conti St. Brick (façade stuccoed and scored to simulate ashlar), rectangular (6-bay front) with semidetached central rear service wing, 2½ stories, gable roof with brick dentil course, double end chimneys with connecting parapet, unusual 2-bay cast-iron entrance porch with balustraded deck extended 1 bay to each side to form cantilevered balconies, 2-tiered wooden gallery along each side of rear wing; double entrance with side-hall plan in each unit. Built 1858, apparently as rental property for Roman Catholic Diocese of Mobile; erroneously referred to as Durand House, after early French family who owned lot; razed by diocese in 1975 and reerected in Fort Condé Village. 8 ext. photos (1936–37), 3 int. photos (1937), 2 ext. photos (1963); 2 data pages (1937), 1 data page (1963). *See also* FBJ (J7-ALA-1282 and 1282-A).

Double House (Reingard Double House) (AL-25), 8–10 N. Jackson St. Brick with stucco scored to simulate ashlar, rectangular (7-bay front with bisecting carriageway), 2 stories, gable roof, continuous 2-tiered cast-iron gallery across front; side-hall plan in each unit, Greek Revival interior trim. Originally identical brick dependencies in rear courtyard. Tradition says house built ca. 1820 in Blakely, across Mobile Bay; dismantled and moved to Mobile in 1829 by C. Reingard. Architectural evidence suggests that house assumed present form during ownership (1842–60) of John B. Toulmin, or at later date; demolished. ½ sheet filed as AL-12 (1934, ironwork detail only); 4 ext. photos (1934–35), 6 int. photos (1935); 2 data pages (1936). *See also* FBJ (J7-ALA-1337).

Douglas-Huger Double House. *See* Lloyd Bowers Double House (AL-60), 109, 111 S. Conception St.

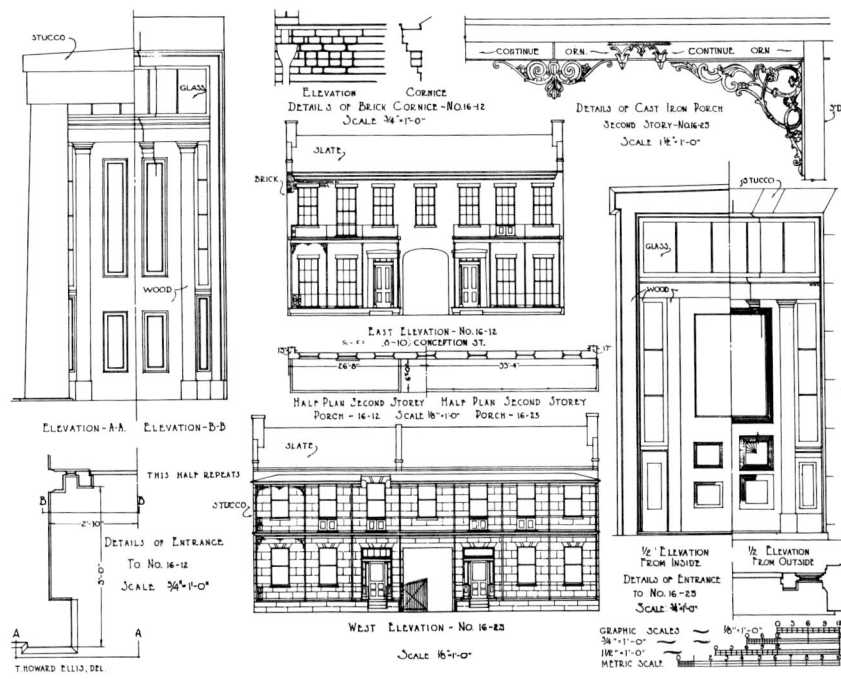

Top center: Chamberlain and Rapier Double House, Mobile (1852).
Above center: Double House, 8–10 N. Jackson Street, Mobile (mid-19th century, demolished).

DuMont House. *See* Bunker-DuMont House (AL-28), 157 Church St.

Durand House. *See* Double House (AL-59), 308–310 Conti St.

Elkus, Isaac, House (AL-7Y), 50 S. Franklin St. Brick, rectangular (3-bay front) with ell, 2 stories, gable roof with brick dentil course, recessed doorway with battered jambs, wrought-iron second-story balcony supported by scrolled brackets; side-hall plan. Built 1854. 1 photo (1934, balcony only).

Ellis-Lyons House (Lyons House) (AL-40), 168 S. Royal St. Brick (façade stuccoed and scored to simulate ashlar), 3-bay front with offset 1-bay side wing, 2½ stories, gable roof, double end chimneys with parapet, brick dentil course, cast-iron gallery with deck; side-hall plan. Cast-iron fence. Reputedly built between 1853 and 1857 for Robert Ellis (described as "bricklayer" in 1850 census); Ellis and partner, Jonathan Kirkbride, probably builder-architects; demolished. 3 ext. photos (1936); 2 data pages (1937).

Emanuel, Jonathan, House (AL-3), 251 Government St. (SW corner Government and Joachim sts.). Brick with stucco scored to simulate ashlar, main block 36'4" (5-bay façade) X 55'4", 1-story W wing with projecting bay, 3 stories, shallow hipped roof concealed by blocking course above cornice, 1-story distyle Doric entrance porch with deck enclosed by ironwork balustrade employing motifs from Asher Benjamin, recessed Ionic order doorways above and below, decorative iron window grilles; center-hall plan, double drawing room (E side) with elaborate pendant archway resting on scrolled consoles, marble mantels, Greek Revival interior woodwork and ornate plaster trim, mahogany doors, silver-plated hardware. Semidetached 2-story dependency in rear; notable iron fence with anthemia cresting and fretwork motif. Built ca. 1836 for English-born merchant; attributed to James Gallier. Interior elaborated and side wing added ca. 1860; used as headquarters for Order of the Mystic Shrine 1923–35; demolished 1936. One of Alabama's most outstanding early urban residences. 9 sheets (1934, including site plan, plans, details, ironwork); also 1 sheet of wrought-iron fence and balustrade filed as AL-7H; 3 ext. photos (1934), 4 int. photos (1934); 2 data pages (1936). See also FBJ (J7-ALA-1296 and 1297).

Eslava, Celestine, House. *See* Marshall-Eslava House (AL-6), 152 Tuthill Ln. (Spring Hill).

Eslava, Miguel, Jr., House (J. J. McMahon House, French Creole House) (AL-21A), 456 St. Francis St. Raised Creole cottage, frame with clapboarding, rectangular (5-bay front) with ell, rear brick and frame offset, 1½ stories above brick ground floor, gable roof, segmentally arched dormers, 2 interior end chimneys, full-length balustraded gallery with turned posts, secondary basement entrance beneath front of gallery; center-hall plan, casement windows onto gallery. Federal period interior trim with mid-to-late-19th-C. modifications. Built ca. 1834; demolished. Miguel Eslava, Jr., was son of Don Miguel Eslava, Mobile official during Spanish period (1780–1813). 5 ext. photos (1934–36), 11 int. photos (1934–36); 2 data pages (1936).

Fences, Iron. *See* Gates and Fences.

Finch House. *See* House, 301 N. Joachim St. (AL-9F).

Finnigan, Capt. Owen, House (AL-9Z), 752 Government St. Brick, 3-bay front, 2 stories, 2-tiered cast-iron gallery with floor-length windows; side-hall plan. Built ca. 1870; demolished. Finnigan was captain of steamer *Selma*. 1 ext. photo (1936, portion of façade only).

Fire Station No. 5. *See* Washington Fire Engine Company No. 8 (AL-2), 7 N. Lawrence St.

Foote, Charles K., House (Trammell House) (AL-9H), 255 N. Conception St. Brick, approx. 29' (3-bay front) X 100' including long rear ell, 2½ stories, gable roof with curtain wall at each end, brick dentil course, cast-iron gallery with deck, 2-tiered 2-level L-shaped wooden gallery at rear; side-hall plan, double parlors. Built ca. 1856 for Charles K. Foote, "Grocer and Dealer in Western Produce"; interior adapted for apartments. 2 ext. photos (1936, ironwork only).

Ford House. *See* Hall-Ford House (AL-46), 165 St. Emanuel St.

Forsyth House (Four Sisters). *See* Tardy-Thorp House (AL-17), 112 S. Conception St.

Fort Condé-Charlotte House. *See* Jonathan Kirkbride House (AL-14), 104 Theatre St.

Four Sisters House. *See* Tardy-Thorp House (AL-17), 112 S. Conception St.

Franklin Street Methodist Episcopal Church (Beehive Church) (AL-26), SW corner Franklin and St. Michael sts. Brick, approx. 65' X 90' with rectangular apse, 1 story above full ground floor, gable roof with pediment surmounted by 2-stage domed cupola, originally raised distyle in antis Doric portico on heavy piers with main entrance beneath, brick pilasters and entablature; open plan with 2 aisles, horseshoe-shaped gallery in rear reached by twin spiral stairways. Built 1848–49; Dougherty, architect, and Richard Redwood, contractor. Nicknamed Beehive Church because of mission and educational activity of congregation. Renovation ca. 1875 included enclosure of portico, addition of apse, installation of new gallery stairs, art glass windows, pipe organ in arched apse; 1890 sold to black congregation and became Franklin Street Baptist Church; demolished 1971. 1 ext. photo originally filed as AL-7S (1934, wrought-iron wall bracket only), 3 ext. photos (1934–36), 13 int. photos (1936); 3 data pages (1936).

Frascatti (AL-71), near Mobile Bay on Yeend St., 0.2 mi. E of Baker St. and due S of Hamilton St. Frame with clapboarding, rectangular main block (3-bay front) with long 13-bay side wing, 2 stories (side wing 1 story), gable roof extending over full-length 2-tiered gallery, decorative bargeboards beneath eaves and at each gable end, continuous gallery along side wing; center-hall plan (main block), Greek Revival interior trim, decorative plasterwork. Two-story main block built ca. 1855 as residence, 1-story side wing added ca. 1870; main block demolished ca. 1940, wing shortened 9' and remodeled for commercial use. Summer home for many years of Martin Horst, mayor of Mobile; later center of popular turn-of-the-century recreational park known as Frascatti. 9 ext. photos (1936–37), 3 int. photos (1937); 2 data pages (1937).

Gaillard, S. P., House. *See* Beal-Gaillard House (AL-107), 111 Myrtlewood Ln.

Gas Lamps. *See* Street Furnishings (AL-36).

Gates and Fences, Ironwork.
215 S. Conception St. (AL-8X). Cast-and-wrought-iron gate and iron fence; gate design centers upon stylized sunflower topped by double scroll terminating in openwork fleur-de-lis. Probably mid-19th C.; gate and fence removed when house demolished 1968 for urban renewal. 1 photo (1936).
456 S. Conception St. (AL-8CX). Cast-and-wrought-iron gate and fence; approx. 4' high; gate design consists of elaborated sunflower design topped by double scroll and open fleur-de-lis, latticework panel beneath; flanking openwork cast-iron piers with molded caps and bases, urnlike finials, shaft embellished by open guilloche motif; fence consists of series of cast-iron palings enriched beneath by frieze-band of continuous circlets. Erected 1878 in front of Battle-Ross House (AL-9V) for William Ross; moved 1920s to 456 S. Conception St. (Andrew Coffin House); moved again 1963 (gate to 1802 Old Government St., fence to 3333 Rivière du Chien Rd.) when Andrew Coffin House razed. 1 photo (1936).
201 Government St. (AL-9BA7). Cast-iron fence and double-leaf gate, approx. 3'6" high; gate design consists of cusped iron palings set above horizontal panels embellished by concentric Ionic scrolls; flanking openwork cast-iron piers, each articulated by cap with double quatrefoil motif and foliated finial. Erected ca. 1850 in front of Murray Forbes Smith residence, childhood home of Mrs. William K. Vanderbilt (later Mrs. O. H. P. Belmont), née Alva Smith. Gate removed to 1758 Spring Hill Ave. after Smith house razed ca. 1936; moved again to 3609 Rivière du Chien Rd. in 1970. 1 photo (1936).
453 Government St. (AL-7XXV). Wrought-iron double-leaf vehicular gate, approx. 3' high, design consists of stylized sunflower topped by double scroll terminating in patera and open fleur-de-lis; box lock. Probably erected mid-19th C. as carriageway gate for now-demolished Samuel Acre House; destroyed. 1 photo (1934).
605 Government St. (AL-8U). Wrought-iron gate, approx. 3' high, design consists of stylized sunflower topped by double scroll terminating in patera and open fleur-de-lis; cast-iron newels with fluted shafts and conical caps adorned with crockets and finials. Probably mid-19th C.; destroyed. 1 photo (1936).
800 block St. Anthony St. (AL-9A), S side St. Anthony between N. Bayou and N. Jefferson sts. Cast-iron fence, approx. 3'6" high; design consists of series of cusped ogival arches above continuous row of quatrefoil; cast-iron posts with octagonal bases, foliated shafts, and urn-like finials. Probably mid-19th C.; destroyed. Good example of Gothic Revival motifs rendered in cast-iron. 1 photo (1936).
251 St. Joseph St. (AL-8TC), NW corner St. Joseph and State sts. Wrought-and-strap-iron fence and gate, approx. 4'6" high; fence has spiked palings above strap-iron latticework panels studded with paterae and surrounded by scrollwork border; gate design composed of lyre motif topped by double scroll. Probably mid-19th C.; destroyed. Panels of fence utilize same design as that found in fence and carriage gate at adjacent 253 St. Joseph St. 1 photo (1936).
253 St. Joseph St. (AL-8TM). Wrought-and-strap-iron fence and carriage gate, approx. 4'6"

high; fence has spiked palings above strap-iron latticework panels studded with paterae and surrounded by scrollwork border; double-leaf gate topped by double scroll and fleur-de-lis. Probably mid-19th C.; destroyed. Panels of fence and gate utilize same design as that found in fence at adjacent 251 St. Joseph St. Portion reerected in garden at 3703 Old Shell Rd. 1 photo (1936).

153–155 St. Louis St. (AL-7C). Wrought-iron pedestrian gate and double-leaf carriage gate, approx. 4' high swung between openwork cast-iron piers with molded caps and bases, shafts embellished by open guilloche motif; design of gates consists of stylized sunflower motif topped by double scroll terminating in paterae and open fleur-de-lis. Probably erected mid-19th C. for William L. Truit House; destroyed. 1 sheet (1934); 2 photos (1934).

See Appendix B for complete listing of structures included in 1934–36 ironwork survey.

Gates-Daves House (AL-799), 1570–1572 Dauphin St. Frame with clapboarding (gallery plaster over hand-split lath), approx. 57' (7-bay front) x 27' plus 2 parallel rear wings, 1 story, gable roof extending over full-length balustraded gallery with chamfered posts, 2 exterior end chimneys (plus 2 additional chimneys), French doors flanking central entrance; center-hall plan, simple interior woodwork, box locks. Built 1842 for Hezekiah Gates; E rear wing added ca. 1960 to match earlier wing. Excellent example of early-19th-C. Gulf Coast cottage; originally a country residence. 3 ext. photos (1966); 6 data pages (1966, 1972). NR. See also FBJ (J7-ALA-1286).

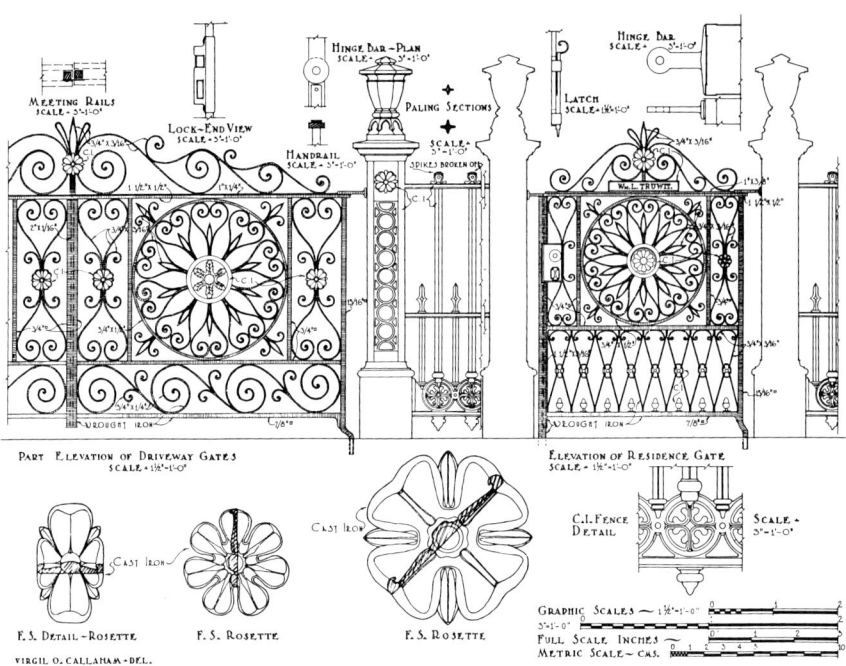

Gates and fence, 153–155 St. Louis Street, Mobile (mid-19th century, destroyed).

Gazzam, Audley H., House (AL-53), 1255 Government St. (S side Government St. between Ann St. and Georgia Ave.). Frame with clapboarding, rectangular (5-bay front) with ell, 2½ stories, gable roof (broken in rear) with dormers, 2-tiered pedimented tetrastyle Doric portico with wheatsheaf balustrade, full-length 2-tiered jalousied gallery across rear; center-hall plan with side stairhall, notable interior woodwork. Semidetached ell with flounder roof service wing (frame with clapboarding, rectangular, 2 stories) at rear. Built ca. 1838; demolished ca. 1940 and portico incorporated into subsequent structure on site. 31 ext. photos (1936), 18 int. photos (1936); 2 data pages (1937).

Gee-Barrow House (AL-825), originally at 253 Monroe St.; reconstructed at 251 St. Anthony St. Brick 25'2" (3-bay front) x 78'6" including rear ell, 2½ stories, gable roof with brick dentil course; side-hall plan. Built ca. 1852 for Gideon Gee. Dismantled 1970 and rebuilt at new location with alterations, including elimination of rear wing, heightening of roof and brick parapets at each gable end, also addition of cast-iron gallery and deck. 1 ext. photo (1966); 4 data pages (1966).

George, Elizabeth, House (AL-9K), 159 Monroe St. Pressed brick, rectangular (3-bay front) with ell, 2½ stories, cast-iron gallery with deck and floor-length windows; side-hall plan. Built ca. 1860; demolished. 1 ext. photo (1936, portion of façade only).

Georgia Cottage (Hardaway-Evans-Wilson House) (AL-826), 2564

Spring Hill Ave. (in old Summerville). Frame with cypress clapboarding (plastered on gallery), 54'8" (5-bay front) x 64'0" including gallery plus flanking offset rear wings (18'3" wide, 3 bays), 1 story, hipped roof extending over full-length balustraded gallery with 6 piers supporting classic style entablature (identical gallery once at rear), similar 3-bay galleries fronting wings, jib windows opening onto main porch; center-hall plan, Greek Revival interior woodwork, silver-plated hardware and simple decorative plasterwork. Built 1840 for Col. John Murrell as gift to his daughter, Mrs. William A. Hardaway. Home (1857–68) of 19th-C. romantic novelist Augusta Evans Wilson (see also Ashland, AL-68), who purchased the house in the name of her father, Matthew R. Evans, with proceeds from her first novel, *Inez; A Tale of the Alamo* (1855). At Georgia Cottage, as she named the house, Mrs. Wilson wrote *Macaria* (1864) and *St. Elmo* (1866). 4 ext. photos (1963), 3 int. photos (1963); 6 data pages (1972). NR. *See also* FBJ (J7-ALA-1344 and 1345).

Gibbons-Torrey House (C. J. Torrey House) (AL-43), 60, 62 S. Conception St. Brick with marble trim, rectangular (3-bay front) with ell, 3½ stories (ell 2 stories), gable roof, double end chimneys with curtain wall, wrought-iron balcony at second-floor level with floor-length windows, 2-tiered gallery in rear; side-hall plan with principal floor at second-story level (piano nobile arrangement), interior woodwork probably adapted from Minard Lafever, double drawing room. Wrought-iron carriage gate. Built ca. 1855 for Judge Lyman Gibbons; balcony removed and first floor altered for commercial purposes. 8 ext. photos (1936–37), 19 int. photos (1936–37, including privy); 2 data pages (1937).

Gilmore-Gaines-Quigley House (AL-9C), 751 Government St. (SW corner Government and Scott sts.). Brick, rectangular (3-bay front) with offset rear wing, 2 stories, low hipped roof, wide bracketed cornice, 2-tiered cast-iron gallery, floor-length windows, 2-tiered wooden gallery at rear; side-hall plan, notable interior woodwork. Built 1864 for George W. and Carolyn F. Gilmore; rear gallery later partially enclosed. Home 1866–84 of Dr. Edmund Pendleton Gaines (1824–84), Confederate surgeon and head of the Alabama Medical Association; later residence of son-in-law, Judge Oliver J. Semmes, state legislator and son of Adm. Raphael Semmes of the Confederate Navy. 3 ext. photos (1936), 5 ext. photos (1963), 2 int. photos (1963); 1 data page (1963).

Girard Double House. *See* Chamberlain and Rapier Double House (AL-12), 56, 58 S. Conception St.

Gliddon, John S., House (AL-18), 400 St. Anthony St. (NW corner St. Anthony and N. Franklin sts.). Frame with clapboarding above stuccoed brick first floor scored to simulate ashlar, 42'6" (5-bay façade) x 28'3", 2 stories, hipped roof with wooden shingles, 2 exterior end chimneys, cantilevered full-length covered balcony at second-story level with turned colonnettes and wooden balustrade, upper and lower doorways possibly adapted from Asher Benjamin, second-story loggia at rear; modified center-hall plan. Masonry wall along Franklin St. to rear. Built ca. 1840 for wealthy English-born blacksmith Gliddon. Said to have been 1 story originally; rear loggia later enclosed; demolished. Replicated 1980 at NW corner Congress and Joachim sts. for Mobile Historic Development Commission; Nicholas Holmes, Jr., AIA, architect. Unique example in Mobile of West Indian–type residence. 3 sheets (1936, including plans, elevations, section, details); 8 ext. photos (1936), 8 int. photos (1936); 2 data pages (1936). *See also* FBJ (J7-ALA-1303 and 1304).

Goelet-Randlette-Beck House (Beck House, Randlette House) (AL-855), 1005 Augusta St. Frame with clapboarding, rectangular (5-bay front) with rear wing, 1½ stories, high gable roof extending over full-length balustraded gallery with square wooden columns (molded caps and bases), floor-length gallery windows; center-hall plan, original architrave moldings and fireplaces. E side (3 bays) built 1868 for Virginia Goelet. W parlors added and present appearance assumed ca. 1878–80, following purchase of house in 1875 by Columbia E. Randlette. 6 ext. photos (1974), 1 int. photo (1974).

Goldsby, Judge Joel, House (AL-9W), 452 Government St. Brick with stucco, main block basically T-shaped with stem projecting forward to form massive central pavilion flanked by lateral cast-iron galleries and fronted by 2-story semioctagonal bays with flanking corner pilasters, main block approx. 52' x 55' overall, 2½ stories, steeply pitched central gable toward street embellished with bargeboard trim; central chimney with corbeled cap, cast-iron window grilles, hood molds above windows; entrance at W side into lateral hall, interior features once included curved stairway, double drawing room, dining room with archway into breakfast alcove, library; notable Gothic Revival style cast-iron fence. Built ca. 1855; severely altered for commercial use ca. 1955, including destruction of first-floor façade to build 1-story business structure in front; demolished 1982. Rare example in Alabama of Gothic Revival style employed for domestic architecture. 2 ext. photos (1936, principally cast-iron details); 1 ext. photocopy (ca. 1900).

Goldsmith, Meyer, House. *See* Griffin-Goldsmith House (AL-76), 408 Conti St.

Gonzales, Mrs. Margaret, House. *See* House, 352 State St. (AL-9E).

Government Street Methodist Church (Government Street United Methodist Church) (AL-853), 901 Government St. (SW corner Government and Broad sts.). Brick with rough stucco, basically rectangular (approx. 70′ × 140′ overall), 3-bay front with slightly advanced corner pavilions, modified apsidal end, tiled roof with low clerestory dome resting on pendentives over nave, elaborate neo-Churrigueresque façade executed in sculptured mortar and embellished with Christian symbolism surrounding great central doorway and rose window directly above; formerly semicircular auditorium with "Akron-plan" seating arrangement of turn-of-the-century Protestantism, focusing upon central pulpit and choir loft; carved *reja* employed as screen for organ pipes. Built 1889–90, R. D. Price, architect; extensively remodeled to present appearance in 1906, George B. Rogers, architect. Notable local example of neo–Spanish Baroque style. Congregation dates from 1826 and moved to present location in 1890 from Franklin Street Methodist Episcopal Church (AL-26). 6 ext. photos (1974), 3 int. photos (1974).

Government Street Presbyterian Church (AL-1), 300 Government St. (NW corner Government and Jackson sts.). Brick with stucco scored to simulate ashlar, 62′5″ × 98′8″, 1 story over raised basement, temple-type façade with pedimented distyle in antis Ionic portico, anta-like pilasters along side walls, originally 2-stage battered octagonal tower (removed 1852), full entablature with denticulated cornice once surmounted by antefixae; notably intact Greek Revival interior; open plan with 2 aisles, U-shaped gallery and supports based on Plate 48 from *Beauties of Modern Architecture*, pulpit dais backed by pylon-like screen framing engaged Corinthian tetrastyle and topped by antefixae, coffered ceiling, original pews, twin winding stairways from basement to gallery. Built 1836–37; initial plans prepared by firm of James Gallier and Charles Dakin, finished by Charles and James Dakin; Thomas S. James, brick contractor. Burgett Memorial Church School added in 1904, C. L. Hutchisson, Sr., architect. Most outstanding Greek Revival period church in Alabama. 5 sheets (1934, including elevation, plans, details); 5 ext. photos (1934–36), 9 int. photos (1934–36), 3 data pages (1936). NR. *See also* FBJ (J7-ALA-1305 through 1307).

Government Street Stores. *See* Commercial Buildings: Government Street (AL-62 series).

Government Street United Methodist Church. *See* Government Street Methodist Church (AL-853), 901 Government St.

Griffin-Goldsmith House (Meyer Goldsmith House) (AL-76), 408 Conti St. (NE corner Conti and Hamilton sts.). Brick, rectangular (3-bay front) with ell, 2½ stories, gable roof, double end chimneys with curtain wall, deck with wooden balustrade across front (steps at W end), small wrought-iron balcony at second-floor level, plaster sills and splayed lintels, brick dentil course, 2-tiered wooden gallery along W (inner) wall of ell; side-hall plan. Built ca. 1845, probably for Edward Griffin. Later home of Meyer Goldsmith, member of Mobile Jewish community and sometime president of Hebrew Relief Association; demolished 1969 because of deteriorated condition. 4 ext. photos (1936–37); 2 data pages (1937).

Guesnard-Craft House (AL-806), 51 S. Jackson St. (SE corner Jackson and Conti sts.). Brick, rectangular (3-bay front) with offset wing on S side and offset rear ell on N, hipped roof, 2 stories, 2-tiered cast-iron gallery with floor-length windows, wide bracketed cornice with unusual dogtooth brick dentil course beneath, marble sills and lintels; side-hall plan. Cast-iron fence. Built 1859 for tobacconist and jeweler Theodore Guesnard, Jr. Later owned by his son-in-law, Sen. John Craft; acquired and adapted to educational use by Government Street Presbyterian Church in 1965. 3 ext. photos (1963); 1 data page (1963).

Gulf City Hotel (Southern Hotel) (AL-11), 53–65 Water St. (SE corner Water and Conti sts.). Brick with stucco scored to simulate ashlar, L-shaped, approx. 172′ (24 bays) along Water St. x 83′ (12 bays) along Conti St. excluding later addition, 3 stories, combination hipped-and-gable roof concealed by brick parapet, continuous 2-tiered cast-iron gallery with balustraded deck at third-floor level along Water St. front and partially along Conti St. elevation, first floor devoted to commercial use. Built 1837 for Lewis Judson and Philip McCloskey as Gulf City Hotel. Renovations (including addition of cast-iron gallery) after 1865; renamed Southern Hotel 1894; demolished 1960s for Water St. Urban Renewal Project. 1 sheet originally filed as AL-8B (1934, ironwork only); 6 sheets (1935, including plans, elevations, details); 1 ext. photo originally filed as AL-8B (1934, ironwork gallery), 14 ext. photos (1934–35), 12 int. photos (1934–35); 2 data pages (1936).

Gulf, Mobile, and Ohio Passenger Terminal (AL-796), NE corner Beauregard St. and Telegraph Rd. Yellow brick, L-shaped with 15-bay front, 3 stories, hipped red-tile roof, neo–Spanish Baroque structure with raised central pavilion enriched by pseudo-Churrigueresque ornamentation, tiled dome with lantern, continuous 16-bay arcade across façade with curvilinear parapet; central rotunda and ticket area with marble wainscoting, marble stair with cast-iron balustrade to offices on upper floors. Completed 1907; P. Thornton Marye, architect (also designed Terminal Station, Atlanta, and other notable southern railway structures); modified for offices 1959; dome sealed off 1961. 2 ext. photos (1966); 6 data pages (1966). NR.

Hall-Ford House (Ford House) (AL-46), 165 St. Emanuel St. (NE corner St. Emanuel and Monroe sts.). Frame with clapboarding above stuccoed brick first floor, 46′3″ (5 bays) x 40′2″ plus ell, 2½ stories, gable roof with dormers, 4 exterior end chimneys, 2-tiered gallery of superimposed Doric order (stuccoed brick below, wooden above); center-hall plan. Semi-detached brick 2-story dependency off rear gallery on Monroe St. side; cast-iron fence. Built ca. 1836 for Edward Hall, native of Philadelphia and early mayor of Mobile; extensively reconditioned 1977. Unusual instance of raised-basement Creole plan transformed into fully developed first floor. 5 sheets (1966, including site plan, elevations, plans, section, details); 4 ext. photos (1935), 3 int. photos (1935); 2 data pages (1936), 7 data pages (1966, 1972).

Hall-Horst House (Henry Horst House, Clitherall House) (AL-23), 110 St. Emanuel St. (N side of Christ Church). Brick, 5-bay asymmetrical front, 3 stories with 2-story rear service wing, shed roof concealed by brick parapet, façade has semioctagonal 2-story bay on S side with winged wooden balconies at upper level, N bay of façade consists of arched carriageway paved with brick in herringbone pattern; main entrance in carriageway opening onto transverse center hall with flanking parlors and dining room. Built ca. 1850, reputedly for Edward Hall as gift to daughter, Mrs. Clitherall; demolished 1945. 6 ext. photos (1934–36), 9 int. photos (1936); 2 data pages (1936).

Hamilton-Gaillard House. See Church Street Block Study (AL-803).

Hammond-Willoughby House (AL-44), NE corner St. Michael and Hamilton sts. Frame with clapboarding plus brick side wing, (pedimented 3-bay front) with ell, originally 2 stories raised on brick piers (wing 1 story with cellar), gable roof, small asymmetrically placed Doric entrance porch, side wing fronted by 3-bay gallery; side-hall plan (main block), mahogany doors and Greek Revival style interior trim, jib window with sidelights opening onto rear gallery of main block. Frame, 2-story slave quarters. Built 1836–37 for W. P. Hammond. Upper story burned 1934 and house repaired as 1-story structure; demolished. 6 ext. photos (1935), 4 int. photos (1935); 2 data pages (1936).

Hanlein House. See House (AL-21B), 652 St. Francis St.

Hannah Houses. See Robinson Twin Houses (AL-807), 157, 159 N. Conception St.

Hardaway-Evans-Wilson House. See Georgia Cottage (AL-826), 2564 Spring Hill Ave.

Hazard-Semmes House (Judge Oliver J. Semmes House, Andrew Zimlich House) (AL-57), 2828 Dauphin Way. Frame with clapboarding, rectangular (5-bay front), 2 stories, gable roof with 2 exterior end chimneys and 2 interior end chimneys, full-height 4-column portico of modified Doric order with heavy pediment, balustraded galleries at both levels; center-hall plan, simple Greek Revival style interior woodwork, decorative plaster. Built ca. 1835 for Charles C. Hazard. Later rear additions; demolished ca. 1947. Residence 1865–70 of S. Spence Semmes, Mobile lawyer and son of Adm. Raphael Semmes, who lived here briefly at end of Civil War until his arrest by Union authorities. 7 ext. photos (1936–37), 12 int. photos (1937); 2 data pages (1937).

Hellen-Croom House (AL-808), 1001 Augusta St. (SW corner Augusta and Charles sts., S side Washington Sq.). Frame (heart pine) with clapboarding, 25'9" (3-bay front) X 54'6" plus offset wing (15'0" X 48'5") at SE rear with attached 1-story ell, 2 stories, low hipped roof with bracketed eaves extending over full-height portico composed of 4 slender square columns, upper and lower galleries enclosed by flatwork wooden balustrade, floor-length windows at both levels; side-hall plan, double parlors. Built 1870 for Mariah H. Hellen. Rear porch enclosed 1920; ell originally containing kitchen and indoor privy now converted into apartment. 3 ext. photos (1963), 1 int. photo (1963); 2 data pages (1963).

Henderson, Dr., House. *See* Bates-Henderson House (AL-22A), 12 N. Jackson St.

Hitchcock, Henry, House. *See* House (AL-24), 301 Church St.

Hitching Posts. *See* Street Furnishings (AL-36).

Home Industry Foundry (*Hunley* Building) (AL-809), 250 N. Water (SE corner N. Water and State sts.). Brick, rectangular main block (5-bay front, 8 bays deep) with wing along N. Water St., 1 story with clerestory windows along SW (front) elevation, half-hipped roof topped by monitorlike ventilator, pilastered façade, large central archway on SW front. Built 1884 for Augustus Kling, who produced industrial and decorative ironwork; dismantled 1965 and materials stored for re-erection; May 1978 City of Mobile committed itself to reconstruction of foundry at NE corner of Church and S. Franklin sts. as part of Museum of the City of Mobile complex. Confederate submarine *Hunley* built at earlier foundry on same site. 2 ext. photos (1963); 1 data page (1963).

Horst, Henry, House. *See* Hall-Horst House (AL-23), 110 St. Emanuel St.

Horst, Martin, House (AL-776), 407 Conti St. (SE corner Conti and Hamilton sts.). Brick, 50'2" (5-bay front) X 38'10" plus offset rear wing (53'2" X 20'0"), 2 stories, shallow hipped roof concealed by paneled brick parapet (low gable roof over wing), bracketed cornice, elaborate 4-bay cast-iron gallery with deck, segmentally arched door and windows with ornate cast-iron sills, lintels, grilles. L-shaped 2-tiered wooden gallery partially enclosed with jalousies at rear; center-hall plan, interior woodwork shows late Greek Revival influence, notable plasterwork including segmentally arched opening between east parlors embellished with keystone busts of Confederate heroes Robert E. Lee and Stonewall Jackson; notable cast-iron fence and gate. Built 1867–68 at cost of $26,000; George W. Cox, brick contractor. Restored late 1960s (major interior changes in wing, 1-story dependency veneered with brick and attached to rear gallery). One of Mobile's most outstanding postwar residences. First owner, German-born Martin Horst, became mayor of Mobile in 1871. 8 sheets (1966, including site plan, plans, elevations, section, details); 9 data pages (1972). NR.

Horta-Semmes House (Admiral Raphael Semmes House) (AL-56), 802 Government St. Brick, 29'3" (3-bay front) X 39'6" plus offset rear wing (14'6" X 27'0"), 2 stories, gable roof, 2 pairs of double end chimneys with brick dentil course, cast-iron gallery with deck (floor-length windows at both levels) and recessed doorway, 2-tiered wooden gallery at rear; side-hall plan. Cast-iron fence. Built 1859 for Peter Horta; cast-iron gallery added 1870s. Purchased by popular subscription in 1871 as home for southern naval hero Adm. Raphael Semmes (1809–77), commander of Confederate raider *Alabama*. Educational annex to adjacent First Baptist Church since 1946; exterior subsequently painted and interior modified. 9 sheets (1936, including plans, elevations, sections, details); 13 ext. photos (1936), 18 int. photos (1936); 2 data pages (1937). NR.

House (Three Sisters House) (AL-24), 301 Church St. (SW corner Church and S. Jackson sts.). Frame with clapboarding on brick piers, rectangular (3-bay front), 8 bays deep including long ell parallel to Jackson St., gable roof, pedimented tetrastyle portico of modified Doric order with cast-iron balustrade at both levels, floor-length windows, double wooden stairway to gallery; side-hall plan. Large rear lot with brick dependencies enclosed by brick wall. Reputedly built 1835–36 for Henry Hitchcock as one of 3 adjoining houses (hence Three Sisters); demolished 1964 for urban renewal. Cast-iron balustrade identical, and architecture very similar, to those of House (AL-8C) at 203 N. Conception St. ½ sheet of cast-iron balustrade detail filed as AL-8C (1934); 3 ext. photos (1934–36); 2 data pages (1937).

House (Brooks House) (AL-7B), 108-110 N. Conception St. (E side Conception St., approx. 60' s of intersection with St. Louis St.). Brick with stucco, approx. 45' (5-bay front) x 40' plus ell (approx. 18' x 50'), 2½ stories, gable roof with double end chimneys and curtain wall, monumental tetrastyle pedimented modified Doric portico with upper and lower galleries and wrought-iron balustrade, quarter-round windows in gable ends; center-hall plan. Built ca. 1835–40; later alterations included addition of outside stairway to façade; demolished. 1 sheet (1934, ironwork detail and partial façade only); 2 photos (1934, ironwork and partial façade).

House (AL-8C), 203 N. Conception St. (W side Conception, just N of St. Anthony St.). Frame with clapboarding, rectangular (3-bay front), 2 stories, gable roof, pedimented tetrastyle portico of modified Doric order with cast-iron balustrade at both levels, recessed doorway; side-hall plan. Cast-iron fence, hitching post patterned after small tree trunk. Built ca. 1836; Charles Dakin possibly architect. Pediment later modified with fish-scale shingling; demolished before 1960. Compare with House, 301 Church St. (AL-24). ½ sheet (1934, ironwork detail only); 1 ext. photo (1934).

House (AL-828), 303 N. Conception St. *See* Parmly Houses.

House (AL-8SR), 207 S. Conception St. Brick and stucco, rectangular (3-bay front), 2 stories, 2-tiered cast-iron gallery with slender fluted posts below and trelliswork above, simulated quoins, lintels, and frieze of stucco; side-hall plan. Built mid-19th C.; demolished 1960s for urban renewal. 1 ext. photo (1936).

House (AL-8X), 215 S. Conception St. *Under* Gates and Fences, *see* 215 S. Conception St.

House (AL-8CX), 456 S. Conception St. *Under* Gates and Fences, *see* 456 S. Conception St.

House (AL-7E), 250 Government St. (NW corner Government and S. Joachim sts.). Brick, rectangular (3-bay front), 2 stories, gable roof, cast-iron gallery with deck; brick 2-story rear dependency; side-hall plan, curved stairway. Built 1850s; demolished ca. 1955. Occupied 1870s by Daniel Perrin Bestor, Jr., who sold it in 1881 to Felix McGill, Mobile philanthropist. ½ sheet (1934, ironwork detail only); 1 ext. photo (1934, fence and balustrade detail only).

House (AL-7XXV), 453 Government St. *Under* Gates and Fences, *see* 453 Government St.

House (AL-8U), 605 Government St. *Under* Gates and Fences, *see* 605 Government St.

House (James Riley House) (AL-50), 8 N. Hamilton St. Brick with ashlar trim, rectangular (3-bay front) with ell, 2½ stories, gable roof, recessed entrance with battered architrave and denticulated cornice, cantilevered wrought-iron balcony (middle bay of second floor), 2-tiered jalousied gallery at rear with outside stair; side-hall plan. Built ca. 1850; demolished before 1960. 1 photo originally filed as AL-7XB (1936, balcony and partial façade), 6 ext. photos (1936), 4 int. photos (1936); 2 data pages (1937).

House (Tom Riley House) (AL-9Q), 256 N. Jackson St. Brick, rectangular (3-bay front), 2 stories, cast-iron gallery with grilled vents beneath and steps at N end, recessed doorway with Greek Revival architrave; side-hall plan. Marble walk. Built ca. 1850; demolished. 2 ext. photos (1936, portion of gallery and grilled vent only).

House (Finch House) (AL-9F), 301 N. Joachim St. Brick (gallery stuccoed and scored to simulate ashlar), 3-bay front, 2 stories, cast-iron gallery with steps at either end, recessed doorway and floor-length windows; side-hall plan. Built ca. 1855; demolished. 1 ext. photo (1936, portion of façade only).

House (AL-786), 204 S. Joachim St. Frame with clapboarding, 26'4" (3-bay front) x 30'3" plus ell and small S side addition, 1½ stories (ell 2 stories), gable roof with dormers extending over full-length balustraded gallery, floor-length windows, bracketed cornice; side-hall plan. Probably built ca. 1860; renovated ca. 1875, including addition of dormers, paneled front door, enlargement of rear wing to 2 stories; demolished 1969 for construction of I-10. Excellent example of Creole cottage. 3 sheets (1966, including site plan, plans, elevations, section); 2 ext. photos (1966); 6 data pages (1966, 1972).

House (AL-787), 208 S. Joachim St. Frame with cypress clapboarding, L-shaped main block (3-bay front with asymmetrically projecting s bay) plus ell, approx. 38′0″ × 62′11″ overall including ell, 2 stories, shallow gable roof with front cross-gable, bracketed cornice, 1-story entrance porch with scroll-cut trim set into angle of façade, adjacent semioctagonal bay with cast-iron window grilles, L-shaped gallery in rear; center-hall plan with side stairhall, molded plaster arch between double parlors. Built ca. 1865–70; demolished 1969 to make way for I-10. Good local example of post–Civil War Victorian style. 6 sheets (1966, including site plan, plans, elevations, section, detail); 2 ext. photos (1966), 1 int. photo (1966); 7 data pages (1966, 1972).

House (AL-7X), 350 Monroe St. Brick, rectangular (2 bays first floor, 3 bays second floor), 2 stories, gable roof, brick dentil course, balcony at upper level with wrought-iron balustrade, unusual wrought-iron lamp bracket at corner of building. Probably built ca. 1840, with first floor originally devoted to commercial use, living quarters upstairs; demolished 1963. 2 ext. photos (1936).

House (Barker House, Spanish Dwelling) (AL-21D), 109 St. Anthony St. Brick (gallery stuccoed and scored to simulate ashlar), L-shaped (6-bay) front set back from street with forward projecting 2-bay pavilion, 1-story late 19th-C. wooden porch (probably replacing earlier one). Possibly built ca. 1835 for John B. Toulmin, although traditionally assigned earlier date; demolished 1940–41. 1 ext. photo (1934).

House (AL-15), 161 St. Anthony St. *See* Smith-Clarke House.

House (iron steps only) (AL-7R), 256 St. Francis St. Brick, rectangular (3-bay front) with offset rear wing, 2 stories, cast-iron gallery with iron steps at E end; side-hall plan. Built ca. 1850; demolished. 1 ext. photo (1936, steps and railing only).

House (Hanlein House) (AL-21B), 652 St. Francis St. Brick, rectangular (4-bay front consisting of 2 units of 2 bays each), 1 story, gable end toward street with brick parapet and coping, full-length wooden gallery. Built 19th C.; demolished 1934. Possibly erected as dependency of larger structure. 1 ext. photo (1934).

House (AL-8TC), 251 St. Joseph St. *Under* Gates and Fences, *see 251 St. Joseph St.*

House (AL-8TM), 253 St. Joseph St. *Under* Gates and Fences, *see 253 St. Joseph St.*

House (AL-7C), 153, 155 St. Louis St. *Under* Gates and Fences, *see 153, 155 St. Louis St.*

House (AL-9), 154 St. Louis St. Brick with stucco scored to simulate ashlar, rectangular (3-bay front), 2½ stories, gable roof with end chimneys, 2-tiered cast-iron gallery with floor-length windows; side-hall plan. Cast-iron fence, semidetached brick 2-story dependency. Built ca. 1850; demolished. 2 sheets (1934, elevation and details); 3 ext. photos (1934); 1 data page (1936, ironwork only).

House (AL-45), 256 St. Louis St. Frame with clapboarding, rectangular (4-bay front) with ell, 1½ stories, gable roof extending over full-length balustraded gallery, 2 segmentally arched front dormers, lean-to across rear; probably 2-room plan, some Greek Revival style trim. Built ca. 1835; demolished 1935. 3 ext. photos (1935); 1 data page (1936).

House (AL-39), 351 St. Michael St. *See* Vanroy-Barnewall House.

House (Tate House) (AL-9P), 304 State St. Brick, rectangular (3-bay front), 2 stories, shallow hipped roof, 2-tiered cast-iron gallery; side-hall plan. Built mid-19th C.; demolished ca. 1950 because of deteriorated condition. 1 ext. photo (1936).

House (Walsh House) (AL-9N), 350 State St. Brick, rectangular (3-bay front) with offset rear wing, 2 stories, gable roof, double end chimneys with curtain wall, 2-tiered cast-iron gallery with curved cast-iron steps at E end; side-hall plan. Built mid-19th C., demolished 1957. 1 ext. photo (1936).

House (Mrs. Margaret Gonzales House) (AL-9E), 352 State St. Brick, rectangular (3-bay front), 2 stories, gable roof, brick dentil course, 2-tiered cast-iron gallery, curved steps at end of porch (cast-iron balustrade), recessed doorway; side-hall plan. Built mid-19th C. Demolished 1957 to make way for funeral home. 1 ext. photo (1936). *See also* FBJ (J7-ALA-1308).

Huger, Charles L., House (AL-9BA5), 154 S. Conception St. Brick, 3-bay front, 2 stories, cast-iron gallery with deck, marble steps; side-hall plan. Built mid-19th C. First owner, Huger, was one-time president of Mobile Cotton Press Association. Demolished 1960s for urban renewal. 2 ext. photos (1936, gallery only).

Huger-Douglas Double House. See Lloyd Bowers Double House (AL-60), 109, 111 S. Conception St.

Hunley Building (AL-809). See Home Industry Foundry, 250 N. Water St.

Iron Gate, Fence, and Railing, 250 Government St. See House (AL-7E), 250 Government St.

Iron Gates and Fence (AL-7C), 153, 155 St. Louis St. *Under* Gates and Fences, *see 153, 155 St. Louis St.*

Iron Hitching Posts. See Street Furnishings (AL-36).

Iron Lace. See Charles Richards House (AL-810), 256 N. Joachim St.

Ironwork ("Early Period Ironwork," "Middle Period Ironwork," "Later Period Ironwork"). 1934–36 survey of Mobile's cast-iron and wrought-iron work; includes all structures originally assigned survey numbers in AL-7 series ("Early Period Ironwork"), AL-8 series ("Middle Period Ironwork"), and AL-9 series ("Later Period Ironwork"); for example, AL-7A, AL-8B, AL-9CA7. Details of cast-iron and wrought-iron balconies, galleries, fences, gates, lamp posts, etc. For individual listing of all structures included in survey *see* Appendix B. See *also* Church Street Cemetery Ironwork (AL-845), Magnolia Cemetery Ironwork (AL-8, AL-9), Street Furnishings (AL-36), and Gates and Fences.

Jacobson House. See Vanroy-Barnewall House (AL-39), 351 St. Michael St.

James, Thomas S., Double House (Augustine-Ottenstein House, Ottenstein House) (AL-27), 207, 209 N. Jackson St. Brick with stucco scored to simulate ashlar, 58'2" (6-bay front composed of 2 3-bay units) x 45'5" plus central rear wing with flanking dependencies, 2½ stories, gable roof (slate) with dormers, 2 pairs of double end chimneys with curtain wall, 2-tiered full-length gallery composed of superimposed Doric pillars surmounted by double raked parapets; side-hall plan in each unit (entries occupying 2 center bays of portico). Stables at rear. Built ca. 1836 (possibly as speculative or rental property) by James, an early Mobile builder-architect; later addition at sw rear. Very notable example of Mobile double-house tenement; demolished ca. 1940. 13 sheets (1936, including plans, section, details); 14 ext. photos (1934–36), 17 int. photos (1934–36); 3 data pages (1936).

Jordon House. See Rider House (AL-38), 303 Conti St.

Kennedy, Joshua, House (Barnewall-Mitchell House) (AL-800), 607 Government St. (SE corner Government and Dearborn sts.). Brick with stucco scored to simulate ashlar, rectangular (3-bay front) with long offset rear wing, 2 stories, gable roof with single cross-gable, wide bracketed eaves, full-height pedimented 4-column portico reflecting transition between Greek Revival and Italianate, arched openings with hood molds, bay window on w side, L-shaped wooden gallery in rear; side-hall plan, ornate interior woodwork, curved stair with statuary niche, denticulated plaster cornice. Notable cast-iron fence. Built 1857. Later Seamen's Bethel; American Legion Headquarters since 1947; later addition to rear wing. Outstanding local example of late antebellum architectural eclecticism. 4 ext. photos (1963), 2 int. photos (1963); 1 data page (1963).

Ketchum, Dr. George A., House. See Silver-Ketchum House (AL-798), 257 St. Francis St.

Ketchum, William H., House (Bishop's Residence) (AL-9U), 400 Government St. (NW corner Government and Franklin sts.). Brick with ashlar trim, irregular square (7 bays by 5 bays) with massive rear service wing, projecting 3-story central block with flanking 2-story (2-bay) pavilions, bracketed cornice surmounted by blocking course, quoined corners, molded stone belt course and architraves, elaborate 1-story cast-iron gallery with Tudor-esque arches and marble floor, terminating on Franklin St. side with porte cochère, main entrance from Franklin St.; center-hall plan, 60' drawing room, ornate plasterwork, marble mantels, winding stair from basement to third floor. Elaborate cast-iron fence along street frontage. Built 1860; C. T. Lernier possibly architect. Ketchum was a planter and cotton merchant, later major in Confederate army. Commandeered as headquarters of Union occupation force in 1865; residence of Roman Catholic bishops of Mobile since 1906. Rear wing remodeled for use as garage. 7 ext. photos (1936, gallery and fence only). *See also* FBJ (J7-ALA-1270).

Kilduff-Ray House (AL-849), 200 George St. (SW corner George and Church sts.). Frame with clapboarding, basically L-shaped with steeply gabled 2-bay projecting front, 1 story on high foundation, gallery with slender paired wooden columns (tripled at corners) and flatwood balustrade, cusped bargeboards and pierced brackets in scroll design, double-leaf paneled and glazed doorway; side-hall plan, neoclassical interior trim contrasting with late Victorian exterior, decorative plasterwork. Built 1892 for William J. Kilduff; restored 1940. 4 ext. photos (1974), 2 int. photos (1974).

Kirkbride, Jonathan, House (Fort Condé-Charlotte House) (AL-14), 104 Theatre St. Museum. Brick with stucco, irregular rectangle approx. 45′0″ × 35′5″ (5-bay front) with long ell and connected stables and carriage house, 2½ stories, gable roof, double end chimneys, 2-tiered gallery of modified classic design (Doric order below, Corinthian order with wheatsheaf balustrade above); center-hall plan. Built ca. 1845 incorporating portions of ca. 1822 city jail; east bay and upper portion of gallery added ca. 1850 by Kirkbride and Robert Ellis, masterbuilders. Home of Kirkbride, born in New Jersey, and his descendants 1853–1926; restored 1940 as museum house of Historic Mobile Preservation Society. Occupies part of site of 18th-C. Fort Condé (later Fort Charlotte). 4 sheets (1934, including plans, elevations, section, details); 9 ext. photos (1934–36), 5 ext. photos (1963), 5 int. photos (1934–36), 2 int. photos (1963); 3 data pages (1936). NR. *See also* FBJ (J7-ALA-1314 through 1316).

Kling House. *See* Butt-Kling House (AL-820), 254 N. Jackson St.

LaClede Hotel (AL-811), 150–160 Government St. (NW corner Government and St. Emanuel sts.). 3 adjoining units dating from different periods (overall length approx. 156′6″), brick with portion of side and rear stuccoed and scored to simulate ashlar, each unit 3 stories, with gable roof and brick dentil course. E section (nos. 150, 154) 7 bays long with 2 interior party walls, middle and W units together 14 bays long with inner party wall, continuous 2-tiered cast-iron gallery along front and St. Emanuel St. elevations extending over sidewalk with slender cast-iron supports at street level; first floor devoted to commercial use, second and third floors used as hotel. Nos. 150, 154 built 1855 to house fruit and liquor business of Joseph Peter; nos. 156, 158 built 1855–56 as family residence of Caleb Price. Both sections incorporated into LaClede Hotel in 1871; enlarged 1940 (J. H. Hutchisson, architect) by addition of no. 160 (W 25′) matching older portion. One of most important antebellum commercial structures surviving in downtown Mobile. 4 ext. photos (1963); 1 data page (1963).

Lamp Posts. *See* Street Furnishings (AL-36).

Larrouil-Arresijac House (AL-812), 252 S. Claiborne St. Frame with clapboarding (gallery plastered) on brick piers, rectangular (5-bay front), 1½ stories, gable roof extending over balustraded gallery with 6 turned posts; center-hall plan, enclosed stair. Brick bake-oven and dependencies formerly in rear. Built ca. 1840 for Toulouse-born confectioner Pascal Larrouil; demolished 1963 for municipal auditorium and urban renewal. Good example of small mid-19th-C. Mobile dwelling. 3 ext. photos (1963); 1 data page (1963). *See also* FBJ (J7-ALA-1317 and 1318).

LeLoupe House. *See* Weldon-LeLoupe House (AL-20), 107 St. Emanuel St.

LeVert House and Office (AL-29), 151, 153 Government St. (SW corner Government and St. Emanuel sts.). Dwelling and medical office of Dr. Henry Strachy LeVert and his wife, Madame Octavia Walton LeVert, leader of antebellum Mobile society.

House, 151 Government St. Brick, 34′0″ (3-bay front) × 42′6″ with offset rear wing (partially stuccoed) and attached irregularly shaped service dependency, 2 stories, shallow hipped roof, brick dentil course, recessed door with eared and battered architrave, 2-tiered cast-iron gallery on side wing; side-hall plan. Cast-iron fence. Built 1847; Thomas S. James, Lewis Judson, and William H. Pratt, builders. Extensively altered late 19th C. including neo-Romanesque façade, rear additions, and cast-iron side gallery; demolished 1965. 7 sheets (1935, including site plan, front and W elevation before alteration, cast-iron details); 1 ext. photocopy (n.d., showing original façade), 1 ext.

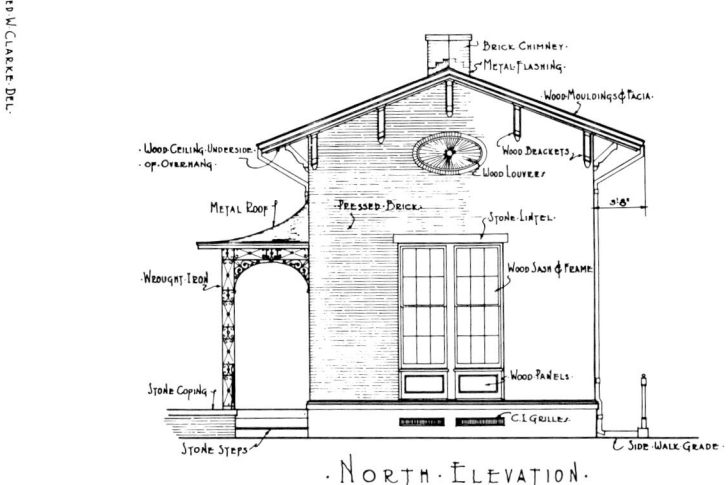

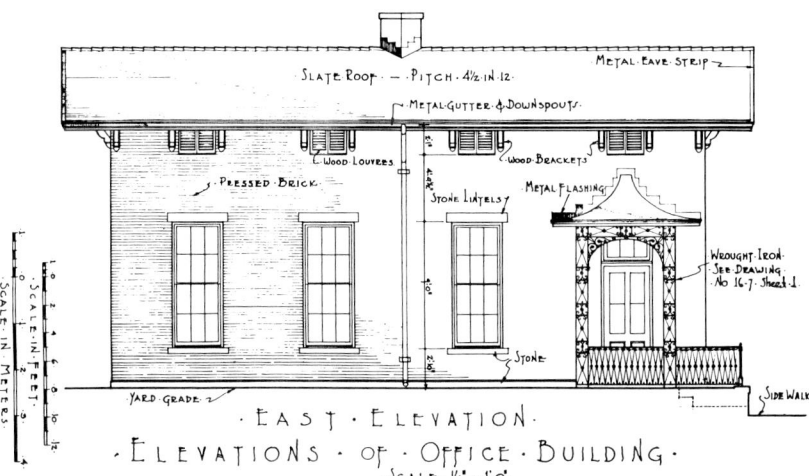

Dr. Henry LeVert Office, Mobile (1856).

photo (1934, side elevation only); 2 data pages (1936).
Office (Office and Studio), 153 Government St. Brick, approx. 20′10″ (1-bay front) × 43′4″, 1 story, rectangular, gable roof, side entrance framed by small cast-iron porch with marble floor, louvered attic vents beneath wide bracketed eaves; 2-room plan. Studio to rear (brick, irregular rectangular, 1 story). Built 1856; studio demolished 1977 to make way for courthouse annex. 2 sheets (1935, plans, elevations), also ½ sheet originally filed as AL-7G (1934, cast-iron porch only); 2 ext. photos originally filed as AL-7G (1934, cast-iron porch only).
See also FBJ (J7-ALA-1321).

Lott, William, House (AL-851), 160 Rapier Ave. (NW corner Rapier Ave. and Church St.). Frame with clapboarding, basically rectangular (3-bay front), 2 stories, hipped roof with bracketed eaves, Palladian dormer, tetrastyle piered portico with Ionic capitals, curvilinear balcony resting on scrolled consoles, floor-length French windows with transoms; modified center-hall plan, paneled interior. Built 1907; C. L. Hutchisson, Sr., architect. S porch added ca. 1921; restored 1978. 6 ext. photos (1974), 3 int. photos (1974).

Ludlow House (AL-41), 1113 Church St. Frame with clapboarding, rectangular (3-bay front) with offset rear wing, 2 stories, low hipped roof with bracketed cornice extending over full-height portico composed of attenuated octagonal wooden columns with corbeled caps, balustraded galleries above and below, similar portico with exterior stairway in rear (intersecting 2-tiered gallery of wing), jib windows; side-hall plan. Built 1875 for Mobile plumber Noel K. Ludlow; demolished 1973 because of deteriorated condition. Details of portico and overall design similar to those of Bragg-Mitchell House (AL-30). 7 ext. photos (1936), 10 int. photos (1936); 1 data page (1937).

Lyons House. *See* Ellis-Lyons House (AL-40), 168 S. Royal St.

Lyons, Patrick J., House (AL-9S), 300 State St. Brick, rectangular (3-bay front), 2 stories, shallow hipped roof with bracketed cornice, cast-iron gallery with deck on rough-cast concrete foundation, cast-iron steps, recessed door with Greek Revival style architrave, floor-length windows, 2-tiered wooden gallery at rear; side-hall plan. Cast-iron fence and Venetian fountain in yard. Built mid-19th C.; demolished 1950 for apartment construction (fountain moved to 2166 Old Shell Rd.). Once home of Lyons, longtime mayor of Mobile. 3 ext. photos (1936).

McDowell, Withers & Company (AL-784), 50–52 N. Commerce St. (NE corner N. Commerce and St. Francis sts., occupying lot extending S to Front St.). Brick and cast-iron parallelogram (determined by lot shape), approx. 60′0″ (similar 8-bay E and W fronts) × 80′9″ (9-bay side), 3 stories, paired hipped roofs partially concealed by paneled brick parapet above brick dentil course, trabeated first story (both E and W fronts) with cast-iron pilasters embellished with cartouches and supporting cast-iron entablature with egg-and-dart molding, first-floor bays originally contained double-leaf glazed doors, segmentally arched second- and third-story windows with cast-iron lintels, covered sidewalk along Front St. with continuous second-story balustraded deck (formerly covered) resting on slender cast-iron posts; interior bisected longitudinally by 19″ party wall. Built 1860–63 for McDowell, Withers & Co., cotton factors; demolished 1972 for Water Street Urban Renewal Project. Notable local example of mid-19th-C. commercial architecture utilizing cast-iron elements. 9 sheets (1966, including site plan, plans, elevations, section, details); 8 data pages (1966, 1972).

McGill Institute (Daniel Chandler House, Maybrick House) (AL-77), 252 Government St. (between Jackson and Joachim sts.). Brick with rusticated façade, 7-bay front including projecting (3-bay) W pavilion, 3 stories, flat roof, full-length giant-order colonnade of Roman Doric order (advanced to front of W pavilion), cast-iron balconies, pedimented windows at second-floor level, main doorway of W pavilion has battered architrave; cast-iron Greek Revival style fence with masonry piers capped by urns. W pavilion built ca. 1850 as private residence for Chandler, an attorney; originally rectangular (3-bay front) with full-height tetrastyle Greek Doric portico, approx. 35′ × 50′ plus long 2-story ell with 2-tiered wooden galleries; side-hall plan. Extensively altered and enlarged to later appearance after 1896, when it became McGill Institute, including set-back E addition and rebuilding of portico after Roman Doric order (rear ell also razed and replaced by large 2-story structure); demolished 1953. Polish patriot Louis Kossuth entertained in original Chandler House in 1856. McGill Institute founded through endowment of Arthur McGill for free education of "Catholic young men" of Mobile. ½ sheet of ironwork detail only filed as AL-7D (1934); 2 ext. photos (1934–36). See also FBJ (J7-ALA-1327).

McGowin-Creary House (AL-852), 1151 Government St. (SW corner Government and Roper sts.). Ashlar, rectangular (5-bay front) with slightly advanced pedimented pavilion on E side, rounded bay on W, 2 stories, hipped roof with deck breaking into pediment above central bay of façade and side pavilions, modillioned cornice, 1-story semicircular Ionic entrance porch with flanking bays surmounted by balustraded deck, recessed central loggia at upper level, triangular pediments with scrolled relief carving above second-story windows, porte cochère with balustraded deck on E side, 1-story porch on W; center-hall plan, notable woodwork and paneling throughout. Built 1904 for J. F. McGowin, lumber magnate. 9 ext. photos (1974), 7 int. photos (1974).

McKeon House. See Azalea Grove (AL-54), 55 S. McGregor Ave.

McMahon, J. J., House. See Miguel Eslava, Jr., House (AL-21A), 456 St. Francis St.

McMillan House. See Charles G. Richards House (AL-810), 256 N. Joachim St.

Macy-Adams House (AL-813), 1569 Dauphin St. Frame (board and batten), 38′6″ (3-bay front) × 35′2″, 1½ stories, shallow jerkinhead roof with subordinate cross-gable above middle bay of façade, 2 interior chimneys, 3-bay porch with chamfered posts and connecting cusped trelliage (repeated in side stoop), scalloped bargeboards beneath eaves, lozenge window in each gable end, hood molds above second-story end windows; center-hall plan, dining room walls have unusual rounded corners. Built 1867–68 for Robert C. Macy, auctioneer and commission merchant; possibly adapted from Plate 16 ("A Bracketed Farm-House of Wood") in A. J. Downing's *Architecture of Country Houses*. Rear porch enclosed ca. 1940, minor interior changes. Unusual occurrence in Mobile of Carpenter Gothic style. 2 ext. photos (1963), 2 int. photos (1963); 1 data page (1963).

Magnolia Cemetery Ironwork (AL-7-JP), N side Virginia St. between Ann and Gayle sts. Examples of wrought-iron and cast-iron fences enclosing private burial plots. Stylistic themes represented include Greek and Gothic Revival motifs, as well as specifically funerary motifs such as the weeping willow. Ironwork ranges in date from ca. 1835 to ca. 1900. Plots include those of Judge Henry Hitchcock (1795–1839) and early Mobile builder B. F. Scattergood, as well as those of Gazzam, Tarleton, Battle, and other eminent families. Magnolia Cemetery established as municipal burial ground in 1827. 37 photos originally filed as AL-7, AL-8, AL-9 series (1936, part of general ironwork survey). *See also* Pomeroy Family Tomb (AL-785), Hope H. Slatter Family Tomb (AL-860), and Church Street Graveyard Ironwork (AL-845).

Magnolia Cotton Warehouse (Cotton Warehouse) (AL-74), NE corner Lipscomb and Magnolia sts. (extending along Magnolia St. to Beauregard St.). Brick, approx. 215′ x 300′ overall, 2 parallel rectangular buildings (approx. 50′ x 300′) with large court between enclosed at each end by high brick wall pierced by arched gateways to Lipscomb and Beauregard sts.; each building has gabled roof with stepped parapets at either end, star-shaped iron tie-rods. Built 1866 for M. H. Bloodgood to replace 1854 cotton warehouse destroyed in explosion of nearby ordnance depot on 25 May 1865; modified ca. 1965, including replacement of arched doorways by square-headed sliding doors. Lone survivor of once-numerous waterfront cotton warehouses. 3 ext. photos (1937).

Marine Hospital. *See* U.S. Marine Hospital (AL-781), 800 St. Anthony St.

Marshall-Eslava House (Celestine Eslava House) (AL-6), 152 Tuthill Ln., N of Old Shell Rd. (Spring Hill). Frame with clapboarding (gallery plastered), T-shaped with rectangular (5-bay) front and flanking 2-bay wings, 1 story on raised basement, shallow hipped roof with half-hip over wings, full-length balustraded gallery with 6 fluted Doric columns, similar 2-bay galleries fronting each wing, Doric loggia in rear; Ionic order main doorway; center-hall plan with folding louvered doors between front and rear hallway area, Greek Revival style woodwork. Notable grounds with circular drive and formal gardens. Built 1853 for Benjamin F. Marshall, cotton factor from South Carolina, on site of 1828 wooden church. 8 sheets (1935–36, including site plan, plans, elevations, sections, details); 11 ext. photos including fountain and cast-iron fence (1935), 5 int. photos (1935); 2 data pages (1936).

Marx, Isaac, House (Tuthill House) (AL-778), originally at 113 Church St. (SE corner Church and St. Emanuel sts.); reconstructed on campus of University of South Alabama at 307 University Blvd. Brick 29′1″ (3-bay front) x 47′0″ with lateral offset (14′5″ x 20′8″) and semidetached rear wing parallel to St. Emanuel St. and at obtuse angle with main block, 2 stories, shallow hipped roof with cast-iron brackets and paneled soffits, 2-tiered cast-iron gallery, 2-tiered wooden gallery at rear partially enclosed by jalousies; side-hall plan, notable interior plasterwork, segmental arch between parlors. Cast-iron fence. Built ca. 1870; dismantled 1968 to make way for I-10 and rebuilt with modifications at new location; wing and second floor adapted for classroom use. 5 sheets (1966, including site plan, plans, elevations, section); 7 data pages (1972).

Mastin, Dr. Claude, House. *See* Phillippi-Mastin House (AL-816), 53 N. Jackson St.

Maybrick House. *See* McGill Institute (AL-77), 252 Government St.

Middleton-Boulo House (AL-42), 13 N. Cedar St. (NE corner Cedar and St. Francis sts.). Frame with clapboarding (matched boarding on gallery), rectangular (5-bay front), 1½ stories, gable roof extending over full-length gallery, 4 interior end chimneys, bracketed cornice, floor-length windows, ornate front door with raised panels; center-hall plan. Reputedly built ca. 1855 for Louis Middleton; demolished. 3 ext. photos (1935); 1 data page (1936).

Miller-O'Donnell House (AL-814), 1102 S. Broad St. Raised cottage, frame with clapboarding on high brick basement, 48′6″ (5-bay front) x 30′3″, 1½ stories over full ground floor, gable roof, 4 interior end chimneys, central pedimented gallery with wooden balustrade on high brick piers, lunette in tympanum; center-hall plan. Built 1837 for James P. Miller as country residence on what was then Dog River Rd. Present roof with splayed eaves probably early 20th C.; modern concrete steps to porch. 2 ext. photos (1963); 1 data page (1963).

Mobile City Hall. *See* City Hall and Southern Market (AL-5), 111 S. Royal St.

Mobile City Hospital. *See* City Hospital (AL-13), 850 St. Anthony St.

Mobile and Ohio Railroad Office Building (AL-794), 409 N. Royal St. Brick with stucco deeply scored to simulate ashlar, 54′8″ (8-bay front) × 84′6″ including later addition, 3 stories, roof composed of shallow parallel gables concealed by parapet surmounting cornice, arcuated ground floor on E front with slender fluted cast-iron colonnettes (originally full-length cast-iron balcony above); central hall flanked by interconnecting irregularly sized rooms. Built 1860. Extensively remodeled ca. 1907 (brick walls stuccoed, E front altered); demolished 1968. 1 sheet (1966, tracing of floor plans drawn 1916 by Charles Hays, architect); 2 ext. photos (1966), 2 int. photos (1966); 8 data pages (1966–72).

Mohr, Dr. Charles H., House. *See* Bush-Mohr House (AL-9J), 254 St. Anthony St.

Moreland House. *See* Robert S. Bunker House (AL-802), 157 Monroe St. (reconstructed at 201 S. Warren St.).

Mounting Block, Government St. *See* Street Furnishings (AL-36).

Noble, Annie B., House. *See* Bunker-DuMont House (AL-28), 157 Church St.

Number 5 Fire Station. *See* Washington Fire Engine Company No. 8 (AL-2), 7 N. Lawrence St.

Oakleigh (Denniston House) (AL-47), 350 Oakleigh Pl. House museum. Elaboration of raised-cottage style, frame with clapboarding on stuccoed brick basement, T-shaped (overall dimensions 66′3″ × 69′9″) with projecting 3-bay front and identical flanking 2-bay wings, 1 story over full ground floor, central gable (half-hips over wing) breaking into raised prostyle pedimented portico of modified classic design with square wooden piers and unsupported semispiral wooden stairway from ground level to main floor, wings also galleried; side-hall plan, Greek Revival style woodwork, jib windows. Built ca. 1833–38 for merchant James W. Roper (1801–56), born in South Carolina, who was reputedly his own architect. Damaged by fire and modified ca. 1840; minor exterior and interior alterations late 19th and early 20th C. Restored 1955 by City of Mobile as house museum. 12 sheets (1935, including site plan, plans, elevations, section, details); 9 ext. photos (1934–35), 5 ext. photos (1963), 8 int. photos (1935), 4 int. photos (1963); 2 data pages (1936). NR.

Dependency (slave quarters), SW rear. Frame with clapboarding, irregular rectangle, 50′4″ (7-bay front) × 18′3″ overall, 1 story, gable roof cantilevered over front as protective overhang. Built mid-19th C. 1 sheet (1935, plans, elevations, section); 1 ext. photo (1935).

Odd Fellows Hall (Second American Theater) (AL-16), 17 S. Royal St. (E side Royal between Conti and Dauphin sts.). Brick with stucco, approx. 78′ (5-bay front) × 110′, 3 stories, flat roof, street façade composed of slightly projecting 3-bay center section with 4 fluted Corinthian pilasters flanked by corner antae, denticulated cornice surmounted by low brick parapet; shops and Odd Fellows meeting rooms occupying ground floor, theater with gallery on upper 2 floors, frescoed ceiling, monumental stairway at rear. Built ca. 1850; interior altered and exterior modified in late 19th C. when it became Adam Glass Furniture Warerooms. Severe additional alterations during 1950s, including removal of cornice and Corinthian pilasters, fenestrational changes; demolished 1978. 1 ext. photo (1934).

Old City Hospital. *See* City Hospital (AL-13), 850 St. Anthony St.

Old Mobile Cemetery, Ironwork. *See* Church Street Cemetery Ironwork (AL-845).

Old Southern Hotel. *See* Gulf City Hotel (AL-11), 53–65 Water St.

Otis-Allen House (AL-854), 1050 Palmetto St. Frame with clapboarding, rectangular (5-bay front) with ell, 1 story, hipped roof extending over full-length front gallery carried on slender square supports, 2 pairs of transomed French doors flanking central entry topped by segmentally arched transom, pier foundation enclosed with latticework; center-hall plan. Built ca. 1897. 3 ext. photos (1974).

Ottenstein House. *See* Thomas S. James Double House (AL-27), 207, 209 N. Jackson St.

Palmetto Hall. *See* Azalea Grove (AL-54), 55 S. McGregor Ave. (Spring Hill).

Parmly Houses (AL-815), 303, 305, 307 N. Conception St. Two dwellings (including 1 double house) built for Dr. Ludolph Parmly in mid-19th C.

Nos. 303, 305 (double house). Brick, rectangular (6-bay front composed of 2 3-bay units), 2½ stories, gable roof with dormers, brick dentil course, both units probably identical as originally constructed. No. 303 (S unit) has small central wrought-iron balcony at second floor; no. 305 (N unit) has 2-tiered cast-iron gallery; side-hall plan in each unit; twin dependencies formerly in rear; built 1842; later modifications and rear additions, including addition of gallery to no. 305; interior damaged by fire 1973.

No. 307 (single-family dwelling). Brick, 29'5" (4-bay front) × 79'0" including long ell, 3 stories (ell 2 stories), gable roof, double end chimneys with curtain wall, brick dentil course, recessed doorway with battered jambs and slightly pedimented architrave, side passage to rear, balconies formerly at second- and third-floor levels; side-hall plan, continuous 3-flight stairway with skylight. Cast-iron fence. Built 1852 as Parmly residence; interior damaged by neglect.

No. 303 restored 1964; nos. 305 and 307 restored 1977–78. Parmly, born in Vermont, was prominent antebellum dentist of Mobile. ½ sheet filed under AL-7A (1934, balcony detail of no. 303 only); 1 ext. photo originally filed as AL-7A (1934, ironwork of no. 303), 4 ext. photos (1963, including 2 general views, detail of no. 303, ell of no. 307), 2 int. photos (1963, including Eastlake style mantelpiece in no. 305, stairway of no. 307); 1 data page (1963).

Perdue House. *See* Carolina Hall (AL-10), 76 S. McGregor Ave.

Phillippi-Mastin House (Dr. Claude Mastin House, Antoine Pinto House) (AL-816), 53 N. Jackson St. Brick, rectangular (4-bay front) with ell, 2 stories, gable roof, brick dentil course, 2-tiered cast-iron gallery extending over sidewalk, carriage entrance at left (S) side with late-19th-C. cantilevered semioctagonal bay above, recessed doorway with battered jambs; side-hall plan. Built ca. 1850 for Antonio Phillippi; later modifications include conversion of carriageway to garage. 2 ext. photos (1963); 1 data page (1963).

Phoenix Fire Company No. 6 (AL-7Z), originally at 154 S. Franklin St.; reconstructed at 203 S. Claiborne St. Museum. Brick with ashlar trim, approx. 35'6" (3-bay front) × 45'6" with slightly projecting center bay and offset rear stable wing, 2 stories, shallow hipped roof surmounted by octagonal cupola, bracketed cornice, quoined corners, 3 large engine doors, full-length cantilevered balcony above enclosed by wrought-iron balustrade; open plan. Built 1859 for volunteer fire company organized in 1838. Dismantled early 1960s to make way for municipal complex and rebuilt minus stable wing at new location; opened as Phoenix Fire Station Museum on 9 Oct. 1964, with dedication by Mrs. Lyndon B. Johnson. Good example of structure which served both utilitarian and social function in 19th-C. life of Mobile. 2 ext. photos (1936, façade only).

Pinto, Antoine, House. *See* Phillippi-Mastin House (AL-816), 53 N. Jackson St.

Planters and Merchants Insurance Company (AL-777), 60 St. Michael St. Brick (façade faced with limestone), 21'0" × 64'5", 2 narrow bays flanking wider central bay, first floor of façade centers on Romanesque arch embellished with engaged columns and bas-relief carving, cast-iron balcony above flanked by floor-length casements with grilles, decorative parapet with sculptured shield bearing construction date and stylized cotton bale; open plan (originally), paneled wainscoting, glazed skylight. Built 1896; Rudolph Benz, architect; demolished 1968. Good example of commercial work of German-born architect active in Mobile during late 19th C. 4 sheets (1966, including site plan, plans, elevation, section, details); 6 data pages (1966).

Pollock Building (Commercial Building) (AL-48), 51 S. Royal St. (SE corner Royal and Conti sts.). Brick with stucco, approx. 95' × 85', 3 stories, flat roof concealed by parapet above cornice-line, post-and-lintel first story (fluted Doric columns between each bay, terminated at corners by masonry piers), cast-iron window grilles at second-story level, simulated quoining. Built 1859–60 for Richard Lee Fearn. Later known as Pollock Building; apparently remodeled ca. 1900; south end of building used as Mobile Theater (gutted by fire 1913); demolished. 4 ext. photos (1936, partial elevation only); 2 data pages (1937).

Pomeroy, P. B., Family Tomb (AL-785), Magnolia Cemetery (Lots 72 and 89, Square 5, N side Virginia St. between Ann and Gayle sts.). Mausoleum, brick faced with cast-iron on raised granite base, rectangular (7'6" × 10'3" above marble foundation, 7'10" from grade to cornice), slightly battered walls, single entrance bay to burial vault, surface treatment simulates rustication, with vermiculated quoins framing inset panels, full entablature with frieze bearing bas-relief representations of classical funerary motifs including burial urn and griffins, cornice surmounted by highly ornate parapet; door to vault has bas-relief representation of inverted torch, inscription above doorway. Erected ca. 1860 for Porter B. Pomeroy, Mobile feed merchant; cast-iron plate possibly from foundry of Robert Wood & Co., Philadelphia. One of 2 nearly identical tombs in cemetery; see also Hope H. Slatter Family Tomb (AL-860). Outstanding example of use of cast-iron elements in funerary architecture. 4 sheets (1966, including plot plans, plans, elevations, details); 2 photos (1974); 4 data pages (1966, 1972). *See also* Magnolia Cemetery Ironwork (AL-844) and Church Street Graveyard Ironwork (AL-845).

Portier, Bishop Michael, House (AL-37), 307 Conti St. Frame with clapboarding (gallery plastered), 46'4" (5-bay front) × 57'6", 1½ stories, gable roof extending over full-length galleries front and rear, 2 interior chimneys, ornate dormers (segmentally arched pediments, denticulated cornice, engaged Tuscan-order colonnettes), balustraded gallery with slender Tuscan style colonnettes, main doorway framed by full Tuscan-order architrave, leaded sidelights and transom; center-hall plan, notable Federal period interior woodwork, curved stair with unusual arrow-shaped balusters, rare use in Alabama of casement windows. Stuccoed brick underground cistern in back yard. Built or remodeled into present form ca. 1834 for Portier (1795–1859), first bishop of Roman Catholic Diocese of Mobile; French-born Claude Beroujon, architect; restored 1958. Best surviving example in city of Creole cottage with Federal period detail. Home during 1870s of Fr. Abram J. Ryan, "Poet-Priest of the Confederacy." 9 sheets (1934–35, including site plan, elevations, plans, section, details); 5 ext. photos (1935), 4 ext. photos (1963), 12 int. photos (1935), 3 int. photos (1963); 3 data pages (1936). NR.

Kitchen and Servants' Quarters. Brick 64'9" (6 irregular bays) × 21'9", 2 stories, shed roof with stepped parapet, 2-tiered wooden gallery with exterior stair. Antebellum, demolished ca. 1950. 1 sheet (1934–35, including site plan, elevations, plans, section, details); 2 ext. photos (1935).

Cistern. Stuccoed brick, circular structure. Antebellum; filled 1930s. 1 ext. photo (1935).

See also FBJ (J7-ALA-1334 through 1336).

Private School. *See* Ayers House (AL-49), 57 S. Hamilton St.

Protestant Orphans' Asylum (AL-33), 911 Dauphin St. Brick, approx. 49'6" (5-bay front) × 50'5" with long offset rear wing (approx. 25'6" × 88'10"), 2 stories above full ground floor, low hipped roof, 4 interior end chimneys (main block), brick dentil course, cast-iron balustraded gallery with canopy roof at first-floor level resting on slender fluted cast-iron posts, similar L-shaped 2-tiered cast-iron gallery at rear (partially enclosed); center-hall plan. Cornerstone laid 4 July 1845; Henry Moffat of Philadelphia, architect. Minor alterations late 19th C.; rear portion altered 1924, further renovation 1950. Erected for Protestant Orphans' Asylum Society chartered in wake of 1839 yellow fever epidemic. 3 ext. photos (1934–35), 2 int. photos (1935); 2 data pages (1936). NR.

Quigley, Albert, House. *See* Gilmore-Gaines-Quigley House (AL-9C), 751 Government St.

Quigley Twin House (AL-9D), 258 Congress St. Brick, 29'0" (3-bay front) × 80' including ell, 2 stories, low gable roof, double end chimneys with curtain wall, 2-tiered cast-iron gallery, recessed doorway with battered jambs and slightly pedimented architrave, stucco lintels; side-hall plan. Built 1856 for A. M. and S. B. Quigley as 1 of 2 identical residences (second house at 260 Congress St. not included in HABS survey). Post–World War II frame 2-story rear addition; extensive interior alterations for apartment use. 1 ext. photo (1936).

Randlette House. *See* Goelet-Randlette-Beck House (AL-855), 1005 Augusta St.

Ravesies, Frederick P., House. *See* Church Street Block Study (AL-803).

Redwood, Richard H., House (AL-9T), 260 St. Louis St. (NE corner St. Louis and N. Jackson sts.). Brick with granite trim, rectangular (5-bay front), 2½ stories, flat roof, notable 2-tiered 4-bay cast-iron gallery (Tudoresque arches resting on slender coupled colonnettes, open tracery in spandrels), denticulated cornice, recessed entrance with Greek Revival style architrave; center-hall plan. Cast-iron fence. Built ca. 1860. Sash windows replaced by casements early 20th C.; demolished. Redwood was a local builder and the chief contractor for construction of City Hall and Southern Market (AL-5) in 1856–57. 1 ext. photo (1936).

Reingard Double House. *See* Double House (AL-25), 8–10 N. Jackson St.

Revault-Maupin-Shawhan House (Mrs. Narcissa M. Shawhan House) (AL-9G), 254 N. Conception St. Brick, 25'0" (3-bay front) × 96'0" including rear ell, 2 stories, shallow hipped roof, brick dentil course, cast-iron gallery with deck, wooden gallery in rear; side-hall plan, double parlors. Built 1856 for Alexander Revault, commission merchant and cotton factor. Later home of Narcissa Tayloe Maupin, well-known parliamentarian. Very similar to Charles K. Foote House (AL-9H), at 255 N. Conception St., built same year. 1 ext. photo (1936). *See also* FBJ (J7-ALA-1338).

Richards, Charles G., House (Richard McMillan House, Iron Lace) (AL-810), 256 N. Joachim St. House museum. Brick, main block rectangular (3-bay front) with rear offsets terminating in semioctagonal bays, shallow hipped roof, bracketed cornice with paneled soffit, elaborate cast-iron gallery and deck with marble and granite floor and ironwork incorporating allegorical figures of the Four Seasons motif, floor-length windows; side-hall plan, curved stairway, marble mantels, ornamental plasterwork, original bronze chandeliers, etched glass in sidelights and transom; notable cast-iron fence. Built 1860; renovated 1947 for office use; opened as municipally owned museum in 1972. One of Mobile's best preserved and most elaborate examples of mid-19th-C. urban domestic architecture. 5 ext. photos originally filed as AL-9B (1936, ironwork only), 4 ext. photos (1963), 2 int. photos (1963); 1 data page (1963). *See also* FBJ (J7-ALA-1328 through 1331); Tebbs (T3-ALA-434085 and 434086).

Rider House (Conti House, Jordon House) (AL-38), 303 Conti St. Brick, 24'4" (3-bay front) × 35'4" plus ell, 2 stories, gable roof, double end chimneys with curtain wall, brick dentil course, tall French windows opening onto full-length iron-railed second-floor balcony; side-hall plan. Supposedly built for English-born Mrs. Elizabeth Rider in 1843. Originally raised house with high wooden stoop; renovated, with addition of balcony, in mid-19th C. 8 sheets (1935, including site plan, elevations, plans, section, details); 1 ext. photo originally filed as AL-21C (1934, balcony only), 2 ext. photos (1934–36), 5 int. photos (1935); 2 data pages (1936).

Dependency. Brick, 53'7" (7-bay first floor, 6-bay second floor), 2 stories, shed roof with parapet, 2-tiered wooden gallery with exterior stair; 3 end-to-end rooms. Referred to as "slave quarters" although may have contained dining room and extra sleeping rooms, as well as kitchen and service areas. Partially collapsed in 1935. 2 sheets (1935, including plans, elevation).

Dependency razed in 1948; house, in 1952. *See also* FBJ (J7-ALA-1310 and 1311).

Riley, James, House. *See* House (AL-50), 8 N. Hamilton St.

Riley, Tom, House. *See* House (AL-9Q), 256 N. Jackson St.

Robert, Madame Paul, House. *See* Ayers House (AL-49), 57 Hamilton St.

Roberts, James F., Houses. *See* Robinson Twin Houses (AL-807), 157, 159 N. Conception St.

Robinson Twin Houses (Clarke House, Hannah Houses, James F. Roberts Houses) (AL-807), 157, 159 N. Conception St. (SW corner St. Anthony St.). Brick, 2 freestanding units, approx. 28' (3 bays each) × 48' with connecting central rear wing (approx. 32' × 23'), 3 stories, gable roof, double end chimneys with curtain wall, brick dentil course, cast-iron galleries with deck; side-hall plan, egg-and-dart plaster molding, chandelier medallions. Cast-iron fence. Built 1852–53 for Cornelius Robinson, commission merchant. Kitchen possibly as early as 1834; cast-iron gallery added ca. 1900 to no. 159; both structures renovated (including addition of identical cast-iron gallery to no. 157) and joined at rear for single office use in 1963. Rare example of twin house construction. 1 ext. photo (1934), 2 ext. photos (1963), 1 int. photo (1963); 1 data page (1963).

Ross, William H., House. *See* Battle-Ross House (AL-9V), 602 Government St.

St. Michael Street Stores. *See* Commercial Buildings: St. Michael Street (AL-64 series).

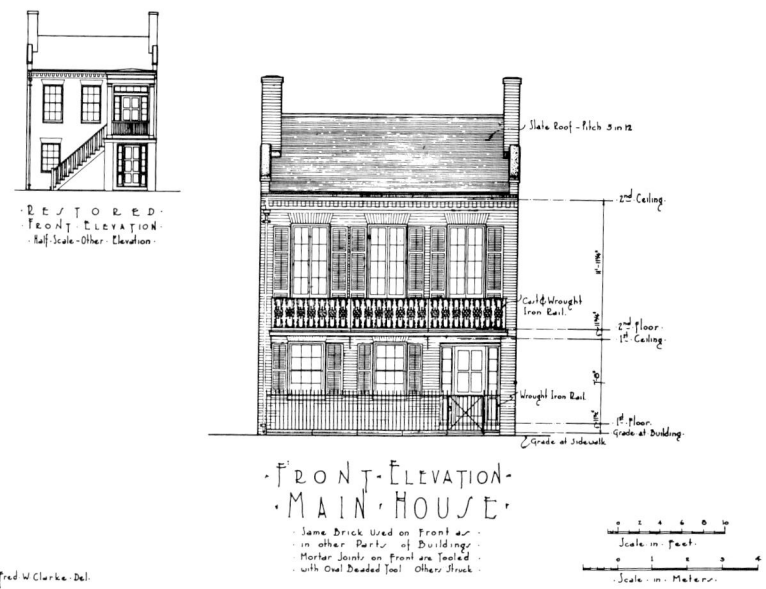

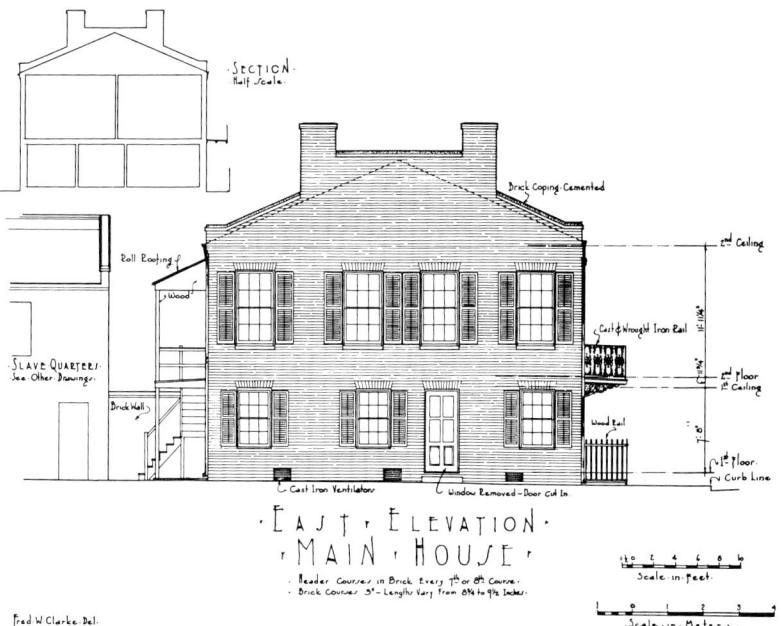

Elizabeth Rider (Conti) House, Mobile (1843 with later alterations, demolished 1952).

cornice with brick dentil course (dogtooth cornice in rear), cast-iron second-floor balcony with floor-length jib windows; interior divided into 3 units of 3 bays each. Built ca. 1835, probably for Thaddeus Sanford (1790–1867), businessman born in Connecticut and owner-editor of *Mobile Register*; cast-iron balcony later; demolished. Unusual triple-unit variant of conventional Mobile double house. 7 ext. photos (1936), 11 int. photos (1935–36); 2 data pages (1936).

Servants' Quarters, connected to dwelling by brick wall along Hamilton St. Brick, rectangular (5-bay front), 2 stories, gable roof, central open passage containing privy and stair to upper floor, corner fireplace. Contemporary with house; demolished. 4 ext. photos (1936), 8 int. photos (1936).

Sanford-Thompson House (AL-817), 1621 Spring Hill Ave. Frame with clapboarding raised on brick piers with latticework between, irregular rectangle (5-bay front) with extensive lateral wings and rear ell, 1½ stories, gable roof with dormers, broad balustraded gallery across front and along either side, slender turned colonnettes with modified Doric entablature, floor-length windows, "welcoming arms" stairway; center-hall plan. Situated in extensive live oak grove. Built ca. 1855 for James Sanford; extensively remodeled in 1920s by Mobile architect George B. Rogers; demolished 1965. One-time home of Frederick Ingate Thompson, editor of *Mobile Register*. 5 ext. photos (1963); 1 data page (1963).

Sanford-Staylor House (William Staylor House, John Craft House) (AL-22), 451, 453 St. Francis St. (SW corner St. Francis and Hamilton sts.). Brick, rectangular (9-bay front), 2½ stories, gable roof, double end chimneys with curtain wall (also 2 interior chimneys), corbeled

Schieffelin-Sledge House (Sledge House) (AL-72), 52, 54 S. Jackson

St. Brick, rectangular (3-bay front), 2½ stories, gable roof, double end chimneys with curtain wall, 2-tiered cast-iron gallery, 2-tiered wooden gallery at rear, recessed doorway; side-hall plan. Cast-iron fence with carriage gate. Built ca. 1848 for New York–born George Schieffelin of firm of Schieffelin and Crozier, Sailmakers; cast-iron gallery added later; demolished. 7 ext. photos (1937, including cast-iron details). *See also* FBJ (J7-ALA-1339).

Schley-Rutherford House (AL-857), 1263 Selma St. (SE corner Selma and S. Ann sts.). Frame with clapboarding, basically rectangular (3 irregularly spaced bays), 2½ stories, pyramidal roof with large central dormer, denticulated cornice, continuous gallery with fluted Ionic colonnettes and denticulated cornice across front and along E and W sides, balustraded deck at second-story level, neoclassical doorway with beveled glass sidelights and transom framed by Ionic pilasters, 1 original mantelpiece. Built 1905; interior renovated ca. 1945 in Early American style. 5 ext. photos (1974), 3 int. photos (1974).

Seamen's Bethel (AL-779), originally at 75 Church St. (between Water and Royal sts.); reconstructed on campus of University of South Alabama, 307 University Blvd. Brick, 40'0" (3-bay front) × 60'0", 1 story, low gable roof, bracketed cornice, slightly projecting central bay with pointed-arch doorway and rose window above; flanking 2-part pointed windows, wooden belfry originally; single aisle plan with pulpit platform at front. Built 1860 as chapel and meeting hall for trustees of the adjoining Seamen's Home, a philanthropic organization chartered by state legislature in 1845 to care for spiritual and physical welfare of Protestant mariners. Brick addition in 1901 to E; 1909 extensively altered (including removal of belfry, installation of windows flanking doorway and at rear of pulpit platform); 1923 sold to Little Theatre of Mobile; dismantled 1968 and reconstructed at new location. 5 sheets (1966, including site plan, plans, elevations, section, roof structure); 5 data pages (1966, 1972).

Second American Theatre. *See* Odd Fellows Hall (AL-16), 17 S. Royal St.

Semmes, Admiral Raphael, House. *See* Horta-Semmes House (AL-56), 802 Government St.

Semmes, Judge Oliver J., House. *See* Hazard-Semmes House (AL-57), 2828 Dauphin Way.

Sewall, Judge Kiah B., House. *See* Briarwood (AL-69), Dauphin Way and Mobile sts.

Shawhan, Mrs. Narcissa M., House. *See* Revault-Maupin-Shawhan House (AL-9G), 254 N. Conception St.

Shippers' Exchange Saloon (AL-789), 50 S. Commerce St. (SW corner Commerce and Conti sts.). Brick, approx. 20'0" × 50'2" with truncated NW and NE corners, 2 stories, cast-iron entablature with bracketed and denticulated cornice topped by paneled parapet, arcuated corner entrances, 3-bay façade (E elevation) with engaged cast-iron Corinthian colonnettes, plaster voussoirs, fluted keystones, heavily paneled doors; open interior plan, enclosed stairway, skylight above second-floor hallway. Built ca. 1902 for Mobile saloon-keeper Timothy Crowley. Closed during Prohibition and subsequently passed through various hands; demolished 1967 for Water Street Urban Renewal Project. Good example of ca. 1900 commercial architecture. 1 ext. photo (1935, detail only), 3 ext. photos (1966), 2 int. photos (1966); 5 data pages (1966, 1972).

Shops. *See* Commercial Buildings (under specific locations).

Silver-Ketchum House (Dr. George A. Ketchum House) (AL-798), 257 St. Francis St. E half of original double house; brick, 26'11" (3-bay front) × 39'3" excluding demolished rear wing, 2½ stories over raised basement, gable roof, double end chimneys with curtain wall, brick dentil course, originally 2-tiered raised wooden galleries along front (N) and both sides connecting to rear galleries; side-hall plan, double parlors, Greek Revival interior trim. Built 1845 by architect Joseph Silver, born in Maryland, for speculative purposes. Wooden galleries removed late 19th C.; raised cast-iron gallery with deck added to E half; W half obscured by modern front addition; interior alterations. Residence 1852–69 of Ketchum, a prominent Mobile physician. 4 ext. photos (1966), 4 int. photos (1966); 8 data pages (1966, 1972).

Slatter, Hope H., Family Tomb (AL-860), Magnolia Cemetery (Lots 28 and 61, Square 15), N side Virginia St. between Ann and Gayle sts. Mausoleum, brick faced with cast-iron on raised granite base, rectangular with slightly battered walls, single entrance bay to burial vault, surface treatment simulates rustication with vermiculated quoins framing inset panels, full entablature with frieze bearing bas-relief representations of classical funerary motifs including burial urn and griffins, cornice surmounted by highly ornate parapet, door to vault has bas-relief representation of inverted torch. Lot surrounded by cast-iron fence swung between tall paneled piers; fence design consists of series of cusped lancet arches above continuous row of quatrefoil, ogee-arched gateway with crockets and finials. Tomb and fence erected ca. 1860 for cotton factor Hope Hull Slatter; cast-iron plate from foundry of Robert Wood & Co., Philadelphia. One of 2 nearly identical tombs in Magnolia Cemetery (see also Pomeroy Family Tomb, AL-785). Outstanding example of use of cast-iron in funerary architecture. 1 photo originally filed as AL-9CA4 (1934, cast-iron fence only), 7 photos (1974). *See also* Magnolia Cemetery Ironwork (AL-844) and Church Street Cemetery Ironwork (AL-845).

Sledge House. *See* Schieffelin-Sledge House (AL-72), 52, 54 S. Jackson St.

Smith, Sidney, House (AL-9BA8), 203 Government St. Brick with stucco scored to simulate ashlar, rectangular (5-bay front), 2 stories, bracketed cornice, 3-bay cast-iron gallery with deck, recessed entrance, molded architraves framing doors and windows. Cast-iron fence. Built ca. 1860; demolished. 1 ext. photo (1936, portion of façade only).

Smith-Clarke House (Clarke House, House) (AL-15), 161 St. Anthony St. (SE corner St. Anthony and N. Conception sts.). Brick, square (5-bay front) with long ell, 2 stories, roof concealed by paneled brick parapet, brick dentil course, 3-bay cast-iron gallery with deck, notable Greek Revival doorway with eared and battered architrave framing inset Ionic colonnettes (possibly adapted from Minard Lafever), jalousied 2-tiered L-shaped wooden gallery at rear; center-hall plan, spiral stairway with statuary niches, paneled overdoors, marble mantels. Built 1853 for William A. Smith; demolished. ½ sheet originally filed as AL-8E (1934, cast-iron detail only); 5 ext. photos (1934–35), 3 int. photos (1935); 1 data page (1936).

Southern Hotel. *See* Gulf City Hotel (AL-11), 53–65 Water St.

Southern Market. *See* City Hall and Southern Market (AL-5), 111 S. Royal St.

Spanish Dwelling. *See* House (AL-21D), 109 St. Anthony St.

Spring Hill College (AL-34), 4307 Old Shell Rd. at end of College Ln. (Spring Hill). Four buildings: Old Main Building (destroyed), Main Building (now Administration Building), Infirmary, and Sodality Chapel, ranging in date from 1830 to 1869. Founded in 1830 as Roman Catholic seminary by the Rev. Michael Portier, Spring Hill College is Alabama's oldest institution of higher learning. 6 general data pages (1936). NR.
Old Main Building. Brick, rectangular (29-bay front) with pilastered 4-bay advanced end pavilions, 4 stories, shallow hipped roof with parapet, full-height octastyle Tuscan portico with projecting 3-bay pedimented center section, wooden galleries at upper levels and flanking covered walkways with balustraded deck, square 2-stage belfry with clock. Erected ca. 1830–31; Claude Beroujon, builder-architect; enlarged mid-19th C.; burned 4 Feb. 1869. 1 ext. photocopy of ground plan (1839), 1 ext. photocopy (n.d.), 1 ext. photocopy (1869, ruins only).
Main Building (Administration Building). Brick, approx. 381′6″ (25-bay front) × 67′6″ with advanced 3-bay center and end pavilions, gable roof with cross-gable over each pavilion, 2-stage octagonal belfry with cupola and cross, center pavilion arcaded at first-floor level, S front originally had 2-tiered gallery with cast-iron balustrade and deck; center-hall plan with cross hall, galleried and domed rotunda at second- and third-floor levels. Built April–Dec. 1869; James Freret of New Orleans, architect. Original cupola destroyed by 1906 hurricane; reinforced concrete galleries and iron-pillared arcades replaced 2-tiered frame galleries on S front (1909), also single-story concrete parapeted gallery added to N elevation facing inner courtyard. 5 sheets (1935–36, including plans, elevations, sections); 2 ext. photocopies (ca. 1900), 25 ext. photos (1934–36), 14 int. photos (1936).
Infirmary. Brick, rectangular (3 bays wide, 10 bays long), 2 stories, hipped roof with brick dentil course. Built 1866; later interior modifications; used as offices in 1970s. 1 ext. photo (1935).

Sodality Chapel. Frame with clapboarding, rectangular (1 bay wide, 3 bays long), gable roof, central doorway with semicircular transom. Built ca. 1850; oldest extant building on campus. 1 ext. photo (1935).
See also Tebbs (T3-ALA-434077 through 434079).

Staples House. *See* Calef-Staples House (AL-51), 1614 Old Shell Rd.

Staylor, William, House. *See* Sanford-Staylor House (AL-22), 451, 453 St. Francis St.

Store Buildings. *See* Commercial Buildings (under specific locations).

Street Furnishings (Carriage Block, Hitching Posts, Lampposts, Street Lamps) (AL-36 series). Includes 19th-C. mounting block or carriage mount, examples of iron hitching posts, and lampposts formerly found throughout older sectors of Mobile.
Carriage Block (AL-36A), SE corner Lawrence and Government sts. Ashlar, rectangular (approx. 3′ high) with flight of 5 steps to mounting platform edged with coping terminated in sculpted allegorical figureheads; base embellished with bas-relief tendril motif. Probably erected ca. 1860 in conjunction with Wheeler residence. Later residence of Col. E. L. Russell, president of the Mobile and Ohio Railroad; destroyed ca. 1955. 1 photo (1934).
Hitching Posts (AL-37B). Examples of iron hitching posts found throughout 19th-C. Mobile. Includes simple rounded wrought-iron shafts with attached hitching rings of early 1800s (especially in commercial district on water-

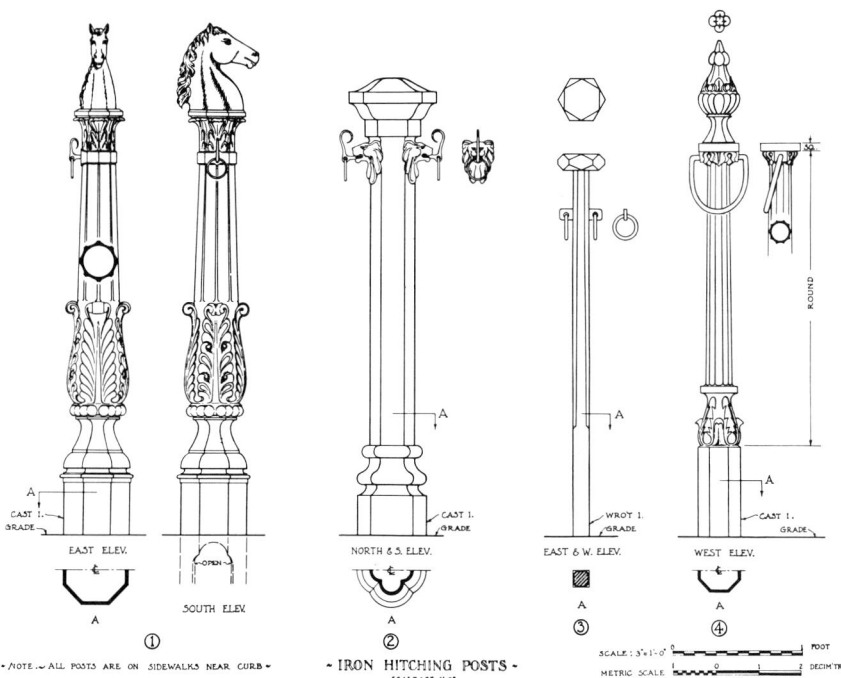

Iron hitching posts, Mobile (19th century, destroyed).

front) and elaborate mid-to-late 19th-C. hitching posts found principally in residential areas, employing such motifs as horse heads, acanthus-leaf, and other neoclassical adornment, simulated miniature tree trunks and characteristic iron stableboy. Most of these artifacts have been removed or destroyed. 1 sheet (1935); 15 photos (1935); 2 data pages (1936, including information on street lamps described below).
Lampposts (Gas Lamps, Street Lamps) (AL-36C). Four iron street lamps located respectively at 156 St. Anthony St., 1357 Spring Hill Ave. (150′ E of Garnet St.), N side of State St. intersection with Lawrence St., and E side Commerce St. 100′ N of intersection with Government St.; faceted or fluted shafts topped by sconces and glass shields. Erected mid-to-late 19th C. as part of municipal gas-lighting system; all but Spring Hill Ave. lamp destroyed in 1975. 1 sheet (1935, showing details); 4 photos (1936); 2 data pages (1936, including information on hitching posts described above).
Street Lamps. See Street Furnishings (AL-36).

Tacon-Gordon House (AL-848), 1216 Government St. (NE corner Government St. and Georgia Ave.). Frame with clapboarding, irregular rectangular with offset (3-bay) front, 2½ stories, steeply pitched irregular hipped roof with ornate balconied dormers, 2-stage corner turret from second floor with tall onion-shaped roof, very elaborate Queen Anne style porch with balustraded deck along front and W side; center-hall plan, late Victorian interior with ca. 1905 wallpaper on first floor, original electrical system and marble and brass plumbing fixtures. Built 1899–1901 for Henry Tacon, secretary and treasurer of the Mobile and Ohio and the Bay Shore railroads. 10 ext. photos (1974), 9 int. photos (1974).

Tardy, Balthasar, House. *See* Tardy-Thorp House (AL-17), 112 S. Conception St.

Tardy-Thorp House (Four Sisters House, Balthasar Tardy House) (AL-17), 112 S. Conception St. (NW corner Conception and Church sts.). Frame with clapboarding (first-floor gallery walls plastered), rectangular (3-bay façade) with detached brick dependency, 2 stories, hipped roof extending over gallery, bracketed cornice, partially encircled by full-height colonnade with square wooden columns and 2-tiered balustraded gallery; side-hall plan. Reputedly built ca. 1835–40 for Balthasar Tardy, auctioneer and commission merchant. Stylistic elements indicate later date or extensive remodeling (possibly when acquired in 1856 by livery stable owner E. R. Thorp). Name Four Sisters derives from 3 similar houses that once stood on same block. Sometime residence of John Forsyth (1812–79), U.S. minister to Mexico 1856–58 and editor of *Mobile Register*; demolished. 3 ext. photos (1934–36); 2 data pages (1936). *See also* FBJ (J7-ALA-1298).

Tarleton, George W., House (Dawson Creole House) (AL-21), 101 N. Hamilton St. Raised cottage, frame with clapboarding over brick basement, rectangular (4-bay front), 1½ stories over full ground floor, gable roof with segmentally arched dormers extending over balustraded gallery, 2 interior end chimneys, steps at N end of gallery, secondary entrance at ground level beneath gallery; side-hall plan. Built 1835–36; demolished. 1 ext. photo (1934); 1 data page (1936). *See also* FBJ (J7-ALA-1287).

Tate House. *See* House (AL-9P), 304 State St.

Texas House. *Under* Dargan-Waring House (AL-19), 351 Government St., *see* Waring "Texas," 110 S. Claiborne St.

Three Sisters House. *See* House (AL-24), 301 Church St.

Torrey, C. J., House. *See* Gibbons-Torrey House (AL-43), 60, 62 S. Conception St.

Toulmin House (AL-106), originally at 552 Wilson Ave. (E side of Old St. Stephens Rd. in former village of Toulminville); reconstructed on campus of University of South Alabama, 307 University Blvd. Frame with flush boarding on raised basement, 78′10″ (9-bay front) X 32′0″ plus rear wing, 1 story over full brick ground floor, gable roof (2 interior end chimneys) with broad kick-off extending over full-length balustraded gallery and around either side to cover end bays, gallery rests on brick piers; center-hall plan, Greek Revival interior trim. Built ca. 1828–29 for Gen. Theophilus Toulmin (1796–1866) near what was then road to Saint Stephens. Gallery renovated late 19th C. with substitution of coupled chamfered supports for original wooden piers; house partially dismantled 1974 and rebuilt (with restoration of gallery) at new location under supervision of Nicholas H. Holmes, Jr., AIA; new foundation faced with brick from old. Gen. Toulmin was son of first U.S. judge of the Tombigbee District (1804) as well as early state legislator and Mobile postmaster. 6 ext. photos (1937), 9 ext. photos (1974), 7 int. photos (1937), 7 int. photos (1974).

Townsend-Foreman Building (Coley Building) (AL-805), 56 St. Francis St. Brick with partial cast-iron façade, rectangular (6-bay façade), 2 stories, high brick parapet at each end enclosing mansardlike roof, cast-iron first-floor commercial front composed of engaged Corinthian columns supporting denticulated cornice embellished with consoles, cast-iron bracketed entablature. Portion of walls reputedly date from ca. 1836. Extensively renovated to present form ca. 1870 for Edwin Townsend; rear wing added 1930; remodeled 1959–60, Harry Inge Johnston, architect. Occupied as bank ca. 1900. 3 ext. photos (1963); 1 data page (1963).

Trammell House. *See* Charles K. Foote House (AL-9H), 255 N. Conception St.

Tuthill House. *See* Isaac Marx House (AL-778), 113 Church St.

U.S. Custom House and Old Post Office (AL-830), SW corner Royal and St. Francis sts. Regular ashlar over brick, 86′4″ (5 bays) X 145′10″ (9 bays) with advanced 3-bay central pavilion on each street façade, 3 stories, shallow hipped roof, bracketed cornice, vermiculated stone facing at ground floor (also vermiculated quoining), triple entrances on each façade framed by architraves studded with paterae; balcony above resting on scrolled consoles; piano nobile arrangement (ground floor devoted to postal services, public lobby, and appraiser's room and storage; custom house and U.S. courtroom on second and third floors respectively), twin 3-story cast-iron stairways in Royal St. vestibule, skylight above third-floor courtroom. Built 1853–56; Ammi B. Young, architect; Daniel Leadbetter, superintendent of construction; demolished 1963. Notable example of Renaissance Revival style, work of leading 19th-C. federal architect. U.S. emblems from gates on display at Museum of the City of Mobile, 355 Government St. 7 photocopies of original plans (1852, including plans, elevations, sections, details), 1 photocopy of proposed post office interior layout (1855), 7 photocopies of proposed alterations and improvements (1872), 3 photocopies of plans (1877); 5 ext. photos (1963), 1 int. photo (1963); 2 data pages (1963).

U.S. Marine Hospital (Marine Hospital) (AL-781), 800 St. Anthony St. (N side St. Anthony between Jefferson and Bayou sts.). Brick with stucco, 161'6" (15-bay front) X 62'0" overall with 5-bay central pavilion flanked by recessed 5-bay colonnaded wings, 2 stories on raised basement, low longitudinal gable concealed by brick parapet with broad cross-gable over central pavilion breaking into formal pediment with lunette in tympanum, raised 1-story tetrastyle Doric entrance portico with balustraded deck, flanking loggia-like colonnades of modified Tuscan design terminating with square end piers and enclosed by wrought-iron balustrade; center-hall plan with transverse secondary corridors. Built 1839–42; Frederick Bunnell, architect; John H. Collins, supervising architect; Robert Williamson, contractor. Opened April 1843; roof reconstructed after 1906 hurricane; T-shaped rear wing added 1931 (Warren, Knight, and Davis of Birmingham, architects), necessitating removal of N portico; second renovation 1955; other exterior alterations include replacement of direct flight of stairs to front portico by divided flight, glazing of bays between colonnades of end pavilions. 5 sheets (1966, including plans, elevations, sections); 4 ext. photos originally filed as AL-7U (1936, wrought-iron details only); 2 photocopies of plot plans (1884, 1887), 1 photocopy of floorplans (1894); 8 data pages (1972). NR.

U.S. Post Office Building (AL-797), NW corner St. Joseph and St. Michael sts. Italian Renaissance style structure of reinforced concrete faced with white marble, 2-story rectangular main block (9 bays by 5 bays) over basement, 1-story (7-bay) service wing across rear, ceramic-tile hipped roof with wide overhanging eaves resting on carved brackets, façade distinguished by 7-bay vaulted loggia set between blind end-bays embellished with Corinthian pilasters and inset with pedimented aediculae, upper floor half as high as first floor (according to classical rubric) and articulated by cornice band between first and second floors, sculptured ornamentation, entrance steps flanked by classical balustrade; main floor interior arranged around U-shaped public lobby enclosing work area, marble floor, coffered ceiling, marble stairway with bronze balustrade, second-floor offices with bisecting lateral corridor. Built 1914–16; Oscar Wenderoth, supervising architect; demolished 1968 for new Federal Building. Mobile's best example of *beaux arts* neo-Renaissance style. 2 ext. photos (1966), 1 int. photo (1966); 5 data pages (1972).

Vanroy-Barnewall House (House, Jacobson House) (AL-39), 351 St. Michael St. (SW corner St. Michael and Claiborne sts.). Brick with ashlar trim, rectangular (3-bay front) with offset wing, 2 stories plus raised attic, shallow hipped roof, brick cornice and dentil course, recessed entrance with battered architrave, frieze windows above second story enframed by applied cast-iron garlands, 2-tiered L-shaped wooden gallery at rear; side-hall plan, ornate plasterwork. Two-story brick dependency at rear of lot which is enclosed by brick wall. Built 1841–42 for John Vanroy; demolished. 3 ext. photos (1935), 6 int. photos (1935); 1 data page (1936).

Vincent-Walsh House (Walsh House) (AL-70), 1664 Spring Hill Ave. Raised cottage, frame with clapboarding, rectangular, 1 story over basement, gable roof breaking into shallow hipped roof extending over surrounding galleries, central chimney; center-hall plan. Center portion of house built ca. 1830 as country residence of Capt. Benjamin Vincent, owner of coastal steam packet plying between Mobile Bay and New Orleans. Basement originally open with wide central steps leading up to front gallery; remodeled 1902, including enclosure of basement; C. L. Hutchisson, Sr., architect. Outside front stairway removed and extensions built to either side in 1927, when again renovated to assume appearance of raised Louisiana or West Indian cottage. 2 ext. photos (1936); 2 data pages (1937). See also FBJ (J7-ALA-1346 and 1347).

Visitation Convent. See Convent and Academy of the Visitation (AL-73), 2300 Spring Hill Ave.

Walsh House. See Vincent-Walsh House (AL-70), 1664 Spring Hill Ave.

Walsh House. See House (AL-9N), 350 State St.

Waring House. See Dargan-Waring House (AL-19), 351 Government St.

Waring "Texas." *Under* Dargan-Waring House (AL-19), 351 Government St., *see* Waring "Texas" (110 S. Claiborne St.).

Washington Fire Engine Company No. 8 (No. 5 Fire Station) (AL-2), 7 N. Lawrence St. Brick, 32′2″ (3-bay front) x 45′0″ excluding later rear addition; 2 stories, gable roof, 2-tiered pedimented façade composed of distyle in antis Doric loggia at lower level (sheltering side entrance bay and 2 engine doors) with pilastered upper story, floor-length windows at upper level originally opening onto cantilevered balcony with wrought-iron balustrade; open plan with Greek Revival interior trim. Built ca. 1851 for private engine company; acquired by city in 1888 and designated as No. 5 Fire Station; balcony removed and loggia partially enclosed, interior extensively altered for commercial purposes. 2 sheets (1934, including plan, elevation, section, details); 5 ext. photos (1934–36), 1 photocopy of early exterior view (n.d.), 5 int. photos (1934–36); 2 data pages (1936). See also Tebbs (T3-ALA-434083).

Water Street Stores. See Commercial Buildings: Water Street (AL-65 series).

Weldon-LeLoupe House (LeLoupe House) (AL-20), 107 St. Emanuel St. Brick, rectangular (3-bay front), 2 stories, hipped roof, façade flush with sidewalk, covered walkway in front of house with cast-iron supports (later wooden deck above); side-hall plan, Greek Revival interior trim. Detached 2-story dependency at rear. Built 1850–52 for merchant John Weldon who lived upstairs, maintained dry goods store on first floor; demolished. 3 ext. photos (1936), 2 int. photos (1936); 2 data pages (1936). See also FBJ (J7-ALA-1319 AND 1319A).

Wilson, Augusta Evans, House. See Ashland (AL-68), S of Springhill Ave.; *also* Georgia Cottage (AL-826), 2564 Springhill Ave.

Wilson-Gibbs House (AL-856), 1012 Palmetto St. (NE corner Palmetto and Chatham sts.). Frame with clapboarding, L-shaped (4-bay) front with 2-story projecting semi-octagonal bay window on W and 2-tiered gallery, 2 stories, gable roof, gallery embellished with scroll-cut flatwood balustrade and trim, also rear ell with 2-tiered bracketed gallery; center-hall plan, curving stair, decorative plaster medallions and trim, original gas chandeliers and drop globe electric fixtures. Built before 1878 for a Mr. Wilson of New Orleans, reputedly as wedding present for his bride. Later rear additions. 4 ext. photos (1974), 4 int. photos (1974).

Worker's House (AL-821), 457 Eslava St. Frame with clapboarding, rectangular (2-bay front), 1½ stories, high gable roof (broken in rear) extending over 2-bay gallery with square wooden posts, central chimney, ground-level gallery (later enclosed at rear) abutted by rectangular gabled dependency (probably kitchen); 2 rooms deep. Antebellum; 1 house in row of 4 small mid-19th-C. dwellings. Demolished ca. 1963 for Church Street Urban Renewal Project. Important example of antebellum working-class dwelling. 3 ext. photos (1963); 1 data page (1963).

Wrought-iron Work. See Ironwork.

Zimlich, Andrew, House. See Hazard-Semmes House (AL-57), 2828 Dauphin Way.

Mobile Vicinity

Mobile Light No. 6639 (Middle Bay Light) (AL-780), middle of Mobile Bay, approx. 14 mi. S/SE of City of Mobile and 6 mi. due E of mouth of Fowl River and approx. equidistant between E and W shores of Mobile Bay. Frame superstructure on metal pilings, hexagonal (18′8″ on either side, excluding surrounding deck), 1½ stories topped by platform and beacon mast (18′8″), peaked hexagonal slate-covered roof with dormers; foundation rests in approx. 12′ of water and consists of central metal pipe surrounded by outward sloping metal legs secured by turnbuckle tie-rods; wooden platform and deck of keeper's quarters and light approx. 16′ above water surface; keeper's quarters consist of 4 rooms grouped about wooden cylindrical interior stair ascending to beacon platform. Built 1905 for U.S. Coast Guard. Light automated and keeper's quarters unoccupied since 1935. 5 sheets (1966, including site plan, plans, elevation, section, details); 5 data pages (1966, 1972).

Mon Louis Island

Boat Repair Yard (Old Boat Repair Yard) (AL-189), E bank of Fowl River just S of confluence with Mobile Bay and N of Faustinas Beach; approx. 0.5 mi. NE of Ala. 163 and 10 miles S of Mobile. Wooden ramp or boatway with horse-powered winch to draw boats up from river. Windlass reinforced with iron straps and anchored to timber platform with massive iron bolts. Yard established ca. 1830 by black creole Maximilien Colin; timbers replaced periodically through years until abandonment of boatyard in 1965; surviving remnants of machinery badly deteriorated by 1975. 4 photos (1937).

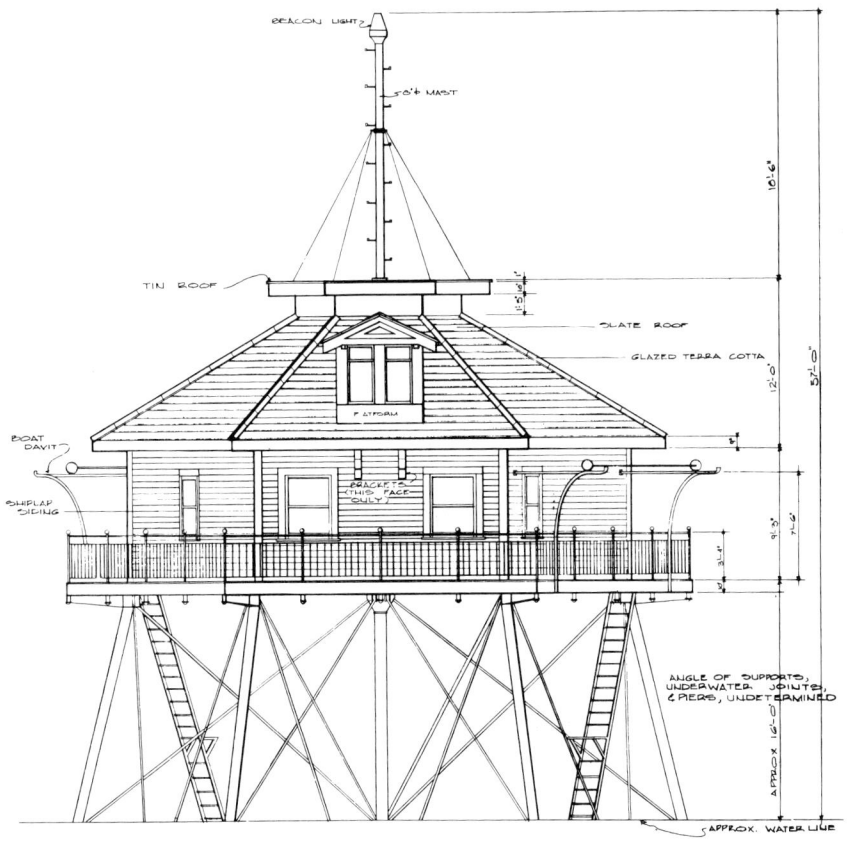

Mobile Light No. 6639 (Middle Bay Light), Mobile vicinity (1905).

Mount Vernon

Beasley House. *See* Cooper-Beasley House (AL-117), Co. 96.

Cooper-Beasley House (Beasley House) (AL-117), S side Co. 96 (Old Saint Stephens Rd.), approx. 0.5 mi. W of intersection with U.S. 43. Nucleus of house a dogtrot structure of sawn logs (later enlarged and sheathed with clapboarding), rectangular (5-bay front), open central passage, gable roof (broken at rear) extending over porch with enclosed bay at each end, 4 exterior end chimneys. Built early 19th C. Purchased 1865 by John Albert Cooper, who is probably responsible for renovation and enlargement; demolished 1959. Cooper came to Mount Vernon Arsenal in 1859 from Richmond, Va., to supervise powder manufacture. 4 ext. photos (1937); 2 data pages (1937).

Curry, L. B., House. *See* Rogers-Curry House (AL-124), Co. 96.

Fall, Nelias, House (AL-162), approx. 0.1 mi. N of Co. 96 (Old Saint Stephens Rd.), 0.8 mi. W of intersection with U.S. 43. Frame with clapboarding, 40′6″ (6-bay front) X approx. 32′ including gallery, 1½ stories, gable roof extending over full-length porch with 6 square wooden supports, 2 interior end chimneys; center-hall plan, beaded flush boarding in hallway. Built ca. 1850, rear addition ca. 1935; front extensively altered 1938 including enclosure of W 2 bays of gallery, replacement of wooden posts with heavy concrete piers and coping, addition of large shed dormer; addition to E side 1959, rear utility room 1972. 3 ext. photos (1937), 1 int. photo (1937); 1 data page (1937).

Indian Schoolhouse (AL-125), approx. 0.1 mi. S of Co. 96 (Old Saint Stephens Rd.) on W side of road to Searcy Hospital (old Mount Vernon Arsenal), just outside old arsenal walls and W of main gate. Frame with vertical siding (fish-scale shingles in gable ends), rectangular with lean-to entrance porch at S end, gable roof; bisected laterally by open passage with single large room to each side. Built ca. 1888 for U.S. government as schoolhouse for Apache tribesmen incarcerated at Mount Vernon between 1887 and 1894; later used as recreation hall; destroyed by storm 1936. Indians sheltered in log cabins outside arsenal walls. 3 ext. photos (1935).

Mount Vernon Arsenal (Mount Vernon Barracks) (AL-105), S side of Co. 96 (Old Saint Stephens Rd.), 0.6 mi. W of intersection with U.S. 43 at Mount Vernon. Mid-19th-C. U.S. military complex situated on 2,150-acre tract and including arsenal building, barracks, officers' quarters, and workshops plus ancillary structures arranged in semicircle around parade ground. Principal buildings encircled by "ring road" beyond which were originally located gardens, pastures, stables, and gunsheds. Entire 47-acre area formed nucleus of original reservation enclosed by circumferential brick wall approx. 1.0 mi. in length; powder magazines outside walls to S. Buildings subsequently altered and ground plan extensively modified to accommodate new structures and 20th-C. use as hospital. U.S. cantonment established on site in 1811; federal arsenal at Mount Vernon authorized by Congress 24 May 1828; main buildings erected ca. 1830–40. Arsenal seized by state militia during Civil War; 1873 arsenal complex converted to barracks use, with some subsequent structural changes. Apache chieftain Geronimo and followers imprisoned here 1888–89. Deactivated as U.S. military post and conveyed to State of Alabama in 1895; became Searcy Hospital, a state mental institution for blacks, in 1900; in 1980s continued as part of state mental health system. Ground plan extensively modified and buildings variously altered in 20th C. 2 data pages (1937). See below for records on individual structures.

Gates (AL-105A). West Gate (opening onto former Saint Stephens Rd., approx. 300 yds. N of arsenal building in NW section of perimeter wall); brick, segmentally arched gateway with flanking pedestrian entrances, paneled brick parapet above; built ca. 1840 as secondary entrance, demolished prior to 1935. South Gate (approx. 250 yds. SW of arsenal building in SW segment of perimeter wall): brick, segmentally arched gateway approx. 11' wide, raised parapet above, heavy wooden gates of diagonally set batten construction; built ca. 1840 to provide access to powder magazines beyond arsenal walls. 2 photocopies of West Gate (1914), 2 photos of South Gate (1935).

Inner Wall (Old Retaining Wall) (AL-105B). Horseshoe-shaped wall encompassing former parade ground and connecting 7 major structures of original arsenal complex arranged in semicircle around main building; brick with ashlar foundation, topped by wooden palings set between brick piers; vehicular gateways flanked by pedestrian entries. Erected ca. 1830–35. 6 photos (1935).

Administration Building (Commissary and Guardhouse) (AL-105C), approx. 900' E of old arsenal building on site of former main gate to arsenal and incorporating earlier flanking structures. Center pavilion (occupying site of original main gate to arsenal) frame with clapboarding, approx. 44' (3-bay front) X 68' including portico, 2 stories, gable roof, pedimented Tuscan style portico with cupola, flanking 1-story gable brick wings approx. 48' (4 bays) X 35'; segmentally arched gates to either side. Wings erected mid-19th C. (N wing as guardhouse, S wing as commissary); center section and gates built ca. 1905 following conversion of arsenal to hospital; numerous interior alterations, portico partially enclosed after 1935. 3 ext. photos (1935), 2 int. photos (1935).

Arsenal Building (Barracks Building) (AL-105D), on SE side of old parade ground. Brick, approx. 115' (10-bay front) X 48', 3 stories, hipped roof, projecting 5-story hexagonal central tower on front (SE) elevation with crenellated observation deck, segmentally arched casement windows; open interior plan with double row of pier supports on first and second floors, stairway in tower; also detached N flanker approx. 60' (6 bays long) X 40', gable roof. Main structure built ca. 1835 as nucleus of complex; 3-tiered gallery added to SE elevation (probably after 1873); subsequent interior modifications including complete renovation for hospital use 1977–78; galleries also partially enclosed. N flanker built ca. 1880 replacing original gunsheds. 4 ext. photos (1935), 1 int. photo (1935, stairway only).

Officers' Quarters (Subaltern's Quarters, Barracks Building) (AL-105E), one of 2 identical buildings roughly on axis and 70′ from main arsenal building. Brick, approx. 21′ (1 bay) × 35′ (4 bays), 2 stories, hipped roof, continuous 2-tiered porch around 3 sides with superimposed brick piers, unusual divided outside stairway on gallery; 2-room plan with central chimney; brick (rectangular) 2-room semidetached kitchen to NW rear. Built ca. 1835, gallery partially enclosed 20th C., rear frame addition, interior modifications. 3 ext. photos (1935).

Workshop (Officers' Quarters) (AL-105F), southwesternmost of 4 formerly similar structures arranged in quarter-circle to either side of main barracks building and facing parade ground. Brick, approx. 56′ (6-bay front with double entrance) × 29′, hipped roof, 2 interior chimneys, gallery across front. Probably built 1830–40; renovated for barracks use 1872–82, later brick and frame additions. Used as carpenter shop during arsenal period (1828–73). 2 ext. photos (1935).

Barracks (Officers' Quarters) (AL-105G), NW of arsenal building at apex of semicircle of structures originally facing parade ground. Brick, approx. 62′ (5-bay front) × 32′ overall, 2 stories, hipped roof partially encircled by 2-tiered porch with superimposed brick piers, projecting 4-story hexagonal tower with arched windows and pyramidal roof on NW (rear) elevation; center-hall plan (2 rooms on either side) with rear stairhall partially contained in tower. Built ca. 1835; gallery partially enclosed, interior modifications. 1 photocopy of plans, elevations, section (1840); 2 ext. photos (1935).

Laboratory and Office (Old Officers' Quarters) (AL-105H), approx. 700′ due S of arsenal building. Brick, approx. 18′6″ (3-bay front) × 30′6″, 1 story, gable roof, pedimented wooden porch on E front. Built ca. 1835 as one of 4 small laboratory structures (2 of brick) with furnace inside for casting shot; officers' quarters after 1873; later used as morgue. Companion structures demolished. 2 ext. photos (1935).

Paymaster's Office (AL-105J), directly in front and approx. 110′ SE of arsenal building on original semicircular drive leading from old main gate. Brick, approx. 20′ (3-bay SE front) × 35′, 2-story SE elevation (structure set into hillside), 1-story NW elevation, gable roof, wooden porch (SE front) raised on square brick piers with outside stair, projecting wooden bay on NW front, scalloped bargeboard; 2-room plan. High brick retaining wall extending to either side and parallel to original semicircular roadway. Built 1830–40 (porches formerly at each end). Renovated ca. 1872; 20th-C. changes include frame-and-brick addition to SW side. 1 photocopy of plans, elevations (1840, also including blacksmith shop); 4 ext. photos (1935), 4 int. photos (1935).

Stables (Barn) (AL-105K), approx. 250′ SE of old parade ground to rear of W range of workshops (see above, AL-105F). Brick, rectangular (5 bays long), 1 story plus hayloft, gable roof. Built ca. 1840; struck by lightning and burned 1942. 2 ext. photos (1935).

Workshop (Officers' Quarters) (AL-105L), N side of parade ground E of barracks building, one of 4 originally similar structures. Brick, rectangular (5-bay front), 1 story, hipped roof, porch across front; center-hall plan. Built 1830–40 as one of arsenal workshops. Remodeled as officers' quarters ca. 1873; later frame addition at rear. 2 ext. photos (1935).

Mess Hall (AL-105M), E of arsenal building. Brick, rectangular (13 bays long), 1 story, widely overhanging gable roof with monitor, irregularly spaced entrance bays. Built ca. 1880. 1 ext. photo (1935).

Mount Vernon Barracks. *See* Mount Vernon Arsenal (AL-105), Co. 96.

Rogers-Curry House (L. B. Curry House) (AL-124), N side of Co. 96 (Old Saint Stephens Rd.), approx. 100′ W of intersection with old U.S. 43. Frame with clapboarding, 41′ (3-bay front) × 40′, 1½ stories, gable roof with 3 dormers extending over full-length balustraded wooden gallery; center-hall plan. Built ca. 1850 for Thomas Rogers; original detached kitchen connected to house by enclosed passageway early 20th C. 2 ext. photos (1935), 1 int. photo (1935).

MONROE COUNTY

Burnt Corn Vicinity

Watkins House (AL-112), approx. 1.5 mi. N of Burnt Corn community on W side of Ala. 30 (Old Federal Road) forming boundary between Monroe and Conecuh counties. Frame with clapboarding, rectangular (3-bay front), 2½ stories with 1-story lean-to extension across rear, gable roof with broad kick-off extending over porch, 2 exterior end chimneys, full-length 2-tiered porch partially screened by latticework at upper level, stairway on porch to second floor; unplastered interior, simple Federal period mantelpieces and trim. Rectangular 1-story semi-detached dining wing off SW corner of house. Built ca. 1820 for Dr. John Watkins (ca. 1785–1853) from Appomattox County, Va. 2 ext. photos (1934), 1 int. photo (1934); 2 data pages (1936).

Claiborne

Deer's Store (AL-104), S side of U.S. 84, approx. 0.8 mi. SE of Alabama River Bridge. Frame with clapboarding, 26'1" (3-bay front first story, 2 bays second story) × 60'5", 2 stories, gable roof with pedimented gable ends, originally wooden steps at front; large room below with post office and stair at rear. Built ca. 1850; housed community post office and store from date of construction until abandoned in 1971; demolished spring 1979. 1 sheet (1934, including plans, elevations, section); 2 ext. photos (1934), 1 int. photo (1934); 2 data pages (1936).

Dellet, James, House (AL-121), at end of private lane, approx. 0.4 mi. N of U.S. 84 (Ala. 12), approx. 1.0 mi. SE of Alabama River Bridge. Frame with clapboarding, rectangular (5-bay front), 2 stories with 1-story lean-to extension across rear, gable roof, 2 interior chimneys, 2-tiered pedimented tetrastyle Doric portico, 3-bay loggia at rear, lunettes in each gable end; center-hall plan, Greek Revival style interior woodwork, marble mantel in parlor. Built ca. 1835–40; one "Campbell" reputedly architect-builder. Dellet (1788–1848), first owner, born in Philadelphia, was a noted early Alabama lawyer and legislator. 2 ext. photos (1934), 1 int. photo (1934); 1 data page (1936). *See also* FBJ (J7-ALA-1251 through 1253).

Travis, William B., House (AL-882). Relocated to Perdue Hill. *See listing under Perdue Hill.*

Franklin Vicinity

Gin House (Mule Gin) (AL-141), W side Ala. 41, approx. 0.8 mi. NW of Flat Creek Bridge, approx. 12.4 mi. NW of Monroeville, and 5.0 mi. S of Franklin community. Frame partially covered with rough clapboarding, 1 story with loft space, gable roof covered with shakes, open shed at E end; ground floor open, containing wooden gin machinery, cotton stored in loft above. Built ca. 1850; originally located on Garland Goode plantation at hilltop site approx. 2 mi. W; moved to site on what is now Ala. 41 in late 19th C. as more central location; demolished ca. 1955. 1 ext. photo (1936), 3 int. photos (1936, gin machinery).

Monroeville Vicinity

House (W. T. Andrews House) (AL-122), NW side of Ala. 21-47 NE of Limestone Creek between Monroeville and Peterman community. Log (saddle-notch construction) on wood pilings, rectangular, 1 story, gable-roof broken to extend over full-length front porch and rear lean-to, 1 stone exterior end chimney (brick stack above ridge line), porch enclosed at 1 end; presumably open-passage (dogtrot) plan originally. Built early to mid-19th C. Good example of folk dwelling in lower Alabama–Tombigbee area. 1 ext. photo (1934).

Mount Pleasant.

See Uriah Vicinity.

Perdue Hill

House (John Daniels House) (AL-123), S side U.S. 84 (Ala. 12), approx. 2 mi. E of intersection with Co. 1 at Perdue Hill. Frame with clapboarding, rectangular (5-bay front), 1 story, broken gable roof extending over full-length front porch, rear lean-to, 4 ashlar exterior end chimneys, porch roof extends beyond balustraded porch itself and rests on 4 square wooden supports springing from ground-level brick piers; center-hall plan. Built ca. 1860. Scroll-cut porch balustrade possibly later; demolished 1965–66. 1 ext. photo (1934).

Masonic Hall (AL-103), between U.S. 84 (Ala. 12) and Co. 1, approx. 200' W of junction at Perdue Hill. Frame with clapboarding, rectangular (7-bay E front, 3-bay S front), 2 stories, gable roof, small 1-story pedimented porch with scroll-cut trim sheltering doorway on E front; open plan with 2 small rooms and stair at S end, assembly room first floor, lodge room second floor with raised dais at N end, original furnishings include paneled pulpit beneath freestanding elliptical arch supported by fluted colonnettes. Built ca. 1825 in village of Claiborne (approx. 2 mi. NW on Alabama River) for Alabama Masonic Lodge No. 3; John Parks, superintendent of construction. Building moved ca. 1865 to Perdue Hill; acquired ca. 1930 by Woman's Club of Perdue Hill as clubhouse and community meeting place. Building reputedly dedicated by Marquis de Lafayette during 1825 visit. 2 sheets (1934, including plans, elevations, section, details); 2 ext. photos (1934), 3 int. photos (1934); 1 data page (1936).

Travis, William B., House (AL-882), between U.S. Hwy. 84 (Ala. 12) and Co. Rd. 1 W of junction at Perdue Hill, adjacent to old Masonic Hall. Frame with beaded clapboarding, rectangular (3-bay front), 1 story, gable roof, 1 ashlar exterior end chimney; interior subdivided by beaded-board partitions into 3 rooms (1 large room 16' × 17', with 2 small front and rear chambers adjoining); Federal-period detailing includes molded chairrail and Adamesque mantelpiece. Built ca. 1820–28. Originally located approx. 0.5 mi. S of village of Claiborne; moved to Perdue Hill in 1984 for preservation and restoration under supervision of Mobile architect Nicholas H. Holmes, Jr. Rare surviving example in lower Alabama of small early-19th C. frame dwelling. Historically significant as home of William Barrett Travis (1809–36), who later emigrated to Texas and commanded American forces at the Battle of the Alamo. 1 sheet (1983, including plan, elevations, sections, details).

Uriah Vicinity

Ferrell House (Judge Ferrell House) (AL-114), E side of FAS 16 (Eureka Landing Rd.), approx. 0.1 mi. N of intersection of Co. 1 and Co. 8 in Eliska community, near old Mount Pleasant community. Frame with clapboarding, rectangular (6-bay front), 2 stories with 1-story lean-to extension across rear, gable roof, 2 exterior end chimneys, full-length 1-story porch. Built early 19th C.; demolished early 1950s. 1 ext. photo (1934).

MONTGOMERY COUNTY

Montgomery

Alabama State Capitol (First Confederate Capitol) (AL-601), E end of Dexter Ave. Open to public. Original portion brick with stucco scored to simulate ashlar, 152'0" (11-bay front) × 69'8" with 5-bay advanced center pavilion and wing (50'10" × 40'1") at middle rear, 3 stories, full-height hexastyle portico with Corinthianesque cast-iron capitals from Plate 11 of Minard Lafever's *Beauties of Modern Architecture,* iron-railed balconies at second and third stories, pedimented clock surmounting entablature, main pavilion capped by wood and cast-iron dome resting on drum encircled by Corinthian colonnade (12-sided lantern crowns dome); interior arranged around axial rotunda (open from second floor to dome) entered through antechamber, twin unsupported spiral stairways flank main door and ascend through third floor, Senate wing to N, House to S, Supreme Court chamber once in E (rear) wing, interior details drawn from Minard Lafever. Built 1850–51 on foundation of previous structure (erected 1846–47, burned on 14 Dec. 1849) designed by Stephen D. Button; present edifice apparently based on design by Daniel Pratt, itself a modification of Button plan for 1846–47 capitol; Barachias Holt, superintending architect; John P. Figh and James D. Randolph, principal contractors; Nimrod E. Benson and Judson Wyman, supervisors. Rear (judiciary) wing extended 6 bays in 1885, according to plan of W. T. Walker; 6-bay setback wings added to each side in early 1900s (S side 1906–7, N side 1911–12) with Frank Lockwood as architect, in consultation with Charles Follen McKim (also interior renovations to original structure). Further interior renovation, including rotunda murals by Roderick MacKenzie, 1926–30; E and S wing interior renovations 1940: Warren, Knight, and Davis, architects; exterior restoration 1978–80 including replacement of stucco: Nicholas H. Holmes, Jr., architect. Meeting place of Confederate Congress Feb.–May 1861, prior to removal of Confederate capital to Richmond. 8 sheets, original portion only (1934, including plans, elevations, section, details); 6 ext. photos (1934), 5 int. photos (1934); 11 data pages (1936). NHL. *See also* FBJ (J7-ALA-1030 through 1032); Tebbs (T3-ALA-428171 through 428177).

Arrington House. *See* Bibb-Goldthwaite-Arrington House (AL-611), 203 Church St.

Ball, Charles P., House. *See* Seibels-Ball-Lanier House (AL-612), 407 Adams Ave.

Barnes School. *See* Figh-Pickett House (AL-626), 14 Clayton St.

Bibb-Goldthwaite-Arrington House (Arrington House) (AL-611), 203 Church St. (SW corner Church and Moulton sts.). Brick (façade Flemish bond), approx. 55′ (5-bay front) × 44′ plus transverse rear extension, 2 stories (extension 1 story), shallow hipped roof, bracketed cornice, 1-story 3-bay Italianate style entrance porch; center-hall plan, curving stair, Greek Revival style woodwork possibly adapted from Minard Lafever, decorative plaster, marble mantels (also some Federal period woodwork and mantelpieces). Cast-iron gate; 2 brick dependencies (kitchen and servants' house). Built ca. 1835 reputedly for Benajah Smith Bibb (1796–1884), lawyer, planter, legislator; extensively remodeled ca. 1850 and 1876, including removal of original semicircular portico; demolished 1948. 7 ext. photos (1934–35), 18 int. photos (1935); 2 data pages (1936).

Branch, E. W., House. *See* Ray-Branch House (AL-609), 730 S. Court St.

Davis, Jefferson, House. *See* First White House of the Confederacy (AL-624), 625 Washington St.

Figh-Pickett House (Barnes School, Pickett House) (AL-626), 14 Clayton St. Brick, rectangular (5-bay front) with central extension at rear and long slightly offset service ell, 2 stories over high basement (ell 1 story over ground floor formed by rearward slope of lot), shallow hipped roof terminating in small louvered cupola, bracketed cornice, 4 interior end chimneys, 3-bay wooden porch with scroll-cut balustrade and trim, unusual lattice-enclosed passage cantilevered over service court along rear ell (latticework pierced by elliptical openings screened with louvers); center-hall plan, dining room floor paved with granite blocks from first State Capitol (burned 1849) at Montgomery. Built ca. 1838–40 by John P. Figh, local contractor and brickyard owner, as family residence; later enlarged and remodeled in Italianate style; mutilated by alteration for commercial purposes ca. 1960. Purchased in 1858 by Albert J. Pickett, first historian of Alabama. Later Barnes School for Boys. 7 ext. photos (1934–35).

First Confederate Capitol. *See* Alabama State Capitol (AL-601), E end of Dexter Ave.

First White House of the Confederacy (Jefferson Davis House) (AL-624), originally located at SW corner Bibb and Lee sts., moved to 625 Washington St. (SW corner Washington and Union sts.). House museum. Frame with clapboarding, 52′8″ (5-bay front) × 36′8″, also large irregularly shaped transverse rear extension (73′0″ × 20′4″ overall), 2 stories (wing 1 story), hipped roof with bracketed cornice and wide frieze-band pierced by circular cast-iron ventilator grilles, 4 exterior end chimneys (main block), 3-bay 1-story porch with façade beneath scored to simulate rustication; center-hall plan, early to mid-19th-C. woodwork (including paneled dado, Adamesque mantels, and heavy early Victorian bannister and newel post); some furnishings from 1861 period. Built 1833 for William Sayre, merchant who was born in New Jersey; A. M. Bradley, contractor; extensively altered ca. 1855 in Italianate style for John G. Winter. Residence March–May 1861 of Confederate Pres. Jefferson Davis and family; acquired by State of Alabama 1919, moved to present site, and dedicated as museum 3 June 1921. Restored to 1861 appearance in 1976. 7 sheets (1935, including plans, elevations, section, details); 2 ext. photos (1934), 4 int. photos (1934); 5 data pages (1936). NR.

Fitzpatrick-Saffold House (Saffold House) (AL-617), 442 S. McDonough St. (SW corner McDonough and High sts.). Brick, main block 28'10" (3-bay front) X 56'10" plus offset rear wing (20'7" X 45'10"), 2 stories above English basement, hipped roof, continuous 1-story wooden porch along front, S side, and rear with scroll-cut balustrade and trim, bracketed cornice; side-hall plan, double parlors, full basement with service area (including original kitchen). Ornate cast-iron fence. Built 1859 for Elmore Fitzpatrick; renovated for apartment use ca. 1935; razed 1986. 6 sheets (1935, including plans, elevations, section, details); 7 ext. photos (1935), 5 int. photos (1935); 2 data pages (1936).

Garrett-Hatchett House (Hatchett House) (AL-630), 313 Catoma St. Frame with flush siding, 52'11" (3-bay front) X 51'9" plus transverse rear porch (79'0" X 13'8") linking offset parallel service wings at rear to main block, 2 stories (wings 1 story), hipped roof with cupola, bracketed cornice, 6 interior end chimneys, ornate arcuated 3-bay porch with applied foliation in spandrels, recessed entrance with louvered blinds, quoined corners; center-hall plan, elaborate formal interior with carved woodwork, decorative plaster, marble mantels. Built 1860 for John B. Garrett; demolished ca. 1964. Notable example of frame Italianate style dwelling. 6 sheets (1935, including plans, elevations, section, details); 3 ext. photos (1934), 4 int. photos (1934); 3 data pages (1936).

Gerald-Bethea House (St. Mary's of Loretto Academy) (AL-604), 203 S. Lawrence St. (SE corner S. Lawrence St. and Adams Ave.). Brick with stucco scored to simulate ashlar, 54'3" (5-bay front) X 48'9" including portico, also parallel rear service wings (each 12'3" wide X 30'6" long), 2 stories over raised basement (wings 1 story), shallow hipped roof partially concealed by false entablature, raised full-height hexastyle Corinthian portico across front approached by double flight of curving steps with cast-iron balustrade (portico has marble floor, cast-iron balcony above doorway), 3-bay Doric loggia at rear; center-hall plan, ornate interior with Greek Revival-style woodwork and decorative plaster cornices and ceilings. Cast-iron fountain in front of house. Built 1851 for Perley Gerald (1800–66), Indian trader, businessman, and "Forty-Niner" who was born in New York; Roman Catholic academy 1872–1964, during which time rear wings were replaced by 2-story addition; demolished Feb. 1964. House reputedly erected with fortune made by Gerald in California gold rush of 1849. 4 sheets (1934, including plans, elevations, section, details); 5 ext. photos (1934), 4 int. photos (1934); 2 data pages (1936). *See also* FBJ (J7-ALA-1024).

Gerald-Dowdell House (Kenneworth House, Moffatt House) (AL-614), 405 S. Hull St. Raised cottage, frame with clapboarding over stuccoed-and-scored brick ground floor, rectangular (5-bay front), hipped roof with bracketed cornice, 2 interior chimneys, full-length porch with scroll-cut balustrade and trim resting on brick piers (ground-floor entrance area beneath screened by latticework); center-hall plan. Built ca. 1858 for Perley Gerald (see also Gerald-Bethea house, AL-604). Notable application of Italianate design to smaller house. 4 ext. photos (1934–35), 4 int. photos (1935). NR.

Gilmer-Shorter-Lomax House (Lomax House) (AL-607), 235 S. Court St. (NE corner S. Court and Alabama sts.). Brick (portico stuccoed), rectangular (5-bay front), 2½ stories, gable roof, double end chimneys with parapet, full-height pedimented tetrastyle modified Doric portico with marble floor, cast-iron railed balcony above door; center-hall plan, continuous spiral stairway to third floor. Built ca. 1844–47 by local contractor John P. Figh who sold house to James J. Gilmer in latter year; large rear wing added 1939; renovated and restored 1972. Offices of Preferred Life Insurance Co. since 1929. 5 ext. photos (1934–35), 6 int. photos (1935); 2 data pages (1936).

Graves, Gov. Bibb, House. *See* Taylor-Ponder-Graves House (AL-644), 511 S. McDonough St.

Harris-Smith House (Smith House) (AL-610), SE corner Church and Catoma sts. Brick with stucco scored to simulate ashlar, rectangular (5-bay front) with transverse rear extension terminating in rounded end bays, 2 stories (extension 1 story), shallow hipped roof with widely overhanging bracketed cornice, 4 interior end chimneys, Palladian-style doorway sheltered by ornate cast-iron entrance porch, window above set into blind elliptical arch, cast-iron lintels employing palmette motif; center-hall plan, very ornate interior including trompe l'oeil ("fresco") painting in main hallway, curving stair. Brick 2-story servants' quarters at rear;

cast-iron fence. Built ca. 1855 for Nathan Harris; demolished 1946. Notable local example of mid-19th-C. eclecticism, with both Italianate and some late Greek Revival elements. 6 ext. photos (1934–35), 12 int. photos (1935).

Hatchett House. *See* Garrett-Hatchett House (AL-630), 313 Catoma St.

Hilliard, Henry, House (AL-613), E side of Jackson St. facing E end of Washington St. Brick, 2 stories (1-story transverse rear wing with rounded end bays). Built ca. 1855; extensively altered ca. 1905; demolished 1959. Henry Washington Hilliard (1808–92) was lawyer, Methodist minister, U.S. ambassador to Brazil 1877–81. 2 data pages (1936).

Housman House. *See* Oliver-Housman House (AL-635), SW corner Wilkerson and Montgomery sts.

Kenneworth House. *See* Gerald-Dowdell House (AL-614), 405 S. Hull St.

Lomax House. *See* Gilmer-Shorter-Lomax House (AL-607), 235 S. Court St.

McBryde-Screws-Tyson House (Tyson House) (AL-608), 423 Mildred St. Frame with clapboarding, rectangular (5-bay front) with advanced 3-bay entrance pavilion and offset rear wing, 2 stories (wing 1 story), shallow hipped roof concealed at front by paneled parapet, denticulated cornice, 4 exterior end chimneys, full-height tetrastyle portico with square columns, full-length balcony; center-hall plan with transverse entrance hall. Believed to have been built ca. 1855 for Mrs. Anne (Allen) McBryde, later Mrs. Benjamin Thiess; E porch added along with rear additions in late 19th C.; Victorian-period renovations inside; damaged by fire in February 1985. Home 1885–90 of Maj. William Wallace Screws, editor of *Montgomery Advertiser*. 5 ext. photos (1934–35), 9 int. photos (1935). NR.

Moffatt House. *See* Gerald-Dowdell House (AL-614), 405 S. Hull St.

Murphy, John H., House (AL-603), 22 Bibb St. (NE corner Bibb and Coosa sts.). Open to public. Brick (façade stuccoed and scored to simulate ashlar), main block 57′2″ (5-bay front) × 49′6″ including portico, originally transverse rear extension (20′0″ × 77′2″) projecting 1 bay beyond each side of main block, 2 stories (extension 1 story), shallow hipped roof concealed by brick parapet, full-height hexastyle Corinthian portico across front with marble floor, recessed doorway flanked by engaged Corinthian colonnettes, cast-iron balcony above, cast-iron lintels; center-hall plan, ornate interior including large drawing room with elaborate plaster ceiling, marble mantels, brass chandeliers. Built 1850s; renovated 1927–34 including replacement of transverse rear wing by 2-story addition, again renovated and restored 1969–70 to house Montgomery Water Works and Sanitary Service Board. Original owner, Murphy, was a cotton broker. Headquarters in April 1865 of Union provost marshall following capture of city by U.S. forces at end of Civil War. 3 sheets (1934, including plans, elevations, section, details); 5 ext. photos (1934–35), 13 int. photos (1934–35); 3 data pages (1936).

Oliver-Housman House (Housman House) (AL-635), SW corner Wilkerson and Montgomery sts. Brick, 50′11″ (5-bay front) × 46′6″ plus offset rear service wing (15′0″ × 30′0″), 1 story, hipped roof extending over full-length porch with fluted Doric colonnettes, bracketed cornice; center-hall plan. Built ca. 1850 for Dr. Mack Oliver; frame additions to rear; demolished during winter of 1934. 3 sheets (1934, including plan, elevations, section, details); 2 ext. photos (1934), 1 int. photo (1934); 3 data pages (1936).

Owens-Teague House (Teague House) (AL-606), 440 S. Perry St. (NW corner S. Perry and High sts.). Open to public. Brick, 51′10″ (5-bay front) × 53′0″ including portico, 2 stories, hipped roof, 4 interior end chimneys, full-height hexastyle Ionic portico across front with denticulated cornice, 3-bay cast-iron balcony; center-hall plan. Brick dependency connected to main block by frame breezeway and containing kitchen and servants' quarters. Built 1848 for Berry Owens; minor alterations and additions later (including early 20th-C. doorway); adaptively restored 1982–83 (columns re-stuccoed, interior refurbished, breezeway glassed in). Headquarters of Gen. James Wilson, USA, 12–14 April 1865, upon occupation of Montgomery by Union forces at end of Civil War. Became offices of Alabama State Chamber of Commerce in 1955. 3 sheets (1934, including plans, elevations, section, details); 6 ext. photos (1934–35), 11 int. photos (1934–35); 2 data pages (1936). NR.

Pickett House. *See* Figh-Pickett House (AL-626), 14 Clayton St.

Pollard, Col. Charles Teed, House (AL-605), 117 Jefferson St. (NW corner Jefferson and Lawrence sts.). Brick with stucco scored and marbleized, 55'6" (5-bay front) × 64'3" including portico, also transverse rear extension (72'10" × 33'6") projecting 1 bay beyond each side of main block, 2 stories (extension 1 story), shallow hipped roof concealed by brick parapet, full-height hexastyle Corinthian portico across front with marble floor and decorative plaster ceiling, cast-iron balcony over doorway, small cast-iron porches at side, 3-bay arcaded loggia at rear; center-hall plan, elaborate formal interior with marble floor in hallway, decorative plaster ceilings, marble mantels, twin service stairs at rear. Completed 1853; Stephen D. Button possibly architect; B. F. Randolph, contractor; late-19th-C. modifications including Eastlake style front door; demolished ca. 1938. Home 1853–76 of Charles Teed Pollard, early Alabama industrial and railroad entrepreneur. One of most elaborate of Montgomery's mid-19th-C. mansions. 6 sheets (1934, including plans, elevations, section, details); 8 ext. photos (1934–35), 16 int. photos (1934–35, including basement); 2 data pages (1936). *See also* Tebbs (T3-ALA-426180).

Ray-Branch House (E. W. Branch House) (AL-609), 730 S. Court St. Frame with clapboarding, rectangular (5-bay front), shallow hipped roof concealed by paneled parapet, denticulated and modillioned cornice, full-height hexastyle Corinthian portico across front with wrought-iron balcony on scrolled brackets above doorway; center-hall plan. Built 1854 for William O. Ray, cotton merchant; portico added and other renovations ca. 1900; demolished 1968, columns and other materials incorporated into Ray McBride House approx. 5 mi. w of Prattville, Ala., on S side of Ala. 14. 1 ext. photo (1934).

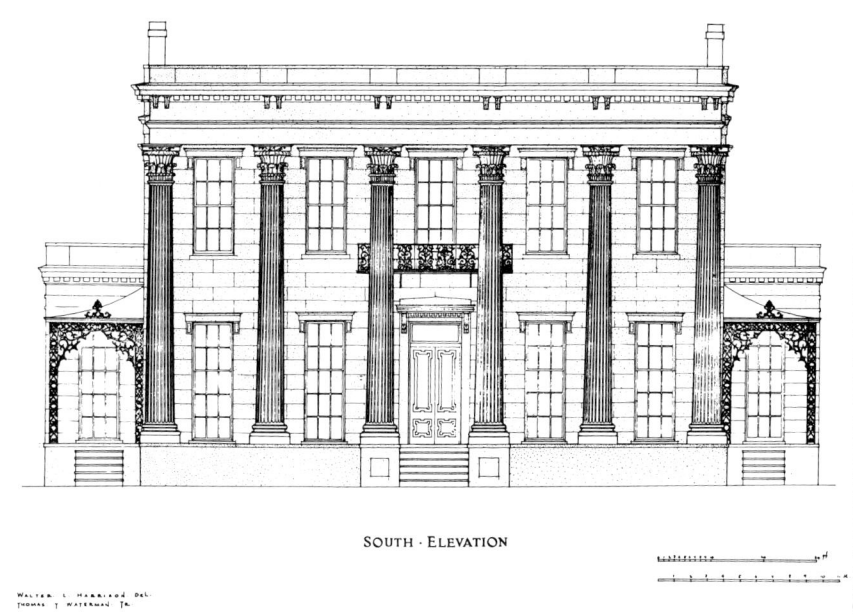

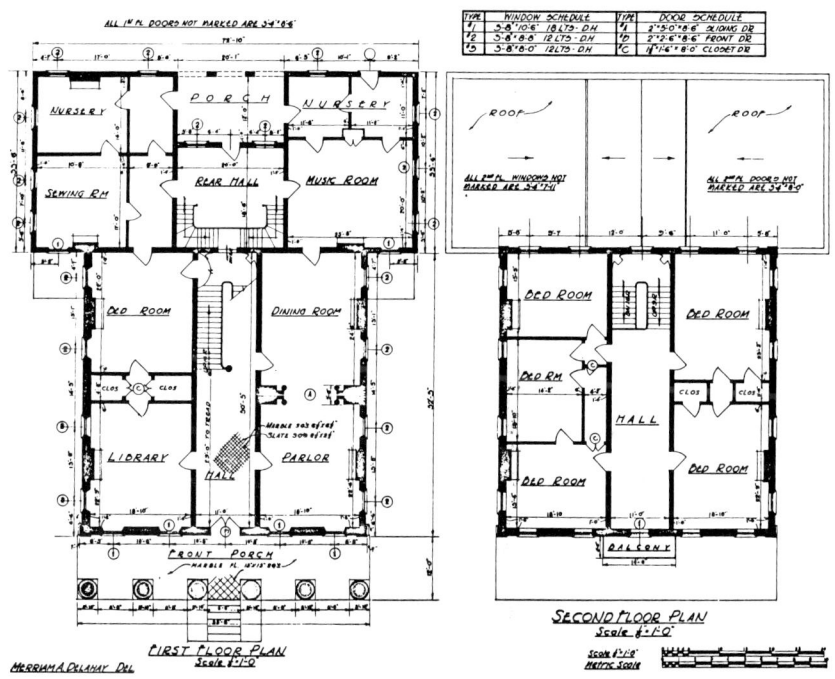

Col. Charles Teed Pollard House, Montgomery (1853, demolished ca. 1938).

Saffold House. *See* Fitzpatrick-Saffold House (AL-617), 442 S. McDonough St.

St. John's Episcopal Church (AL-643), 113 Madison Ave. (NE corner Madison Ave. and Perry St.). Brick with stucco, rectangular nave with chancel, tower at SW corner, façade dominated by large traceried window surmounted by trefoil, buttressed 4-stage square entrance tower crenelated above belfry and breaking into octagonal broached spire pierced by lucarnes with gablets; open plan (3 aisles), choir and organ gallery at rear, stenciled ceiling. Built 1854–55; Frank Wills and Henry Dudley, architects; B. F. Randolph, contractor; renovated 1869, including construction of chancel to accommodate choir and altar, installation of trussed wooden ceiling, stenciling of walls and chancel window facings; further alterations in 1962 included placement of choir and organ once again in gallery; stenciled ceiling restored 1983. Notable example of Gothic Revival in Alabama. 1 ext. photo (1934), 1 int. photo (1934); 2 data pages (1936). *See also* Tebbs (T3-ALA-441248).

St. Mary's of Loretto Academy. *See* Gerald-Bethea House (AL-604), 203 S. Lawrence St.

Sayre-Troy House (Troy House) (AL-641), SE corner Adams Ave. and Jackson St. Frame with clapboarding, rectangular (5-bay front) with rear wings, 1 story, shallow hipped roof extending over full-length balustraded porch with square columns, 4 exterior end chimneys; center-hall plan, simple Late Greek Revival style woodwork; late-19th-C. mantels. Built ca. 1850 for Philemon D. Sayre; 2-room addition to W side ca. 1885; demolished 1940s. 3 ext. photos (1934–35), 8 int. photos (1934–35); 2 data pages (1936).

Seibels-Ball-Lanier House. *See* Samuel Swan House (AL-612), 407 Adams Ave.

Smith House. *See* Harris-Smith House (AL-610), SE corner Church and Catoma sts.

Swan, Samuel, House (Seibels-Ball-Lanier House, Charles P. Ball House) (AL-612), 407 Adams Ave. (NE corner Adams Ave. and Hull St.). Brick with stucco, irregular main block with L-shaped street façades, 2 stories, shallow hipped roof with projecting half-hips, cupola, arcuated porches on W and S (street) façades, quoined corners, bracketed cornice; elaborate interior including curved stairway with statuary niche, decorative arches resting on scrolled acanthus-leaf consoles, marble mantels. Dependencies include 2-story brick servants' house and frame (board-and-batten) carriage house; high retaining wall along street sides of lot. Built ca. 1854–55 for Samuel Swan, publisher. Purchased 1857 by Col. John J. Seibels. Originally oriented W to Hull St.; reoriented toward Adams Ave. ca. 1906, when street lowered. Greatly altered after acquisition by Scottish Rite Temple of Montgomery in 1948 (including removal of porches, cupola, major interior alterations); interior heavily vandalized 1979–83; derelict in 1984. Carriage house moved to North Hull Street Historic District 1981. Formerly one of Alabama's best examples of Italianate style residential architecture. Second owner, Col. Seibels, was appointed U.S. minister to Belgium in 1855. 3 ext. photos (1934, including servants' quarters), 5 int. photos (1934); 3 data pages (1936). *See also* Tebbs (T3-ALA-428178, gate only).

Taylor-Ponder-Graves House (Gov. Bibb Graves House) (AL-644), 511 S. McDonough St. Frame with clapboarding, rectangular (5-bay front) with side and rear additions, 2 stories, hipped roof, full-height hexastyle portico across front composed of paneled square columns with Composite capitals, denticulated cornice; center-hall plan, both Federal and Greek Revival period trim. Built ca. 1835, possibly for William Henry Taylor (some sources say John Goldthwaite); later neoclassical renovations include addition of colonnade; incorporated into Downtown Nursing Home ca. 1960 and subsequently altered beyond recognition. Home of David Bibb Graves, governor of Alabama 1927–31 and 1935–39. 4 ext. photos (1934–35), 7 int. photos (1934–35). *See also* FBJ (J7-ALA-1025).

Teague House. *See* Owens-Teague House (AL-606), 440 S. Perry St.

Troy House. *See* Sayre-Troy House (AL-641), SE corner Adams Ave. and Jackson St.

Tyson House. *See* McBryde-Screws-Tyson House (AL-608), 423 Mildred St.

Winter Building (AL-602), 2 Dexter Ave. (SE corner Dexter Ave. and S. Court St.). Brick, 64'0" (6-bay N front) × 66'2" (8-bay W front), 3 stories, shallow hipped roof with bracketed cornice and wide frieze-band, stone lintels, later cast-iron and wood porch along N and W fronts; center-hall plan with cross hall to Court St. front, some Greek Revival style interior trim. Built ca. 1840–43 as commercial edifice for John Gindrat; bracketed cornice and porches added later (porches removed 1948); first floor extensively altered in 20th C. From second-floor offices of Southern Telegraph Co., housed here in 1861, orders sent from Confederate government to fire on Fort Sumter. 2 sheets (1934, including plan, elevations, section, details); 1 ext. photo (1934); 2 data pages (1936). NR.

Montgomery Vicinity

Stone-Young House (AL-650), S side of Co. 54 (Old Selma Rd.) 0.3 mi. E of intersection with Co. 17, approx. 3.5 mi. E of Pintlalla Creek (Montgomery–Lowndes County boundary line) and 1.2 mi. due S of Catoma Creek. Brick with stucco scored to simulate ashlar, 54′9″ (5-bay front) x 66′4″ including portico and small flanking offset rear wings, 2 stories (wings 1 story), roof concealed by false entablature, full-height hexastyle Doric portico across front with entablature embellished by applied laurel-wreath motif, recessed doorway with cast-iron balcony above, flanking 1-bay side porches, Doric loggia at rear; center-hall plan. Brick 1-story smokehouse and ruinous brick kitchen to rear; entire complex originally enclosed by brick wall. Built 1856 for Dr. Barton Stone (1800–1884) as seat of large plantation; second and fourth columns of portico removed ca. 1939 and fluting of other columns replaced by smooth stucco in course of repair work; loggia also enclosed; renovated and reconditioned 1972–73. One of 3 extant Greek Revival style structures built by Stone family in area, including Stone-McCarty-Robinson House (AL-652) and Burkville United Methodist Church, both in Lowndes County. 9 sheets (1936, including plot plan, plans, elevations, section, details, dependencies); 18 ext. photos (1934–36), 15 int. photos (1934–36); 2 data pages (1936).

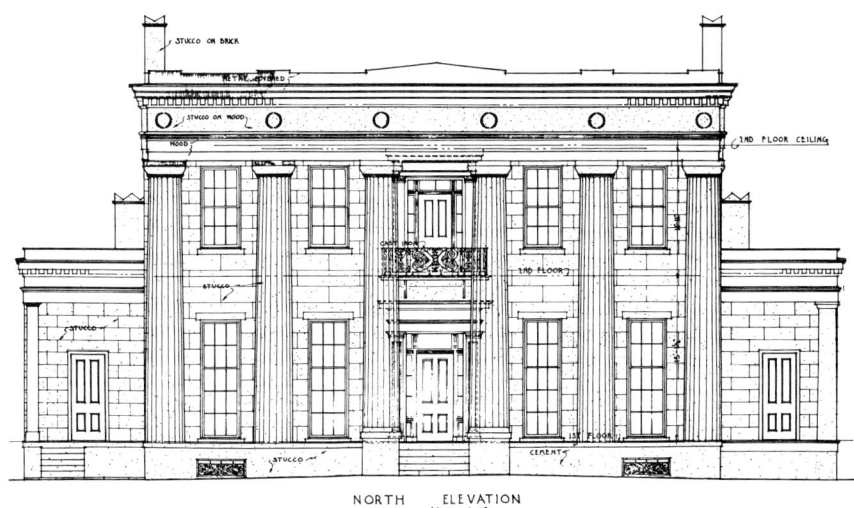

Stone-Young House, Montgomery vicinity (1856).

MORGAN COUNTY

Decatur

Bank Building. *See* Decatur Branch, State Bank of Alabama (AL-348), SW corner Bank St. and Wilson Ave.

Decatur Branch, State Bank of Alabama (Bank Building) (AL-348), SW corner Bank St. and Wilson Ave. Brick (Flemish bond) on granite foundation, 43'9" (4-bay front) x 61'11" including portico, 2 stories, prostyle building with unusual 5-column granite pedimented portico (modified Tuscan order with unusual square capitals), arched window with Gothic tracery piercing tympanum (removed during 1979–80 reconditioning), "eaves cornice" trim adapted from Asher Benjamin's *American Builder's Companion* (1827), granite sills and bull's-eye lintels, fan transoms over doorways; banking room across front with vault in recess framed by Roman Doric architrave; side entrance to second-floor living quarters. Built 1834–36; narrow 1-bay addition at S side (late 19th C.); roof extensively rebuilt after 1870s fire; reconditioned 1934 under WPA, including construction of Jeffersonian serpentine wall (demolished 1975) enclosing rear garden; again reconditioned as tourist bureau 1979–84 including razing of S side addition and partial interior restoration plus reconstruction of rear frame-and-brick dependency on original foundations. One of 5 Decatur buildings to survive Civil War. 8 sheets (1935–36, including plot plan, plans, elevations, details); 5 ext. photos (1934–35, including 1 photo before WPA renovation), 1 int. photo (1934); 3 data pages (1936). NR. *See also* FBJ (J7-ALA-1102 through 1104).

McEntire House. *See* Rhea-Burleson-McEntire House (AL-364), 120 Sycamore St.

Rhea-Burleson-McEntire House (McEntire House) (AL-364), 120 Sycamore St. (SE corner Sycamore and Market sts.). Brick (façade Flemish bond), rectangular (5-bay front) with ell, 2 stories, truncated hipped roof formerly surmounted by open balustraded observatory, full-height tetrastyle portico across front with paneled square piers and balcony carried on cast-iron brackets above main doorway, window openings have granite sills and bull's-eye lintels; 2-tiered porch originally along inside of rear ell; center-hall plan with exceptionally fine interior woodwork including paneled dado in main halls and doors framed with engaged columnar architraves (most original mantelpieces now gone); lawn enclosed by mid-19th-C. iron fence. House built 1836 for merchant John Sevier Rhea, grandson of Tennessee Gov. John Sevier. Home in 1850s of Dr. Aaron A. Burleson, who may have replaced original porch with present portico and balcony. Renovated again during late 19th century including addition of 2 bays to ell and removal of original 12-over-12 and 9-over-9 sashing. Last major renovation (1938) included razing of ell addition as well as story-and-a-half gabled kitchen dependency directly behind, which were replaced by garage addition. House served as headquarters for both Union and Confederate forces during Civil War and was reputedly 1 of only 5 Decatur buildings to survive war. Girlhood home during post–Civil War years of Grace Hinds, afterward the second Lady Curzon, Marchioness of Kedleston. 5 ext. photos (1936), 7 int. photos (1936). NR. *See also* FBJ (J7-ALA-1098 through 1101).

Somerville

Morgan County Courthouse, Old (AL-861), W side of Bluff City Rd. approx. 0.2 mi. N of intersection with Ala. 67, occupying middle of original court square in village of Somerville. Brick on ashlar foundation, approx. 50'4" (5-bay front) x 40'4", 2 stories, hipped roof surmounted by 2-stage cupola with octagonal belfry and dome topped by weathervane, 4 interior end chimneys; center-hall plan on first floor, large courtroom and 2 adjacent chambers on second floor, original Federal style mantelpieces and chairrails. Built 1837; reconditioned 1934 with WPA funds, including removal of original double stairway as well as other interior modifications. Morgan County courthouse 1837–91; later high school and community center. Oldest extant courthouse in Alabama. 1 ext. photo (1978). NR.

Rice, Judge Green P., House (AL-864), approx. 0.2 mi. E of Bluff City Rd. and 0.4 mi. N of Ala. 67; 0.2 mi. due W of Joiner Branch. Brick (Flemish bond) on ashlar foundation, rectangular (5-bay front) with 2-room ell, 1½ stories, gable roof, 3 exterior end chimneys, very unusual molded brick cornices, granite doorsills, main block has modified 2-room plan (narrow room between) with double entrance; 2 additional rooms in ell; paneled wainscoting and naïve Adamesque mantelpieces throughout; enclosed stair from rear porch to upper floor. Built ca. 1835 possibly for Matthew C. Houston as home for Houston's brother-in-law, the Rev. Robert Gillespie, Presbyterian minister. Residence 1840–1900 of Judge Green Pryor Rice, early state legislator, and his descendants. Notable for exceptionally fine brickwork. Restoration of house begun in 1981 after long period of abandonment, including removal of 20th-C. central dormer and porch. 3 ext. photos (1978), 1 int. photo (1978).

PERRY COUNTY

Marion

Courthouse. *See* Perry County Courthouse (AL-766), public square bounded by Washington, Pickens, Jefferson, and Green sts.

Edwards, W. H., House. *See* House (AL-824), Edwards Rd.

Elmcrest. *See* Judge John Moore House (AL-770), Judson College campus.

Ford House. *See* Lowrey-Ford House (AL-822), Washington St.

Hanna, Dr. R. C., House. *See* Whitsett-Hurt-Hanna House (AL-713), 110 W. Lafayette St.

House (W. H. Edwards House) (AL-824), E side of Edwards Rd., approx. 0.1 mi. N of intersection with Lafayette St. Frame with clapboarding, rectangular (6 bays below, 4 bays above), 2 stories with 1-story shed extension at rear projecting beyond lateral walls of main block, gable roof, 4 exterior end chimneys, shed porch across front and along each side abutting against rear extension; 2-room plan (main block) with enclosed stairway between. Built 1830–35; later additions at rear; demolished 1973–74. Unusual variant on typical rear-shed plan and one of earliest frame houses in area. 3 ext. photos (1936), 3 int. photos (1936).

King, Judge Porter, House (AL-772), 1001 Washington St. Frame with clapboarding, rectangular (5-bay front), 2 stories, shallow hipped roof partially concealed by paneled parapet at front and sides, 4 interior end chimneys, full-height hexastyle portico across front with slender fluted Doric columns and paneled corner pilasters, balcony with wire-grille balustrade above doorway; center-hall plan. Built 1856; minor additions to rear ca. 1900. 3 ext. photos (1935), 3 int. photos (1935); 1 data page (1936).

Outbuildings. Kitchen and Servants' Houses (both structures: frame with clapboarding, rectangular, gable roof, 1 interior chimney, 2-room plan); kitchen connected to main house by latticed covered way. Carriage House (frame with clapboarding, rectangular, gable roof, pair of segmentally arched doorways). All structures probably contemporary with main house. 2 general ext. photos (1935).

Lowrey-Ford House (Ford House) (AL-822), W side of Washington St. (Co. 45), 0.8 mi. S of intersection with Murfee Ave. Frame with clapboarding, rectangular (3-bay front) with ell and long galleried wing on N side, 2 stories (side wing 1 story), hipped-and-gable roof; main block has 2 exterior end chimneys, full-height hexastyle portico composed of stucco-covered brick piers with molded caps and bases, full-length upper gallery with cast-iron balustrade, similar L-shaped colonnade at rear; center-hall plan. Built ca. 1858; house damaged by tornado in 1961. 5 ext. photos (1935), 4 int. photos (1935).

Kitchen, W of house. Brick, rectangular (1-bay front), gable roof, 1 exterior end chimney. 2 ext. photos (1935).

Marion Female Seminary (Old Perry County High School) (AL-771), NW corner Monroe and Centreville sts. Brick, approx. 80′ (9-bay front) × 40′, 3 stories, hipped roof, full-height tetrastyle pedimented portico of modified Doric order (slightly wider central bay). Built 1836–37 by Methodists and Presbyterians of Marion; 1884 schematic plan of school shows frame, 1-story rear wing, plus 1-story rectangular dining room with detached kitchen immediately W of main building; extensively remodeled in 1930 for use as public high school (including fenestrational alteration and rebuilding of interior as 2 instead of 3 stories, construction of brick 3-story rear wing). 1 ext. photocopy (n.d.) prior to alterations; 2 ext. photos (1935), 1 photo of page from 1903 annual; 1 data page (1936). NR.

Moore, Gov. Andrew Barry, House (AL-767), N side of Ala. 14, 0.6 mi. W of Courthouse Square at Washington and Green sts. Frame with clapboarding, rectangular (5-bay front), 2 stories, gable roof, 2 exterior end chimneys, pedimented 2-tiered central portico with pair of heavy square wooden columns above and below; center-hall plan. Built ca. 1840; porch later extended full length of house by addition of flanking 1-story bays; original ell also replaced in early 20th C. Restored 1955, flanking porches removed, new addition at rear. Home of Moore, governor of Alabama 1857–61. 1 ext. photo (1934); 1 data page (1936).

Moore, Judge John, House (Elmcrest) (AL-770), H. G. Williams Circle, E of Bibb (Judson) St., between Lafayette and DeKalb sts., on Judson College campus. Frame with clapboarding, rectangular (3-bay front), 2 stories, hipped roof, full-height pedimented central portico composed of 2 pairs of square columns, flanking double windows, balcony above doorway, bracketed cornice. 1 dependency (frame, rectangular, 2-bay front, gable roof). Built ca. 1858; acquired by Judson College in 1920 (interior remodeled and rear wing added); roof damaged by fire after 1935 and rebuilt in gabled form, chimneys removed. Boyhood home of John Trotwood Moore (1858–1929), southern historian and poet, later state archivist of Tennessee. 3 ext. photos (1935), 4 int. photos (1935); 1 data page (1936).

Perry County Courthouse (AL-766), public square bounded by Washington, Pickens, Jefferson, and Green sts. Brick, 69′7″ (5-bay front) × 88′0″, 2 stories, gable roof, amphiprostyle structure (pedimented hexastyle Ionic porticoes at E and W ends with corresponding pilasters), full-length cast-iron balcony on W front with clock in tympanum above dentiled cornice, originally bowed pavilions midway of lateral walls to accommodate twin spiral stairways; center-hall plan with cross hall (first floor), large courtroom on second floor. Built 1855–56, B. F. Parsons, architect; James Didlake, builder; altered and enlarged 1954 (2-story wings added concealing semicircular bows, original stairways removed and other interior changes). 12 sheets (1936, including plot plan, plans, elevations, sections, details); 13 ext. photos (1934–37, including photo of Nicola Marschall marker on lawn), 11 int. photos (1934–37); 1 data page (1936).

Siloam Baptist Church (AL-774), NW corner Washington and Early sts. Brick, rectangular (5 bays deep) above raised basement, gable roof, pedimented distyle in antis portico of modified Doric order with flanking pilasters (lateral walls also pilastered), 2-stage steeple with louvered belfry and octagonal spire; auditorium plan, 2 aisles, originally side and rear galleries. Built 1848–49; interior renovated 1905–1906 (original galleries and pews removed, present rear gallery with curvilinear balustrade erected, art glass replaced original sash windows); original steeple damaged by lightning in July 1949 and subsequently replaced. 2 ext. photos (1935), 2 int. photos (1935); 1 data page (1936). NR.

Whitsett-Hurt-Hanna House (Dr. R. C. Hanna House) (AL-773), 110 W. Lafayette St. Frame with clapboarding, rectangular (5-bay front) plus narrow 1-bay setback end pavilions, low hipped roof terminating in balustraded deck, 4 inside end chimneys, tetrastyle Doric portico, full entablature with dentiled cornice, balcony above entrance; center-hall plan, decorative plasterwork. Also small brick outbuilding NE of house. Reputedly built ca. 1858 for Joseph Whitsett, conveyed to David Scott 1863; occupied by Hurt and Hanna families 1885–1947; later additions to rear. 2 ext. photos (1935), 3 int. photos (1935); 1 data page (1936).

Marion Vicinity

Carlisle Hall (AL-765), 0.1 mi. N of Ala. 14 (Greensboro Rd.) at end of private lane, 0.2 mi. W of intersection with Washington St. (Co.

45) in Marion. Brick with brownstone trim, irregular plan, 2½ stories plus tower, basically shallow hipped roof with subordinate projecting gables, wide bracketed eaves, semirecessed entrance porch abutting asymmetrically placed 5-stage tower with second-floor canopied balcony, arched brownstone hood molds above windows, arcuated porch across rear linking main block with kitchen; basically center-hall plan, very elaborate interior with branched main stairway and continuous open-well elliptical secondary stair from first to third floor, heavily molded woodwork, decorative plaster cornices and medallions, marble mantels. Residential complex also includes brick hipped-roof kitchen and smokehouse, brick cistern, latticed wellhouse, and frame barn. Built 1858–61 for Edward Kenworthy Carlisle, Mobile cotton factor and Perry County planter; Richard Upjohn & Son, architects. Original arcuated entrance porch removed ca. 1900; back porch removed after 1935; house vacant and heavily vandalized 1943–55, including destruction of balustrades, mantels, and original stained glass windows; partially restored since. Outstanding example in Alabama of Italian villa style. 11 ext. photos (1934–36), 11 int. photos (1934–36), 1 photo each of smokehouse interior and barn (1937); 2 data pages (1936).

Cocke-Crenshaw House. See Jones-Cocke-Crenshaw House (AL-823).

Edwards, W. H., House. *Under Marion, see* House (AL-785), Edwards Rd.

Ford House. *Under Marion, see* Lowrey-Ford House (AL-777), Washington St.

Jones-Cocke-Crenshaw House (AL-823), E side of Co. 45 (Washington St.) 1.2 mi. S of intersection with Murfee Ave. Frame with clapboarding, rectangular (5-bay front) with long ell at N rear, 2 stories, originally gable roof with 2 interior end chimneys (main block) and 1 interior chimney (ell); full-height tetrastyle portico across front composed of stucco-covered brick piers with molded caps and bases supporting upper gallery (balustrade removed), also recessed L-shaped rear porch with brick piers; center-hall plan, interior has both Late Federal and Greek Revival style woodwork. Nucleus of house reputedly built 1838 for Mrs. Rachel Jones and originally located on old stage road; moved to present site in mid-19th C. and enlarged and remodeled, including addition of porches; damaged by tornado 1961–62 (gable roof subsequently rebuilt as hipped roof, asbestos siding added). 5 ext. photos (1935), 8 int. photos (1935).

Osborne-Jones House (AL-788), 0.4 mi. E of Co. 45 (Washington St.) 0.7 mi. S of intersection with Murfee Ave. Frame with clapboarding, rectangular (3-bay front) with ell at S rear, 2 stories, gable roof, 2 exterior end chimneys (main block), 2-tiered pedimented tetrastyle entrance portico composed of modified Tuscan colonnettes flanked by triple windows; center-hall plan, grained interior woodwork. Also covered well and frame, rectangular dependency to S of main building. Built ca. 1830; later modifications to rear; razed 1961–62. One of earliest frame houses in area. 4 ext. photos (1936), 4 int. photos (1936), 1 photo of well and outbuilding (1936).

Uniontown

Masonic Hall (AL-768), NE corner Water Ave. and North St. Frame with clapboarding, 28'5" (1-bay front) X 54'4", 2 stories, gable roof, 2-tiered porch across front with exterior stairways at each end to upper level and scroll-cut balustrade, single lodge room upper floor. Built mid-19th C. for Union Lodge No. 50, organized in 1839. Porch enclosed with asbestos siding ca. 1950. 2 ext. photos (1935).

Pitts' Folly (AL-267), S side of Ala. 21 approx. 0.2 mi. SE of Southern Railroad crossing and 1.1 mi. SE of intersection with U.S. 80. Frame with clapboarding, rectangular (3-bay front), 2 stories, gable roof, full-height semiperipteral portico across N (front) and along E side composed of 14 stuccoed brick columns after rudimentary Doric order, full-length second-floor gallery, cornice surmounted on N by low paneled parapet, recessed doorway with in antis Doric colonnettes; center-hall plan. Notable gardens surrounding house. Built 1851–52 for Philip Henry Pitts (1816–84), Virginia-born planter; later additions at rear. Notable example of improvisational "country Greek Revival." Still occupied by descendant of builder in 1978. 11 ext. photos, including 3 photos of grounds (1935–36), 6 int. photos (1936); 2 data pages (1937). NR.

Summerhouse (Gazebo). Small frame octagonal structure with low conical roof and enclosed by diagonally placed boards. Probably

built late 19th C.; destroyed. 1 ext. photo (1936).
Kitchen and Wellhouse. Kitchen is frame with clapboarding, rectangular (2-bay front), 1 story, gable roof, 1 interior chimney; 2-room plan. Adjacent wellhouse open structure with pyramidal roof upheld by 4 rough corner posts. Built ca. 1850; destroyed. 3 ext. photos (1936).
Dairy (Old Cooler). Frame with clapboarding, small rectangular structure with inset at NE corner, W end latticed (over large underground storage room). Built ca. 1850; destroyed. 1 ext. photo (1936).
Playhouse. Frame covered with split logs, rectangular (1 bay), 1 story, gable roof with wooden shakes, mud-and-stick exterior end chimney encased with split logs. Probably built late 19th C.; chimney rebuilt in brick ca. 1940; ruinous in 1978. 1 ext. photo (1936).

Westwood (AL-769), facing S on E side of Ala. 61 approx. 0.7 mi. N of intersection with U.S. 80. Frame with clapboarding, basically rectangular (6-bay front) with advanced 2-bay pedimented center pavilion, shallow gable roof with subordinate cross-gable, small asymmetrical entrance porch fronting center pavilion with adjacent bay window to E, flanking recessed 1-story cast-iron porches, end elevations of house each have narrow 2-story elliptically arched loggia set between narrow 1-bay square corner "turrets" surmounted by paneled parapet, 1-bay pedimented off-center extension at rear (with later kitchen addition), denticulated cornice encircling house; asymmetrical plan with high-ceilinged formal rooms flanking entrance hall. Built ca. 1850 for James Lewis Price, Virginia-born lawyer and planter, as seat of 4,700-acre estate on outskirts of Uniontown; later acquired by son-in-law Alexander Caldwell Davidson (1826–97). Naïve expression of romantic eclecticism combining neoclassical and picturesque elements. 3 ext. photos (1935), 6 int. photos (1935). NR.

PICKENS COUNTY

Aliceville

Hughes, Benjamin, House. *See* Ingleside (AL-395), Ala. 14 (Second St.).

Ingleside (Benjamin Hughes House) (AL-395), E side of Ala. 14 (Second St.) approx. 0.5 mi. S of railroad crossing and 1.3 mi. N of Lubbub Creek Bridge, in large oak grove on southern edge of Aliceville. Frame with clapboarding, 48′4″ (5-bay front) x 38′8″, 2½ stories, gable roof, 4 exterior end chimneys, full-height tetrastyle portico with slender freestanding square columns, second-floor balcony originally resting on slender wooden supports, 2-tiered porch at rear; center-hall plan, unusual stair arrangement with reverse-flight stairway in front hall, formerly linked at landing with partially enclosed stair from SE (dining) room, paneled dado, some grained woodwork (now painted over). Early dependencies included frame kitchen (SE rear) and smokehouse (NE rear), log "cook's house," board-and-batten carriage house. Built 1848–52 for Benjamin Jolly Hughes, merchant-farmer born in Camden District, S.C.; semidetached "new" kitchen added to S side rear of house ca. 1900 (razed when second kitchen-wing addition built at rear during 1950s); post-1946 renovations include removal of sliding doors between rooms on both sides of main hall, overlaying of original floor, removal of dining room stair, concrete-and-tile porch floor. All dependencies except carriage house destroyed. Hughes's store formerly stood beside main road SW of house. Still owned and occupied by descendants of builder in 1978. 8 ext. photos (1937, including old kitchen, smokehouse, and cook's house), 3 int. photos (1937).

Aliceville Vicinity

Hughes, Dr. William, House (AL-396), approx. 0.4 mi. due N of Hughes Creek at point approx. 5.0 mi. E of Ala. 14 (E by SE of Aliceville); S side of unnamed dirt road approx. 3.6 mi. SE of road's juncture with Ala. 2 at point 1.4 mi. E of intersection of Ala. 2 and Ala. 14 S of Aliceville; also approx. 1.2 mi. SE of Bethany Cemetery. Frame with clapboarding, rectangular (5-bay front), 2 stories, gable roof (broken at rear), 4 exterior end chimneys; central 2-tiered pedimented tetrastyle portico with Doric colonnettes and frieze, portico ceiling embellished with decorative plasterwork including acanthus-leaf centerpiece and denticulated cornice; center-hall plan, elaborately plastered interior, main hall bisected by elliptical arch resting on scrolled consoles, curving stair, marbleized baseboards. Dependencies include frame smokehouse and "buggy house." Built ca. 1845–50 for physician born in Camden District, S.C.; plasterwork reputedly executed by Italian artisans; razed ca. 1939. Unusually ornate treatment of simple frame dwelling. 6 ext. photos (1937, including smokehouse and "buggy house"), 13 int. photos (1937).

Carrollton

Methodist Church (First United Methodist Church) (AL-394), NE corner Tuscaloosa (Ala. 86) and Scott sts. Brick, rectangular (3-bay front, 4 bays deep), gable roof, pedimented façade surmounted by belfry with tall, slender octagonal spire, tall Greek Revival style central doorway; open plan with 3 blocks of slip pews, slave gallery at rear. Built 1855–57; James Pearce, contractor; subsequent changes included 2-story rear addition (ca. 1900) and renovation of pulpit area, with installation of choir loft behind; razed 1949 for new structure. 3 ext. photos (1937), 7 int. photos (1937, including 2 photos of plaques listing pastors and presiding elders, 1854–1934).

Pettus, Edmund Winston, House (AL-372), E side Ala. 17 approx. 0.3 mi. N of courthouse square at Carrollton. Frame with clapboarding, approx. 46'3" (5-bay front) X 20'0" plus ell (40'2" X 17'0") on S side and parallel N rear wing, 1 story on brick piers, gable roof, 2 exterior end chimneys (main block), central pedimented entrance porch with 2 pairs of square columns; center-hall plan, paneled dado. Built ca. 1850; later addition at NE rear. First owner, Pettus (1821–1907), was lawyer and circuit judge for Pickens County; moved 1858 to Selma and subsequently became U.S. senator (1897–1907). 3 ext. photos (1937), 1 int. photo (1937).

Phoenix Hotel (AL-393), N side of courthouse square on E side of Phoenix St. Frame with clapboarding, L-shaped with irregularly spaced bays at both upper and lower levels, 2 stories, hipped roof extending over full-length double veranda along S (front) and W sides supported by 13 slender square columns; center hall with rooms to either side; 1-story wing at central rear (N). Built 1841 for Benjamin F. Roper, sheriff of Pickens County, to replace burned hostelry; minor modifications in late 19th C.; razed 1968 to make way for county office building (some of columns re-used in modern portico of Parks E. Ball house near Aliceville). Phoenix Hotel was important relay stop on Mobile-Columbus, Miss., stage road. 9 ext. photos (1937), 6 int. photos (1937).

Memphis

Boykin, Will, House (AL-870), in rural community on W bank of Tombigbee River, E side of Co. 1 approx. 5.1 mi. N of intersection with Ala. 32 about 10 mi. SW of Aliceville. Frame (vertical siding over wood studs) on cast concrete and stone piers, rectangular (4-bay front) with ell and parallel lean-to at rear, 1 story, gable roof (cross-gable over ell), 2 exterior end chimneys, shed-roof porch across front; main block had 2 rooms with single ell room and shed room behind; pair of pilastered mantelpieces of naïve Federal design may have been taken from another structure. Construction date of house unknown; moved from undetermined previous site and reconstructed ca. 1940 by Will Boykin, black farmer. Acquired 1975 by U.S. government and subsequently razed as part of Tennessee-Tombigbee Waterway project. 4 sheets (1978, including plot plan, plan, elevations, details); 4 ext.

photos (1978), 4 int. photos (1978); 8 data pages (1978).

Charity, Tom, House (AL-871), in rural community on W bank of Tombigbee River, W side of Co. 1 approx. 5.0 mi. N of intersection with Ala. 32 about 10 mi. SW of Aliceville. Frame with clapboarding on brick and concrete piers, overall dimensions 22'4" (3-bay front) X 33'10", 1 story, gable roof, 2 exterior end chimneys, shed-roof porch across front and along one side, second porch at rear; main block has single room with smaller room at rear turned perpendicular to main block; mantelpieces in house represent naïve folk interpretation of neoclassical elements. Built ca. 1885–1900; longtime domicile of Tom Coleman (alias "Tom Charity"), local black bootlegger. Acquired 1975 by U.S. government and subsequently razed as part of Tennessee-Tombigbee Waterway project. 4 sheets (1978, including plot plan, plan, elevations, details); 7 ext. photos (1978), 1 int. photo (1978); 2 photos of outbuildings (1978); 8 data pages (1978).

Memphis Community (AL-869), general historical and architectural information on rural village located on W bank of Tombigbee River, along Co. 1 approx. 5.0 mi. N of intersection with Ala. 32 about 10 mi. SW of Aliceville. First settled in 1841 and developed as small trading center in rich cotton-growing area. Town site partially flooded by Gainesville Reservoir of Tennessee-Tombigbee Waterway in early 1980s. 35 data pages (1978). *See also* preceding entries for Will Boykin and Tom Charity houses.

Pickensville

Baptist Church (AL-342), approx. 0.1 mi. SE of intersection of Ala. 86 and Ala. 14; N side Bonner Mill Rd. (Bluff St. on Pickensville plat) facing S. Frame with clapboarding (façade flush boarding), rectangular (2-bay front, 4 bays deep), 1 story, gable roof, modified temple-type tetrastyle portico with square columns resting on low brick stylobate, 3-stage belfry with short octagonal spire; very plain auditorium-type interior with three blocks of slip pews and "Amen" corners. Built ca. 1850 for congregation organized in 1847; later modifications include fish-scale shingling in tympanum of portico; razed 1958. 3 ext. photos (1937), 2 int. photos (1937).

Ferguson, William C., House (Gus Long House) (AL-386), approx. 0.2 mi. E of Ala. 14 and approx. 0.3 mi. S of Ala. 86; E side of Chopitoulas St. just SE of Methodist church on Pickensville plat. Frame with clapboarding, rectangular (5-bay front), 2½ stories, gable roof, 4 exterior end chimneys, central tetrastyle pedimented portico with paired square columns supporting upper porch, wheatsheaf balustrade, small pedimented porch on S side and shed porch at rear; center-hall plan. Built ca. 1850 for James Chalmers as gift to daughter, Mrs. Ferguson; 1-story kitchen ell added ca. 1900; razed 1966. Said to have been prototype for nearby Dr. A. M. Wilkins House (AL-378) and other dwellings in Pickensville area. 5 ext. photos (1937), 3 int. photos (1937).

House (Sanders House, Henry Williams House) (AL-392), approx. 0.1 mi. SE of intersection of Ala. 86 and Ala. 14; NW corner of Bonner Mill Rd. (Bluff St.) and Ferguson St. on Pickensville plat. Frame with clapboarding, L-shaped with 6-bay street fronts on S and E sides, 1 story, hipped roof extending along street sides, L-shaped gallery at rear; unusual in having no center hall (3 rooms end-to-end along S and E fronts). Traditionally dated 1841 (first owner unknown); razed 1972–73 to make way for new house on same site. 5 ext. photos (1937, including well), 4 int. photos (1937).

Long, Gus, House. *See* Ferguson House (AL-386), 0.2 mi. E of Ala. 14.

Methodist Church (AL-387), approx. 0.1 mi. SE of intersection of Ala. 86 and Ala. 14; E side of Ferguson St. on Pickensville plat. Frame with clapboarding (façade flush boarding), approx. 40'4" (2-bay front) X 60'9" (including portico 10'5" deep), 1 story, gable roof, temple-type pedimented hexastyle Doric portico, 2-stage belfry capped by low-pitched pyramidal roof; auditorium-type interior with 3 blocks of slip pews and "Amen" corners, semicircular rail-enclosed pulpit dais. Built 1842; post-1937 modifications include partitioning of area to either side of pulpit dais, replacement of original brick foundation with cinderblock. 3 ext. photos (1937), 2 int. photos (1937).

Sanders House. *See* House (AL-392), near intersection of Ala. 86 and Ala. 14.

Store ("Peterson Building") (AL-309), NW corner of intersection of Ala. 14 and Ala. 86; Broad Ave.

and Main St. on Pickensville plat. Frame with clapboarding, rectangular (5-bay E front, 4-bay S front), 2 stories, hipped roof; lower floor used for commercial purposes, living quarters upstairs, some simple Federal period woodwork. Built ca. 1840; razed ca. 1965. Owned by merchant Albert Peterson (1833–95) during riverboat era of late 19th C. 3 ext. photos (1937), 5 int. photos (1937).

Wilkins, Dr. A. M., House (AL-378), approx. 0.1 mi. SW of intersection of Ala. 86 and Ala. 14; W side of courthouse square on old Pickensville plat, due S of Ferry Rd. Frame with clapboarding, approx. 49'0" (5-bay front) × 37'4", 2½ stories, gable roof, 4 exterior end chimneys, central pedimented tetrastyle portico with paired square columns supporting second-floor porch, wheatsheaf balustrade; center-hall plan. Dependencies. Built ca. 1850; late-19th-C. offset wing to SW rear; used as hunting lodge until 1973; subsequently abandoned and stripped; ruinous in 1978. 7 ext. photos (1937, including 1 dependency), 2 int. photos (1937).

Williams, Henry, House. *See* House (AL-392), intersection of Ala. 86 and Ala. 14.

PIKE COUNTY

Orion

Alabama College. *See* Orion Male and Female Institute (AL-574), old U.S. 231.

Baptist Church (AL-562), E side of old U.S. 231 approx. 0.2 mi. S of junction with Co. 37. Frame with clapboarding, rectangular (2-bay front, 4 bays deep), 1 story, gable roof, pedimented façade with 2 narrow doors, square belfry, modified Greek Revival detail; open plan with 2 aisles, slip pews with central divider to separate men and women worshipers. Built 1858 for Missionary Baptist congregation. 3 ext. photos (1935), 2 int. photos (1935).

Chancey, John, House. *See* William C. White House (AL-572), old U.S. 231.

Hanchey-Pennington House (AL-563), E side of old U.S. 231 approx. 0.2 mi. N of junction with Co. 37 and approx. 0.3 mi. S of Montgomery County line. Frame with clapboarding, rectangular (5-bay front), 1 story, hipped roof, central pedimented distyle portico with slender square wooden pier-supports; center-hall plan, modified Greek Revival interior trim. Built ca. 1850, possibly for Martin Hanchey; breezeway and garage added to N side in 20th C. 2 ext. photos (1935), 1 int. photo (1935).

Henderson House. *See* McCullough-Henderson House (AL-596), unmarked road off old U.S. 231.

McCullough-Henderson House (Henderson House) (AL-596), approx. 0.3 mi. SE of old U.S. 231 on N side of unmarked paved road that intersects old U.S. 231 approx. 0.4 mi. S of junction with Co. 37 at Orion. Frame with clapboarding, rectangular (5-bay front) with ell, 2 stories (ell 1 story), gable roof, 2 exterior end chimneys, central pedimented tetrastyle portico with square columns and upper gallery; center-hall plan, unplastered interior. Built 1854–55 for William Thomas McCullough; later 1-story rear additions; chimney rebuilt, aluminum siding added, columns modified by addition of brick base. 1 ext. photo (1935), 2 int. photos (1935).

Orion Male and Female Institute (Alabama College) (AL-574), W side old U.S. 231, 0.2 mi. N of junction with Co. 37, which is approx. 11 mi. N of Troy town square. Frame with clapboarding, rectangular (3-bay front, 4-bay sides), 2 stories, gable roof, pedimented portico with 4 square columns, belfry, modified Greek Revival trim. Built ca. 1850 for Baptist-related educational institution incorporated in 1848 (sometimes known as Orion Academy); building materials contributed by Solomon Siler; later became public high school; demolished 1953; 2 ext. photos (1935).

Siler, Solomon, House (AL-597), W side old U.S. 231, approx. 0.1 mi. S of junction with Co. 37, which is approx. 11 mi. N of Troy town square. Frame with clapboarding, rectangular (5-bay front) with flanking offset rear wings (3 bays each), 2 stories (wings 1 story), hipped roof, 4 exterior end chimneys (main block), tall central pedimented portico with 2 pairs of tapering square columns flanking doorway, upstairs porch with lattice balustrade; center-hall plan, curving stair with turned newel and marbleized risers. Built ca. 1850; later rear additions. Moved W in 1953 to make way for widening of highway (N wing then demolished). Siler (1788–1854) was a wealthy planter, benefactor of Orion Male and Female Institute. 5 ext. photos (1935), 10 int. photos (1935).

White, William C., House (John Chancey House) (AL-572), W side of old U.S. 231 approx. 0.1 mi. S of Montgomery-Pike county line and 0.3 mi. N of U.S. 231 intersection with Pike Co. 37 (China Grove Rd.). Frame with clapboard (façade rabbeted), rectangular (5-bay front), 1 story, hipped roof, central tetrastyle portico composed of 2 pairs of columns with fluted shafts and unusual molded box-like bases and capitals, denticulated architrave with soffit embellished by mutules, fluted window surrounds with paneled cornerblocks and keystones, unusual door combining naïve Adamesque and neoclassical elements; center-hall plan. Built ca. 1850; moved approx. 50′ W of original site about 1935, when highway widened. Subsequent alterations include rear addition, asbestos siding over clapboarding, numerous interior modifications. 1 ext. photo (1935), 1 int. photo (1935).

RUSSELL COUNTY

Cottonton Vicinity

Cotton Gin and Well Sweep, Cliatt Plantation (Mule Cotton Gin, Well Sweep) (AL-552). Part of 19th-C. plantation complex developed by William Cliatt around his extant (1979) house on W side of Ala. 165, approx. 0.2 mi. S of junction with Co. 12; approx. 2.4 mi. S of Hatchechubbee Creek Bridge and 2 mi. W of Chattahoochee River. 2 general data pages (1936).
Cotton Gin, located approx. 0.8 mi. W of dwelling on S side of Co. 12. Frame superstructure (approx. 30′ × 30′), 1 story with loft, gable roof, open below with board-and-batten sheathing above; structure sheltered cotton gin consisting of mule-powered horizontal wheel linked by series of gears to ginning machinery mounted in loft. Built mid-19th C.; destroyed. At top capacity, gin could produce 6 to 7 bales of cotton in 12-hour day. 2 sheets (1936, including plans, elevations, details); 2 ext. photos (1936), 3 int. photos (1936).
Well Sweep, W of dwelling (exact site unknown). Slender 22′-long pole fashioned from wild cherry and mounted on tall post (18″ in diameter) hewn from longleaf pine; chain and bucket at end of pole. Probably erected late 19th C.; destroyed. 1 sheet (1936, including ground plan, elevation, section); 2 photos (1936).

Mule Cotton Gin, Cliatt Plantation. *See* Cotton Gin and Well Sweep (AL-552), Ala. 165.

Crawford

Tuckabatchee Masonic Lodge No. 863 (AL-515), S side of U.S. 80 immediately E of and opposite junction with Co. 79. Frame with clapboarding, 28′6″ (3-bay front) × 40′4″, 2 stories, gable roof extending forward to form pedimented portico with 4 slender square columns, center columns carry small second-floor entrance gallery reached by "dogleg" stairway in W bay of porch. Built ca. 1848; lower floor originally used as school; asbestos shingles applied to exterior ca. 1950. 3 ext. photos (1935), 3 int. photos (1935).

Fort Mitchell Vicinity

Crowell, Col. John, House. *See* Crowell-Cantey-Alexander House (AL-578), near Ala. 165.

Crowell-Cantey-Alexander House (Col. John Crowell House) (AL-578), approx. 1 mi. E of Ala. 165 approx. 3.2 mi. due N of Uchee Creek Bridge; W ½ of Section 22, Township 16 N, Range 30 E. Frame with clapboarding, rectangular (5-bay front) plus large offset wing at NW rear corner, 1 story, gable roof, 2 interior chimneys, continuous balustraded deck-like porch across front and along each side covered by widely overhanging roof with slender square columns resting on freestanding circular brick bases; center-hall plan. Dependencies included 3 log structures (slave house, "gardener's house," and "old woodshed") plus plantation cemetery. Nucleus of structure was house built for Col. John Crowell, Sr. (1785–1846); renovated and en-

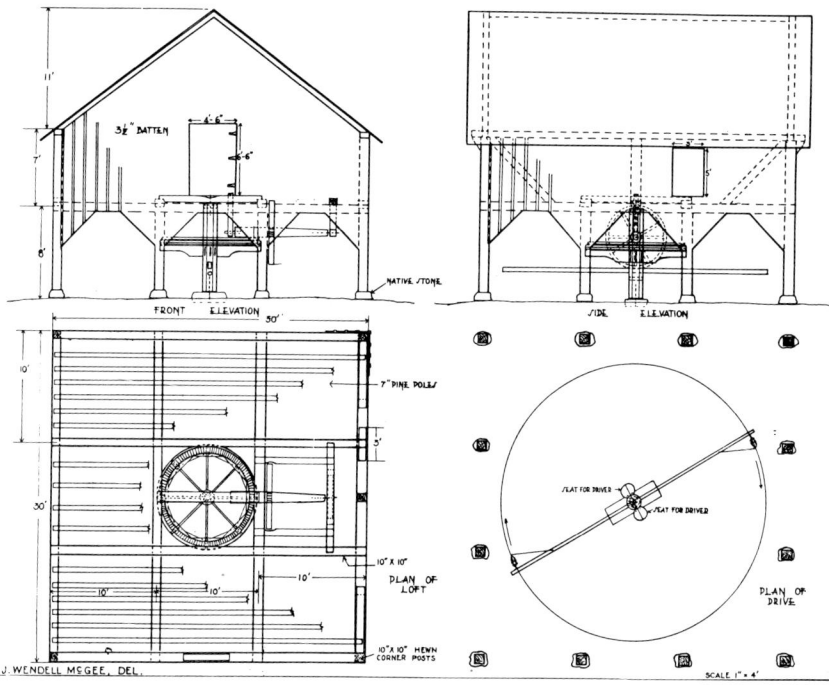

Cotton gin on Cliatt plantation, Cottonton vicinity (mid-19th century, destroyed).

larged in late 19th C., including addition of wing; burned ca. 1970. Crowell was last U.S. agent to Creek Indian Nation (1821–36) and only delegate to Congress from Alabama Territory (1818–19). House later residence of Confederate Brig. Gen. James Cantey (1818–74). 11 ext. photos (1935, including 4 photos of dependencies), 4 int. photos (1935).

Post Office, Old (E. Johnson House) (AL-594), exact location undetermined. Frame with clapboarding, rectangular (5-bay front), 1 story, gable roof, 1 exterior end chimney and 1 interior chimney, crude shed porch enframing entrance to open dogtrot-type hall, unglazed windows each covered by single batten shutter; 2 rooms to either side of central passage. Built ca. 1840, possibly for Enoch Johnson; destroyed. 2 ext. photos (1935), 2 int. photos (1935).

Glennville.

See Pittsview Vicinity.

Pittsview Vicinity

Glennville Plantation. See Americus Mitchell House (AL-570), U.S. 431.

Mitchell, Americus, House (Elmoreland, Glennville Plantation) (AL-570), W side of U.S. 431 approx. 5.1 mi. S of Hatchechubbee Creek Bridge; approx. 5.5 mi. S of U.S. 431 intersection with Co. 4 at Pittsview. Frame with clapboarding (façade novelty siding), 52′6″ (5-bay front) × 49′5″, 2 stories, shallow hipped roof extending over full-length hexastyle Doric portico with corresponding entablature, slightly wider intercolumniation at center bay, recessed main doorway framed by classical architrave, similar doorway directly above opening onto small balcony enclosed by turned wooden balustrade; center-hall plan, broad semielliptical archway between foyer and wider stairhall at rear containing curved stair; notable Greek Revival style mantelpieces, wood trim, and decorative plasterwork (plaster centerpieces in parlor now destroyed); 1-story porch formerly across rear of house, extending beyond main structure as covered way to flanking dependencies. S dependency is large octagonal chamber (now dining room) with 2-room wing at rear, N dependency (destroyed) believed to have been kitchen; additional elements of complex include frame servants' house, formal garden, and grape arbor. House built 1842–44; S octagonal dependency added ca. 1850–60. Complex restored in early 1920s, including enlargement of rear porch, creation of formal garden; again refurbished ca. 1937, when paneled wainscoting installed in stairhall; subsequent changes minor. Called Glennville Plantation since about 1937 to perpetuate name of dead antebellum planting community of which estate was a part. 15 sheets (1936, including plot plan, plans, elevations, section, details); 14 ext. photos (1935–36, including 1 photo of servants' house, 2 photos of grounds), 14 int. photos (1935–36); 2 data pages (1936).

Quarles, W. T., House. *See* Richardson-Quarles-Comer House (AL-514), unmarked road off U.S. 431.

Richardson-Quarles-Comer House (W. T. Quarles House) (AL-514), 0.4 mi. W of U.S. 431 on S side of unmarked dirt road approx. 5.9 mi. S of Hatchechubbee Creek Bridge; 0.5 mi. due S of Glennville Plantation at SW edge of old community of Glennville. Frame with clapboarding (novelty siding at front and sides), original dimensions approx. 52'4" (5-bay front) x 40'0" including L-shaped porch across W (front) and N side, 1 story, hipped roof extending over porch supported by fluted Doric columns, double-leaf doorway adapted from Plate 29 of Asher Benjamin's *Practice of Architecture* (1833), flanking floor-length windows; center-hall plan, notable plasterwork including hall ceiling medallion (reproduction of original) and oakleaf frieze in NW room. Built ca. 1845–50 for Walker Richardson; restored and enlarged ca. 1950, including addition of flanking wings and extension of porch along S side, utilizing columns removed from N porch when wings added; several interior modifications. 3 ext. photos (1936), 2 int. photos (1936).

Seale

Dudley Hotel (AL-531), SE corner Railroad and Main sts., facing N toward old Seaboard Coastline Railroad tracks and former courthouse square; approx. 0.1 mi. E of U.S. 431. Frame with clapboarding, basically L-shaped, 2 stories, intersecting gable roofs with bracketed cornice and bargeboard trim, 2-tiered balustraded porches on N and W elevations; irregular interior plan. Built 1882 for Charles Hammond Dudley, incorporating mid-19th-C. structure moved from NE corner of Main and Glennville sts.; destroyed by fire 19 Sept. 1940. 3 ext. photos (1936).

Seale Vicinity

Bass-Perry House (Magnolia Green, Mott House) (AL-588), NW side of U.S. 431 approx. 2.4 mi. SW of Uchee Creek Bridge and 2.2 mi. NE of junction with Ala. 169 at Seale. Frame with clapboarding (façade flush siding), rectangular (3-bay front), 2 stories, hipped roof extending over tetrastyle Doric portico with full-length balcony, 2 interior chimneys, wide double-leaf doors on both levels flanked by long 3-part windows, fluted door and window surrounds, originally 1-story central pedimented portico at rear; center-hall plan, simple Greek Revival style interior woodwork. Begun ca. 1840 for planter Hartwell Bass (1797–1843), born in Virginia, who died prior to completion; architect believed to be same as that for Americus Mitchell House (AL-570), Pittsview Vicinity; semidetached 1-story gabled wing added at NE corner in late 19th C.; renovated and restored ca. 1938, including addition of carport on W, solarium on E, reconstruction of rear entrance porch and replacement of full-length upper gallery with small iron-railed balcony. 7 ext. photos (1935), 13 int. photos (1935).

Magnolia Green. *See* Bass-Perry House (AL-588), U.S. 431.

Mott House. *See* Bass-Perry House (AL-588), U.S. 431.

Vilula

Birds' Nest, The (Martin House) (AL-545), E side of U.S. 43 in Vilula community, approx. 2.0 mi. S of Silver Run Creek Bridge and 2.4 mi. S of intersection with Ala. 26 at Seale. Frame with clapboarding, square (5-bay front), 1 story with half-basement at rear, shallow hipped roof breaking into broad full-length shed porch, 2 interior chimneys, pilastered doorway, unusual "split" blinds at windows; center-hall plan, late Greek Revival style interior woodwork. Built ca. 1845–55 for a Mr. Billups; reconditioned ca. 1935, including rebuilding of raised back porch; extensive additions at front and sides (1940s) entailing enclosure of porches. Named The Birds' Nest ca. 1870 when it became home of Lyman Waddell Martin family. Restaurant (The Vilula Tea Garden) since 1945. 5 ext. photos (1935), 5 int. photos (1935).

Martin House. *See* The Birds' Nest (AL-545), U.S. 43.

SHELBY COUNTY

Harpersville Vicinity

Chancellor, William, House (AL-435), at Chancellor Crossroads approx. 4.0 mi. SE of Harpersville and 1.4 mi. due N of Coosa River; immediately SE of Ala. 76 intersection with unmarked road to Harpersville. Frame with clapboarding, approx. 52′10″ (5-bay front) × 17′10″ plus ell approx. 18′11″ × 40′4″, 1 story, gable roof extending over L-shaped porch at rear, 3 exterior end chimneys, central gabled entrance porch; center-hall plan with cross hall between main block and ell, stippled and grained interior woodwork. Built mid-19th C. 2 ext. photos (1935); 1 data page (1936).

Eastis House. *See* Rock House (AL-447), U.S. 280.

Rock House, The (Eastis House) (AL-447), at end of farm lane on N side of U.S. 280 (Ala. 38) approx. 1.3 mi. E of intersection with U.S. 23 (Ala. 25) in Harpersville. Regular ashlar (limestone), approx. 32′6″ (4-bay front) × 21′1″, 2 stories, gable roof, 2 interior end chimneys, simply molded box cornice, 2 doorways (each with elliptical transom and deeply paneled reveals); 2-room plan, enclosed stairway, simple Federal style interior woodwork. Built ca. 1835 (possibly for James McCollum); present frame ell and front porch ca. 1900. Possibly unique in Alabama as surviving example of ashlar construction in antebellum domestic architecture. 2 ext. photos (1935), 1 int. photo (1935); 1 data page (1936).

Helena Vicinity

Cotton Press (Mule Cotton Press) (AL-422), in Hillsboro community on W side of Co. 17 approx. 1.1 mi. S of intersection with Ala. 261 in Helena. Heavy timber framework (approx. 8′0″ × 8′0″ × 14′0″ high) enclosing wooden screw (17″ in diameter) of white oak mounted on cross pieces. Originally protected by gable roof covered with wooden shingles. Machine utilized to compress cotton bales for bagging and shipment. Built 1869 in conjunction with cotton gin owned by Robert Thomas Dunnam; abandoned and ruinous 1936; subsequently removed (possibly to museum). 2 sheets (1936, including plot plan, plan, elevation, details).

Mule Cotton Press. *See* Cotton Press (AL-422), Co. 17.

Montevallo

King, Edmund, House (AL-438), NW of intersection of Highland and Bloch sts. on University of Montevallo campus. Brick, approx. 46′6″ (5-bay front) × 23′9″, 2 stories, gable roof, 2 exterior end chimneys, molded brick watertable; center-hall plan, chair-rails, Federal period mantels. Built 1823; house partially stuccoed and scored to simulate ashlar in mid-19th C.; 3-bay porch with scroll-cut balustrade added, frame 1-story ell and rear porch ca. 1900. Extensively reconditioned 1973–74 as university guest house, including dismantling and reconstruction of interior (using original woodwork); stucco removed and exterior veneered with "antique brick" manufactured at Williamsburg, Va.; Gene Jones, AIA, architect; Nicholas Holmes, AIA, consultant; Lewis Mason, contractor. 2 ext. photos (1934), 2 int. photos (1934); 2 data pages (1936). NR.

Montevallo Male Institute (Reynolds Hall, University of Montevallo) (AL-427), N side of Highland St. between Middle and Vines sts. on campus of University of Montevallo. Brick, 71′8″ (7-bay front) × 51′6″, 2 stories, shallow hipped roof concealed by parapet, pilastered façade with full entablature and central tetrastyle Ionic portico (originally surmounted by paneled parapet and 3-stage octagonal cupola), upper windows of façade arcuated; center-hall plan (first floor), large central assembly room on second floor. Built 1851 according to plans drawn by Gen. C. M. Shelley (George R. Allen, master-carpenter); subsequent alterations include removal of wooden parapet and replacement of cupola with triangular pediment (prior to 1896); addition of low 2-story wings at rear (early 20th C.). Extensively renovated 1970 including addition of double iron stairway at front, gutting of interior. 1 ext. photo (1934); 3 data pages (1936).

SUMTER COUNTY

Brewersville.

See listings under Coatopa Vicinity.

Coatopa Vicinity

Brewersville Methodist Church (AL-295), E side of Ala. 28 in old community of Brewersville, approx. 2.7 mi. N of junction with Co. 23 at Coatopa; 5.0 mi. N of Ala. 28 intersection with U.S. 80 S of Coatopa. Frame with clapboarding, 32'4" (2-bay front) X 40'4" (3 bays deep), 1 story, gable roof, pedimented façade with twin double-leaf doorways; little-altered interior with 2 aisles, original slip pews, pulpit dais and flanking lampstands with flatwood Communion rail in front, slave gallery at sides and rear. Built ca. 1850; subsequent changes include 20th-C. translucent window sashing, cinderblock foundation (replacing original open-work brick foundation), 1957 frame addition at rear. 4 ext. photos (1935), 5 int. photos (1935).

House (Henson House) (AL-293), E side of Ala. 28 in old community of Brewersville approx. 2.6 mi. N of junction with Co. 23 at Coatopa; approx. 4.9 mi. N of Ala. 28 intersection with U.S. 80 S of Coatopa. Frame with clapboarding, rectangular (5-bay front), 1½ stories, saltbox-type gable roof with low shed across rear, 4 exterior end chimneys, central modified Greek Revival style pedimented portico with paired square columns; center-hall plan with enclosed stair; random-width flush-board walls of heart pine; frame wellhouse. Built ca. 1840; ell added much later; portico removed ca. 1938; heavily altered in 1975 including brick veneer, replacement sashing, extensive interior changes. 3 ext. photos (1936, including wellhouse), 2 int. photos (1936).

Lee Haven (AL-290), E side of Co. 21 approx. 1.6 mi. S of Ponkabia Creek Bridge and 2.6 mi. S of junction of Co. 21 with Ala. 28 between Livingston and Coatopa; approx. 3.2 mi. N of junction of Co. 21 with U.S. 80 near Bellamy. Frame with clapboarding, main block approx. 48'4" (5-bay front) X 33'2" plus semidetached central rear wing approx. 70' long, 2 stories with 1-story shed across rear (wing also 1 story), gable roof, 4 exterior end chimneys (main block), central distyle pedimented portico, unusually large glazed double-leaf doorway with balcony above; center-hall plan, paneled dado. Dependencies include plantation office; extensive landscaped grounds. Built 1852 for Col. James Madison Lee from Louisa County, Va.; early-20th-C. alterations include addition of terraces flanking portico, renovation of rear wing with enclosure of open passage between wing and main block. 5 ext. photos (1935, including office), 5 int. photos (1935); 2 data pages (1937).

Patton, Joseph E., House (AL-292), W side Ala. 28 in old community of Brewersville approx. 2.2 mi. N of junction with Co. 23 at Coatopa; approx. 4.2 mi. N of junction of Ala. 28 with U.S. 80 S of Coatopa. Frame with clapboarding, approx. 48'6" (5-bay front) X 48'9" including porches, 1½ stories raised on brick piers, gable roof extending over full-length balustraded porches front and rear, 4 exterior end chimneys; originally open central hall with straight-run stair at rear ascending from back toward front, enclosed secondary stair in NE front room to "girls' room" above, simple "country Federal" style woodwork. Log smokehouse (approx. 9'0" X 11'0", dovetail notching) at NW rear of house; also garçonnière or "boys' house" (destroyed) at rear. Built between 1833 and 1840; Patton recorded as first settler in Sumter County (1831); subsequent changes include enclosure of hall and back porch, addition of kitchen wing at NW rear (ca. 1900), removal of NW chimney, "boxing-in" of original front-porch supports, and removal of balustrade after 1935. Still owned and occupied by descendants of builder in 1978. 3 ext. photos (1936, including smokehouse), 2 int. photos (1936).

Livingston

Arrington-Chapman House (Livingston Hotel, Old Inn) (AL-285), 207 W. Main St.; S side W. Main St. between Spring and Tuxedo sts. approx. 70 yds. W of Spring St. intersection. Frame with clapboarding over raised brick basement, rectangular (5-bay front), 1½ stories above ground floor, gable roof with dormers, 2 interior chimneys, full-length shed porch raised on brick piers; center-hall plan. Late-19th-C. wellhouse at SW rear. Built ca. 1855 for Dr. Hal Arrington, early Livingston physician; ca. 1900 additions at rear; later used as hotel-apartment house; demolished 1950. 3 ext. photos (1936, including wellhouse), 4 int. photos (1936).

Episcopal Church. *See* St. James' Episcopal Church (AL-294), Spring and Monroe sts.

Gulley, Mrs. Ellen B., House. *Under Coatopa Vicinity, see* Lee Haven (AL-290).

Harris-Ennis-White House (T. V. White House) (AL-264), N side of W. Main St. just E of Upton St. Frame with clapboarding, approx. 48'7" (5-bay front) X 33'0" (main block) plus ell and rear additions, 1 story, gable roof, central pedimented tetrastyle portico with paired Doric columns and scroll-cut balustrade; center-hall plan, simple Greek Revival style interior woodwork. Built ca. 1840 for Henry H. ("Chub") Harris, merchant; Hiram W. Bardwell (?), master-builder; ell slightly later; rear porch enclosed and kitchen moved from end of ell to NW rear early 20th C. 4 ext. photos (1936, including well), 1 int. photo (1936).

House (W. G. Little House) (AL-262), SW corner W. Main and Spring sts. Frame with clapboarding, 50'7" (5-bay front) X 34'7" (main block), 1½ stories, gable roof (broken at front and rear) extending over full-length front porch with fluted Doric colonnettes, 4 exterior end chimneys; center-hall plan, Greek Revival style mantel in NW room probably based on Plate LI of Asher Benjamin's *Practical House Carpenter* (1830). Nucleus of structure believed to be log house built as an inn by a Mr. Rains; greatly enlarged into present structure ca. 1840; subsequent alterations include large 3-bay shed dormer both front and rear (early 20th C.), also rear additions and extensive interior alterations. 3 ext. photos (1936, including late wellhouse), 3 int. photos (1936).

Lakewood (James L. Parker House) (AL-284), E side U.S. 11 (Washington St.) approx. 0.3 mi. N of intersection with Ala. 28 (North St.). Frame with clapboarding over raised brick basement, rectangular (5-bay front), 1½ stories over ground floor, gable roof, 2 interior chimneys, pilastered façade with denticulated cornice, raised central pedimented tetrastyle Doric portico (wheatsheaf balustrade) approached by double curved wrought-iron stairway, arched dormers; center-hall plan, some faux bois graining, late-19th-C. pressed-tin cornice in hall. Dependencies include 20th-C. wellhouse. Built ca. 1840 for Joseph Lake; Hiram W. Bardwell (?), master-builder; iron stairs added later, porch built onto N side and rear porch partially enclosed as kitchen ca. 1900, original wooden shingles replaced by asbestos after 1936. Julia Tutwiler, noted state educator, lived at Lakewood 1881–1910, while president of Livingston State Normal School (now Livingston University). 4 ext. photos (1936, including wellhouse), 9 int. photos (1936).

Lee Haven. *See Coatopa Vicinity.*

Little, W. G., House. *See* House (AL-262), W. Main and Spring sts.

Livingston Hotel. *See* Arrington-Chapman House (AL-285), 207 W. Main St.

McMahon House. *See* Price Williams House (AL-263), 100 W. Main St.

Old Inn. *See* Arrington-Chapman House (AL-285), 207 W. Main St.

Parker, James L., House. *See* Lakewood (AL-284), U.S. 11.

Pleasant Ridge. *See* Price Williams House (AL-263), 100 W. Main St.

St. James' Episcopal Church (Episcopal Church) (AL-294), SW corner Spring and Monroe sts. Frame with clapboarding, nave approx. 30'0" (3-bay front) X 40'0" (3 bays deep) plus projecting board-and-batten narthex (approx. 9'3" X 5'8") and shallow chancel recess, gable roof, pedimented façade with Doric frieze, 2-stage louvered belfry with pyramidal roof; open plan interior with 2 aisles and 3 blocks of original slip pews (formerly grained), recessed chancel enclosed by late-19th-C. Communion rail, originally had rear slave gallery. Built 1841–42 (probably fronted by Doric portico originally); extensive alterations 1870s including extension of façade, installation of memorial windows, construction of narthex and flanking pointed windows, chancel and vestry added to rear. 3 ext. photos (1936), 2 int. photos (1936), also 1 photo (1936) of cast-iron horsehead hitching post and wellhouse adjacent to church on S.

White, T. V., House. *See* Harris-Ennis-White House (AL-264), W. Main St.

Williams, Price, House (McMahon House, Pleasant Ridge)

(AL-263), 100 W. Main St. Frame with clapboarding, 54'6" (5-bay front) × 19'6" plus offset ell at E rear (19'6" × 21'3"), 2 stories, gable roof, 2 exterior end chimneys (main block), central 2-tiered pedimented Doric portico; center-hall plan. Built 1842 for local merchant; Hiram W. Bardwell (?), master-builder; rear porch glazed ca. 1949, replaced by den and bath in early 1960s. 2 ext. photos (1936), 6 int. photos (1936).

Livingston Vicinity

Oak Manor (AL-257), approx. 0.4 mi. SW of Ala. 28 at end of private lane, which enters W side Ala. 28 approx. 3.8 mi. SE of Ala. 28 intersection with U.S. 11 in Livingston, or 1.0 mi. SE of Ala. 28 junction with Bluffport Rd. Frame with clapboarding (façade novelty siding), approx. 53'0" (5-bay front) × 20'6" plus large central rear wing, 2 stories (wing 1 story), gable roof, 2-tiered porch across front (hipped roof breaking into pediment above middle bay), floor-length windows, bracketed eaves, large bracketed belvedere atop roof, rear wing originally semidetached (linked to main block by full-length open porch), octagonal conservatory flanking S side of rear wing; center-hall plan with continuous stairway from first floor to belvedere, colored glass in sidelights and transom. House surrounded by large deer park. Built ca. 1860 for I. James Lee; 20th-C. additions and modifications to wing. Decorative elements reflect transition between neo-Classic and Italianate forms. 9 ext. photos (1935–36, including deer park and well), 17 int. photos (1936).

Sherard-Tartt House (R. H. Sutherland House, Ruby Pickens Tartt House) (AL-283), N side of Ala. 28 on knoll just E of intersection with Whitfield Ave.; approx. 0.6 mi. E of Ala. 28 junction with U.S. 11 in Livingston, or 0.5 mi. E of railroad underpass. Frame with clapboarding, rectangular (7-bay front) with rear ell, 2 stories (ell 1 story), gable roof, 2 exterior end chimneys, 3-bay pedimented tetrastyle Doric portico, iron-railed balcony above main door, small pedimented Tuscan porch on E side; center-hall plan with cross hall between main block and ell, paneled dado, scenic wallpaper in dining room. Built ca. 1845 as plantation residence for John H. Sherard from North Carolina; destroyed by tornado Feb. 1945. Last occupant, Mrs. Tartt, was noted folklorist, short story writer, and painter. 4 ext. photos (1936, including well), 12 int. photos (1936).

Sutherland, R. H., House. *See* Sherard-Tartt House (AL-283), Ala. 28.

Tartt, Ruby Pickens, House. *See* Sherard-Tartt House (AL-283), Ala. 28.

TALLADEGA COUNTY

Alpine

Alpine (Welch House) (AL-433), N side of Co. 46 at Alpine, approx. 3.6 mi. W of intersection with Ala. 21 (Alt. U.S. 231) N of Winterboro community; 0.5 mi. due S of Talladega Creek. Frame with clapboarding on regular ashlar foundation, approx. 60'0" (3-bay front) × 30'5" plus ell, 2 stories with 1-story L-shaped shed extension at rear, gable roof, 2 interior end chimneys (main block), 1 interior end chimney (ell), central pedimented tetrastyle Doric portico with denticulation and fluted pilasters, balcony over doorway with cast-iron balustrade, portico flanked by 3-part windows; center-hall plan, marbleized mantels in parlor and guest bedroom, large brick-paved basement dining room with built-in cabinets and pie safe across E wall. Frame rectangular dependencies at rear. Built 1858 for planter Nathaniel Welch; Almarion Devalco Bell, master-builder; rear porch enclosed and carport added off end of ell in 1970. Occupied by Welch family until 1970. 6 ext. photos (1937, including photos of dependencies), 6 int. photos (1937).
Kitchen, N of main house. Frame with clapboarding, 32'4" (3 bays) × 24'1", gable roof extending over porch along E elevation, large stone chimney with brick stack; 2-room plan. Built ca. 1858. 1 ext. photo (1937).
Smokehouse and Storehouse, NE of main house. Each structure frame, rectangular (1-bay front), 1 story, gable roof. Built

mid-19th C.; storehouse razed 1970 and framing used in construction of carport. 1 ext. photo showing both buildings (1937).

Welch House. *See* Alpine (AL-433), Co. 46.

Alpine Vicinity

Jenkins-Carlton-Autrey House (AL-449), N side of Co. 52 facing W toward L&N Railroad right-of-way approx. 0.8 mi. E of Co. 52 junction with old Talladega-Sylacauga highway (Co. 11). Clapboarding over log, approx. 58′9″ (5-bay front) × 20′6″ plus (formerly) rear shed extension, 1½ stories, gable roof, 2 exterior end chimneys, central pedimented tetrastyle Tuscan portico, wide double-leaf doors with sidelights and transom; center-hall plan, interior finished with flush boarding, paneled dado in hall. Dependencies include frame kitchen, smokehouse (later converted into garage). Built as large log house ca. 1836 for Robert Jenkins; logs probably covered with clapboarding soon afterward with addition of portico and rear shed extension; reconditioned 1967–71, including new foundation, replacement of shed extension by central gabled rear wing, reconstruction of chimneys, and replication of original deteriorated front doors. Good example of log structure evolving into house with formal architectural elements. 5 ext. photos (1937, including 2 photos of kitchen and smokehouse), 4 int. photos (1937).

Lawler-Whitney House. *See* Orange Vale (AL-443), Co. 11.

Mallory House. *See* Selwood (AL-448), near Ala. 76.

Morriss, John, House. *See* Morriss-Holmes House (AL-459), Ala. 76.

Morriss-Holmes House (John Morriss House) (AL-459), S side of Ala. 76 approx. 0.7 mi. W of junction with Ala. 21 (Alt. U.S. 231) at Winterboro community; 0.2 mi. W of Greasy Head Branch. Frame with clapboarding, approx. 52′6″ (3-bay front) × 32′6″, 2 stories with 1-story shed extension across rear, gable roof, 2 pairs of exterior end chimneys, central pedimented tetrastyle portico supported by octagonal columns, recessed doorways above and below with balcony at upper level enclosed by picket balustrade, denticulated frieze, flanking double windows; center-hall plan, marbleized woodwork. Built mid-19th C. for Simon Morriss (1792–1874); renovated ca. 1962, including rear additions, aluminum siding, and concrete porch floor. Traditional "I"-type house in form, with mid-19th-C. stylistic embellishments. 3 ext. photos (1937), 2 int. photos (1937).

Mount Ida (Reynolds House) (AL-442), W side of old Talladega-Sylacauga highway (Co. 11) approx. 0.2 mi. NW of bridge over Wewoka Creek near junction with Winterboro Rd., approx. 1.6 mi. E of Ala. 21 at Winterboro; house on terraced knoll facing E toward Talladega Mountain. Frame with clapboarding, rectangular (5-bay front) plus large ell, 2 stories, deck-like roof, 2 pairs of exterior end chimneys (main block), 54′-long hexastyle portico across front supported by fluted columns with marble bases resting on brick pedestals (unusual inverted bell-like molded capitals), full-length balcony enclosed by cast-iron balustrade, floor-length windows above and below, heavy denticulated entablature at front and sides, recessed doorway with paneled reveals and flashed glass in sidelights; center-hall plan, notable interior woodwork including paneled wainscoting, marbleized baseboards and mantelpieces, straight-run stair from rear of hall with statuary niche beneath, plaster ceiling medallions. Covered walkway connecting ell to frame kitchen. Built for planter Walker Reynolds (1799–1871) from Warren County, Ga. House represents two periods of construction: earlier rear portion (ca. 1840) is conventional L-shaped 2-story dwelling with gable roof, front tier of rooms and colonnade finished 1859; restored 1949 for R. B. Kent; struck by lightning and burned Aug. 1956; ruined colonnade marked site in 1979. 9 ext. photos (1935, including covered way and kitchen), 5 int. photos (1935); 2 data pages (1936).

Spinning House, W of main dwelling. Brick, rectangular (2-bay front), 2 stories, gable roof, 1 exterior end chimney; probably single room above and below. Built mid-19th C.; destroyed. 1 ext. photo (1935).

Smokehouse, approx. 30′ S of main house. Frame with clapboarding, rectangular (1 bay), gable roof; probably single room with loft space. Built mid-19th C.; destroyed. 1 ext. photo (1935).

Plantation Cemetery, approx. 0.2 mi. N of house on neighboring hilltop, oriented E toward Talladega Mountain. Reynolds family burial plot (37′9″ × 57′0″) surrounded by 4′-high brick wall; notable 19th-C. funerary monuments including marble rectangular mausoleum with battlemented parapet and Tudor-arched entrance formerly protected by iron grating (built ca. 1840 to hold remains of Reynolds's first wife). 1 photo (1935).

Orange Vale (Lawler-Whitney House) (AL-443), W side of old Talladega-Sylacauga highway (Co. 11) just N of junction with Co. 46, which is approx. 0.9 mi. E of intersection of Co. 46 and Ala. 21; 0.1 mi. due S of Greasy Head Branch. Frame with clapboarding, approx. 54′1″ (5-bay front) X 42′0″, 2 stories, shallow hipped roof, 2 interior chimneys, full-length hexastyle portico composed of fluted columns with unusual molded capitals and bases, paneled entablature surmounted by paneled parapet, balcony with cast-iron balustrade, 4-bay 1-story porch with deck at rear; center-hall plan, decorative plasterwork in hall and SE first-floor room, grained woodwork. Identical frame 1-story dependencies flanking rear. Built 1852–54 for Gen. Levi Welbourne Lawler, planter and Mobile commission merchant; large 1-story porch added to S side of house in 1912 (later removed); restored and renovated 1971–75 for Dr. Richard Bliss family, under supervision of Helen Davis, AIA, of Davis Speake Associates, Birmingham (rear porch extended full length of house with second-story addition above, flanking wings built at SW and NW rear). 7 ext. photos (1935, 1937, including 1 photo of kitchen), 9 int. photos (1937); 1 data page (1936). *See also* FBJ (J7-ALA-1034).

Riser House. *See* Wewoka (AL-429), Riser Mill Rd.

Selwood (Mallory House) (AL-448), 0.5 mi. S of Ala. 76 between Childersburg and Winterboro community and 0.2 mi. due E of Bryant Branch on unmarked dirt road approx. 6.5 mi. NE of Ala. 76 intersection with U.S. 280 at Childersburg; house faced W toward Bryant Branch. Frame with clapboarding (rear portion logs covered with clapboarding), rectangular (5-bay front) plus low ell and semidetached service rooms, 1 story, gable roof, 2 pairs of exterior end chimneys, 3-bay pedimented tetrastyle portico supported by octagonal columns, unusual sawtooth fascia board; center-hall plan. Semidetached kitchen at rear, also frame wellhouse and dairy or "milk house." House built 1851–52 for James Mallory, planter from Madison County, Va., who settled in Talladega County in Oct. 1834. As recorded in Mallory's journal, dwelling cost "$1150 exclusive of finding workmen, lumber gotten by our own hands." Wellhouse and dairy or "milk house" built 1846, kitchen and "negro quarters" erected 1849. Complex demolished early 1970s and part of materials from house used in O. V. Hill residence at 1015 Cloverdale Cir., Talladega. 5 ext. photos (1937, including 1 photo of wellhouse and dairy), 4 int. photos (1937).

Wewoka (Riser House) (AL-429), about 3 mi. SW of Winterboro on Riser Mill Rd. (Co. 31), approx. 2.5 mi. SW of junction with Ala. 76, which is 1.1 mi. W of Winterboro; 0.6 mi. NW of bridge over Wewoka Creek just NE of unmarked dirt road over Riser Mountain to site of Selwood (AL-448); main dwelling stood approx. 100 yds. from Riser Mill Rd. facing SE toward creek. Frame with clapboarding, rectangular (5-bay front) with semidetached ell, 2 stories with 1-story rear shed extension and ell, gable roof, 2 exterior end chimneys, 1-story central pedimented tetrastyle portico, double-leaf doors with latticed sidelights; center-hall plan, matched-board interior walls, paneled dado and other Federal style woodwork. Built ca. 1835–40 for George Riser (1805–75) from Newberry, S.C. Main doorway, interior doors, and paneled dado removed ca. 1950 and incorporated into A. Olin Riser residence approx. 1.1 mi. to SW (off Riser Mill Rd.); subsequently burned by vandals ca. 1965. Wewoka plantation originally adjoined Selwood (AL-448), the Mallory plantation, to W. 6 ext. photos (1937), 6 int. photos (1937). *Store,* SE of main house at junction of Riser Mill Rd. with unmarked dirt road W over Riser Mountain. Frame with clapboarding, rectangular, 1-story front portion, 2 stories at rear, gable roof. Built mid-19th C. as part of Wewoka plantation complex; destroyed. 1 ext. photo (1937). *Grist Mill,* 0.1 mi. NE of main house on W bank of Wewoka Creek and on E side of Riser Mill Rd. Frame with clapboarding on stone piers, rectangular, 2 stories, entrance at N gable end; millrace ran underneath building to turn water-powered turbine. Built ca. 1845; demolished in 1960s. 1 ext. photo (1937).

Eastaboga Vicinity

Covered Bridge (AL-445), on Co. 93 (old Talladega-Eastaboga Rd.) where it crosses Choccolocco Creek, approx. 7.0 mi. N of junction with Ala. 21; approx. 2.8 mi. S of I-20.

Frame (Town lattice truss secured with pegs) resting on ashlar abutments, board-and-batten sheathing, gable roof. Built ca. 1850; Baldwin M. Fluker possibly contractor; collapsed Nov. 1945, shortly before scheduled demolition following completion of new bridge a few yards downstream (W). Locally known as "the old peg bridge." 5 ext. photos (1935), 2 int. photos (1935).

Munford

Old Academy. *See* Spence House (AL-463), Ala. 21.

Spence House (Old Academy) (AL-463), S side of Ala. 21 immediately W of intersection with Co. 105 (road to Cheaha State Park). Frame with clapboarding, T-shaped with semidetached rear wing forming stem, 1 story, gable roof extending over inset porch across rear (connecting main block to wing), subordinate cross-gable at front, early-20th-C. porch along front (N) and E side. Built ca. 1870; used as academy in early 20th C., later residence; demolished ca. 1940 to make way for new highway. 4 ext. photos (1937).

Sylacauga

Cook House. *Under Sylacauga Vicinity, see* Bledsoe-Cook House (AL-439).

Fluker, Baldwin M., House (AL-454), E side of old Talladega Hwy. between Willowood St. on S and Machen Dr. on N, E of old L&N Railroad tracks. Frame with clapboarding, rectangular (5-bay front), 1 ½ stories, gable roof extending over full-length front porch supported by octagonal columns, unusual raised monitor along ridge of roof to accommodate upper story (monitor broken at front by narrow hipped-roof central dormer), 2 interior chimneys, recessed doorway; center-hall plan, marbleized mantel in parlor, some decorative plasterwork. Built 1858; demolished ca. 1940. Baldwin Madison Fluker (1811–91) was early Talladega County builder, contractor in 1845 for bridge over Tallasseehatchee Creek between Sylacauga and Talladega. 2 ext. photos (1935), 3 int. photos (1935); 1 data page (1936).

Sylacauga Vicinity

Bledsoe-Cook House (Cook House) (AL-439), E side of Ala. 21 (Alt. U.S. 231) approx. 4.8 mi. N of intersection with U.S. 280 (Ft. Williams St.) in Sylacauga; 0.2 mi. N of Tallasseehatchee Creek. Frame with clapboarding, rectangular (5-bay front) with ell and rear shed extension, 2 stories (ell and shed 1 story), gable roof with pedimented gable ends, 2 exterior end chimneys, central 2-tiered pedimented tetrastyle portico with slender wooden piers, denticulated cornice; center-hall plan, flush board interior walls with chair-rail, severe white marble mantel in parlor (probably from local quarry). Dependencies include wellhouse and smokehouse. Built ca. 1840 for Benjamin Bledsoe (1788–1847) from Franklin County, N.C.; barn built around remains of house ca. 1960. Family cemetery (ruinous) due N of house. 3 ext. photos (1935, including 1 photo of dependencies), 1 int. photo (1935); 1 data page (1936).

Bledsoe-Kelly House. *See* Mountain Spring (AL-428), Ala. 21.

Cook House. *See* Bledsoe-Cook House (AL-439), Ala. 21.

Kelly House. *See* Mountain Spring (AL-428), Ala. 21.

Mallory House. *Under Alpine Vicinity, see* Selwood (AL-448).

Mountain Spring (Bledsoe-Kelly House, Kelly House) (AL-428), E side of Ala. 21 (Alt. U.S. 231) approx. 2.7 mi. N of intersection with U.S. 280 (Ft. Williams St.) in Sylacauga. Frame with clapboarding, approx. 46′ 3″ (5-bay front) x 30′ 5″ plus ell (originally 20′ x 17′ approx.), 1 story, gable roof broken at rear to extend over shed rooms (also unusual catslide gable roof covering ell), 2 exterior end chimneys, central pedimented tetrastyle portico supported by 2 pairs of fluted Doric colonnettes, recessed doorway; center-hall plan, beaded chair-rail in hall and flanking front rooms identical to that in school at Samuel Mardis House (AL-460). Built ca. 1850 for Samuel Bledsoe; ell extended approx. 16′ in early 20th C. Birthplace of Maude McClure Kelly (1887–1977), lawyer, feminist, and first woman attorney to practice before the U.S. Supreme Court. 5 ext. photos (1937), 2 int. photos (1937).

Reynolds House. *Under Alpine Vicinity, see* Mount Ida (AL-442).

Riser House. *Under Alpine Vicinity, see* Wewoka (AL-429).

Selwood. *See Alpine Vicinity.*

Wewoka. *See Alpine Vicinity.*

Talladega

Alabama Institute for Deaf and Blind. *See* East Alabama Masonic Female Institute) (AL-446), 205 E. South St.

Chambers House. *See* Huey-Stone-Chambers House (AL-457), 301 N. East St.

East Alabama Masonic Female Institute (Alabama Institute for Deaf and Blind, Manning Hall, Masonic Female Institute) (AL-446), 205 E. South St. (s side of South St. opposite intersection with Astrid Pl.). Brick, approx. 103' (7-bay front) X 52', 2½ stories over raised basement, gable roof with pedimented gable ends and cross-gable projecting over pedimented giant-order semirecessed raised hexastyle Ionic portico (full-length balcony at upper level enclosed by ornate cast-iron balustrade), denticulated cornice, frieze or "eyebrow" windows screened by cast-iron grilles, portico flanked by large 3-part windows above and below; H-shaped interior plan with center section containing assembly rooms on 2 main floors flanked by hallways from front to back with 2-room end pavilions beyond, Greek Revival style interior woodwork. Cornerstone laid 12 April 1850; completed 1851; Gen. Hiram H. Higgins of Athens, Ala., architect. Became Methodist-related Talladega Conference Female Institute in 1855 and state-related school for deaf-mutes in 1858 (blind pupils admitted 1867); now Alabama Institute for Deaf and Blind. Portico columns (damaged during Civil War) replaced in 1868 and 2 sets of exterior steps replaced by single 3-bay wide flight with cast-iron balustrades; dormitory wing and shed porch added ca. 1890 (demolished 1957), also interior changes; further interior renovation for administrative offices in 1975 and front steps again replaced by double flight of curving steps with fountain between. Notable example of use of Greek Revival in institutional architecture. Named Manning Hall in 1929 in honor of Dr. Frederick Haughton Manning, former head of school. 12 sheets (1935–37, including plot plan, plans, elevations, section, details); 15 ext. photos (1935, 1937), 13 int. photos (1935, 1937); 1 data page (1936). *See also* FBJ (J7-ALA-1035 and 1036).

Huey-Stone-Chambers House (Chambers House) (AL-457), 301 N. East St. (w side of East St. opposite intersection with Brignoli St.). Frame with clapboarding, basically U-shaped with 5-bay front and asymmetrical parallel rear wings, 2 stories, 4-bay tetrastyle portico with attenuated Corinthian columns, balcony over doorway, heavy denticulated entablature across front and along sides concealing inward-sloping shed roof; center-hall plan. Built ca. 1840 for James Grandison Leroy Huey, merchant, planter, and state senator; extensively altered ca. 1860 including addition of colonnade and other Greek Revival elements; interior refurbished ca. 1935; annex of Trinity United Methodist Church 1956–67; demolished 1967 to make way for church educational building. 5 ext. photos (1935, 1937), 8 int. photos (1935, 1937); 1 data page (1936).

Isbell, James, House (AL-455), 108 E. North St. Frame with clapboarding, rectangular (5-bay front), 2 stories, full-length hexastyle portico with attenuated Doric columns carrying heavy denticulated entablature, recessed doorway with balcony above; center-hall plan. Built ca. 1850; demolished in 1947. First owner, James Isbell (1806–71), was local merchant and banker whose late-19th-C. banking house still stands (1985) adjacent to house site. 6 ext. photos (1935, 1937, including 1 photo of servants' house), 4 int. photos (1935, 1937); 1 data page (1936).

Carriage House (Old Barn), at rear of house. Frame with clapboarding, rectangular (2-bay front), 2 stories, hipped roof with subordinate cross-gable, 2 large double doors; open interior plan with loft. Built ca. 1900; demolished. 1 ext. photo (1935).

See also FBJ (J7-ALA-1033).

Manning Hall. *See* East Alabama Masonic Female Institute (AL-446), 205 E. South St.

Masonic Female Institute. *See* East Alabama Masonic Female Institute (AL-446), 205 E. South St.

Plowman, T. L., House. *See* Plowman-Elliott House (AL-456), 511 S. East St.

Plowman-Elliott House (T. L. Plowman House) (AL-456), 511 S. East St. Frame with clapboarding, approx. 47'6" (5-bay front) X 38'6", 2 stories, shallow hipped roof concealed by heavy cornice, 3-bay tetrastyle Doric portico, recessed doorway, full-length balcony, full entablature encircling house, 2-tiered shed porch across rear; center-hall plan. Dependencies include brick rectangular 1-story kitchen (approx. 26'0" X 14'2") later joined to main dwelling and frame servants' house (approx. 20'3" X 17'9") at SW rear. Built ca. 1848 for Judge George Paris Plowman, merchant, farmer, legislator, and prominent Unionist during Civil War; sunporch added to S side of house early 20th C.; Queen Anne style double-leaf glazed doors have replaced originals. Restored 1941 for Julian Elliott, Sr. (rear porch partially enclosed, minor interior changes). Home in late 19th C. of Idora McClellan Plowman-Moore, who under pseudonym "Betsy Hamilton" was author of folk stories reflecting plantation and hill life, black folk culture. 7 ext. photos (1935, 1937, including dependencies), 3 int. photos (1935, 1937), also 1 photo (1937) of column-base on lawn from county courthouse which burned in 1925; 1 data page (1936).

Talladega Vicinity

Burt House. *See* J. L. M. Curry House (AL-472), Ala. 21.

Curry, J. L. M., House (Burt House) (AL-472), NW side of Ala. 21 just E of junction with Co. 93 approx. 3.2 mi. NE of courthouse square in Talladega. Raised cottage, frame with clapboarding on brick piers, rectangular main block (5-bay front) with flanking offset 2-bay wings, 1 story with partial basement beneath, deck roof (originally inward-sloping shed roof) with half-gable across rear, continuous balustraded porch along front and sides terminating against flanking wings, heavy entablature with wide frieze pierced by louvered vents; center-hall plan, Greek Revival style interior woodwork. Two-room gabled dependency with central chimney at rear. Reputedly built mid-19th C. for Jackson Curry, then sold to brother, Hon. J. L. M. Curry; kitchen ell added late 19th C., also bathroom to end of S wing; further renovations in 1947 included partial enclosure of rear porch, partitioning of rear of center hall, removal of jib window onto S porch from SW rear room. Second owner, Jabez Lamar Monroe Curry (1825–1903), was noted southern educator, U.S. and Confederate congressman, Baptist minister, and U.S. minister to Spain. 3 ext. photos (1937), 1 int. photo (1937). NHL.

Hardie-Lewis House. *See* Thornhill (AL-441), private drive off Ala. 21.

King House (AL-462), at S edge of suburban Bemiston community on Frank St.; 0.2 mi. S of intersection with W. Parkway and U.S. 231 (Ala. 21); just N of Talladega Creek. Frame with clapboarding originally on brick piers with latticework between, 52'6" (5-bay front) X 19'6" plus ell (17' X 19'), 2 stories, hipped roof, 2 interior end chimneys (main block), 1 interior end chimney (ell), 2-tiered 5-bay porch across front; center-hall plan; also frame rectangular 1-story servant house. Built ca. 1860; renovated and restored ca. 1965 including grading of lot and construction of new foundation, ell widened approx. 3'6", rear porch removed, sunroom added to N end of house. 5 ext. photos (1937, including 1 photo of servant house), 2 int. photos (1937).

Lawler-Whitney House. *Under Alpine Vicinity, see* Orange Vale (AL-443).

Mardis House. *See* Mardis-Batchelor House (AL-460), U.S. 231.

Mardis-Batchelor House (Mardis House) (AL-460), in Mardisville community approx. 4.9 mi. SW of Talladega; house site on NW side of U.S. 231 approx. 0.2 mi. S of junction where old U.S. 231 forks to W; 2.0 mi. SW of Talladega Creek Bridge. Frame with clapboarding, rectangular (5-bay front) with ell, 1 story, gable roof, 2 exterior end chimneys (main block), central gabled porch with paired wooden columns, double-leaf door flanked by wide latticed sidelights; center-hall plan. Dependencies include frame barns and frame rectangular (2-bay) 1-story private schoolhouse or office. Built ca. 1834; later additions at rear; S chimney rebuilt after 1937; house demolished spring 1978 except for S chimney; school extant but ruinous in March 1979. One of earliest frame houses in Talladega County. First owner, Samuel W. Mardis (1800–1836), was lawyer and U.S. congressman (1831–35). 4 ext. photos (1937, including 2 photos of dependencies), also 1 photo (1937) of marker located across U.S. 231 approx. 100 yds. SW of house commemorating 1813 Jackson Trace and erected in 1918 by Andrew Jackson Chapter, Daughters of the American Revolution, near site of first Talladega land office (1832).

Thornhill (Hardie-Lewis House) (AL-441), 0.2 mi. W of Ala. 21 (Alt. U.S. 231) at end of private drive approx. 0.6 mi. S of Talladega Creek Bridge. Frame with clapboarding, approx. 54'4" (5-bay front) X 20'6" plus wide ell, 2 stories, gable roof with pedimented gable ends, 2 exterior end chimneys (main block), 1 exterior end chimney (ell); center-hall plan, paneled dado and other Federal period woodwork; dependencies include frame rectangular (2-bay) 1-story gabled office and frame barns, family cemetery. Built ca. 1835–40 for John Hardie (1797–1848), Scottish-born planter; renovated and restored in 1959, including installation of modern kitchen in ell, enclosure of rear porch for library, construction of new chimney and carport at end of ell. 5 ext. photos (1935, including 3 photos of outbuildings and cemetery), 2 int. photos (1935); 2 data pages (1936). *See also* FBJ (J7-ALA-1037 through 1040).

Winterboro.

See Alpine Vicinity.

TALLAPOOSA COUNTY

Dadeville

Dennis Hotel. *See* United States Hotel (AL-511), N. Broadnax and E. Green sts.

Lane House. *See* Mitchell-Lane House (AL-510), 311 W. Columbus St.

Mitchell-Lane House (Lane House) (AL-510), 311 W. Columbus St. (S side of Columbus St. approx. 0.2 mi. W of courthouse square). Frame with clapboarding (portico flush siding), rectangular (3-bay front), 2 stories, gable roof breaking into shed at rear, pedimented gable ends, 2 pairs of exterior end chimneys, central pedimented tetrastyle portico with slender fluted Doric columns, semielliptical lunette in tympanum, large balcony above doorway with wheatsheaf balustrade, semielliptical fanlight doorways above and below; center-hall plan, paneled dado in hall and flanking rooms. Early history unclear (reputedly built ca. 1837 for M. Shackelford, owned in mid-19th C. by William Mitchell), 2-tiered shed porch and 1-story offset rear wing added late 19th C; 1953–54 alterations included concrete porch floor, rebuilding of narrow interior stair, and consequent moving of door between hall and dining room; late-19th-C. kitchen ell altered and enlarged in 1958. Architecturally similar to Benjamin L. Goodman House (AL-535) in nearby Lafayette. Known at one time as Little Huntington. 7 ext. photos (1935), 7 int. photos (1935).

United States Hotel (Dennis Hotel) (AL-511), NE corner N. Broadnax and E. Green sts. Frame with clapboarding, L-shaped (7-bay W front approx. 65' long) plus ell at NE rear, 2 stories (ell 1 story), gable roof extending over full-length 2-tiered porch with outside stair and triple doorways, large central chimney and 2 exterior end chimneys. Built ca. 1842 for Samuel Dennis, planter and hotel proprietor from York District, S.C.; renamed Dennis Hotel in late 19th C.; converted to rooming house ca. 1900; demolished 1956. Southern humorist and local editor Johnson Jones Hooper (1815–62) reputedly wrote *Some Adventures of Captain Simon Suggs* (1846) here. 3 ext. photos (1935), 8 int. photos (1935).

Dadeville Vicinity

Black-Gilling House. *See* Gregory House (AL-548).

Gardner, William A., House (AL-529), E side of Lafayette Hwy. (Co. 75) approx. 1.2 mi. NE of Central of Georgia Railroad crossing at N edge of Dadeville; about 2.5 mi. NE of courthouse square. Frame with clapboarding (flush siding on porch) raised on brick piers, approx. 48'2" (3-bay front) X 42'6", 1½ stories, gable roof extending over porch at front and each side with rectangular supports linked by scroll-cut balustrade, broad 3-part windows flanking unusual divided doorway enframed by continuous transom and sidelights; 2 large rooms at front with separate entrances, 3 rooms originally across back, paneled dado. Built ca. 1850 over 2-year period; Wash Smith, contractor; Henry Shepherd, chimney-builder; small gabled wing ("stove room" or kitchen) added to NW rear in late 19th C.; renovated 1962 including brick lean-to addition across rear, modifications of interior plan, replacement of original front-room mantelpieces by Victorian-period mantels, replacement of windows in each gable end. Architecturally similar to nearby Gregory House (AL-548) built by same contractor. Still occupied by Gardner family in 1979. 5 ext. photos (1935), 6 int. photos (1935).

Gregory House (Black-Gilling House) (AL-548), S side of Co. 44 (Dudleyville Rd.) approx. 0.4 mi. E of junction with Co. 75 (Daviston Rd.) in Easton community; about 5 mi. NE of Dadeville. Frame with clapboarding (façade flush siding), rectangular (3-bay front), 1½ stories, gable roof extending over full-length front porch, originally 2 pairs of stone and brick exterior end chimneys, wide double-leaf doorway flanked by 3-part windows; center-hall plan, interior walls wide flush boarding, chair-rail and simple Federal period interior woodwork. Probably built ca. 1850; Wash Smith, contractor; demolished ca. 1970. Architecturally similar to nearby William A. Gardner House (AL-529), also built by Smith. 4 ext. photos (1935), 5 int. photos (1935).

TUSCALOOSA COUNTY

Bucksville

Tannehill Furnace (AL-276), S side of Mud Creek in Tannehill State Park, approx. 3.0 mi. SE of I-59 Bucksville Exit. Charcoal blast furnaces constructed of local sandstone with rubble fill; Furnace no. 1 approx. 30' x 30' x 32' high, Furnaces nos. 2 and 3 (double-hearth) approx. 56' x 40' x 32' high; battered ashlar casing encloses brick-lined hearth and stack; large cast-iron waterwheel located on creek to N of furnaces. Furnace no. 1 built 1855 under supervision of iron-master Moses Stroup (at site of forge erected in 1830 by Daniel Hillman, later owned by Col. Ninian Tannehill); Furnaces nos. 2 and 3 built 1863 with aid of Confederate bonds after acquisition of works by William L. Saunders & Co. (steam engine also installed); produced pig iron for Confederacy; partially destroyed on 31 March 1865 by Union forces. State park since 1969 (furnaces restored 1975–76, nos. 2 and 3 partially reconstructed after vandalism; brick smokestack, charging bridge, and casting shed also reconstructed). 7 photos of furnace ruins (1936). NR.

Tuscaloosa

Alabama State Capitol, 1829–46 (Old Capitol) (AL-867), facing E in Capitol Park, W end of Broad St. at Twenty-eighth Ave. Brick and locally quarried sandstone, cross-shaped, approx. 120' x 80' overall (9-bay front with 3-bay advanced center pavilions front and rear), 3 stories, low parapeted hipped roof breaking into pedimented cross-gable over central pavilion, dome terminating in lantern-cupola, rusticated first floor (ashlar facing, rubble in-fill) with arched windows, central pavilion embellished by engaged Ionic columns, small 1-story Greek Doric entrance porches at N and S ends; central rotunda with flanking legislative chambers occupying upper 2 floors. Ionic order utilized in House chamber, Corinthian order in circular Senate chamber. Built 1828–30; William Nichols, architect. Housed Alabama Central Female College after state capital moved to Montgomery in 1846; separate 4-story dormitory erected to SW rear in 1861; entire complex destroyed by fire in 1923. 3 ext. photocopies (n.d.), 1 int. photocopy of old House chamber (ca. 1919). See also FBJ (J7-ALA-1146 and 1147, ruins only).

Bagby, Gov. Arthur P., House. See James Dearing House (AL-230), 421 Queen City Ave.

Battle, Alfred, House. See Battle-Friedman House (AL-226), Greensboro Ave.

Battle-Friedman House (Alfred Battle House) (AL-226), W side Greensboro Ave. between Bryant Dr. and Eleventh St. House museum. Brick (façade stuccoed, scored, and marbleized), rectangular (5-bay front) with rear wing, 2 stories, truncated hipped roof, hexastyle portico across front with paneled square columns and entablature surmounted by wheatsheaf balustrade, fanlight doorway with balcony above enclosed by wheatsheaf balustrade, 2-tiered rear gallery; center-hall plan with cross hall containing stair, elaborate original plasterwork in N and S parlors, ca. 1900 plasterwork in hallway. One-story brick dependency (originally 2-story) at rear formerly linked to house by covered way; formal gardens and greenhouse on S side. Built ca. 1835–40 for Alfred Battle (1801–77), merchant who was born in North Carolina; house originally T-shaped structure with central rear wing; renovated ca. 1875 for Bernard Friedman family (2-story brick addition at SW rear, portico flagged with marble, granite steps added); formal gardens also developed late 19th C.; again renovated ca. 1900 including opening of parlor across front, addition of grapevine-motif plaster frieze in main hallway and rear cross hall, installation of present stair (original probably located in front hall). Acquired by City of Tuscaloosa in 1965. 6 ext. photos (1934, 1936), 7 int. photos (1934, 1936); 1 data page (1936). NR. *See also* FBJ (J7-ALA-1127 and 1128).

Capitol, Old. *See* Alabama State Capitol, 1829–46 (AL-867), Broad St.

Christ Episcopal Church (AL-249), 605 Twenty-fifth Ave. (SE corner Twenty-fifth Ave. and Sixth St.).
Original Building. Brick covered with stucco, rectangular with shallow apsidal end, 1 story, gable roof, pedimented façade composed of unusual "pseudo" distyle in antis Ionic portico (blind center bay with arched niche flanked by recessed entrance bays), 2-stage pilastered belfry, arched windows along each side of church with inset decorative panels above; open interior plan, semicircular Communion rail enclosing pulpit and small altar flanked by doors to rear vestryroom (Decalogue, Lord's Prayer, and Apostles' Creed on front wall above altar). Built 1829–30; William Nichols, architect; new edifice built on site in 1882 incorporating portions of old. 3 ext. photocopies (ca. 1880), 1 int. photocopy (ca. 1880).
Second Building. Brick with stucco, basically rectangular (3-bay front) with nave and chancel, steeply pitched gable roof, buttressed walls, lancet windows, projecting entrance porch, small 3-stage tower at SW corner; modified Gothic Revival; center-aisle plan, scissor-truss roof, triple windows above altar, chancel lighted by shallow stained-glass dome. Built 1882 incorporating walls of previous church (above); chapel and parish hall added 1952–53: Lawrence Whitten, architect; church repaired 1954. 2 ext. photos (1936), 4 int. photos (1936); 2 data pages (1936).

Cochrane, William, House (Stillman Institute) (AL-217), 3600 Fifteenth St. (U.S. 11/43), S of Fifteenth St. and E of Fosters Ferry Rd. in center of present Stillman College campus. Brick covered with stucco and scored to simulate ashlar, rectangular (5-bay front), 2 stories, flat roof, massive hexastyle Corinthian portico with heavy denticulated cornice across front, full-length balcony enclosed by iron balustrade; center-hall plan, elaborate plasterwork, marble mantels on first floor. Built ca. 1850 for lawyer born in New York who came to Alabama in 1837; became main building of black Presbyterian college, Stillman Institute (now Stillman College), in 1898 with subsequent 2-story addition across rear, interior alterations; demolished 1964 (Corinthian column capitals utilized in colonnade of college library built on same site). 4 ext. photos (1934, 1936), 3 int. photos (1934); 1 data page (1936). *See also* FBJ (J7-ALA-1162).

Collier, Gov. Henry W., House (AL-268), 905 Twenty-first Ave. (SE corner Twenty-first Ave. and Ninth St.). Frame with clapboarding (façade stuccoed), main block approx. 63'6" (5-bay front) x 21'6" plus central wing at rear, 2 stories, shallow hipped roof extending over full-length hexastyle portico composed of paneled square piers, wider intercolumniation at center bay which carries large balcony with wheatsheaf balustrade, notable Greek Revival doorway probably adapted from Asher Benjamin; center-hall plan, spiral stairway, black marble mantels in two rooms. Built ca. 1835–40, possibly to designs of William Nichols, Jr.; rear wing incorporates earlier 1½-story structure built ca. 1825 for James Walker (this portion of house raised to 2 full stories 1934–36); house reconditioned and restored 1974: Edward Vason Jones, architectural consultant, including addition of pedimented gable to rear wing. Henry Watkins Collier, first owner, was state governor 1849–53. 5 ext. photos (1934, 1936), 7 int. photos (1934, 1936). NR. *See also* FBJ (J7-ALA-1163).

Deal, Dr. Seaborn, House. *See* Dearing, James, House (AL-230), 421 Queen City Ave.

Dearing, Alexander, House (Dearing-Swaim House) (AL-228),

2111 Fourteenth St. (SW corner Fourteenth St. and Queen City Ave.). Brick covered with stucco, rectangular (5-bay front) with semidetached central rear wing, 2 stories, hipped roof extending over U-shaped portico encircling front and sides of house (colonnade composed of 16 slender Ionic columns, center bay carries upper balcony with wheatsheaf balustrade); center-hall plan, spiral stairway, Greek Revival style decorative plasterwork, 32'-long drawing room with pair of marble mantels on E side of hall. Built ca. 1838 for local merchant; rear wing late 19th C. (possibly built on site of previous wing); ca. 1888 renovations include leaded-glass front doors and alteration of stair in Eastlake manner; ca. 1920 changes include replacement of wooden portico floor with concrete, also frame additions at rear; stairway partially restored to original appearance ca. 1950. 3 ext. photos (1934), 6 int. photos (1934, 1936); 1 data page (1936). See also FBJ (J7-ALA-1130 and 1131).

Dearing, James, House (Dr. Seaborn Deal House, "Governor's Mansion," University Club) (AL-230), 421 Queen City Ave. (NE corner Queen City Ave. and University Blvd.). Brick covered with stucco, basically T-shaped with stem formed by rear wing, 5-bay front, 2 stories (rear wing originally 1 story), truncated hipped roof originally terminating in balustraded deck, full-length hexastyle Ionic portico (once surmounted by turned and paneled balustrade), center columns originally supported balcony with wheatsheaf balustrade, semielliptical fanlight doorways above and below set into deep paneled reveals, 1-story Tuscan-order shed porch along S side of rear wing; center-hall plan, much of original woodwork replaced in 1920s by Colonial Revival style trim, some decorative plasterwork. Brick dependency at rear. Built ca. 1834–35, possibly to designs by William Nichols; John J. Webster, master-builder; renovated ca. 1922 for Dr. Seaborn Deal, including shortening of rear wing and addition of second story, also 1-story arcuated solarium on S side of main block, reduction and rebuilding of balcony; simultaneous interior changes encompassed moving back of stairway and replacement of balustrade (using original handrail), coffered ceiling, and arched French doors in dining room; further rear additions 1957. First owner, Dearing, was merchant and riverboat captain. House considered "wonder of the town" when built. Home of Gov. Arthur P. Bagby 1838–43. University Club since 1944. 6 ext. photos (1934, 1936, including 2 photos of dependency and brick garden wall), 4 int. photos (1934); 2 data pages (1936).

Dearing-Swaim House. See Alexander Dearing House (AL-228), 2111 Fourteenth St.

Drish, Dr. John R., House (AL-201), 2300 Seventeenth St. (in traffic circle at intersection of Seventeenth St. and Twenty-third Ave.). Brick covered with stucco, 61'2" (5-bay front) × 67'10" overall, 2 stories, hipped roof extending over full-length porticoes front and rear, bracketed cornice with egg-and-dart ovolo molding, applied paterae on frieze, N elevation (front) dominated by 3-story arcuated tower breaking from center of full-height Ionic portico (tower embellished with Greek Revival style detail and bracketed cornice), hexastyle Tuscan colonnade across rear; semidetached rectangular 1-story service wing (approx. 41'11" × 20'3") on E side; center-hall plan, originally branched stairway to second floor, elaborate plasterwork throughout. Erected early 1830s; shows influence of William Nichols. Considerably altered ca. 1855 with addition of Italianate tower, cast-iron grillwork, and other decorative elements. Mansion originally stood at end of tree-lined lane extending to now-demolished gate and porter's lodge at present Twenty-third Ave.–Fifteenth St. intersection. House mutilated early to mid-20th C., including gutting of interior (removal of original stair, plasterwork, and most interior trim), stripping away of cast iron, demolition of service wing; now sandwiched between modern construction on E and W. Once remarkable example of combination of Greek Revival and picturesque elements. Dr. Drish, builder-owner, was Tuscaloosa physician and erstwhile building contractor and owner of skilled slave craftsmen who evidently executed much early decorative plasterwork in Tuscaloosa. House was Jemison School 1906–25; Southside Baptist Church annex in 1983. 5 sheets (1934, including plot plan, plans, elevations, details); 1 ext. photocopy (ca. 1907), 5 ext. photos (1934, 1936), 3 int. photos (1934, 1936); 2 data pages (1936). See also FBJ (J7-ALA-1132 through 1135); Tebbs (T3-ALA-339183 and 339184).

Duffie's Tavern. See Old Tavern (AL-224), 2800 28th Ave.

Eddins House. *See* Price-Eddins-Rosenau House (AL-204), Greensboro Ave. and Bryant Dr.

Foster, Charles M., House. *See* Foster-Shirley House (AL-216), 1600 Dearing Pl.

Foster-Shirley House (Foster House) (AL-216), 1600 Dearing Pl. Frame with clapboarding (originally on raised brick basement), rectangular (5-bay front), 2½ stories, gable roof with pedimented gable ends (dormers on rear slope), 2 pairs of interior end chimneys, 2-tiered 3-bay pedimented tetrastyle portico (Tuscan order below, Ionic above) with denticulated cornice, 2-tiered shed porch across rear; center-hall plan, spiral stairway, elaborate plasterwork throughout first floor, some Victorian period marble mantelpieces. Built ca. 1830–40 possibly for Charles M. Foster, tanner and bootmaker born in Philadelphia. House originally faced W toward Queen City Ave. at end of 100-yd.-long avenue of trees (present Dearing Pl.); when Dearing Pl. opened in late 1920s, house moved approx. 100' N and turned to face S toward new street (raised basement eliminated). 2 ext. photos (1934), 8 int. photos (1934, 1936); 1 data page (1936). *See also* Tebbs (T3-ALA-339072 and 339073).

Friedman House. *See* Battle-Friedman House (AL-226), Greensboro Ave.

Gluck House. *See* Martin-Comegys-Gluck House (AL-225), 2021 Seventh St.

Gorgas House. *See* University of Alabama, Gorgas House (AL-203), Ninth Ave. and Capstone Dr.

Governor's Mansion. *See* James H. Dearing House (AL-230), 421 Queen City Ave.

Guild, Dr. LaFayette, House. *See* Ormond-Little House (AL-202), 325 Queen City Ave.

Jemison, Sen. Robert, House (Jemison–Van de Graaf–Burchfield House) (AL-205), 1305 Greensboro Ave. (SE corner Greensboro Ave. and Thirteenth St.). Brick covered with stucco and scored to simulate ashlar, basically rectangular (5-bay front) with slightly advanced central pavilion and 1-story demioctagonal side bays, long offset service wing at rear, 2 stories over full basement, shallow hipped roof surmounted by large glazed cupola, bracketed cornice, encircling arcuated porch (gabled 2-tiered center bay with flanking 1-story shed porches), glazed conservatory wing at SE corner; center-hall plan with segmentally arched opening into rear stairhall, 18' high ceilings, inlay woodwork fashioned of various types of wood (walnut, light oak, chinaberry) from Jemison plantations. Built 1860–62 for State Sen. Robert Jemison (1802–71); John Stewart, formerly of Philadelphia firm of Sloan and Stewart, architect; private gas plant originally in basement; restored 1945 for J. P. Burchfield; renovated 1955–57 for use as Friedman Memorial Library, including removal of some interior partitions and trim, installation of steel and concrete substructure in rear basement to support stack area; adaptive restoration for office use underway in 1983. Rare survival in service wing of mid-19th-C. bathroom. 2 ext. photos (1934), 2 int. photos (1934); also 1 view of remnants of brick wall along Thirteenth St. (1934); 2 data pages (1936).

Servants' House, at NE rear of main dwelling (now 2302 Thirteenth St.). Brick covered with stucco and scored to simulate ashlar, rectangular (3-bay front), shallow hipped roof breaking into gable above middle bay, 1-story porch across front with scroll-cut trim; center-hall plan. Built 1860–62; restored as residence, 1976–77. 1 ext. photo (1934).

Jemison–Van de Graaf–Burchfield House. *See* Sen. Robert Jemison House (AL-205), 1305 Greensboro Ave.

Martin-Comegys-Gluck House (Gluck House) (AL-225), 2021 Seventh St. (SE corner Seventh St. and Twenty-first Ave.). Brick covered with stucco and scored to simulate ashlar (irregular ashlar foundation), main block approx. 51'0" (5-bay front) × 47'0" overall plus 2-bay E side wing (approx. 32'0" × 19'1"), 2½ stories (wing 1 story), gable roof, 2 pairs of end chimneys, full-length hexastyle portico with paneled square columns, balcony above doorway, bracketed cornice; center-hall plan, decorative Victorian period plasterwork. Built 1841 for Peter Martin (1797–1862), lawyer and brother of Gov. Joshua Lanier Martin; subsequent renovations include probable addition of portico, heavily paneled late-19th-C. doorway; demolished ca. 1940. Home for a time of Dr. Burwell B. Lewis, congressman and president of University of Alabama. 3 sheets (1934, including plot plan, plans, elevations, section, details); 2 ext. photos (1934), 1 int. photo (1936); 2 data pages (1937).

Martin-Marlowe House (AL-223), 816 Twenty-second Ave. (W side Twenty-second Ave. between Eighth and Ninth sts.), originally oriented N toward Eighth St. Brick, basically T-shaped (5-bay original front) with stem formed by rear wing, 2 stories, gable roof, 2 interior end chimneys (main block), originally 1-story porch with deck; center-hall plan with cross hall in wing. Brick dependencies and frame wellhouse. Built ca. 1840 for Joshua Lanier Martin (1799–1856), governor of Alabama 1845–47; early-20th-C. renovations included reorientation of front toward E (Twenty-second Ave.), 1-story Colonial Revival porch with balustraded deck added to new front, extensive interior alterations in Colonial Revival style; demolished 1964. Home during Reconstruction period of Ryland Randolph, local editor and head of Ku Klux Klan. 6 ext. photos (1936, including 2 photos of dependencies), 4 int. photos (1936); 1 data page (1936).

Moody, Washington, House. *See* Scott-Moody House (AL-227), 1925 Eighth St.

Observatory Building. *See* University of Alabama, Observatory Building (AL-231), Stadium Dr. and Fifth St.

Ormond-Little House (Dr. Lafayette Guild House) (AL-202), 325 Queen City Ave. Brick, basically T-shaped (5-bay front) with rear wing forming stem, 2 stories, gable roof, 2 interior end chimneys (main block), bracketed cornice, 3-bay 1-story porch with Ionic colonnettes (originally narrow 2-tiered central porch); center-hall plan with rear cross hall containing secondary stair, plaster chandelier medallions and ornate plaster frieze employing palmette motif in parlor. Built ca. 1835 for Judge John J. Ormond (1795–1866), early State Supreme Court justice; subsequent renovations include construction of present porch (1852), bracketed cornice and replacement of roof and sashing (1860). 5 sheets (1934, including plot plan, plans, elevations, section, details); 5 ext. photos (1934, 1936), 6 int. photos (1934); 2 data pages (1936).

Peck, Samuel Mintern, House. *See* Snow-Peck House (AL-222), Eighteenth St. and Thirtieth Ave.

President's Home, University of Alabama. *See* University of Alabama, President's House (AL-207), University Blvd.

Price-Eddins-Rosenau House (Eddins House) (AL-204), NE corner Greensboro Ave. and Bryant Dr. Brick covered with stucco and scored to simulate ashlar, approx. 67′2″ (3-bay front) × 40′1″ overall, 2 stories, shallow hipped roof concealed by balustraded parapet, full-height semiperipteral Tuscan colonnade across front and along each side, balcony above doorway, cast-iron lintels; center-hall plan, elaborate Greek Revival style interior plasterwork. Nucleus of house possibly built before 1833 as the Washington & LaFayette Academy for Prof. William Price; renovated in mid-19th C. (with probable addition of colonnade) and again in early 20th C. (installation of leaded glass door and windows, frame additions at rear); demolished Sept. 1954. Scrolled balcony brackets identical to those of Magnolia Grove (AL-219) in Greensboro. Home ca. 1850–1900 of local physician, Dr. Simeon J. Eddins. 3 sheets (1934, including plot plan, plans, elevations, section, details); 4 ext. photos (1934, 1936), 3 int. photos (1934); 4 data pages (n.d.).

Kitchen and Storeroom, at SE rear. Brick with stucco, 43′9″ × 16′9″ overall, 1 story, gable roof, 2 rooms with connecting woodshed and recessed porch between. ¼ sheet (1934, including plan, elevations); 2 ext. photos (1934).
See also FBJ (J7-ALA-1138 and 1139).

Prince, Oliver Thomas, House (Student's Masonic Building) (AL-248), S side University Blvd. just W of intersection with Seventeenth Ave. Frame (flush boarding at front and sides, clapboarding at rear), rectangular (5-bay front) with ell, 2 stories (ell 1 story), semiperipteral colonnade with paneled square columns across front and along each side, bracketed cornice surmounted by low parapet, 3-bay balcony at upper level with cast-iron balustrade; center-hall plan. Built ca. 1858–61; contractors, Jemison and Sloan; late-19th-C. renovations included rear additions, leaded sidelights and transom, Eastlake style screen in main hall; demolished ca. 1960 to make way for Prince Apts. (portion of balcony balustrade reused in new building). University Masonic Club early 20th C. 4 ext. photos (1934), 5 int. photos (1934, 1936); 2 data pages (1936).

Scott-Moody House (Washington Moody House) (AL-227), 1925 Eighth St. (SE corner Eighth St. and Twentieth Ave.). Open by appointment. Brick with frame wing, main block rectangular (3-bay front) with

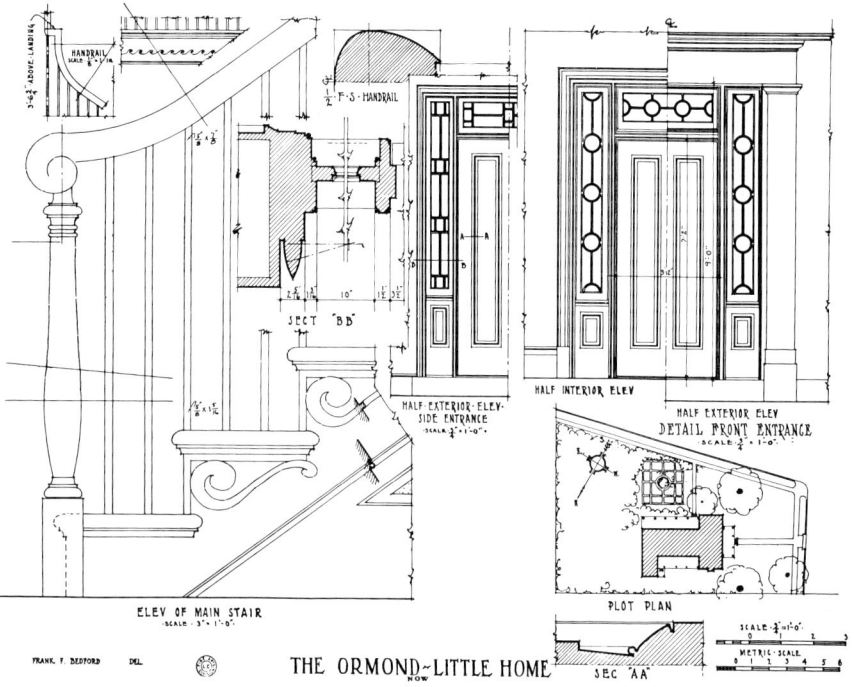

Stair and doorway details, Ormond-Little House, Tuscaloosa (ca. 1835).

low wing on E side, 2½ stories (wing 1 story), gable roof, 2 interior end chimneys, full-length tetrastyle porticoes at front and rear with paneled square columns; side-hall plan (main block), original Carpenter & Co. locks. Built ca. 1835 for David Scott (1803–68), merchant and entrepreneur (wing believed to be earlier); porticoes reputedly added after 1883 for Hester family; subsequent changes (ca. 1925) include sunporch at rear, tile porch floors, some Colonial Revival style interior woodwork; renovated and restored 1977 for David Warner Foundation. House called Janus Place ca. 1900, when occupied by Dr. George Little, because of nearly identical N and S fronts. 3 ext. photos (1934, 1936), 6 int. photos (1934, 1936); 1 data page (1936).

Snow, E. N. C., House (Wesleyan Female Academy) (AL-206), 2414 Eighth St. Brick covered with stucco, basically T-shaped (5-bay front) with rear wing forming stem, 2 stories, shallow hipped roof extending over full-length hexastyle portico with attenuated Ionic columns, balcony across second floor with scroll-cut balustrade; 1-story porch with Doric colonnettes along E side of rear wing; center-hall plan, "corkscrew" stairway with mahogany balustrade at rear of main hall, curving secondary stair to attic. Built ca. 1835 as Wesleyan Female Academy (later converted to private residence); extensively altered mid-19th to early 20th C. including Ionic colonnade, interior stairway and woodwork, decorative plasterwork, leaded glass doorway; demolished 1964 to make way for new Tuscaloosa County courthouse. Sometime residence of James Hogan (1792–1851), early merchant, and Prof. Michael Toumey, first state geologist. 6 ext. photos (1934, 1936), 5 int. photos (1934, 1936); 2 data pages (1936). *See also* FBJ (J7-ALA-1159).

Snow-Peck House (Samuel Mintern Peck House) (AL-222), located near what is now SW corner of Eighteenth St. and Thirtieth Ave. (facing N toward Eighteenth St.). Raised cottage, frame with clapboarding on raised brick basement, rectangular (5-bay front), 1½ stories over ground floor, high gable roof broken front and rear to extend over full-length balustraded porches, dormer windows, 2 pairs of interior end chimneys, raised covered way (E side) connecting house and detached kitchen; center-hall plan. Dependencies include kitchen, smokehouse, servants' house; picket fence at front. Reputedly built 1837 for Henry Adams Snow, merchant who was born in Massachusetts; demolished ca. 1960. Later home of Elisha Wolsey Peck (1799–1888), born in New York, a lawyer and chief justice of Alabama Supreme Court 1867–74 who was a prominent Unionist during Civil War; also home of son, Samuel Mintern Peck (1854–1938), Alabama poet and author. 5 ext. photos (1934, 1936, including 2 photos of outbuildings and fence), 6 int. photos (1934, 1936); 2 data pages (1936).

Stillman Institute. *See* William Cochrane House (AL-217), 3600 Fifteenth St.

Student's Masonic Building. *See* Oliver Thomas Prince House (AL-248), University Blvd.

Tavern, Old (erroneously called Duffie's Tavern) (AL-224), 2800 Twenty-eighth Ave. (in Capitol Park W of Twenty-eighth Ave. intersection with Broad St.); originally located at 2512 Broad St. (N side Broad St. approx. 50' W of Twenty-fifth Ave.). Museum. Brick (formerly covered with stucco and scored to simulate ashlar), rectangular (4-bay front) with 3-bay wing on W side at original site, 2 stories (wing 1 story), gable roof with raked parapets, 1 interior end chimney and chimneys on rear slope of main block and wing, covered wooden balcony with scroll-cut balustrade across second-floor front, 1-story shed porch with trellis supports formerly at rear and on E side; side-hall plan with adjacent keeping room, smaller chambers at rear, simple Federal period woodwork, kitchen and service area in basement. Early history obscure; reputedly built ca. 1827 for William Dunton, innkeeper (wing possibly later than main block); balcony probably late-19th-C. replacement of earlier one. Building originally adjoined by "Brick Row" (range of additional guest chambers extending depth of lot). Hostelry for many notables while Tuscaloosa was state capital. Masonry exterior walls dismantled and side wing demolished in 1966 when frame substructure of tavern moved to Capitol Park site by Tuscaloosa County Preservation Society; modifications in reconstructed edifice include elimination of original basement kitchen and side wing, rear porches, exterior stucco wall-covering (interior restored). Opened as museum on 13 Oct. 1968. 4 ext. photos (1934, 1936), 7 int. photos (1936); 2 data pages (1936). *See also* FBJ (J7-ALA-1136 and 1137).

University Club. *See* James Dearing House (AL-230), 421 Queen City Ave.

University of Alabama, Gorgas House (Gorgas House) (AL-203), NW of intersection of Ninth Ave. and Capstone Dr. on University of Alabama campus. Raised cottage, brick (front and sides Flemish bond), 53'0" (5-bay front) X 42'1" plus frame wing at rear, 1 story over ground floor, hipped roof, 4 interior end chimneys, raised 3-bay tetrastyle Doric portico on arcuated base with twin flights of curving steps, cast-iron balustrade; center-hall plan, simple Federal period interior woodwork and chair-rail. Two-story brick dependency formerly at rear. Built 1829 as University of Alabama dining hall and steward's residence (ground floor originally contained large dining room and pantry, steward's quarters upstairs); William Nichols, architect. Discontinued as steward's hall in 1847 and remodeled as a professor's residence, including partitioning of ground floor; center bay of portico added 1853 (date of curving steps uncertain); portico extended 1 bay to each side in 1896 (Watkins and Hardaway, contractors), with curved steps being moved at that time and additions made to cast-iron balustrade. House restored 1953 as museum, with subsequent landscaping and enclosure of grounds. Prototype for several mid-20th-C. Alabama residences. 4 sheets (1934, including plot plan, plans, elevations, details); 4 ext. photos (1932, 1936), 5 int. photos (1934); 3 data pages (1936). NR. *See also* FBJ (J7-ALA-1141 through 1143); Tebbs (T3-ALA-339177 and 339178).

University of Alabama, Observatory (AL-231), NW corner Stadium Dr. and Fifth St. on University of Alabama campus. Brick, basically T-shaped (5-bay front) with rear wing forming stem, 1 story, pilastered front section has gable roof with entablature and pedimented gable ends, brick architraves with corbeled cornices; rear wing (original section) composed of domed center block housing telescopic equipment, with flanking hyphens (E hyphen forms link to later front section). Built 1844, largely at instigation of Prof. Frederick A. P. Barnard (later president of Columbia University and founder of Barnard College), who provided plan and specifications; pilastered front section added in 1858; interior heavily remodeled during 20th C. 2 ext. photos (1934, 1936), 1 int. photo (1934, showing telescope and dome); 2 data pages (1936).

University of Alabama, President's House (AL-207), S side of University Blvd. between Sixth and Ninth aves. on University of Alabama campus. Brick covered with stucco to simulate ashlar, 65'3" (5-bay front) X 57'4" excluding rear porch, 2 stories over full ground floor, slightly raked flat roof, raised full-length hexastyle Ionic portico on elliptically arched base with twin flight of curving steps to center bay, notable doorway framed by engaged Doric colonnettes, 3-bay balcony above, entablature of portico has unusual pulvinated frieze with modillioned cornice originally surmounted by balustraded parapet, raised 2-tiered 3-bay porch on arcuated base at rear; center-hall plan, spiral stairway, elaborate interior plasterwork, silver-plated hardware. Built 1839–41 according "to the plan of a building . . . furnished by . . . Mr. [Michael] Barry" (also shows influence of William Nichols); Dr. John R. Drish, plaster contractor; second-story porch balustrade added 1853, exterior stair railing added 1887. House completely remodeled in 1907 by state architect Frank Lockwood; changes included removal of all original floors and mantels, installation of central heating, restoration of plaster friezes; house also completely restuccoed on exterior and painted solid white, destroying original polychromy. Subsequent changes include glazing of rear porch, restuccoing of exterior. House saved from destruction when university burned during Civil War through personal intervention of president's wife, Mrs. Landon Cabell Garland. 11 sheets (1934–35, including plot plan, plans, elevations, details); 23 ext. photos (1934–36, including 2 views of grounds, 1 view of drive), 22 int. photos (1934–35); 2 data pages (1936).

Dependencies (two on each side, at rear of house). Two outermost buildings were servants' quarters. Innermost building to SE served as kitchen and smokehouse. Innermost building to SW contained well and dairy. Each structure is brick, rectangular, 1 story, with gable roof. Built 1840–41; subsequently altered. 4 sheets (1935–36, including plans, elevations, details); 3 ext. photos (1935).

See also FBJ (J7-ALA-1153 through 1158).

Wesleyan Female Academy. *See* E. N. C. Snow House (AL-206), 2414 Eighth St.

WASHINGTON COUNTY

McIntosh

Andrews Chapel (AL-866), E side of U.S. 43 (Ala. 13) immediately N of and opposite junction with Co. 35 (W) and approx. 0.4 mi. due E of Birch Branch. Hewn-log construction (square-notch locking joints) resting on wood pilings, 25'9" (1 middle entrance bay) x 36'0", gable roof covered by shakes; open interior plan with original slip pews, Communion rail. Built ca. 1860; small gabled entrance porch added; brick piers reinforce original foundation. 1 sheet (1976, plan, elevations, details).

Saint Stephens

Old Washington County Courthouse (Masonic Lodge) (AL-111), E side of Co. 34 just S of junction with unmarked road to Old Saint Stephens. Frame with clapboarding, rectangular (3-bay front), gable roof, pedimented 2-tiered 3-bay porch, twin reverse-flight stairways to second floor at each end of porch; originally county offices below, large courtroom upstairs. Built 1853; later 1-bay rear extension; courthouse 1853 to 1907 when county seat moved to Chatom; subsequently sold to Saint Stephens Masonic Lodge No. 81; original exterior stairs and superimposed colonnettes removed 1948. 2 ext. photos (1934), 1 int. photo (1934); 2 data pages (1936).

WILCOX COUNTY

Allenton

Fitzgerald House. *See* Tavern (AL-191), Co. 24.

Grace, Joshua B., House. *See* Grace-Chesnut House (AL-190), Co. 24.

Grace-Chesnut House (Joshua B. Grace House) (AL-190), S side of Co. 24 approx. 1.1 mi. E of junction with Ala. 21, which is 1.6 mi. N of Ala. 21 intersection with Ala. 10 at Oak Hill. Frame with clapboarding, approx. 50'9" (5-bay front) x 33'6" overall, 2 stories with 1-story rear shed extension, gable roof (pedimented gable ends), 2 pairs of exterior end chimneys, tall central pedimented portico with 2 square columns, balcony at second floor partially supported by iron braces secured to columns; center-hall plan, paneled dado throughout, ornate acanthus-leaf medallion and molded cornice in parlor (NW room); also log smokehouse (rectangular, 1-story gable roof) at rear. Built 1852 for planter Joshua Betts Grace (1802–75), once an overseer for James Asbury Tait of Dry Forks (see Coy Vicinity); semidetached kitchen added to SW rear in late 19th C.; house abandoned and badly deteriorated in 1985. 3 ext. photos (1937), 3 int. photos (1937); 1 data page (1937).

Tavern (Fitzgerald House) (AL-191), N side of Co. 24 approx. 0.8 mi. E of junction with Ala. 21, which is 1.6 mi. N of Ala. 21 intersection with Ala. 10 at Oak Hill.

Frame with clapboarding, 2 sections consisting of 4-bay 2-story W wing (32′6″ × 30′7″ including 1-story shed extension at rear) and 2-bay 1-story E wing (18′0″ × 16′3″) with 10′5″ open hall between, gable roofs over both sections, 2 exterior end chimneys, full-length 1-story shed porch across front; enclosed stairway between two lower rooms of W wing leads directly from porch to second story, simple paneled dado in single room of E wing; detached kitchen behind W wing formerly joined to main building by covered way. Reputedly built ca. 1828 for a "Mr. Sauerhaver"; later expansions and alterations included incorporation of detached kitchen as ell extension of main structure, probably in early 20th C.; abandoned and ruinous in June 1979. Operated as hotel by Fitzgerald family in late 19th C. 5 ext. photos (1937, including 1 photo of old well), 3 int. photos (1937); 1 data page (1937).

Camden

Bagby House. *See* Bagby-Liddell House (AL-133), Broad St.

Bagby-Liddell House (Bagby House) (AL-133), W side of Broad St. (Ala. 28) approx. 0.1 mi. NW of intersection with Whiskey Run Rd.; 0.8 mi. NW of courthouse square. Frame with clapboarding, 48′6″ (5-bay front) × 36′4″, 2 stories, gable roof, 4 exterior end chimneys, central pedimented portico with 2 paneled square columns, balcony over doorway; center-hall plan, double parlors on N side with sliding doors between. Built 1853 for Arthur Pendleton Bagby (1794–1858); Henry F. Cook, contractor; renovated late 19th C. including extension of eaves and application of brackets and other embellishment, 1-story bay window on N side of portico and 1-story porch extension on S plus other exterior and interior changes; restored ca. 1940 including removal of Victorian additions. First owner was governor of Alabama 1837–41, U.S. senator 1841–48, and U.S. minister to Russia 1848–49 (moved from Camden to Mobile in 1856). 6 ext. photos (1936), 7 int. photos (1936).

Baptist Church (AL-169), NE side of Broad St. (Ala. 28) just NW of Camden Cemetery; approx. 0.4 mi. NW of courthouse square. Frame with clapboarding, rectangular (2-bay front, 4 bays long), 1 story, gable roof, modified temple-type façade with pedimented tetrastyle portico composed of 4 paneled square columns with full entablature, double entrance doors, segmentally arched windows along each side; open interior plan; 2 aisles, segmentally arched ceiling, Victorian period pews and pulpit furnishings. Built ca. 1855; demolished 1972 following completion of new church immediately W of old structure in 1969. 4 ext. photos (1937), 2 int. photos (1937).

Beck, Franklin King, House (AL-132), 312 Clifton St. Frame with clapboarding, main block approx. 38′6″ (4-bay front) × 34′6″ plus front and rear porches and flanking 2-bay wings, 1½ stories, central section covered by broad gable roof extending over porch to form pedimented façade with 6 slender pier-supports and connecting balustrade, lunette in tympanum, rear elevation originally very similar to front; unusual interior arrangement with 2 large formal rooms across front connected by sliding doors, jib windows opening onto porch, center stair hall to rear of double front rooms, with flanking chambers. Built ca. 1845; rear porch subsequently enclosed and bay window added to rear, glazed door installed at front, extensive wings erected to either side; reconditioned and restored 1967–69, including removal of later glazed front door and rearrangement of fenestration to create symmetrical 4-bay façade, construction of additional bay window at rear; side additions also razed and "quilting room" (dependency E of house) adaptively restored. Col. Beck (1814–64) was lawyer, delegate to Secession Convention of 1861, and Confederate officer killed during Civil War at Resaca, Georgia, October 1864. 7 ext. photos (1936, 1937), 4 int. photos (1936, 1937).

Bloch, Daniel, House (AL-171), 101 Hill St. (SW corner Hill and Water sts., one block SE of courthouse square). Frame with clapboarding (façade flush siding), 40′2″ (6-bay front) × 30′2″, 1 story over brick basement, gable roof with front slope broken to extend over full-length porch supported by 6 freestanding square columns resting on brick pedestals, 2 exterior end chimneys; 2-room interior plan with separate entrances, simple Federal period woodwork; brick-enclosed well to E of house. Built ca. 1840; rear wing (raised on brick piers) added early 20th C. One of earliest extant frame houses in Camden area; good example of distinctive vernacular dwelling-type brought to area from South Carolina. Bloch was Jewish merchant. 4 ext. photos (1937, including 2 photos of well), 2 int. photos (1937).

Bloch, Maurice, Store. *Under* Store Buildings, *see* Store (AL-175A), Water St.

Coates-Kilpatrick House (AL-168), SE side of Bridgeport Rd. (Co. 37) immediately S of intersection with Camden Bypass (Ala. 10) and 0.3 mi. NE of Bridgeport Rd. intersection with Broad St. Frame with clapboarding, main block 52'5" (3-bay front) X 38'3" plus 2-room semidetached ell at SE rear, 1½ stories, gable roof with 2 exterior end chimneys, full-length porch with 6 pier-supports on freestanding brick pedestals, large 3-part windows flanking central doorway, recessed central porch at rear; center-hall plan. Dependencies include frame kitchen, smokehouse, and office. Built ca. 1860–70; abandoned and deteriorated in 1985. Birthplace of Dr. Emmett Kilpatrick, interpreter for President Woodrow Wilson at Versailles Conference. 6 ext. photos (1937, including 2 photos of dependencies), 1 int. photo of kitchen (1937).

Corzelius-McMillan House (McMillan House) (AL-182), E side of Broad St. (Ala. 28) just SE of junction with Bridgeport Rd. (Co. 37); approx. 1.0 mi. NW of courthouse square and 0.5 mi. SE of Camden Bypass (Ala. 10). Frame with clapboarding 49'9" (5-bay front) X 40'6", 1 story, gable roof, 2 interior chimneys, full-length balustraded porch with 6 paneled square columns (possibly central porch originally), also full-length inset porch formerly across rear; center-hall plan, sidelights flanking front door decorated with hand-painted figures of birds each surrounded by gilded oval border. Built ca. 1860 for Frank Corzelius, carriage manufacturer; rear porch enclosed and small ell added later (possibly following acquisition by Dr. William T. Moore in 1904). 2 ext. photos (1937); 1 data page (1937).

Coster House. *See* Henry Kaster House (AL-184), Broad and Hill sts.

Courthouse. *See* Wilcox County Courthouse (AL-172), courthouse square.

Dale Lodge No. 25 (Masonic Lodge) (AL-131), SW side of Broad St. (Ala. 28) in triangle formed by Broad, Clifton, and Union sts.; approx. 0.2 mi. NW of courthouse square. Frame with clapboarding (façade flush boarding), approx. 40'3" (3-bay front) X 62'8" overall, 2 stories, gable roof, temple-type façade with pedimented tetrastyle Doric portico, double-leaf doorway surmounted by semielliptical fanlight with motif repeated above in 3-part window topped by semielliptical transom; first floor has single large room bisected longitudinally by row of 4 fluted Doric colonnettes, enclosed stairway to upper floor in SE rear corner. Built 1847 for lodge originally chartered in 1827 as Lafayette Lodge, Daletown (subsequently relocated at Camden); William T. Mathews, designer and builder. Minor interior modifications to structure in 20th C. Served as courthouse during construction of present structure. 7 ext. photos (1936), 6 int. photos (1936). *See also* FBJ (J7-ALA-1256).

Dunn, Thomas, House. *See* Dunn-Fairley-Bonner House (AL-176), Broad St.

Dunn-Fairley-Bonner House (Thomas Dunn House) (AL-176), E side of Broad St. opposite intersection with Clifton St. and facing Dale Masonic Lodge No. 25; approx. 0.2 mi. NW of courthouse square. Frame with clapboarding incorporating log dogtrot, 42'2" (5-bay front) X 32'3" plus porch, 2½ stories, high gable roof, 2 pairs of exterior end chimneys, full-length 2-tiered porch with 6 slender pier-supports carrying balustraded upper gallery; center-hall plan, dado and molded chair-rail, Victorian period mantelpieces. Built ca. 1825–30 for Thomas Dunn (front portion possibly oldest section of house); extensive late-19th-C. alterations included heightening of roof (to accommodate half-story) and extension of eaves, rear shed addition, replacement of mantelpieces, and other interior modifications. Reputedly oldest house in Camden; badly deteriorated in 1985. First owner donated land for site of Camden to encourage establishment there of county seat. 2 ext. photos (1937); 1 data page (1937).

Episcopal Church. *See* St. Mary's Episcopal Church (AL-135), 302 Clifton St.

Fail-McIntosh House (McIntosh House) (AL-151), W side of Fail St. opposite and approx. 40' N of intersection with Caldwell St. Frame with clapboarding, approx. 48'4" (5-bay front) X 42'7" overall (as originally built), 1 story on high brick foundation, broken gable roof extending over recessed porch and flanking shed rooms at front and shed extension at rear, 2 exterior end chimneys; originally open hall through center with paneled walls; lot formerly enclosed by massive brick wall. Built ca. 1835–40 reputedly for Whitmell William Rives; wall added by later owner, Jeremiah Fail, prior to 1860; hall enclosed ca. 1860–70 and early porch supports replaced by scroll-cut trellis supports, 1-room ell addition at SW rear; offset rear wing added ca. 1890 and NW shed room enlarged in early 20th C. Demolished 1983 (brick wall razed ca. 1951–1960s). Notable example of vernacular house-form brought to Alabama from Carolina and Georgia. 10 ext. photos (1937, including 2 photos of brick walls), 2 int. photos (1937); 1 data page (1937). *See also* FBJ (J7-ALA-1257).

Female Academy. *See* Wilcox Female Institute (AL-170), Broad St.

Handley-Felts House (AL-128), 209 Caldwell St. (S side of Caldwell St. between Union and Fail sts.). Frame with clapboarding, 50′3″ (5-bay front) × 28′4″ including original shed extension across rear, 1 story, gable roof (broken at rear), 2 exterior end chimneys, 3-bay pedimented tetrastyle portico with octagonal columns, denticulated cornice, jib windows; center-hall plan. Built possibly as early as 1830s for blacksmith Gabriel Handley, with subsequent Greek Revival style modifications; rear shed extended after 1937. 2 ext. photos (1937), 3 int. photos (1937); 1 data page (1937).

Jones, Heustis, House. *See* Jones-Liddell House (AL-178), Broad St.

Jones, Gen. R. C., House. *See* Jones-McIntosh House (AL-180), Broad St.

Jones-Liddell House (Heustis Jones House) (AL-178), W side of Broad St. approx. 0.1 mi. SE of intersection with Bridgeport Rd. (Co. 37) and 1.0 mi. NW of courthouse square. Frame with clapboarding, original dimensions approx. 46′6″ (5-bay front) × 37′0″ plus semi-detached central rear dining wing, 1 story, 2 pairs of exterior end chimneys, 3-bay pedimented central porch with 4 freestanding square columns on brick pedestals; originally open center passage with 1 large room to either side and small room directly behind each, porch across rear connecting main block and dining room (brick outside kitchen). Small law office on lawn. Built ca. 1850 for Col. Edward Nathaniel Jones; open center passage later enclosed; extensively altered 1926 including enclosure of back porch and additions at side and rear, removal of interior partitions; small law office also converted to guest house. 2 ext. photos (1937).

Jones-McIntosh House (Gen. R. C. Jones House) (AL-180), W side of Broad St. approx. 0.2 mi. SE of intersection with Bridgeport Rd. (Co. 37) and 0.9 mi. NW of courthouse. Frame with clapboarding, main block 48′2″ (5-bay front) × 36′0″ plus rear wing, 1 story, hipped roof, 3-bay central pedimented tetrastyle portico with paneled rectangular columns and connecting balustrade, jib windows flanking central doorway; center-hall plan. Dependencies included 2-room schoolhouse at rear (frame, 35′3″ × 12′1″, 1 story, gable roof) and octagonal latticed gazebo. Built ca. 1860; later renovations and additions at rear; gazebo demolished. Home of Richard Channing Jones (1841–1903), president of University of Alabama (1890–97) and brigadier general in state militia (1876–90). 6 ext. photos (1937, including 2 photos of dependencies), 5 int. photos (1937); 1 data page (1937).

Jones Office. *Under* Law Offices, *see* Law Office (AL-173C), Court and Water sts.

Kaster, Henry P., House (Coster House) (AL-184), NE corner Broad and Hill sts., one block S of courthouse square. Raised cottage, brick covered with stucco and scored to simulate ashlar, 46′3″ (5-bay front) × 44′0″ including 12′-deep porch, 1½ stories over partially sunken ground floor, hipped roof extending over raised full-length balustraded porch latticed beneath and supported by 4 octagonal colonnettes, 2 exterior end chimneys, dormers on lateral slopes of roof; center-hall plan. Built ca. 1860; later additions and alterations include frame wing at rear, large shed-dormer at front; razed 1982 by Camden National Bank to make way for new quarters. Original owner, Kaster (1818–78), was merchant from Vreden, Hanover (Germany). 2 ext. photos (1937).

Kilpatrick House. *See* Coates-Kilpatrick House (AL-168), Bridgeport Rd.

Law Offices (AL-173 series, AL-174), 4 frame 1-story structures typical of several in vicinity of Camden courthouse square, dating from mid-19th C. and later used for variety of commercial purposes.
Law Office (AL-173A) (Gov. B. M.

Miller Law Office), SW corner Planters and Water sts., one block N of courthouse square. Frame with clapboarding, 24'4" (narrow 3-bay front) X 40'3", 1 story, gable roof, pedimented portico with 4 square columns (inner columns later removed and subsequently replaced), flanking shed extensions at rear covering porch on E side and shed room on W, façade of both front and side porches finished in smooth stucco with chair-rail, Greek Revival style trim; 2 rooms with chimney between. Built ca. 1850 possibly for Franklin K. Beck; unoccupied in fall 1985. Good example of Greek Revival style as applied to small commercial structure. Office of Benjamin Meek Miller (1864–1944), governor of Alabama (1931–35). 2 ext. photos (1937), 2 int. photos (1937).

Law Office (AL-173B) (Dr. W. W. Moore Office), N side Court St. approx. 40' W of Water St. intersection, facing S to courthouse square. Frame with clapboarding, 18'3" (narrow 3-bay front) X 42'3", 1 story, gable roof, pedimented porch with slender square supports and balustrade; 2 rooms with chimney between. Built ca. 1860–70; sometime law office of Col. Edward N. Jones (later medical office of Dr. Moore); ruinous in 1985. 2 ext. photos (1937), 1 int. photo (1937). *See also* FBJ (J7-ALA-1254).

Law Office (AL-173C) (Jones Office), NW corner Court and Water sts., facing S to courthouse square. Frame with clapboarding, 18'5" (narrow 3-bay front) X 53'10", 1 story, gable roof, pedimented porch with turned bracketed supports and fish-scale shingling in tympanum, latticed porch at rear; 2 rooms. Probably built ca. 1850, with late-19th-C. renovations; metal siding applied and rear porch enclosed in 1977. Sometime law office of Gen. Richard Channing Jones (1841–1903), president of University of Alabama 1890–97. 2 ext. photos (1937), 1 int. photo (1937). *See also* FBJ (J7-ALA-1254).

Law Office (AL-174) (Old Newspaper Plant), N side of Planters St. in middle of block between Broad and Water sts. Frame with clapboarding (façade flush siding), rectangular with narrow 3-bay front, 1 story, gable roof, pedimented portico with 4 square columns and connecting balustrade, lean-to addition on W side; probably 2-room plan originally. Built ca. 1845–50; later (until 1960) housed printing equipment of the *Wilcox Progressive Era*; demolished 1961. Sometime law office of state legislator John Wells Bridges. 1 ext. photo (1937), 2 int. photos (1937).

Masonic Lodge, *See* Dale Lodge No. 25 (AL-131), Broad St.

Matheson-Weir-Moore-McLeod House (S. D. Moore House) (AL-127), 310 Broad St. (facing SE on N side of Broad St. approx. 0.6 mi. NW of courthouse square). Frame with clapboarding, original section approx. 36'3" X 43'6" including 12'-wide porch, 1½ stories, gable roof slightly broken at front to extend over porch, 2 exterior end chimneys; 2-room plan with separate entrances and enclosed stair between, shed rooms behind two main rooms; later shed-porch extension across front and S side, irregular additions on N side (including semidetached 1-story square dependency situated at right-angle to front porch). Earliest part of house reputedly built ca. 1835 for Dr. Alexander C. Matheson; purchased by the Reverend John Calvin Weir, ca. 1870. Frame gabled 1-story dependencies subsequently moved and joined to N side of main house; hipped roof "office" structure with bracketed eaves also added ca. 1875; kitchen addition built 1930 (razed 1979). 2 ext. photos (1937); 2 data pages (1937).

McIntosh House. *See* Fail-McIntosh House (AL-151), Fail St.

McMillan House. *See* Corzelius-McMillan House (AL-182), Broad St.

McWilliams House. *See* Sterrett-McWilliams House (AL-134), 400 Clifton St.

Miller, Gov. B. M., Law Office. *Under* Law Offices, *see* Law Office (AL-173A), Planters and Water sts.

Moore House. *See* Matheson-Weir-Moore-McLeod House (AL-127), 310 Broad St.

Moore Office. *Under* Law Offices, *see* Law Office (AL-173B), Court St.

Newson-Sharp House (Newson House) (AL-113), N side of Ala. 10 just E of intersection with Old Selma Rd. (Co. 31), approx. 0.6 mi. E of courthouse square. Frame with clapboarding, rectangular, 1 story, catslide gable roof, 2 pairs of exterior end chimneys, central pedimented portico with 4 paneled square columns, shed porch across rear. Built ca. 1860 for jeweler and silversmith Alfred A. Newson; offset hipped-roof ell added late 19th C., lean-to sleeping porch added to E side early 20th C.; destroyed by fire ca. 1970. 2 ext. photos (1937); 1 data page (1937).

Newspaper Plant. *Under* Law Offices, *see* Law Office (AL-174), Planters St.

Presbyterian Church (AL-185), S side of Broad St. (Ala. 28) about 40 yds. NW of intersection with Union St.; approx. 0.3 mi. NW of courthouse square. Frame with clapboarding, 40′1″ (3-bay front) × 50′0″ with projecting central tower, 1 story, steeply pitched gable roof with bracketed cornice, pointed windows at front and sides, heavy corner pilasters, entrance through each side of tower with window at front, open shingle-covered belfry with "stick-style" trim and bracketed cornice; open interior plan, 2 aisles, walls originally decorated with trompe l'oeil (simulated Gothic apse behind pulpit dais, painted pilasters). Built 1885 to replace 1854 structure destroyed by fire; steeple added 1893; educational annex built at rear and interior altered after 1936, including enlargement of pulpit platform and removal of trompe l'oeil painting. 2 ext. photos (1936), 1 int. photo (1936); 2 data pages (1937).

St. Mary's Episcopal Church (Episcopal Church) (AL-135), 302 Clifton St. (N side of Clifton St. just W of intersection with Fail St.). Frame (board and batten), 35′10″ (3-bay front) × 46′10″ (4 bays long) plus projecting central tower and chancel extension, 1 story, shallow gable roof, tower pierced by single louvered lancet above doorway and capped by octagonal needle spire, louvered lancet windows in nave and lateral walls of tower; open interior plan with center aisle, plain slip pews, recessed chancel with large Gothic stained glass window above altar, hanging brass lamps. Erected 1855–56; Alexander J. Bragg, builder; renovated for residential use in 1943 (spire removed and tower reduced to gabled open porch, chancel razed, and interior partitioned). 2 ext. photos (1937), 2 int. photos (1937).

Spurlin, R. L., Store. *Under* Store Buildings, *see* Store (AL-175B), Broad St.

Sterrett-McWilliams House (McWilliams House) (AL-134), 400 Clifton St. Frame with clapboarding, basically T-shaped with "stem" formed by slightly lower rear wing, main block 42′10″ (3-bay front) × 30′3″ with wing 18′3″ × 36′2″, 2 stories, hipped roof over main block with 2 exterior end chimneys, full-height portico with 4 trellis-like supports and long balcony at upper level enclosed by scroll-cut balustrade, cornice of portico trimmed with scalloped fascia and surmounted by unusual scroll-cut decorative parapet; entrance hall with twin spiral cantilevered stairways opens at rear into double drawing room with folding doors between, Greek Revival style woodwork, ornamental plaster moldings and ceiling medallions, unusual double-arched doorway from upper hallway onto balcony. Built 1851 for Col. David W. Sterrett (construction date on rain-water heads); acquired ca. 1870 by merchant Richard Ervin McWilliams, who is said to have added scroll-cut trim to porch and extended rear wing by construction of 1-story addition. Notable example of mid-19th-C. architectural eclecticism employing Greek Revival and Italianate elements. 6 ext. photos (1936), 13 int. photos (1936).

Store Buildings (AL-175 series), 3 frame 1- and 2-story commercial structures typical of several which formerly surrounded courthouse square and lined Broad, Claiborne, and Water sts.

Store (AL-175A) (Maurice Bloch Store), E side of Water St. approx. 50′ N of Claiborne St. intersection, facing W to courthouse square. Frame with clapboarding, rectangular with narrow 3-bay front, 2 stories, with 1-story lean-to across rear, gable roof, 2-tiered shed porch, doorway flanked by large 12-light display windows with paneled shutters. Probably built mid-19th C.; second floor housed early motion picture theater; demolished ca. 1950. 3 ext. photos (1937).

Store (AL-175B) (R. L. Spurlin Store), E side of Broad St. in middle of block approx. 90′ N of intersection with Court St. Frame with clapboarding, rectangular (3-bay front), 1 story, gable roof, pedimented façade, batten doors and shutters; open interior plan with flush board finish. Built ca. 1850; predecessor to brick store constructed ca. 1940 by merchant Spurlin; demolished. 2 ext. photos (1937), 1 int. photo (1937).

Store (AL-175C) (Black Store No. 2, later McMillan Store), W side of Broad St. approx. 40′ N of intersection with Planters St. Frame with clapboarding, rectangular with narrow front (3 bays first story, 2 bays second), 2 stories, gabled roof with stepped frame parapet at front, corner pilasters with encircling entablature and simple Greek Revival style detailing, central door flanked by 6-light display windows; open interior plan. Built ca. 1850, display windows late 19th C.; demolished ca. 1960. 2 ext. photos (1937), 1 int. photo (1937).

Wilcox County Courthouse (Courthouse) (AL-172), courthouse square, bounded by Broad St. (Ala. 28), Claiborne St. (Ala. 10), Court and Water sts. Brick, 50'1" (5-bay front) X 82'1" (7 bays long), 2 stories, shallow hipped roof with subordinate 3-bay cross-gables at each elevation, full entablature, heavily bracketed cornice with turned pendents, full-height pedimented tetrastyle Doric portico on W (front) elevation with bracketed cornice, double flight of balustraded cast-iron steps in each end-bay of portico leading to second-floor central doorway, each elevation pilastered; bisecting center hall on first floor with offices to each side, large courtroom on second floor with 2 antechambers at E end (splayed window reveals enframed by eared architraves with battered jambs), mid-19th-C. cast-iron records vault on first floor. Built 1858–59; Alexander J. Bragg, architect; small 1-story 3-bay vestibule addition to E front ca. 1930, interior considerably modified; flanking wings (24'4" X 48'3") built on N and S sides of E end in 1963: Sherlock, Smith, and Adams, Inc., architects and engineers. 8 ext. photos (1937), 9 int. photos (1937).

Wilcox Female Institute (Old Female Academy) (AL-170), S side of Broad St. (Ala. 28) just W of intersection with Fail St.; approx. 0.4 mi. NW of courthouse square. Brick, 70'2" (5-bay front) X 36'1" with large central rear wing, 2 stories, hipped-roof with subordinate cross-gables (main block), gabled wing, main block has 2 pairs of interior end chimneys, central pedimented portico with 2 modified Doric columns, second-floor balcony suspended by iron rods, roof surmounted by 2-tiered frame cupola with pilastered belfry and raked parapet; center-hall plan (main block), retardataire Adamesque mantelpieces. Erected 1849 (Institute chartered 1850); deeded to State of Alabama in 1908 for use as public school; rear wing demolished ca. 1965; main block restored 1978–79. 6 ext. photos (1937), 2 int. photos (1937).

Wilcox Hotel (AL-136), W side of Broad St. (Ala. 28) approx. 100' N of intersection with Caldwell St.; 0.1 mi. N of courthouse square. Brick, rectangular (5-bay front) with large ell on N side, 2 stories over high basement, hipped roof, continuous porch across front (E) and around N side (2-tiered along N side); central hall, Greek Revival style grained woodwork. Built ca. 1848–50 as one of town's first brick structures for James Asbury Tait; Archibald Bigger possibly master mason; demolished ca. 1960 to make way for motel. 6 ext. photos (1936), 8 int. photos (1936–37).

Camden Vicinity

Burford, Leonard M., House (AL-129), in field approx. 1.3 mi. SW of unmarked dirt road intersecting Co. 33 at point 1.0 mi. S of Co. 33 junction with Ala. 10 in Possum Bend community, which is approx. 5.5 mi. W of courthouse square in Camden on Ala. 10. Site located in Section 32 of Township 12N, Range 7E. Frame with clapboarding, rectangular (5-bay front) with large ell separated from main block by open hall, 2½ stories, gable roof with pedimented gable ends, 3-bay 2-tiered pedimented tetrastyle portico composed of superimposed square columns with connecting balustrade, central doorways above and below flanked by floor-length windows; center-hall plan with 2 rooms to either side, eared architraves and other late Greek Revival style interior woodwork throughout. Dependencies include small gabled structure of square logs; also family cemetery enclosed by brick wall with arched gateway. Built as plantation residence ca. 1855; ruinous in 1937 and subsequently demolished (cemetery extant but ruinous in 1984). 8 ext. photos (1936–37, including 1 photo each of log outbuilding and cemetery gate), 1 ext. photocopy (1921), 10 int. photos (1936). *See also* FBJ (J7-ALA-1255).

Capell House (AL-166), W side of Ala. 41 approx. 2.3 mi. S of junction with Ala. 221 and about 3 mi. SW of Camden; 1.8 mi. S of Pursley Creek Bridge, in Pebble Hill community. Frame with clapboarding, approx. 69'7" (5-bay front) X 50'5" overall, 2 stories, unusual "umbrella"-type hipped roof, deeply overhanging upper story and extending over broad continuous porch at front and sides supported by slender widely spaced columns on brick pedestals (outer columns square, inner columns octagonal), roof breaks into subordinate gable enframing wide segmental arch above center bay of colonnade, denticulated cornice, 2 interior chimneys, narrow semielliptical fanlight over main doorway with balcony above, floor-length casement windows flanking doorway; center-hall plan. Built ca. 1850; attributed to local builder William T. Mathews; ell added at NW rear ca. 1900; renovation and restoration begun 1979, including enlargement of ell. Highly unusual expression of plantation-house architecture. 5 ext. photos (1937, including 1 photo of old syrup mill), 3 int. photos (1937).

Clifton Ferry Landing. *Under Clifton Ferry, see* Store and Ferry Landing (AL-167A).

Clifton House. *Under Clifton Ferry, see* House (AL-167).

Cook Store. *Under Clifton Ferry, see* Store and Ferry Landing (AL-167A).

Countryside. *See* Tait-Ervin, House (AL-139), on private lane off Co. 33.

Dawson, Col. Reginald, House (AL-126), W side of Co. 31 approx. 0.3 mi. N of junction with Co. 43 (Old Selma Rd.); approx. 1.2 mi. NE of intersection of Old Selma Rd. and Ala. 10 on eastern edge of Camden. Frame with clapboarding, cruciform in shape with narrow 3-bay front, 1 story, gable roof with cross-gable front and rear, narrow continuous inset U-shaped balustraded porch at front, central double-leaf paneled doorway with narrow sidelights; unusual interior arrangement with 3 large rooms grouped around central entrance hall. Built ca. 1850; wing (approx. 18′ × 23′) added to N side in late 19th C.; porch partially enclosed and minor modifications to rear ca. 1950. Rare use of cruciform plan in Alabama vernacular architecture. 2 ext. photos (1937); 1 data page (1937).

Dry Forks Plantation. *Under Coy Vicinity, see* Dry Forks (AL-137).

Ervin House. *See* Tait-Ervin House (AL-139), on private lane off Co. 33.

Kilpatrick House. *Under Camden, see* Coates-Kilpatrick House (AL-168).

Liberty Hall (McDowell House) (AL-164), W side of Ala. 221 approx. 1.1 mi. S of junction with Ala. 10, which is W of Camden. Frame with clapboarding, 56′5″ (5-bay front) × 36′3″ plus semi-detached central rear wing, 2 stories (wing 1 story), hipped roof with modillioned cornice, 2 interior chimneys, full-height pedimented 3-bay tetrastyle portico composed of 2 paneled outer piers and 2 fluted inner columns of Ionic order, long cantilevered balcony at upper level, semielliptical fanlight doorways above and below, floor-length windows flanking main doorway, windows of façade framed by unusual segmentally arched architraves, rear wing formerly encircled by open porch; center-hall plan, Greek Revival style woodwork with notable eclectically derived carved mantelpiece in parlor, ornamental plaster cornices and ceiling medallions, main hallway opens onto transverse rear porch with dining wing beyond, original French windows open from dining room onto surrounding porch. Built ca. 1845 for planter John Robert McDowell (1813–97); rear wing extended ca. 1900, resulting in partial enclosure of porch. 4 ext. photos (1937), 6 int. photos (1937). NR.

McDowell House. *See* Liberty Hall (AL-164), Ala. 221.

Miller, Dr. George, House. *Under Canton Bend and Vicinity, see* Miller-Smith House (AL-179).

Newson House. *Under Camden, see* Newson-Sharp House (AL-113).

Tait, Felix, House. *See* Tait-Starr House (AL-138), Co. 23.

Tait, James Asbury, House. *Under Coy Vicinity, see* Dry Forks (AL-137).

Tait, Robert, House. *See* Tait-Ervin House (AL-139), on private lane off Co. 33.

Tait-Ervin House (Countryside, Ervin House, Robert Tait House) (AL-139), at end of long private lane on W side of Co. 33 approx. 1.1 mi. S of junction with Ala. 10 at Possum Bend community 4 mi. W of Camden. Frame with clapboarding, T-shaped with 2-story main block (approx. 60′0″ × 23′) and massive 1½ story rear extension, hipped roof covering main block, gable over rear wing, continuous 10′-wide 1-story porch across front and partially along each side with widely spaced paneled square columns resting on freestanding brick piers, balustraded porch across rear; formal interior with 78′-long axial hallway and wide cross hall, intersection of halls faced with 4 elliptical arches springing from scrolled consoles, double drawing-rooms across front with foyer between and connecting sliding doors, marble mantels, Greek Revival style woodwork, ornamental plaster cornices and ceiling medallions. Original dependencies include log smokehouse, "ironing house," and barn.

Built ca. 1855 for planter Robert Tait, son of James Asbury Tait of Dry Forks (see Coy Vicinity); builder-architect possibly Alexander J. Bragg. One of the finest and least altered of area plantation houses. 6 ext. photos (1936, including 1 photo each of smokehouse and toolhouse), 5 int. photos (1936).

Tait-Starr House (Felix Tait House, White Columns) (AL-138), E side of Co. 23 approx. 1.9 mi. S of junction with Ala. 10 at Possum Bend community, which is approx. 5 mi. SW of Camden. Frame with clapboarding (principal façades rabbeted), irregular L-shape, 2 stories, hipped roof with heavily bracketed cornice, asymmetrically composed 5-bay W façade with 2-bay setback, full-height tetrastyle porticoes on both W and S façades with octagonal columns and scroll-cut balustrade, 2-tiered L-shaped porch at rear; asymmetrically arranged interior plan with bisecting E-W main hallway intersecting S crosshall containing principal stairway, sliding doors connect main hall to flanking formal rooms, late Greek Revival style grained woodwork. Dependencies formerly included 2-story colonnaded frame kitchen, brick smokehouse, frame wellhouse, and privy. Built 1859–60 for planter Felix Tait (1822–99), son of James Asbury Tait of Dry Forks (see Coy Vicinity); Alexander J. Bragg, architect; most of dependencies razed, house itself little altered. Outstanding example of eclecticism in late antebellum period architecture. 10 ext. photos (1936, including 6 photos of dependencies), 3 int. photos (1936). *See also* FBJ (J7-ALA-1263 and 1264).

White Columns. *See* Tait-Starr House (AL-138), Co. 23.

Canton Bend and Vicinity

Bethea, Truet, House. *See* Bethea-Strother House (AL-186), Ala. 28.

Bethea-Strother House (Truet Bethea House) (AL-186), W side of Ala. 28 immediately NW of junction with Co. 19 S of Canton Bend community; approx. 5.3 mi. SE of J. Lee Long Bridge over Alabama River. Brick with frame rear wing, 54'0" (5-bay front) x 20'3" plus frame ell at SW rear, 2 stories (ell 1 story), gable roof with pedimented gable ends and 2 interior end chimneys, soffit of cornice embellished with mutules, full-height central pedimented portico framing wide segmentally arched fanlight doorways at both first- and second-story levels, cantilevered balcony at upper level; center-hall plan with single large room to either side, molded chair-rail, ornamental plaster moldings and ceiling medallions; 2-room ell at rear edged by porch on N side, frame rectangular kitchen at right angle off end of porch. Other dependencies formerly included 2 wells and plantation store. Built ca. 1844 for Tristram Benjamin Bethea (1810–54); ell modified at later date; unoccupied and deteriorated in summer of 1979. One of 2 examples in county of brick construction in antebellum domestic architecture. 6 ext. photos (1937, including 2 photos of wells and plantation store), 6 int. photos (1937); 1 data page (1937). NR.

Mathews-Tait House. *See* Youpon (AL-130), Co. 19.

Miller-Smith House (Dr. George Miller House) (AL-179), at end of lane on E side of Ala. 28 approx. 0.2 mi. SE of junction with Ala. 221 at Canton Bend community; approx. 5.9 mi. SE of J. Lee Long Bridge over Alabama River and 4 mi. NW of Camden. Frame with clapboarding (façade flush siding), 53'0" (5-bay front) x 42'8", 1½ stories, gable roof with pedimented dormers extending over full-length porch with modillioned cornice and 8 fluted Doric columns resting on freestanding brick piers, semielliptical fanlight doorway, shed porch across rear; center-hall plan, narrow stairway (formerly enclosed) leads from rear of hall to second floor, notable woodwork possibly derived from Asher Benjamin. Built ca. 1840–45 for Dr. Abijah Miller, graduate of the University of Edinburgh; attributed to William T. Mathews, local builder; kitchen wing added to SE rear (replacing earlier detached brick kitchen), other rear additions ca. 1900; house renovated 1949 including replacement of rear additions with new construction, also installation of rear dormers; wing added to N side 1969–70. 2 ext. photos (1937); 1 data page (1937). *See also* FBJ (J7-ALA-1258 and 1259).

Strother Store. *Under Millers Ferry, see* William Henderson Store (AL-194).

Tait, Frank, House. *See* Youpon (AL-130), Co. 19.

Youpon (Mathews-Tait House, Frank Tait House) (AL-130), at end of circular drive on E side of Co. 19 approx. 1.8 mi. S of junction with Ala. 28 at Canton Bend community; about 5 mi. NW of Camden. Frame with clapboarding on raised brick basement, 55'7" (5-bay front) × 41'0" plus porches, 2 stories over full basement, hipped roof with modillioned cornice, 2 pairs of interior end chimneys, raised 3-bay pedimented tetrastyle Doric portico with full-length cantilevered balcony at upper level enclosed by wheatsheaf-style balustrade (semielliptical fanlight doorways above and below, main doorway flanked by jib windows), raised 1-story shed-roof porch across rear; center-hall plan, 2 rooms to either side connected by sliding doors, notable Greek Revival style woodwork, ornamental plaster cornices and ceiling medallions, basement kitchen, storage areas, and wine cellar. Formerly 2 octagonal dependencies (kitchen and guest house). Built ca. 1847–48 for planter and local builder William T. Mathews, under direction of contractor George Lynch from Maryland; detached octagonal kitchen burned ca. 1900 and remaining octagonal dependency moved and joined to SE corner of rear porch as kitchen; rear porch fully enclosed in 1978 and wooden decking of portico replaced by concrete slab resting on cinderblock infill between original brick foundation piers. Name Youpon derives from species of holly bordering circular entrance drive. Plantation formerly called "Mimosa." 6 ext. photos (1936, 1937), 10 int. photos (1936). *See also* FBJ (J7-ALA-1266 through 1268).

Capell.

See Camden Vicinity.

Clifton Ferry

House (Clifton House) (AL-167), W bank of Alabama River on Clifton Ferry access road (exact site undetermined) E of junction with Ala. 162, which is approx. 8.4 mi. S of Ala. 162 intersection with Ala. 28 W of Millers Ferry and J. Lee Long Bridge. Frame with clapboarding, rectangular (5-bay front), 2 stories, gable roof, 2 exterior end chimneys, 3-bay pedimented 2-tiered tetrastyle portico with square columns; center-hall plan. Built ca. 1835 possibly for Francis Bridges, Jr.; destroyed. 1 ext. photo (1936), 1 int. photo (1936).

Store and Ferry Landing (Cook Store) (AL-167A), facing E on W bank of Alabama River, on S side of Clifton Ferry access road 0.7 mi. E of junction with Ala. 162, which is approx. 8.4 mi. S of Ala. 162 intersection with Ala. 10. Frame with clapboarding, 29'6" (3-bay front) × 46'9" plus porch, 1 story, gable roof projecting over front to form pedimented porch with 4 square columns; open interior plan. Built ca. 1850 to serve community and rural region around ferry landing; porch replaced by metal shed in mid-20th C. and structure used for agriculture storage in 1979. 1 ext. photo (1936), 2 photos of ferry and ferry landing (1936).

Coy Vicinity

Dry Forks (James Asbury Tait House) (AL-137), at end of private lane on N side of Co. 12 approx. 0.3 mi. E of intersection with Ala. 41 near Gulletts Bluff; about 8 mi. SW of Camden. Frame with clapboarding, 48'2" (5-bay front) × 38'4" plus front and rear porches, 2 stories, gable roof, 2 pairs of exterior end chimneys, cornice embellished by "i"-dentil fascia board, central 2-tiered pedimented portico with 4 square columns at each level (upper porch enclosed by wheatsheaf-type balustrade), 1-story shed porch across rear; center-hall plan, notable Federal style mantelpieces and woodwork, jib windows from NE room onto rear porch. Dependencies included two 2-room frame structures, stable, and chicken house; also family cemetery. Built 1834–35 for James Asbury Tait by hired slave carpenters 'Kiah and 'Lijah; deteriorated in 1979 (rear chimneys removed, wheatsheaf balustrade partially destroyed, dependencies razed). 9 ext. photos (1936, including 4 photos of dependencies, 1 photo of cemetery), 10 int. photos (1936). *See also* FBJ (J7-ALA-1265).

Millers Ferry and Vicinity

Henderson House. *See* Sellers-Henderson House (AL-147), Ala. 28.

Henderson, William, Store (AL-194), in Canton Bend community, on S side of Ala. 28 approx. 1.8 mi. SE of J. Lee Long Bridge over Alabama River and immediately NE of Sellers-Henderson House (AL-147). Frame with clapboarding, rectangular with narrow 3-bay front, 2 stories, gable roof, central battened door flanked by large 6-over-6 sash windows with solid shutters, loft entrance in front gable end. Built 1858; burned 1940s. 2 ext. photos (1937), 2 int. photos (1937); 1 data page (1937).

Mathews House. *See* Rosemary (AL-150), unmarked road off Ala. 28.

Mathews-Cade House. *See* Rosemary (AL-150), unmarked road off Ala. 28.

Rosemary (Mathews House, Mathews-Cade House) (AL-150), E side of unmarked road 1.1 mi. s of intersection with Ala. 28 at point 0.2 mi. w of J. Lee Long Bridge; sw of Millers Ferry Lock and Dam. Frame with clapboarding on high brick foundation, 56'6" (5-bay front) × 42'3" plus porches and ell, 2 stories, gable roof, 2 pairs of exterior end chimneys, 1-story full-length porch with balustraded deck, 2-tiered porch at rear; center-hall plan, branched stairway with bay window at landing. Built mid-19th C. for Peter Early Mathews as 1-story raised cottage; second story added 1905 and house extensively renovated. 8 ext. photos (1937, including 1 photo of commissary), 3 int. photos (1937); 1 data page (1937).
Commissary Store, exact location unknown. Frame with clapboarding, rectangular with narrow 3-bay front, 1 story, gable roof breaking into cantilevered hipped roof at front over raised wooden platform. Built late 19th C.; destroyed. 1 ext. photo (1937).
See also FBJ (J7-ALA-1262).

Sellers House. *See* Sellers-Henderson House (AL-147), Ala. 28.

Sellers-Henderson House (Henderson House, Sellers House) (AL-147), sw side of Ala. 28 approx. 1.8 mi. SE of J. Lee Long Bridge over Alabama River. Frame with clapboarding raised on brick piers, 50'4" (5-bay front) × 28'4", 1 story, catslide gable roof, 2 very notable exterior end chimneys with diaperwork composed of glazed brick, central pedimented portico with 2 pairs of attenuated colonnettes; originally open-hall plan with single large room to each side and smaller rooms directly behind, hall embellished with vertical paneling. Built 1839 for Calvin C. Sellers from South Carolina; long ell added probably in late 19th C., other rear additions; abandoned and deteriorated in early 1980s. Significant for rare occurrence in Alabama of diapering as decorative pattern in brickwork. 2 ext. photos (1937), 1 int. photo (1937); 1 data page (1937).
Smokehouse, SE rear of dwelling. Brick, 22' × 26' with single doorway, gable roof, notable openwork to provide ventilation. Probably contemporary with house; destroyed ca. 1981. 1 ext. photo (1937).

Oak Hill

Fox, Dr. Daniel J., House. *See* Fox-Harris-Jones House (AL-148), Ala. 21.

Fox-Harris-Jones House (Dr. Daniel J. Fox House) (AL-148), E side of Ala. 21 approx. 0.7 mi. NE of intersection with Ala. 10. Frame with clapboarding, main block 48'3" (7-bay front) × 36'7" plus porch and ell, 1 story, gable roof, formerly 2 pairs of exterior end chimneys, full-length porch at front, central double-leaf door with single door in middle bay to each side; center-hall plan, Eastlake style interior trim; also advanced semi-detached wings formerly flanking main block at right angle to façade, extant s wing (41' × 26') is 6 bays long with 2-bay pedimented gable end toward front, inset balustraded full-length porch along N side; 2 rooms with sliding doors between, Greek Revival style interior trim. Covered well at NE corner of house. Main block of dwelling built ca. 1840–45 for Dr. Daniel J. Fox; flanking wings added ca. 1855; main block extensively altered ca. 1890 including extension of porch around NW corner of house, replacement of early woodwork and window sashing, N wing also razed and kitchen ell added to NE rear. 5 ext. photos (1937, including 1 photo of well), 4 int. photos (1937); 1 data page (1937).

Ramsey, Rev. Abiezer Clarke, House (AL-108), s side of Ala. 10 facing w and approx. 0.3 mi. E of intersection with Ala. 21. Frame with clapboarding, 52'6" (5-bay front) × 20'2" plus parallel rear wings (20'5" × 40'0"), 2 stories (wings 1 story), gable roof with 2 exterior chimneys at gable ends of main block, 1-story shed porch across front supported by 6 square columns on freestanding brick piers, jib windows flanking central doorway, U-shaped porch between rear wings (inner court formed by wings later roofed over to create carriage-shed, enclosed with latticework); center-hall plan, unusual 4-leaf folding doors at each end of lower hallway. Dependencies included frame smokehouse, barn, and wellhouse. Built 1837–38; 1-story gabled kitchen wing added to s side in late 19th C. Oldest house in Oak Hill. Ramsey was early Methodist circuit-rider. 6 ext. photos (1937, including 1 group photo of dependencies),

2 int. photos (1937); 1 data page (1937).

Pine Apple

Hawthorn, Col. Joseph R., House (AL-119), W side of Co. 59 (Broad St.) approx. 0.5 mi. N of intersection with Ala. 10 and 0.1 mi. S of Co. 59 junction with Co. 7. Frame with clapboarding, approx. 48′0″ (5-bay front) x 34′0″ plus front and rear porches, 2½ stories, gable roof with pedimented end gables pierced by lunettes, 2 pairs of interior end chimneys, central 2-tiered pedimented portico with 4 square pillars above and below (wheatsheaf-style balustrade, lunette in tympanum), wide Palladian style doorway with semielliptical transom and flanking 8-over-8 sashed sidelights; center-hall plan with 16′-wide passage, unusual triple-leaf doors at each end, grained woodwork. Frame servants' house, log smokehouse, and wellhouse at rear. Built ca. 1854; Ezra Plumb, architect/builder. Servants' house burned and smokehouse demolished in mid-20th C. Hawthorn was planter, state legislator. House was also boyhood home of Brig. Gen. John Herbert Kelly (1840–64), orphaned grandson of Hawthorn's third wife and one of youngest officers in Confederate army. 8 ext. photos (1937, including 3 photos of dependencies), 10 int. photos (1937); 1 data page (1937). NR.

Glossary of Architectural Terms

Note: In addition to standard architectural terms, this glossary includes a number of colloquial expressions the use of which may be confined to a specific region or locale.

ABACUS. The topmost portion of a column capital, on which the entablature, or object supported, rests; esp. the square topmost member of a Doric capital.

ACANTHUS LEAF MOTIF. A stylized neoclassical motif based on the leaves of the acanthus, a common Mediterranean plant; characteristic decorative element of the Corinthian and Composite orders.

ACROTERIA. Ornaments at the peak or extremities of a classical pediment (*sing.*: ACROTERION).

ADAMESQUE. In the manner of the delicate, classically derived style of the brothers Robert and James Adam (English, 18th C.); said of motifs used in the American Federal period, which were themselves drawn from builders' guides such as those of William Pain, Asher Benjamin, and Owen Biddle, all based on the work of the Adams.

AEDICULA. A niche, door, or window framed by columns or pilasters and capped with a pediment.

AKRON PLAN. A fluid interior layout devised in the late 19th C. for non-liturgical Protestant churches, whereby the adjacent Sunday School rooms can be joined by means of folding or sliding doors to the main church assembly room; also often characterized by a fan-shaped arrangement of pews away from the pulpit area.

ALTO-RELIEVO. A sculptured or raised plaster ornamental surface in which the decorative detail is undercut or otherwise shaped so as to project boldly from the surface; decorative plaster interior cornices and moldings of the period ca. 1850–80 were often executed in alto-relievo; opposite of bas-relief.

AMPHIPROSTYLE. A temple-type structure with columns across each end.

ANTA (*pl.*: ANTAE). A pier or pilaster, formed by a thickening of a wall; frequently used in Greek Revival architecture to frame a recessed colonnade (an in antis porch).

ANTEFIX. In Classic architecture, a decorated upright ornament, generally in the form of a palmette or anthemion, used in series along the ridge of a roof, or atop the cornice of an entablature.

ANTHEMION. A classical decorative motif based on the honeysuckle or palmette (palm leaf).

ANTIS. *See* IN ANTIS.

APRON. A fixed panel beneath a window.

APSE. The rounded or semipolygonal area terminating one end of a church and historically intended to contain the altar; adaptations of the apsidal form to nonliturgical Protestant churches also occurred during the late 19th C.

ARABESQUE. An intricate, geometric decorative pattern combining animal, plant, and occasionally human forms, used in Roman, Renaissance, and Moorish architecture; also, any species of flat ornament of infinite variety.

ARCHITRAVE. (1) The lowest part of a classical entablature, resting directly on the capital of columns or piers and supporting the frieze and cornice. (2) The molding, trim, or casing around a door or window opening.

ARCHIVOLT. The innermost molding or facing around an arch, corresponding to the straight architrave of an entablature; an ornamental molding or band of moldings on the face of an arch, following the outer curve (extrados) visible on the facings of an arch.

ARCUATED. Having a series of arches, corresponding with trabeated (having a series of square-headed openings).

ART GLASS. A form of colored or stained glass popular during the late 19th and early 20th C.

ASHLAR. Squared stonework.

ASTRAGAL. In general, a half-round or convex molding with a fillet on one or both sides, as the ring molding sometimes found at the top of a column shaft (*ex.*: in the Tuscan order).

BALLOON FRAME. A frame for a structure constructed of small members nailed together rather than heavy timbers joined by mortises and tenons.

BALUSTER. An upright, often vase-shaped support for a handrail or coping; a series of balusters, together with the rail or coping, forms a balustrade.

BALUSTRADE. A railing system (as along the edge of a balcony, stair, terrace, or porch) composed of a series of balusters supporting a rail or coping.

BARGEBOARD. A board, often ornately curved or sawn, attached to the projecting edge of a gable; also called a vergeboard.

BARREL VAULT. A masonry, wood, or metal arching vault which describes a semicylinder and is used to roof an elongated space, such as the nave of a church; the barrel vault is derived from Roman classical architecture.

BASE COURSE. The lowest layer of masonry in a wall.

BASILICA PLAN. The traditional form of an early Christian church, consisting of a nave, transepts, and an apse, creating an overall cruciform shape.

BAS-RELIEF. A sculptured or raised plaster ornamental surface in which the projection of the ornament is only slight, as opposed to alto-relievo.

BASTION. A defense work projecting from the wall of a fortification to defend the flanking walls.

BATTEN DOOR, BATTEN SHUTTER. A door or window shutter constructed of vertical boards fastened together by two or more horizontal members.

BATTER. The receding upward slope of a wall, framing, or support which deviates from the perpendicular; hence, in architecture, "battered" means sloping inward from the base.

BAY. In architecture, any of a series of major divisions or units in a structure, as window, door, or archway openings, or the space between columns or piers. As used in the HABS catalogs, referring commonly to the number of openings (doors and windows) across the principal elevation or elevations of a structure.

Glossary of Architectural Terms

BAY WINDOW. A window projecting from the main wall plane; usually semioctagonal, although sometimes circular or rectangular.

BEAD AND REEL. A classical ornamental molding which consists of a continuous band of small half-spheres (sometimes elongated into a capsule-like form) alternating with small disks (reels), singly or in pairs.

BEADED CLAPBOARD. A clapboard the exposed side of which has a narrow decorative bead molding; much used in 18th-C. Virginia, Maryland, and the Carolinas, and found occasionally in early 19th-C. Alabama architecture.

BEAD MOLDING. A semicircular molding.

BELL-CAST ROOF. A curved roof profile flaring out or splayed at the bottom.

BELLCOTE. A small open construction, usually a vertical extension of a wall itself, which contains a bell; sometimes the bellcote may be corbeled out from the plane of the wall. A feature of some small Gothic Revival chapels and churches.

BELT COURSE. A narrow, slightly raised decorative band running horizontally along the exterior walls of a building and usually defining the interior floor divisions, or sometimes simply marking a division in the exterior wall plane. Also called a band course.

BELVEDERE. A rooftop observatory.

BLIND ARCH, BLIND ARCADE. An arch or series of arches applied to a wall as decoration, or to frame a smaller opening; hence, not open through.

BLIND ARCHITRAVE. A classical enframement consisting of pilasters supporting a top member (entablature) which is applied for decorative purposes against a wall; during the Greek Revival period in Alabama and elsewhere, such blind architraves were often placed behind the pulpit platform or altar area of a church, or the judge's dais of a courtroom.

BLINDS. Window shutters with louvers.

BLOCKING COURSE. A plain finished course of masonry (or a similar construction in wood) surmounting a cornice, as a parapet.

BOARD AND BATTEN. Wall sheathing in which vertical boards are used, the joints between being covered with narrow wooden strips (*ex.*: St. Andrew's Church, Prairieville).

BOLECTION MOLDING. A raised molding of ogee profile, often covering a joint and encircling a panel or opening.

BOND. In masonry, the pattern in which bricks or stones are laid. *See also* COMMON BOND, FLEMISH BOND.

BOX PEW. Church pew with a hinged gate.

BOX STAIR. A stairway enclosed by walls, often with a door at or near the foot of the stair and sometimes at the head as well.

BRACKET. A support element under eaves, shelves, or other overhangs, often more decorative than functional; an especially common feature of the Italianate style.

BROACHED SPIRE. An octagonal spire surmounting a square tower, the transition being made by a half-pyramid, or broach, above each corner of the tower.

BROKEN GABLE. A gable roof of which one or both slopes are "broken" so as to form a shallower angle of pitch, usually in order to extend out over a porch or shed room; typically associated with vernacular dwellings.

BROKEN PEDIMENT. A pediment which is split apart at its apex, the resulting gap often being filled by an ornamental urn or finial.

BROKEN SCROLL PEDIMENT. A curvilinear pediment split apart at its apex, each half being scrolled; also called a swan's neck pediment; a feature of Georgian and neo-Georgian architecture.

BULL'S-EYE. (1) A round or oval aperture, glazed, louvered, or open. (2) An ornament of raised or incised concentric circles as sometimes found at either end of a lintel.

BUTTERFLY ROOF. A roof consisting of a main gable with a smaller gable behind and parallel to it, so that the resulting trough between forms a catchment for water which is piped into a cistern; an occasional feature on the Gulf Coast (*ex.*: Worker's Cottage, Mobile).

BUTTRESS. An abutting support which strengthens or stabilizes a wall; esp. characteristic of Gothic architecture.

CAMBER. A flattened arch, usually curved only slightly upward over the space it spans.

CAMPANILE. A belltower, usually a freestanding one.

CANOPY ROOF. A roof, usually covering a porch or a balcony, which simulates the concave curvature of a cloth canopy; also called a pagoda-type roof.

CANTILEVERED. Supported only at one end or one side by projecting beams.

CAPITAL. The topmost part, or cap, of a column, pilaster, anta, etc.; usually molded or otherwise decorated as with volutes (Ionic order) and acanthus leaves (Corinthian order).

CAROLINA PORCH. A colloquial term for a porch the supporting posts or piers of which rise directly from ground level and stand free and in front of the porch itself, which consists of a deck (usually railed) behind the row of supports; ordinarily, the supporting posts or columns rest on pedestal-like bases; porch so-called from supposed place of origin on the South Atlantic seaboard, from which it was brought to Alabama by early settlers; esp. common in southern Alabama.

CARTOUCHE. An ornamental shield, scroll, oval, circle, etc., often bearing an inscription.

CASEMATE. A vault or chamber in a defense bastion, having openings for the firing of weapons.

CASEMENT. A window that swings open on hinges, as opposed to a sash, which is raised and lowered.

CASTELLATED. Having the external fortification elements of a castle, as battlements (crenellation), towers, etc., for ornamentation.

CAST IRON. An iron alloy, shaped by pouring the molten metal into a mold; cast iron is brittle, hard, and cannot be welded, but it lends itself to intricate raised surface patterns because of its process of manufacture.

CAST-IRON FRONT. A load-bearing façade composed of prefabricated cast-iron units, much used in American commercial architecture ca. 1850 to 1890.

Glossary of Architectural Terms

CATSLIDE ROOF. A double-pitched or gable roof one slope of which is shallower and longer than the other so as to extend out over a shed room or porch.

CAVETTO. A concave molding.

CENTER-HALL PLAN. Consisting of a bisecting central passage with rooms symmetrically disposed to either side. *See diagram p. 391.*

CENTERPIECE. An ornamental plaster, wood, or metal plaque affixed to a ceiling, often from which a chandelier is suspended.

CHAIR-RAIL. A broad molding, normally wooden, around the walls of a room (or in Alabama sometimes across the outside wall of a house beneath the sheltering porch) at the height of a chair back.

CHAMFER. The beveled corner of a post or other structural element; also, the act of cutting such a bevel.

CHANCEL. That portion of a church reserved for clergy, choir, and altar.

CHEVRON. A V-shaped decoration generally used as a continuous molding.

CHINKING. The clay, plaster, or wood infill found in the cracks between the logs of a log wall.

CHORAGIC MONUMENT OF LYSICRATES. One of the most widely imitated monuments of the classical world (also called Demosthenes' lantern), distinguished by a circular peristyle with a low peaked roof rimmed with antefixes; its form was liberally copied for cupolas and gazebos (*ex.*: old Madison County courthouse, Huntsville; gazebo at Gaineswood, Demopolis).

CLAPBOARD. A board with one edge thicker than the other, so as to facilitate horizontal overlapping to form a weather-proof wall sheathing; also known as a weatherboard.

CLERESTORY. The upper part of the walls of the nave, transepts, and choir of a church, above the side aisles, containing windows; any similar upper zone of wall pierced with windows to admit light into a lofty space; a row of windows high in the wall.

CLIPPED GABLE. *See* JERKINHEAD ROOF.

CLOSED STRINGER STAIR. A stair in which the treads, or steps themselves, are concealed by the diagonally running stringer.

COFFER. A recessed panel in a flat or vaulted ceiling; an esp. popular treatment in Classic architecture and its derivatives, such as Renaissance and Greek Revival.

COLLAR BEAM. A horizontal wood or metal beam which ties together two rafters that form the triangular truss of a roof; short diagonal supporting pieces underneath the collar beam itself are called collar braces.

COLONNETTES. Small, slender columns.

COLOSSAL ORDER. *See* GIANT ORDER.

COMMON BOND. Brickwork consisting of bricks laid end-to-end with the long side exposed (as stretchers), the inner and outer courses themselves being bonded every few rows by a single row of bricks laid crosswise with only the end exposed (as headers). *See also* FLEMISH BOND.

COMPOSITE ORDER. The last of the five Classic orders, a Roman elaboration of the Corinthian order combining the acanthus leaf motif of the

Corinthian capital with the volutes of the Ionic order, among other embellishments. *See diagram p. 377.*

CONSOLE. A decorative support or bracket usually in the form of a vertical or horizontal scroll.

CORBEL. Masonry built out from a wall so as to support a cornice, beam, etc.

CORBIESTEP. Same as stepped; a parapet having a stepped outline.

CORINTHIAN ORDER. The most ornate of the three main Classic orders, characterized by a bell-shaped capital embellished with acanthus leaves, and by a slender shaft, usually fluted. *See diagram p. 377.*

CORNER BLOCKS. Square blocks, frequently carved, at the corner of door or window frames.

CORNICE. (1) In Classic architecture, the topmost projecting part of an entablature, resting on the frieze and composing the base of the pediment. (2) The horizontal projecting member at the top of a wall or building. (3) Any molded projection which crowns or finishes the part to which it is affixed. *See also* RAKING CORNICE.

CORONA. The greatest projection of a cornice, designed mainly to throw off rain from the roof.

COTTAGE ORNÉ. A picturesque country or suburban dwelling, usually contrived to look informal and rustic; in Alabama, the concept of the *cottage orné* was introduced through the works of A. J. Downing and other contemporary architectural writers during the 1840s and 1850s.

CRENELLATION. A parapet with repeated indentations; battlemented.

CREOLE COTTAGE. A colloquial term referring to a type of folk domestic architecture on the coast of the Gulf of Mexico popularly believed to have evolved from French colonial house-forms; most frequently used with reference to a story-and-a-half gabled house in which the front or both slopes of the high-pitched roof extend over a full-length porch, or gallery.

CRESTING. The ornamental finish at the ridge of a roof, or at the top of a wall, screen, canopy, etc.

CROCKET. In Gothic architecture, a projecting ornament in the shape of stylized foliage that decorates the edges of spires, gables, and pinnacles.

CROSS-GABLE. A gable, usually a secondary one, turned at right angles to the main roofline.

CROWSTEP. A parapet having a stepped outline; corbiestepped.

CRUCIFORM PLAN. In the shape of a cross, especially a Latin cross with one long and three short arms; usually with reference to the layout of a church.

CUDDY. A colloquial term referring to the attic space above a porch, directly beneath the slope of the roof; usually reached through a crawl space.

CUPOLA. A terminal structure (observatory, belvedere, lantern, etc.) rising above a main roof.

CURTAIN WALL. (1) A parapet wall between two chimneys. (2) A nonloadbearing wall between columns or piers. (3) The wall between two bastions of a fortification.

CUSHIONED. *See* PULVINATED.

Glossary of Architectural Terms

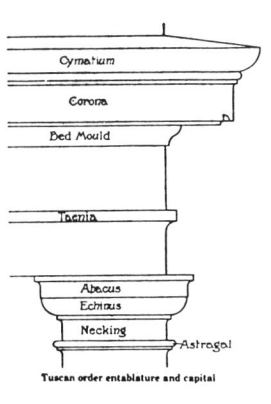
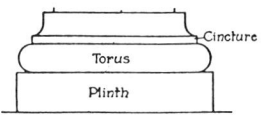

TUSCAN

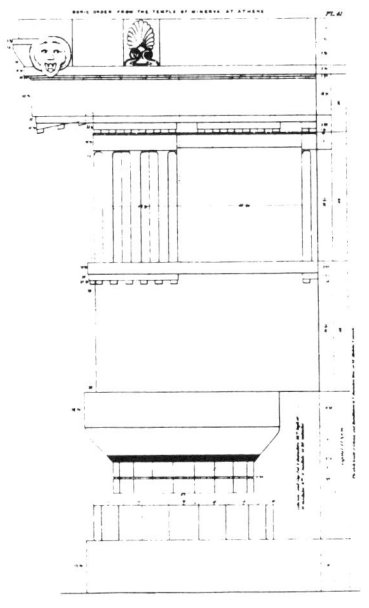

DORIC

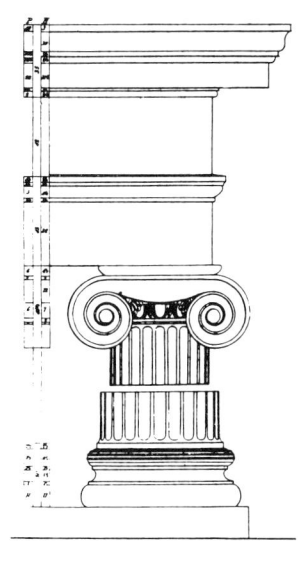

IONIC

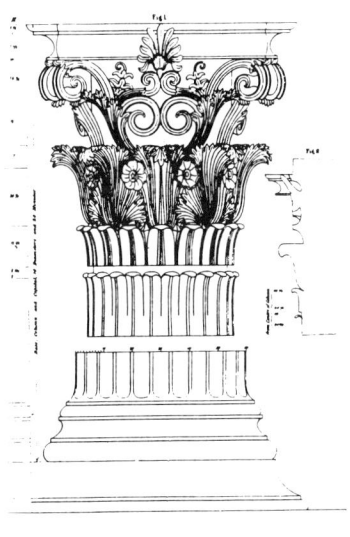

CORINTHIAN

COMPOSITE

TOWER OF THE WINDS
CORINTHIAN

The Classical Orders

CUSP. Projecting point formed by intersecting Gothic window tracery.

CYLINDRICAL STAIR. One which rises in corkscrew fashion around a central post; sometimes used in the mid-19th C. for ascent to a rooftop belvedere (*ex.*: Sturdivant Hall, Selma; James Watkins House, Huntsville; Walton-Bruce House, Dayton); also called a screw stair or vice stair.

DADO. Decorative or protective paneling applied to the lower part of the walls of a room above the baseboard; occasionally also used in early Alabama architecture as an exterior decorative element for porches or galleries (*ex.*: Moore-Whatley House, Auburn Vicinity).

DAIS. Raised platform at the end of a large room or meeting hall containing, in a church, the pulpit and sometimes the organ and choir.

DECK. A roofless porch, or, as in the Carolina porch, a raised porch-like sitting area sheltered by a roof carried on freestanding supports.

DENTICULATION. A decorative row of dentils, or small blocks, forming part of a classical entablature.

DENTIL. *See* DENTICULATION.

DIAPERWORK, DIAPERING. A pattern, esp. of brickwork, in which a design is repeated on a rectangular or diagonal grid; usually associated with colonial architecture in America; found very rarely in early 19th-C. Alabama (*ex.*: Sellers-Henderson House, Millers Ferry; Jacob Green House, Ashville Vicinity).

DISTYLE. Having two columns.

DISTYLE IN ANTIS. In Greek architecture, a portico with two columns set between the piers (antae) of the flanking end walls; an especially popular façade treatment for churches during the Greek Revival period.

DOGLEG STAIR. A stair rising first in one direction then in another, usually in reverse flight.

DOGTOOTH. A pattern of diagonally laid brick forming a serrated profile, as in some brick corbel courses and decorative string courses; sawtooth.

DOGTROT. A colloquial reference to the open-ended passage or breezeway often found between the two main rooms of early Alabama log (and sometimes frame) houses; such dogtrot houses were the characteristic yeoman dwelling of 19th-C. Alabama.

DORIC ORDER. The oldest and simplest of the three main Classic orders, with a simple rounded column capital and, properly, an entablature with a frieze composed of triglyphs and metopes; both Greek and Roman versions of Doric occur. *See diagram p. 377.*

DORMER. A window that projects through the slope of a roof.

DOUBLE LOG HOUSE. An early-19th-C. term used generally to describe a house consisting of two log pens, or rooms, with an open passage between.

DOUBLE PEN. Primarily a folklorist's term to describe a dwelling the main block of which consists of two side-by-side rooms (pens), each with a separate front door; log houses of this type consisted of two abutting log enclosures, or "pens"; frame, and sometimes even brick, versions of this house-type also occurred.

DOUBLE PILE. House two rooms deep; usually associated with colonial architecture.

DOVETAIL NOTCH. *See* NOTCHING.

DRIP CORBELING. Corbeling distinguished by regularly spaced pendants which drop from the continuous main masonry course; particularly associated with early neo-Romanesque, or Norman style, architecture (ca. 1855–75 in Alabama); sometimes called Lombard detail because of supposed roots in the Romanesque architecture of Lombardy.

DRIP MOLDING. Any raised molding around an opening so formed and arranged as to throw off rain; dripstone.

DRUM. (1) The vertical supporting wall for a dome. (2) One of the stone cylinders forming the shaft of a column.

DRYMOAT. A below-ground-level excavated space or trench around the base of a structure, designed to provide light and air to the cellar area; also depressed area around fortification.

EARED ARCHITRAVE. A door or window architrave which breaks into side projections at the upper corners (also called Greek ears); a popular Greek Revival device.

EASTLAKE. A type of elaborate late-19th-C. wood ornamentation (sometimes copied in metal) which was the product of the lathe, chisel, and gouge; after Charles Eastlake, an English architect whose ideas on craftsmanship the ornamentation supposedly expressed, although Eastlake disavowed the excesses that earmarked this style in America.

ECHINUS. The curved molding immediately beneath the abacus of a Doric capital, or the corresponding element on another column, supporting the abacus.

ECLECTIC. In architecture, the use of features, elements, or characteristics from several different stylistic sources, based on personal preference; also, the imitation of several different styles at the same time.

EGG AND DART. A standard classical decorative motif composed of alternating egg-shaped and dart-shaped elements, used to enrich a band of molding on an entablature; also, for ornamental interior plasterwork during the Greek Revival period. In the egg-and-anchor, egg-and-arrow, and egg-and-tongue molding, the dart-like ornament is varied in form.

EGYPTIAN DOOR. A colloquial term used, in Alabama especially at Mobile, to refer to a door opening framed by a shouldered (eared) architrave, usually with battered jambs and sometimes with a shallow pedimented molding above; also called a Greek key door.

ELL. A secondary wing or extension of a building at right angles to the principal block, sometimes separated from the main structure by an open passage in early Alabama architecture, and generally containing the dining room.

EMBRASURE. A deeply recessed opening, often with splayed sides.

ENCEINTE. The line of works enclosing a fortification.

END CHIMNEY. A chimney occurring at the gable end or side wall of a building, as opposed to rising from somewhere inside a structure; an exterior end chimney extrudes from the main wall plane, while an interior end chimney is flush with the main wall plane.

ENGAGED COLUMN. A column attached to a wall or pier.

ENTABLATURE. In classical architecture, the ornamented horizontal beam carried by the columns, divided into the architrave (below), the frieze (middle), and the cornice (topmost section); a similar feature as the crown of a wall. *See* ORDER.

ENTASIS. The slight outward curve, or convex profile, of the shaft of a column; used in order to correct the optical illusion of concavity which would result from a straight-sided column.

ETCHED GLASS. Glass treated with an incised decorative pattern.

EYEBROW WINDOWS. (1) A low dormer with no sides, the roof of which is carried over it in a curve. (2) Any small secondary window above a main one, such as the frieze windows found in some Greek Revival structures.

FAÇADE. A principal exterior face of a building, usually the front, and oftentimes distinguished by elaboration of architectural details and treatment.

FALSE GRAINING. *See* GRAINING.

FANLIGHT. A semicircular or semielliptical window, with radiating muntins or tracery, set over a door or sometimes another window; a popular motif of the Federal period.

FASCES. A symbol of Roman authority consisting of a bundle of rods with a projecting axe blade; sometimes used as a classical ornament, as in a fence post, etc.

FASCIA. Any flat horizontal facing or molding used in a cornice or beneath eaves, etc.

FAUX BOIS. Literally "false wood," French term for the artificial wood graining popular in the U.S. esp. during the mid-19th C. *See* GRAINING.

FENESTRATION. The arrangement of windows in a structure.

FESTOON. A carved, molded, or painted garland of fruit, flowers, or leaves suspended between two points; a frequent motif of Adamesque and Federal period decor; also called a swag.

FIELD. Raised center of a panel, hence a "fielded panel."

FILLET. A term loosely applied to almost any rectangular molding, usually used in conjunction with or to separate other moldings; often narrow, flat, and square in section.

FINIAL. An ornament on top of a spire, gable, post, etc.

FISH-SCALE SHINGLES. Decorative shingles the exposed end of which are rounded as in a fish scale; a popular late-19th-C. motif.

FLASHING. Metal strip used to prevent rain from entering a building at a roof intersection.

FLAT ARCH. An arch with a horizontal or nearly horizontal intrados; also called a jack-arch or straight arch.

FLATWORK. Flat (as opposed to turned) decorative woodwork, executed with a scrollsaw or jigsaw.

FLÈCHE. A slender rooftop spire usually at the intersection of the nave and transepts of a church.

FLEMISH BOND. Brickwork consisting of bricks laid alternately lengthwise (exposing the long side) and endwise (exposing the short side); the bricks laid lengthwise are called stretchers, and those laid crosswise, headers. As a decorative form of bricklaying, Flemish bond was popular during the 18th and early 19th C. In Alabama, it occurs most frequently in the Tennessee Valley. Ordinarily used on the front or main elevations; other surfaces were laid in the simpler common bond pattern. *See also* COMMON BOND.

FLEUR-DE-LIS. Stylized lily ornamentation, the French royal lily.

FLEURON. Any small flower-like ornament, but specifically that at the center of each side of a Corinthian abacus.

FLUSH SIDING. Wooden wall sheathing applied so that the resulting surface is completely smooth and the boards do not overlap; generally used for wall surfaces protected from the weather, as for the area sheltered by a porch; sometimes used as an interior wall finish in early Alabama. In a few cases (*ex.*: Adustin Hall, Gainesville) flush siding is used as an exterior finish in combination with antae or pilasters, to create the smooth surfaces valued during the Greek Revival period.

FLUTED. Having regularly spaced, parallel grooves (flutes), as on the shaft of a column or pilaster; also, fluting.

FOLIATED. Decorated with leaf-like ornamentation.

FRENCH DOORS. Glazed door opening, as a window, onto a porch or terrace.

FRESCO WORK. A form of mural painting using water-based colors on plaster; in Alabama, used colloquially to refer to the decorative painting of walls and ceilings, often with reference to trompe l'oeil. *See* TROMPE L'OEIL.

FRET. A classical ornamental form consisting of short lines intersecting at right angles in a maze-like pattern and usually forming a continuous band; also called a Greek key, or meander; fretwork can refer to this or similar ornamental patterns; in Greek Revival architecture the open metal or wooden grilles covering frieze windows were sometimes sawn or cast in this pattern.

FRIEZE. The central part of an entablature, between the architrave below and the cornice above; may be plain or ornamented.

FRIEZE WINDOW. A window, usually one in a series, which pierces the frieze of an entablature; especially popular motif during the Greek Revival period.

FRONTISPIECE ENTRANCE. A decorative entrance or doorway treatment, usually with flanking pilasters or columns, and an entablature.

FROSTED GLASS. *See* ETCHED GLASS.

GABLE. The triangular well segment beneath the double-pitched slopes of a gable roof.

GABLE ROOF. A roof having two pitched slopes. *See diagram p. 382.*

GALILEE PORCH. Narthex or vestibule at west end of a church, communicating with outside.

GALLERY. (1) Colloquially, a porch or veranda; esp. one that functions as an outdoor living space (from the Fr. *galerie*). (2) In houses of worship, the upper tier of seats at the rear and sometimes along each side of the nave for the accommodation of additional worshipers (also incorrectly referred to as a balcony); in early Alabama churches, the gallery or a por-

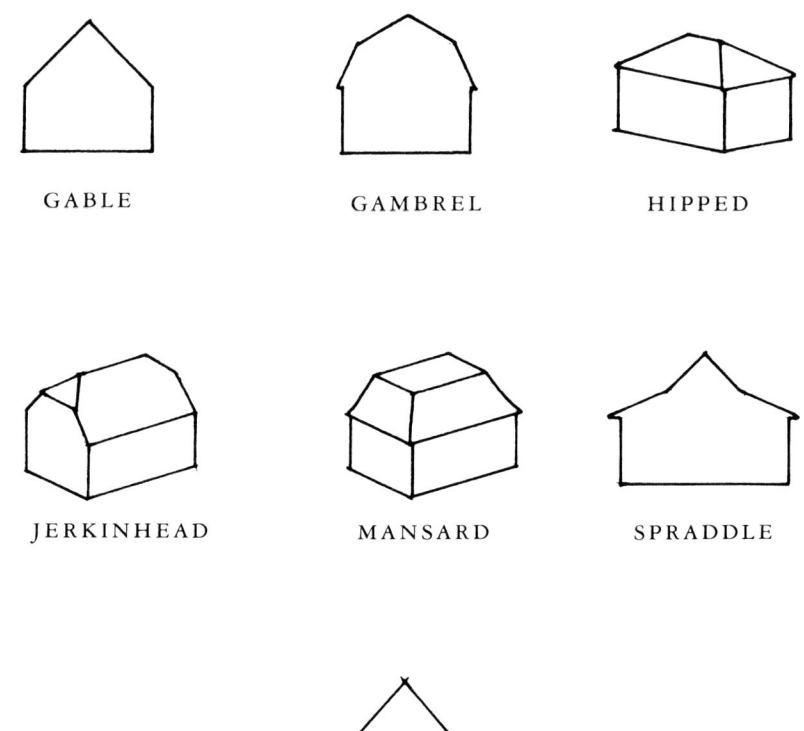

Roof Types

tion of it was customarily set aside for slaves and black worshipers; choir and organ were also located in the gallery.

GAMBREL. A variant on the double-pitched gable roof in which each slope is broken into two planes, the lower plane having a steeper pitch than the upper plane. *See diagram above.*

GARÇONNIÈRE. Separate living quarters set apart from the main house for the accommodation of the young men of the family; bachelor quarters. A Gulf Coast practice especially, based on French custom.

GAUGED AND RUBBED BRICK. Brickwork in which bricks are cut or sawn to achieve a precise shape and then rubbed to an exact size and smooth finish; an especial characteristic of 18th- and early-19th-C. brickwork.

GAZEBO. A garden house or summer house, usually open at the sides.

GIANT ORDER. Columns rising through two or more stories; also called colossal order.

GLACIS. A sloped embankment in front of a fortification.

GLAZED BRICK. Bricks fired so as to have a thin, glossy, glass-like finish.

GRAINING. Decorative painting technique which simulates wood graining; an esp. popular ornamental element during the mid-19th C.

GRECIAN CROSS. A plan in the shape of a Grecian cross, i.e., four equilateral arms.

GREEK EARS. Projections near the top of the enframements to doors of the Greek Revival period.

GREEK KEY DOOR. *See* EGYPTIAN DOOR.

GROUT. Primitive concrete.

GUILLOCHE. A typical classical ornament composed of intertwining curvilinear bands.

GUTTAE. The row of peg-like ornaments fringing the taenia of a classical entablature or occurring on the mutules of a Doric frieze.

HALF-DOVETAIL NOTCH. *See* NOTCHING.

HALL-AND-PARLOR PLAN. A floorplan rooted in medieval English domestic folk design, consisting of two main rooms—the "hall" (main room) and the adjacent "parlor" (private room); the plan, brought to Alabama from the Atlantic seaboard, occurs from time to time in some of the state's earliest examples of domestic architecture. *See diagram p. 391.*

HAMMERBEAM. A short horizontal beam at the base of one of the two rafters composing an exposed roof truss, which acts as a support for the rafter itself and for the attached collar braces.

HEADER. A brick or squared stone laid crosswise in a wall, so that its short end is exposed. *See also* STRETCHER.

HEXASTYLE. A row of six columns.

HIPPED ROOF. A roof with four uniformly pitched sides. *See diagram p. 382.*

HONEYSUCKLE ORNAMENT. Common term for the anthemion, a standard Grecian decorative motif.

HOOD MOLD. The projecting molding over a door or window; known as a label mold, if extending horizontally over a square opening and vertically downward a short distance, parallel to either side of the opening.

HYPHEN. A small connecting structure forming the link between the major blocks of a large building, esp. between the center pavilion and the end pavilions of a longitudinally disposed edifice.

"I"-DENTIL. Ornament composed of a row of dentils with a pierced hole above, thus simulating in appearance the letter "i"; primarily a Federal period motif.

IMBRICATION. A decorative pattern of shaped and overlapping tiles or shingles.

IMPOST BLOCK. A block, often tapered, atop the capital of a column, placed to receive the thrust of the lintel or spandrel above; similar to a stilt block.

IN ANTIS. In Greek architecture, the type of portico recessed between end walls, which are themselves defined by antae; most commonly, such porticoes have two freestanding columns, hence, distyle in antis.

INTERCOLUMNIATION. The clear space between two adjacent columns.

INTRADOS. The soffit or undersurface of an arch.

IONIC ORDER. One of the Classic orders used in Greek and Roman architecture and its derivatives, characterized by its scroll-like capitals (volutes). *See diagram p. 377.*

JALOUSIE. A blind or sunscreen consisting of diagonally positioned fixed or movable slats; often used on porches and galleries in 19th-C. Alabama, as at Bluff Hall, Demopolis.

JAMB. The vertical member to either side of a door or window opening.

JERKINHEAD ROOF. A double-pitched roof form, the gable ends of which have been "clipped" diagonally so as to form a partially hipped configuration from the ridge downward a short distance; a popular feature during the Queen Anne period (ca. 1880–1900). *See diagram p. 382.*

JIB WINDOWS. (1) Sash windows with hinged panels beneath, which open so as to allow egress and ingress when the sash is raised. (2) A floor-length sash window, the sashes of which can be raised to permit egress and ingress; jib windows were especially popular during the mid-19th C.

JIGSAW WORK. Decorative flat woodwork, usually in intricate patterns, executed with a jigsaw; popularly associated with the period ca. 1850–1900 and found especially as porch and balustrade trim.

KEYSTONE. The wedge-shaped central stone or masonry unit of an arch; a decorative element which simulates such a stone, as in the wooden trim around an interior arch.

KING POST. The vertical post from the tie beam to the apex of a triangular truss.

LABEL MOLDING. A squared-off drip molding. *See* DRIP MOLDING.

LAMB'S TONGUE. A tapering tongue-shaped molding frequently used to terminate the bevel of a chamfered post, esp. from the pre-Revolutionary period through the early 19th C. in American folk-building practice.

LANCET. The narrow, sharply pointed window used in the earliest phase of English Gothic (ca. 1150–1250) and favored by the Gothic Revivalists of the mid-19th C.; may be used singly or in groups.

LANTERN. A rooftop construction with windowed sides, esp. on top of a dome.

LEADED GLASS. Small panes of glass held in place with lead strips; the glass may be clear or stained.

LEAN-TO. A wing or extension, usually having a single pitched roof, abutting the main block of a structure; frequently found across the rear, though sometimes at the front or sides, of many folk dwellings in Alabama.

LIGHTS. With reference to a window, same as windowpanes.

LINTEL. The supporting horizontal member spanning an opening.

LOGGIA. A roofed open gallery or arcade in the side of a building, esp. one facing an open court or recessed into the main block of the structure (latter more specifically called an umbrage).

LOTUS CAPITAL. A capital having the shape of a stylized lotus bud (also called a lotiform capital); an ancient Egyptian motif.

LOUVER. One in a series of overlapping horizontal slats, tilted so as to admit air but exclude rain, snow, or heavy sunlight; louvers may be fixed or movable (usually fixed on early-19th-C. exterior window blinds).

LOZENGE. A diamond-shaped decorative motif.

LUNETTE. A half-moon or semicircular window, esp. one which decoratively pierces the tympanum of a neoclassical pediment; also, the wall space beneath an arch or vault.

MANSARD. A roof having short, steep slopes on at least two (and usually all four) sides, with a much shallower pitched, or nearly flat, platform-like roof above; after French Renaissance architect François Mansart; characteristic of the Second Empire style (ca. 1870–90 in Alabama). *See diagram p. 382.*

MARBLEIZE (also MARBELIZE). Process of decoratively painting a surface, esp. wood or stucco, to imitate marble; a popular ornamental technique for both interior and exterior treatment in 19th C. (*ex.*: Alfred Battle House, Tuscaloosa).

MATCHED BOARDING, MATCHED SIDING. *See* FLUSH BOARDING.

MEANDER. The Greek fret or key pattern. *See* FRET.

MEDALLION. An ornamental plaque, usually round, oval, or square, bearing a decorative relief design; esp. an ornamental plaster, wood, or metal ceiling centerpiece from which is often suspended a chandelier; also known as a centerpiece.

METOPE. The panel between the triglyphs in a Doric frieze; most generally plain in American Greek Revival architecture.

MODILLION. An ornamental bracket or console used in series under or as part of a classical cornice; distinguished from a dentil in that it is somewhat larger, elaborated of form, and more widely spaced.

MOLDING. A long strip of material having a definite profile used for decorative purposes.

MONITOR. A raised central portion of a roof, as along a gable or at the top of a hipped roof, having small windows or louvers to provide light and air; found in both industrial and residential architecture (in the latter, sometimes surmounted by a cupola or deck as at Kirkwood, Eutaw).

MORTISE AND TENON. An early form of frame construction in which heavy timbers were fit together by means of mortises (holes or grooves) cut into one member to receive the tenons (corresponding projecting pieces) of another, the resulting joint then being secured by wooden pegs driven through both members. In Alabama, this mode of construction was gradually supplanted by balloon frame construction from the mid-19th C. onward.

MULLION. A vertical dividing member, or support, between the sections of a multipart window or door.

MUNTIN. The bar-like vertical and crosswise members, usually of wood or metal, separating the glass panes of a window or door sash; also called glazing bars.

MUTULE. One of the sloping flat blocks on the soffit of a Doric cornice, usually decorated with guttae.

NARTHEX. Vestibule leading to the nave of a church.

NAVE. The main body of a church.

NECKING. On a classical column, the space between the bottom of the capital and the top of the shaft, marked at the juncture with the shaft by a sinkage or a ring of raised (astragal) moldings; also, any ornamental band at the lower part of a capital.

NEWEL. The main post at the base or head of a stair railing.

NOGGING. The brick or rubble material that is used to fill the spaces between the studs and posts of a wooden frame; a primitive form of insulation and fire retardant.

NOSING. That part of the tread of a stair which projects over the riser.

NOTCHING. In log construction, the various methods by which two logs are joined together; the hewn notches can be of various types: dovetail, half-dovetail, saddle, square, "V"-notch. In Alabama, the half-dovetail is perhaps the most common. *See diagram p. 387.*

NOVELTY SIDING. Boards with a continuous horizontal concave or squared groove on the face of the upper part, and a rabbet (or rebate) on the back of the lower part, the rabbet to receive the groove of the board beneath; when in place, the boards are in a vertical plane—as with flush siding—and the horizontal joints are emphasized by the squared or concave grooves. Also called simply rabbeted siding in the 19th C. Novelty siding was used as a decorative finish for walls beginning in the mid-19th C. in Alabama (*ex.*: Llewellyn Cato House, Eufaula).

OBELISK. A four-sided shaft that is tapered, terminating with a pyramidal point.

OCTASTYLE. A row of eight columns.

OCULUS. (1) An opening at the top of a dome. (2) A small circular window (also bull's eye, roundel).

OGEE. Having an outline composed of a double curve.

OGEE ARCH. A pointed arch composed of reversed curves, the lower concave and the upper convex.

OPEN PLAN. An interior arrangement without any major divisions.

ORDER. A column together with its entablature and base, esp. one of the five standard orders of Classic architecture; the Greeks used three orders—Doric, Ionic, and Corinthian—from which the Romans evolved derivatives, besides adding the Tuscan and Composite orders. *See diagrams p. 377.*

ORIEL. Usually a bay window corbeled out from the wall of an upper story; also, a projecting bay forming the extension of a room.

OVERDOOR. Decorative cabinetwork above a door opening, often in the form of a blind transom.

OVERMANTEL. Decorative cabinetwork above a mantelshelf, usually in the form of paneling.

OVOLO MOLDING. A rounded convex molding, usually a quarter-circle in Roman architecture but flatter in Grecian work.

PALLADIAN OPENING. An arched opening flanked by smaller square-headed openings; also called a Venetian or Serlian opening; a motif much used by the Italian Renaissance architect Andrea Palladio (1508–80) and associated with the Federal style in America. A modified Palladian opening usually refers to a three-part window or door in which the wide center opening is squared instead of arched.

PARAPET. A low wall at the edge of a roof, porch, or terrace.

PARGETING. Ornamental plaster relief decoration.

PARQUETRY. A pattern of inlaid wood, often of two or more kinds and colors.

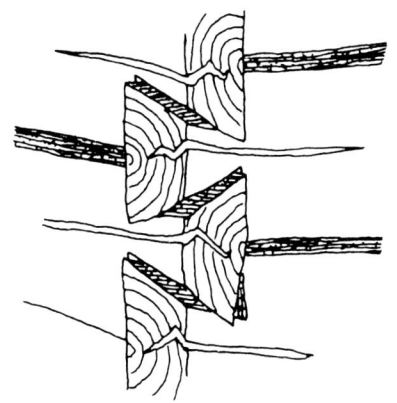
DOVETAIL NOTCH

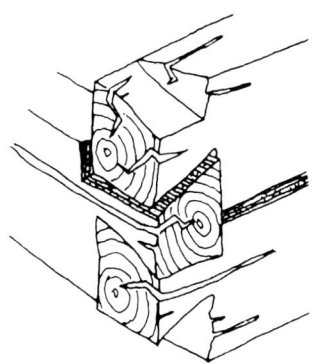
HALF-DOVETAIL NOTCH

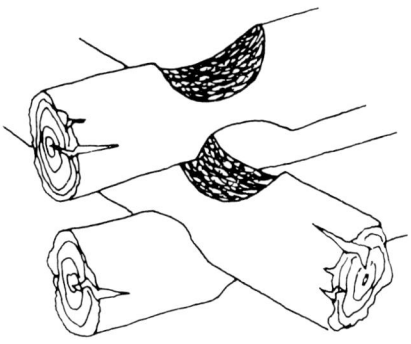
SADDLE NOTCH

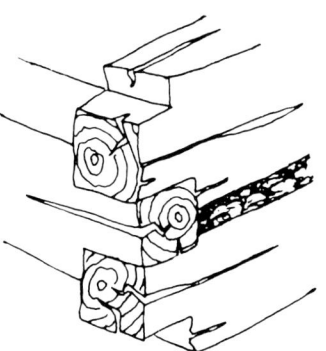
SQUARE NOTCH

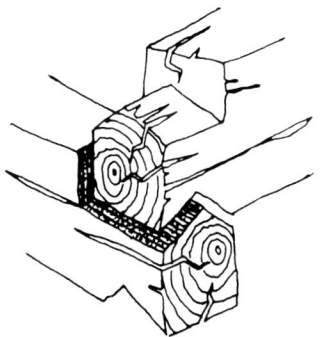
"V" NOTCH

Notching

PATERA. A standard classical decorative element consisting of a round or oval disk or medallion bearing a bas-relief ornamental design, often a sunburst or stylized floral motif.

PAVILION. The major subdivision(s) of a building, usually referring to projecting central and/or end blocks.

PEDESTAL. A base or small foundation, often with moldings at top and bottom.

PEDIMENT. In Classic architecture esp., the triangular face of a roof gable; also, any similar triangular crowning element used over doors, windows, niches, etc.

PEN. A four-sided log enclosure, forming a room.

PENT. A narrow shed-roof projection from the gable end of a house, ordinarily abutting or placed between chimneys, and serving as a closet; a feature primarily of 18th-C. Virginia and Maryland architecture carried over only rarely in Alabama, as at Bride's Hill, Wheeler Vicinity (Lawrence County), and Ivy Green, Tuscumbia.

PERGOLA. An arbor usually constructed of a double row of supports carrying an open framework.

PERISTYLE. An encircling colonnade, one completely surrounding a building or open area.

PIANO NOBILE. The principal story in a house, usually one flight above ground; esp. characteristic of Renaissance architecture and its derivatives (*ex.*: U.S. Custom House and Barton Academy, Mobile).

PIAZZA. In U.S., a colloquial term meaning porch.

PIER. A column serving as a principal support, whether freestanding, as part of a porch, or a thickened part of a wall (in both cases, a pier is usually one in a regularly spaced series). The term normally refers to a support, square or rectangular, often with molded cap and base though not necessarily related to a specific Classic order.

PIERCED WORK. Refers to decorative treatment, usually woodwork, which consists of patterns that are bored or sawn out; a form of gingerbread work.

PILASTER. A shallow, flattened rectangular upright, applied to a wall and treated like a column, with base, shaft, and capital.

PILASTRADE. A row of pilasters.

PINNACLE. In Gothic architecture, a small ornamental shaft or peak.

PLATE. A horizontal beam carrying or receiving the ends of joists, rafters, posts, etc.

PLATE GLASS. Rolled sheet glass (post–Civil War period).

PLINTH. The pedestal-like square or rectangular support on which a column rests; also, the base block at the juncture of a baseboard and the trim around an opening.

PODIUM. A raised base or platform; in architecture esp. a formal terrace upon which an edifice may rest in order to give the structure greater visual monumentality.

POINTING. The mortar in a brick or stone wall.

POLYCHROMY. The use of many colors in decoration; polychromatic roofs and walls were a popular feature of the High Victorian period.

PORTE COCHÈRE. A carriage porch or similar covered vehicular entrance.

PORTICO. A porch, usually treated in a formal manner, consisting of a roof supported by columns.

PRESSED METAL. Thin sheets of metal, often tin, which are molded or stamped into decorative designs and used to cover ceilings and interior walls; a popular late-19th-C. feature.

PROSTYLE. A temple-type structure with columns across only the front.

PULVINATED. Bulging out or cushion-shaped, convex in profile, as in the rounded frieze of some Ionic orders.

PUNCHEON. A split log, often serving as a floor joist.

QUATREFOIL. A roughly cloverleaf-shaped Gothic ornamental motif consisting of four lobes; a pattern frequently to be seen in Gothic Revival period tracery or pierced work.

QUEEN POST. One of two parallel posts running up from the tie beam to the rafters of a triangular truss.

QUOIN. One of the units of stone or brick accentuating the corners, angles, or openings of a wall. Sometimes a quoined treatment is simulated in raised stucco or plaster.

RABBET. A channel, groove, or recess cut along the edge of a board so that the edge fits against the overlapping edge of an adjacent board. *See* NOVELTY SIDING.

RAKED. Inclined, as a raked cornice (along the slope of a pediment).

RAKING CORNICE. A cornice that follows the slope of a gable, pediment, or roof.

RANDOM ASHLAR. Ashlar masonry in which rectangular stones are set seemingly without a continuous pattern of mortar joints.

REEDING. A series of narrow parallel convex moldings, the opposite of fluting; reeded panels are a frequent characteristic of Federal-period woodwork.

REENTRANT ANGLE. Interior angle of a wall, as the juncture between the façade and a projecting wing.

REJA. A grille (Sp.), as an ornamental grille in a church screening organ pipes, etc.

REREDOS. An ornamental screen behind an altar.

REVEAL. The side of an opening (door, window) cut through the wall; in the 19th C., reveals were often paneled (*ex.*: James Dearing House, Tuscaloosa).

REVERSE-FLIGHT STAIR. A stair rising to a landing, then in an opposite direction to the floor above.

RINCEAU. A band of ornament, esp. in Classic architecture, consisting of undulant and intertwining foliage.

RISER. The vertical front plane of a step, beneath the tread.

ROODSCREEN. Ornamental screen separating nave from chancel of a church (*ex.*: St. Paul's Church, Lowndesboro).

ROSETTE. An ornamental disk ornament, esp. in Classic architecture, with a stylized leaf or floral pattern usually in relief.

ROSE WINDOW. *See* WHEEL WINDOW.

ROUNDEL. A small circular window or panel.

RUBBED BRICK. *See* GAUGED AND RUBBED BRICK.

RUBBLEWORK. Masonry composed of rough or irregular stones.

RUNNING ORNAMENT. Any ornament in which the design is continuous, with intertwined or flowing lines as waves, foliage, fretwork; esp. common beneath stair treads.

RUSTICATION. Cut stone or imitation stone having strongly emphasized beveled or recessed joints and roughly textured or smooth faces; a popular Renaissance and neo-Renaissance treatment for the exterior facing of the ground or basement floor esp.

SADDLEBAG HOUSE. Descriptive of a dwelling type, esp. log, consisting of two rooms (or log pens) with a common chimney between (*ex.*: Beaty-Mason House slave quarters, Athens); rare in Alabama.

SADDLE NOTCH. *See* NOTCHING.

SALTBOX. A two-story gabled-roof dwelling in which the rear slope of the roof extends downward in an unbroken plane to cover a one-story extension across the back.

SAWTOOTH. *See* DOGTOOTH.

SCALLOPED. Having a wavy edge.

SCISSORS TRUSS. A roofing truss in which the braces for the rafters cross, resembling a pair of open scissors.

SCORED. Marked off on a plaster, stuccoed, or sometimes wood surface so as to resemble stone coursing or rustication.

SCROLL-CUT. Cut with a scroll-saw (jigsaw); said esp. of the gingerbread trim popular ca. 1850–1900.

SECRET ROOM. Colloquial term for the garret room directly above the open central passage in a dogtrot log house, sometimes entered only through a cubbyhole from one or the other adjacent garret chambers.

SEGMENTAL ARCH. Any rounded arch of less than a semicircle, thus a segment of a semicircular arch.

SHAFT. The main part of a column, between the base and the capital.

SHAKE. A thick, hand-split shingle, formed by splitting a short leg into radial sections.

SHED ROOM. A secondary room abutting the main block of a house, as a lean-to; also called a side room; characteristic of Alabama folk dwelling-types.

SHIPLAP, SHIPLAP SIDING. Wood sheathing in which one edge of each horizontally laid board has been channeled or grooved so as to accommodate the adjacent overlapping board.

SHOULDERED ARCHITRAVE. *See* EARED ARCHITRAVE.

SIDE-HALL PLAN. Consisting of hall with a room or rooms only to one side. *See diagram p. 391.*

SIDELIGHTS. The narrow windows flanking a door and often topped by the same transom or fanlight surmounting the door opening; an esp. common feature of the Federal and Greek Revival periods.

SILL. (1) The horizontal bottom member, usually wood, stone, or brick, of a door or window frame. (2) A horizontal timber at the bottom of the frame of a wood structure, resting directly on the foundation masonry or piers and often carrying the floor joists (as a plate), as well as the posts and studs of the frame above.

SINGLE PEN. Primarily a folklorist's term used to describe a dwelling the main block of which consists of a single room (pen); the most primitive version was the domicile consisting of a single log enclosure, or pen,

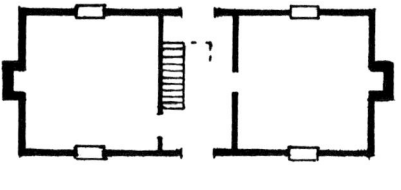
CENTER HALL

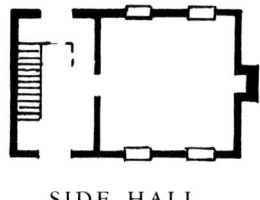
SIDE HALL

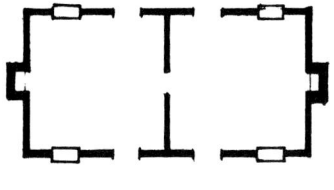
TWO ROOM

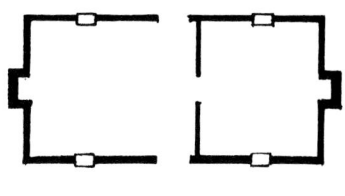
HALL AND PARLOR

Plan Types

sometimes with a low half-story above. Frame versions of the single-pen dwelling also occurred.

SINGLE PILE. House one room deep; usually associated with colonial architecture.

SLIP PEW. A church pew with no hinged gate (as with an old-fashioned box pew) forming one in a series of regularly arranged seats.

SOFFIT. The exposed undersurface of a cornice, eaves, balcony, or other projection.

SPANDREL. The basically triangular space between the left or right exterior curve of an arch and the rectangular framework surrounding it; the space between adjacent arches and the horizontal molding or cornice above them. Also, in skeleton-frame construction, the horizontal panels below and above windows between the continuous vertical supports.

SPINDLE. (1) A turned decorative piece, esp. wood, as in a spindle frieze. (2) A baluster.

SPINDLE FRIEZE. A decorative openwork frieze or screen composed of a series of ornamentally turned members; esp. characteristic of Queen Anne, Eastlake, and other late Victorian-period modes; also called a spool frieze.

SPIRE. A tapering roof surmounting a steeple.

SPOOL FRIEZE. *See* SPINDLE FRIEZE.

SPRADDLE ROOF. A roof having two pitched slopes, the lower parts of which are broken or splayed outward. *See diagram p. 382.*

SQUARE NOTCH. *See* NOTCHING.

STEAMBOAT GOTHIC. A vague colloquial term referring to the ornately trimmed residences of the period ca. 1850–80, esp. those with elaborate wooden porches, cupolas, etc.

STEPPED PARAPET. The stepped profile of a parapet wall masking the gable end of a roof; also known as a corbiestep, crowstep, or catstep.

STILT BLOCK. A block atop the capital of a column, placed to receive the thrust of the lintel or spandrel above.

STIPPLED. A form of folk painting in which a surface is embellished by the application of a series of dots or flicks; stippling.

STRAIGHT-RUN STAIR. A stair rising in a single straight flight to the floor above.

STRETCHER. A brick or squared stone laid lengthwise in a wall, so that its long end is exposed. *See also* HEADER.

STRING COURSE. A molding or decorated band, usually masonry, running horizontally along the exterior wall of a building.

STRINGER. The continuous supporting beam at the end or beneath the treads of a stair. *See also* CLOSED STRINGER STAIR.

STYLOBATE. A continuous base or plinth on which a row of columns is set.

SUNBURST. An ornamental pattern formed by radiating lines, usually reeded or channeled, resembling the rays of the sun; a popular Federal period motif (*ex.*: Leroy Pope House, Huntsville).

SWAG. *See* FESTOON.

TAENIA, TENIA. A narrow raised band or fillet, esp. that separating the frieze of an entablature from the architrave below.

TEMPLE-TYPE FAÇADE. A façade having the general form of a classical temple, that is, a full-width pediment with entablature, and usually regularly spaced columns or pilasters; said of many Greek Revival period buildings (*ex.*: Magnolia Hall, Greensboro).

TEMPLE WITH WINGS. A standard Greek Revival period house-form, rarely appearing in Alabama, which consists of a pedimented two-story central block (usually three bays wide) with flanking one-story wings (*ex.*: Kenan House, Selma Vicinity).

TERRA COTTA. A hard-baked, unglazed clayware used as architectural ornament esp. in the latter half of the 19th C.

TETRASTYLE. A row of four columns.

TIE BEAM. The horizontal beam tying together the two rafters and forming a triangular truss.

TIERED PORCH. A porch of two or more stories.

TORUS MOLDING. A large convex molding, as that forming part of the base of an Ionic or Corinthian column.

TOWER OF THE WINDS ORDER. A variation on the Corinthian order. *See diagram p. 377.*

TOWN LATTICE. A type of covered-bridge truss consisting of a lattice-like network of overlapping triangles, so-called because patented by Ithiel Town in 1820; the most popular type of bridge truss in 19th C. Alabama because of the ease with which it was erected (*ex.*: Buzzard Roost Bridge, Cherokee Vicinity).

TRABEATED. Post-and-lintel construction; thus, for example, a series of square-headed openings as opposed to arched openings.

TRACERY. The open patternwork in a Gothic window.

TRANSEPT. The short arms of a cross-shaped church, at right angles to the main axis.

Glossary of Architectural Terms

TRANSOM. A window over a door or sometimes over another window; usually rectangular.

TREAD. The flat, horizontal topmost part of a step.

TREFOIL. A roughly cloverleaf-shaped Gothic ornamental motif consisting of three lobes; a pattern frequently to be seen in Gothic Revival period tracery and pierced work.

TRELLIS-WORK. In architecture, latticed or scroll-cut wooden porch supports, or similar openwork metal supports; esp. popular in U.S. after 1840 through the influence of A. J. Downing and others who advanced the concept of the *cottage orné* in domestic building. Trellis-work may also be referred to as trellage or treillage.

TRIANGULAR ARCH. An arch the top of which is a triangle formed by two diagonals, instead of being pointed or rounded; sometimes used in the Gothic Revival and High Victorian Gothic periods (*ex.*: St. Alban's Church, Gainesville; Waldwic, Gallion).

TRIGLYPH. Characteristic ornament of Doric-order frieze consisting of a slightly raised block with V-shaped grooves; the triglyphs alternate with plain or sculptured panels called metopes.

TROMPE L'OEIL. Literally, deception of the eye; in architecture, with reference to kind of wall and ceiling painting executed so as to suggest three-dimensional elements such as doorways, pilasters, columns, coffers, and paneling; esp. popular in the third quarter of the 19th C. in Alabama. Often colloquially called fresco work.

TRUNCATED. Squared off at the top, or angled at the corner.

TUDOR ARCH. A low-pitched, very shallow pointed arch.

TURNED WORK. A round member (porch support, etc.) that has been turned on a lathe.

TUSCAN ORDER. One of the Classic orders used in Roman and other Italian architecture; derived from the Doric order but of greater simplicity, with a plain frieze and unfluted column shaft. *See diagram p. 377.*

TWO-ROOM PLAN. Consisting of two equal-sized adjoining rooms. *See diagram p. 391.*

TWO-TIERED PORCH. A porch of two stories.

TYMPANUM. The triangular space enclosed by the sloping (raking) and horizontal cornices of a pediment, or a similar arched space.

UMBRAGE. An open area or porch recessed into the main body of a building and protected by the roof or floor above; also more generally classified as a loggia.

VERANDA. A porch; a colloquial reference in the South to an unusually ample one, often running the length of one or more sides of a structure.

VERGEBOARD. *See* BARGEBOARD.

VERMICULATED. *See* VERMIFORM RUSTICATION.

VERMIFORM RUSTICATION. A worm-like pattern carved in a masonry surface; same as vermiculated work.

VESTIBULE. An anteroom or small foyer leading into a larger space.

VITRUVIAN SCROLL, VITRUVIAN WAVE. A common classical ornament consisting of a series of scrolls connected by a wave-like band; also called a wave scroll or running dog; a common motif for the running ornament beneath the treads of a stair.

"V"-NOTCH. *See* NOTCHING.

VOLUTE. A spiral scroll-like motif such as that used, in pairs, as part of the Ionic capital; also used with reference to the coil terminating a bannister or handrail.

VOUSSOIR. One of the wedge-shaped masonry units which form an arch and terminate at the keystone above and at the two impost blocks where the arc begins below.

WAINSCOT. Wood paneling, most often sheathing lower part of a wall.

WATERTABLE. The projecting base course of an exterior masonry wall, usually from ground-level to first-floor level, which is beveled or molded at the top for weathering.

WEATHERBOARDING. Clapboarding, any overlapping siding.

WEATHERING. The slope, usually stepped, which forms the transition between the broad lower part and the narrower upper part of a chimneystack.

WHEATSHEAF DESIGN. An ornamental balustrade design in which a single upright support is criss-crossed diagonally by two others, usually with a short horizontal piece at the point of intersection, so as to resemble a bound sheaf of wheat; also known as a crow's foot balustrade. Most commonly used for balcony and porch railings in antebellum Alabama.

WHEEL WINDOW. A large circular window with radiating tracery, as the spokes of a wheel; also, a rose window.

WINDER. The tapered tread at the curve of a flight of steps.

WROUGHT IRON. Iron made by puddling, which is then hammered and forged into the desired shape.

Brief Bibliography for Alabama Architecture

Scholarly research on Alabama architecture is just beginning. Most of the titles listed below are, therefore, only incidentally related to historic architecture and, oftentimes, fall more into the realm of antiquarian literature. Still, in the absence of more analytical source materials for many locales, pictorial histories and works of the "old homes and families" variety can at least offer a clue as to the type of architectural resources that exist in counties and communities across the state. Listed first are works with a statewide focus, then those that are multi-county or regional in scope, and finally a county-by-county breakdown.

Works with a Statewide Focus

Alabama Chapter, American Institute of Architects. *A History of The Practice of Architecture in the State of Alabama.* 1941.

Alabama Council, American Institute of Architects. "Alabama Courthouses" (audiovisual presentation). 1976.

———. "150 Years of Architecture in Alabama" (audiovisual presentation). 1975.

———. "Religious Architecture in Alabama" (audiovisual presentation). 1977.

Alabama Historical Commission. *Alabama Ante-Bellum Architecture: A Scrapbook View from the 1930's.* 1976.

———. *Alabama Register of Landmarks & Heritage.* 1978.

———. *Alabama's Tapestry of Historic Places: An Inventory.* 1978.

———. *The National Register in Alabama.* 1978.

———. *Preservation Report* (periodical). 1970–.

Allen, Richard Sanders. *Covered Bridges of the South* (chapter V on Alabama). Brattleboro, Vt.: Stephen Greene Press, 1970, pp. 22–27.

Bayer, Linda, "Commercial Brick was 20th c. small business style," *Preservation Report,* vol. 12, no. 1 (July–Aug. 1984).

Bowsher, Alice, "Industrial towns are part of State's heritage," *Preservation Report,* vol. 11, no. 3 (Nov.–Dec. 1983).

Brannon, Peter F. *Adventures on the Highroad.* Montgomery: Paragon Press, 1930.

———. *Bypaths in Alabama.* Montgomery: Paragon Press, 1929.

———. *Historic Highways in Alabama.* Montgomery: Paragon Press, 1929.

———. *Little Journeys to Interesting Points in Alabama.* Montgomery: Paragon Press, 1930.

———. *Mile Stones Along Alabama's Pathway.* Montgomery: Paragon Press, 1931.

———. *Turning the Pages in Alabama History.* Montgomery: Paragon Press, 1932.

Burkhardt, Ann. "Craftsman style a reaction to Victorian extravagance," *Preservation Report,* vol. 11, no. 1 (July–Aug. 1983).

Burkhardt, E. Walter, and Varian ("Varian Feare"). Articles in *Birmingham News-Age-Herald* on antebellum Alabama architecture, 1934–37. (See above, Alabama Historical Commission, *Alabama Ante-Bellum Architecture.*)

Gamble, Robert S. "Black builders left their mark in antebellum Alabama," *Preservation Report,* vol. 12, no. 6 (May–June 1985).

———. "Double Dogtrot was frontier mansion," *Preservation Report,* vol. 11, no. 5 (Mar.–April 1984).

———. "Early Alabama builders designed for a hot climate," *Preservation Report,* vol. 11, no. 2 (Sept.–Oct. 1983).

———. "HABS: Documenting Alabama's vanishing legacy," *Preservation Report,* vol. 11, no. 4 (Jan.–Feb. 1984).

———. "Plantation Plain: The 'I'-type house was popular early farm dwelling," *Preservation Report,* vol. 12, no. 2 (Sept.–Oct. 1984).

———. "Tidewater-type cottage disappearing from Alabama," *Preservation Report,* vol. 10, no. 6 (May–June 1983).

Hammond, Ralph. *Ante-Bellum Mansions of Alabama*. New York: Architectural Book Co., 1951.
Holmes, Nicholas H., Jr. "The Capitols of the State of Alabama," *Alabama Review*, vol. 32, no. 3 (July 1979), pp. 163–71.
——— . "State exhibit celebrates HABS 50th Birthday," *Preservation Report*, vol. 11, no. 4 (Jan.–Feb. 1984).
Jenkins, William H. "Alabama Forts, 1700–1838." *Alabama Review*, vol. 12, no. 3 (July 1959), pp. 163–79.
Lancaster, Clay. "Greek Revival Architecture in Alabama." *Alabama Architect*, vol. 4, no. 1 (Jan.–Feb. 1968), pp. 6–19.
Live-In-A-Landmark Council of Alabama (periodical), intermittent since 1978–.
National League of American Pen Women, Alabama Members. *Historic Homes of Alabama and Their Traditions*. Birmingham: Birmingham Publishing Co., 1935.
Orr, Henry P. "Decorative Plants Around Historic Alabama Homes." *Alabama Review*, vol. 11, no. 1 (Jan. 1958), pp. 5–30.
Patrick, James. "The Architecture of Adolphus Heiman" (two-part article). *Tennessee Historical Quarterly*, vol. 38, nos. 2 and 3 (Summer and Fall 1979).
Peatross, C. Ford. "Architect of a Region, William Nichols," *Society for the Fine Arts Review*, vol. 4 (Summer 1982), pp. 6–10.
——— , and Robert Mellown. *William Nichols, Architect*. University: University of Alabama Art Gallery, 1979.
Prince, A. G. *Alabama's Covered Bridges*. Privately published, 1972.
Sangster, Tom and Dess L. *Alabama's Covered Bridges*. Montgomery: Coffeetable Publications, 1980.
Scully, Arthur F., Jr. *James Dakin, Architect: His Career in New York and the South*. Baton Rouge: Louisiana State University Press, 1973.
Sulzby, James, F., Jr. *Historic Alabama Hotels and Resorts*. University: University of Alabama Press, 1960.
Thompson, Alan Smith. "Gothic Revival Architecture in Ante-Bellum Alabama." Ph.D. diss., University of Alabama, 1963.
Wilson, Eugene M. *Alabama Folk Houses*. Montgomery: Alabama Historical Commission, 1976.
——— . "Folk Houses of Northern Alabama." Ph.D. diss., Louisiana State University, 1969.
——— . *A Guide to Rural Houses of Alabama*. Montgomery: Alabama Historical Commission, 1975.

Multi-County and Regional Publications

Art Work of Central Alabama Cities. Chicago: Gravure Illustration Co., 1907.
Birmingham Regional Planning Commission. *A Historic Site Survey of Blount, Chilton, Shelby, St. Clair, and Walker Counties*. Birmingham: A. H. Cather Publishing Co., Inc., 1975.
Central Alabama Regional Planning and Development Commission. *Historic Places in Central Alabama* (Autauga, Elmore, Montgomery counties). Montgomery, 1973.
Curtis, Nathaniel C. "Ante-bellum Houses of Central Alabama" (Auburn and Tuskegee area). *AIA Journal*, vol. 8 (November 1920), pp. 388–98.
East Alabama Regional Planning and Development Commission. *Historic Sites: Survey–Evaluation–Re-Inventory* (Calhoun, Chambers, Cherokee, Clay, Cleburne, Coosa, Etowah, Randolph, Talladega, Tallapoosa counties). Anniston, June 1972.

Jeane, D. Gregory, and Douglas Clare Purcell. *The Architectural Legacy of the Lower Chattahoochee Valley in Alabama and Georgia* (Barbour, Chambers, Dale, Henry, Houston, Lee, Russell counties). University: University of Alabama Press, 1978.

Kennedy, J. Robie, Jr. "Examples of the Greek Revival Period in Alabama" (Tuscaloosa area). *The Brickbuilder,* vol. 13 (June–July 1904).

———. "Greek Revival of the Far South" (Tuscaloosa area). *Architectural Record,* vol. 17 (May 1905).

North Central Alabama Regional Council of Governments. *Regional Historic Preservation Survey* (Cullman, Lawrence, Morgan counties). Decatur, 1979.

Robinson, Willard B. "Military Architecture at Mobile Bay." *Journal of the Society of Architectural Historians,* vol. 30, no. 2 (May 1971).

Student Writers Club of Selma. *Some Old Churches of the Black Belt.* Birmingham: Banner Press, 1962.

Tennessee Valley Historical Society. *Historic Muscle Shoals: A Guide to Places of Historic Interest in Colbert and Lauderdale Counties, Alabama.* Sheffield: Standard Print, 1962.

———. *Historic Muscle Shoals: Buildings and Sites* (Colbert and Lauderdale counties). Published as vol. 10 of the *Journal of Muscle Shoals History,* 1983.

———. *Journal of Muscle Shoals History, Bicentennial Issue* (Colbert and Lauderdale counties), vol. 4, 1976.

Top of Alabama Regional Council of Governments (TARCOG). *Preliminary Historical-Architectural Survey* (DeKalb, Jackson, Limestone, Madison, Marshall counties). Huntsville, 1974.

West Alabama Planning and Development Council. *Inventory of Historic Sites and Structures* (Bibb, Fayette, Greene, Hale, Lamar, Pickens, Tuscaloosa counties). Tuscaloosa, 1977.

Wilson, Samuel, Jr. *Gulf Coast Architecture.* Pensacola: Historic Pensacola Preservation Board, 1971, 1977.

County-by-County Publications

Asterisk indicates listings also to be found under multi-county and regional publications.

Autauga County
  Bank of Prattville, *Historic Prattville and Autauga County,* 1975.
*Baldwin County
  Olsen, Susan C., ed. *Archeological Investigation at Fort Mims.* (Archeological Completion Report Series, No. 4), Washington: Department of the Interior, 1975.
  Scott, Florence D. and Richard J. *Battles Wharf and Point Clear.* Mobile: Interstate 2, 1971.
  ———. *Daphne.* Mobile: Jordan Publishing Co., Inc., 1965.
  ———. *Montrose.* Mobile: privately published, 1960.
*Barbour County
  Eufaula Heritage Association. *Historic Eufaula: A Treasury of Southern Architecture, 1827–1910.* Eufaula, 1972.
  Matlack, Carol. "Eufaula." *American Preservation.* (October–November 1978).
  Orr, Henry P. "Ornamental Plantings in Eufaula." *Alabama Review*, vol. 16, no. 4 (October 1963).

Bullock County
- South Central Alabama Development Commission. *Historic Assets: Bullock County, Alabama.* Montgomery, 1978.

*Calhoun County
- First National Bank of Jacksonville. *The Jacksonville Story . . . An Enduring Heritage.* Jacksonville, 1977.
- Gen. John H. Forney Chapter United Daughters of the Confederacy. *Historic Jacksonville.* Jacksonville, 1952.

*Chambers County
- Davidson, William H. *Pine Log and Greek Revival.* Alexander City: Outlook Publishing Co., 1964.

*Colbert County
- Kirk, Mary Wallace. *Locust Hill.* University: University of Alabama Press, 1972.

*Cullman County
- Graf, Dot. *If Walls Could Talk.* Birmingham: Oxmoor Press, 1977.

*Dallas County
- Greene, Elisabeth Y. *Old Homes of Richmond, Carlowville, and Minter.* Privately published, 1978.
- Neville, Bert and Nellie. *A Glance at Early Selma: Scenes of Selma, Alabama, 1820–1920.* Selma: Selma Printing Service, 1968.
- ———. *A Glance at Old Cahawba.* Selma: Selma Printing Service, 1961.
- Peoples Bank and Trust Co. *Historic Selma and Dallas County* (pictorial history and historic site tour guide). 1976.
- Selma and Dallas County Sesquicentennial Committee. *Selma and Dallas County: 150 Years.* 1969.

*DeKalb County
- Landmarks of DeKalb County, Inc. *Landmarks: A Pictorial History of DeKalb County.* Collegedale, Tenn.: College Press, 1971.

Elmore County
- Brooms, Bascom McDonald, and James W. Parker. *Fort Toulouse: Phase III.* Montgomery: Alabama Historical Commission, 1980.
- Thomas, Daniel H. "Fort Toulouse—In Tradition and Fact." *Alabama Review,* vol. 13, no. 3 (July 1960), pp. 243–57.
- Waselkov, Gregory A., Brian M. Wood, and Joseph M. Herbert. *Colonization and Conquest: The 1980 Archaeological Excavations at Fort Toulouse and Fort Jackson, Alabama* (Auburn University Archaeological Monograph 4). Montgomery: Auburn University at Montgomery, 1982.

*Greene County
- Black Belt Pilgrimage Association. "Eutaw Walking Tour" (brochure). 1976.
- Greene County Historical Society. *A Goodly Heritage: Memories of Greene County.* Clarksville, Tenn.: Josten's, 1977.
- ———. *A Look at Early Eutaw.* 1969.
- Houseman, Robert. "A Great Revival" (Eutaw architecture). *House Beautiful,* vol. 125, no. 3 (March 1983).
- Lancaster, Clay. *Eutaw: The Builders and Architecture of an Ante-Bellum Southern Town.* Eutaw: Greene County Historical Society, 1979.
- Moseley, Franklin S., and Mrs. Ralph Banks, Sr. "Ante-Bellum Homes of Greene County." *Greene County Democrat* (6 April 1961–12 August 1965).
- Roper, James H. "Eutaw: A Treasury of Greek Revival Architecture Distinguishes this Alabama Community." *American Preservation* (November–December 1979).

*Hale County
  Cobbs, Nicholas Hamner. "Historic Homes of Hale County." Series in *Greensboro Watchman* (6 October 1941–11 June 1942).
  Greensboro Community Council. *Ante-Bellum Greensboro* (brochure). Greensboro, n.d.
  Spencer, William M. "St. Andrew's Church, Prairieville." *Alabama Review*, vol. 14, no. 1 (January 1961).
*Jackson County
  Carmichael, Flossie, and Ronald Lee. *In and Around Bridgeport*. Collegedale, Tenn.: College Press, 1969.
  Hammer, Walt. *A Pictorial Stroll Thru Ol' High Jackson*. Collegedale, Tenn.: College Press, 1967.
Jefferson County
  Art Work of Birmingham, Alabama. Chicago: Gravure Illustration Co., 1907.
  Art Work of Birmingham, Alabama. Chicago: Gravure Illustration Co., 1923.
  Atkins, Leah Rawls. *The Valley and the Hills*. Woodland Hills, Calif.: Windsor Publications, 1981.
  Birmingham Historical Society. *Southside-Highlands Report: Architectural and Historic Resources*. 1981.
  Birmingham Regional Planning Commission. *Historic Site Survey, Jefferson County, Alabama*. 1972.
  Burkhardt, Ann McCorquodale, and Alice Meriwether Bowsher. *Town Within a City: The Five Points South Neighborhood 1880–1930*. Special Issue of the *Journal of the Birmingham Historical Society*, vol. 7, nos. 3 and 4 (November 1982).
  Datnow, Claire-Louise. *Downtown—An Outdoor Classroom*. Birmingham: Birmingham Publishing Co., 1978.
  Erdreich, Ellen Cooper. "Birmingham Craftsman: An Introduction." *Journal of the Birmingham Historical Society*, vol. 8, no. 1 (December 1983).
  McMillan, Malcolm C. *Yesterday's Birmingham*. Miami: E. A. Seemann Publishing, Inc., 1975.
  Satterfield, Carolyn G. *Historical Sites of Jefferson County, Alabama*. Birmingham: Gray Printing Co., Inc., 1976.
  White, Marjorie L. *The Birmingham District: An Industrial History and Guide*. Birmingham: Birmingham Publishing Co., 1981.
  ———. *Downtown Birmingham: An Architectural and Historical Walking Tour Guide*. Birmingham: Birmingham Publishing Co., 1977.
  ———, ed. (for The Birmingham Historical Society). *Downtown Discovery Tour*. Birmingham: Birmingham Publishing Co., 1978.
*Lee County
  Lee County Area Council of Governments. *Cornerstones: Historic Preservation Analysis of Lee County, Alabama*. 1979.
  Logue, H. E., and John D. Simms. *Auburn, a Pictorial History of the Loveliest Village*. Norfolk, Va.: The Donning Co., 1981.
*Limestone County
  Axford, Faye Action, and Chris Edwards. *The Lure and Lore of Limestone County*. Tuscaloosa: Portals Press, 1978.
  Dunnavant, Bob. "Architect's Legacy Survives in Community Buildings" (Hiram H. Higgins). *Athens News Courier* (27 March 1977).
  Jones, Virgil C. (Pat). "Historic Athens Homes." *Huntsville Times* (5 May 1935–15 July 1935).
  "Vivid Restatement of Southern Neo-Classicism" (John Wallace House). *Architectural Record*, vol. 137 (May 1965), p. 58 passim.

*Lowndes County
  Lowndesboro Heritage Society. *Lowndesboro's Picturesque Legacies*. Lowndesboro, 1979.
  South Central Alabama Development Commission. *Historic Assets: Lowndes County, Alabama*. Montgomery, 1975.
*Macon County
  "Chapel for Tuskegee by Rudolph." *Architectural Record*, vol. 146 (November 1969), p. 117 passim.
  Howard, Annette. *Truths and Traditions of Old Tuskegee*. Tuskegee: *Tuskegee News*, ca. 1935.
  Meadors, Mrs. J. H. *Homes, Buildings, and Gardens, Tuskegee, Alabama*. n.d.
  South Central Alabama Development Commission. *Historic Assets: Macon County, Alabama*. Montgomery, 1975.
*Madison County
  Bayer, Linda. "Edgar Lee Love." *Historic Huntsville Quarterly of Local Architecture and Preservation*, vol. 8, no. 2 (Winter 1982), pp. 2–3.
  ———. "George Steele: Huntsville's Antebellum Architect." *Historic Huntsville Quarterly of Local Architecture and Preservation*, vol. 5, no. 3 (Spring 1979), pp. 3–22.
  Haagen, Victor B. *The Pictorial History of Huntsville, 1805–1865*. Meriden, Conn.: Meriden Gravure Co., 1963.
  Historic Huntsville Quarterly of Local Architecture and Preservation, 1977–.
  Huntsville Chapter, American Association of University Women. *Glimpses Into Ante-Bellum Homes* (enlarged and revised edition). Huntsville: Hicklin Printing Co., 1976.
  Huntsville City Planning Commission. "Bicycle Tour of Huntsville's Historical Districts" (brochure). 1977.
  Jones, Harvie P. "The Bungalow and Other 20th Century Residential Styles in Huntsville: An Overview." *Huntsville Historical Review*, vol. 13, nos. 3 and 4 (July–October 1983), pp. 3–20.
  ———. "Constitution Hall Park—Architectural Notes." *Historic Huntsville Quarterly of Local Architecture and Preservation*, vol. 8, no. 3 (Spring 1982), pp. 8–21.
  ———. "Federal Period Residential Architecture in Huntsville and Madison County, 1805–1835." *Historic Huntsville Quarterly of Local Architecture and Preservation*, vol. 7, no. 1, pp. 3–24.
  ———, and Martha Simms. "George Steele." *ART gallery* (special issue). Huntsville: Huntsville Museum of Art, 1978.
  Jones, Virgil Carrington (Pat). "Historic Homes of Madison County." *Huntsville Times*, 28 August 1932–27 August 1933 passim.
  Lagenbach, Randolph (edited by Linda Bayer). "Downtown Huntsville." *Historic Huntsville Quarterly of Local Architecture and Preservation*, vol. 5, no. 2 (Winter 1979), pp. 3–18.
  Martz, John. "Early American Architecture Related to Constitution Hall Park." *Huntsville Historical Review*, vol. 1, no. 2 (April 1971), pp. 18–33.
  Ryan, Patricia. *"Cease Not to Think of Me": The Steele Family Letters* (related to architect George Steele). City of Huntsville, 1979.
  Simms, Martha H. "Greek Revival Period Architecture in Huntsville and Madison County, 1830–1845." *Historic Huntsville Quarterly of Local Architecture and Preservation*, vol. 7, no. 4 (Summer 1981), pp. 2–20.
*Marengo County
  Marengo County Historical Society. *Historic Demopolis* (brochure). n.d.
  Nielson, Jerry J. *Limited Archaeological Investigations at Gaineswood, Demopolis,*

Alabama. University: University of Alabama (Department of Anthropology), 1973.

　　Patton, Walter S., and J. Glenn Little. "Gaineswood: Research for Preservation." *Southern Antiques and Interiors* (Fall 1972).

　　Smith, Winston, and Gwyn Collins Turner. "History in Towns: Demopolis, Alabama." *Antiques*, vol. 117, no. 2 (February 1980), pp. 402–13.

　　"The Story of Gaineswood: Details of the Building of a Famous Alabama Plantation House." *House and Garden*, vol. 76, no. 5 (November 1939), pp. 40–43.

　　Whitfield, Jesse G. *Gaineswood and Other Memories*. Privately published, 1938.

*Mobile County

　　Glennon, John F. and Rosemary. *Where Time Bears Witness to Sound Building*. Mobile: First National Bank, 1935.

　　Gould, Elizabeth B. *From Fort to Port: An Architectural History of Mobile, Alabama, 1711–1918*. University: University of Alabama Press, forthcoming.

　　———. "Port city commerce builds rich legacy." *Preservation Report*, vol. 13, no. 1 (July–Aug. 1985).

　　———. "Transition and Adaption in Mobile Architecture." *Antiques*, vol. 112, no. 3 (September 1977), pp. 466–69 and 473–75.

　　Hamilton, Peter J. *Art Work of Mobile and Vicinity*. Chicago: W. H. Parish Publishing Co., 1894.

　　Harris, Donald A., and Jerry J. Nielson. *Archaeological Salvage Investigations at the Site of the French Fort Conde, Mobile, Alabama*. University: University of Alabama (Department of Anthropology), 1972.

　　Higginbotham, Jay. *Old Mobile: Fort Louis de la Louisiane, 1705–1711*. Mobile: Museum of the City of Mobile, 1977.

　　Ingate, Margaret Rose. "History in Towns: Mobile, Alabama." *Antiques*, vol. 85, no. 3 (March 1964), pp. 294–309.

　　———. "The Marshall-Hixon House." *Antiques*, vol. 112, no. 3 (September 1977), pp. 492–95.

　　———. "Mobile Ironwork." *Antiques*, vol. 92, no. 3 (September 1967), pp. 354–59.

　　Junior League of Mobile, Inc. *Historic Mobile: An Illustrated Guide*. 1974.

　　McLaurin, Melton A., and Michael V. Thomason. *Mobile: American River City*. Mobile: Easter Publishing Co., 1975.

　　———. *Mobile: The Life and Times of A Great Southern City*. Woodland Hills, Calif.: Windsor Publications, 1981.

　　Mobile City Planning Commission. *Nineteenth-Century Mobile Architecture: An Inventory of Existing Buildings*. Mobile, 1974.

　　Mobile Writers' Workshop. *Historic Churches of Mobile*. 1971.

　　Nelson, Lucy. *The History of Oakleigh, An Ante-Bellum Mansion in Mobile*. Mobile: Gill Printing and Stationery Co., 1956.

　　Watson, Bama Wathan. *History of Barton Academy*. Mobile: Haunted Book Shop, 1971.

　　Young, Dwight. "Historic Preservation in Mobile." *Antiques*, vol. 112, no. 3 (September 1977), pp. 460–65.

Montgomery County

　　Art Work of Montgomery and Vicinity. Chicago: H. W. Kennicott & Co., 1894.

　　Flynt, Wayne. *Montgomery: An Illustrated History*. Woodland Hills, Calif.: Windsor Publications, 1980.

　　Gamble, Robert S., and Thomas W. Dolan. *The Alabama State Capitol: Architectural History of the Capitol Interiors*. Montgomery: Alabama Historical Commission, 1984.

Hole, Donna C. "The Alabama State Capitol in Montgomery: An Architectural and Political History." M.A. thesis, Auburn University, 1979.

———. "Daniel Pratt and Barachias Holt: Architects of the Alabama State Capitol?" *Alabama Review*, vol. 37, no. 2 (April 1984), pp. 83–97.

Junior League of Montgomery, Inc. *A Guide to the City of Montgomery*. Montgomery: Walker Printing Co., Inc., 1969.

Keene, Elizabeth Katherine. "Domestic Architecture of Montgomery, Alabama before 1860." M.A. thesis, University of Colorado, 1945.

Montgomery Museum of Fine Arts. *Spaces and Places: Views of Montgomery's Built Environment*. Montgomery: Walker Printing Co., Inc., 1978.

Napier, Cameron Freeman, *The First White House of the Confederacy* (revised edition). Montgomery: Brown Printing Co. for The First White House Association, 1978.

Seale, William. *Restoration of the Alabama State Capitol: An Historical Perspective for Renovation and Restoration of the Interior*. Montgomery: Alabama Historical Commission, 1983.

Society of Pioneers of Montgomery. *A History of Montgomery in Pictures*. Montgomery: publisher unknown, 1963.

Tintagil Club of Montgomery. *Official Guide to the City of Montgomery*. Montgomery: Paragon Press, 1948.

*Morgan County

Sentell, Lee, ed. *Historic Decatur Picture Book*. Decatur: Morgan County Historic Preservation Society, 1976 (reprinted 1985).

Perry County

Auburtin, Mary G. (for City of Marion). *Ante-Bellum Marion* (brochure). Birmingham and Mobile: Graphics, Inc., 1960.

Harris, W. Stuart. *A Short History of Marion, Perry County, Alabama, Its Homes and Its Buildings*. Camden: Alabama-Tombigbee Regional Planning Commission, 1975.

Randolph County

Jeane, Gregory. *Archival and Field Survey of McCosh's Mill, West Point Lake, Alabama*. Auburn: Auburn University, 1979.

Russell County

Chase, David W. *Fort Mitchell: An Archaeological Exploration in Russell County, Alabama*. Moundville: The Alabama Archaeological Society, 1974.

*Shelby County

Everse, Janice and Marty. *Celebrating an Era: 19th Century Montevallo Architecture*. Montevallo: University of Montevallo, 1979.

Johnson, Golda W. *The Lives and Times of Kingswood in Alabama, 1817 to 1890*. Montevallo: University of Montevallo, 1976.

Meroney, Eloise. *Montevallo: The First One Hundred Years*. Montevallo: Times Printing Co., 1977.

Sumter County

Livingston Bicentennial Committee. *Historic Sumter County* (brochure). 1976.

Sumter County Preservation Society. *Sumter Heritage* (brochure). 1977.

Talladega County

Blackford, Randolph F. *Fascinating Talladega County*. Talladega: Brannon Publishing Co., 1957.

Elliott, Wilmary Hitch. *East Street, South: Pen and Ink Drawings of Historic Talladega and North Talladega County Homes*. Talladega: Brannon's, Inc., 1975.

Lee, Mary Welch. "Old Homes in Talladega County." *Alabama Historical Quarterly* 10 (1948).

*Tuscaloosa County
  Brooms, Bascom McDonald. *Collier-Boone House: A Study in Historical Archaeology.* University: University of Alabama (Department of Anthropology), 1976.
  Mellown, Robert O. "The President's Mansion at the University of Alabama." *Alabama Review,* vol. 35, no. 3 (July 1982), pp. 200–29.
  Oldshue, Jerry C. "Historical Archaeology on the University of Alabama Campus." *Alabama Review,* vol. 30, no. 1 (January 1977), pp. 266–75.
  Smyth, Sydnia Keene. "The Ante-bellum Architecture of Tuscaloosa." M.A. thesis, University of Alabama, 1929.
  Tuscaloosa County Preservation Society. *Past Horizons.* Tuscaloosa, 1978.
  Wolfe, Suzanne Rau. *The University of Alabama: A Pictorial History.* University: University of Alabama Press, 1983.
*Walker County
  Pennington, Martha, and Dot Graf. *Walking through Walker County.* Cullman: Modernistic Printers, 1981.
Wilcox County
  Jones, William J., and Joyce Carothers. *Oak Hill, Alabama: Its Houses and People.* Privately published, 1978.

Historic American Buildings Survey Sites in Alabama as of 1985.

Appendixes

APPENDIX A
Status of HABS-Recorded Structures in Alabama, 1985

County	Number of structures represented in HABS collection	Number destroyed	Number moved and/or reconstructed	Number abandoned or ruinous according to latest information
Autauga	7	3	0	0
Baldwin	5	0	0	1
Barbour	8	0	1	0
Bullock	7	1	1	3
Butler	12	6	0	0
Calhoun	18	4	0	2
Chambers	4	3	0	0
Clarke	2	1	0	0
Cleburne	1	1	0	0
Colbert	34	12	0	2
Crenshaw	1	1	0	0
Dallas	46	15	0	0
Elmore	14	6	0	0
Fayette	1	1	0	0
Greene	33	10	2	9
Hale	28	7	1	2
Henry	6	5	0	1
Houston	5	4	0	0
Jefferson	3	2	0	0
Lamar	2	1	0	0
Lauderdale	15	5	0	0
Lawrence	6	3	0	0
Lee	16	10	0	1
Limestone	17	3	0	0
Lowndes	15	3	0	0
Macon	13	0	1	2
Madison	23	5	0	1
Marengo	13	4	0	0
Marion	1	0	1	0
Mobile	177	138	7	4
Monroe	9	4	1	0
Montgomery	23	10	0	2
Morgan	4	0	0	2
Perry	15	2	0	1
Pickens	14	10	0	1

(*continued*)

APPENDIX A (*Continued*)

County	Number of structures represented in HABS collection	Number destroyed	Number moved and/or reconstructed	Number abandoned or ruinous according to latest information
Pike	6	1	0	1
Russell	9	4	0	0
Shelby	5	1	0	1
Sumter	12	2	0	1
Talladega	20	10	0	0
Tallapoosa	4	2	0	0
Tuscaloosa	23	8	1	0
Washington	2	0	0	0
Wilcox	48	12	0	8
Total	727	321	16	45

APPENDIX B
Mobile Ironwork Survey

Below is a list of structures included in a 1934–36 survey of Mobile Ironwork (*see* "Ironwork" under Mobile section of the main catalog text). This survey was part of the overall HABS recording effort in Mobile during the Depression years. For the most part, the records consist of photographs of ironwork details only. Rather arbitrarily, the material was divided into "Early Period," "Middle Period," and "Late Period" ironwork—classified respectively as the AL-7, AL-8, and AL-9 series. Most of the structures treated have also been recorded as individual buildings or objects in the general survey. The following listing presents the ironwork survey as it was originally organized within the three broad categories. The original survey number assigned each structure is followed by the later survey number if the records were subsequently reclassified.

"Early Period" Ironwork (AL-7 Series)

Butt-Kling House,[1] 254 N. Jackson St. (AL-7WG; now AL-820)
Church Street Cemetery: Crothers Lot (AL-7U; now AL-845), Thaddeus Sanford Lot (AL-7T; now AL-845), Unidentified Lot (AL-7F; now AL-845), Unidentified Lot (AL-7V; now AL-845)
Elkus, Isaac, House, 50 S. Franklin St. (AL-7Y)
Emanuel, Jonathan, House, 251 Government St. (AL-7H; now AL-3)
Franklin Street Methodist Episcopal Church, SW corner Franklin & St. Michael sts. (AL-7S; now AL-26)
Gate, 453 Government St. (AL-7XXV)
Gates, 153–155 St. Louis St. (AL-7C)
Griffin-Goldsmith House, 408 Conti St. (AL-7W; now AL-76)
House, 108 N. Conception St. (AL-7B)
House, 250 Government St. (AL-7E)
House, 8 N. Hamilton St. (AL-7XB; now AL-50)
House, 350 Monroe St. (AL-7X)
LeVert, Dr. Henry, Office, 153 Government St. (AL-7G; now AL-29)
McGill Institute, 252 Government St. (AL-7D; now AL-77)
Magnolia Cemetery: Henry Goldthwaite Lot (AL-7P; now AL-844), Johnson-Garbo Lot (AL-7N; now AL-844), William G. Jones Lot (AL-7L; now AL-844), Jacob Mitchell Lot (AL-7J; now AL-844), B. F. and M. Y. Scattergood Lot (AL-7M; now AL-844), G. W. Tarleton Lot (AL-7K; now AL-844)
Parmly House, 303 N. Conception St. (AL-7A; now AL-815)
Phoenix Fire Company No. 6, 154 S. Franklin St.; now moved to 203 S. Claiborne St. (AL-7Z)
U.S. Marine Hospital, 800 St. Anthony St. (AL-7US; now AL-781)

---

[1]Additional photograph under "Later Period" Ironwork.

"Middle Period" Ironwork (AL-8 Series)

Church Street Graveyard: John Herpin Lot (AL-8S; now AL-845), Jeunedot Lot
(AL-8R; now AL-845)
Gate, 215 S. Conception St. (AL-8X)
Gate, 456 S. Conception St. (AL-8CX)
Gate, 605 Government St. (AL-8U)
Gate, 251 St. Joseph St. (AL-8TC)
Gate, 253 St. Joseph St. (AL-8TM)
Gulf City Hotel, 53–65 Water St. (AL-8B; now AL-11)
House, 301 Church St. (AL-8D)
House, 203 N. Conception St. (AL-8C)
House, 456 S. Conception St. (AL-8CX)
House, 161 St. Anthony St. (AL-8E)
Magnolia Cemetery: James Battle Lot (AL-8J; now AL-844), John A. M. Battle Lot
(AL-8J; now AL-844), H. C. Brewer Lot (AL-8G; now AL-844), Catonnet Lot
(AL-8E; now AL-844), Henry P. Ensign Lot (AL-8P; now AL-844), Florian and
Muller Lot (AL-8N; now AL-844), Charles Gascoigne Lot (AL-8F; now AL-844),
Henry Hitchcock Lot (AL-8D; now AL-844), Jewish Lot (AL-8M; now AL-844),
Martin Robbins Lot (AL-8L; now AL-844), Charles Walsh-Amos R. Manning
Lots (AL-8K; now AL-844),

"Later Period" Ironwork (AL-9 Series)

Batre-Bernheimer-Saad House, 155 Monroe St. (AL-9M; now AL-801)
Battle-Ross House, 602 Government St. (AL-9V)
Bester, Daniel Perrin, Jr., House, 208 Government St. (AL-9X)
Brown, Milton S., House, 108 S. Conception St. (AL-9BA; now AL-78)
Bunker, Robert S., House, 157 Monroe St. (AL-9L; now AL-802)
Bush-Mohr House, 254 St. Anthony St. (AL-9J)
Butt-Kling House,[2] 254 Jackson St. (AL-9R; now AL-820)
Fence (see "Gates and Fences"), 800 block St. Anthony St. between N. Jefferson &
N. Bayou sts. (AL-9A)
Finnigan, Capt. Owen, House, 752 Government St. (AL-9Z)
Foote, Charles K., House, 255 N. Conception St. (AL-9H)
Gate, 201 Government St. (AL-9BA7)
George, Elizabeth, House, 159 Monroe St. (AL-9K)
Goldsby, Judge Joel, House, 452 Government St. (AL-9W)
House, 256 N. Jackson St. (AL-9Q)
House, 301 N. Joachim St. (AL-9F)
House, 154 St. Louis St. (AL-9)
House, 304 State St. (AL-9P)
House, 350 State St. (AL-9N)
House, 352 State St. (AL-9E)
Ketchum, William H., House, 400 Government St. (AL-9U)
Lyons, Patrick J., House, 300 State St. (AL-9S)
Magnolia Cemetery: Fred P. Brown Lot (AL-9CA7; now AL-844), John Burden

---

[2] Additional photograph under "Early Period" Ironwork.

Lot (AL-9BA9; now AL-844), James Coyles Lot (AL-9CA9; now AL-844), John Foster Lot (AL-9DA; now AL-844), F. C. Frazier Lot (AL-9Y1; now AL-844), Gazzam Family Lot (AL-9CA3; now AL-844), Emanuel Green Lot (AL-9CA6; now AL-844), William F. James Lot (AL-9CA9; now AL-844), R. A. Nicoll Lot (AL-9CA2; now AL-844), Edwin F. Shields Lot (AL-9BA2; now AL-844), B. S. Skaats Lot (AL-9CA1; now AL-844), Hope H. Slatter Lot (AL-9CA4; now AL-860), Stephen Twelves and Jarvis Turner Lot (AL-9CA5; now AL-844), G. Yuille Lot (AL-9Y; now AL-844), Charlotte V. Yver Lot (AL-9DA4; now AL-844), Unidentified Lot (AL-9Y2; now AL-844), Unidentified Lot (AL-9Y3; now AL-844)

Redwood, Richard H., House, 260 St. Louis St. (AL-9T)

Revault-Maupin-Shawhan House, 254 N. Conception St. (AL-9G)

Richards, Charles, House, 256 N. Joachim St. (AL-9B; now AL-810)

Smith, Sidney, House, 203 Government St. (AL-9BA8)

APPENDIX C
Mobile Structures Arranged by Street Address

Structures for which there is no street number are listed at end of numerical listing

A

1001 Augusta St. *See* Hellen-Croom House
1005 Augusta St. *See* Goelet-Randlette-Beck House
320 Avalon St. *See* Batre-Hamilton House

B

1102 S. Broad St. *See* Miller-O'Donnell House
Beauregard St. at Telegraph Rd., NE corner. *See* Gulf, Mobile, and Ohio Passenger Terminal

C

13 N. Cedar St. *See* Middleton-Boule House
300 Chatham St. *See* Conn-Meriwether House
6 Church St. *See* Commercial Buildings, Miscellaneous
75 Church St. *See* Seaman's Bethel
113 Church St. *See* Isaac Marx House
157 Church St. *See* Bunker-DuMont House
301 Church St. *See* House ("Three Sisters House")
401, 403, 405, 407 Church St. *See* Church Street Block Study
1113 Church St. *See* Ludlow House
Church St. at Scott St. *See* Church Street Graveyard
4 S. Claiborne St. *See* Cathedral of the Immaculate Conception
110 S. Claiborne St. *See* Dargan-Waring House (Waring "Texas")
203 S. Claiborne St. *See* Phoenix Fire Co. No. 6 (originally at 154 S. Franklin St.)
252 S. Claiborne St. *See* Larrouil-Arresijac House
7 N. Commerce St. *See* Commercial Building
8 N. Commerce St. *See* Commercial Building
9 N. Commerce St. *See* Commercial Building
15 N. Commerce St. *See* Commercial Building
16 N. Commerce St. *See* Commercial Building
50, 52 N. Commerce St. *See* McDowell, Withers Company
104 N. Commerce St. *See* Commercial Building
114 N. Commerce St. *See* Commercial Building
117 N. Commerce St. *See* Commercial Building
150 N. Commerce St. *See* Commercial Building
N. Commerce at Goverment, E side (lamppost). *Under* Street Furnishings, *see* Lampposts.

12, 55, 58 S. Commerce St. *See* Commercial Buildings: Commerce St.
50 S. Commerce St. *See* Shippers Exchange Saloon
157, 159 N. Conception St. *See* Robinson Twin Houses
203 N. Conception St. *See* House
251 N. Conception St. *See* Decatur C. Anderson House
254 N. Conception St. *See* Revault-Maupin-Shawhan House
255 N. Conception St. *See* Charles K. Foote House
265 N. Conception St. *See* Calvert-Webster House
303, 305, 307 N. Conception St. *See* Parmly Houses
56, 58 S. Conception St. *See* Chamberlain and Rapier Double House
60, 62 S. Conception St. *See* Gibbons-Torrey House
108 S. Conception St. *See* Milton S. Brown House
111 S. Conception St. *See* Lloyd Bowers Double House
112 S. Conception St. *See* Tardy-Thorp House
154 S. Conception St. *See* Charles L. Huger House
207 S. Conception St. *See* House
215 S. Conception St. *See* Gates and Fences
456 S. Conception St. *See* Gates and Fences
258 Congress St. *See* Quigley Twin House
303 Conti St. *See* Rider House
307 Conti St. *See* Bishop Michael Portier House
308–310 Conti St. *See* Double House
407 Conti St. *See* Martin Horst House
408 Conti St. *See* Griffin-Goldsmith House

D

2 Dauphin St. *See* Commercial Buildings: Dauphin St.
12 Dauphin St. *See* Commercial Buildings: Dauphin St.
51 Dauphin St. *See* Daniels, Elgin and Company
56 Dauphin St. *See* Commercial Buildings: Dauphin St.
715 Dauphin St. *See* Commercial Buildings: Dauphin St.
911 Dauphin St. *See* Protestant Orphans Asylum
1569 Dauphin St. *See* Macy-Adams House
1570, 1572 Dauphin St. *See* Gates-Daves House
2828 Dauphin Way. *See* The Anchorage
Dauphin Way at Mobile St., NW of intersection. *See* Briarwood

E

457 Eslava St. *See* Worker's House

F

50 S. Franklin St. *See* Isaac Elkus House
154 S. Franklin St. *See* Phoenix Fire Co. No. 6

Franklin St. at St. Michael St., sw corner. *See* Franklin Street Methodist Episcopal Church

G

200 George St. *See* Kilduff-Ray House
9 Government St. *See* Commercial Buildings: Government St.
51–73 Government St. *See* Commercial Buildings: Government St.
66 Government St. *See* Commercial Buildings: Government St.
67, 69 Government St. *See* Commercial Building
71, 73 Government St. *See* Commercial Buildings: Miscellaneous
110 Government St. *See* Commercial Buildings: Government St.
112, 114 Government St. *See* Commercial Buildings: Government St.
150–160 Government St. *See* LaClede Hotel
151–153 Government St. *See* LeVert House and Office
201 Government St. *See* Gates and Fences
203 Government St. *See* Sidney Smith House
208 Government St. *See* Daniel Perrin Bester, Jr., House
250 Government St. *See* House
251 Government St. *See* Jonathan Emanuel House
252 Government St. *See* McGill Institute
300 Government St. *See* Government Street Presbyterian Church
351 Government St. *See* Dargan-Waring House
400 Government St. *See* William H. Ketchum House
452 Government St. *See* Judge Joel Goldsby House
453 Government St. *See* Gates and Fences
504 Government St. *See* Barton Academy
602 Government St. *See* Battle-Ross House
605 Government St. (gate). *See* Gates and Fences
607 Government St. *See* Joshua Kennedy House
751 Government St. *See* Gilmore-Gaines-Quigley House
752 Government St. *See* Capt. Owen Finnigan House
802 Government St. *See* Horta-Semmes House
901 Government St. *See* Government Street Methodist Church
1151 Government St. *See* McGowin-Creary House
1209 Government St. *See* Burgess-Maschmeyer House
1216 Government St. *See* Tacon-Gordon House
1255 Government St. *See* Audley H. Gazzam House
Government St. at S. Lawrence St., SE corner (carriage block). *Under* Street Furnishings, *see* Carriage Block.

H

8 N. Hamilton St. *See* House
101 N. Hamilton St. *See* George W. Hamilton House
57 S. Hamilton St. *See* Ayers House

J

8–10 N. Jackson St. See Double House
12 N. Jackson St. *See* Bates-Henderson House
53 N. Jackson St. *See* Phillippi-Mastin House
207, 209 N. Jackson St. *See* Thomas S. James Double House
254 N. Jackson St. *See* Butt-Kling House
256 N. Jackson St. *See* House
51 S. Jackson St. *See* Guesnard-Craft House
52, 54 S. Jackson St. *See* Schieffelin-Sledge House
256 N. Joachim St. *See* Charles G. Richards House
301 N. Joachim St. *See* House
204 S. Joachim St. *See* House
208 S. Joachim St. *See* House

L

Lanier Ave., S end (Spring Hill). *See* Ashland
7 N. Lawrence St. *See* Washington Fire Engine Co. No. 8
S. Lawrence St. at Government, SE corner (carriage block). *Under* Street Furnishings, *see* Carriage Block
62 Lipscomb St. *See* Magnolia Cotton Warehouse

M

55 S. McGregor Ave. (Spring Hill). *See* Azalea Grove
76 S. McGregor Ave. (Spring Hill). *See* Carolina Hall
155 Monroe St. *See* Batre-Bernheimer-Saad House
157 Monroe St. *See* Robert S. Bunker House
159 Monroe St. *See* Elizabeth George House
253 Monroe St. *See* Gee-Barrow House
306, 308, 310 Monroe St. *See* Bloodgood's Row
350 Monroe St. *See* House
111 Myrtlewood Ln. (Spring Hill). *See* Beal-Gaillard House

O

350 Oakleigh Pl. *See* Oakleigh
1802 Old Government St. (gate). *Under* Gates and Fences, *see* 456 S. Conception St.
1614 Old Shell Rd. *See* Calef-Staples House
3703 Old Shell Rd. (fence). *Under* Gates and Fences, *see* 251, 253 St. Joseph St.
4307 Old Shell Rd. *See* Spring Hill College

P

1012 Palmette St. *See* Wilson Gibbs House
1115 Palmette St. *See* Cox-Deasy House

R

160 Rapier Ave. *See* William Lott House
3333 Riviere du Chien Rd. (fence). *Under* Gates and Fences, *see* 456 S. Conception St.
3609 Riviere du Chien Rd. (gate). *Under* Gates and Fences, *see* 201 Government St.
364 N. Royal St. *See* Commercial Building
409 N. Royal St. *See* Mobile and Ohio Railroad Office Building
N. Royal St. at St. Francis St., SW corner. *See* U.S. Custom House and Old Post Office
17 S. Royal St. *See* Odd Fellows Hall
23 S. Royal St. *See* Commercial Buildings: Miscellaneous
51 S. Royal St. *See* Pollock Building
109 S. Royal St. *See* City Hall and Southern Market
168 S. Royal St. *See* Ellis-Lyons House

S

109 St. Anthony St. *See* House
156 St. Anthony St. *See* Cluis-Rubira House; *under* Street Furnishings, *see also* Lampposts
161 St. Anthony St. *See* Smith-Clarke House
254 St. Anthony St. *See* Bush-Mohr House
400 St. Anthony St. *See* John S. Gliddon House
800 St. Anthony St. *See* U.S. Marine Hospital; *also* Gates and Fences
850 St. Anthony St. *See* City Hospital
107 St. Emanuel St. *See* Weldon-LeLoupe House
110 St. Emanuel St. *See* Clitherall-Horst House
114 St. Emanuel St. *See* Christ Episcopal Church
165 St. Emanuel St. *See* Hall-Ford House
56 St. Francis St. *See* Townsend-Foreman Building
256 St. Francis St. *See* House
257 St. Francis St. *See* Silver-Ketchum House
451, 453 St. Francis St. *See* Sanford-Staylor House
456 St. Francis St. *See* Miguel Eslava, Jr., House
652 St. Francis St. *See* House
251, 253 St. Joseph St. *See* Gates and Fences
St. Joseph St. at St. Michael, NW corner. *See* U. S. Post Office Building
153, 155 St. Louis St. *See* Gates and Fences
154 St. Louis St. *See* House
256 St. Louis St. *See* House

260 St. Louis St. *See* Richard H. Redwood House
7 St. Michael St. *See* Commercial Building
10 St. Michael St. *See* Commercial Buildings, St. Michael St.
56, 58 St. Michael St. *See* Commercial Buildings, St. Michael St.
57 St. Michael St. *See* Commercial Buildings, St. Michael St.
60 St. Michael St. *See* Planters and Merchants Insurance Co.
67 St. Michael St. *See* Commercial Buildings, St. Michael St.
74, 76 St. Michael St. *See* Commercial Buildings, St. Michael St.
78 St. Michael St. *See* Commercial Buildings, St. Michael St.
351 St. Michael St. *See* Vanroy-Barnewall House
St. Michael at Hamilton, NE corner. *See* Hammond-Willoughby House
1263 Selma St. *See* Schley-Rutherford House
1357 Spring Hill Ave. (lamppost). *See* Street Furnishings
1621 Spring Hill Ave. *See* Sanford-Thompson House
1664 Spring Hill Ave. *See* Vincent-Walsh House
1906 Spring Hill Ave. (old Summerville). *See* Bragg-Mitchell House
2300 Spring Hill Ave. (old Summerville). *See* Convent and Academy of the Visitation
2564 Spring Hill Ave. (old Summerville). *See* Georgia Cottage
300 State St. *See* Patrick J. Lyons House
304 State St. *See* House
350 State St. *See* House
352 State St. *See* House
State St. at Lawrence, N side (lamppost). *Under* Street Furnishings, *see* Lampposts

T

104 Theatre St. *See* Jonathan Kirkbride House
152 Tuthill Lane. *See* Marshall-Eslava-Hixon House

U

307 University Blvd. *See* Isaac Marx House; Seaman's Bethel; Toulmin House

V

Virginia St., N side between Ann and Gayle. *See* Magnolia Cemetery Ironwork; *also* P. B. Pomeroy Family Tomb, Hope H. Slatter Family Tomb

W

201 S. Warren St. *See* Robert S. Bunker House
3 N. Water St. *See* Commercial Building
4, 19–21, 55, 106, 108, 110, 112, 116 N. Water St. *See* Commercial Buildings: Water St.

250 N. Water St. *See* Home Industry Foundry
N. Water St. at Conti, SE corner. *See* Gulf City Hotel
4, 12, 16, 54, 64–66 S. Water St. *See* Commercial Buildings: Water St.
552 Wilson Ave. *See* Toulmin House

Y

Yeend St., E of Baker. *See* Frascati

APPENDIX D
Alabama Properties Recorded by the Historic American Engineering Record (HAER) as of 1985

Autauga County: Prattville

Continental Gin Company Factory (AL-5). W bank of Autauga Creek opposite spillway. Outgrowth of factory founded by Daniel Pratt to manufacture cotton gins. Photos (1974). (Under HABS listings, *see also* Prattville, Daniel Pratt Factory Complex.)

Jackson County: Bridgeport

Bridgeport Swing Span Bridge (AL-7). Spans Tennessee River 1.5 mi. NE of Bridgeport. Single-track steel railroad bridge with swing span to accommodate river traffic; built 1890–92 by Nashville, Chattanooga, and St. Louis Railway. Field notes (1980); photos (1980).

Jefferson County: Bessemer Vicinity

Woodward Iron Works (AL-4). W of Co. Rd. 57, E of Opossum Creek. Largest independent manufacturer of pig iron in the U.S.; built 1883 and later. Demolished 1974–75. Photos (1974).

Jefferson County: Birmingham

Sloss Blast Furnaces (AL-3). SE side of First Ave., W of Thirty-second St. Furnace no. 1 is oldest surviving blast furnace in Birmingham area, and perhaps in U.S. Dates 1902–64. Measured drawings (1976); data pages (1976); photos (1974). NR, NHL.

Montgomery County: Montgomery

Union Station (AL-2). NW side of Water St. opposite Lee St. Romanesque style, built by Louisville and Nashville Railroad in 1897–98. 1 photocopy of architect's original drawing (1896); 1 photocopy of ext. photograph (date unknown); photos (1974). NR, NHL.
Union Station Train Shed (AL-1). NW side of Water St. opposite Lee St., along Alabama River. One of twelve known long-span, trussed-roof train sheds surviving in the U.S.; built 1897–98. Field notes (1974); 2 photocopies of ext. photographs (dates unknown); photos (1974). NR.

Talladega County: Sylacauga Vicinity

Gantts Quarry (AL-6). Quarry Rd., 2.5 mi. SW of Sylacauga. One of principal marble quarries in Alabama and Southeast. Photos (1974).

Index

Structures included in the Historic American Buildings Survey are normally listed in the index *only* under their primary names. Other names by which the structure may be known are cross-referenced under the appropriate locale.

Abbeville, 244
Abbeville District, S.C., 207
Abernathy, Dr. Robert T., 214
Abingdon Place, Huntsville, 97
Academic revival, 159–68
Academies. *See* Schools
Adam, Robert and James, 44
Adamesque influence, 27, 44, 48, 53
Adams, Richard H., 34
Aderholdt's Mill, Jacksonville vicinity, 205
Adustin Hall, Gainesville, 71
Akron, Ala., 237
"Akron plan," 128, 298
Alabama, C.S.S., 300
Alabama Centennial Commission, 218
Alabama Central Female College, Tuscaloosa, 351
Alabama Conference Female College (Tuskegee Female College), Tuskegee, 84, 265
Alabama Historical Commission, 177, 185, 195, 212, 223
Alabama Medical College, 282
Alabama Polytechnic Institute (Auburn University), 178
Alabama Power Company, Birmingham, 158
Alabama River, 5, 6, 186, 193, 223, 367
Alabama State Capitols: Cahaba, 218, 262; Montgomery (first), 67, 72; Montgomery (second), 6, 7, 141, *144,* 323–24; Tuscaloosa, 46, 52, 135, 351; move to Montgomery, 10
Alabama Theater, Birmingham, 160
Alamo, Battle of the, 323
Albemarle, Courtland vicinity, 33
Albert Hotel, Selma. *See* Hotel Albert
Alexander, Dr. Abram F., 230
Alexander, Judge Lewis, 267
Alexander-Hurt-Whatley house, Tuskegee vicinity, 267

Alexander-Webb house, Eutaw, 230
Alexandria, 202
Aliceville, 334–35
Allen, George R., 341
Allen, William W., 287
Allenton, 358–59
"Alley, Mr.," 227
Allred, Jim, 229
Allsboro, 209
Alpine (house), Alpine community, 27, 344–45
Altwood, Faunsdale vicinity, 34
American Architect and Building News, 122, 127, 148
American Builder's Companion, The (Benjamin), 45, 49, 248, 330
American Institute of Architects (AIA), xix, 178, 185
"American Renaissance," the, 138
Andalusia, 159, 234
Anderson, Decatur C., house, Mobile, 280
Anderson, Nelson, 213
Anderson, Pelham J., 110
Andrews, Mark, 207
Andrews-Allen house, Lafayette, 207
Andrews Chapel, McIntosh, 358
Anniston, 10, 114, 116, 122, 123, 128–29, 131, 132, 133, 134, 139, 159
Anonymous architecture. *See* Folk architecture
Anthony, David Rinehart, 230, 231, 232; house, Eutaw, 230–31
Apache Indians, 320
Appalachians, 16–17
Appomattox County, Va., 322
Apprenticeship tradition, 11, 33
Architect, The (Ranlett), 237
Architects, builders, contractors, engineers, 11–13, 178–80; George R. Allen, 341; "Mr. Alley," 227; Nelson Anderson, 213; Pelham J.

(Architects, continued)
Anderson, 110; David Rinehart Anthony, 230, 231, 232; Erastus Bardwell, 278; Hiram W. Bardwell, 343, 344; James Barnes, 285; Michael Barry, 52, 358; Almarion Devalco Bell, 344; Asher Benjamin, 12, 13, 45, 49, 69, 71, 194, 195, 196, 223, 228, 233, 247, 274, 278, 330, 340, 343, 352, 366; Rudolph Benz, 11, 139, 309; Simone Bernard, 195; Claude Beroujon, 50, 285, 310, 314; Archibald Bigger, 364; J. Hardy Bossong, 151; A. M. Bradley, 324; Alexander J. ("Sandy") Bragg, 11, 78, 282, 363, 364, 366; James M. Brundidge, 258; Frederick Bunnell, 317, 354; Cary Butt, 285; Stephen D. Button, 11, 67, 100, 102, 323, 327; ——— Campbell, 322; Weatherly Carter, 160; Fred W. Clarke, 179; C. K. Colley, 270; John H. Collins, 287, 317; Henry F. Cook, 359; George Woodward Cox, 291, 300; Ralph Adams Cram, 160, 161, 162; Thomas J. Crutchfield, 204, 205; Charles and James Dakin, 11, 57, 58, 281, 285, 288, 298, 301; Helen Davis, 346; Thomas Dial, 211; James Didlake, 332; ——— Dougherty, 294; Walter T. Downing, 11, 134; John R. Drish, 78, 79, 239, 353, 358; Henry Dudley, 80, 328; Robert Ellis, 294, 304; William Ellis, 256; Aymar Embury II, 166, 167; George M. Figh, 231; John P. Figh, 323, 324, 325; John Fitch, 201; Baldwin M. Fluker, 245, 347; Telford Forsyth, 201; James Freret, 11, 314; James Gallier, 11, 57, 58, 281, 294, 298; C. Frank Galliher, 136; William George, 287; Capt. John F. Gibbs, 85; J. H. Giles, 102; Joe Glasgow, 244; Willis H. Green, 219; Charles Sumner Greene and Henry Mather Greene, 145; George W. Gregory, 287; Ino Griffiths and Son, 155; Alex Price Hamilton, 259; Harrod and Andry, 128; Charles Hays, 308; Adolphus Heiman, 84, 241, 249; Thomas Hibben, 170; Hiram H. Higgins, 11, 15, 62, 69, 252, 258, 260, 348; James Hill, 285; Ira E. Hobbs, 258; Nicholas H. Holmes, Jr., 35, 185, 287, 316, 323, 324, 341; Barachias Holt, 323; Richard Morris Hunt, 128; C. L. Hutchisson, Sr., 11, 298, 305, 317; J. H. Hutchisson, 285, 304; Thomas S. James, 298, 303, 304; Gene Jones, 341; Harvie Jones, xvi, 271, 273; "Kiah" and "Lijah" (slaves), 367; Horace King, 11; Jonathan Kirkbride, 294, 304; Minard Lafever, 12, 58, 60–61, 67, 68, 73, 209, 224, 261, 314, 323, 324; Daniel Leadbetter, 317; Tilman Leak, 227; Peter Lee, 244; Thomas Helm Lee, 223, 274; Charles T. Lernier, 99, 303; "Lev" and "Griff" (slave builders), 206; Frank Lockwood, 11, 141, 165, 324, 358; Sprott Long, 236; Edgar Love, 11, 179; Earl Guthrie Lutz, Jr., 179; George Lynch, 367; Charles Follen McKim, 141, 324; McKim, Mead, and White, 133, 141; Edward C. Marty, 179; P. Thornton Marye, 151, 152, 299; Lewis Mason, 341; William T. Mathews, 360, 365, 366, 367; Bernard Maybeck, 145; Miller and Martin, 146; Elbert Green Morris, 205; Mullins and Hall, 241; Col. James T. Murfee, 85; William Nichols, 11, 46, 50–52, 54, 135, 251, 351, 352, 353, 357, 358; William Nichols, Jr., 352; William Parham, 260; John Parks, 366; Benjamin F. Parsons, 60, 240, 274, 332; James Pearce, 335, 391; Simeon Perry, 255; Ezra Plumb, 369; E. T. Potter, 115; William H. Pratt, 304; R. D. Price, 298; B. F. Randolph, 327, 328; James D. Randolph, 323; George E. Redwood, 284; Richard H. Redwood, 287, 294, 310, 311; H. H. Richardson, 113, 127–28; James Robertson, 285; George B. Rogers, 11, 142, 152, 179, 283, 284, 298, 312; Fenton L. Rousseau, 119; Paul Rudolph, 169; B. F. Scattergood, 287, 307; Gen. C. M. Shelley, 341; Shelton and Williams, 255; Henry Shepherd, 350; Sherlock, Smith, and Adams, 364; Edouard Sidel, 119; Samuel Sloan, 11, 12, 84, 87, 93–94, 97, 98, 99, 100, 107, 202, 203, 223, 275; Sloan and Stewart, 267, 354; Benjamin Bosworth Smith, 128, 160; Wash Smith, 78, 350, 351; William Smoot, 212, 217; George Steele, 11, 14, 57, 59, 63–64, 67, 84, 177, 269–73; Edward Stegar, 213; John Stewart, 11, 84, 93, 98; Charles Stuart, 199; J. T. Terrell, 274; J. G. Totten, 279; Ithiel Town, 58; Richard Upjohn, 11, 80, 97–98, 109, 218, 234, 244, 263; Richard Upjohn and Son, 333; Richard M. Upjohn, 11, 97; E. B. Van Keuren, 260; Daniel Wade, 252; W. T. Walker, 324; Thomas U. Walter, 12, 70; Thomas U. Walter III, 134; H. Langford Warren, 160; William T. Warren, 11, 151, 179; Warren, Knight, and Davis, 158, 162, 179, 317, 324; Watkins and Hardaway, 357; Watson, Watson, and Rutland, 174; Weary and Kramer, 128; John J. Webster, 353; William Leslie Welton, 148; Oscar Wenderoth, 317; William C. Weston, 141, 155; Lorenzo B. Wheeler, 11; Harry B. Wheelock, 11; D. O. Whilldin, 162; Lawrence Whitten, 352; Robert Williamson, 317; Frank Wills, 80, 328; Frederick C. Withers, 115; Henry Wolters, 11; William Halsey Wood, 129; Frank

Lloyd Wright, 21, 145, 169, 171; Ammi B. Young, 102, 106, 317
Architectural Record, The, 5, 145, 147, 152, 157, 172
Architecture of Country Houses, The (Downing), 90, 93, 107, 306
Arlington (The Grove), Birmingham, 61, 247
Arrington, Dr. Hal, 342
Arrington-Chapman house, Livingston, 342–43
Arsenals, 320–21
Arts and Crafts movement, 145–47, 165
Ashe Cottage, Demopolis, 89–90
Ashland, Mobile, 280
Ashville, 26
Athens, Ala., 11, 15, 61, 62, 69, 80, 81, 169, 177, 258–60, 348
Athens, Greece, 57, 59
Athens Female Institute (now Founders Hall), Athens, 69, 258
Atkinson, Octavia, *181,* 199
Atkinson, Saul, 198
Atkinson, Thomas, house, Tensaw vicinity, 37, 195
Atlanta, 11, 122, 134, 151, 152; Cotton States Exposition, 138
Atlantic seaboard, influence on folk architecture, 4, 23, 33–34, 41. *See also* Carolinas, Maryland, Virginia
Auburn, 62, 65, 100, 104, 179, 180, 183, 254–55
Auburn University, 100; and HABS, 178
Autauga County, 6, 100; HABS listings, 193–94. *See also* Autaugaville, Prattville
Autauga County courthouse, Prattville, 100
Autaugaville, 6
Aycock, John Henry, 212
Aycock house, Tuscumbia, 212
Ayers, Andrew, house, Mobile, 280
Azalea Grove, Mobile, 280

Badger, D. D., Co., 102
Bagby, Gov. Arthur P., 353; house, Camden, 359

Bagby-Liddell house, Camden, 359
Baldwin County, HABS listings, 195. *See also* Tensaw
Baldwin houses, Montgomery, 116, *118*
Ball, Parks E., house, Aliceville vicinity, 335
Bank buildings, 53, 57, 64, 69, 102, *104,* 169, *173,* 196, 224, 269–70, 330
Bankhead, George, house, Crews, 30, 247
Bankhead, James Greer, house, Sulligent, 30, *31,* 247–48
Bankhead, Sen. John Hollis, 247, 248
Bankhead, Tallulah, 31, 247, 248
Bankhead, William Brockman, 247, 248
Bankhead-Crews house. *See* George Bankhead house
Bankhead Hotel, Birmingham, 159
Baptist Church, Camden, 359
Baptist Church, Eufaula, 196
Baptist Church, Loachapoka, 256
Baptist Church (and Masonic Hall), Newbern, 242
Baptist Church, Orion, 64, 70, 337
Baptist Church, Pickensville, 336
Barbour County, HABS listings, 196–97. *See also* Clayton, Eufaula
Bardwell, Erastus, 278
Bardwell, Hiram W., 343, 344
Barker, "Shoestring," 217
Barker-Kirkpatrick house, Cahaba, 217
Barnard, Prof. Frederick A. P., 357
Barnard College, 357
Barner, John W., 211
Barnes, James, 285
Barns. *See* Farm buildings
Barracks, 195, 279, 320–21
Barry, Michael, 52, 358
Barton, Armistead, 209
Barton, Clark T., 216
Barton Academy, Mobile, 57, 281
Barton Hall, Cherokee vicinity, 64, *68,* 209–10
Bass, Hartwell, 340
Bass-Perry house, Seale vicinity, 340

Bates, James F., 281
Bates-Henderson house, Mobile, 281
Bath, England, 11, 50, 52
Bath houses, 197
Batre, Charles and Mary, 281
Batre-Bernheimer-Saad house, Mobile, 281
Battle, Alfred, 352
Battle, James, house, Mobile, 282
Battle, John, 282; house, Point Clear, 195
Battle-Friedman house, Tuscaloosa, 61, 351–52
Battle house, Tuscaloosa, 97
Battle House Hotel, Mobile, 159
Battle-Ross house, Mobile, 281–82, 295
Bauhaus movement, 169
Bavaria, 280
Bay Minette, 128
Bay Shore Railroad, 316
Bazemore community, 229
Beal, Gustavus, 282
Beal-Gaillard house, Mobile, 282
Beaty, Robert, 258
Beaty-Mason house, Athens, 61, 62, 258
Beauford District, S.C., 220
Beauties of Modern Architecture, The (Lafever), 58, 68, 209, 298, 323
Beaux arts influence, 134, 138–45, 160
Beck, Franklin King, 362; house, Camden, 359
Bedford County, Va., 268
Beecher, Leonard T., house, Birmingham, 146, *148*
Beehive Church, Mobile, 294–95
Behrens, William F., & Co., 283
Beirne, George P., 268
Belfast, Ireland, 280
Belgium, 328
Belize, 37
Bell, Abram, 212
Bell, Almarion Devalco, 344
Bell, John, 212
Bell Building, Montgomery, 156
Bell Factory, Madison County, 6, 7

Bell-Prout-Edwards house, Tuscumbia, 212
Belle Mina (Belmina), Limestone County, 45, 260
Belle Mina community, 260
Belle Mont, Tuscumbia vicinity, 53, 56, 212, 215
Belmont, Mrs. O. H. P. (Alva Smith), 88
Benjamin, Asher, 12, *13*, 45, 49, 69, 71, 194, 195, 196, 223, 228, 233, 247, 274, 278, 330, 340, 343, 352, 366
Benson, Nimrod E., 323
Benton, 261
Bentwood Park, Boligee vicinity, 11
Benz, Rudolph, 11, 139, 309
Bernard, Simone, 195
Bernheimer, Leah, 281
Beroujon, Claude, 50, 285, 310, 314
Berry, Mastin, house, High Ridge, 198
Bessemer, 30, 32, 122, 134, 417
Bestor, Daniel Perrin, Jr., 282, 301; house, Mobile, 301
Bethea, Tristram Benjamin, 366
Bethea-Strother house, Canton Bend, 178, 366
Bethsalem Presbyterian Church, Boligee vicinity, 229
Bexar, 182, 279
Bibb, Benajah Smith, 324
Bibb, Rev. Peyton Dandridge, 226
Bibb, Gov. Thomas, house: Belle Mina, 260; Huntsville, 12, *14*, 268
Bibb-Bradley-Beirne house, Huntsville, 268
Bibb County, 6. See also Centreville
Bibb-Goldthwaite-Arrington house, Montgomery, 324
Bicknell's Village Builder, 119
Biddle, Owen, 12, 45
Big Bear Creek Covered Bridge, Allsboro vicinity, 209
Bigger, Archibald, 364
Biggin, Dean Frederick Child, 178
Billups, Mr., 340
Bird, William, log house, Lawrence County, 27

Birdseye maple graining, 207. See also Graining
Birds' Nest, Vilula, 340
Birmingham, 5, 10, 11, 61, 102, 114, 116, 119, 120, 122, 124, 128, 129, 130, 132, 134, 135, 137, 139, 141, 142, 144, 146, 147, 148, 150-51, 152, 154, 155-59, 160-68, 247, 417; and HABS recording, 179, 182, 183-84, 186
Birmingham Country Club, old, 146, *147*
Birmingham News, HABS articles in, 182-83, 185
Birmingham Public Library, 142
Birmingham-Southern College, 88, 162, *164*, 241. See also Southern University, Greensboro
Black Belt, 9, 24, 57, 181, 183
Black builders and craftsmen, 11, 206, 210, 244, 367
Black churches, 111, *113*
Blacksmith shops, 195, 224, 266
Black Warrior River, 5
Blake, Samuel R., house, Selma, 221
Blakely, 293
Bland, Ezra, 220
Bland-Chesnut house, Orrville vicinity, 30, *31*, 220
Bledsoe, Benjamin, 347
Bledsoe, Samuel, 347
Bledsoe-Cook house, Sylacauga vicinity, 347
Bliss, Dr. Richard, family, 346
Bloch, Daniel, house, Camden, 359-60
Bloodgood, John, 282
Bloodgood, M. H., 307
Bloodgood's Row, Mobile, 282
Blue Lake United Methodist Assembly, 234
Bluff Hall, Demopolis, 46, 275
Boat Repair Yard, Mon Louis Island, 319
Boiling Spring, Oxford vicinity, 205-06
Boligee, 11, 67, 229-30
Boligee Hill, Boligee vicinity, 230
Booneville, Miss., 279

Borders, John, 206
Borders-Blackman house, Oxford vicinity, 206
Borton-Chenault house, Decatur, 122, 123, *126*
Bossong, J. Hardy, 151
Boston, Mass., 12, 122, 128, 129, 133, 160
Bowdon, Arthur J., 246
Bowdon, Lewis, 246
Bowdon, Samuel, house, Gordon, 246
Bowers, Lloyd, Double House, Mobile, 282
Boxwood, Talladega, 90
Boykin, Will, house, Memphis, 335-36
"Bracketed Greek Revival," 70-71, 78, 79, 103
"Bracketed style." See Italianate style
Braden, Andrew, 216
Bradford, Henry C., 273
Bradford, James, 226
Bradford house, Birmingham, 122
Bradford-Stowe house, Wetumpka, 226
Bradley, A. M., 324
Bradley, Mrs. James, 268
Bragg, Alexander J. ("Sandy"), 11, 78, 282, 363, 364, 366
Bragg, Gen. Braxton, 282
Bragg, Judge John, 78. See also Bragg-Mitchell house
Bragg-Mitchell house, Mobile, 78, 282-83
Brahan, Gen. John, 250
Branch house, Livingston, 18
Brandon, Thomas, 268
Brandon-Read-Burritt house, Huntsville, 268
Brannon, Peter, 229
Brantley (St. James) Hotel, Selma, 222-23
Braune, Charles H., 232
Braune, Gustave, 232
Bray-Barron house, Eufaula, 62
Brewer, Judge Samuel, house, Tuskegee, 152, *154*
Brewersville Methodist Church, Coatopa vicinity, 342

Brewton, 128
Briarwood, Mobile, *18*, 283
Brick community, 209
Bride's Hill, Courtland vicinity, 33, 34, 35, 178, 252
Bridgeport, 122, 152
Bridges. *See* Transportation and transportation facilities
Bridges, Francis, Jr., 367
Bridges, John Wells, 362
Brierfield, 107, 108
Brisk and Jacobson Co., 291
Britt-Williams-Bowdon house, Gordon, 246
Brooklyn, N.Y., 58, 109
Brown, Milton S., house, Mobile, 283
Brundidge, James M., 258
Brunswick County, Va., 254
Bryan, Col. and Mrs. James R. II, 278
Bryce Hospital, Tuscaloosa, 100, *103*
Buck house, Tuscaloosa, 89
Bucksville, 351
Buell house, Greenville, *91*
Buena Vista, Prattville vicinity, 194
Builders. *See* Architects, builders, contractors, engineers
Builder's Guide, The (Hills), 12, *14*
Bullard, John, 229
Bullard, Gen. Robert Lee, 208
Bullock, William H., 235
Bullock County, 181; HABS listings, 198–99. *See also* Union Springs
Bullock County Courthouse, Union Springs, *119*
Bungalow, 145–49
Bunker, Robert S., house, Mobile, 283
Bunker-DuMond house, Mobile, 283
Bunnell, Frederick, 317, 354
Burchfield, J. P., 354
Burford, Leonard M., house, Camden vicinity, 364
Burgess, David R., house, Mobile. *See* Burgess-Maschmeyer house
Burgess-Maschmeyer house (David R. Burgess house), Mobile, 139–40, *142*, 283–84

Burkhardt, E. Walter, 178–80, 182–85
Burkville, 261
Burleson, Dr. Aaron A., 330
Burnett, William, 200
Burnett-Dunklin-Smith house, Greenville, 200
Burns-Bell house, Selma, 221
Burnt Corn, 322
Bush, Alex, 179
Bush, J. G., and Thomas, 284
Bush-Mohr house, Mobile, 284
Butler County, 181; HABS listings, 200–02. *See also* Greenville
Butt, Cary, 285
Butt, Cary W., Jr., 284
Butt-Kling house, Mobile, 284
"Butterfly" roof, 38
Button, Stephen D., 11, 67, 100, 102, 323, 327
Buzzard Roost Covered Bridge, 210
Byrd, Judge William McKendree, 221
Byrd-Pitts house, Selma, 221
"Byzantine" style. *See* Romanesque Revival

Cabaniss, Septimus D., 272
Cabinet makers. *See* Andrew Braden, Westwood Wallace James
Cahaba, 83, 217–18, 262
Cain, Elisha Milton, 228
Caldwell, John M., house, Birmingham, 139
Caldwell Hotel, Birmingham, 155
Caledonia plantation, Courtland vicinity, 45
Calef, John F., 284
Calef-Staples house, Mobile, 37, *40*, 284
Calhoun County, 30; HABS listings, 202–07. *See also* Anniston, Jacksonville, Oxford, Weaver
Calhoun County Courthouse, Anniston, 139
California bungalow. *See* Bungalow
California gold rush, 325
Calvert-Webster house, Mobile, 284
Cambridge University, 160

Camden, 11, 16, 41, 53, 78, 177, 182, 359–66
Camden District, S.C., 334, 335
Campbell, ———, 322
Canada, 37, 57
Cantelou, Lamar, 227
Cantey, Gen. James, 339
"Cape Cod" cottages, 163
Capell house, Camden vicinity, 364–65
Capitols. *See* Alabama State Capitols, United States Capitol
Caribbean influence, 37–38
Carlisle, Edward Kenworthy, 101, 333
Carlisle Hall (Kenworthy Hall), Marion vicinity, 97–98, *101*, 184, 332–33
Carlowville, 41
Carnegie Library, Montgomery, 139, *140*
Carolina Hall, Mobile, 284
"Carolina" porch, 41, *43*
Carolinas, architectural influence from, 4, 23, 29, 34, 37, 41, 43, 361. *See also* North Carolina, South Carolina
Carpenter's handbooks. *See* Patternbooks
Carr, W. B., house, Tuskegee, 265
Carriage block, 315. *See also* Mounting blocks
Carriage factories, 215, 216
Carriage houses, 241, 273, 275, 348
Carroll, George W., 212
Carroll-Johnson house, Tuscumbia, 212
Carrollton, Ala., 100
Carrollton, Ga., 265
Carter, Weatherly, 160
Carver, Dr. George Washington, 266
Cassey, N. B., 234
Cast iron. *See* Ironwork (ornamental)
"Castellated" style, 15
Cathedral of the Immaculate Conception, Mobile, 284–85
Cato, Lewis Llewellyn, house, Eufaula, 196
Catoma Street Church of Christ, Montgomery. *See* Temple Beth-Or
Caver, Thomas J., 206

Cedar Grove, Faunsdale vicinity, 277
Cedars, The, Athens, 258
Cedarwood, Moundville vicinity, 34, 242, *243*
Cemeteries, 7, 8, 200–01, 276, 286, 306–07; private, 194, 251, 252, 345–46, 350. *See also* Grave houses, Mausoleums
Centenary Institute, Summerfield, 224, *225*
Centennial of 1876, 122, 257; influence on Colonial Revival, 133
Center Star, 248
Central Bank of Alabama, Montgomery, 102, *104*
Central Plank Road, 229
Centreville, 46
Chalmers, James, 336
Chamberlain, Henry, 285
Chamberlain and Rapier Double House, Mobile, 285, *293*
Chambers County, HABS listings, 207–08. *See also* Lafayette
Chancellor, William, house, Harpersville vicinity, 341
Chandler, Daniel, house. *See* McGill Institute
Chantilly, Greensboro, 107, *108*
Charity, Tom, house, Memphis, 336
Charles City County, Va., 278
Charleston, S.C., 45
Charlottesville, Va., 53
Chastang, Zeno, house, Chastang, 279
Chatom, 358
Chattahoochee River, 5, 245
Chattahoochee Valley, 41, 245
Chaudron house, Claiborne, 35
Cherokee, 64, 68
Chesapeake Bay region, 33–34
Cheshire-Webb Building, Demopolis, 132
Chewacla Lime Works, Opelika vicinity, 182, 256
Chicago, 122, 155, 160; World's Fair of 1893, 138, 151
Chickasaw Indians, 210
Childers, George, 224
Childers-Tate house, Summerfield, 224–25

Childress, Thomas B., 239
Chimney builders, 350–51
Chimney pent, 34, 35, 252
Chittey, Howell, house, Shorterville, 245
Choccolocco Valley, 207
Choragic Monument of Lysicrates, 59, 270
Christ Episcopal Church, Mobile, 285, 286
Christ Episcopal Church, Tuscaloosa, 46, 352
Christian, Archibald S., 213, 216
Christian, John T., 213
Christian-Lindsay house, Tuscumbia, 213
Chunnennuggee Ridge, 181, 198–99
Churches. *See* Religious architecture
Church of the Ascension, Montgomery, 161, *162–63*
Church of the Nativity, Huntsville: first, 80; second, 80, *82–83*
Church of the Visitation, Huntsville, 110
Church Street Block Study, Mobile, 285
Church Street Cemetery, Mobile, 286
Church Street Urban Renewal Project, Mobile, 318
Cincinnati, 283
Cisterns, 310
Citronelle, 279
City halls: Mobile, 100, *104*, 286–87; Montgomery, 119
City Hospital, Mobile, 53, 287
Civic center complexes, 157, 169
Civil War, 8, 9, 11, 21, 57, 78, 80, 97, 100, 103, 109, 111, 114, 133, 181, 195, 210, 212, 216, 222, 223, 232, 238, 252, 260, 268, 270, 281, 303, 320, 326, 330, 348, 351, 356, 359
Civil Works Administration, 179, 257
Claiborne, 35, 40, 177, 322
Clapp, Avery T., 256
Clark Hall, University of Alabama, 115–16, *117*
Clarke, Fred W., 179
Clarke, Mrs. William, 268

Clarke County, HABS listings, 208
Clarke-Fackler house, Huntsville, 268
Classical architecture. *See* Neoclassical architecture, Neoclassicism
Classical orders, *380–81*
Clay, J. Withers, 273
Clayton, 15, 91
Cleaveland and Backus, 107
Cleburne County, HABS listing, 209
Cleburne County Courthouse, Edwardsville, 209
Cleveland, Pres. Grover, 221
Cliatt, William, 338
Cliatt plantation, Cottonton vicinity, 338
Clifton Ferry, 367
Climate, effect on Alabama architecture, 16–19
Clinton, 64, 70, 230
Clitherall, Mrs. 299
Cloverdale, 163
Club Florentine, Birmingham, 162, *164*
Clubs, 146, *147*, 162, *164*, 166, *167*
Cluis, Frederick V., house (Cluis-Rubira house), Mobile, 95, 287
Coalter, George, 45, 248
Coalter-McFarland house, Florence, 45, 49, 248–49
Coastal defense system, 195, 279
Coates, Gideon, house, Gadsden vicinity, 78
Coates-Kilpatrick house, Camden, 360
Coatopa, 43, 342
Cochran, Claudius M., 220
Cochran-Crumpton house, Orrville vicinity, 220
Cochrane, William, house, Tuscaloosa, 70, 75, 352
Coe, George, 193
Coe-Swift-Fay house (T. A. Fay house), Prattville, 35, 193
Coffeeville, 208
Colbert, Chief George, house, Cherokee vicinity, 210
Colbert County, HABS listings, 209–17. *See also* Cherokee, Leighton, Tuscumbia
Coleman, Tom ("Tom Charity"), 336

Colin, Maximilien, 319
Colleges and universities. *See* Schools
Collegiate Gothic, 160–61
Colley, C. K., 270
Collier, Gov. Henry W., house, Tuscaloosa, 61, 64, 352
Collins, John H., 287, 317
Colonial period in Alabama, 29, 33–34
Colonial Revival, 133–38, 160; affinity with antebellum neo-classicism, 134; later phase, 163, 166
Columbia, 244–45, 246
Columbia University, 141, 178, 357
Coman, Joshua P., 259
Commercial architecture, 64, 69, 100, 102, *104, 105, 119, 120, 132, 155–59,* 160, 162, 163, *173, 174,* 213, *215,* 216, 234, 287–90, 291, 313, 316, 328–29, 336–37. *See also* Bank buildings, Hotels and inns, Industrial architecture, Law offices, Medical offices, Skyscrapers, Store buildings, Transportation and transportation facilities
Commercial Row, Tuscumbia, 213
Commissaries, 195, 203, 256, 368
Confederacy, 222, 300, 324, 349, 351
Confederate Congress, 324
Confederate hospital, 195
Conn, Annie, 291
Conn-Meriwether house, Mobile, 290–91
Connecticut, 312
Construction techniques, 4–5, 102, 155
Continental Gin Company Factory, Prattville, 417. *See also* Pratt, Daniel, factory complex
Contractors, 241, 255, 256, 274, 285. *See also* Architects, builders, contractors, engineers
Convent and Academy of the Visitation, Mobile, 128, 291
Cook, Henry F., 359
Cook, Thomas, 207
Cook-Johnson house, White Plains, 207

Coons, J. W., 213
Coons-Steele-Armistead house, Tuscumbia, 213
Cooper, John Albert, 319
Cooper-Beasley house, Mount Vernon, 319
Coosa River, 5
Corey. *See* Fairfield
Corncribs. *See* Farm buildings
Cornyn, Gen. Florence N., 216
Corzelius, Frank, 360
Corzelius-McMillan house, Camden, 360
Cottage orné, 92, 107–09
Cottage Residences (Downing), 90
Cotton, impact on architecture, 9–10
Cotton gins, 257, 322, 338, *339;* cotton gin factory, 7, 193–94; cotton press, 341; gin house, 322
Cotton Hill, Athens vicinity, 260
Cotton States Exposition, 138
Cottonton, 338
Country clubs. *See* Clubs
Courthouses, 9, 57, *59,* 60, 70, 75, 78, 100, 102, 128, *129,* 133, 139, 209, 231, 252, 270, 278, 330, 332, 358, 364
Courtland, 9, 33, 45, 176–77, 178, 184, 252
Courtview, Florence, 249
Covered bridges. *See* Transportation and transportation facilities
Cowan, Dr. William L., 196
Cowan-Ramser house, Eufaula, *13,* 196
Cowikee Mills Foundation, 197
Cox, George, Jr., 268
Cox, George Woodward, 291–300
Cox-Deasy house, Mobile, 291
Cox-White house, Huntsville, 268
Coy, 367
Craft, Sen. John, 298
Craftsman, The, 146
Craftsman style, 5, 145–51, 153
Craig-Wilson house, Orrville, 219
Cram, Ralph Adams, 160, 161, 162
Crawford, 338
Creek Indians, 257, 339
Creek Indian War, 197

Crenshaw, Judge Anderson, house, Butler County, 201
Crenshaw, Walter Henry, plantation complex, Butler County, 201
Crenshaw County, HABS listings, 217
Creole cottage, 23, 24, 37–41, 43, 182; Mobile examples (HABS), 282, 294, 299, 301, 310
Crews, 247
Cripple Deer Creek Covered Bridge, Allsboro vicinity, 209
Crocheron, Henry, 218
Crocheron-Mathews house, Cahaba, 218
Croom, Isaac, 239
Crossland, John V., 231
Cross ventilation, 16
Crowan Cottage, Anniston, 122
Crowell, Col. John, Sr., 338
Crowell-Cantey-Alexander house, Fort Mitchell vicinity, 338–39
Crowley, Timothy, 313
Crutchfield, Thomas J., 204, 205
Cullman, 24, 102
Cullman County Courthouse, 102
Cunningham, Col. C. J. L., 198
Cunningham-Atkinson house, Union Springs vicinity, 198
Curry, Jackson, 349
Curry, J. L. M., house, Talladega vicinity, 349
Curzon, Lady, Marchioness of Kedleston, 330
Custom houses, 102, *106,* 316–17
Cypress Factory, Florence, 6

Dadeville, 75, 350–51
Dairies, 272–73, 334, 346
Dakin, Charles and James, 11, 57, 58, 281, 285, 288, 298, 301
Dale County. *See* Ozark
Dale Lodge No. 25, Camden, 360
Dallas County, 30, 186; HABS listings, 217–25. *See also* Cahaba, Martin's Station, Orrville, Pleasant Hill, Selma, Summerfield
Dancy, Francis W., house, Decatur, 46, 50
Dandridge, Mrs. Elizabeth, 252

Daniel, Emile B., 289
Daniel, Mr., 264
Daniels, Elgin and Company Building, Mobile, 102, *105*, 291
Dargan, Judge Edmund Spann, 292
Dargan-Ledyard house, Mobile, *108*
Dargan-Waring house, Mobile, 63, 66, 182, 291–92
Daugette, Dr. Clarence W., 203
Dauphin Island, 279
Davidson, Alexander Caldwell, 334
Davis, Alexander Jackson, 58, 84–85, 90
Davis, Helen, 346
Davis, Jefferson, 275, 324
Davis Speake Associates, 346
Dawson, Elodie Todd, 221
Dawson, John C., 281
Dawson, Nathaniel H. R., 221
Dawson, Col. Reginald M., house, Camden vicinity, 365
Dawson, William A., 284
Dawson-Vaughan house, Selma, 221
Dayton, 274–75
Deaf and Blind, State Institute for, Talladega. *See* East Alabama Masonic Female Institute
Deal, Dr. Seaborn, 353
Dean Hall, Eufaula, 93
Dearing, Alexander, house, Tuscaloosa, 352–53
Dearing, James, house, Tuscaloosa, 51, *55*, 353
Decatur, 4, 9, 46–47, 50, 53, 119, 121, 122, 123, 124, 126, 127. *See also* Morgan County
Decatur Branch, State Bank of Alabama, 53, 330
Deer park (Oak Manor, Sumter County), 344
Deer's Store, Claiborne, 177, 322
Delamier house, Mobile, 285
Dellet, James, house, Claiborne, 322
Demopolis, 11, 45–46, 70, 76–77, 89–90, 132, 180, 275–76, 285
Dennis, Samuel, 350
Department of the Interior, 178, 188
Dependencies and outbuildings, 207, 210, 235, 238, 258, 269, 271, 272, 273, 275, 308, 311, 331, 344–45, 358, 365–66. *See also* Farm buildings, Gazebos, Kitchen buildings, Plantation complexes, Playhouses, Privies, Servant and slave quarters, Smokehouses, Stables, Wellhouses
Depots. *See* Transportation and transportation facilities
Depression, the Great, 159, 167, 169, 178, 181
DeYampert, Col. L. Q. C., 241
Dial, Thomas, 211
Diapering (diaperwork), 368
Dicksonia, Lowndesboro vicinity, 264
Didlake, James, 332
Dixons Mills, 181, 276
Doges, Palace of the, 114
Dogtrot house: basic, 23, 24, 25–29, 198, 229, 234, 248, 251; "improved," 26, 27, *28*, 345
Donelson, Cathy, 185
Donnell, Robert, house (Pleasant Hill), Athens, 177, 259
Dothan, 141
Dothan Opera House, 141
Double houses, 282, 285, 293, 303, 308–09, 312. *See also* Row houses, Twin houses
Double-pen log houses, 24, 25, *26*, 198, 201, 229–30, 236, 248, 251, 252; two-story, 26, 27
Double-pile house, 33
Double-square building formula, 33, 34
Dougherty, ———, 294
Dowdell, James, 208
Dowdell, Lewis F., house, Tuskegee, *20*, 264
Dowdell-Mathews-Bullard house, Oak Bowery, 208
Downing, Andrew Jackson, 12, 90–91, 93, 107, 145, 257, 306
Downing, Walter T., 11, 134
Drake, Dr. Gaston, 238
Drake, Dr. John Hodges, 254
Drake-Northrup house, Greensboro, 238
Drake-Samford house, Auburn, 254

Drish, John R., 239; house, Tuscaloosa, 78, *79*, 353, 358
Dry Forks, Coy vicinity, 358, 366, 367
Duane Street Methodist Church, Brooklyn, N.Y., 58
Dudley, Charles Hammond, 340
Dudley, Henry, 80, 328
Dudley Hotel, Seale, 340
Duke of Gloucester Street, 33, 36
DuMont, Mrs. Alphonse, 283
Dunklin, Daniel G. and Susan Burnett, 200
Dunklin, Maj. James Hilliard, 200
Dunklin, William A. J., 200
Dunklin-Beeland house, Greenville, 200
Dunklin-Beeland-Kendrick house, Greenville, 200
Dunn, Thomas, 360
Dunn-Fairley-Bonner house, Camden, 360
Dunnam, Robert Thomas, 341
Dunton, William, 357
Durand house, Mobile, 293
"Dutch Colonial," 133

Eastaboga, 346–47
East Alabama Male College, Auburn, 100, *104*
East Alabama Masonic Female Institute, Talladega, 62, 69, 348
Eastern Bank of Alabama, Eufaula, 102, 196
East Lake, 146
Ebenezer Presbyterian Church, Clinton, 64
Ecclesiastical architecture. *See* Religious architecture
Ecclesiological movement, 80
Eclecticism in Alabama architecture, 12–13, 15–16, 21; *cottage orné* as expression of, 107–08
Ecole des Beaux-Arts, 139, 140
Eddins, Dr. Simeon J., 355
Educational institutions. *See* Schools
Edwards, John C., house, Opelika, 90, 257
Edwardsville, 209

Elizabethan influence, 15, 160
Elkus, Isaac, house, 293
Elliott, Julian, Sr., 349
Elliott, Mr., 211
Ellis, Benjamin F., 220
Ellis, Robert, 294, 304
Ellis, William, 256
Ellis-Lyons house, Mobile, 293–94
Elm Bluff, Selma vicinity, 64, 186
Elmore, Gen. John Archer, 226
Elmore community, 226
Elmore County, 16; HABS listings, 226–29. *See also* Wetumpka
Elyton, 61
Emanuel, Jonathan, house, Mobile, 294
Embury, Aymar II, 166, 167
Emmanuel Church, Pittsburgh, Pa., 129, 132
Empire Building, Birmingham, *157,* 157–58
Engineers. *See* Architects, builders, contractors, engineers
Engineers, military, 195, 279
English influence, 4–5, 9, 11, 29, 33, 80
Erie, old, 230
Erswell house, Birmingham, *165*
Erwin, Col. John, 238
Eslava, Miguel, 286, 294
Eslava, Miguel, Jr., house, Mobile, 37, 294
Etowah County. *See* Gadsden
Eufaula, 5, 9, 13, 62, 93, 97, 98, 100, 102, 107, 114, 115, 119, 122, 134, 135, 196–97
Eutaw, 67, 78, 80, 181, 230–33
Eutaw Female Academy, 231
Evans, Matthew R., 297
Evergreen, Jefferson vicinity, 278
Evergreen Bower, Union Springs vicinity, 199
Exchange Hotel, Montgomery, 159
Expositions, 122, 133, 138, 151
"Extended I house." *See* I-house with sheds

Fackler, John J., 268
Factories, 6–7, *7,* 193–94

Fail, Jeremiah, house (Fail-McIntosh house), Camden, 41, *42,* 360–61
Fair Hill (Perrin-Willis house), Forkland vicinity, 235
Fairfield, 147, 150–51
Fairfield District, S.C., 230
Fall, Nelias, house, Mount Vernon, 319
False-plate construction, 5
Fambro, Judge William W., 218
Fambro-Troy house, Cahaba, 218
Farm buildings: barns, 201, 212, 230, 237, 248, 252; corncribs, 201; gin houses, 322; wheat houses, 205. *See also* Blacksmith shops, Dependencies and outbuildings, Plantation complexes
Farm Security Administration, 181
Fatima community, 25
Faunsdale, 18, 34, 107, 277–78
Fay, T. A., house (Coe-Smith-Fay house), Prattville, 35, 193
Fayette County, HABS listings, 229
Fearn, Richard Lee, 309
Fearn, Dr. Thomas, 269
Fearn-Garth house, Huntsville, 269
Federal buildings, 135, 139; Birmingham, 128, *129,* 142; Mobile, 102, *106,* 139, *141,* 316–17; Tuscaloosa, 135, *138*
Federal Emergency Relief Administration, 180
Federal period, 21, 27, 37, 44–56; and Colonial Revival, 133–34
Fences. *See* Freestanding walls, Gates and fences
Ferguson, William C., house, Pickensville, 336
Ferrell house, Uriah vicinity, 30, 323
Ferries. *See* Transportation and transportation facilities
Figh, George M., 231
Figh, John P., 323, 324, 325
Figh-Pickett house, Montgomery, 324
Figures, John W., 208
Figures-York house, Coffeeville, 208
Finnigan, Captain Owen, house, Mobile, 294
Fireplaces, *42. See also* Mantelpieces

Fire stations, *70,* 100, 309, 318
First Baptist Church, Selma, 115, *117*
First Baptist Church, Wetumpka, 227
First Christian Church property, Selma, 222
First Methodist Church, Birmingham, 128, *130*
First Methodist Church, Huntsville, 111
First Methodist Church, Jasper, 141
First Methodist Church, Oxford, 113
First Methodist Church, Sylacauga, 167
First Methodist Church, Tuscumbia, 213
First Methodist Church, Tuskegee, 110, *111*
First Methodist Church, Wetumpka, 227
First National Bank, Andalusia, *159*
First Presbyterian Church, Birmingham, 114, *116*
First Presbyterian Church, Eufaula, 114, *115*
First Presbyterian Church, Eutaw, 231
First Presbyterian Church, Florence, 249
First Presbyterian Church, Huntsville, 84
First Presbyterian Church, Jacksonville, 110–11, *112,* 202
First Presbyterian Church, Montgomery, 80, *81*
First Presbyterian Church, old, Selma, 112
First Presbyterian Church, Talladega, 110–11, *113*
First Presbyterian Church, Tuscumbia, 80, 213–14, *215*
First Presbyterian Church, Wetumpka, 84, *87,* 227
First White House of the Confederacy, Montgomery, 324
Fitch, John, 201
Fitzpatrick, Gov. Benjamin, house, Elmore vicinity, 16, 226
Fitzpatrick, Elmore, 325
Fitzpatrick, Kelly, 228

Fitzpatrick-Saffold house, Montgomery, 325
Five Oaks, New Market, 274
Floor plans, 18; hall-and-parlor, 5, 33, 35, 43
Florence, 6, 33, 45, 47, 49, 51, 54, 84, 119, 122, 139, 161, 169, 171, 178, 248–51
"Flounder" roof, 262
Flowers Hall, Huntingdon College, 160–61, *161*
Fluker, Baldwin M., 347; house, Haleburg vicinity, 245; house, Sylacauga, 347
Folk architecture, 3–5, 23–43
Foote, Charles K., house, Mobile, 294, 311
Forest Field, Huntsville, 271
Forest Hill, Demopolis, 89
Forest Park, 146
Forkland, 25, 61, 83, 233–37
Forks of Cypress, Florence vicinity, 51, 54, 169, 250–51
Forsyth, John, 316
Forsyth, Telford, 201
Fort Condé (Fort Charlotte), Mobile, 304
Fort Dale Cemetery, Butler County, 200–01
Fort Gaines, Dauphin Island, 279
Fortifications, 195
Fort Mitchell, 338–39
Fort Morgan, Gulf Shores vicinity, 195, 279
Fort Payne, 122
Fort Sumter, S.C., 329
Foster, Charles M., 354
Foster, George Washington, 249
Foster, Henry, 255
Foster, Robert Savidge, house, Tuscaloosa County, 46, 51
Foster, Dr. Sterling Johnston, 198
Foster, Col. Wilbur, 265
Foster-Cobb-Laslie house, Tuskegee, 264–65
Foster-Shirley house, Tuscaloosa, 354
Founders Hall (old Athens Female Institute), Athens, 69, 258

Foundries, 6, 8, 10, 266, 300, 417
Fountains, cast-iron, 17
"Four Sisters" house, Mobile, 316
Fowler, Orson Squire, 13
Fox, Dr. Daniel J., 368
Fox-Harris-Jones house, Oak Hill, 368
France, 118. *See also* French colonial influence
Frances Benjamin Johnston Collection, 190, 191
Francis, Dr. J. C., office, Jacksonville, 69
Franklin, 322
Franklin County, N.C., 347
Franklin Street Methodist Church, Mobile, 294–95, 298
Frascatti, Mobile, 295
Fraternal orders (meeting halls). *See* Masonic halls, Odd Fellows Hall
Frazer, Addison, 255
Frazer, Sen. Thomas Sidney, 199
Frazer-Brown house, Auburn, 255
Fredericksburg, Va., 236
Freestanding walls, 320, 361
French colonial influence, 37–39
Freret, James, 11, 314
Funerary architecture, 7, *8,* 276

Gadsden, 78, 124, 139, 180
Gaines, Edmund Pendleton, 286, 297
Gainesville, 40, 67, 69, 71, 78, 186
Gaineswood, Demopolis, 3, 70, 76–77, 180, 275–76
Gallier, James, 11, 57, 58, 281, 294, 298
Galliher, C. Frank, 136
Gallion, 89, 90, 237
Garçonnieres, 292, 342
Gardendale, 169, 170
Gardens. *See* Landscaping
Gardner, William A., house, Dadeville vicinity, 350–51
Garland, Mrs. Landon Cabell, 358
Garland Hall, University of Alabama, 117
Garrett, John B., 325
Garrett-Hatchett house, Montgomery, 93, 96, 325

Gas lamps. *See* Street furnishings
Gates, Hezekiah, 296
Gates-Daves house, Mobile, 296
Gates and fences, 7, *17,* 233, 275, 281, 292, 295, *296,* 314, 320. *See also* Freestanding walls
Gayle, Gov. John, 238, 239
Gayle, Col. Rees D., house, Cahaba, 218
Gayle-Hobson-Tunstall house, Greensboro, 238
Gazebos (summer houses), 182, 276, 333. *See also* Dependencies and outbuildings
Gazzam, Audley H., house, Mobile, 296
Gee, Gideon, 296
Gee-Barrow house, Mobile, 296
Geneva, Ala., 27
George, Elizabeth, house, Mobile, 296
George, William, 287
George Washington Lodge No. 24, Clinton, 230
Georgia, 9, 29, 34, 41, 177, 194, 198, 201, 224, 225, 233, 277, 345, 359, 361; architectural influence, 29, 34, 41
Georgia Cottage, Mobile, 61, *64,* 296–97
"Georgian Gothick," 214
Georgian style, influence of, 4–5, 20, 23, 29, 44, 133–34, 159, 160, 162
Gerald, Perley, 325
Gerald-Bethea house (Perley Gerald house), Montgomery, 70, *74,* 325
Gerald-Dowdell house, Montgomery, 325
German immigrants, 24
Germany, 361
Geronimo, 320
Gibbons, Judge Lyman, 297
Gibbons-Torrey house, Mobile, 297
Gibbs, Capt. John F., 85
Giles, J. H., 102
Gillespie, Rev. Robert, 331
Gilmer, James J., 325

Gilmer-Shorter-Lomax house, Montgomery, 325
Gilmore, George W. and Carolyn F., 297
Gilmore, Thomas, 234
Gilmore-Gaines-Quigley house, Mobile, 297
Gindrat, John, 329
Gins. *See* Cotton gins
Girard (now Phenix City), 11
Glasgow, Joe, 244
Glen Alpine, Forkland vicinity, 235
Glencairn, Greensboro, 238
Glennville Plantation, Pittsview vicinity, 61, *62,* 339
Gliddon, John S., house, Mobile, 177, 297
Glover, Allen, 276; house, Demopolis, 45–46, *50*
Glover, Cato, 234
Glover, Mary Ann Diven, 276
Glover, Virginia, house, Forkland, 233
Glover, William, 234
Glover, Williamson Allen, 234, 235
Glover, Dr. Wylie, house, Weaver vicinity, 206
Glover Mausoleum, Demopolis, 276, 277
Godey's Lady's Book, 107
Goelet, Virginia, 297
Goelet-Randlette-Beck house, Mobile, 297
Gold Hill, 255–56
Goldsby house, Mobile, 88, 177, 297–98
Goldsmith, Meyer, 298
Goode, Garland, 322
Goodloe, John Calvin, house, Cherokee vicinity, 210
Goodman, Benjamin L., house, Lafayette, 207–08, 350
Gordon community, 246
Gorgas, Amelia Gayle, 238
Gorgas house, Tuscaloosa, 357
Gosse, Philip, 24
Gothic influence, 160. *See also* Gothic Revival

Gothic Revival, 13, 15, 21, 80–92, 107, 109, 114, 177, 219, 237, 244, 298, 306
Gould, William Procter, 230
Government buildings. *See* Federal buildings
Government Street, Mobile, 16, *17,* 133, 140
Government Street Methodist Church, Mobile, 152, *153*
Government Street Presbyterian Church, Mobile, 57, *58,* 298
Grace Episcopal Church, Anniston, 114, *116*
Grace Episcopal Church, Mount Meigs, 83
Grace-Chesnut house, Allenton, 358
Grace, Joshua Betts, 358
Gracey, Mr. and Mrs. Minor Winn, 237
Gracey, Robert Sinclair, 237
Graining, 30, 177, 201, 207, 212, 217, 257, 341, 346, 364. *See also* Marbleizing, Painting (decorative), Stippling, Trompe l'oeil
Granaries (wheat houses). *See* Farm buildings
Grant, Basil, house, Jefferson vicinity, 278
Grave houses, 200, 201, 217. *See also* Cemeteries, Mausoleums
Graves, Gov. David Bibb, 328
Graves-Haigler house, Lowndes County, 34
Graymont, 146
Greek Revival, 3, 11, 12, 14, 15, 21, 23, 27, 37, 46, 53, 57–79, 103, 141; confusion with "Colonial," 133–34
Green, Jacob, 202
Green, Willis H., 219
Green-Woodruff house, Alexandria, 202
Greene, Charles Sumner and Henry Mather, 145
Greene County, 30, 43, 63; HABS listings, 229–37. *See also* Boligee, Clinton, Eutaw, Forkland

Greene County Courthouse and Probate Office, Eutaw, 231
Greene County, Ga., 198
Greenlawn, Huntsville, 269
Greenly, D., 212
Greensboro, 18, 34, 46, 57–58, 60, 78, 84, 88, 89, 97, 100, 107, 108, 122, 146, 181, 186, 237–42, 355
Greenville, 91, 200–01
Greenwood, Hale County, 240
Gregory, George W., 287
Gregory house, Dadeville vicinity, 351
Grenier, 37
Grey Columns, Tuskegee, 266–67
Griffin, Edward, 298
Griffin-Goldsmith house, Mobile, 298
Griffiths, Ino, and Son, 155
Grist mills, 205, 229, 256–57, 346
Grove, The, Birmingham. *See* Arlington
Guesnard, Theodore, Jr., 298
Guesnard-Craft house, Mobile, 298
Gulf City Hotel, Mobile, 298–99
Gulf coast, 17, 23, 37, 40, 42
Gulf, Mobile, and Ohio Passenger Terminal, Mobile, 151, *152,* 299
Gulf Shores, 195
Guntersville, 173
Gup, Benjamin and Marcus, tailor shop, 289

H-shaped plan, 18, 254, 258, 348
HABS. *See* Historic American Buidings Survey
HAER. *See* Historic American Engineering Record
Haleburg, 245
Hale County, 19, 90; HABS listings, 237–44. *See also* Greensboro, Gallion, Prairieville
Hall, Edward, 299
Hall-and-parlor plan, 5, 33, 35, 43
Hall-Ford house, Mobile, 299
Hall-Horst house, Mobile, 299
Hamilton, Alex Price, 259
"Hamilton, Betsy." *See* Idora McClellan Plowman-Moore
Hamilton, Thomas A., 281, 285

Hamilton-Gaillard house, Mobile, 285
Hammond, W. P., 299
Hammond-Willoughby house, Mobile, 299
Hampton house, Huntsville vicinity, 186
Hanchey, Martin, 337
Hanchey-Pennington house, Orion, 337
Hancock County, Ga., 225
Hand, John, Building, Birmingham. *See* Jefferson County Savings Bank
Handley, Gabriel, 361
Handley-Felts house, Camden, 361
Hannah, Dr. Robert C., house, Greensboro, 238
Hardaway, Mrs. William A., 297
Hardie, John, 350
Harpersville, 341
Harper's Weekly, 6
Harris, Edmund S., 256
Harris, Henry H. ("Chub"), 343
Harris, Nathan, 326
Harris, Norfleet, house, Faunsdale vicinity, 107
Harris, Page, 237
Harris, Peter Coffee, 265
Harris, Dr. Sidney J., 274
Harris, W. K., 265
Harris-Ennis-White house, Livingston, 343
Harris-Smith house, Montgomery, 325–26
Harris-Wadsworth house, Tuskegee, 265
Harrison, Benjamin, 278
Harrison, "Colonel," 264
Harrison, Dr. Kirkland, 223
Harrison-Hunter-Harper house, Selma vicinity, 223
Harrod and Andry, 128
Hart, John, 196
Hart-Milton house, Eufaula, 196
Hartford, Conn., 12
Hartley, Joseph, 201
Harwell Goodwin Davis Library, Samford University, *168*
Hassinger house, Birmingham, *166*
Hatchett, W. T., 229

Haviland, John, 12
Hawkins, Wiley T., 249
Hawkins-Sample house, Florence, 249
Hawthorn, Col. Joseph R., house, Pine Apple, 16, 369
Haynes, Aaron, 204
Hayneville, 75
Hays, Charles (architect), 308
Hays, Charles (planter-politician), 230
Hazard, Charles C., 299
Hazard-Semmes house, Mobile, 299–300
Heiman, Adolphus, 84, 241, 249
Helen Keller Library, Tuscumbia, 216
Helena, 341
Hellen, Mariah H., 300
Hellen-Croom house, Mobile, 300
Henderson, William, Store, Millers Ferry, 367
Henry, Judge John, house, Centreville, 46
Henry, John Kelly, 200
Henry-Beeland-Stanley house, Greenville, 200
Henry County, 42, 192–93; HABS listings, 244–45
Hibben, Thomas, 170
Higgins, Hiram H., 11, 15, 62, 69, 252, 258, 260, 348
High, William M., house, Forkland vicinity, 231
High Ridge, 198
High styles, 44–168
High Victorian Gothic, 80, 113, 114–18
Highland, Talladega, 89, 90
Highland Avenue, Birmingham, 122, 186
Highland Golf and Country Club, Birmingham, 146, *147*
Hill, James, 285
Hill of Howth, Boligee, 11, 229–30
Hilliard, Henry, house, Mobile, 326
Hillman, Daniel, 351
Hills, Chester, 12, 14
Hinds, Grace, 330
Historic American Buildings Survey (HABS), xiii, xix–xx, 3, 177–91; in Alabama, xv–xvii, 177–87, 405–

06; "discard" photographs, 184; use of HABS catalog, 188–91
Historic American Engineering Record (HAER), xix, 191, 417–18
History of Alabama (Pickett), 226
Hitchcock, Judge Henry, 287, 288, 300, 307
Hitching posts, 17, 210, *315*. *See also* Carriage block, Mounting blocks, Street furnishings
Hobbs, Ira E., 258
Hobson, Col. Edwin, 238
Hobson, Matthew, 238
Hobson, Richmond Pearson, 239
Hogan, James, 356
Hoke, John D., house, Jacksonville, 202–03
Holman, J. D., house, Ozark, 134, *136*
Holmes, Nicholas H., Jr., 35, 185, 287, 316, 323, 324, 341
Holmes, Nicholas H., Sr., xvii
Holmes, Nicholas H. III, xvii
Holt, Barachias, 323
Home Bank, The, Guntersville, *173*
Home for All, A (Fowler), 13
Home Industry Foundry, Mobile, 284, 300
Homes for the People (Wheeler), 107
Homestead Architecture (Sloan), 99
Homewood, Eufaula, 93, 98
Hood, James, 251
Hooper, Johnson Jones, 350
"Hoover Wagon," 181, 277
Hopkins, Arthur Francis, 271
Horst, Martin, 295, 300; house, Mobile, 300
Horta, Peter, 300
Horta-Semmes house, Mobile, 300
Horton, Rhoda, 269
Horton-McCracken house, Huntsville, 269
Hospital for the Insane. *See* Bryce Hospital
Hospitals, 53, 100, *103*, 287, 317, 320. *See also* Infirmaries
Hotel Albert, Selma, 114
Hotels and inns, 114, *119, 120*, 124, 127, 155, *159*, 197, 201, 203,

222–23, 228, 234, 247, 250, 261, 267, 298–99, 304, 335, 340, 350, 357, 358–59, 364
Hough, John Baugh, 198
Hough-Roughton house, High Ridge, 198
Houmas House, La., 169
House Beautiful, 145
Houston, Gov. George S., house, Athens, 258
Houston, Matthew C., 331
Houston-Abernathy-Minor house, Tuscumbia, 214
Houston County, HABS listings, 246
Huey, James Grandison Leroy, 348
Huey-Stone-Chambers house, Talladega, 348
Huger, Charles L., house, Mobile, 302–03
Hughes, Benjamin Jolley, 334
Hughes, Dr. William, house, Aliceville vicinity, 335
Hundley house, Mooresville, 35, *36*
Hunley (submarine), 300
Hunt, Richard Morris, 128
Hunter, Dr. J. W., 265
Hunter, Perrin P., house, Jasper, 152, *154*
Hunter-Callaway house, Tuskegee, 265
Hunter Street Baptist Church, Birmingham, 167
Huntingdon, Elmore vicinity, 226
Huntingdon College, Montgomery, 160–61, *161*
Huntsville, 5, 7, 9, 10, 11, 12, 14, 45, 46, 48, 57, 59, 63–64, 67, 80, 81, 82–83, 84, 91, 97, 102, 110–11, 122, 134, 159, 177, 179, 180, 186, 268–73
Huntsville Branch, State Bank of Alabama, 57, 269–70
Huntsville Democrat, 273
Huntsville Female Seminary, 84, 273
Hurricane Frederick, 177, 287
Hutchisson, C. L., Sr., 11, 298, 305, 317
Hutchisson, J. H., 285, 304

I-house with sheds, 29–32
Icehouses, 252, 271
Ihagee plantation, Russell County, 16
Imperial Hotel, Montgomery. *See* LeGrand Building
Independent Presbyterian Church, Birmingham, 162
Indians, 210, 257, 339
Indian Schoolhouse, Mount Vernon, 320
Industrial architecture, 6, 7, 9, *10,* 193–94, 256, 300, 417. *See also* Factories, Grist mills
Industrial development (and Alabama architecture), 6–10, 122, 146
Infirmaries, 314. *See also* Hospitals
Ingleside, Aliceville, 334–35
Inn, Forkland, 234
Inns. *See* Hotels and inns
International style, 169
Interstate Highway, 10, 185, 301, 302, 307
Iron-front buildings, 102, *105,* 291
Iron manufacture, 6–8, 351
Ironwork (ornamental), 7, *17,* 286, 303, 306–07, 315; Mobile survey of, 407–09
Iron works, 417
Irvine, James Bennington, 250; house, Florence, *47,* 249
Irwin, Gen. William, 245
Irwin-McAllister house, Henry County, *192, 193,* 245
Irwinton Inn, 197
Isbell, James, house, Talladega, 348
Isolation, factor in Alabama architecture, 6, 9
Italianate style, 3, 8, 13, 21, 78, 92–106, *107*
Ivy Creek Methodist Church, Mulberry, *193,* 226
Ivy Green, Tuscumbia, 214–15

Jackson, Andrew, 211
Jackson, James, 251
Jackson, Dr. Reuben H., 239
Jackson, Stonewall, 300
Jackson-Locke house, Greensboro, 239

Jackson Street Presbyterian Church, Mobile, 84
Jackson Trace, 349
Jacksonville, 69, 83, 86, 93, 97, 98, 110–11, 112, 161, 202–05
Jails, 304
James, Thomas S., 298, 303, 304
James, Thomas S., Double House, Mobile, 303
James, Westwood Wallace, 252; house, Courtland, *176–77,* 252
Janney foundry, 7
Japanese architecture, 145
Japonica Path, Greensboro, 239
Jasper, 141, 152, 154
Jefferson, Thomas, 44, 52–53, 60, 212
Jefferson community, 278
Jefferson County, HABS listings, 247. *See also* Bessemer, Birmingham, Gardendale
Jefferson County Courthouse, Birmingham: 1873 building, 101–02; 1889 building, 128
Jefferson County Savings Bank, Birmingham, *156*
Jeffersonian influence, 44–45, 52–53, 55–56, 254
Jeffries, Dr. Algernon, 223
Jemison, Robert, house, Tuscaloosa, *93, 97,* 354
Jemison, Robert IV, house, Birmingham, *134, 137*
Jemison and Company, Birmingham, 162
Jenkins, Robert, house (Jenkins-Carlton-Autrey house), Alpine vicinity, *27, 28,* 345
Jervis house, Decatur, 122
John XXIII, Pope, 285
John Hand Building, Birmingham. *See* Jefferson County Savings Bank
Johnson, Enoch, 339
Johnson, John, house, Leighton vicinity, *33, 34,* 35
Johnson, Mrs. Lyndon B., 309
Johnson-Abercrombie-Lamar house, Tuskegee, 265
Johnston, Burr, 265

Johnston, Thomas M., 239
Johnston-Torbert house, Greensboro, 46, 239
Jones, Lt. Catesby ap R., 222
Jones, Dudley E., 250
Jones, Col. Edward Nathaniel, 361, 362
Jones, Edward Vason, 232, 352
Jones, Gene, 341
Jones, Harvie, xvi, 271, 273
Jones, Dr. Haywood, 259
Jones, Hugh, 253
Jones, Mrs. Rachel, 333
Jones, Richard Channing, 361, 362
Jones, Samuel, 215
Jones-Cocke-Crenshaw house, Marion vicinity, 333
Jones-Coman-Westmoreland house, Athens, 258–59
Jones-Liddell house, Camden, 361
Jones-McIntosh house, Camden, 361
Jones-Winston-Rand house, Tuscumbia, 215
Judson, Lewis, 299, 304
Judson Female Institute (Judson College), Marion, 119, *120*, 332

Kaster, Henry P., house, Camden, 177, 361
Keller, Captain Arthur, 213, 214
Keller, David and Mary Fairfax, 214
Keller, Helen, 213, 214
Keller, Helen, Library, Tuscumbia, 216
Kelly, Gen. John Herbert, 369
Kelly, Maude McClure, 347
Kelly, Simon, house, Weaver, 30, 206–07
Kelly-Bland-Ward house, Orrville vicinity, 220
Kenan, Mary Rand, 224
Kenan house, Selma vicinity, 58, 60, 61, 223–24
Kendall Manor, Eufaula. *See* Homewood
Kennedy, Joshua, house, Mobile, 303
Kennedy, Mr., 240
Kennedy-Sims house, Montgomery, 122, *124*

Kennon, William, 242
Kent, R. B., 345
Kentucky, 248; architectural influence, 23
Kenworthy Hall (Carlisle Hall), Marion vicinity, 97–98, *101*, 332–33
Ketchum, William H., house, Mobile, 97, 99, 303
Key West, Fla., 37
"Kiah" and "Lijah" (slaves), 367
Kidd, James W., 254
Kidd-Halliday-Cary house, Auburn, 62, *65*, 254
Kilduff, William J., 304
Kilduff-Ray house, Mobile, 304
Kilns, 256
Kilpatrick, Dr. Emmett, 360
Kimbrough house, Old Erie, 186
King, Edmund, house, Montevallo, 341
King, Edward, house, Newport, 98
King, Horace, 11
King, Judge Porter, house, Marion, 331
King, William B., 222
King house, Talladega vicinity, 349
King-Welch house, Selma, 177, 222
Kirk, Mary Wallace, 216
Kirkbride, Jonathan, 294; house, Mobile, 304
Kirkbride plan, 100, *103*
Kirkpatrick, Clifton, 217
Kirkpatrick, Dr., house, Selma, 221–22
Kirksey, Foster M., 232
Kirkwood, Eutaw, 43, 78, 231–32
Kitchen buildings, 182, 198, 203, 206, 209–10, 210, 212, 213, 214–15, 235, 238, 239, 241, 255, 268–69, 273, 310, 331, 344, 355, 366. *See also* Dependencies and outbuildings
Kitchen, Col. William, 195
Kitchen-McMillan house, Stockton, 195
Kling, Augustus, 284, 300
Knox, William, house, Montgomery, 67, 73
Knox County, Tenn., 270

Koger, William, house, Lauderdale County, 33
Kossuth, Louis, 306
Ku Klux Klan, 355

L-shaped plan, 18
Laboratories, 321
LaClede Hotel, Mobile, 304
Ladies' Home Journal, 145
Lafayette, 139, 207–08
Lafayette, Marquis de, 323
Lafever, Minard, 12, 58, 60–61, 67, 68, 73, 209, 224, 261, 314, 323, 324
Lake, Joseph, 343
Lakewood, Livingston, 343
Lamar County, 30; HABS listings, 247–48. *See also* Sulligent
Lambuth Memorial Church, Forkland, 234
Lampkin, Griffin, 261
Lampposts, 315
Landscaping, 216, 239, 307, 339
Lane, Gen. James, house, Athens, 15
Larrouil, Pascal, 304
Larrouil-Arresijac house, Mobile, 304
Lathrop house, Birmingham, 134
Latin tradition (and Mission style), 151
Lauderdale County, HABS listings, 248–51. *See also* Florence
Laurel Hill, Union Springs, 198
Lawler, Levi Welbourne, 346
Law offices, 64, 201, 233, 240–41, 259, 361–62. *See also* Medical offices, Offices, Plantation complexes
Lawrence County, 27, 33, 34, 35; HABS listings, 252–54. *See also* Courtland, Moulton, Town Creek
Lawrence County Courthouse, Moulton, 252–53, *253*
Leadbetter, Daniel, 317
Leak, Tilman, 227
Leckey, Hugh C., house, Leighton, 97, 99, 210
Lee, I. James, 344
Lee, James Madison, 342
Lee, Peter, 244
Lee, Robert E., 169, 300

Lee, Thomas Helm, 223, 274
Lee County, 30, 90–91, 177; HABS listings, 254–57. *See also* Auburn, Opelika
Lee Haven, Coatopa vicinity, 342
Legare, Amelia Walton, 183
LeGrand Building, Montgomery, *119*
Leighton, 33, 34, 97, 99, 210–11
Leipzig, 178
Lenlock, Weaver vicinity, 206
Lernier, Charles T., 99, 303
LeSueur, Howard Grady, 256
LeSueur's Mill, Notasulga vicinity, 256
"Lev" and "Griff" (slave builders), 206
LeVert, Dr. Henry Strachy, 304
LeVert, Octavia Walton, 304
LeVert House and Office, Mobile, 304–05
Levy, J. L., 234
Levy-Glover Store, Forkland, 234
Lewis, Mrs. Ann, house, Forkland, 234
Lewis, Burwell Boykin, 354
Lewis, Sen. Dixon Hall, 262
Lewis, Francis, house, Lowndesboro, 262
Lewis, John H., 273
Lewis-Cilley-Howard house, Lowndesboro, 262
Lewis-Hall-James house, Lowndesboro, 262
Liberty Hall, Camden vicinity, 365
Libraries, 139, *140*, 142, *168*
Library of Congress, xix–xx, 183, 184, 190
Lighthouses, 318–19, *319*
Limestone County, 15; HABS listings, 258–61. *See also* Athens, Mooresville
Limestone Democrat, The, 15
Lime works, 256
Lincoln, Mary Todd, 221
Lincolnton, N.C., 203
Linden, 278
Lindsay, Gov. Robert B., 213
Linley, John, 41
Little, Dr. George, 356

Little Huntington. *See* Mitchell-Lane house
Living hall, 123, *126*
Livingston, 10, 18, 114, 117, 342–44
Livingston State Normal School, 343
Loachapoka, 256
Locke, James Whitehead, 239
Lockwood, Frank, 11, 141, 165, 324, 358
Locust Hill, Tuscumbia, 215–16
Log construction, 3, 11, 24–28, 32, 198, 211, 229–30, 234, 237, 248, 251, 252, 258, 280, 342, 345, 375
"Lombard" style. *See* Romanesque Revival
Long, Sprott, 236
Looney, John, house, St. Clair County, 26, 27
Lott, William, house, Mobile, 134, *137*, 305
Louisa County, Va., 342
Louisiana plantation houses (compared with Alabama's), 61
Louisville, Ky., 11
Louisville and Nashville Railroad, 417
Louisville and Nashville Station, Bridgeport, 152
Love, Edgar, 11, 179
Lowell, Mass., 9
Lowndesboro, 262–64
Lowndesboro Female Institute (President's House), Lowndesboro, 263
Lowndes County, HABS listings, 261–64
Lowrey-Ford house, Marion, 331
Ludlow, Noel K., house, Mobile, 305
Ludwell-Paradise house, Williamsburg, 29
Lutz, Earl Guthrie, Jr., 179
Lyceum, The, University of Alabama, 50
Lynch, George, 367
Lyon, Francis Strother, 275
Lyon, George Gaines, 276
Lyon Hall, 276
Lyons, Patrick J., house, Mobile, 305–06

Mabry, Dr. Albert Gallatin, 222
Mabry-Jones house, Selma, 222
McAlpine, William, 235
McBride, Ray, house, Prattville vicinity, 327
McBryde, Anne Allen, 326
McBryde-Screws-Tyson house, Montgomery, 326
McCaa house, Anniston, 122
McCaleb, Tyler, 229
McCaleb's Mill, 229
McCampbell, James, 203
McCampbell-Martin house, Jacksonville, 203
McCloskey, Philip, 299
McClung, Col. James W., 270
McClung-Watkins house, Huntsville, 270
McCollum, Gwaltney, 239
McCollum, James, 341
McCormick, G. B., house, Birmingham, *165*
McCrary, David F., 240
McCrary, J. W., 241
McCullough, William Thomas, 337
McCullough-Henderson house, Orion, 337
McDonald, Alexander, 197
McDonald-Smartt house, Eufaula, 196–97
McDowell, John Robert, 365
McDowell, William, 270
McDowell, Withers & Co., Mobile, 306
McDowell-LeVert-Chase house, Huntsville, 270
McElhaney, F. G., 255
McElhaney house, Auburn, 254–55
McEntire house. *See* Rhea-Burleson-McEntire house
McGehee-Stringfellow house, Greensboro vicinity, 186
McGill, Arthur, 306
McGill, Felix, 301
McGill Institute, Mobile, 306
McGowin, J. F., 306
McGowin-Creary house, Mobile, 306
McIntire, Samuel, 45
McIntosh, 358

McKee, Col. John, 230
MacKenzie, Roderick, 324
McKim, Charles Follen, 141, 324
McKim, Mead, and White, 133, 141
McKinley, John, 273
McKinley, Pres. William, 265
McKleroy house, Anniston, 122
McLemore, Ulysses T., 230
McMillan, Lewis, house, Orrville vicinity, 177, 220
McNab, John, 196
McNamee, Thomas, 208
McNamee-Kinsey-McLemore house, Lafayette, 208
Macon County, 128, 129, 133; HABS listings, 264–67. See also Tuskegee
Macon County Courthouse, Tuskegee, 128, 129, 133
McQueen house, Tuscaloosa, 146, 149
McQueen House ("Tavern"), Wetumpka, 177, 228
McWilliams, Richard Ervin, 363
Macy, Robert C., 306
Macy-Adams house, Mobile, 306
Madison County, 6; HABS listings, 268–74. See also Huntsville
Madison County Courthouse, Huntsville, 57, 59, 270
Madison County, Va., 346
Madison Square Presbyterian Church, N.Y., 141
Magnolia Cemetery, Mobile, 8, 306–07
Magnolia Cotton Warehouse, Mobile, 307
Magnolia Grove, Dayton, 274
Magnolia Grove, Greensboro, 58, 239, 355
Magnolia Hall, Greensboro, 58, 60, 240
Magnolias, The, Jacksonville, 97, 203
Mail-order houses, 149
Maine, 283
Mallory, James, 346
Malone, James Henry, 258
Manchester, 9
Manning, Dr. Frederick Haughton, 348
Manning, W. N., 180

Manning Hall, Talladega. See East Alabama Masonic Female Institute
Manningham, 201
Mansard roof, 119–20
Mantelpieces, 20, 46, 71, 126. See also Fireplaces
Manufacturing, 6–8
Mapleton (Coalter-McFarland house), Florence, 45, 49, 248–49
Marbleizing, 200, 201, 206, 221, 257, 345, 351. See also Graining, Painting (decorative), Stippling, Trompe l'oeil
Mardis, Samuel W., 349
Mardis-Batchelor house (Samuel Mardis house), Talladega vicinity, 177, 347, 349
Mardisville, 177, 349
Marengo County, 49, 181; HABS listings, 274–78. See also Demopolis, Faunsdale
Marengo County Courthouse, Linden, 278
Marengo County Historical Society, 275
Marine Hospital, Mobile. See United States Marine Hospital
Marion, 8, 60, 97, 101, 107, 112, 113, 119–20, 331–32
Marion County, 182; HABS listing, 279
Marion Female Seminary, Marion, 332
Market houses, 100, 104, 286–87
Marks, Col. John R., 221, 222
Marks, William M., house, Montgomery vicinity, 34
Marks-Plattenburg house, Selma, 222
Marschall, Nicola, 332
Marshall, Benjamin F., 307; house, Mobile, 61, 307
Marshall-Atchison house, Orrville, 122, 126
Marshall County. See Guntersville
Marshall-Eslava house (Benjamin F. Marshall house), Mobile, 61, 307
Marshall house, Selma, 91
Martin, Gov. Joshua Lanier, 354, 355
Martin, Lyman Waddell, family, 340

Martin, Peter, 354
Martin-Barnes house, Montgomery, 34, 35
Martin-Comegys-Gluck house, Tuscaloosa, 354
Martin-Marlowe house, Tuscaloosa, 355
Martin's (Martins) Station (now Martin), 85, 218–19
Marty, Edward C., 179
Marx, Isaac, house, Mobile, 307
Marx, Otto, house, Birmingham, 152, 165
Marye, P. Thornton, 151, 152, 299
Maryland, 4, 23, 33, 212, 252, 261, 280, 313, 367; architectural influence, 4, 23, 33
Mason, Capt. John, 258
Mason, Lewis, 341
Masonic halls: Athens, 80, 81, 259; Benton, 261; Camden, 53, 360; Claiborne, 322–23; Clinton, 230; Crawford, 338; Huntsville, 81; Newbern, 242; Perdue Hill, 322–23; Saint Stephens, 358; Uniontown, 333
Massachusetts, 60, 246, 356
Matheson, Dr. Alexander C., 362
Matheson-Weir-Moore-McLeod house, Camden, 362
Mathews, Peter Early, 368
Mathews, Col. Thomas, 218
Mathews, William T., 360, 365, 366, 367
Matthews, Luke, 260
Maupin, Narcissa Tayloe, 311
Mausoleums, 7, 8, 276, 309–10, 313–14. See also Cemeteries, Grave houses
Maybeck, Bernard, 145
Mazange, Ovid, 287
Meadows-Powell house, Lowndesboro, 262
Means, Dr. John David, 230
Mecklenburg County, N.C., 244
Medical offices, 64, 69, 279, 304, 305. See also Law offices, Offices, Plantation complexes
Mellon house, Oxford, 122

Memphis and Charleston Railroad Depot, Huntsville, 102
Memphis community, 335–36
Mental hospitals. *See* Bryce Hospital, Searcy Hospital
Merchants National Bank, Mobile, 158
Meriwether, Joseph, house, Springfield, 232
Meriwether, Dr. Willis, 232
Meriwether-Clark-Malone house, Eutaw, 232
Merrick, William M., 10
Merrimac, 222
Mesopotamia Academy, Eutaw, 232
Methodist Church, Burkville, 261, 329
Methodist Church, Cahaba, 218, *219*
Methodist Church, Carrollton, 335
Methodist Church, Dayton, 274
Methodist Church, Forkland, 234
Methodist Church, Gainesville, 78
Methodist Church, Livingston, 114, 117
Methodist Church, Loachapoka, 256
Methodist Church, Lowndesboro, 262
Methodist Church, Pickensville, 336
Methodist Church, Robinson Springs, 226
Methodist Church, Summerfield, 64, 225
Methodist Parsonage, Forkland, 234
Methodist Parsonage, Robinson Springs, 226
Mewhinney, Philip S., 179
Meyer, Franz, Co. (Munich), 285
Middle Bay Light, Mobile Bay, 185, 318–19, *319*
Middleton, Louis, 307
Middleton-Boulo house, Mobile, 307
Milhous-Albritton house, Orrville, 219
Military architecture, 195, 279–80, 320–21
Milledgeville, Ga., 194
Miller, Dr. Abijah, 366
Miller, Gov. Benjamin Meek, law office, Camden, 362
Miller, Earl Hart, 223
Miller, James P., 307

Miller and Martin, 146
Miller-O'Donnell house, Mobile, 307
Millers Ferry, 367–68
Miller-Smith house, Canton Bend, 366
Mills. *See* Factories, Grist mills
Mimosa, Canton Bend vicinity. *See* Youpon
Minge, David, 278
Minor, Dr. William Tompkins, 261
Minor-Hundley house, Mooresville, 261
Mission style, 151–55
Mississippi, 10, 11, 243, 279
Mississippi River, 169
Mitchel, Gen. Ormsby M., 270
Mitchell, Dr. Alexander W., 212
Mitchell, Americus, house (Glennville Plantation), Pittsview vicinity, 339–40
Mitchell, Archelus Hughes, 225
Mitchell, William, 350
Mitchell-King house, Summerfield, 225
Mitchell-Lane house, Dadeville, 350
Mobile, xvi, 5, 7, 8, 9, 10, 11, 16, 17, 18, 37, 39, 50, 53, 57, 58, 61, 63, 64, 67, 70, 72, 78, 80–81, 84, 88–89, 93, 95, 97, 99–100, 102, 104–06, 107–08, 111, 113, 122, 125, 128, 133, 134, 137, 139–40, 142, 151–53, 156–59, 162, 163, 177, 179, 181–82, 198, 333, 346, 359; HABS listings, 280–318, 407–16
Mobile and Girard Railroad, 199
Mobile and Ohio Railroad, 280, 283, 315, 316; railroad office building, Mobile, 308
Mobile Bay, 37, 40, 140, 185, 195, 279, 285, 293, 317
Mobile City Hall and Southern Market, 100, *104,* 286–87
Mobile County, HABS listings, 279–321. *See also* Mobile, Whistler
Mobile County Courthouse, *139*
Mobile Historic Development Commission, 297
Mobile Light No. 6639. *See* Middle Bay Light

Mobile Register, 312
Mobile Steam Cotton Press and Building Co., 288
Mobility (and early Alabama architecture), 10–11
Model Architect, The (Sloan), 84, 87, 93–94, 97, 98, 202, 203, 223
Modern Builder's Guide, The (Lafever), 58, *60,* 224
Moffatt, Henry, 310
Moffitt, Capt. Henry, 257
Moffitt's Mill, Opelika vicinity, 256–57
Molett, John Ulmer, 221
Molett, William Page, 220
Molett houses, Orrville vicinity, 220–21
Molton Hotel, Birmingham, 159
Monitor, 222
Mon Louis Island, 319
Monroe County, 30; HABS listings, 322–23. *See also* Claiborne, Perdue Hill
Monroeville, 322
Montebrier, Brierfield, 107, *108*
Montevallo, 341
Montevallo Male Institute, 341
Montgomery, 5, 6, 7, 9, 10, 11, 27, 29, 34, 35, 67, 70, 72–75, 80, 81, 93–98, 102, 104, 109–10, 116, 118, 119, 122, 124, 128, 130, 134, 135, 139, 140, 141, 144, 155, 156, 159, 160–63, 165, 174, 179, 186, 323–29, 417
Montgomery, William, 194
Montgomery Advertiser, 326
Montgomery City Hall, 119
Montgomery County, HABS listings, 323–29. *See also* Montgomery, Mount Meigs
Montgomery County Courthouse, 70, 75, 139
Montgomery Ward Company, 149
Moore, Gov. Andrew Barry, house, Marion, 332
Moore, Austin Osborne, 255
Moore, Dr. Clement Billingslea, 225
Moore, Judge John, house, Marion, 332

Moore, John Trotwood, 332
Moore, Sydenham, house, Greensboro, 240
Moore, Dr. William T., 360, 362
Moore-Hudson house, Summerfield, 225
Mooresville, 35, 36, 45, 261
Moore-Whatley house, Auburn vicinity, 255
Moorman, Dr. A. L., office, Bexar, 182, 279
Morgan, Calvin, 270
Morgan, Gen. John Hunt, 271
Morgan, Sen. John T., 223
Morgan, Sarah, 213
Morgan County, 4; HABS listings, 330–31. *See also* Decatur
Morgan County Courthouse, Somerville, 330
Morgan house, Tuscumbia, 213
Morgan-Neal house, Huntsville, 270
Morris, Elbert Green, 205
Morris Building, Birmingham, 119, *120*
Morriss, Simon, 345
Morriss-Holmes house, Alpine vicinity, 345
Moseley, Lewis B., 221
Moseley, William, house, Decatur, 119, *121*
Moseley-Seale house, Orrville vicinity, 221
Moses Building, Montgomery, *155*
Moulton, 252–53
Moundville, 242
Mount Ida, Talladega County, 345–46
Mount Jefferson Methodist Church, Opelika vicinity, 257
Mount Meigs, 83
Mount Olive Estates, 169, *170*
Mount Pleasant Baptist Church, Leighton vicinity, 211
Mount Pleasant Cumberland Presbyterian Meeting House, Leighton vicinity, 211
Mount Vernon, Ala., 319–21
Mount Vernon Arsenal, 319, 320–21
"Mount Vernon" portico, 165, 167

Mountain Brook, 160, 163
Mountain Brook Club, Birmingham, 166, *167*
Mountain Spring, Sylacauga, 347
Mountain Terrace, 146
Mounting blocks, 210. *See also* Carriage block, Street furnishings
Mudd, William S., 247
Mulberry community, 193
Mullins and Hall, 241
Munford, 347
Munger Memorial Hall, Birmingham-Southern College, 162, *164*
Munich, 285
Murfee, Col. James T., 85
Murphey, Dr. William, house, Decatur vicinity, 4–5
Murphy, John H., house, Montgomery, 70, 326
Murrah, James K., 259
Murrell, Col. John, 297
Muscle Shoals, 9
Myrtle Hall, Boligee vicinity, 230

Napoleon III, 118
Nash County, N.C., 254
Nashville, Tenn., 84, 241, 249, 270
Natchez, 223
Natchez Trace, 210
Nathan house, Sheffield, 122
National Historic Landmark Program, 190, 191
National Park Service, xv, xvi, 178, 184, 188, 266, 267
National Register of Historic Places, 186, 190
Neal, George W., 270
Nelson, Frank, house, Birmingham, 146
Nelson, Gideon, house, Greensboro, 97, *100*
Neoclassical architecture, 44–79, 133–45
Neoclassicism: influence of handbooks on, 12–16; Federal and Jeffersonian, 44; "new," 138–39
Neo-Renaissance, 138
Newbern, 242–43

Newberry, S.C., 198, 346
New Decatur, 122
New England, 6–7, 45
New Hampshire, 194
New Harmony Presbyterian Church, Lowndesboro, 263
New Jersey, 304
New Louvre, Paris, 119
New Market, 274
New Orleans, 11, 128, 314, 317, 318
Newport, R.I., 88, 122
New York, 8, 11–13, 57, 58, 102, 105, 129, 141, 160, 233, 313, 325, 352, 356; architectural influence, 11–12, 57, 58
New York Wire Railing Co., 287
Newson, Alfred A., 362–63
Newson-Sharp house, Camden, 362–63
Nichols, William, 11, 46, 50–52, 54, 135, 251, 351, 352, 353, 357, 358
Nichols, William, Jr., 352
Nininger house, Anniston, 122, *123*
Nisbet, Dr. John, 203
Nisbet-Weaver house, Jacksonville, 203
Noble guest cottage, Anniston, 122, *123*
Norfolk, Va., 33
"Norman" style. *See* Romanesque Revival
Norris, Calvin, 239
North Alabamian (office), 213
North Carolina, 11, 52, 203, 211, 229, 239, 244, 245, 246, 254, 261, 344, 347, 352; architectural influence, 23, 52. *See also* Carolinas
North Hull Street Historic District, 27, 29, 34, 328
North River Yacht Club, 69, 244
Northrup, John, 228
Northrup-Bateman house, Wetumpka, 58, 227–28
Norwood, 146
Norwood plantation house, Faunsdale vicinity, 18, 277–78
Notasulga, 256
Nunley, Mr., 263, 264

Oak Bowery, 208
Oak Grove, Elmore vicinity, 226
Oak Hill community, 43, 368–69
Oaklawn, Huntsville, 271
Oakleigh, Mobile, 67, 72, 308
Oakleigh Garden Historic District, Mobile, 185, 291
Oakman, 122, 126
Oak Manor, Livingston vicinity, 344
Oak Place, Huntsville, 64, 67, 271
Oaks, The, Leighton vicinity, 210–11
Oaks, The (Booker T. Washington house), Tuskegee, 122, 266
Oates, Gov. William Calvin, 244
Oates-Danzey house, Abbeville, 244
Observatory, University of Alabama, 357
Octagonal houses, 13, 15
Odd Fellows Hall, Mobile, 308
Offices, 201, 233, 258, 304. See also Law offices, Medical offices, Plantation complexes
Old Brick Presbyterian Church, Leighton vicinity, 211
"Old English" style, 121, 124
Oliver, Dr. Mack, 326
Oliver-Housman house, Montgomery, 326
Olmsted, Frederick Law, 6
O'Neal, Gov. Emmet, 249
Opelika, 30, 75, 90, 139, 182, 256–57
Open-hall plan, 3, 16, 32. See also Dogtrot house
Orange Vale, Talladega County, 177, 346
Orders. See Classical orders
Organs, 214, 244
"Oriental" style, 15
Orion, 64, 70, 337–38
Orion Male and Female Institute, 337, 338
Ormond, Judge John J., 355
Ormond-Little house, Tuscaloosa, 355, 356
Orphanages, 224, 310
Orrville, 30, 122, 126, 177, 219–21
Orrville Male Academy, 219

Osborne-Jones house, Marion vicinity, 333
Otey, William Madison, 269
Otis-Allen house, Mobile, 308
Outbuildings. See Dependencies and outbuildings
Outhouses. See Privies
Owen, Marie Bankhead, 229
Owens, Berry, 326
Owens-Teague house, Montgomery, 326
Oxford, Ala., 41, 89, 113, 122, 203, 205–06
Oxford University, 160
Ozark, 134, 136

Painting (decorative), 177, 227. See also Graining, Marbleizing, Stippling, Trompe l'oeil
Palings, The, Greenville vicinity, 201
Palladian influence, 44–45, 47, 52–53, 60, 69, 79, 212, 254
Palladio, Andrea, 44
Palmetto Hall, Mobile. See Azalea Grove
Panama Canal, 223
Parham, William, 260
Parker, Duncan T., house, Anniston, 132–33, 133
Parker Memorial Baptist Church, Anniston, 114, 116
Parks, John, 366
Parmly, Dr. Ludolph, 309
Parmly houses, Mobile, 308–09
Parsonages, 226, 234
Parsons, Benjamin F., 60, 240, 274, 332
Parsons, Gov. Lewis, house, Talladega. See Highland
Patternbooks, 12, 13, 14, 45, 49, 58, 60, 68, 83, 84, 86, 87, 90, 93, 94, 97, 98, 107, 119
Patton, Joseph E., house, Coatopa, 43, 342
Patton, Gov. Robert, 177, 250
Patton-Perry house, Florence, 249–50
Paul Hayne School, Birmingham, 116
Pearce, James, 335, 391

Peck, Elisha Wolsey, 356
Peck, Samuel Mintern, 356
Peebles, Robert and Sophia (Withers), 261
Peebles-Zeitler-McCrary house, Mooresville, 261
Pent. See Chimney pent
Percy, Walker, house, Birmingham, 124
Perdue Hill, 43, 322–23
Period architecture, 159–68
Periodicals, influence on Alabama architecture, 5, 107, 122, 145–47
Peripteral colonnade, 61, 251
Perkins, Col. Peter, 271
Perkins, William, 232
Perkins-Spencer house, Eutaw, 232
Perkins-Winston-Orgain house, Huntsville, 271
Perrin, Dr. George, 235
Perrin-Willis house, Forkland vicinity, 235
Perry, J. T., family grave plot, Greenville, 200
Perry, Simeon, 255
Perry-Cauthen house, Auburn, 255
Perry County, 60; HABS listings, 331–34. See also Marion
Perry County Courthouse, Marion, 60, 332
Perry Street, South, Montgomery, 124, 186
Peter, Joseph, 304
Peterson, Albert, 337
Peterson, Charles, xv
Pettus, Edmund Winston, house, Carrollton, 335
Petty, Benjamin F., house, Clayton, 15
Phenix City, 11
Philadelphia, 8, 11, 12, 155, 160, 299, 310, 314, 354
Phillippi, Antonio, 309
Phillippi-Mastin house, Mobile, 309
Phoenix Fire Station No. 6, Mobile, 100, 309
Phoenix Hotel, Carrollton, 335
Pickens, Gov. Israel, 240

Pickens, Samuel, 244
Pickens County, 100, 102; HABS listings, 334–37. *See also* Carrollton
Pickens County Courthouse, Carrollton, 100–01
Pickensville, 336–37
Pickett, Albert, 226, 324
Picturesque movement, 107–08
Pike County, 64; HABS listings, 337–38. *See also* Orion, Troy
Pine Apple, 16, *18,* 369
Pine Crest Cemetery, Greenville, 200
Pines, The, Anniston, 134
Pines, The, Greensboro, 146
Pitts, Philip Henry, 333
Pitts' Folly, Uniontown, 333–34
Pittsburgh, Pa., 129, 132
Pittsview, 339
Planing mills, 6
Planned communities, 147, *150–51,* 169, *170*
Plantation complexes, 201, 206, 209–10, 210–11, 212, 214–15, 230, 235–37, 244, 250–51, 252. *See also* Dependencies and outbuildings
Planters and Merchants Insurance Company, Mobile, 309
Playhouses, 284, 334
Pleasant Hill (Donnell house), Athens, 177, 259
Pleasant Hill community, Dallas County, 24
Plowman, George Paris, 349
Plowman-Elliott house, Talladega, 348–49
Plowman-Moore, Idora McClellan, 349
Plumb, Ezra, 369
Point Clear, 195
Pollard, Charles T., 256, 327; house, Montgomery, 70, 327
Pollock Building, Mobile, 309
Pomeroy, P. B., family tomb, Mobile, 309–10
Pope, Dr. Edgar A., 193
Pope, Leroy, house, Huntsville, 45, 48, 271–72
Pope-Alexander-Golson house, Prattville, *48,* 193

Pope's Tavern, Florence, 250
Poplar Grove, Huntsville, 272
Population of Alabama, 5; mobility in nineteenth century, 10–11; agrarian character, 6, 9, 10
Porches, cast-iron, 7, *17*
Port-au-Prince, 38
Porter's lodge (Gaineswood), 276
Portier, Bishop Michael, 285; house, Mobile, 37, *39,* 310, 314
Post offices, 128, *129,* 135, *138, 139, 141,* 316, 317, 339
Post-modernism, 174
Potter, E. T., 115
Powell School, Birmingham, 116
Practical House Carpenter (Benjamin), 19, 195, 233, 247, 343
Practice of Architecture (Benjamin), 13, 69, 196, 340
Prairie-style house, 145
Prairieville, 83, 84, 184, 243–44
Pratt, Daniel, 6, 193–94, 323; house, Prattville, 194; factory complex, 6, 7, 193–94. *See also* Continental Gin Company Factory
Pratt, William H., 304
Prattville, 6, 7, 35, 48, 100, 128, 193–94, 327
Prefabricated iron fronts, 102
Presbyterian Church, Camden, 182, 363
Presbyterian Church, Gainesville, 78
Presbyterian Church, Lowndesboro, 263
Presbyterian Church, Marion, 112, *113*
Presbyterian Church, Newbern, 242
Presbyterian Church, Union Springs, 114
President's House, University of Alabama, 357
Price, James Lewis, 334
Price, R. D., 298
Price, Prof. William, 355
Price-Eddins-Rosenau house, Tuscaloosa, 355
Price house, Lamar County, 30
Prince, Oliver Thomas, house, Tuscaloosa, 355

Prince William County, Va., 216
Privies, 182, 212, 251, 275, 292, 366. *See also* Dependencies and outbuildings
Progressive Farmer, 149
"Prophet's chamber," 30
Protestant Orphans' Asylum, Mobile, 310
Protestant Union Church, Mobile, 80, 81
Pryor, Luke, house, Athens, 259
Pulaski County, Ga., 277
Pullman Hotel, Citronelle, 279
Purdy, Alexander, 283
Purefoy house, Talladega, 122
Putnam County, Ga., 201

Quarries, 347, 418
Queen Anne style, 3, 117, 121–27, 135, 138, 145, 146, 186
Quigley, A. M. and S. B., 310
Quigley twin house, Mobile, 310
Quill house, Mobile, 133

Ragsdale house, Talladega, 122
Railroad architecture. *See* Transportation and transportation facilities
"Rains, Mr.," 343
Raised houses, 213
Raised-plate construction, 5
Rammed-earth houses, 169, *170*
Ramsey, Rev. Abiezer Clarke, house, Oak Hill, 368–69
Randlette, Columbia E., 297
Randolph, B. F., 327, 328
Randolph, James D., 323
Randolph, Ryland, 355
Ranlett, William H., 237
Rapier, Charles W., 285
Rather, Capt. John Taylor, 216
Ravesies, Frederic, house, Mobile, 285
Ray, William O., 327
Ray-Branch house, Montgomery, 327
Read, Col. John, 268
Reconstruction era, 9, 230, 355
Rectories. *See* Parsonages
Redmont Park, 163, 166
Redwood, George E., 284

Redwood, Richard H., 287, 294, 311; house, Mobile, 310–11
Reese, Edwin, 232
Reese-Lucius house, Eutaw, 232
Religious architecture: churches, 6, 9, 46, 57, 58, 64, 70, 78, 80, *81, 82–87*, 109, *110–13*, 114, *115–17*, 128–29, *130, 131*, 132, 141, *144*, 152, *153*, 161, *162–63*, 167, 169, *172*, 193, 196, 202, 211, 213–14, 218–19, 225, 226, 227, 229, 231, 234, 242, 243, 249, 256, 257, 262, 263, 274, 284–85, *286*, 294, 298, 313, 315, 328, 329, 332, 335, 336, 337, 342, 343, 352, 358, 359, 363; convents, 128, 291; temples (Jewish), 109, *110*, 141, *144*. See also Slave galleries
Resaca, Ga., 359
Resettlement Administration, 169, 170
Revault-Maupin-Shawhan house, Mobile, 311
Reynolds, Walker, 345
Rhea, James W., 216
Rhea, John S., 47, 330
Rhea-Burleson-McEntire house, Decatur, *47*, 330
Rice, Judge Green P., house, Somerville, 330–31
Richards, Charles G., house, Mobile, 311
Richardson, H. H., 113, 127–28
Richardson, Walker, 340
Richardson, William, house, Athens, 259
Richardson-Quarles-Comer house, Pittsview vicinity, 340
Richardsonian Romanesque, 127–33
Richmond, Va., 45, 238, 319, 324
Ricks, Abraham, 210
Rider, Elizabeth, house, Mobile, 311, *312*
Ridgeville, 201–02
Riser, George, 346
Rives, Whitmell William, 361
Roach-Cabaniss house, Huntsville, *272*, 272–73

Roach, John C., 272
Roane County, Tenn., 205
Robertson, James, 285
Robertson, G. J., house, Birmingham, 146, *148*
Robinson, John, 271
Robinson, Toddy, 226
Robinson, Maj. William, 262
Robinson Springs, 226
Robinson twin houses, Mobile, 311
"Rock House," the, Harpersville vicinity, 341
Rocky Hill, Lawrence County, 184, 253
Rogers, George B., 11, 142, 152, 179, 283, 284, 298, 312
Rogers, Thomas, 321
Rogers-Curry house, Mount Vernon, 321
Rogersville, 251
Rolfe, John, house, Va., 34
Romanesque Revival, 109–13
Roof types: Creole cottage, 37; butterfly, 38; spraddle, 41; mansard, 119
Roosevelt, Pres. Franklin, 181
Roper, Benjamin F., 335
Roper, James W., 308
Rose, Col. Howell, 228
Rose Hill, Forkland vicinity, 231
Rosemary, Millers Ferry vicinity, 368
Rosemount, Forkland vicinity, 43, 61, *63*, 183, 235
Rosenbaum house, Florence, 169, *171*
Rosewood, Lowndesboro vicinity, 264
Ross, William H., 282, 295
Rotunda, University of Alabama, 50
Rousseau, Fenton L., 119
Row houses, 282, 308–09. See also Double houses, Twin houses
Rudolph, Paul, 169
Rural Architecture (Upjohn), 83, 86, 218, 234, 244, 263
Ruskin, John, 114, 115–16
Russell, Col. E. L., 315
Russell, E. W., 180
Russell County, 16, 61, 62, 199; HABS listings, 338–40

Russell-Turrentine house, Gainesville, 40
Russia, 57, 359
Rutledge, 217
Ryan, Father Abram J., 310

Sacred Heart Chapel, Mobile, 128
Saddlebag-type log house, 251, 258
Sadler, Isaac Wellington, house, Bessemer vicinity, 30, *32*
St. Andrew's Episcopal Church, Prairieville, 83, *84*, 184, 242–43
St. Clair County, 27. *See also* Ashville
St. Francis Street Baptist Church, Mobile, 111
St. James' Episcopal Church, Livingston, 343
St. James Hotel, Selma, 222–23
St. John's Episcopal Church, Forkland, 83, 234
St. John's Episcopal Church, Montgomery, 6, 80, 328
St. Luke A.M.E. Church, Eufaula, 196
St. Luke's Episcopal Church, Dallas County, 83, *85*, 218–19
St. Luke's Episcopal Church, Jacksonville, 83, *86*
St. Mary's Episcopal Church, Camden, 363
St. Michael and All Angels Episcopal Church, Anniston, 128–29, *131*
St. Paul's Cathedral, Birmingham, 114, *116*
St. Paul's Episcopal Church, Lowndesboro, 263
St. Paul's Episcopal Church, Selma, 114
St. Peter's Catholic Church, Montgomery, 109
St. Stephen's Episcopal Church, Eutaw, 80
Saint Stephens, 358
Saloons, 313
Samford, Gov. William James, 254
Samford University, Birmingham, 167, *168*
Sanford, James, 312
Sanford, Thaddeus, 286, 312

Sanford-Staylor house, Mobile, 312
Sanford-Thompson house, Mobile, 312
Sash, door, and blind factories, 6, 193–94
Sauerhaver, Mr., 359
Saunders, James Edmonds, 253
Saunders, Turner, house (Saunders-Goode-Hall house), Town Creek vicinity, 10, 53, 55, 253–54
Savannah, Ga., 45
Sawyerville, 244
Sayre, Philemon D., 328
Sayre, William, 324
Sayre-Troy house, Montgomery, 328
Scattergood, B. F., 287, 307
Schieffelin, George, 313
Schieffelin-Sledge house, Mobile, 312–13
Schiffman Building, Huntsville, *132*
Schley-Rutherford house, Mobile, 313
Schools, 9, 50, 51–52, *53*, 64, *69*, 84–85, *88*, 100, *104*, 115–16, *117*, 119, *120*, 140–41, *143*, 160, *161*, *162*, *164*, 167, *168*, 219, 224, 230, 231, 232, 235, *236*, 241, 244, 256, 258, 263, 273, 281, 291, 320, 332, 337, 341, 347, 348, 351, 352, 355, 356, 357–58, 364
Scott, David, 332, 356
Scott, Sir Walter, 80
Scott-Moody house, Tuscaloosa, 355–56
Scottsville, 6
Screws, William Wallace, 326
Seale, 199, 340
Seale, Arnold, 199
Seale-Mosley house, Union Springs vicinity, *178*, 199
Seaman, George, 228
Seaman-Airey house, Wetumpka, *177*, 228
Seamen's Bethel, Mobile, 313
Searcy Hospital, Mount Vernon, 320
Sears Company, 149
Seay, Gov. Thomas, house and offices, Greensboro, 240–41
Second Empire style, 117, 118–21

Seibels, John J., 328
Seibels house (Samuel Swan house), Montgomery, 98, *102*, 328
Self, Dr. Raymond, 198
Sellers, Calvin C., 368
Sellers-Henderson house (Sellers house), Millers Ferry, *178*, 368
Selma, 5, 7, 9, 10, 58, 60, 64, 74, 91, 112, 114, 115, 116, 117, 122, 139, 165, 177, 186, 221–24, 241, 274, 335
Selma, Battle of, 222
Selma and Rome Railroad, 203
Selwood, Talladega County, 346
Semmes, Judge Oliver, 297
Semmes, Adm. Raphael, 297, 300
Semmes, S. Spence, 299
Servant and slave quarters, 24–25, *25*, *182*, 195, 201, 203, 206, 209–11, 212, 235, 236, 237, 238, 239, 241, 249, 258, 268–69, 271, 283, 292, 308, 312, 331. *See also* Dependencies and outbuildings
Seven Lamps of Architecture, The (Ruskin), 114
Sevier, Gov. John, 330
Sewall, Judge Kiah B., 283
Sewanee, Tenn., 239
Shackelford, M., 350
Shackelford, Robert D., 241
Shackelford-McCrary-Otts house, Greensboro, 241
Shaw, Edward, 12
Shawver, George W., 233
Shawver-Coleman-Banks house, Eutaw, 232–33
Sheffield, 122, 180, 211–12
Shelby County, HABS listings, 341
Shelley, Gen. C. M., 341
Shelton and Williams, 255
Shepherd, Henry, 350
Sherard, John H., 344
Sherard-Tartt house, Livingston vicinity, 344
Sherlock, Smith, and Adams, 364
Sherman, Gen. William T., 268
Shiloh Baptist Church, Sardis, 222
Shingle style, 21, 124

Shippers Exchange Saloon, Mobile, 313
Shorter, Eli, house, Eufaula, 134
Shorter, Gov. John Gill, 246
Shorterville, 245
Sidel, Edouard, 119
Siler, Solomon, 337; house, Orion, 337–38
Siloam Baptist Church, Marion, 332
Silver, Joseph, 313
Silver-Ketchum house, Mobile, 313
Simpson, John, 250; house, Florence, 250
Simpson-Irvine house, Florence, 250
Single-pile house, 33
Sinnige, H. H., house, Birmingham, 134, *135*
Skinner, Dr. Marcus, house, Selma, *165*
Skyscrapers, 155–59
Slatter, Hope H., family tomb, Mobile, *8*, 313–14
Slave builders, 206, 244, 367. *See also* Black builders and craftsmen
Slave galleries, 70, 211, 218, 226, 227, 335, 342
Slave population, 5
Slave quarters. *See* Servant and slave quarters
Sloan, Samuel, 11, 12, 84, 87, 93–94, 97, 98, 99, 100, 107, 202, 203, 223, 275. *See also* Sloan and Stewart
Sloan and Stewart, 267, 354
Sloss, James Withers, 260
Sloss Blast Furnaces, Birmingham, 417
Sloss-Pettus house, Athens, 259–60
Sloss-Sheffield Furnace, Birmingham, 260
"Smart bucket," *181*, 199
Smith, Bartlett, house, Henry County, 41, *42*, 245
Smith, Benjamin Bosworth, 128, 160
Smith, F. Patterson, 160
Smith, McQueen, stables, Prattville, 194
Smith, Murray Forbes, house, Mobile, 88–89, 295

Smith, Sidney, house, Mobile, 314
Smith, Wash, 350, 351; house, Selma, 78
Smith, William A., 314
Smith-Clarke house, Mobile, 314
Smith Hall, University of Alabama, 143
Smithsonian Institution, 109
Smith-Sutton house, Orrville, 219–20
Smokehouses, 182, 206, 210, 211, 213, 217, 223, 224, 230, 233, 242, 243, 249, 251, 252, 255, 269, 271, 273, 274, 275, 278, 280, 342, 344, 345, 366, 368. *See also* Dependencies and outbuildings
Smoot, E. L., house, Wetumpka, 228
Smoot, William, 212, 217
Snow, Dudley, house, Oxford, 41, 205
Snow, E. N. C., house, Tuscaloosa, 356
Snow, Fielding, 203
Snow, Henry Adams, 356
Snow-Arnold-Rowan house, Jacksonville, 203
Snow-Peck house, Tuscaloosa, 356
Sodality Chapel (Spring Hill College), Mobile, 315
Somerville, 330–31
South Carolina, 43, 198, 201, 207, 220, 230, 247, 307, 308, 334, 335, 346, 368; architectural influence, 43, 359–60. *See also* Carolinas
South Highlands, 146
Southern Architecture Illustrated, 165
"Southern Colonial" style, 133–34, *136, 137,* 163, *165,* 167
Southern Market, Mobile. *See* Mobile City Hall and Southern Market
Southern University, Florence, 119
Southern University, Greensboro, 84, 88, 238, 241; Chancellor's house, 78, 241. *See also* Birmingham-Southern College
Southers, Gillan, 202
Southside Baptist Church, Birmingham, 141
Southwest, Old, 10

Spain, 349
Spanish American War, 195, 239, 252
Spanish colonial period, 37
Spanish Colonial style, 3, 160, 163, *165;* and Mission Revival, 152–53
Spearman, M. D. L., house, Bexar, 279
Spence house (Old Academy), Munford, 347
Spinning houses, 345
Spring Hill, 162–63
Spring Hill College, Mobile, 50, 53, 314–15
Spring Valley, 212
Spring Villa, Opelika vicinity, 90, 257
Stables, 182, 194, 237, 256, 292, 321. *See also* Dependencies and outbuildings
Stagecoach Inn, Tuskegee vicinity, 267
Stairways, 45, *47, 48, 49,* 65, 68, 74, *102, 125, 126,* 148
State Bank, Decatur. *See* Decatur Branch, State Bank of Alabama
State Bank, Huntsville. *See* Huntsville Branch, State Bank of Alabama
State Capitols. *See* Alabama State Capitols
State Hospital for the Insane. *See* Bryce Hospital
State Institute for the Deaf and Blind, Talladega, 69
State Street A.M.E. Church, Mobile, 111, *113*
Statehouses. *See* Alabama State Capitols
Steele, George, 11, 14, 57, 59, 63–64, 67, 84, 177, 269–73
Steele, John, 193
Steele, John A. and Martha Winston, 213
Stegar, Edward, 213
Steiner Bank, Birmingham, 132
Stephenson, Dr. H. W., house, Oakman, 122, *126*
Sterrett, David W., 363
Sterrett-McWilliams house, Camden, 363

Steward's House, Huntsville Female Seminary, 273
Stewart, John, 11, 84, 93, 98. *See also* Sloan and Stewart
Stewart, Patrick Henry, 194
Stick style, 21
Stickley, Gustav, 146
Stickney, Joseph Blodgett, 242
Stillman College, 352
Stippling, 177, 341. *See also* Graining, Marbleizing, Painting (decorative), Trompe l'oeil
Stockton, 195
Stone, Dr. Barton, 329
Stone, Warren T., 261
Stone-McCarty-Robinson house, Burkville vicinity, 261
Stone-Young house, Montgomery vicinity, *329*
Stonecroft, Tuscumbia, 216
Stones of Venice, The (Ruskin), 114
Store buildings, 206, 234, 278, 336–37, 346, 363–64, 367, 368. *See also* Commercial architecture
Stratford Hall, Va., 169
Strawberry Hill, Forkland vicinity, 235–36
Street furnishings, 315
Stroup, Moses, 351
Stuart, Charles, 199
Sturdivant, Robert, 225
Sturdivant, Robert D., 223
Sturdivant Hall, Selma, 70, 74 223
Sturdivant-Moore-Hartley house, Summerfield, 225
Stuttgart, 139
Suburbs, 107, 146, 160, 162–63
Sugarberry Hill, Wetumpka vicinity, 228–29
Suggsville, 208
Sulligent, 31, 247–48
Summerfield, 64, 224–25
Summer homes, 40, 195, 199, 295
Summer houses. *See* Gazebos
Sumter County, 43, 186; HABS listings, 342–44. *See also* Coatopa, Gainesville, Livingston

Sunnybrook, Courtland vicinity. *See* Bride's Hill
Sunnyside, Talladega vicinity, 16
Sussex County, Va., 260
Swan, Samuel, house (Seibels house), Montgomery, 98, *102*, 328
Swann house, Birmingham, 166
Sweetwater, Florence, 45, 177, 250
Swift, Wiley Pope, 225
Swift-Moore-Cottingham house, Summerfield, 225
Sylacauga, 167, 347
Syrian arch, 128, 133

T-shaped plan, 18, 67, 267, 282, 308, 352, 353, 355, 356
Tacon, Henry, 316
Tacon-Gordon house, Mobile, *ii,* 122, *125,* 315–16
Tait, Felix, 366; house, Camden vicinity, *78,* 366
Tait, James Asbury, 358, 364, 366, 367; house, Coy vicinity, 367
Tait, Robert, 366; house, Camden vicinity, 16, 365–66
Tait-Ervin house (Robert Tait house), Camden vicinity, 16, 365–66
Tait-Starr house (Felix Tait house), Camden vicinity, *78,* 366
Talladega, 16, 28, 47, 62, 69, 89, 90, 102, 110–11, 113, 122, 117, 348–50
Talladega County, 177, 229; HABS listings, 344–50. *See also* Talladega
Talladega County Courthouse, 102
Tallapoosa County, HABS listings, 350–51
Tallapoosa River, 5, 6
Tallassee, 6
Tanglewood, Akron vicinity, 237
Tannehill, Ninian, 351
Tannehill Furnace, Bucksville, 351
Tardy, Balthasar, 316
Tardy-Thorp house, Mobile, 316
Tarleton, George W., house, Mobile, 316
Tartt, Ruby Pickens, 344
Tate-Thompson house, Tuskegee, 265

Tavern (Crow Building), Jacksonville, 203–04, *204*
Tavern, Allenton, 358–59
Tavern, Mooresville, 261
Tavern, Wetumpka, 228
Tavern, Old, Tuscaloosa, 357
Tavern, The, Decatur, 124, *127*
Tavern, The, Eufaula, 197
Taverns. *See* Hotels and inns
Tayloe, Henry A., 244
Taylor, Benjamin, 248
Taylor, John Burt, 246
Taylor, Robert R., 266
Taylor, William Henry, 328
Taylor-Cunningham houses, Center Star vicinity, 248
Taylor-McGriff house, Columbia, 246
Taylor-Ponder-Graves house, Montgomery, 328
Teague-Riegel house, Columbia, 246
Tebbs, Robert, Collection, 190, 191
Technology, impact on Alabama architecture, 5, 6–7, 12, 15, 16, 23–24, 44, 102, 111
Temple, N.H., 194
Temple Beth-Or, Montgomery, 109, *110*
Temple Emanu-El, Birmingham, 141, 144
Temple-front houses, 57, 60
Temples (Jewish). *See* Religious architecture
Temple Theater, Birmingham, 142
Temple-with-wings form, 57, 60–61, 227
Tennessee, 9, 23, 205, 270, 330; architectural influence, 23
Tennessee River, 5, 9, 210
Tennessee-Tombigbee Waterway, 335–36
Tennessee Valley, 9, 10, 23, 42, 45, 52–53, 181, 186
Ten Oaks, Jacksonville, 97, *98,* 203
Tensaw, 37
Terminal Station, Atlanta, 152
Terminal Station, Birmingham, 152
Terra Firma farm, 207
Terrell, J. T., 274

Texas, 10
Textile factories, 6, 7
Theaters, 141, 142, 160, 308
Thigpen house, Montgomery, 134, *135*
Thimbleton, Florence, 119
Thomas, "Squire" George, 263
Thomas, Micajah, 258
Thomas-Hagood house, Lowndesboro, 263
Thomas Jefferson Hotel, Birmingham, 159
Thompson, Frederick Ingate, 312
Thorn Hill, Talladega County, *47,* 349–50
Thornhill, Forkland vicinity, 25, 61, 236–37
Thornton, David, 229
Thornton, James Innes, 236
Thoroughgood, Adam, house, Va., 33
Thorp, E. R., 316
"Three Sisters" house, Mobile, 300
Tidewater-type cottage, 21, 23, 33–36, 186, 212, 261
Timmerman Building, Andalusia, *159*
Tinker, Robert, 242
Tinker house, Greensboro vicinity, 242
Todd, Elodie (Mrs. N. H. R. Dawson), 221
Tombigbee River, 5, 40, 183
Tool houses, 235
Totten, J. G., 279
Toulmin, John B., 293, 302
Toulmin, Theophilus, house, Mobile, 316
Toulouse, France, 304
Toumey, Michael, 356
Town, Ithiel, 58
Town Creek, 53, 55, 253–54
Town lattice truss, 209, 347
Townsend, Edwin, 316
Townsend-Foreman Building, Mobile, 316
Traditionalism, persistence of, 169–70
Train stations. *See* Transportation and transportation facilities

Transportation and transportation facilities: bridges, 347, 417; covered bridges, 209, 210, 346–47; ferries, 367; railroad offices and workshops, 9, *10*, 308; railroad stations, 102, 128, *130*, 151, *152*, 299, 417. See also Hotels and inns
Travis, William Barrett, house, 323
Treatise on Landscape Gardening (Downing), 107
Tredegar Ironworks, 238
Trimble, Benjamin, 228
Trimble-Fitzpatrick house, Wetumpka, 228
Trinity Episcopal Church, Boston, Mass., 129
Trinity Episcopal Church, Mobile, 80
Trompe l'oeil, 227, 268, 325, 363. See also Graining, Marbleizing, Painting (decorative), Stippling
Troy, 9, 91, 122
Troy, Col. Daniel, 218
Truit, William L., house, Mobile, 296
Tuckabatchee Masonic Lodge, Crawford, 338
Tucker, Rev. Eppes, 257
Tuck house, Greene County, 30
Tudor influence, 3, 15, 160, 163, 165. See also Elizabethan influence, Gothic influence, Gothic Revival
Tunstall house, Tensaw vicinity, 195
Turner, Wiley, 264
Turner-Dickson house, Lowndesboro, 264
Tuscaloosa, 5, 46, 51, 55, 61, 64, 69, 70, 75, 78, 79, 84–85, 89, 91, 93, 97, 100, 103, 115–16, 135, 138, 159, 163, 169, 173, 179, 351–58
Tuscaloosa County, 51; HABS listings, 351–58. See also Tuscaloosa
Tuscaloosa County Preservation Society, 357
Tuscan style, 13. See also Italianate style
Tuscumbia, 9, 53, 80, 212–17
Tuscumbia, Courtland, and Decatur Railroad, 9, 213

Tuskegee, 18, 20, 62, 75, 84, 91, 110, 111, 122, 128, 152, 154, 164, 172, 264–67
Tuskegee Female College (Alabama Conference Female College), Tuskegee, 84, 265
Tuskegee Institute, 265–66
Tuskegee Institute Chapel, 169, *172*
Tutwiler, Herbert, house, Birmingham, *165*
Tutwiler, Julia, 343
Tutwiler Hotel, Birmingham, 159
Twin houses, 310, 311. See also Double houses, Row houses
Tyler, Edward, house, Anniston. See The Pines (Anniston)
Tyson, Archibald, house, 263
Tyson-Maner house, Montgomery, 98

U-shaped plan, 18, *19*, 212, 235, 244, 265, 278
Ulster, 250, 251
Umbria, Hale County, 18, *19*, 244
Union Depot, Birmingham, 128
Union District, S.C., 247
Union Female College, Eufaula, 100
Union Springs, 114, 119, 198–99
Union Station, Montgomery, 128, *130*, 417; train shed, 417
Uniontown, 333–34
United States Capitol, 70
United States Custom House, Mobile, 102, *106*, 316–17
United States Hotel, Dadeville, 350
United States Marine Hospital, Mobile, 317
United States Post Office Building, Mobile, 317
United States post offices. See Federal buildings, Post offices
United States Supervising Architect, 139
Universities. See Schools
University of Alabama, 46, 50, 54, 84–85, 115–16, *117*, 140, *143*, 237, 357–58, 361, 362; Lyceum and Rotunda, 50; President's House, 51–52, 357–58

University of Montevallo, Reynolds Hall. See Montevallo Male Institute
University of the South, 239
Upjohn, Richard, 11, 80, 97–98, 109, 218, 234, 244, 263. See also Richard Upjohn and Son
Upjohn, Richard, and Son, 333
Upjohn, Richard M., 11, 97. See also Richard Upjohn and Son
Urban renewal, 285, 287, 288, 299, 306, 313, 318
Uriah, 323
Usonian concept, 169, 171

Van Antwerp Building, Mobile, 156, *157*
Vanderbilt-Belmont, Alva Smith, 88, 295
Van Keuren, E. B., 260
Vanroy, John, 317
Vanroy-Barnewall house, Mobile, 317
"Varian Feare" (Mrs. E. Walter Burkhardt), 183
Varner, William, 267
Varner-Alexander house, Tuskegee, 78, 266–67
Vasser, Richard W., 260
Vaux, Calvert, 12
Vermont, 309
Vernacular building. See Folk architecture
Versailles Conference, 360
Village and Farm Cottage (Cleaveland and Backus), 107
Vilula, 340
Vincent, Captain Benjamin, 317
Vincent-Walsh house, Mobile, 317–18
Vine and Olive Colony, 285
Vining, Thomas, 260
Vining-Wood-Vasser house, Athens, 260
Vinson, Drury, house, Leighton vicinity, 211
Violet Hall, Tuscumbia, 216
Virginia, 4, 10, 23, 33, 34, 44, 177, 213, 214, 216, 236, 252, 254, 260, 261, 268, 271, 278, 322,

(Virginia, continued)
333, 334, 342, 346; architectural influence, 4–5, 23, 33–35, 44, 252
Virginia (ironclad), 222
Virginia Military Institute, 85
Vogtner, George, farm, Dawes, 280

Wade, Daniel, 252
Wade, David, house, Huntsville, 273
Waldwick, Gallion, 89, 90, 237
Walker, Charles and Margaret Jemison, 277
Walker, James, 352
Walker, Col. Luther, 199
Walker, Merritt Warren, 199
Walker, Judge Thomas A., 203
Walker, W. T., 324
Walker, William Augustus, Sr., 247
Walker, Judge William Harrison, house, Athens, 260
Walker County. *See* Jasper, Oakman
Walker-Frazer house, Union Springs vicinity, 199
Walker-Smith house, Birmingham, 247
Wallace, John, house, Athens, 169
Wallpaper, scenic, 344
Walls. *See* Freestanding walls
Walter, Thomas U., 12, 70
Walter, Thomas U. III, 134
Walthall, Leonidas, 8
Walthall, Margaret Hill, 243
Walthall, Robert K., 243
Walthall house, Newbern, 242–43
Walton, John T., 274
Walton, Justina Gennerick, 235
Walton, William, 235
Walton-Bruce house, Dayton, 274–75
Warehouses, 307
Waring, Moses, 292
Waring "Texas" house, Mobile, 292
Warren, H. Langford, 160
Warren, Knight, and Davis, 158, 162, 179, 317, 324
Warren, William T., 11, 151, 179
Warren County, Ga., 345
Washington, Booker T., house, Tuskegee, 122, 266

Washington, D.C., 70, 109, 183, 184, 188, 216
Washington and LaFayette Academy, Tuscaloosa, 355
Washington County, HABS listings, 358
Washington County Courthouse, Saint Stephens, 358
Washington County, Ga., 224
Washington Ferry, 193
Washington Fire Engine Company No. 8, Mobile, 70, 318
Washington State University, 178
Water mills. *See* Grist mills
Water Street Urban Renewal Project, Mobile, 287, 288, 299, 306, 313
Watkins, James L., 270
Watkins, Dr. John, house, Burnt Corn, 322
Watkins and Hardaway, 357
Watson, Watson, and Rutland, 174
Watts, Edward, house, Selma. *See* Sturdivant Hall
Watts, Thomas Hill, house, Montgomery, 97
Watts Building, Birmingham, *158*, 160
Weary and Kramer, 128
Weaver, 30, 206–07
Weaver, Adam, house, Rogersville, 251
Weaver, Mrs. Lucinda, 207
Weaver, William, house, Selma, 116
Weaver-Rowe house, Weaver, 207
Webb, J. H. Y., house, Greensboro, 78, 241
Webb, William P., law office, Eutaw, 233
Webster, John J., 353
Weeden, Howard, 273
Weeden house, Huntsville, 46, 273
Weir, Rev. John Calvin, 362
Welch, Nathaniel, 344
Weldon, John, 318
Weldon-LeLoupe house, Mobile, 318
Wellborn, Dr. Levi Thomas, house, Eufaula, 197

Wellhouses, 182, 197, 198, 230, 236, 237, 244, 258, 272–73, 334, 346, 366. *See also* Dependencies and outbuildings, Wellsweeps
Wellsweeps, 338
Welton, William Leslie, 148
Wemyss house, Greensboro vicinity, 89
Wenderoth, Oscar, 317
Wesleyan Female Academy, Tuscaloosa, 356
Wesleyan University, Florence, 84
West End, 146
West Indian architectural influence, 18, 37, 38, 177, 297
Weston, William C., 141, 155
Weston plantation, Boligee vicinity, 230
Westwood, Uniontown, 334
Wetmore, Thomas Badger, 223
Wetmore-Morgan-Agee house, Selma, 223
Wetumpka, 58, 84, 87, 177, 226–29
Wewoka, Talladega County, 346
Weyanoke, Marengo County, 49
Wheat, Moses, 257
Wheat houses (granaries). *See* Farm buildings
Wheat-Tucker-Fincher house (Moses Wheat house), Opelika vicinity, 30, 177, 257
Wheeler, Gervase, 12, 107
Wheeler, Gen. Joseph, house, Courtland vicinity, 252
Wheeler, Lorenzo B., 11
Wheelock, Harry B., 11
Whilldin, D. O., 162
Whistler, 9, 10
Whitcher house, Bridgeport, 122
White, Asa, 233
White, William C., house, Orion, 338
White Cross, Newbern vicinity, 243
White House of the Confederacy, Montgomery, 93, 95
White-McGiffert house, Eutaw, 233
White Plains, 207
Whitfield, Nathan Bryan, 11, 70, 275

Whitsett, Joseph, 332
Whitsett-Hurt-Hanna house, Marion, 332
Whitten, Lawrence, 352
Wilbergand, Thil, 140, 283
Wilcox County, 25, 43, 78, 178; HABS listings, 358–69. *See also* Camden, Fatima, Oak Hill, Pine Apple
Wilcox County Courthouse, Camden, 78, 364
Wilcox Female Institute, Camden, 364
Wilcox Hotel, Camden, 364
Wiley-Trotman house, Troy, 119
Wilkins, Dr. A. M., house, Pickensville, 336, 337
Williams, Edward, 197
Williams, Col. Thomas Richard ("Dick"), 205
Williams-Bragg house, Lowndesboro, 263–64
Williamsburg, Va., 24, 33, 36, 341
Williams-Greenleaf house, Jacksonville, 204–05
Williamson, Robert, 317
"Willis" (black barber), 214
Willis, Virginia Bullock, 235
Wills, Frank, 80, 328
Wilson, Albert J., house, Suggsville, 208
Wilson, Augusta Evans, 280, 297
Wilson, Catlin, 233
Wilson, Gen. James, 326
Wilson, Lorenzo M., 280
Wilson, Pres. Woodrow, 360
Wilson-Gibbs house, Mobile, 318
Wilson-Herndon-Dunlap house, Eutaw, 233

Windham, William, house, Huntsville, 273
Winston, Anthony, house, Sheffield, 211
Winston, Isaac, 212, 215
Winston, William, house, Tuscumbia, 216
Winter, Benjamin Ricks, 211
Winter, John G., 324
Winter, Joseph S., house, Montgomery, 93, 94, 97
Winter, William Hooe and Catherine (Washington), 216
Winter-Barner house, Sheffield, 211
Winter Building, Montgomery, 328
Winterboro, 229
Wiregrass, 27
Withers, Frederick C., 115
Wolters, Henry, 11
Womack, Jacob Lewis, 202
Womack, T. Augustus, house, Butler County, 201–02
Womack-Crenshaw house, Butler County, 202
Wood, Robert, and Company, 8, 310, 314
Wood, William Halsey, 129
Woodland, Florence vicinity. *See* Woodlawn
Woodland, Moundville vicinity, 242
Woodlands, Claiborne, 40
Woodlawn, Florence vicinity, 45, 49, 251
Woodlawn High School, Birmingham, 161
Woods, Alexander, 205
Woods-Cook-Tredaway house, Jacksonville, 205
Woods Hall, University of Alabama, 84–85

Wood-Spahn house, Troy, 122
Woodward Building, Birmingham, 155–56, *156*
Woodward Iron Works, Bessemer vicinity, 417
Wooten, Dr. Hardy Vickers, 264
Workers' housing, Mobile, 38, 318
Works Progress Administration (WPA), 180, 330
World War I, 5, 24, 142, 149, 153, 157, 208
World War II, 173, 184, 188, 195
Worthington, Benjamin P., house, Birmingham, 247
Wright, Frank Lloyd, 21, 145, 169, 171
Wright, Sarah, 276
Wright-Pearson house, Dixons Mills vicinity, 276
Wrought iron. *See* Ironwork
Wyman, Judson, 323

Yancey, William Lowndes, dogtrot, Montgomery County, 27
Yonge, Penn C., 257
York's Bluff (now Sheffield), 211
Young, Ammi B., 102, 106, 317
Young, Isaac E., 216, 217
Young Carpenter's Assistant, The (Biddle), 45
Young's Carriage Shop, Tuscumbia, 215, 216
Young-Stine house, Tuscumbia, 216–17
Youpon (Mimosa), Canton Bend vicinity, 366–67

Zeitler, Henry, 261

About the Author

Robert Gamble received his bachelor's degree in history from Birmingham-Southern College and his master's from the University of Georgia. He is the senior architectural historian with the Alabama Historical Commission, where he has worked since 1982.

While serving with the Peace Corps in Santo Domingo for two and a half years, Gamble became the first peace corpsman to work with historic preservation when he undertook an architectural survey for the Oficina de Patrimonia Cultural. When he returned to the United States in 1969, he joined the staff of the National Park Service, working initially with the National Register of Historic Places in Washington, D.C., and then with the National Landmarks Program. He has also worked, under the auspices of the United Nations, with several preservation projects in the Caribbean and Central America.